Compared to What?

An
Introduction
to the
Analysis
of Algorithms

Gregory J. E. Rawlins

Computer Science Press
An Imprint of
W. H. Freeman and Company
New York

Compared to What?

An
Introduction
to the
Analysis
of Algorithms

PRINCIPLES OF COMPUTER SCIENCE SERIES

Series Editors
Alfred V. Aho, Bellcore, Morristown, New Jersey
Jeffrey D. Ullman, Stanford University, Stanford, California

Alfred V. Aho and Jeffrey D. Ullman
Foundations of Computer Science

Egon Börger, Editor
Trends in Theoretical Computer Science

Ruth E. Davis
Truth, Deduction, and Computation: Logic and Semantics for Computer Science

A. K. Dewdney
The Turing Omnibus: 61 Excursions in Computer Science

Vladimir Drobot
Formal Languages and Automata Theory

Narian Gehani
Advanced C: Food for the Educated Palate
C: An Advanced Introduction, ANSI C Edition
C for Personal Computers: IBM PC, AT&T PC 6300, and Compatibles

Eitan M. Gurari
An Introduction to the Theory of Computation

Martti Mäntylä
An Introduction to Solid Modeling

Shamim Naqvi and Shalom Tsur
A Logical Language for Data and Knowledge Bases

Christos Papadimitriou
The Theory of Database Concurrency Control

Gregory J. E. Rawlins
Compared to What?: An Introduction to the Analysis of Algorithms

Stuart C. Shapiro
LISP: An Interactive Approach
COMMON LISP: An Interactive Approach

Richard Snodgrass
The Interface Description Language: Definition and Use

James A. Storer
Data Compression: Methods and Theory

Steven Tanimoto
Elements of Artificial Intelligence
Elements of Artificial Intelligence Using COMMON LISP

Jeffrey D. Ullman
Computational Aspects of VLSI
Principles of Database and Knowledge-Base Systems, Volume I: Classical Database Systems
Principles of Database and Knowledge-Base Systems, Volume II: The New Technologies
Theory of Relational Databases

Library of Congress Cataloging-in-Publication Data

Rawlins, Gregory J. E.
    Compared to what? : an introduction to the analysis of algorithms
  / by Gregory J. E. Rawlins
        p.   cm.
    Includes bibliographical references and index.
    ISBN 0-7167-8243-X
    1. Computer algorithms.   I. Title.
  QA76.9.A43R39   1991
  005. 1--dc20   91-30850
                                                        CIP

Printed in the United States of America

Computer Science Press
An imprint of W. H. Freeman and Company
The book publishing arm of *Scientific American*
41 Madison Avenue, New York, NY 10010
20 Beaumont Street, Oxford OX1 2NQ, England

1 2 3 4 5 6 7 8 9 0   RRD   9 9 8 7 6 5 4 3 2

This candle is for you, the beginner.
Turn it into a flame.

What comes from the heart, goes to the heart.

Samuel Taylor Coleridge, *Table Talk*

CONTENTS

LIST OF ALGORITHMS

LIST OF TABLES

FOREWORD

I am very pleased to have this new book in the Aho/Ullman series *Principles of Computer Science.* I see this book as a major step toward making computer science theory accessible to the wide range of students who need to know the subject. It covers a good segment of the classical material on data structures and algorithms, but it does so in a spritely way that involves and challenges the student at every turn of the page. I think you will be amused and challenged by the original examples and applications of these ideas.

The book concludes with an accessible introduction to the modern ideas in complexity theory. These include cryptography, complexity classes related to randomness, and interactive proofs. I hope the reader wil enjoy and profit from this book as I did.

Jeffrey D. Ullman
Stanford, California
September 1991

PREFACE

When I hear somebody sigh, 'Life is hard,'
I am always tempted to ask, 'Compared to what?'

Sydney J. Harris, *Majority of One*

Designing efficient programs requires some way to compare different methods of doing the same thing; it's hard to tell if something is good without comparing it to something else. One way to compare two programs solving the same problem is to run them on some representative inputs. But this only tells us how they behave on those inputs, leaving a number of questions unanswered. How will the programs do if run on other inputs? What is their worst performance? Their best performance? Their average performance? Which program is best?

These questions then lead to general questions about program design. What happens to a program's efficiency if we modify the program? What changes give the most improvement? What principles help in designing good programs in the first place? What is the best possible program for solving the problem? Is there a best program for the problem? Does every problem have a good program? Finally, how can we design the best program without wasting time writing, debugging, and running many duds? Analysis helps us answer all of these questions.

Well then, with all this talk of programs, what's an algorithm? An algorithm is a computational recipe: a general way to do something that is so specific that everyone—including our literal-minded friends, computers—can follow it. Every program is a particular instance of some algorithm, so an algorithm is a way of talking about a whole class of programs without worrying about machine-specific details. If you like, the algorithm is the thing that stays the same whether the program is in Pascal running on a Cray in New York or is in BASIC running on a Macintosh in Kathmandu.

Analyzing algorithms means working out the computational resources needed by problems and the algorithms that solve them, and using that information to design better algorithms. This book will help you to learn how to analyze algorithms.

TO THE STUDENT

> A book is a machine to think with.
>
> I. A. Richards, *Principles of Literary Criticism*

This book is about problem solving. Each chapter begins with a problem and progresses to a good solution while asking several questions. I divide these questions into pauses, exercises, problems, and research. Further, there are three types of pauses (pause, long pause, and very long pause) appearing throughout the chapter; pauses suggest the kinds of questions you should ask yourself as you read. I've left some pauses unsolved to keep you thinking, but I've solved most of them in the text, usually within a page or two. The three other types of questions appear at the end of the chapter. Exercises are usually harder than pauses, problems are difficult or require specialized knowledge, and, as far as I know, research problems are all unsolved.

Although it seems like extra work, you should try to solve as many problems as you can—even the solved ones. (Virgil said to beware programmers bearing proofs, didn't he?) Analysis is not a spectator sport; you learn things about yourself, particular problems, and problem solving in general, only by trying to solve problems. Along the same lines, you should program some of the algorithms in the language of your choice and attempt to improve the program further. Each algorithm should be easily programmable in Pascal, C, or Modula-2. (Virgil also may have said to beware theorists bearing programs.)

I want this book to help you solve computational problems but I have no magic problem-solving wand to give you. Students sometimes think that their instructor has a secret way to solve every problem and that they could never guess this secret. Well no technique solves all problems (a good thing too, otherwise we would all be out of a job). Don't defeat yourself before you begin by assuming that you can't solve a problem. Always remember that every solved problem was once a virgin; no matter how clever its current solution, *at one time no one knew how to solve it.*

I hope this book helps you produce efficient algorithms. I also hope it shows you something of the beauty of mathematics, and the power and clarity of thought it can give you. I've tried to make this book interesting, challenging, and fun. I hope you like it.

TO THE INSTRUCTOR

> Houses are built to live in and not to look on;
> therefore let use be preferred before uniformity,
> except where both may be had.
>
> Francis Bacon, *Essays: On Building*

I hope this book is easy to teach with, easy to learn from, and easy to read. While writing, three kibitzers helped me stick to that goal: an instructor, a student, and a general reader. The general reader was the easiest to please. He wanted a readable book telling him what's happening on the frontiers of analysis and suggesting some interesting unsolved problems. It wasn't hard to write for him since he is a computer professional, so I could count on his expertise. The instructor, too, knows what's what. She wanted me to cover certain topics and to include certain questions. Our biggest fights were over my unconventional presentation. Of the three, the student was the only one seeing this material for the first time; so I've tried hard to please the student. Here are four of the guidelines I followed, and my reasons for following them.

First, I put how-come before how-to. I develop each idea through a sequence of approximations to optimal solutions instead of posing a problem, stating the best known result, and then moving on to the next topic. Presenting only the best ideas makes students feel that they aren't smart enough to find something new. Further, students who are less involved with the material are less motivated to work with it. We need both Socrates and Aristotle in the search for knowledge, but in education today there is too much Aristotle and too little Socrates.

Second, I structured the book around problems, not techniques. For example, there is no chapter on divide and conquer, but it shows up several times as a solution strategy suggested naturally by the problem. It's difficult to motivate a strategy without first telling students what it's for. Rather than giving them a hammer and having them search for nails, I ask them to build a table and have them search for something hammer-like. After banging their thumbs with their shoes for a while students quickly come to appreciate the power and precision of good tools.

Third, to avoid distracting details I assume that algorithms are to be run on large inputs and that inputs can fit comfortably in fast memory. Both of these assumptions are distortions; in practice we have to worry about paging and block sizes, files and access protocols. Nonetheless, I stress the idea behind the algorithm and possible improvements, not programming concerns; it is best to confuse only one issue at a time. I do pay some slight attention to programming to prevent students believing that theoretically interesting algorithms are usable as is, or that the presented version of a popular algorithm (like quick sort) is the last word in efficiency.

Finally, I tried not to lose any students. I develop material in detail early in each chapter, particularly in the first two chapters, to make sure that the basics are understood. Each chapter gets more difficult as it progresses, but every student should be able to follow at least the first three sections of every chapter. With such a detailed treatment you have the option of teaching at almost any level of detail, knowing that students can fill in whatever they may have missed in class. If you deem material elementary you can assign it as home reading with some confidence that students can master it themselves. Overall, I've tried to help students understand why something is done and how they may have come up with that solution themselves—one day they will have to.

A FEW WORDS ABOUT USE

> Education is what survives when what
> has been learnt has been forgotten.
>
> B. F. Skinner, *"Education in 1984,"*
> *New Scientist, 484, 21 May 1964*

We usually advise students to do as many problems as possible; we know from hard experience that this is the best way to learn. But students, lacking that experience, don't see why they should do what looks like extra work. The solution that works for me is to construct assignments with some questions from the book, and to have open-book exams also with some questions from the book (or a research problem in a take-home exam). This way everyone wins because students want to solve as many questions as possible, and instructors have an almost ready-made set of assignments and exams. Open-book exams tend to emphasize thought over rote so this scheme also encourages students to really engage with the material. (Giving students only drill questions is like teaching them penmanship for four years, and then asking them to become novelists upon graduation.) Few of the end of chapter questions have been explicitly solved in other texts so open-book exams should be fair. Almost all questions are original and I have given references for every non-original exercise and problem.

To stop the book from growing even larger than it is I dropped search data structures (including hash arrays), amortized analysis, data compression algorithms, string algorithms, geometric algorithms, on-line algorithms, distributed algorithms, and parallel algorithms. The worst omission is probably parallel algorithms and I apologize for leaving it out, but a careful treatment of that topic alone would have doubled the book. The further readings section at the end of each chapter lists references to related material.

Even with the omissions, this book covers more material than is usually taught in a one-semester course. I have used it for a junior-level course by covering the appendices, the early parts of the first four chapters, and highlights of the last three chapters; for a middle-level course by sampling topics from most of the chapters; and for an advanced or graduate course by covering some topics in depth and tackling a few research problems. I recommend that all variations at least cover parts of chapters 1, 2, 6, and 7. Chapter 1 touches on most of the important analysis ideas; chapter 2 discusses some of the more prominent ideas through a specific example (the searching problem); chapter 6 contains an introduction to cryptology and tomography; and chapter 7 develops infeasibility and concludes at the frontiers of analysis.

Although earlier chapters are necessary to understand any chapter fully, I arranged the material so that later sections of each chapter are not necessary to understand early sections of the next chapter. I use a magnifying glass icon to signal subsections that go into greater mathematical detail; they may be skipped on a first reading. Finally, the problem treated in each chapter increases in computational cost. Roughly speaking: chapter 2 (searching) is logarithmic, chapter 3 (selection) is linear, chapter 4 (sorting) is sub-quadratic, chapter 5 (graphs) is quadratic, chapter 6 (arithmetic) is sub-exponential, and chapter 7 (infeasibility) is (perhaps!) exponential.

MY THANKS

> You may depend on my bare word, reader,
> without further guarantee, that I wish this book,
> this offspring of my brain, were as ingenious,
> sprightly, and accomplished as you could desire;
> unfortunately I could not avoid that decree of
> Nature requiring that like beget like.
>
> Miguel de Cervantes Saavedra, *Don Quixote*

This book is a record of my travels through the continent of analysis over the past six years. It is a distillate of my course notes for graduate and undergraduate classes on foundations of computing, data structures, theory of computation, and analysis of algorithms, taught at the University of Waterloo and at Indiana University from 1986 to 1991. This book was a lot of fun to write, particularly because it was a joint effort with a lot of fun people, who I now thank.

First, I thank my parents for making it possible; without their experience and uncritical support nothing would be possible. And I thank Benton Leong, Ian Munro, Gaston Gonnet, Arto Salomaa, and Derick Wood, for giving me the theory bug; this book is a result of their infectious enthusiasm. I especially thank Derick for too much to mention here; this book would not have been possible without him.

I thank Joe Culberson at the University of Alberta, John Franco at the University of Cincinnati, and Greg Shannon at Indiana University, for class-testing the book before publication. They put up with an apparently endless succession of drafts, and their comments helped to shape the book. I thank my own classes for foolishly allowing me to experiment on them, and I thank my department for providing the services I used to complete the book from a multitude of scattered files and even more scattered notes. I thank Stephen Ryner, Jr. who did an excellent job drawing the cartoons, and I thank Indiana University's Center for Innovative Computer Applications who provided technical support for his artwork. I thank Terry Jones and Lisa Thomas for their amazing job collaborating on the crosswords. I typeset the book using LaTeX, thanks to the heroic efforts of John Sellens at Waterloo, and Steve Hayman, Caleb Hess, and Bruce Shei at Bloomington.

I have benefited enormously from the comments of early readers at Bell Northern Research, Carnegie-Mellon University, Dartmouth College, the Georgia Institute of Technology, Indiana University, the University of Alberta, the University of British Columbia, the University of Chile, the University of Cincinnati, the University of Illinois, the University of Manitoba, and the University of Waterloo. I profusely thank:

> Angela Allen, Ricardo Baeza-Yates, Phil Bradford, Jon Buss, Dave Chalmers, Mert Cramer, Rob Day, Ruth Eberle, Dave Forsey, Dan Friedman, Dave Goldberg, Mayer Goldberg, Judy Goldsmith, Merav Harris, Brian Heck, Dan Jacobson, Rick Kazman, Sushil Louis, Marek Lugowski, Xiaoyang Luo, Gary McGraw, Lisa Meeden, Jon Mills, Raymundo Morado, Octavian Nicoliou, John Nienart, Paul Van Oorschot, Jacqueline Pulliam, Paul Purdom, Darrell Raymond, Brian Ridgely, Mary Rodes, Steve Ryner, Peter Shirley, Raja Sooriamurthi, John Stasko, Neelakantan Sundaresan, Gek Woo Tan, Yufeng Tsui, Dedaimia Whitney, and David Wise.

Each of them read various portions of various stages of the manuscript and clearly explained to me why it was all wrong. I especially thank Joe Culberson and Terry Jones for their many ideas and for steadfastly wading through so very many iterations.

I thank my consulting editor, Jeffrey D. Ullman at Stanford University, for valuable discussions on the structure and content of the book, and I thank my reviewers for their thorough and insightful comments:

> Susan Anderson-Freed at Illinois Wesleyan University, Susanne Hambrusch at Purdue University, Ming Kao at Duke University, Peter A. Ng at the New Jersey Institute of Technology, M. V. Ramakrishna at Michigan State University, Ivan Rival at the University of Ottawa, Violet R. Syrotiuk at the University of Manitoba, and Robert A. Walker at Rensselaer Polytechnic Institute.

Last, I thank my editor Nola Hague for putting up with me; somehow she endured the hundreds of hours this book took to get from prospectus to publication with patience, diligence, and wit. I further thank the other wonderful people at Freeman for doing such a great job producing the book. I cannot forget the intriguing combination of vivacity and charm coupled with dedication and professionalism of Freeman president Linda Chaput, Mark Dazzo, Greg Edwards, Christine Kempski, and the many others who made this such an enjoyable experience.

This book will never be finished, only published. To the extent that it is good, thank the readers. In closing, I thank you for acquiring this book. I hope that it is useful to you and I hope you enjoy it as much as I enjoyed writing it.

G. J. E. R.
rawlins@iuvax.cs.indiana.edu

CONVENTIONS

"What's the good of Mercator's North Poles and Equators,
Tropics, Zones, and Meridian Lines?"
So the Bellman would cry: and the crew would reply
"They are merely conventional signs!"

Lewis Carroll, *The Hunting of the Snark*

To begin with we need some special symbols. Theorists have a shorthand language to set them apart from everyone else. To become a member of the club you have to learn the mathematical equivalent of a secret handshake.

Write this	Say this
$\forall$	for all, *or* for every, *or* for each
$\exists$	there exists, *or* there is, *or* for some, *or* for at least one
$\in$	is an element of, *or* is in, *or* in
$\implies$	implies, *or* only if, *or* is sufficient for
$\iff$	implies and is implied by, *or* if and only if, *or* is necessary and sufficient for

Any symbol with a diagonal stroke through it is the *negation* of the symbol. Thus, $\neq$ means "not equal," $\not\implies$ means "does not imply." These conventions apply everywhere; the ones that follow are specific to this book.

Integers

The symbols i, j, k, l, m, and n will always be integer variables and the symbols a, b, c, and d will always be integer constants.

Reals

The symbols w, x, y, and z will always be real variables and the symbols r, s, t, u, and v will always be real constants. The symbols p and q are also real variables but they are reserved for probabilities.

Functions

The symbols f, g, and h will always be functions. In this book functions almost always map positive integers to positive reals, and are nondecreasing (that is, $n \geq m \implies f(n) \geq f(m)$).

integer constants	functions	integer variables	probabilities	real constants	real variables
$a\,b\,c\,d$	$f\,g\,h$	$i\,j\,k\,l\,m\,n$	$p\,q$	$r\,s\,t\,u\,v$	$w\,x\,y\,z$

Pause | What letters don't have a default type?

Subscripts

A subscripted symbol is of the same type as the unadorned symbol. For example, since f is always a function then f_1, f_2, and f_3, are also functions.

Statements

By default all variables are greater than zero. Thus, the statement "$\forall n$" (or i, j, k, l, or m) is shorthand for "$\forall$ positive integers n." To specifically include zero we say "$\forall n \geq 0$." Similar rules apply to the reals.

Icons

Several subsections throughout the book are marked with one of three icons. The first icon identifies subsections that introduce material of general interest that is specifically useful for analysis. The second icon identifies subsections that introduce an idea widely applicable when fashioning algorithms. The third icon identifies subsections that are in more mathematical detail than the previous text, and can safely be skipped on a first reading.

'What is the use of a book,' thought Alice,
'without pictures or conversations?'

Lewis Carroll, *Alice's Adventures in Wonderland*

Our first aim has been to write an
interesting book, and one unlike other
books. We may have succeeded at
the price of too much eccentricity, or
we may have failed; but we can
hardly have failed completely, the
subject matter being so attractive that
only extravagant incompetence
could make it dull.

G. H. Hardy and E. M. Wright,
An Introduction to the Theory of Numbers

A great man quotes bravely, and will not
draw on his invention when his memory
serves him with a word as good.

Ralph Waldo Emerson,
"Quotation and Originality," Letters and Social Aims

A facility for quotation covers
the absence of original thought.

Dorothy L. Sayers, *Gaudy Night*

Ridentem dicere verum, quid vetat.
[What forbids us to tell the truth, laughing?]

Horace, *Satires, I.24*

1

OVERVIEW

First I'll instruct thee in the rudiments,
And then wilt thou be perfecter than I.

Christopher Marlowe, *Doctor Faustus*

H OW CAN we decide in advance how long a program will take to run? Suppose we're writing a large graphics program to produce and display an animated movie on a bitmapped screen—a screen with more than a million directly addressable points, called pixels (picture elements). To fool the human eye into believing the motion is continuous, the program must generate at least thirty new images every second. So the program needs to do at least thirty million operations per second. Further, each of these operations can be quite complex depending on the complexity of the movie—for example, a black-and-white movie of a bouncing ball versus a full-color animation of Bugs Bunny.

It isn't sensible to run the program to see if it's too slow. If it's too slow we have to change it to speed it up. But, with no guiding principles to aid prediction, every time we change the program we have to rerun it to find out how long it takes after the change. This is frustrating, it wastes our time, and it wastes computer resources. Worse, it isn't even guaranteed to make the program fast enough. On the other hand, if the program is fast enough for the current movie we still won't know if it will be fast enough for more complex movies. In both cases we need a way to predict—based on the time it takes to produce simple scenes—how much time it will take to produce complex scenes. We need a yardstick to measure the program's performance as a function of the movie's complexity. To clarify what this yardstick should be like, let's consider two commonplace problems—washing dishes and reading books.

Suppose we want to find out about, say, llamas, from one of several books on llamas. Which book should we read? To choose, we need a measure of the books' reading complexity: a "book difficulty" yardstick. Four possible ones are: book length, average word length, average sentence length, and vocabulary size divided by the number of pictures. There is a relation between the sizes of each of these numbers and a book's difficulty—the larger the number, the harder the book is to read. But not all are good difficulty measures because they're not equally easy to compute, and they're not equally good at prediction. A convenient measure should have at least four characteristics:

- it should measure effort we care about;

- it should be quantitative, so that it's easy to compare two books;

- it should be easy to compute, so that computing it isn't as hard as simply reading the books; and

- it should be a good predictor, so that it's easy to predict a new book's difficulty.

Let's see how these ideas work with a household problem—dishwashing. To analyze this problem we have to select a measure of the size of the problem and a measure of the work needed to solve it. First, the number of dirty dishes seems like a good measure of problem size—the larger the number, the more work we have to do. But there are other plausible measures. For example, some of the dirty dishes could be large pots, or we could have fine china that we have to wash separately. So we could also use size or fragility to measure problem size. Second, the amount of time we take seems like a good measure of effort. But, again, there are other plausible measures: for example, the amount of water we use, or the amount of kitchen counter space we use; in a drought or a kitchenette each of these could be more important than time. Thus this example shows that we can measure both problem size and solution effort in many ways.

In general, to analyze a problem we need to pick a measure of problem size and a measure of solution effort, then see how they relate; the measure of solution effort should have at least the four properties itemized above. In the book-reading problem, the two measures could be book length and reading time. Having found how they relate we can look at a new problem instance, find its size, and plug that into the relation we've previously derived to estimate the work needed to solve the new instance. For example, in the dishwashing problem we may estimate that one dish takes one minute, so tonight's dinner party will take half an hour. Further, if someone suggests a new way of washing dishes (for example, buying a dishwasher) we have a way to compare the two methods.

Now let's apply our insights from these two common problems to programs. Time, as they say, is money, so let's assume that only a program's speed matters. How can we measure a program's speed without running it? We cannot compare two programs simply by running them, because their run times depend on the programmer, language, compiler, operating system, and machine. But if we have no particular language or machine in mind, how can we tell how fast each program is? Can we even talk about programs when we don't have a particular language in mind? Instead of thinking of a particular program we should consider the idea behind the program, the *algorithm*—the language- and machine-independent strategy the program uses. Algorithms are to programs like plots are to novels.

Now how can we compare the speeds of two algorithms solving the same problem? Guided by our two household examples, we see that we need a function of the problem instance that reflects the work the algorithm must do to solve the problem for that instance. This will be a good measure of how fast the algorithm is. Specifically, we can count some set of operations that the algorithm performs, then we can derive a rough estimate of the number of such operations required as inputs increase in size. With such a function we can predict how long the algorithm will take on large problem instances, and we can compare two or more algorithms solving the same problem to find the most efficient one.

Let's see how this works with a simple programming example. For simplicity let's assume that:

- assigning a value to a variable takes a fixed time, and
- all other operations take no time.

Let's call these two assumptions the *model* that we use to analyze the problem.

Now look at the three code fragments in figure 1.1. The first code fragment performs one assignment, the second performs $n+1$ assignments, and the third performs n^2+1 assignments. Suppose that all three fragments do the same thing to the variable *sum*.

$\boxed{Pause}$ Do they?

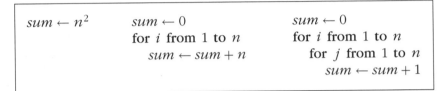

Figure 1.1   Three code fragments

If we had to choose a fragment based on speed alone, we would surely pick the first over the second, and the second over the third. Under our simplifying assumptions (our model), assignments are the only operations that matter. (This is false if squaring n takes longer than doing n additions.) *Within this model,* the first fragment is cheaper than the second, and the second is cheaper than the third. And this is independent of the actual cost of an assignment.

What's more, there is a big difference between the first and second fragments. No matter what n is, the first fragment always does a fixed amount of work. However, as n grows, the second fragment does work proportional to n (see figure 1.2). Thus, the ratio of the work done by the second fragment to the work done by the first fragment is *unbounded.* The second fragment does roughly n times as much work as the first, and n can, we presume, become arbitrarily large.

Further, the same relation holds between the second fragment and the third; n^2 grows much faster than n. To see this, imagine extrapolating the numbers in table 1.1 out to the problem sizes that computers usually deal with. For example, if n is a million, then n^2 is a million times larger than n. As n increases, the ratio of the run times of the third to the second (or the second to the first) grows without bound. The *growth rates* of the three code fragments are different.

Think about growth rates in terms of the change in the amount of work the fragments do when the input doubles in size. If we double the input (n), the first fragment's run time stays the same, the second fragment's run time doubles, and the third fragment's run time quadruples!

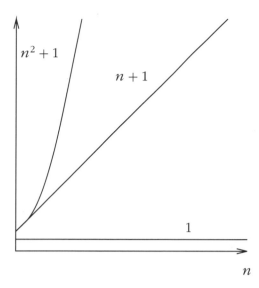

Figure 1.2 Number of assignments the three fragments execute

So if deep in our graphics program we have to square n once per pixel, and if our simplistic model is reasonable, then we should pick the first fragment.

n	1	2	3	4	5	6	7	8	9	10
1	1	1	1	1	1	1	1	1	1	1
$n+1$	2	3	4	5	6	7	8	9	10	11
n^2+1	2	5	10	17	26	37	50	65	82	101

Table 1.1 Comparison shopping

Pause If the run time grows like n^3, what happens if we double the input?

In this book we're going to explore a continent—the continent of analysis. Geographic explorers wanted adventure, trade, or fortune; knowledge, land, or freedom. We want to use our machines effectively, to solve our problems efficiently, and to find the limits of the possible. The territory we're about to explore is mostly uncharted but for a few settlements here and a number of outposts there. Often we will be on the frontier;

at times we will be pioneers. To gear up for the trek we will need tools and weapons—pathfinding through difficult country is rough work. This chapter gives you the tools every pioneer started with, and the next six chapters take you on treks through different parts of the continent.

Each problem is a river to ford, a ravine to cross, a mountain to climb, but we will attack all of them in the same way. Here's our plan:

- We start by recognizing a *problem*. This problem must be of the restricted kind that we can solve on digital computers.

- First, we build an abstract *model* so that we can talk about the problem and decide between different solutions to it. One way to cross a mountain range is to fly over it, but that's not a valid solution if we happen not to have a plane. The model is an inventory of the tools at our disposal to solve the problem, and it determines the yardstick we use to choose between alternate valid solutions to the problem.

- Next, we design an *algorithm* to solve the problem within the model. An algorithm is some way to solve the problem, using only the tools allowed by the model, that is clear enough that even a computer can follow it.

- Then, we *analyze* both the algorithm and the problem within the model.

  - Analyzing the algorithm gives us an *upper bound* on the work sufficient to solve the problem within the model.

  - Analyzing the problem gives us a *lower bound* on the work necessary to solve the problem within the model.

- Finally, we compare the upper and lower bounds to see if the solution is good enough. If it isn't, then either we redesign the algorithm or we try to prove a better lower bound. If that doesn't work we change the model. And if *that* doesn't work we change the problem!

During the first five sections of this chapter we will explore these stages using one problem as an example. Then, in sections 1.6 and 1.7 we will stock our knapsacks with some tools and weapons. The tools will help us reason about growth rates, and the weapons will help us tame wild functions. Finally, in section 1.9 we will encounter some important hard problems.

Now let us begin.

1.1   Problems

> And there's a dreadful law here—it was made
> by mistake, but there it is—that if anyone asks
> for machinery they have to have
> it and keep on using it.
>
> Edith Nesbit, *The Magic City*

We want to identify computationally solvable problems, and for each such problem we want bounds on the computation cost. First we only consider problems that are well-defined enough to be solved on computers. Then we restrict ourselves further to problems that we can divide into **sizes**. For each size there may be many **instances** of the problem. For example, every time we wash dishes we're solving an instance of the dishwashing problem; each instance is different, if only in time, but many of them may have the same size (say, the number of dishes).

To solve an instance of the problem we first code the instance to form an input to an algorithm. We then feed this input to the algorithm and the algorithm produces some output. Then we decode this output into an answer for the problem instance. To **solve** a problem we must show that we can go through this process for any instance of the problem.

One nice thing about digital computers is that once we find a solution for all instances of a problem of one size, we can use it for instances of any size. Further, it is usually not interesting to solve a problem for small sizes; those are often solved faster by hand. So we're interested in well-defined problems whose instances we can group by size, and we want efficient solutions when those sizes are large.

Grouping problem instances by size is like grouping books by their page length (or word count, or any other quantitative measure). For example, using length as our size measure, the set of all fifty page books is the set of instances of the book-reading problem of size fifty. Note how arbitrary this notion of size is; in the introduction we considered using page count *itself* as a measure of the reading difficulty of a book. In effect, we pick one "natural" measure, then see how another measure relates to it.

Selecting a natural measure is not always easy to do. For example, suppose we want to arrange some books by height. One natural size for this problem is the number of books, since the more books there are to arrange the more work there is to do. But this assumes that one book is much like another. If one of the books is as big as the Encyclopædia Britannica then we should take weight into account as well.

Okay, pretend we have a reasonable measure of input size. Now we have to estimate the difficulty of each instance of the problem in terms of its size. We want a function of the problem's size that reflects the effort necessary to solve the problem. So far we have assumed that the first thing to look at is the program's speed. But, our machine may have little memory, so we could look for programs that use the least memory. Similarly, it could be important to reduce the number of disk accesses, the number of comparisons, the number of assignments, or the number of multiplications. In general, there are an infinite number of combinations of program attributes we could try to improve.

We could also choose among programs using more intangible properties. For example: how hard they are to write, how hard they are to modify, and how hard they are to understand. However, lacking a formal definition of these important properties let's leave these measures of program cost to software engineering. This is like trying to measure the difficulty of writing a book, not reading it.

Thus, our aim is to solve problems with as little *computational effort* per problem instance as possible. Sometimes to reduce computational effort we expend great conceptual effort; we only do the conceptual work once but the resulting program does the computational work every time we run it.[1]

One more thing: to do this analysis we need mathematics. Some people confuse mathematics with mere symbol manipulation, but mathematics is much more about critical thinking than it is about symbols. Thinking mathematically forces us to identify our assumptions and so deal with the unusual. As a corollary, we shouldn't be surprised if we derive counter-intuitive results using mathematics; in a way, that's what it's for. It's especially dangerous to rely only on intuition when designing algorithms since computers typically deal with huge problem sizes, and we don't. Intuition is a product of everyday experience and most of us don't think about things with many parts every day. For example, we have a hard time appreciating the effects predicted by quantum theory—we call quantum effects "counter-intuitive." A ball in a bucket does not spontaneously jump through the wall of the bucket, yet this is precisely what electrons do in potential wells, their analogues of buckets.

Similarly, when designing an algorithm we tend to think of the algorithm working on about ten items when in fact we're going to use it on a million items. As we have seen, any display program producing graphics on a bitmapped screen must look at about a million pixels just to process one screenful. And this is not even counting the work the program must do per pixel. Anything being repeated a million times per screenful must be

---

[1]Besides being a great poet Yeats was obviously a great programmer: "A line will take us hours maybe/ Yet if it does not seem a moment's thought,/ Our stitching and unstitching has been naught." W. B. Yeats, *Adam's Curse*.

as fast as possible. Further, even if any one problem instance is small, when there are a million instances even small improvements per instance magnify into large savings.

In sum, the Holy Grail of analysis is to put our computational resources to the best possible use. Given the choice between a ten-second solution and a ten-hour solution we would be crazy to choose the ten-hour solution. Of course, the ten-hour solution is perfectly acceptable if we only have to solve the problem once, or if the ten-second solution is hard to program, or is otherwise expensive. But this is just a more general version of the same goal—we are still trying to reduce effort, the only difference is that now "effort" includes more than just the computer resources used in a solution.

Problem Types

We can classify computational problems by problem requirements and problem difficulty.

In terms of problem requirements there are six computational problems:

- Search problems: Find an X in the input satisfying property Y.

- Structuring problems: Transform the input to satisfy property Y.

- Construction problems: Build an X satisfying property Y.

- Optimization problems: Find the best X satisfying property Y.

- Decision problems: Decide whether the input satisfies property Y.

- Adaptive problems: Maintain property Y over time.

Chapters two and three examine search problems; chapters four and five examine structuring problems; chapters five and six examine construction problems; and chapters six and seven examine optimization and decision problems. We will rarely examine adaptive problems even though they are of great practical importance and they include many real systems (such as operating systems, adaptive control systems, and server systems). Adaptive problems involve practical issues beyond the scope of this book.

Instead of tackling a realistic version of a problem we will look at a simplified version—a toy problem. Toy problems do not include memory management issues and other important details. Although unrealistic, toy problems are useful because we can solve them without the clutter attendant on more realistic versions of the same problem. Thus they better expose the problem's inherent difficulty. We can then use lessons learned while solving toy problems to solve more realistic problems—in the same way that law students use old cases.

We can also classify problems by difficulty. There are four categories of hard problems:

- A conceptually hard problem: We don't have an algorithm to solve this problem because we don't understand the problem well enough.

- An analytically hard problem: We have an algorithm to solve this problem, but we don't know how to analyze how long it will take to solve every problem instance.

- A computationally hard problem: We have an algorithm and we have analyzed it, but analysis suggests that relatively small problem instances will take millions of years to solve.
  This category splits into two groups: problems we *know* are computationally hard, and problems we *suspect* are computationally hard.

- A computationally unsolvable problem: We don't have an algorithm to solve this problem because no such algorithm can exist.

We can use these four categories to differentiate among three subfields of computer science: artificial intelligence explores problems in the first and second categories; complexity theory, of which analysis is a part, explores problems in the second and third categories; and computability theory explores problems in the third and fourth categories.

In this book, our central metaproblem revolves around the third category. What does it mean to say that a problem is computationally hard? We will return to this question at the end of this chapter (page 52) and in chapter seven.

Let's use the following toy problem as a running example of the analysis process. After discussing each step in solving an arbitrary problem we'll turn to our example problem to see how the step works in practice. As the analysis proceeds we will see the problem first as conceptually hard, then analytically hard, and finally computationally hard.

The towers of Hanoi problem: Given three pegs and n disks of different sizes placed in order of size on one peg (see figure 1.3), transfer the disks from the original peg to another peg with the constraints that:

- each disk is on a peg,

- no disk is ever on a smaller disk, and

- only one disk at a time is moved.

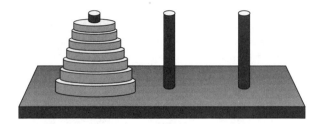

Figure 1.3 The Hanoi problem with seven disks

The towers of Hanoi problem was invented by the French mathematician Édouard Lucas in 1883, and he invented the following story to go with it: it seems that there is a similar three-peg arrangement at the "Tower of Brahma" in Benares, India, except that in Benares there are sixty-four gold disks on three diamond pegs. Legend has it that when the temple priests have moved all the disks to another peg the world will come to an end. If the priests can move a disk from one peg to another in one second, how long does the world have yet to exist?

As you can see, this problem is of great practical importance.

1.2   Models

> A good model represents a well-balanced
> abstraction of a real practical situation—not
> too far from and not too close to
> the real thing.
>
> Arto Salomaa, *Computation and Automata*

Given a problem, we first select a model so that we can talk about the problem sensibly. To tell whether something is a solution to the problem we pick a set of legal operations that solutions can use. And to distinguish between good and bad solutions we pick an operation, or set of operations, in that set to minimize. The set of legal operations is the **environment** and the subset of operations we want to minimize is the **goal**. The environment and the goal together make up the **model**. Choosing an environment includes choosing the kind of machine that solutions will run on, the type of language that solutions will be written in, and the character of the physical environment that the machine runs in. For example, we usually assume, contrary to reality, that cosmic rays will not disrupt the machine.

Choosing a set of operations and restricting attention to only a few is analogous to scientific modelling, in which we abstract some essential feature and examine it alone. A physicist examining falling bodies first assumes that air resistance is negligible and that the body's mass is minuscule compared to the mass of the earth. As she better understands these simple situations she allows drag due to air (and the like) back into the equations of motion until she arrives at a good approximation to the fall of real bodies. As she removes more and more simplifying assumptions, the model behaves more and more like the real system.

The analysis grail is to minimize all resources used. This, like the Holy Grail, is difficult to attain; so to begin we will count the number of times only *one* easily identifiable operation is performed (for example, an addition, a comparison, a disk access). We assume that the chosen operation is proportional to the total computational resources that the problem requires. Our goal then is to attain grace by minimizing the number of times we perform a chosen operation while restricting ourselves to solutions within a well-defined, and small, model. When choosing a model, we will usually assume that the crucial operation is proportional to the run time of the algorithm we choose to solve the problem. Usually the chosen operation is expensive, or frequent, or it otherwise reflects the overall amount of work done.

Here's how this works for the dishwashing problem. Suppose we choose to measure problem size by the number of dishes to be washed. Suppose we want to predict how much time a new problem instance will take (as opposed, say, to how much water it will take). First, we select the set of operations that we can use to solve the problem; for instance, picking up a dish, immersing it, applying soap, and so on. Different choices of legal operations determine different models. For example, one model may assume that we have a dishwasher!

After choosing the legal operations we choose one as a barometer for all the others. For instance, it's likely that drying a dish is no harder than washing a dish. And, since we must dry every dish we wash, we may choose to count only the number of times we wash a dish and ignore drying. Note that we have made the further assumption that overall washing time (the property we're trying to reduce) is proportional to the time taken to wash each dish. Finally, note that we only know that it is proportional, we don't know the actual time it will take. That's good enough because we can compare two or more solutions in the same model based only on proportionality information. Further, we can always find the actual time by running experiments to determine the constant of proportionality.

The two assumptions given for the problem of squaring n (page 3), together with some reasonable assumptions about a suitable machine, constitute a model for that problem. In this model, the goal is to minimize the number of assignments since, by assumption, assignments are the only operations that matter. Further, in this model, the first fragment is the best program for the problem. There is no guarantee, however, that this model captures the real difficulty of the problem. After deciding on a model we have to go back to reality to check its predictive power. Only after checking predictions against reality can we be sure that the model captures the essence of the problem's difficulty.

For instance, suppose we run each of the three fragments with several inputs and discover that their run times are about the same, no matter how large the input is. That tells us that assignments don't matter that much (or that the compiler is changing our code). Alternately, we may find that the run times roughly follow predicted behavior. Now suppose the problem is so frequent, expensive, or important that we need a really good estimate of future run times. Then, *and only then,* should we add more sophisticated measures to our model in an effort to get more accurate time predictions (for example, we may decide that additions should also be counted).

Our default environment will be that we are running our algorithms on errorless, sequential, digital computers, and that we will translate our algorithms into programs in an imperative language (like Pascal). Our environment for the towers of Hanoi problem will be the default environment plus the three constraints defining legal moves (page 10). Our goal will be to reduce the total number of disk moves.

1.3   Algorithms

It has often been said that a person does not really understand something until he teaches it to someone else. Actually a person does not *really* understand something until he can teach it to a *computer.*

Donald E. Knuth,
"Computer Science and Its Relation to Mathematics,"
American Mathematical Monthly, 81, 1974

Having chosen a model for the problem, next we devise an algorithm to solve the problem. This algorithm must use only the operations allowed within the model. Up to this point we haven't seen a formal definition of an algorithm, nor (surprise!) will we see one now. For now, an **algorithm** is a finite sequence of operations, each chosen from a finite set of well-defined operations, that halts in a finite time.

That looks like a definition, but it really isn't. It places some restrictions on what an algorithm can possibly be (for example, it cannot take indefinitely long to describe) but it doesn't say what an algorithm *is*. A really useful definition would allow us to "mechanically" recognize an algorithm whenever we saw one, in the same way that we can recognize alarm clocks. This is hard because algorithms come bundled with the idea of *human purpose;* we intend an algorithm to accomplish some goal. Unfortunately, and unlike alarm clocks, no two algorithms necessarily have the same goal (beyond the complex one of "solving a problem"). To get to a formal definition will take us most of this book. So, for the time being, when you see *algorithm* think *recipe, prescription, procedure, method, strategy, technique,* or *computation.*

∞

All right, now let's design an algorithm solving the towers of Hanoi problem. The first thing to do when confronted with a problem is to solve the problem for its smallest instances. Perhaps there is some insight there that we can generalize to larger instances. For the towers of Hanoi problem the most natural size is the number of disks, n; also, for each size there is only one problem instance. When $n = 1$ or $n = 2$ the problem is easy; however $n = 3$ requires a little thought to minimize the number of moves. Label the three pegs in figure 1.3 [p. 11] A, B, and C, and suppose we have to move the disks from A to C. If we move the smallest disk to B then we will be in trouble when we move the second smallest to C, since C is the eventual destination of the largest disk. Thus, we must move the second smallest, which means that we must move the smallest.

This seems to imply that we should first put the smallest on C, then the second smallest on B, and finally the smallest on top of the second smallest thereby leaving C free for the biggest disk. Now what does this imply when we have n disks? Well, when we're ready to move the biggest disk (which is still sitting patiently on A), there can't be any disks on top of it since we can only move one disk at a time. So, all the smaller disks must be on B. Also, the $n - 1$ disks on B must be stacked in order of size, otherwise some disk must be on top of a smaller one.

Pause Think about this before reading on.

Okay, at some point the biggest disk is alone on A and all $n - 1$ smaller disks are piled neatly on B. There is nothing on C in preparation for the big move. Now observe that all the time the biggest disk was patiently sitting on A, *the other disks were oblivious to it.* Why? Well, the rules say that no disk may be put on a smaller disk, but since the biggest disk is bigger than all others, it is always legal to place any other disk on A if there is nothing on A besides the biggest disk!

If we could only solve the same towers of Hanoi problem but with $n-1$ disks and with a different destination peg (B instead of C) then we could solve our version of the problem! But how, you squeak, can we solve a problem in terms of itself? Isn't this circular reasoning? Well, no. In the reduction of the problem with n disks to one with $n-1$ disks we know that the process will eventually stop since the number of disks is decreasing and we know how to solve one and two disk problems.

Let's go back to the $n = 3$ case. There we realized that we needed to make a tower of the two smallest disks on B before we could move the biggest disk from A to C. So, if only we could solve the $n = 2$ case (but for a different destination peg) then we could solve the $n = 3$ case (try it). But we can easily solve the $n = 2$ case. Thus, when $n = 3$, we first move the top two disks to B (three moves), move the biggest disk to C (one move), then move the two disks on B to C (three moves). So three disks take no more than seven moves. See figure 1.4.

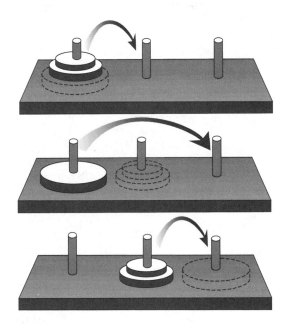

Figure 1.4 Solving the Hanoi problem with three disks

In general, we have n disks and we want to move them from A to C. Our algorithm is to first move the top $n-1$ disks from A to B, move the biggest disk from A to C, then move the $n-1$ disks on B to C. An algorithm that uses itself to solve a problem is called a **recursive** algorithm. See algorithm 1.1; the pegs have been given more meaningful names in the algorithm.

> HANOI (*Start*, *Temp*, *End*, *n*)
>   { Solve the towers of Hanoi problem for $n \geq 1$ disks. }
>
>   **if** $n = 1$
>   **then**
>   move *Start*'s top disk to *End*
>   **else**
>   HANOI (*Start*, *End*, *Temp*, $n - 1$)
>   move *Start*'s top disk to *End*
>   HANOI (*Temp*, *Start*, *End*, $n - 1$)

Algorithm 1.1

How did we find this algorithm? The first ideas came from feeling out the problem for small n. Then we looked at large n and tried to generalize the insights generated from the first phase. Finally we went back to small n to see if the generalized insights made sense.

> ***The forward-backward strategy:*** Solve simple special cases and generalize their solution, then test the generalization on other special cases.

Depending on how insightful we are in the first phase, and how well we generalize in the second phase, this procedure could repeat many times. *Think small, then think big.* This strategy is very handy, but it won't do well on problems whose best solution for large n is not like their best solution for small n.

1.4 Analysis

> When we mean to build,
> We first survey the plot, then draw the model;
> And when we see the figure of the house,
> Then must we rate the cost of the erection.
>
> William Shakespeare, *Henry IV, part 2, III*

Having decided on an algorithm to solve the problem the next step is to analyze both the algorithm and the problem within the model. We want to estimate the resource cost of an algorithm either by itself or in comparison to other algorithms solving the same problem. And we would like to do that without writing, debugging, and then running programs. Further, we want to know if we're wasting time trying to improve the algorithm; perhaps it cannot be improved? In sum, we want to predict how bad an algorithm can get, and we want to determine how hard the problem is.

Upper Bounds

Analysis first involves figuring out bounds on the number of operations an algorithm performs given an input of size n. Usually we will first find its **worst cost,** that is, the maximum number of times it performs the chosen operation. Since the algorithm is proof that we can solve the problem using *at most* that number of operations, even in the worst case, this gives an **upper bound** on the problem's worst cost as a function of n.

We derive an upper bound for the problem within the model by working out the cost of the chosen algorithm on problem instances of a fixed size. The upper bound is a crude measure of the computational effort our algorithm requires. Should we design another algorithm having a smaller cost then, *if our assumptions about real costs are sensible,* we can discard the first algorithm. The worst cost of the algorithm is the worst that could happen, the pessimist's view. We could also be optimistic and find the **best cost** of the algorithm—the least work the algorithm could possibly get away with for some one input of a fixed size.

To put these definitions algebraically, suppose $\mathcal{A}$ is the algorithm we are analyzing and I_n is the set of all possible inputs to $\mathcal{A}$, each of size n. Let $f_{\mathcal{A}}$ be the function expressing the resource cost of $\mathcal{A}$; that is, if I is an input in I_n, then $f_{\mathcal{A}}(I)$ is the resource cost of $\mathcal{A}$ when given input I. Then

$$\text{worst cost}(\mathcal{A}) = \max_{I \in I_n} f_{\mathcal{A}}(I), \quad \text{best cost}(\mathcal{A}) = \min_{I \in I_n} f_{\mathcal{A}}(I)$$

where "$\max_{I \in I_n}$" means "the largest value where I ranges over I_n."

We could also look at the work the algorithm does in the not-so-good case, the tolerably-bad case, and so forth. Instead, observe that for a fixed input size the algorithm's best cost, not-so-good cost, tolerably-bad cost, and worst cost, all occur with some frequency. So, for example, its best cost may occur more often than its worst cost, and we would like a measure reflecting that. To derive this measure we find the algorithm's **average cost,** the average amount of resources the algorithm consumes assuming some plausible frequency of occurrence of each input in I_n.

Figure 1.5 gives resource usage graphs of three fictitious algorithms solving the same problem. In each graph the vertical axis represents the resource cost, f, and the horizontal axis represents I_n. In theory we can draw these graphs by picking a representative input size, running the three algorithms on each possible input of that size, and plotting the resource cost for each input. In practice we can't always do that because not all problems have a "representative" input size.

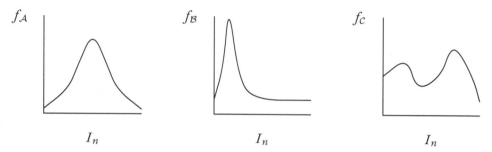

Figure 1.5   Resource usage graphs of three algorithms

In terms of its resource usage graph, an algorithm's worst cost is the highest value, and its best cost is the lowest value. See figure 1.6. The average cost is the average of the values weighted by the frequency of occurrence of the corresponding inputs relative to all inputs in I_n. (The frequency of occurrence of each element of I_n is not shown; it requires a separate computation.)

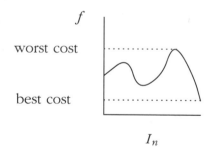

Figure 1.6   An algorithm's best and worst costs

Pause
Can the average cost be worse than the worst cost, or better than the best cost?

In figure 1.5, algorithm $\mathcal{A}$'s worst cost is lower than $\mathcal{B}$'s but higher than $\mathcal{C}$'s. Thus, if it's important to have a good worst cost, then we should pick $\mathcal{C}$. But if the best cost is important, then we should pick $\mathcal{A}$. Finally, $\mathcal{B}$ behaves well for about half of the inputs. Therefore, for some input frequencies, $\mathcal{B}$ should behave better on average than either $\mathcal{A}$ or $\mathcal{C}$.

The average cost is trickier to find than either the best or the worst cost. The only way to judge which of the three algorithms is preferable on average is to figure out with what frequency inputs occur. For example, in terms of the figure, if most of the inputs the algorithms face in practice come from the right-hand half of the input space, then $\mathcal{B}$ is probably best on average. But if most inputs come from the left-hand side, then $\mathcal{A}$ is probably the best on average.

So which algorithm is best? Each of the three complexity measures (best, worst, average) can favor a different algorithm! Now recall that we started off almost arbitrarily picking speed as our performance yardstick. There are an infinite number of other attributes we could use as yardsticks. Each of these yardsticks has a corresponding resource usage graph. For each of these graphs there are an infinite number of complexity measures we can use to judge between them. Finally, there can be an infinite number of algorithms all solving the same problem! As you can see, trying to find the "best" algorithm is insanely complicated. This forces us to ruthlessly pick only a few criteria to judge an algorithm's goodness. So given an algorithm, it's sensible to first find its worst cost; then, if the problem is important enough, its average cost. And that's what we'll do.

∞

The average cost of the towers of Hanoi problem is the same as its worst cost since there is only one problem instance of each problem size. (We've chosen problem size to be the number of disks, n.) So let's find its worst cost only.

We want a function, f, mirroring the total number of times algorithm HANOI (page 16) moves a disk. f should be a function of n since that is the only thing varying in the problem. If we can figure out such a function then we can estimate how the work needed to solve the problem grows as n grows (for example, to see when the priests will finish moving their sixty-four disks).

The simplest thing is to let $f(n)$ be the number of times HANOI moves a disk when solving the problem on n disks. At present we know three things about f: $f(1) = 1$, $f(2) = 3$, and $f(3) = 7$. Further, we can relate the work HANOI does to solve the n disk case *relative to* the work it does for the $n - 1$ case, namely:

$$f(n) = f(n - 1) + 1 + f(n - 1) = 2f(n - 1) + 1 , \quad \forall n \geq 4$$

Now $f(2) = 3 = 2f(1) + 1$ and $f(3) = 7 = 2f(2) + 1$. Thus, we can simplify our four facts to two: $f(1) = 1$ and $f(n) = 2f(n - 1) + 1$, $\forall n \geq 2$. Let's write this as follows:

$$f(n) = \begin{cases} 1 & n = 1 \\ 2f(n - 1) + 1 & n > 1 \end{cases}$$

This is called a **recurrence** because f shows up again (recurs) in its own definition. To find f we must solve the recurrence. That is, we want an easily computable expression that predicts HANOI's cost for any n.

The most obvious thing about the recurrence is that the values at least double if we add a disk ($f(n) > 2f(n-1)$). If we increase the number of disks from 1 to n, then each version of HANOI will take at least twice as long as the last. Now if we start with 1 and double it n times we will end with 2^n. So perhaps the time to solve an n-disk Hanoi is about 2^n (see table 1.2 for the first few powers of two). In fact, looking at the table we see that $f(n)$ is $2^n - 1$. Well that was easy.

n	1	2	3	4	5	6	7	8
2^n	2	4	8	16	32	64	128	256

n	9	10	11	12	13	14	15	16
2^n	512	1024	2048	4096	8192	16384	32768	65536

Table 1.2 Powers of two

Pause | Is this reasoning okay?

Unfortunately we have no reason to believe that the number of disk moves will always be $2^n - 1$ just because that's true for $n \leq 4$. For example, $5n$ is bigger than n^2 for $n \leq 4$, but it's less for all larger n. Fortunately there is an easy way to prove the result—by exploiting the recurrence defining f.

Pause | Do you see how?

We want to show that $f(n) = 2^n - 1$ for all n. Now if $f(n-1) = 2^{n-1} - 1$ and $n > 1$, then from the recurrence we know that

$$f(n) = 2f(n-1) + 1 = 2(2^{n-1} - 1) + 1 = 2^n - 1$$

So *if there is ever an n* for which $f(n) = 2^n - 1$, then from that point on f will always conform to this rule! Now, note that $f(1) = 1 = 2 - 1 = 2^1 - 1$. Therefore f conforms to the rule when $n = 1$; hence f always conforms to the rule.

Thus, when there are n disks, HANOI moves a disk exactly $2^n - 1$ times. Therefore, $2^n - 1$ disk moves is an upper bound on the towers of Hanoi problem. This is a **proof by induction**.

Using induction is like showing that we can climb an arbitrarily high ladder if we can show two things:

- We can climb onto a rung of the ladder. This is the **basis step** of the proof.

- If we can climb to the kth rung then we can climb to the $(k+1)^{th}$ rung. This is the **inductive step** of the proof.

With this understanding, here is the proof again.

Basis step: HANOI makes one disk move when $n = 1$, so $f(1) = 1$. (This is the **boundary condition** of the recurrence). So $f(1) = 2^1 - 1$. Therefore $f(n) = 2^n - 1$ when $n = 1$.

Inductive step: Suppose that for all $k < n$, $f(k) = 2^k - 1$. Then since $n > 1$, from the recurrence we must have that $f(n) = 2f(n-1) + 1$. But $n > n - 1$. Therefore $f(n) = 2(2^{n-1} - 1) + 1 = 2^n - 1$.

Hence, if the inductive assumption is true for all $k < n$ then it is true for n as well. Thus, $f(n) = 2^n - 1$ for all n.

Pause

Transform the recurrence to a new recurrence involving the function g where $g(n) = f(n) + 1$. What is $g(1)$? Does this new recurrence simplify the proof?

To grasp how big 2^n becomes after only a short time, observe that $2^{10} = 1,024$. Thus, ten disks require more than a thousand moves. $2^{20} = 1,048,576$ is more than a million; $2^{30} = 1,073,741,824$ is more than a billion; and $2^{40} = 1,099,511,627,776$ is more than a trillion.[2] In computer memories, 8 bits (binary dig*its*) is a *byte*, 2^{10} bytes is a *kilobyte*, 2^{20} bytes is a *megabyte*, 2^{30} bytes is a *gigabyte*, 2^{40} bytes is a *terabyte*, and 2^{50} bytes is a *petabyte*. Powers of two occur so often in analysis that you should memorize the first ten powers of two.

Pause

Roughly how many digits are there in a petabyte?

Lower Bounds

After finding an upper bound on the problem's difficulty we find the smallest number of operations necessary to solve the problem over all inputs of size n. And, again, usually first for the worst cost. This gives a **lower bound** on the problem's worst cost. A lower bound on the worst cost says that *at least* this much work must be done in the worst case. Note that the lower bound analysis is done *on the problem* and not on the algorithm; a lower bound must apply to all algorithms allowed within the model that solve the problem, not just the one we designed.

----

[2]This book takes a billion as thousand million, and a trillion as a thousand billion.

Long Pause Is a lower bound on the worst cost of the problem the same as the best cost of the algorithm?

For example, consider the dishwashing problem again. Suppose our model of the problem measures effort by the number of dishes we wash. If washing a dish is only a constant times more work than merely handling it then we can find a lower bound on the number of times we handle a dish. Since we must at least handle each dish, this in turn gives us a lower bound on the overall amount of work necessary to solve the problem.

For every problem and model there are an infinite number of algorithms allowed within the model that will solve the problem. This is true even though there are only a finite number of operations to choose from and each algorithm is composed of only a finite number of them. Each of these algorithms has a resource usage graph. Since all of the algorithms halt, each of these graphs has a highest point—its worst cost. If the worst cost for each graph is *at least* L, then L is a lower bound on the problem's worst cost (see figure 1.7). Thus, for example, zero is always a lower bound on the computational cost of any problem. *The* lower bound on the worst cost is the lowest, over all such graphs, of the highest points.

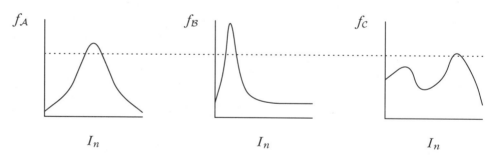

Figure 1.7 A possible lower bound on the worst cost

Long Pause Is this the same as the largest of all lower bounds on the worst cost of the problem?

Lower bounds are harder to find than upper bounds because we can find an upper bound by analyzing *any* algorithm allowed within the model, but to find a lower bound we have to analyze *all* algorithms allowed within the model. An upper bound is a measure of *how bad* a particular algorithm can be; a lower bound is a measure of *how hard* a particular problem is. Lower bounds are like the laws of thermodynamics, they can tell us that a perpetual motion machine is not possible, but they cannot help us build a jet engine.

HODGES DELIGHTED IN FINDING HOLES
IN LOWER BOUND ARGUMENTS

To define the lower bound on the worst cost algebraically, suppose that within the model M, $\mathcal{A}_M$ is the set of all algorithms each of which solve the problem P. Then

$$\text{the lower bound on the worst cost of } P = \min_{\mathcal{A} \in \mathcal{A}_M} \left\{ \max_{I \in I_n} f_{\mathcal{A}}(I) \right\}$$

We can also define the lower bound on the average cost of a problem and, similarly, on the best cost, and so on.

| Very Long Pause | Does every problem have a best (that is, largest) lower bound?

Now we see exactly what the model does for us: *Choosing a model is equivalent to choosing the set of algorithms that solve the problem.* In figure 1.8 P is a problem. For each problem there are an infinite number of models M. For each model there are an infinite number of algorithms $\mathcal{A}$. For each algorithm there are an infinite number of resource measures f. For each resource measure there are an infinite number of complexity measures C (best, worst, average, and so on). And, of course, there are an infinite number of problems, each of which has an infinite number of sizes.

Having found upper and lower bounds, we compare them to decide whether it's worthwhile to look for a more efficient solution than the one we already have. In figure 1.9 suppose that $f(n)$ is the (unknown) worst cost of P. Suppose we have some algorithm $\mathcal{A}$ within M that solves P. Let $g(n)$ be an upper bound on the worst cost of $\mathcal{A}$. Since $\mathcal{A}$ solves P

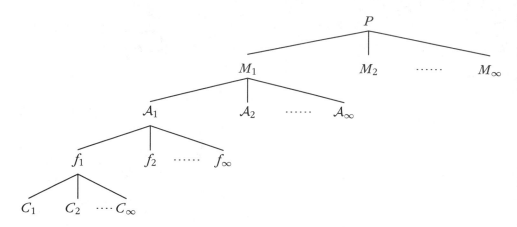

Figure 1.8 The five dimensions of the continent of analysis

and $g(n)$ is an upper bound on $\mathcal{A}$, it is also an upper bound on P. Finally, suppose $h(n)$ is a lower bound on the worst cost of P. Note that $g(n) \geq f(n) \geq h(n)$ only after some point. We only require the inequalities to hold for all inputs larger than some fixed size.

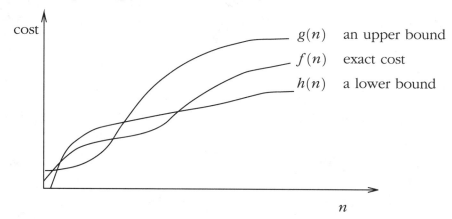

Figure 1.9 Bounds on the worst cost of a problem

If beyond some point $g(n) - h(n) \leq c$, for some constant c, then there is no point looking for a better algorithm; up to a constant, $\mathcal{A}$ is as good a solution as is possible within M. Within M, $\mathcal{A}$ is worst case **optimal** for P.[3] If $g(n) - h(n) \not\leq c$ for any c, even for large n, but beyond some point $g(n)/h(n) \leq c$, for some non-zero constant c then within M, $\mathcal{A}$ is worst case **asymptotically optimal** for P.

---

[3]Optimality depends on the model chosen; within a different model, a previously "optimal" algorithm may be bad since a different model may emphasize different resources or it may allow different operations.

| Pause | So a lower bound can tell us whether an algorithm is optimal; can it tell us whether an algorithm is *not* optimal?

Good lower bounds are usually hard to derive, so why bother with them? First, a lower bound can tell us whether an algorithm is optimal, or asymptotically optimal. (A lower bound cannot tell us whether an algorithm is *not* optimal unless we can show that it is the best possible lower bound.) Second, trying to prove a lower bound—work that must be done—helps us concentrate on what is actually done, and whether it's really necessary. Sometimes we then design improved algorithms because we understand the problem better. Finally, if we happen to derive a lower bound guaranteeing that within our present model no algorithm can do a reasonable job, then it's time to start thinking about whether we really want to solve the problem this particular way. Is there, perhaps, some way to relax the problem or to allow our algorithms more powerful operations by restricting the kinds of inputs we can expect? This observation cuts right to the heart of contemporary analysis; we will rejoin this train of thought at the end of section 1.9.

∞∞

Returning to Hanoi we see that $2n - 1$ is a lower bound on the problem since we must move every disk but the biggest at least twice (why?), and we must move the biggest at least once. But, as we see in table 1.2 [p. 20], this is not very close to our upper bound of $2^n - 1$ when n gets large. What is to blame for the huge difference? A weak lower bound? Or an inefficient algorithm?

Fortunately a stronger lower bound isn't that hard to find. As we've seen, any algorithm solving the problem must move the biggest disk from A to C and, whenever it does, all $n - 1$ other disks must be stacked neatly on B. But moving those disks from A to B using C as a temporary staging area is *at least as hard as solving the problem with $n - 1$ disks.* (Since the biggest disk is bigger than all the others it is effectively invisible to them.) Thus, solving an n-disk problem is at least as hard as solving an $(n - 1)$-disk problem. That is, if $f(n)$ is the number of disk moves necessary to solve an n-disk Hanoi then $f(n) \geq f(n - 1)$. In short, f must be non-decreasing. And this is true regardless of the algorithm used.

Well, you yawn, this isn't news; surely every problem instance is at least as hard as a smaller instance of the same problem. As we shall discover in chapter six, this is plausible—but wrong. Further, f is more than just non-decreasing since there is more work that any algorithm solving an n-disk Hanoi must do: namely, it must move the biggest disk and it must move all those $n - 1$ disks from B to C (on top of the biggest disk). And, again, the $n - 1$ smaller disks can't see the biggest disk. Thus, it must be that $f(1) = 1$ and $f(n) \geq 2f(n-1) + 1$. This forces $f(n)$ to be at least $2^n - 1$. Thus, HANOI is *optimal* (within the model chosen).

Pause | Use induction to show that $f(n) \geq 2^n - 1$.

By the way, if you're worried about the world ending soon, $2^{64} = 18,446,744,073,709,551,616$. If the priests can move one disk a second that's about five hundred and eighty-five billion years (not counting leap years). Let's put this ridiculous number in perspective. The earth is less than five billion years old, and the whole universe is less than fifteen. Fifteen billion years is roughly 4.7×10^{16} seconds. A human lifetime is about 2.2×10^9 seconds. A week is about 6×10^5 seconds. A day is about 86 kiloseconds (8.6×10^4 seconds). Any program taking more than 10^4 seconds (about three hours) is usually judged too slow. Fast computers can perform about one billion operations per second. If a computer could move a disk in a billionth of a second, then the sixty-four-disk Hanoi problem would still take about five hundred and eighty-five years.

1.5 Now What?

> Which, if we find outweighs ability,
> What do we then but draw anew the model
> In fewer offices, or at last desist
> To build at all?
>
> William Shakespeare, *Henry IV, part 2, III*

The sequence of steps outlined in the previous four sections is lovely in theory but, as that sixteenth-century analyst points out, this sequence is often succeeded by the following algorithm, the execution of which is (alas!) beyond the scope of this, and every, book.

> If the upper and lower bounds match,
> then stop,
> else if they're close enough or the problem isn't that important,
>   then stop,
>   else if the model focuses on the wrong thing,
>   then restate it,
>   else if the algorithm is too fat,
>   then generate a slimmer algorithm,
>   else if the lower bound is too weak,
>   then generate a stronger lower bound.
> Repeat to perfection or exhaustion.

Opinion is divided on whether this algorithm terminates.

1.6   Napkin Mathematics

> The advanced reader who skips parts that
> appear to him too elementary may miss more
> than the less advanced reader who skips
> parts that appear to him too complex.
>
> George Pólya,
> *Mathematics and Plausible Reasoning:*
> *Induction and Analogy in Mathematics*

When theorists go to restaurants they invariably talk mathematics. Naturally
they also try to write mathematics. But napkins are small, so they have to
ignore lots of details in their calculations. We will often want to do much
the same thing to get a ballpark figure for the run time of an algorithm. For
example, we've seen that 2^{10} is about 10^3 (let's write this as $2^{10} \sim 10^3$)
with an error of less than three percent. If an algorithm's run time is 2^n,
how long will it run when n is large? For instance, earlier we wanted to
know how many digits there are in a petabyte (2^{50} bytes). To solve this
problem easily we need to recall the idea of a ***logarithm***.

The base x logarithm of y is the power to which we must raise x to
get y. Thus,

$$\log_x y = z \iff x^z = y \iff x^{\log_x y} = y$$

For example, the Richter scale for measuring earthquakes, named after the
American geologist Charles Richter, is a base ten logarithmic scale. Thus,
an earthquake measuring eight on the Richter scale isn't twice as bad as
an earthquake measuring four on the scale, it's ten thousand times as bad.

Because digital computers are binary, base two logarithms are special.
Let's agree to use "lg" to mean the base two logarithm, $\log_2$. See table 1.3.
Also, it is convenient to define the zeroth power of any number (including zero) to be one: that is, $\forall x$, $x^0 = 1$. For example, it would be
nice if $2^0 = 1$ because then HANOI would do nothing when given no disks
($2^0 - 1 = 0$), as it should. Consequently, $\lg 1 = 0$.

n	1	2	3	4	5	6	7	8	9	10
$\lg n$	0	1	1.584	2	2.321	2.584	2.807	3	3.169	3.321

Table 1.3   Base two logarithms (to three decimal places)

Pause   What's $\lg 16$?

The neat thing about logarithms is that instead of multiplying or dividing two numbers we just have to add or subtract their logs since

$$\log_x(rs) = \log_x r + \log_x s \quad \text{and} \quad \log_x \left(\frac{r}{s}\right) = \log_x r - \log_x s$$

$\boxed{Pause}$ Does this make sense for the special case where r and s are integers?

So, for example, in table 1.3,

$$\lg 6 = \lg(2 \times 3) = \lg 2 + \lg 3 = 1 + \lg 3$$

By extension, the logarithm of a power is simple:

$$\lg a^b = b \lg a$$

Now, if $2^n \sim 10^m$ then $\lg 2^n = n \sim \lg 10^m = m \lg 10 \sim 3.321m$. Therefore, $m \sim 0.301n$. So, for example, 2^{50} is about 10^{15}. Thus, a petabyte number of seconds is roughly one forty-seventh of the age of the universe.

$\boxed{Pause}$ Can you estimate the error of this estimate?

2^n is a fast-growing function. Here is another fast-growing function called the **factorial** function:

$$n! = n \times (n - 1) \times \cdots \times 2 \times 1$$

If we have two algorithms whose costs grow like $n!$ and 2^n, which should we use? Looking at table 1.4 we might guess that $n!$ is bigger than 2^n and less than 2^{2n}. But we don't really know. If we had calculated only the first three values we might have thought that $n! < 2^n$; how do we know that if we continue the table for a few more values we won't find that $n! > 2^{2n}$? It could be that once n gets big enough, $n!$ is less than both or $n!$ is greater than both. So far, the only thing we're sure of is that 2^n is slower than 2^{2n}. This teaches us that we can't compare functions based only on their values for small n.

n	1	2	3	4	5	6	7	8
$n!$	1	2	6	24	120	720	5040	40320
2^n	2	4	8	16	32	64	128	256
2^{2n}	4	16	64	256	1024	4096	16384	65536

Table 1.4   Factorials versus powers of two

Although $n! < 2^{2n}$ for $n < 9$, $n!$ grows quite fast. If we increase n to $n + 1$ then $n!$ increases by a factor of $n + 1$ but 2^{2n} only increases by a factor of 4. The appropriate recurrence for 2^{2n} is

$$f(n) = \begin{cases} 4 & n = 1 \\ 4f(n - 1) & n > 1 \end{cases}$$

But the recurrence for $n!$ is

$$f(n) = \begin{cases} 1 & n = 1 \\ nf(n - 1) & n > 1 \end{cases}$$

Intuitively, $n!$ should eventually become larger than 2^{2n}. Let's try to prove that.

Pause   Any idea how?

Well, we could prove this by induction, but it's not clear what the base case should be (any idea?). Instead, let's find a use for the log function. First, $n! \geq 2^{2n}$ if and only if $\lg n! \geq \lg 2^{2n} = 2n$. But

$$
\begin{aligned}
n! &= n \times (n - 1) \times \cdots \times \frac{n}{2} \times \left(\frac{n}{2} - 1\right) \times \cdots \times 2 \times 1 \\
&\geq \frac{n}{2} \times \frac{n}{2} \times \cdots \times \frac{n}{2} \times 1 \times \cdots \times 1 \times 1 \\
&= \left(\frac{n}{2}\right)^{n/2}
\end{aligned}
$$

Therefore,

$$\lg n! \geq \lg \left(\frac{n}{2}\right)^{n/2} = \left(\frac{n}{2}\right) \lg \left(\frac{n}{2}\right)$$

So we only need show that this is eventually bigger than $2n$ and we're done.

$$
\begin{aligned}
\left(\frac{n}{2}\right) \lg \left(\frac{n}{2}\right) &\geq 2n \\
\Longleftrightarrow \qquad \lg \left(\frac{n}{2}\right) &\geq 4 \\
\Longleftrightarrow \qquad n &\geq 32
\end{aligned}
$$

So we're sure that $n! \geq 2^{2n}$ once $n \geq 32$.

Pause   Use induction to prove that $n! \geq 2^{2n}$ for $n \geq 9$.

Factorials occur when we arrange the elements of a set; $n!$ is the number of ways of arranging n people in a row. Factorials also occur when we select elements from a set. For example, the number of ways of selecting m things from n things is $n!/(m!(n-m)!)$; a function that we will meet several times in our trek. This function has a special notation (pronounced "n choose m"):

$$\binom{n}{m} = \frac{n!}{m!(n-m)!}$$

Because of the selection interpretation we sometimes want to talk about the factorial of zero, and also about selecting more things than we have to select from. To make the definitions uniform even for these cases let's define $0!$ to be 1 and define $\binom{n}{m}$ to be 0 if $m > n$.

Factorials make power expansions of two variables easy. For example, multiplying out we see that

$$(x+y)^0 = 1, \quad (x+y)^1 = x+y, \quad \text{and } (x+y)^2 = x^2 + 2xy + y^2$$

These expansions are special cases of the **binomial theorem** ("binomial" means "two terms"):

$$\begin{aligned}
(x+y)^n &= \binom{n}{0}x^{n-0}y^0 + \binom{n}{1}x^{n-1}y + \binom{n}{2}x^{n-2}y^2 + \cdots \\
&\quad + \binom{n}{n-1}x^1 y^{n-1} + \binom{n}{n}x^0 y^n \\
&= x^n + nx^{n-1}y + \frac{n(n-1)}{2}x^{n-2}y^2 + \cdots + nxy^{n-1} + y^n
\end{aligned}$$

Instead of laboriously multiplying out, we can use the binomial theorem to find that

$$(x+y)^3 = x^3 + 3x^2 y + 3xy^2 + y^3 ,$$

$$(x+y)^4 = x^4 + 4x^3 y + 6x^2 y^2 + 4xy^3 + y^4 , \quad \text{and}$$

$$(x+y)^5 = x^5 + 5x^4 y + 10x^3 y^2 + 10x^2 y^3 + 5xy^4 + y^5$$

Although used since ancient times, this neat theorem is credited to the English mathematician Isaac Newton, who generalized it while he was an undergraduate at Cambridge in 1665.

∞∞∞

Here is another toy problem. The greatest European mathematician of the middle ages, the Italian Leonardo Pisano Bigollo, nicknamed, in the present day, Fibonacci ("fib-oh-nah-chee"), posed the following problem in 1202:

> Suppose you have a pair of rabbits and suppose every month each pair bears a new pair that from the second month on becomes productive. How many pairs of rabbits will you have in a year?

This is probably the first ever recursively defined function (although Fibonacci lacked the formalism we have today to state it as a recurrence). Let $f(n)$ be the number of pairs of rabbits alive at month n. The recurrence giving the value of $f(n)$ is

$$f(n) = \begin{cases} 1 & n = 0 \\ 1 & n = 1 \\ f(n-1) + f(n-2) & n > 1 \end{cases}$$

From this recurrence it's easy to write a recursive algorithm finding $f(n)$; see algorithm 1.2. Table 1.5 lists the first few fibonacci numbers.

FIBONACCI(n)
    { Find the nth Fibonacci number where $n \geq 0$. }

    if $n \leq 1$
        then return 1
        else return FIBONACCI($n-1$) + FIBONACCI($n-2$)

Algorithm 1.2

n	0	1	2	3	4	5	6	7	8
$f(n)$	1	1	2	3	5	8	13	21	34

n	9	10	11	12	13	14	15	16	17
$f(n)$	55	89	144	233	377	610	987	1597	2584

Table 1.5 Fibonacci numbers

Although elegant, this recursive algorithm is a bad way to compute the fibonacci numbers since we will compute many numbers many times. For example, as figure 1.10 shows, we compute $f(2)$ three times when finding $f(5)$. Instead we can write a prosaic, but more efficient, iterative algorithm to do the same thing; see algorithm 1.3. This algorithm does work proportional to $3n$.

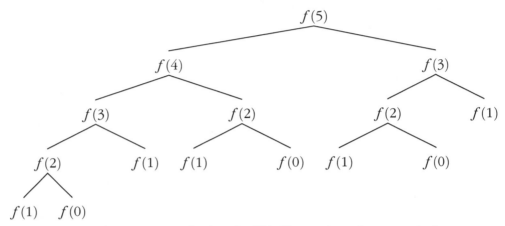

Figure 1.10 Evaluating the fifth fibonacci number recursively

Now how much work does algorithm 1.2 do? This is a surprisingly difficult question, considering how simple the algorithm is. To answer it we will have to develop some more mathematics.

```
FIBONACCI( n )
    { Find the nᵗʰ Fibonacci number where n ≥ 0. }

    past ← 1 ; previous ← 1 ; present ← 1
    for i from 2 to n
        past ← previous ; previous ← present
        present ← previous + past
    return present
```

Algorithm 1.3

To begin with, how much work does the code fragment shown in figure 1.11 do as a function of n? To solve this problem we need a way to manipulate sums of numbers.

$$
\begin{aligned}
&sum \leftarrow 0 \; ; \; inc \leftarrow 0 \\
&\textbf{for } i \textbf{ from } 1 \textbf{ to } n \\
&\quad \textbf{for } j \textbf{ from } 1 \textbf{ to } i \\
&\qquad sum \leftarrow sum + inc \\
&\qquad inc \leftarrow inc + 1
\end{aligned}
$$

Figure 1.11 A double summation

Let's represent the sum of the n real numbers $r_1, r_2, r_3, \ldots, r_n$, by the expression

$$
\sum_{i=1}^{n} r_i
$$

That is,

$$
\sum_{i=1}^{n} r_i = r_1 + r_2 + r_3 + \cdots + r_n
$$

Σ is the Greek letter capital sigma, their form of capital S, and it stands for "the sum of" (the integral sign $\int$ is also an S but it stands for a different kind of sum). Read the expression "$\sum_{i=1}^{n} r_i$" as "the sum of r_i where i ranges from 1 to n." The *sum variable, i*, can be any integer variable; so, for example,

$$
\sum_{i=1}^{n} r_i = \sum_{j=1}^{n} r_j = \sum_{k=1}^{n} r_k = \sum_{l=1}^{n} r_l = \sum_{m=1}^{n} r_m
$$

Also, if the terms are all positive we may add them in any way whatsoever. (This is not true if the numbers can be positive and negative and there are an infinite number of them.) So, for example,

$$
\begin{aligned}
\sum_{i=1}^{100} r_i \;&=\; \sum_{i=1}^{j-1} r_i + \sum_{i=j}^{100} r_i \\[2mm]
&=\; \sum_{i=1}^{j} r_i + \sum_{i=j+1}^{k+3} r_i + \sum_{i=k+4}^{100} r_i \\[2mm]
&=\; \sum_{i \text{ even},\, 1 \le i \le 100} r_i \;+\; \sum_{i \text{ odd},\, 1 \le i \le 100} r_i \\[2mm]
&=\; \sum_{i=1}^{50} r_{2i} + \sum_{i=0}^{49} r_{2i+1}
\end{aligned}
$$

Finally, let's agree that the value of a sum over an empty range is zero. Thus, for example,

$$m > n \implies \sum_{i=m}^{n} r_i = 0$$

Now let's calculate the number of assignments (or equivalently, the number of additions plus two) done in the code fragment in figure 1.11 and use that as an estimate of the work the code fragment does.

The number of assignments done is two plus

$$\sum_{i=1}^{n} (\text{assignments done on repetition } i \text{ of outer loop})$$

The number of assignments done on repetition i of the outer loop is

$$\sum_{j=1}^{i} (\text{assignments done on repetition } j \text{ of inner loop for fixed } i)$$

And for every j, only two assignments are done on repetition j of the inner loop for a fixed i. Thus, the total number of assignments done is two plus

$$\sum_{i=1}^{n} \left(\sum_{j=1}^{i} 2 \right)$$

The value of the inner sum is just $2i$. Therefore, the value of the whole sum is

$$\sum_{i=1}^{n} 2i \quad (= 2 + 4 + 6 + \cdots + 2n)$$

Let's do a little quick napkining to estimate this sum. The largest term is the last term ($2n$) and the smallest term is the first term (2). Since there are n terms in all, the sum is no larger than $2n^2$ and no smaller than $2n$.

We can refine this estimate by observing that the terms are increasing linearly (like on a ramp; see figure 1.12). Thus, the sum will be near the average term times the number of terms, since for each number below the average there is another above the average by the same amount. The average value is near n and there are n terms in all, so the sum should be near n^2. (Warning! This argument will not work unless the terms are linearly increasing. (Why?))

Pause   Use the same idea to estimate $\sum_{i=1}^{n} (ai + b)$.

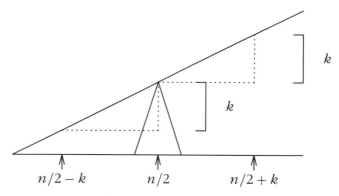

Figure 1.12 Thinking of a linear function like a see-saw

n^2 is a good estimate of the sum, but by rearranging the sum we can get an exact answer. Since every term is doubled, the sum is the same as double the sum of $1 + 2 + 3 + \cdots + n$. Thus,

$$
\begin{aligned}
\sum_{i=1}^{n} 2i &= 2 \sum_{i=1}^{n} i \\
&= 2(1 + 2 + 3 + \cdots + n) \\
&= (1 + 2 + 3 + \cdots + n) + (1 + 2 + 3 + \cdots + n) \\
&= \ \ \begin{array}{ccccccccc} 1 & + & 2 & + & 3 & + & \cdots & + & n \\ + & & & & & & & & \\ n & + & (n-1) & + & (n-2) & + & \cdots & + & 1 \end{array} \\
&= n(n+1)
\end{aligned}
$$

It's depressing to us humans but the eighteenth-century German mathematician Carl Friedrich Gauss discovered this insight before he was ten. To keep the class busy a teacher asked the students to find the sum of a large number of consecutive numbers. Gauss found the above pairing trick and solved what should have been an hour-long question in minutes. Gauss was annoyingly clever.

So now we know that the code fragment in figure 1.11 performs exactly $n(n+1)+2$ assignments. Our napkin estimate of n^2 is off by less than ten percent for n as small as twelve, and it gets even better as n increases.

Mathematics is a search for pattern. Often we have a sum and we want to know its value for large n without doing a lot of calculation. This is only possible if there is some pattern in the terms of the sum (and if we can find the pattern). On the general principle that we can only express things we don't know in terms of things we do know, we have:

The subtract-and-guess or divide-and-guess strategy: To find the value of the sum f, pick a known function g and find a pattern in the terms $f(n) - g(n)$ or $f(n)/g(n)$.

Often it's best to let g be a sum as well, and sometimes we don't even have to know the value of this new sum. For example, consider $f(n) = \sum_{i=1}^{n} i$. There are many things we could try to divide by. Table 1.6 shows division by $g_1(n) = n \ (= \sum_{i=1}^{n} 1)$ and by $g_2(n) = f(n-1)$ (seems like a trick!). We can now find f from either of the guessed patterns,

$$\frac{f(n)}{g_1(n)} = \frac{n+1}{2} \quad \text{or} \quad \frac{f(n)}{g_2(n)} = \frac{n+1}{n-1}$$

n	1	2	3	4	5	6	7	8
$f(n)$	1	3	6	10	15	21	28	36
$g_1(n)$	1	2	3	4	5	6	7	8
$f(n)/g_1(n)$	2/2	3/2	4/2	5/2	6/2	7/2	8/2	9/2
$g_2(n)$	0	1	3	6	10	15	21	28
$f(n)/g_2(n)$		3/1	4/2	5/3	6/4	7/5	8/6	9/7

Table 1.6   How to guess a sum

Pause   What's $\sum_{i=1}^{n} i^2$? (Hint: Try the sum we just found.)

Now, finally, we can get back to Fibonacci and his rabbits. How much work does the recursive FIBONACCI (algorithm 1.2 [p. 31]) do? Let's use additions to estimate the algorithm's cost. After a little thought we see that this cost is proportional to the fibonacci numbers themselves!

Pause   Why is this true? (Hint: See figure 1.10 [p. 32].)

So now the question is: how fast do the fibonacci numbers grow? Applying the divide and guess strategy, table 1.7 lists the ratio of $f(n)$ to $f(n-1)$ to three decimal places. Looking at the table we might guess that $f(n) \sim 1.618 \times f(n-1)$ as n gets large. If that's true then $f(n) \sim 1.618^n$.

n	1	2	3	4	5	6	7
$f(n)$	1	2	3	5	8	13	21
$f(n)/f(n-1)$	1	2	1.5	1.666	1.625	1.615	1.619

n	8	9	10	11	12	13	14
$f(n)$	34	55	89	144	233	377	610
$f(n)/f(n-1)$	1.617	1.618	1.617	1.618	1.618	1.618	1.618

Table 1.7 Ratio of fibonacci numbers

Pause   Suppose we didn't think of $f(n)/f(n-1)$. Compute a table of $f(n)/2^n$ and $f(n)/1.5^n$. How can such tables help us pin down $f(n)$?

Suppose $f(n)/f(n-1)$ is really tending to a fixed number as n tends to infinity. Call it x. What's x? Well, from the recurrence we have that

$$f(n) = f(n-1) + f(n-2)$$

Therefore, if "$\to$" stands for "tends to" then for large n

$$\frac{f(n)}{f(n-2)} = \frac{f(n-1)}{f(n-2)} + \frac{f(n-2)}{f(n-2)} \to x + 1$$

But, for large n

$$\frac{f(n)}{f(n-2)} = \frac{f(n)}{f(n-1)} \frac{f(n-1)}{f(n-2)} \to x^2$$

Therefore if x exists, it must be that

$$x^2 - x - 1 \to 0$$

Setting this quadratic to zero and solving we see that

$$x = \frac{1 \pm \sqrt{5}}{2} = 1.618\cdots \quad \text{or} \quad -0.618\cdots$$

Aha! So if x exists then it must be $1.618\cdots$. The number $1.618\cdots$ has a special symbol, ϕ (this is the Greek letter phi; think of it as standing for the F in Fibonacci, although that isn't why it was first chosen). The second number is just $1-\phi$ (why is this?). Of these two possible solutions only the first is bigger than 1. Therefore as n increases this term will predominate. (Why?) Therefore for some constant r, $f(n) \sim r\phi^n$. It is possible to show that $r = 1/\sqrt{5} \sim 0.447$.

If the first values of f were 1 and ϕ instead of both 1 (that is, if $f(0) = 1$ and $f(1) = \phi$), then $f(n) = \phi^n$ for all n. (Why?) But because of the small change in $f(1)$ all the later values of f are less than half of ϕ^n. This enormous sensitivity to small changes in boundary values is characteristic of fast-growing functions. $f(n)$, 2^n, and $n!$, are all fast-growing functions; in the next section we will develop notation and tools to distinguish between them.

1.7   Growth Rates

> If your wish is to become really a man of
> science, and not merely a petty experimentalist,
> I should advise you to apply to every branch
> of natural philosophy, including mathematics.
>
> Mary Shelley, *Frankenstein*

Now let's make the idea of tossing out constants more precise so that we can do some napkin math on our algorithms. Two functions of n have different **growth rates** if as n goes to infinity their ratio either goes to infinity or goes to zero. If their ratio stays near a non-zero constant then they are asymptotically the same function. Why is this a reasonable view of functions?

The tapestry that's been woven so far gives center place to determining the resource cost of each algorithm as accurately as possible. This is not always easy. To make an analysis as accurate as possible we must include details about the machine the algorithm is to be run on and the language it is to be written in. The more details we include, the more accurate the result becomes, but also the less general the result becomes. By tying the analysis closely to one machine and language we can say little about the speed of the algorithm on a different machine or in a different language.

The second obstacle to complete exactness is that we sometimes develop algorithms whose resource cost is complicated. Sometimes this function is so complicated that it could conceivably take as long to compute the resource cost as it takes to run the algorithm! For example, suppose an algorithm's resource cost is the sum of the first m terms of the sum

$$\sqrt{n} + \sqrt{n + \sqrt{n}} + \sqrt{n + \sqrt{n + \sqrt{n}}} + \cdots$$

The simplest way to evaluate this sum appears to be to evaluate each term and add them! We want to say something about the cost of an algorithm even if we can't express its cost in a simple form. To do that we compare the complicated function to a collection of functions of known growth rates.

Finally, sometimes when we analyze an algorithm we aren't all that interested in the exact time the algorithm takes to run. Often we only want to compare two algorithms for the same problem. The thing that makes one algorithm more desirable than another is its growth rate relative to the other algorithm's growth rate. Given two algorithms with worst costs of $2^{n!}$ and n, respectively, it's clear which to pick *even without thinking of anything else.* Even if the $2^{n!}$ algorithm has a million times less overhead than the n algorithm, as soon as n grows to four or more the n algorithm will far outperform the $2^{n!}$ one in the worst case because $2^{n!}$ grows so much more rapidly than n. (See table 1.8.)

n	1	2	3	4	5	6	7	8	9	10
n	1	1	1	1	1	1	1	1	1	2
n^2	1	1	1	2	2	2	2	2	2	3
2^n	1	1	1	2	2	2	3	3	3	4
$n!$	1	1	1	2	3	3	4	5	6	7
2^{n^2}	1	2	3	5	8	11	15	20	25	31
2^{2^n}	1	2	3	5	10	20	39	78	155	309
$2^{n!}$	1	1	2	8	37	217	1518	12138	109238	1092378

Table 1.8 Functions in terms of the number of decimal digits

Table 1.8 lists some functions in terms of the number of decimal digits needed to express each value—for example, 5! = 120 needs three decimal digits. (The values in the table are near to the base ten log of the function values for each n.) Although all the functions go to infinity, different functions appear to go to infinity at different rates. For example, $2^{n!}$ grows so rapidly that $2^{16!}$ has 6,298,387,349,264 decimal digits! Do all these functions have different growth rates? If we take the ratio of any two of them, does the ratio either go to zero or to infinity? Or does it stay near a non-zero constant?

Well let's first try to answer this for n and n^2. As we saw in the problem of squaring n (page 3) n^2 grows faster than n. n^2 also grows faster than $3n$ (see figure 1.13). Is there a constant so large that if we multiply n by it, the resulting function is always larger than n^2?

Pause   Can you prove this one way or the other?

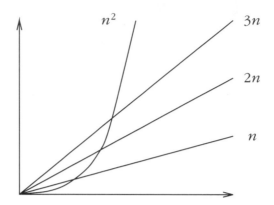

Figure 1.13 Every quadratic beats all linear functions

Instead of trying larger and larger constants suppose there are constants r and s such that $n^2 < rn + s$. Then $n < r + s/n$. But, as n tends to infinity, s/n tends to zero. Thus n is less than something a little bigger than r. But this is silly since n is increasing to infinity. Therefore, there can be no such constants. This is a **proof by contradiction**. The idea is to assume the opposite of what we want to prove, then show that this leads to a contradictory statement; thus what we want to prove cannot be false, and so must be true. (This assumes that every statement is either true or false, but, as we see in chapter seven, when looked at closely there are usually shades of gray.)

We can even tell when n^2 first becomes bigger than $rn + s$. It's bigger for all n larger than the positive root of the quadratic equation $n^2 - rn - s$. That is, for all n larger than $(r + \sqrt{r^2 + 4s})/2$.

$\boxed{\textit{Pause}}$ Check that this value makes $n^2 - rn - s$ zero. Must the quadratic stay positive after this point?

So a bare n^2 eventually grows larger than any linear function of n. Also, given another quadratic function, say $rn^2 + sn + t$, we can always find a constant u such that for all n beyond some point un^2 is bigger than $rn^2 + sn + t$ (for example, $u = r + s + t$). Thus, neither changing the constant multiplying the n^2 term nor adding terms involving only n (or constants) affects the growth rate, we still go to infinity at the same rate as n^2. So n and n^2 have different growth rates.

Now we can order some of the functions in table 1.8. Since n^2 grows faster than n, then 2^{n^2} grows faster than 2^n (exponentiate), n^4 grows faster than n^2 (square), n grows faster than $\sqrt{n}$ (take square roots), and $2\lg n$ grows no slower than $\lg n$ (take logs). Also, on page 29 we saw that $n!$ grows faster than 2^n so now we know five more things:

- $n!!$ grows faster than $2^n!$ (take factorials),
- $2^{n!}$ grows faster than 2^{2^n} (exponentiate),
- $n!^2$ grows faster than 2^{2n} (square),
- $\sqrt{n!}$ grows faster than $\sqrt{2^n}$ (take square roots), and
- $\lg n!$ grows no slower than n (take logs).

And so on. Every relationship we find gives us many more by squaring, taking square roots, exponentiating, taking logarithms, or taking factorials.

$\boxed{Long\ Pause}$ If f grows faster than g, then we can say that f^2 grows faster than g^2 and 2^f grows faster than 2^g. Can we say that $\sqrt{f}$ grows faster than $\sqrt{g}$ and $\lg f$ grows faster than $\lg g$?

We can go on to order the following functions by their growth rates:

$$\lg\lg n \quad \lg n \quad \lg^2 n \quad n^{1/10} \quad \sqrt{n} \quad n \quad n\lg n \quad n^2 \quad 2^n \quad n! \quad 2^{2^n} \quad 2^{n!}$$

$\boxed{Pause}$ Does $n^{1/10}$ really grow faster than $\lg^2 n$? After all, even when n is a trillion $n^{1/10}$ is only about 16 but $\lg^2 n$ is about 1600 (recall that $10^{12} \sim 2^{40}$).

Limits

To prove things about the growth rates of algorithms we need some tools to handle speed. Fortunately there is already a well-developed collection of tools to find growth rates of functions—the differential calculus.[4] It's impossible to compress into a few pages more than two thousand years' worth of ideas about estimating speed. So we will have to skim.

The calculus had been brewing for a long time but it was brought to a boil three centuries ago by Isaac Newton in England and independently by Gottfried Leibniz ("libe-nits") in Germany and it has been enormously useful ever since. Besides the calculus, Newton is famous for many fundamental advances in mathematics, physics, and astronomy; he is probably the most influential mathematician ever to have lived.

The calculus is built around the idea of a *limit* of a function. The statement

$$\lim_{x \to r} f(x) = s$$

is shorthand for the intuitive idea: "$f(x)$ approaches s as x approaches r" but since $f(x)$ also approaches $s - 1$ (as well as all other values less

---

[4]"You are only as rich as the houses you burgle." George Alec Effinger, *Isaac Asimov's Science Fiction Magazine,* July, 1985.

than s), and since f may not be defined at r, we need to be more careful and say that "we can keep $f(x)$ as close to s as we want by keeping x sufficiently close to, but not necessarily equal to, r." Intuitively, no matter how small someone requires the difference between the function value and the limit value to be, we can always find a point near r satisfying that condition (see figure 1.14).

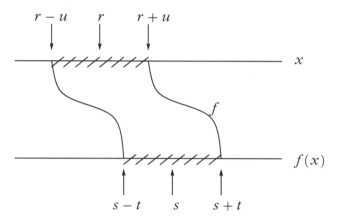

Figure 1.14 $\lim_{x \to r} f(x) = s$ — for every t there is a suitable u

Why the distinction between $f(x)$ near r and $f(r)$? Why not just find $f(r)$ and forget about limits? Well, for one thing f may not be defined at r. For example, people can increase their "reading speed" by skipping words. People who can't read are skipping everything. Does this mean they have an infinite reading speed?

In analysis we want to know how functions behave as their integer arguments increase to infinity. Here's how to define the limit in that case:

$$\lim_{n \to \infty} f(n) = r \iff \forall s > 0 \; \exists c > 0 : \; n > c \implies r + s > f(n) > r - s$$

(":" means "such that"). In words, as n tends to infinity the limit of $f(n)$ is r if, no matter how close we want $f(n)$ to be to r (that is, no matter how small s is), we can always find a big enough n making it that close.

One limit is so important that it has its own name:

$$
\begin{aligned}
e^x &= \lim_{n \to \infty} \left(1 + \frac{x}{n}\right)^n \\
&= 1 + \frac{x^1}{1!} + \frac{x^2}{2!} + \frac{x^3}{3!} + \frac{x^4}{4!} + \cdots \\
&= 1 + x + \frac{x^2}{2} + \frac{x^3}{6} + \frac{x^4}{24} + \cdots
\end{aligned}
$$

The number $e = 1 + 1 + \frac{1}{2} + \frac{1}{6} + \frac{1}{24} + \cdots = 2.71828\cdots$ is so important[5] that base e logarithms have a special symbol, ln.

Order Notation

We use **order notation** to classify functions by their growth rates. Table 1.9 lists the order notations we use in this book. Let's look at one particular one ("O") to see how they all work.

Say that f is	Mean that f is	Write	If
small oh g	slower than g	$f = o(g)$	$\lim\limits_{n\to\infty} f(n)/g(n) = 0$
oh g	no faster than g	$f = O(g)$	$\exists c, r > 0 : \ \forall n > c,$
			$\quad f(n) \leq r\,g(n)$
theta g	about as fast as g	$f = \Theta(g)$	$f = O(g)$ and $g = O(f)$
about g	as fast as g	$f \approx g$	$\lim\limits_{n\to\infty} f(n)/g(n) = 1$
omega g	no slower than g	$f = \Omega(g)$	$g = O(f)$

Table 1.9 Order notations

Suppose your keyboard has a broken "$\leq$" key. Wishing to continue work you decide to use the two keys "$= L$" in its place. But, because "$=$" has such strong associations with equality, after a few uses of "$= L$" in such relations as $1 = L(3)$ and $3 = L(5)$ you naturally start thinking of L as a separate function.

We can think of $L(5)$ as an unspecified number less than 5. This makes it possible to do "arithmetic" with this function. For example, $1 + L(5) = L(6)$, $L(3) + L(1) = L(4)$, and $L(3)L(4) = L(12)$. But this is not the arithmetic we're used to. For example, we cannot say that $L(5) - L(3) = L(2)$ since the indeterminacy about what is really being subtracted could make this almost any number.

Pause   How about $L(6)/L(3)$?

More generally, we can think of L as a set of *functions* (and not just numbers) and thus, $L(g)$ would represent an unspecified function f and the only thing we know (or care) about f is that $f(n)$ is less than $g(n)$ for each n. To use this idea in analysis let's add two more degrees of

_____

[5]Here's a mnemonic sentence to remember the first six digits of e (count the letters): "He studied a treatise on calculus." Ivan Niven, *Maxima and Minima Without Calculus.*

freedom. Since we don't care how a function behaves for small n, we allow the inequality to possibly fail when n is small; we only require that it hold for all n larger than some constant. Also, we only care about growth rates, so the function may be multiplied by any constant.

A function f is O of g if there are positive constants r and c such that $f(n) \leq rg(n)$ for all n bigger than c. We write this relation as: $f = O(g)$, and the intuition is that f goes to infinity no faster than g.

There are four important points to remember about order notations. First, the following analogy helps to keep the notations in table 1.9 straight. o is like "$<$," O is like "$\leq$," Θ is like "roughly equal," $\approx$ is like "$=$," and Ω is like "$\geq$." Since O is like "$\leq$" it does not say how good an algorithm can be, it can only say how bad the algorithm can possibly get. For example, suppose algorithm $\mathcal{A}$ is $O(n)$ and algorithm $\mathcal{B}$ is $O(n^2)$. Is $\mathcal{A}$ better than $\mathcal{B}$? Perhaps; but perhaps neither algorithm has been sufficiently analyzed and $\mathcal{A}$ is in fact $\Theta(n)$ while $\mathcal{B}$ is really $\Theta(\lg n)$.

Second, keep in mind that the O notation, and all other notations in table 1.9, indicate a function's *speed* relative to some other function and not its *size*. Thus, $5n = O(n^2)$ (for example, take $r = 5$, $c = 1$) since n^2 grows faster than n, even though $5n$ is bigger than n^2 when $n < 5$. Further, for all s and t, $sn + t = O(n^2)$ (for example, take $r = s + t$, $c = 1$). Also, for all s, t, and u, $sn^2 + tn + u = O(n^2)$ (for example, take $r = s + t + u$, $c = 1$). Finally, $n^2 \neq O(n)$, as we've already seen (page 40).

Third, $n = O(n^2)$ and $n^2 = O(n^2)$, but we cannot write $O(n) = O(n^2)$. Thus, we cannot treat O like a normal function. Similarly, in the previous example, we can say $L(5) = L(6)$, but not $L(6) = L(5)$; the "equations" are one-way. $O(g)$ is the set of all functions bounded above by some constant times g. Instead of saying that $f = O(g)$ we could say that f is *in* the set $O(g)$. But it's a little clumsier, so we won't. We can extend this set interpretation idea to the other order notations as well.

Finally, for the definitions in table 1.9 recall that, by convention, functions are by default *positive* and *non-decreasing.* We usually only use functions to measure the resource cost of an algorithm, and this will never be negative nor will it decrease as the input increases in size. (This last is not true in general; the performance of algorithms that depend on numerical properties of the input may go up or down as the input increases in size, as we shall see in chapter six.)

Some growth rates occur so often that they have special names (see table 1.10 and figure 1.15). Note that if the resource cost of an algorithm is logarithmic then it only increases by a constant when n doubles; if it's linear, it doubles when n doubles; if it's quadratic, it quadruples when n doubles; if it's exponential, it squares when n doubles!

If f is	say that f is	If f is	say that f is
$\Theta(1)$	constant	$\Theta(n^r), 1 < r < 2$	subquadratic
$\Theta(\lg n)$	logarithmic	$\Theta(n^2)$	quadratic
$\Theta(\lg^c n), c \geq 1$	polylogarithmic	$\Theta(n^3)$	cubic
$\Theta(n^r), 0 < r < 1$	sublinear	$\Theta(n^c), c \geq 1$	polynomial
$\Theta(n)$	linear	$\Theta(r^n), r > 1$	exponential

Table 1.10   Some special orders

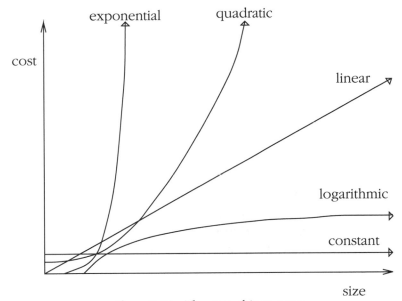

Figure 1.15   The way things grow

Manipulating Order Notation

Now let's use limits to find some orders. First, let's show that

$$\lim_{n \to \infty} \frac{f(n)}{g(n)} = r \Longrightarrow f = O(g)$$

This is a useful way to prove order relations. It's easier to find limits of ratios than to find bounding constants out of thin air.

From the definition

$$\lim_{n\to\infty} \frac{f(n)}{g(n)} = r$$

$$\Longleftrightarrow \quad \forall s > 0 \; \exists c > 0 : \; \forall n > c , \quad r + s > \frac{f(n)}{g(n)} > r - s$$

$$\Longrightarrow \quad \forall s > 0 \; \exists c > 0 : \; \forall n > c , \quad (r + s)g(n) > f(n)$$

Since this is true for all positive s, it is true for $s = 1$ (say). Thus,

$$\exists c > 0 : \; \forall n > c , \quad f(n) < (r + 1)g(n)$$

Therefore,

$$\exists c, r_1 > 0 : \; \forall n > c , \quad f(n) \le r_1 g(n)$$

Thus, $f = O(g)$.

| Pause | Show that $\lim_{n\to\infty} f(n)/g(n) = r > 0 \Longrightarrow f = \Theta(g)$.

We can use this result to show that $n = O(n^2)$ without messing about with bounding constants:

$$\lim_{n\to\infty} \frac{n}{n^2} = \lim_{n\to\infty} \frac{1}{n} = 0$$

Therefore, not only is $n = O(n^2)$ (that is, n is no faster than n^2), but more precisely, $n = o(n^2)$ (that is, n is strictly slower than n^2). Further, we can use the same result to show that $rn + s = o(n^2)$ for all r and s. Thus, every quadratic function is faster than any linear function.

| Pause | Show that $n = o(n^2)$ implies that $n^2 \ne O(n)$.

Differentiation

Now let's look at ways to measure the growth rates of functions. If f is a function of x and we change x by some amount, r, then f changes value from $f(x)$ to $f(x + r)$. If f is "smooth" and r is "small" then the size of this change is a good estimate of the speed with which f changes. The **derivative** of f at x is

$$f'(x) = \lim_{r\to 0} \frac{f(x + r) - f(x)}{r}$$

To find the derivative we **differentiate** the function. This limit, if it exists, measures f's growth rate near x. The steeper f is near x the faster it's increasing and the larger is its derivative, f'. The derivative is also denoted df/dx or d/dx of f since it's the limit of a difference in x divided into the corresponding difference in f (taking d for "difference").

It is possible to show that

$$\frac{d}{dx}x^r = rx^{r-1}, \qquad \frac{d}{dx}e^x = e^x, \qquad \text{and} \qquad \frac{d}{dx}\ln x = \frac{1}{x}$$

So the derivative of a polynomial grows slower than the polynomial. But curious things happen when the function is exponential or logarithmic; if we have an exponential, the only way to get rid of it is to hit it over the head with a log. Finally,

$$\frac{d}{dx}\lg x = \frac{d}{dx}\left(\frac{\ln x}{\ln 2}\right) = \frac{1}{\ln 2}\frac{d}{dx}\ln x = \frac{1}{x \ln 2}$$

Pause   Show that $\log_x y = \log_z y / \log_z x$ by using $y = z^{\log_z y} = x^{\log_x y}$ and $x = z^{\log_z x}$.

$$\infty\infty\infty$$

Now suppose we have two algorithms with growth rates of $\lg n$ and $\sqrt{n}$. Which grows faster? We get nowhere if we try to find $\lim_{n\to\infty}\sqrt{n}/\lg n$ because both functions tend to infinity and nothing cancels. The limit could be anything; it could be zero, a constant, or undefined. Many famous mathematicians have "proved" absurdities through a naive use of infinity. Be wary of infinity.

For example, suppose you have a bag of apples and each one is labelled with one of each of the positive integers. At two minutes to noon you take the first ten apples out of the bag and put them in a convenient box. Then you take the apple labelled "one" out of the box and eat it. At one minute to noon you take the next ten apples out of the bag and put them in the box. Then you take the apple labelled "two" out of the box and eat it. You keep doing this until noon, halving the time interval at each step. How many apples are in the box at noon? One answer is "an infinite number," since you put in nine times as many apples as you ate. Another answer is "zero," since for any i, the apple labelled with i was removed at $4/2^i$ minutes to noon, so there aren't any apples in the box![6]

If two functions go to zero or to infinity, the limit of the ratio of the functions is *indeterminate*. Fortunately sometimes we can find the limit of

---

[6]A third answer is "undefined," since you could never really do this (or perhaps "who cares?," since after eating all those apples you're too sick to care.).

such ratios using the following rule; it is named after a seventeenth-century French nobleman—Guillaume de l'Hôpital ("lop-ee-tal")—but it was developed by Johann Bernoulli ("ber-nu-lee"), one of a famous family of Swiss mathematicians and scientists.

> **l'Hôpital's rule:** If f and g are differentiable, $\lim\limits_{x\to\infty} f(x) = \infty$, $\lim\limits_{x\to\infty} g(x) = \infty$, and $\lim\limits_{x\to\infty} f'(x)/g'(x)$ exists, then
>
> $$\lim_{x\to\infty} \frac{f(x)}{g(x)} = \lim_{x\to\infty} \frac{f'(x)}{g'(x)}$$

We can use l'Hôpital's rule to show that $\lg n = O(\sqrt{n})$. So $\lg n$ is no faster than $\sqrt{n}$.

$$
\begin{aligned}
\lim_{n\to\infty} \frac{\lg n}{\sqrt{n}} &= \lim_{n\to\infty} \frac{\ln n}{\ln 2\sqrt{n}} \\
&= \frac{1}{\ln 2} \lim_{n\to\infty} \frac{\ln n}{\sqrt{n}} \qquad \text{(an undefined limit)} \\
&= \frac{1}{\ln 2} \lim_{n\to\infty} \frac{1/n}{1/(2\sqrt{n})} \qquad \text{(differentiating top and bottom)} \\
&= \frac{1}{\ln 2} \lim_{n\to\infty} \frac{2}{\sqrt{n}} \\
&= 0
\end{aligned}
$$

Thus, not only is $\lg n = O(\sqrt{n})$ but, more precisely, $\lg n = o(\sqrt{n})$. So $\lg n$ grows slower than $\sqrt{n}$. So if we have to choose between two algorithms whose resource costs were $\lg n$ and $\sqrt{n}$ we should choose the $\lg n$ algorithm. More generally, it is possible to show that every sublinear function grows faster than any polylogarithmic function.

Pause   Show that $\lg^2 n = o(n^{1/10})$.

Here's a harder one: which function grows faster, $2^{\sqrt{\lg n}}$ or n^r where $1 > r > 0$? Since both functions go to infinity we could try l'Hôpital's rule.

Pause   Try l'Hôpital's rule now.

That's the trouble with rules—they don't always work. If you depend on rules to replace thought, one day you will be forced to think and you won't know how.

Let's think for a minute. Is there any way to relate these two functions? If we could cast both functions as variants of yet another function then we would at least have a common yardstick and could sensibly compare them.

Let's try the logarithm function. We know that $n = 2^{\lg n}$ (why?), therefore $n^r = 2^{r \lg n}$. So if $2^{r \lg n}$ grows faster than $2^{\sqrt{\lg n}}$, then n^r grows faster than $2^{\sqrt{\lg n}}$.

But 2^x is a one-to-one increasing function; therefore $2^x > 2^y$ if and only if $x > y$ (this is like taking logs of an inequality). So now we only have to show that there is a c such that for all $n > c$, $r \lg n > \sqrt{\lg n}$. Which is easy. $r \lg n > \sqrt{\lg n} \implies \lg n > 1/r^2$.

Pause | So what's c?

So an algorithm whose run time grows like $2^{\sqrt{\lg n}}$, grows slower than every sublinear algorithm.

1.8   Back to Reality

> There's always an easy solution to every problem—neat, plausible, and wrong.
>
> H. L. Mencken

It would be great if once we know that one algorithm's resource cost grows faster than another's then the slower growing one is better. Unfortunately, because we allowed two degrees of freedom in the definition of order notations (the initial constant and the constant multiplier), we have let ourselves in for three possible problems.

First, how big must the input be before it's better to use the slower growing algorithm? For example, we proved that n^2 goes to infinity faster than n, so a linear algorithm is better than a quadratic algorithm. But suppose the constant multipliers of the two algorithms are a million and a millionth, respectively. How big must the input be before the linear algorithm is superior?

Well, we require the smallest n that makes $10^6 n < n^2/10^6$. This is true when $n > 10^{12}$. Thus, the input must be at least a trillion before the linear algorithm is better! Fortunately, in practice constant multipliers are usually within a factor of a hundred of each other. And in that case a linear algorithm is better than a quadratic one.

Second, it can be misleading to perform arbitrary operations on functions. For example, a $\Theta(n^2)$ algorithm is better than a $\Theta(2^{n/10})$ algorithm for any n bigger than 150 (assuming equal constant multipliers). However, a $\Theta(\lg^2 n)$ algorithm is not much better than a $\Theta(n^{1/10})$ algorithm until n is bigger than 2^{150}. And $2^{150} \sim 10^{50}$ is many times larger than the age of the universe in seconds.

Now this is strange because n^2 is to $2^{n/10}$ as $\lg^2 m$ is to $m^{1/10}$ (take $n = \lg m$ to see this). Thus, n^2 should grow relative to $2^{n/10}$ like $\lg^2 n$ grows relative to $n^{1/10}$. And it does; *but not for the input sizes we usually see.* So, taking the logarithm of functions preserves their growth rate difference but distorts their growth rate *relative* differences. This is important because for practical purposes $\lg^2 n$ and $n^{1/10}$ are roughly the same. But this practical equivalence between the functions *does not* hold after we blow up the input exponentially; as soon as we do that, the difference between the two functions' growth rates becomes significant. An exponential change makes a difference because there is a practical limit to the size of our inputs.

Finally, in practice we can only devote a certain amount of time to solving a problem. So what does it mean, in practical terms, to reduce an algorithm's growth rate? If we expect inputs whose sizes are in the million range, then shaving off a factor of n results in *a million-fold saving.* Even if the constant multiplier for overhead increases a thousand-fold we're still way ahead. However, for the same range, shaving off a factor of $\lg\lg n$ results in only a four- or five-fold saving. Typically the constant multiplier increases by at least that much as the algorithm becomes more complicated.

The heart of these three problems is that for any problem we only want to compute on instances up to some fixed size and we only have a finite amount of time to devote to each instance. In short, there is only a small practicality window. Outside of this window either problems of the right size do not occur in practice, or if they did we couldn't afford the resources needed to solve them. Figure 1.16 sketches the practicality window for two pairs of functions; the curves represent the cost of different algorithms, and the dotted lines show the practicality window. We want functions that pierce the practicality window on the right-hand side; if our solution grows like that then if the problem size grows we can afford to solve it. Solutions that pierce the practicality window through the top are effectively useless; no matter how much time we have to devote to the problem we can only afford to increase the size of problem instances by a small amount.

Order notations, the calculus, and asymptotic analysis in general, give information about growth rates as n goes to infinity, not about the shape of curves inside the practicality window. In both cases in figure 1.16 f grows asymptotically faster than g, so in both cases asymptotic analysis would say that g is better than f. But in the second case, g is actually worse than f for all input sizes we see in practice! Asymptotic analysis can be quite misleading.

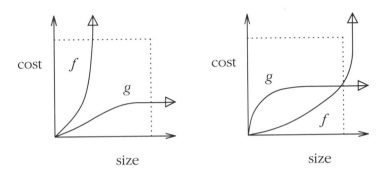

Figure 1.16 Possible ways of leaving the practicality window

Perhaps we should forget about "infinitely growing" inputs entirely? After all, we know that in practice we will never have inputs bigger than 10^{15} or so. Unfortunately this cure is worse than the disease. Table 1.11 gives some values of the $\lg^*$ function. $\lg^* n$ is the *iterated logarithm* of n; it is the number of times we must take the base two logarithm of n to get down to one or less. For all practical purposes we may as well take $\lg^* n$ to be five or less; but what happens when we do? If we bound $\lg^* n$ then we have bounded n. If we bound n then all inputs are constant size. If we only have inputs up to some constant then all our algorithms are constant time. Our whole carefully constructed edifice of analysis crumbles!

n	1	2	3–4	5–16	17–65536	65536–$2^{65536}(\sim 10^{19728})$
$\lg^* n$	0	1	2	3	4	5

Table 1.11 The iterated logarithm function

The moral is that we have to temper justice with mercy and assume (unrealistically) that the input can grow to arbitrarily large sizes just to compare algorithms for reasonably sized inputs. If the input is relatively small then almost any algorithm will do (unless the problem is *very* common or *very* hard), and if the input is ridiculously large then no algorithm will do, so, in practice, we are mostly interested in "reasonably large" problem instances. Growth rates, although applicable only to ridiculously large instances, can say something about performance on reasonably large instances. We use them to try to predict how solutions will behave inside the practicality window by looking at their gross behavior outside the window. Nevertheless, do not be seduced by an algorithm's asymptotic efficiency; in practice we have to vet all algorithms against reality. Asymptopia is a great place to visit, but no one should live there.

1.9   Hard Problems

Good judgment comes from experience,
and experience comes from bad judgment.

Barry LePatner, quoted in Robert Byrne,
The 1,911 Best things anybody ever said

The previous sections sketch the basic topography of the continent of analysis. Now let's look at an important mountain range of hard problems. This last section revolves around the question: what is a hard problem?

Here's a problem: Tess Trueheart decides to hike over a mountain. The reason doesn't matter so let's say that her sweetheart, Richard Tracy, lives on the other side. Tess leaves at eight in the morning and hikes over the mountain in a day. Some days later she again leaves at eight in the morning and, following the same path she used before, she returns home in a day. Prove that there is a point on the path such that Tess passes the point at the same time of day on both trips.

Pause Stop and think about this. Is it even true?

The natural thing to do is to start drawing graphs of distance against time looking for some special point common to all such graphs. But this seems like an infinite process. Fortunately there is an elegant way to prove the result. Imagine *two hikers* walking along the same path from opposite directions. It doesn't matter that the path crosses a mountain or that the hikers start at the same time. At some point they will meet. At that point it will be the same time of day for both hikers (of course!) and the same place (ditto!).

This kind of problem is usually called a puzzle, but in our list of hard problems (page 10) it's a "conceptually hard problem." Puzzles have the special property that they seem difficult until we sneak up on them somehow. However, having done so, it is usually easy to see that the strange strategy solves the problem.

Here's another problem: Given a chessboard and thirty-two dominoes we can cover the board with the dominoes in such a way that every domino covers two chessboard squares and no square is covered by more than one domino (this is easy to do). Suppose we cut off the top left and bottom right squares of the chessboard. Is this mutilated chessboard coverable by thirty-one dominoes?

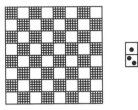

Figure 1.17 A chessboard and a domino

The obvious thing to try is to lay some dominoes on the board and see if thirty-one dominoes can be made to cover the board. At least in this puzzle there are only a finite number of possible ways to cover the board, so we know that we can exhaust all possible coverings. As we try, however, we notice that there are always at least two squares we can't cover (try it on graph paper). Perhaps it cannot be done?

Now observe that since each domino can only cover two squares horizontally or vertically, the two squares it covers must be of different colors. But there are now thirty black squares and thirty-two white squares so there is no way to match the colors up. Also, each possible domino covering corresponds to such a color matching. Thus there is no way to cover the mutilated board with dominoes!

The thing that's special about puzzles is that their solutions are hard to *find* but once given a solution it is usually easy to *check* that it is a solution. Often the only apparent way to solve a puzzle is by a brute force enumeration of all possibilities (or a large proportion of all possibilities). For example, although it isn't a puzzle, we've seen that the function $f(n) = 2^n - 1$ satisfies the towers of Hanoi recurrence. It seems harder to guess that function out of a clear blue sky than to check that the function satisfies the recurrence. A similar thing occurs in computation. There are many problems whose solutions are "easy to check" but seem to be "hard to find."

For example, a **prime** number is a positive integer divisible only by itself and 1 (divisible means that the division leaves no remainder). Thus, 2, 3, 5, 7, 11, 13, 17, 19, and 23 are prime. A number that isn't prime is **composite**. Is 667 prime or composite? It appears harder to *find* the factors of 667 (if it's indeed composite) than it is to *check* that $667 = a \times b$ for some given a and b. To check this, we need only multiply a and b and see if their product is 667. However, to find these factors in the first place seems to require us to test whether 667 is divisible by 2, 3, 5, 7, 9, 11, 13, 17, 19, and 23. (Why can we skip numbers?)

Pause | Why stop at 23?

At a 1903 mathematics meeting, Frank Cole, an American mathematician, presented a paper without saying a single word. Silently he raised two to the 67th power and subtracted one.

$$2^{67} - 1 = 147573952589676412927$$

He then wrote down the number 193,707,721, then the number 761,838,-257,287, and multiplied them.

$$193707721 \times 761838257287 = 147573952589676412927$$

He later said that the factorization took him "three years of sundays" to find, but the gathered mathematicians had only to check his multiplications to see that the factors were correct. There seems to be a big difference between finding and checking!

Pause | How did Cole find 2^{67} so rapidly? (Hint: $x^{2n} = x^n x^n$.)

Even so, the difference between finding and checking might not seem that big a deal. However, the existence of a fast algorithm to factor integers would mean the end of many computer security measures used by banks, industry, the government, and the military. The idea is that because there appears to be a big difference between finding factors and checking factors then factoring can be used as a *trapdoor*. Trapdoors are easy to get out of but hard to get into; going one way is easy, but going the other way is hard unless we know where the secret latch is. As we will see in chapter six, we can use trapdoors to build relatively secure systems. Since some of these trapdoors help guard both your bank account and our military secrets, the distinction between finding and checking can be very important indeed.[7]

We say that a problem has a *fast* solution if we have an algorithm to solve it taking time that is at worst a **polynomial** of the size of the problem. Thus, the time the algorithm takes to solve any instance of the problem is no larger than some constant power of the size of the problem (if the problem is of size n, this is n^c). For example, testing whether an integer is even (divisible by two) is polynomial in the size of the problem, and is hence fast, since the algorithm only need check that the last digit of the number is 0, 2, 4, 6, or 8. Similarly, the complementary problem of deciding whether a number is odd is also polynomial.

_____

[7]In 1940, G. H. Hardy, an English number theorist, wrote that he was happy that the two topics in pure mathematics that he found most elegant had no practical use whatsoever. Those two topics were number theory and the theory of relativity. Poor Hardy.

It might not seem that bad to find that $667 = 23 \times 29$ but cryptology today uses much larger numbers than 667; much larger even than $2^{67} - 1$. The obvious algorithm to test primality—try all smaller primes—is not suitable for large numbers since it takes time that is *not* polynomial in the size of the problem. (The size of the problem is not n, but $\lg n$; we'll find out why in chapter six.) Here's an example of a large factorization problem: is $(2^{353} + 1)/3$ prime?

$$(2^{353} + 1)/3 \ = \ 61159963093068573642955223874722318$$
$$42124173304448749663300236905031794$$
$$336235959488186716141627001830812331$$

This number has one hundred and six digits! Surely this problem is harder than asking whether 667 is prime. Is this question easy or hard? What do we mean when we say that a problem is computationally hard?

Let's separate the difficulty of solving a problem instance just because it's large from the difficulty of finding versus checking. To see why, consider addition. Addition is a well-understood process, yet the addition of two numbers with trillions of digits is a hard problem. Nevertheless it's hard only because the instance is large, not because addition itself is difficult. Since every problem instance of large enough size is hard in that sense we aren't interested in that kind of hardness.

Going by the everyday meaning of the phrase "hard problem," we might say that both the hiker problem and the mutilated chessboard problem are hard, meaning that a random person probably can't solve either of them in under a minute (say). However, this intuition does not apply to computers since the difficulty lies with *us*, not the computer. The hiker problem is *conceptually hard*. The mutilated chessboard problem is not conceptually hard, we can always enumerate all cases, but it, at least initially, appeared to be *computationally hard*.

The current best solutions to thousands of important problems are **exponential** in the size of the problems. Their best solutions take time proportional to a constant raised to the power of the size of the problem (if the problem is of size n, this is r^n, $r > 1$). This is unacceptably long even for fairly small instances of the problem. (As we saw with HANOI, for n as small as sixty-four, the run time can be longer than the age of the universe!) Just what is it about such problems that makes them *intrinsically hard?*

The trouble is that sometimes we really don't know if they are intrinsically hard or not. It's difficult to tell whether a problem with a complex solution is a simple one hiding itself in complexity, or a truly complex one that came by its complexity honestly.

For example, the factoring problem does not yet have a polynomial solution. Does this mean that it doesn't have one or that no one sufficiently clever has tried to find one? We have proved that the towers of Hanoi problem requires an exponential number of moves, but until we proved that lower bound, we had no idea if algorithm HANOI was good or bad; it seemed good, but we weren't sure. At this point you might object that the "real" reason the towers of Hanoi problem is computationally hard is that it takes exponential time just to list the solution. True. Nevertheless there are problems whose outputs are the simplest possible output of "yes" or "no" that still need, or perhaps only appear to need, exponential time. Worse, some problems are so hard that they are *computationally unsolvable,* no algorithm can solve these problems.

OH, I'M NOT SURPRISED YOU COULDN'T
SOLVE THE LAST QUESTION—IT'S UNSOLVABLE.

In chapter seven we will discover that there is a special group of about two thousand apparently computationally hard problems called $\mathcal{NP}$-*complete problems.* They have been proven to be of roughly equivalent difficulty and a polynomial solution to any one would imply a polynomial solution to all others (for more detail see chapter seven, page 424). Since these problems are important in practice and either all polynomially solvable at one stroke or all exponentially solvable, there is intense interest in their solution. One more reason to study these expensive problems is that they are the problems that tie up the computer the most!

The first problem proved to be $\mathcal{NP}$-complete is called the **satisfiability problem:** can a proposition composed of variables that can only have one of two logical values, true or false, ever be true (be *satisfied*)? The only known solution to this problem, as for all other $\mathcal{NP}$-complete problems, is to examine all, or a large fraction, of the exponential number of combinations of possible truth assignments. This is like trying to solve the mutilated chessboard problem by trying all possible ways to lay dominoes on the board. For the past two decades, this brute force solution has been the best solution known for every $\mathcal{NP}$-complete problem.

Solving Hard Problems

If there really are many important problems whose solutions require exponential time and if exponential time algorithms really are useless in practice, then how do we solve these problems?

Well, there are several general techniques we can use. Two of these are *dynamic programming* and *greedy algorithms*. However, while better than blind enumeration, these techniques can still be exponential in the worst case.

To cross this mountain range of hard problems we must be more devious. Since *exact* solutions are so difficult, why not find *approximate* solutions to these problems? In practice, "near" solutions may be sufficient. This idea leads to **approximation algorithms**. There are good approximation algorithms for some of these hard problems that do not guarantee to get the best possible answer, but at least they terminate quickly. Approximation algorithms don't solve the original problem, they solve a relaxed version of it. Instead of climbing the mountain we climb a nearby foothill.

There are other ways to relax the original problem to derive reasonable solutions in a reasonable time. Probably the most surprising of these are **probabilistic algorithms**, which guarantee to work only *most* of the time![8] In the past, algorithms always had to give the right answer; probabilistic algorithms *usually* give the right answer but they always give an answer fast. Instead of climbing the mountain we tunnel through it, accepting the possibility that we may come out at the wrong place. It is worrying that we try to solve these hard problems by writing algorithms that *we know* can lie to us, but desperate times call for desperate measures!

Here is a simple probabilistic algorithm:

Problem: Decide whether

$$(6x^2 + 3x^3 - x)^3 + (6x^2 - 3x^3 + x)^3 = (6x^2(3x^2 + 1))^2$$

Algorithm: Generate a random number and see if it satisfies the equation. If it does, then say that the equation is correct. If it doesn't, then say that the equation is incorrect.

---

[8]In this book we'll call an algorithm that uses random numbers a *randomized algorithm;* as we shall see in chapter three, page 209, a probabilistic algorithm is not necessarily randomized, and a randomized algorithm is not necessarily probabilistic.

Now if this algorithm says the equation is incorrect, the equation is not correct, but if it says the equation is correct, it may be wrong. Of course, if the algorithm is much faster than a non-probabilistic algorithm we can just run it again (and again...). If it says that the equation holds for many random numbers then our confidence that the equation is correct increases. (Actually, if the equation is true for three numbers, it's true for all numbers.)

| Pause | Is the equation correct?

Note the distinction between probabilistic algorithms and normal algorithms that happen to be good on average. Speaking loosely, a probabilistic algorithm is *always fast* but only *mostly right;* a normal algorithm that is good on average is *mostly fast* but *always right.*

1.10 Coda—The Continent of Analysis

> Science is a match that man has just got alight. He thought he was in a room—in moments of devotion, a temple—and that his light would be reflected from and display walls inscribed with wonderful secrets and pillars carved with philosophical systems wrought into harmony. It is a curious sensation, now that the preliminary sputter is over and the flame burns up clear, to see his hands lit and just a glimpse of himself and the patch he stands on visible, and around him, in place of all that human comfort and beauty he anticipated—darkness still.
>
> H. G. Wells, *Essays: The Rediscovery of the Unique*

In the early fifties, when vacuum tubes roamed the earth, there was a lot of controversy over what was the right model for analyzing algorithms. In those prehistoric times people were not even sure what the appropriate model of a computer should be. Have we got it right? Throughout this chapter we've made many assumptions about the appropriate way to analyze problems. Are our results of any practical use? Here are three assurances that they are.

First, we have to start somewhere. We can use any analysis, no matter how rough, to winnow out bad ideas during the design phase. Mindlessly optimizing a program by making small improvements in the code before analyzing its algorithm is like doing carpentry with only sandpaper. It can be done, but using a saw is a lot faster.

Second, we have to make up our own model for each new problem. Studying abstracted problems, like the ones in this book, can only provide examples of how analysis is done. Every new problem, like it or not, could require wholly new tools; it is not enough to amass a large collection of tools that have worked well in the past. The road to heaven is paved with good inventions.

Finally, while we have made many assumptions, some of the broad influences of problem cost are already included in our default model. Run time is always important. It isn't the only important thing, true, but that is no reason to forgo a time analysis. The ancients believed that the earth was flat. We laugh at them today thinking smugly to ourselves that they must have been very stupid. But consider: *the earth is flat to within twelve centimeters in every kilometer.* For many practical purposes the earth *is* flat.

Chock-full of messy and tedious details, reality is an unpleasant place to live; but it's better than the alternative. Being forced to live in reality, we're always forced to approximate. Extending Wells' wonderful analogy: no amount of matches will give light on a windy night. We can't do science if we cannot isolate each variable or, at least, identify its effect. The analysis grail is to minimize all resources used, but that's just not feasible. To progress we're forced to restrict attention to only a few resource costs at a time.

∞∞

We've now seen something of the surface features of the continent of analysis, and we've briefly looked at an unusual mountain range of hard problems somewhere in the interior. We've seen that there are three kinds of hard but solvable problems in computer science: problems can be conceptually, analytically, or computationally hard. Indeed, many problems can be hard in all three senses; artificial intelligence tries to turn conceptually hard problems into merely computationally hard problems.

Next, we will create a detailed map of a small but important state on the continent—the state of comparison-based algorithms. Then we will slowly work our way from the fairly well-understood coast to deep into the interior where things are not so well mapped. But before we go, look at the vast difference in our present levels of understanding of various parts of the continent. As we have seen with Hanoi, we understand some problems so well that we have *exact solutions* (within the model, of course). However we know so little about $\mathcal{NP}$-complete problems that *we don't even know whether they are polynomial.* There is much to do.

Endnotes

Computational Ideas
Complexity measure, problem, problem instance, problem size, model, algorithm, recursive algorithm, resource cost, worst cost, best cost, aver-

age cost, lower bound, upper bound, forward-backward strategy, optimality, order notation, asymptotic behavior, $\mathcal{NP}$-complete problem, approximation algorithm, probabilistic algorithm.

Mathematical Ideas

- Proof by induction: A proof by induction works by establishing the hypothesis for some small integer k (usually 1 or 2) then showing that if the hypothesis is true for any n at least as big as k then it is true for $n + 1$. Therefore the hypothesis is true for all $n \geq k$.

- Proof by contradiction: A proof by contradiction works by assuming the falsity of the hypothesis then showing that this forces an absurdity. Thus the hypothesis cannot be false, and so must be true.

- Using subtract and guess, and divide and guess to find the value of sums.

- Using limits and differentiation to estimate the growth rate of functions.

Definitions

- *recursive algorithm:* A recursive algorithm calls itself with at least one of its parameters decreased.

- *recurrence:* A recurrence is a expression relating the value of a function at some point to its values at other, smaller, points.

- *logarithm:* The base x logarithm of y is the power to which we must raise x to get y.

- *factorial:* The factorial of an integer is the product of all positive integers smaller than or equal to the integer.

- *choose:* n choose m is the number of ways of selecting m things from n things without worrying about their selection order.

- *limit:* The limit of a function, if it exists, is the value the function tends toward as one of the function's parameters tends toward some value.

- *derivative:* The derivative of a function is the limit of the function's growth rate.

- *fibonacci number:* A fibonacci number is the sum of the previous two fibonacci numbers; the first two are both 1.

- *prime number:* A prime number is a positive integer divisible only by itself and one.

- *composite number:* A composite number is a non-prime positive integer.

- *linear function:* A linear function of n is a constant times n plus a constant.

- *polynomial:* A polynomial in n is a sum of terms where every term is a constant times a constant power of n.

- *exponential:* An exponential in n is a constant times a constant raised to a linear power of n.

Constants

- $e = 2.71828\ 18284\ 59045\ 23536\cdots$

- $\phi = 1.61803\ 39887\ 49894\ 84820\cdots$

Notation

- $\sim$ = about the same size as

- $:$ = such that

- $\lg$ = base two logarithm

- $\ln$ = base e logarithm

- $\sum$ = the sum of

- $\rightarrow$ = tends to

- $!$ = the factorial function

- $\binom{n}{m}$ = number of ways of choosing m things from n things.

- $\lim$ = the limit of

- f' = derivative of f

- df/dx = derivative of f with respect to x

- $\max_{x \in S} f(x)$ = the largest value of f where x ranges over the set S

- $\min_{x \in S} f(x)$ = the smallest value of f where x ranges over the set S

Conventions

- $0! = 1$

- $x^0 = 1$

- $\lg 1 = 0$

- $m > n \Longrightarrow \sum_{i=m}^{n} r_i = 0$

- $m > n \Longrightarrow \binom{n}{m} = 0$

Tools

- $2^n - 1$ disk moves are necessary and sufficient to solve the towers of Hanoi problem with n disks

- $\forall x > 1, \quad \log_x y = z \iff x^z = y \iff x^{\log_x y} = y$

- $\forall x > 1, \quad \log_x rs = \log_x r + \log_x s$

- $\forall x > 1, \quad y^{\log_x z} = z^{\log_x y}$

- $\forall x, y > 1, \quad \log_x z = \dfrac{\log_y z}{\log_y x}$

- Solution of quadratics: $rx^2 + sx + t = 0 \Longrightarrow x = \dfrac{-s \pm \sqrt{s^2 - 4rt}}{2r}$

- $\sum_{i=1}^{n} i = \dfrac{n(n+1)}{2}$

- $\forall n \geq m \geq 0, \quad \binom{n}{m} = \dfrac{n!}{m!(n-m)!}$

- $f(n) = \begin{cases} 1 & n = 1 \\ 2f(n-1) + 1 & n > 1 \end{cases} \iff f(n) = 2^n - 1$

- $f(n) = \begin{cases} 4 & n = 1 \\ 4f(n-1) & n > 1 \end{cases} \iff f(n) = 2^{2n} = 4^n$

- $f(n) = \begin{cases} 1 & n = 1 \\ nf(n-1) & n > 1 \end{cases} \iff f(n) = n!$

- $f(n) = \begin{cases} 1 & n \leq 1 \\ f(n-1) + f(n-2) & n > 1 \end{cases} \Longrightarrow f(n) \sim \dfrac{\phi^n}{\sqrt{5}}$

- The binomial theorem: $(x + y)^n = \sum_{i=0}^{n} \binom{n}{i} x^{n-i} y^i$

- $e^x = \lim_{n \to \infty} \left(1 + \dfrac{x}{n}\right)^n = \sum_{i=0}^{\infty} \dfrac{x^i}{i!}$

- $n = O(n^2)$

- $n^2 \neq O(n)$

- $\lim_{n \to \infty} \dfrac{f(n)}{g(n)} = r \implies f = O(g)$

- $\lg n = o(\sqrt{n})$

- $2^{\sqrt{\lg n}} = O(n^r)$

- l'Hôpital's rule: f and g differentiable, $\lim_{x \to \infty} f(x) = \infty$, $\lim_{x \to \infty} g(x) = \infty$, and $\lim_{x \to \infty} \dfrac{f'(x)}{g'(x)}$ exists, $\implies \lim_{x \to \infty} \dfrac{f(x)}{g(x)} = \lim_{x \to \infty} \dfrac{f'(x)}{g'(x)}$

- $f(x) = x^r \implies f'(x) = r x^{r-1}$

- $f(x) = e^x \implies f'(x) = e^x$

- $f(x) = \ln x \implies f'(x) = \dfrac{1}{x}$

- $\forall x \neq 1, \quad \sum_{i=0}^{n} x^i = \dfrac{x^{n+1} - 1}{x - 1}$ (exercise 8, page 69)

Notes

In mathematical circles the number ϕ, also called the *golden ratio*, is named for Phidias, perhaps the most important of the Greek sculptors of antiquity. Phidias was the chief sculptor of the Parthenon, and the ratio between many lengths and widths in the Parthenon is ϕ, said to be the most aesthetically pleasing ratio. Considering that we owe Keats' "On Seeing the Elgin Marbles" and probably also "Ode on a Grecian Urn" to Phidias, there is obviously an intimate connection between recurrences and good poetry.

The broken keyboard analogy for the O notation (page 43) is from *Asymptotic Methods in Analysis,* N. G. de Bruijn, Dover, reprinted 1981. The anecdotes about Gauss' addition and Cole's factoring are recounted in *Mathematics: Queen and Servant of Science,* Eric Temple Bell, Mathematical Association of America, republication, 1987.

The example using the iterated log (page 51) was suggested by a passage in Donald E. Knuth's Blindern lecture notes on computer science,

1972 (unpublished). The polynomial chosen to be tested for equivalence (page 57) is one of Srīnivāsa Rāmānujan's identities; Rāmānujan, a famous Indian mathematician, was probably the most gifted intuitive number theorist ever. Mathematics, like any other human activity, has its folk beliefs: the hiker problem is a folk theorem in real analysis; the mutilated chessboard problem is a folk theorem in combinatorics. Both problems have appeared in many puzzle books. I don't know the original proposers and would appreciate any information you may have.

Exercise 10, page 69, puzzled both Pierre de Fermat and Gottfried Leibniz. Exercise 12, page 70, is adapted from *Playing With Infinity,* Rósza Péter, Dover, 1957. Problem 8, page 75, was suggested by "Computing Fibonacci Numbers (and Similarly Defined Functions) in Log Time," David Gries and G. Levin, *Information Processing Letters,* 11, 68–69, 1980. Problem 9, page 75, appears in *aha! Insight,* Martin Gardner, Scientific American/W. H. Freeman, 1978. This problem is a presentable form of an infamous problem first solved at Yale in the late seventies. The original version was a safe sex puzzle involving a number of men and women and it dates back at least to the late sixties, perhaps much earlier.

The largest known prime cited in research problem 3, page 76, is from Brown, Noll, Parady, Smith, Smith, and Zarantonello, Letter to the editor, *American Mathematical Monthly,* 97, 214, 1990. The factorization of the smaller number mentioned in the problem is the work of Arjen Lenstra, and Mark Manasse, April 1989.

Research problem 4, page 76, is usually called the $3x + 1$ problem. It is also called Ulam's problem, Collatz's problem, Kakutani's problem, the Syracuse problem, Hasse's algorithm, and the Hailstones problem. It is very difficult and has a long history; many people, including me, have wasted lots of time on it. When it was first introduced into America in the fifties some mathematicians called it a Russian plot, since it was soaking up the time of all American mathematicians and no one solved it. One of the greatest living mathematicians, Paul Erdös, is reported to have said that "mathematics is not yet ready for such problems." See "The $3x + 1$ Problem and Its Generalizations," J. C. Lagarias, *American Mathematical Monthly,* 92, 3–23, 1985.

Further Reading

To improve your problem solving ability attack and engulf *How To Solve It,* George Pólya, Princeton University Press, second edition, 1957. This is the best book ever written on developing problem solving skill. See also Pólya's *Mathematics and Plausible Reasoning: Volume 1, Induction and Analogy in Mathematics,* Princeton University Press, 1954, and *Math-*

ematics and Plausible Reasoning: Volume 2, Patterns of Plausible Inference, Princeton University Press, second edition, 1968. To learn about proof techniques using simple examples read *How to Read and Do Proofs,* Daniel Solow, John Wiley & Sons, second edition, 1990. For examples of everyday mathematical thinking try *Thinking Mathematically,* John Mason, Leone Burton, and Kaye Stacey, Addison-Wesley, 1982. To see a concrete example of how mathematicians make everyday thinking more rigorous and also to see something of the limits of rigorous thinking read the excellent *Proofs and Refutations: The Logic of Mathematical Discovery,* Imre Lakatos, Cambridge University Press, 1976.

For more background on the calculus see *A Concept of Limits,* Donald W. Hight, Dover, 1977, and *What is Calculus About?,* W. W. Sawyer, The Mathematical Association of America, 1961. To catch something of the excitement of mathematics read the classic *Men of Mathematics,* Eric Temple Bell, Simon and Schuster, 1937. Although Bell occasionally made factual errors he has excited generations of people to become mathematicians. To find out what's happening today read *The Problems of Mathematics,* Ian Stewart, Oxford University Press, 1987.

For a wide-angle introduction to algorithms and their uses read the wonderful *Algorithmics: The Spirit of Computing,* David Harel, Addison-Wesley, 1987. To help you grapple with recursion see *Thinking Recursively,* Eric S. Roberts, John Wiley & Sons, 1986. For a good introduction to clever programming read *Writing Efficient Programs,* Prentice-Hall, 1982; *Programming Pearls,* Addison-Wesley, 1986; and *More Programming Pearls: Confessions of a Coder,* Addison-Wesley, 1988; all by Jon Louis Bentley. To correct any urges to thoughtlessly hack read the superlative *The Elements of Programming Style,* Brian W. Kernighan and P. J. Plauger, McGraw-Hill, second edition, 1978. For an in-depth study of the art of good programming read *Software Tools in Pascal,* Brian W. Kernighan and P. J. Plauger, Addison-Wesley, 1981.

To find out more about $\mathcal{N}\mathcal{P}$-completeness read *Computers and Intractability: A Guide to the Theory of $\mathcal{N}\mathcal{P}$-Completeness,* Michael R. Garey and David S. Johnson, W. H. Freeman, 1979. For a good non-technical introduction to infeasibility and $\mathcal{N}\mathcal{P}$-completeness plus some history of the field see the wonderful article "Combinatorics, Complexity, and Randomness," Richard M. Karp, in *ACM Turing Award Lectures: The First Twenty Years, 1966–1985,* ACM Press, 1987. For a rigorous way to define and manipulate order notations see "Crusade for a Better Notation," Gilles Brassard, *Sigact News,* 17, 1, 1985. For a large selection of the "good bits" of computer science written in a pleasant style read *The Turing Omnibus,* A. K. Dewdney, Computer Science Press, 1989.

For other presentations of topics touched on in this chapter (and in succeeding chapters) read the excellent *Introduction To Algorithms: A Cre-*

ative Approach, Udi Manber, Addison-Wesley, 1989. For a good all-round introduction to analysis see the well-written *Computer Algorithms: Introduction to Design and Analysis,* Sara Baase, Addison-Wesley, second edition, 1988. For a readable presentation of mostly mathematical algorithms see *Algorithms and Complexity,* Herbert S. Wilf, Prentice-Hall, 1986. For a wide selection of algorithms see *Algorithms,* Robert Sedgewick, Addison-Wesley, second edition, 1988.

For a comprehensive presentation of both algorithms and analysis see *Introduction to Algorithms,* Thomas M. Cormen, Charles E. Leiserson, and Ronald L. Rivest, McGraw-Hill/MIT Press, 1990. *Algorithmics: Theory and Practice,* Gilles Brassard and Paul Brately, Prentice-Hall, 1988, focuses on algorithmic techniques and *Algorithms and Data Structures; Design, Correctness, Analysis,* Jeffrey H. Kingston, Addison-Wesley, 1990, emphasizes correctness. *Design and Analysis of Algorithms,* Jeffrey D. Smith, PWS-Kent, 1989, is an accessible introduction. The following takes a very practical approach: *Algorithms from P to NP: Volume I, Design & Efficiency,* Bernard Moret and Henry Shapiro, Benjamin/Cummings, 1991. For a list of many standard algorithms and exact analyses of their worst and average cases see *Handbook of Algorithms and Data Structures,* Gaston H. Gonnet and Ricardo Baeza-Yates, Addison-Wesley, second edition, 1991.

There are many earlier books on the analysis of algorithms. After Knuth's series of books (listed below) the standard analysis book is the pathbreaking *The Design and Analysis of Algorithms,* Alfred V. Aho, John E. Hopcroft, and Jeffrey D. Ullman, Addison-Wesley, 1974. Also see *Fundamentals of Computer Algorithms,* Ellis Horowitz and Sartaj Sahni, Computer Science Press, 1978. For a large collection of carefully-analyzed algorithms see the three volume *Data Structures and Algorithms,* Kurt Mehlhorn, Springer-Verlag, 1984. Volume 1 is on sorting and searching, volume 2 is on graph algorithms and $\mathcal{NP}$-completeness, and volume 3 is on multi-dimensional searching and computational geometry. *The Analysis of Algorithms,* Paul Walton Purdom, Jr. and Cynthia A. Brown, Holt, Reinhart and Winston, 1985, gives a thorough treatment of mathematical analysis, and *Algorithms: Their Complexity and Efficiency,* Lydia Kronsjö, John Wiley & Sons, second edition, 1987, concentrates on numerical algorithms. See also *Computational Complexity of Sequential and Parallel Algorithms,* Lydia Kronsjö, John Wiley & Sons, 1985.

To see where most of analysis came from you *must* read Donald E. Knuth's massive, and magisterial, trilogy: *The Art of Computer Programming.* Volume 1 (second edition, Addison-Wesley, 1981) concerns fundamental algorithms, volume 2 (second edition, Addison-Wesley, 1981) focuses on numerical algorithms, and volume 3 (Addison-Wesley, 1973) is all about sorting and searching. Knuth is without peer.

Questions

> Be doers of the Word, and not hearers
> only, thus deceiving your own selves.
>
> *Epistle of James, 1:22, The Bible*

Exercises

1. Given a problem, consider the following algorithm: Give the problem to a clever friend to solve.

   (a) Is this an algorithm?

   (b) If not, is it an algorithm if we can apply it recursively?

   (c) Is it optimal?

2. (a) When using space as our resource cost should we count the space needed to represent the input and the output?

   (b) Should we count the program's length? (Hint: Can it ever depend on the size of the input? Think of table-lookup.)

3. We have special names only for the first three powers (line, square, cube; linear, quadratic, cubic; higher powers are derived from Latin) because the Greeks felt that all numbers should have a geometric interpretation. But they couldn't visualize more than three dimensions.

   (a) Examine figure 1.18 then show that $\sum_{i=0}^{n-1}(2i+1) = n^2$.

1   4   9   16

Figure 1.18 Square numbers according to the Greeks

   (b) Use (a) to show that $\sum_{i=0}^{n} i = n(n+1)/2$.

4. The Greeks were also interested in triangular numbers. Two consecutive triangular numbers make up a square. (See figure 1.19.)

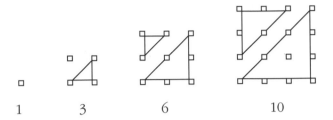

1   3   6   10

Figure 1.19 Triangular numbers

Show that the nth triangular number is $n(n+1)/2$.

5. Consider the code fragment in figure 1.20.

```
sum ← 0
for i from 1 to n
    sum ← sum − 1
    for j from 1 to i
        sum ← sum + 2
```

Figure 1.20 Another code fragment

(a) Does it set *sum* to the same value as the code fragments in figure 1.1, page 4?

(b) How many assignments does it do?

6. What is the final value of *sum* in figure 1.11, page 33? Note that its value is not the same as the number of times it takes part in an assignment.

7. Let $f(n) = \sum_{i=0}^{n-1} 2^i$.

Show that

(a) $f(n) = f(n-1) + 2^{n-1}$.

(b) $f(n) = 2f(n-1) + 1$.

(c) Use (a) and (b) to show that $f(n) = 2^n - 1$.

(d) Use (b) and (c) to show that algorithm HANOI takes $2^n - 1$ steps.

8. Let $f(n) = \sum_{i=0}^{n-1} x^i$.

   Show that

   (a) $f(n) = f(n-1) + x^{n-1}$.

   (b) $f(n) = xf(n-1) + 1$.

   (c) Use (a) and (b) to show that $f(n) = (x^n - 1)/(x - 1)$.

   (d) What is the value of the sum when $x = 1$?

9. (a) Use the square subdivision idea suggested in figure 1.21 to show

   that $\sum_{i=1}^{\infty} 1/2^i = 1$. (Note: Each subsquare is one-quarter of the

   size of the next biggest square.)

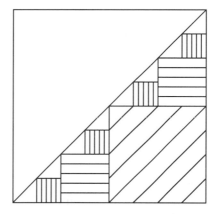

Figure 1.21 Dividing a square into smaller squares

   (b) Construct two more square subdivisions suggesting the same relation.

10. (a) Show that the sum $\sum_{i=1}^{\infty}(-1)^i = -1 + 1 - 1 + \cdots$ does not have a value.

   (b) Suppose we switch on a lamp at one minute to midnight, switch it off at one-half minute to midnight, switch it on again at one-quarter minute to midnight, and so on. Is the lamp on or off at midnight?

   (c) Is infinity even or odd?

11. (a) Use the long division algorithm to divide $(1 - x)$ into 1 to show that $\dfrac{1}{1 - x} = 1 + x + x^2 + x^3 + \cdots$

    (b) Does this mean that $1 - 1 + 1 - \cdots = 1/2$?

12. A chocolate company decides to promote its chocolate bars by including a coupon with each bar. A bar costs a dollar and with c coupons you get a new bar.
    How much chocolate is a dollar worth?

13. Use subtract and guess, or divide and guess, to find the following sums. Once you have found a sum you may use its value in later sums.

    (a) $\displaystyle\sum_{i=1}^{n} i^2$.

    (b) $\displaystyle\sum_{i=1}^{n} i^3$.

    (c) $\displaystyle\sum_{i=1}^{n} i(i + 1)$.

    (d) $\displaystyle\sum_{i=1}^{n} i(i + 1)(i + 2)$.

    (e) $\displaystyle\sum_{i=1}^{n} 1/2^i$.

    (f) $\displaystyle\sum_{i=1}^{n} i2^i$.

    (g) $\displaystyle\sum_{i=1}^{n} i/2^i$.

    (h) $\displaystyle\sum_{i=1}^{n} i^2/2^i$.

14. (a) Use induction to show that $n^2 - n$ is always even.

    (b) Find a one-line proof of the same result.

    (c) Show that $n^3 - n$ is always divisible by three.

    (d) Is $n^5 - n$ always divisible by five?

15. Rewrite HANOI to recurse until there are no disks instead of one disk. Analyze your algorithm.

16. Number the Hanoi disks in order of decreasing size from 0 to $n - 1$. Show that HANOI moves the ith disk 2^i times.

17. FIBONACCI uses the three variables *past*, *previous*, and *present* (excluding the loop index). Rewrite it to use only two variables.

18. Suppose our computer can only represent integers of up to ten decimal digits. Roughly what is the smallest n that will force integer overflow in algorithm 1.3, page 32?

19. Consider the recurrence $f(n) = \begin{cases} 1 & n = 1 \\ f(n-1) + n & n > 1 \end{cases}$

    (a) Guess that $f(n) = rn^2 + sn + t$ and find r, s, and t.

    (b) What happens if we had guessed that $f(n) = rn + s$?

20. (a) Show that the following recurrences all define the same function.

$$f(n) = \begin{cases} 2 & n = 1 \\ f(n-1) + 2 & n > 1 \end{cases}$$

$$f(n) = \begin{cases} 2 & n = 1 \\ 4 & n = 2 \\ 2f(n-1) - f(n-2) & n > 2 \end{cases}$$

$$f(n) = \begin{cases} 2 & n = 1 \\ 4 & n = 2 \\ 6 & n = 3 \\ f(n-1) + f(n-2) - f(n-3) & n > 3 \end{cases}$$

   (b) Show that there are an infinite number of recurrences defining the same function.

   (c) If there are no boundary conditions, are there an infinite number of functions satisfying any recurrence?

21. Let f be the fibonacci number function and assume that f is non-decreasing. By using this fact alone show that

$$\forall n \geq 2, \quad 2^n \geq f(n) \geq \sqrt{2}^{\,n}$$

22. Surprisingly, the binomial theorem for $(1 + x)^r$ holds even for real r, once $1 > x > -1$. Here's how to use the binomial theorem to estimate $\sqrt{1.04}$.

$$
\begin{aligned}
\sqrt{1.04} &= (1 + 0.04)^{1/2} \\
&= 1 + \frac{1}{2}0.04 + \frac{\frac{1}{2}\left(\frac{1}{2}-1\right)}{1 \times 2}0.04^2 + \frac{\frac{1}{2}\left(\frac{1}{2}-1\right)\left(\frac{1}{2}-2\right)}{1 \times 2 \times 3}0.04^3 + \cdots \\
&= 1 + \frac{0.04}{2} - \frac{0.04^2}{8} + \frac{0.04^3}{16} - \cdots \\
&= 1 + 0.02 - 0.0002 + 0.000004 - \cdots \sim 1.019804
\end{aligned}
$$

Although the binomial theorem doesn't apply to $(1 + x)^{1/2}$ if $x > 1$, we can still use it to find square roots of large numbers.
Find the square root of 41600 to five decimal places.

23. Given that $\log_{10} 2 = 0.30102999566 \cdots$ show that $2^{16!}$ has 6,298,387,-349,264 decimal digits.

24. (a) Show that $1 = O(1)$ and that $1 = O(n)$.

    (b) Show that the growth rates of the code fragments in figure 1.1, page 4, are: $O(1)$, $O(n)$, and, $O(n^2)$, respectively.

25. Suppose that $f = O(n)$.

    (a) Show that

        i. $f(n)/n = O(1)$.
        ii. $f(n)/n^2 = o(1)$.

    (b) Characterize $f(n)/n^3$ as exactly as you can.

26. (a) Show that

        i. $5n = O(n \lg n)$.
        ii. $40n \lg n = O(n^2)$.
        iii. $7n \lg n = \Omega(n)$.
        iv. $12n^2 = \Omega(n \lg n)$.

    (b) What can you say about the relative growth rates of n, $n \lg n$, and n^2?

27. Suppose you have five algorithms with worst case run times (in microseconds) of $10000 \lg n$, $1000n$, $100n \lg n$, $10n^2$, and 2^n, respectively, where n is the size of the input.

    (a) What is the worst case fastest algorithm for each value of n?

    (b) Given an hour of computing time, each algorithm can solve the problem only for instances up to a certain size. What is this limiting size for each algorithm?

    (c) Answer (b) for a machine running ten times faster.

28. Complete the following sentence in as many ways as you can: 2^n grows relative to n as — grows relative to $\lg n$.

29. (a) Show that O is *transitive*, that is, show that

$$f = O(g) \text{ and } g = O(h) \Longrightarrow f = O(h)$$

    (b) Are any of the other order notations transitive?

30. Is there anything wrong with any of the following arguments?

(a) $\sum_{i=1}^{n} i = \sum_{i=1}^{n} O(i) = \sum_{i=1}^{n} O(n) = nO(n) = O(n^2)$

(b) $\sum_{i=1}^{n} k^i = \sum_{i=1}^{n} O(k^i) = \sum_{i=1}^{n} O(k^n) = nO(k^n) = O(nk^n)$

(c) $\sum_{i=1}^{n} k^i = \sum_{i=1}^{n} O(k^i) = \sum_{i=1}^{n} k^{O(i)} = \sum_{i=1}^{n} k^{O(n)} = nk^{O(n)}$

31. Suppose that algorithm A runs in time $f(n)$ and that algorithm B runs in time $g(n)$. Answer the following four questions for each of the following five cases.

Questions:

(a) Is A faster than B for all n?

(b) Is B faster than A for all n?

(c) Is A faster than B for all n greater than some c?

(d) Is B faster than A for all n greater than some c?

Cases:

(1) $g(n) = \Omega(f(n) \lg n)$

(2) $g(n) \approx f(n) \lg n$

(3) $g(n) = \Theta(f(n) \lg n)$

(4) $g(n) = O(f(n) \lg n)$

(5) $g(n) = o(f(n) \lg n)$

32. Show that

(a) $f \approx g \quad \Longleftrightarrow \quad f = g + o(g)$.

(b) $f = o(g) \quad \Longrightarrow \quad f = O(g)$.

(c) $f = o(g) \quad \Longleftrightarrow \quad f = O(g)$ and $g \neq O(f)$.

33. Suppose algorithm A has worst cost f and suppose g is the current best lower bound on the problem. The problem's actual cost is unknown. If $f = g + O(h)$ give conditions on h so that A is worst case asymptotically optimal.

34. We have seen that $\lim_{n \to \infty} \dfrac{f(n)}{g(n)} = r \Longrightarrow f = O(g)$. Is the converse true?

35. Describe the following sets of functions in English:

(a) $n^{O(1)}$

(b) $O(n^{O(1)})$

(c) $O(O(n^{O(1)}))$

(d) $n^{\Omega(1)}$

(e) $O(n^{\Omega(1)})$

(f) $O(O(n^{\Omega(1)}))$

36. (a) Show that $2^{n+r} = O(2^n)$.

(b) Show that $2^{2n-r} \neq O(2^n)$.

(c) Is $2^{rn} = O(2^n)$?

37. Show that

    (a) n^r grows faster than n^s for all $r > s$.

    (b) r^n grows faster than s^n for all $r > s > 1$.

38. Let $f \simeq g \iff \lim_{n \to \infty} (f(n) - g(n)) = 0$.

    (a) If f and g are increasing functions, g is non-zero, and $f(n)$ is always at least as large as $g(n)$, show that $f \simeq g \implies f \approx g$.

    (b) Give two reasons why we should use $\approx$ and not $\simeq$ in analysis.

Problems

1. Find a growth rate that cubes the run time when we double the input.

2. (a) Arrange n^2 apples in a square. From each row find the largest one and let A be the smallest of these. From each column find the smallest one and let B be the largest of these. Which apple is bigger, A or B?

   (b) The lower bound on the worst cost of a problem has been defined as

   $$\min_{A \in \mathcal{A}_M} \left\{ \max_{I \in I_n} f_A(I) \right\}$$

   Is this the same as

   $$\max_{I \in I_n} \left\{ \min_{A \in \mathcal{A}_M} f_A(I) \right\}$$

3. For this problem recall that there may be an infinite number of algorithms allowed within a model. Answer the following four questions first for lower bounds on the worst cost then for lower bounds on the average cost. Assume that worst costs are integers.

   (a) Does every problem have a best lower bound?

   (b) Having a representative input size implies that the resource usage graph of an algorithm "looks the same" no matter how large the input is. How could there not be a representative size?

   (c) If the best lower bound exists, must there be a simple relationship between the input size and the resource cost for each input size?

   (d) If the best lower bound exists, must there be a single algorithm achieving this bound for all input sizes? (That is, not one for each size, but one for all sizes.)

4. Which function grows faster:

   (a) n^r or $\lg^c n$ where $1 > r > 0$, and $c \geq 1$?

   (b) $n^{1/n}$ or $\lg n$?

   (c) $n^{\lg n}$ or $\lg^n n$?

   (d) $2^{2^{n \lg n}}$ or $2^{n!}$?

   (e) $2^{\lg n \lg \lg n}$ or $n^{\lg n} e^{\lg \lg n}$?

5. Show that the fibonacci numbers are $f(n) = \dfrac{\phi^n - (1 - \phi)^n}{\sqrt{5}}$.

6. Here is an iterative algorithm to solve the towers of Hanoi problem: Arrange the pegs in a circle. Move the smallest disk to the next peg in clockwise order unless the last move was a move of the smallest disk, in which case, make the only other legal move.
   Show that this iterative algorithm does exactly the same sequence of moves as the recursive algorithm.

7. Find the average number of moves necessary to solve the Hanoi problem starting from an arbitrary legal arrangement if every legal arrangement of n disks distributed on the three pegs is equally likely.

8. Let $f(n)$ be the nth fibonacci number. FIBONACCI finds $f(n)$ in linear time.

   (a) Show that it is possible to find x^n given x in $O(\lg n)$ multiplications.

   (b) Show that f obeys the following matrix recurrence for $n \geq 2$.

   $$\begin{pmatrix} f(n) \\ f(n-1) \end{pmatrix} = \begin{pmatrix} 1 & 1 \\ 1 & 0 \end{pmatrix} \begin{pmatrix} f(n-1) \\ f(n-2) \end{pmatrix}$$

   (c) Show that $f(n + m + 2) = f(n + 1)f(m + 1) + f(n)f(m)$.

   (d) Design an algorithm generating $f(n)$ in logarithmic time.

   (e) Is your algorithm asymptotically optimal?

9. Each of n surgeons must separately operate on each of n patients. However, surgeons don't want to catch the patients' diseases, nor do they want to infect any patient with any other patient's disease. Clinical procedure requires that no glove surface touched by a doctor should touch a patient. Assume that each surgeon refuses to touch a glove surface that another surgeon has touched.

   (a) Show that two surgeons can operate on two patients using only two surgical gloves in all. (Hint: Surgical gloves are made of rubber and so can be everted—that is, turned inside out.)

(b) What is the minimum number of surgical gloves required to accomplish the n^2 operations?

(c) Prove that your algorithm is optimal.

Research

1. Solve problem 9 for n surgeons and m patients.

2. We can generalize the towers of Hanoi problem to more than three pegs. What is the minimum number of disk moves necessary and sufficient to solve the problem when there are $m \geq 4$ pegs?

3. $(2^{353} + 1)/3$ is a product of two primes the smaller of which has 37 digits. This took about a year to decide using a clever algorithm. The largest known prime is $391,581 \times 2^{216193} - 1$. This number has 65,087 digits. How would you test this number for primality?

4. What is the cost of algorithm 1.4?

$$
\begin{array}{l}
\text{STRANGE}(n) \\
\quad \{ \text{ Do something mysterious with } n \geq 1. \ \} \\
\\
\quad \textbf{while } n \neq 1 \\
\quad\quad \textbf{if } n \text{ is even} \\
\quad\quad\quad \textbf{then } n \leftarrow n/2 \\
\quad\quad\quad \textbf{else } n \leftarrow 3n + 1
\end{array}
$$

Algorithm 1.4

5. Find a general way to derive good lower bounds for a wide class of problems.

6. The following crossword is British style; the clues are cryptic references to the answers. Many of the words in the puzzle can be found in this chapter. The number of letters in each word is given in parentheses; every number corresponds to a word. Hyphenations are indicated by a dash. Usually the answers are disguised using bad puns and other double meanings, or are anagrammed or otherwise hidden in the clue. Be wary of misleading punctuation and capitalization.

Across:

1 A slow function sounds like a lumberjack's beat. (9)

5 Color found in a chambermaid's heart. (5)

8 Nothing in Brazil changes. (5)

10 Chain me bewildered—a computer, for example. (7)

13 Farther on in a wardrobe yonder. (6)

16 No light shower. O! Word pun madness! (8)

17 A count is less feeling. (6)

18 Mapping a fly's head in ointment. (8)

21 Is ten ten? Addled but aware. (8)

24 Rich ancestor keeps fortune. (6)

26 Vehicle common for people who lisp. (3)

28 A tree on which your life is written. (4)

30 Micro giant is first temptation. (5)

33 For almost goes with to? (3)

35 Choose one mother; lucky start is best. (7)

37 An example, peeled and chopped, is the biggest. (3)

38 About as fast as the tamale losing its man? (5)

39 Stirring logarithm discovers a recipe. (9)

Down:

1 Loafer's idle remains. (9)

2 Depression from bird. Why? (5)

3 Send up an occasion. (4)

4 Confused acronym forgets New York is big. (5)

6 Smallest mind without end. (3)

7 Happens again about mongrel. (5)

9 A layer then, with no tea? (3)

11 A capital order! The ironic are not included. (5)

12 Feeling a direction and movement. (7)

14 Revolving path but a sphere precedes it? (5)

15 A strange ridge has a mournful air. (5)

18 A seizure is desirable in clothing. (3)

19 Honey found in a dreamy trance. (6)

20 A necessity ruined Eden. (4)

22 A Peron raised a Roman hail. (3)

23 Put in wrong? Gives algorithm food for thought. (5)

25 An odd resort, but Cleo fell upon it, we hear. (3)

26 Enumerate the low ranking nobleman. (5)

27 A letter from Greece cut a rhododendron. (3)

29 Ale drunken with two thousand and a proposition. (5)

31 Might the prisoner of war erode missing poetry? (5)

32 Bound for M.I.T. after '51. (5)

33 Beat up a game. (4)

34 Morning after former spouse is final. (4)

36 Hit it up and get it down. (3)

PART ONE

Fresh Horses

❧❧❧

Shall the contents discover, something rare
Even then will rush to knowledge.
Go; fresh horses;
And gracious be the issue.

William Shakespeare, *The Winter's Tale, III, I*

N OW THAT we've geared up for our trek, let's look at the entire domain we will be exploring. In chapter two we grapple with the problem of searching for things. In chapter three we examine the problem of summarizing things. And in chapter four we look at the problem of arranging things. All three chapters introduce ideas, approaches, and techniques useful beyond their immediate application in the chapter.

2

SEARCHING

> The whole of science is nothing more
> than a refinement of everyday thinking.
>
> Albert Einstein, *Physics and Reality*

N OW LET'S begin solving our computational problems. Our first foray
into the continent of analysis is to search for something; we want to
find a target in a domain by probing elements of the domain. Searching
should be well-understood since we do it every day—we're always looking
for phone numbers, car keys, and good television shows. However, good
search algorithms depend on the search problem since searches vary in
fundamental ways. For example,

- we may probe inaccurately (searching for your only pair of glasses);

- probes may have unequal cost (searching for a pin in the dark);

- domains may be infinite (searching for oil);

- targets may move (searching for an enemy submarine);

- targets may be ill-defined (searching for a good television show);

- search time may be bounded (searching for a gas leak); or

- searches may be all of the above (searching for meaning in life).

Let's simplify and assume that: we are searching for a well-defined and fixed target; we have an unbounded time to find it; the domain is static and finite; all probes cost the same; we never make a mistake when probing; and, we never forget any information gathered during the search.

Further, in the computer world we don't search for something, we search for its **key**. Often, the domain is complicated so we make up a set of simple keys and associate each element of the domain with a key. The point is to make each key, presumably a simple object, stand for an element, perhaps a complex object. For example, in a database with records dozens of fields long it's sensible to index the records by a numerical key (say, their position in a list).

We use keys every day. For example, your friend Terry is a complicated organism. If every time you wanted to find Terry you had to describe him completely, you and Terry would be quickly estranged! Fortunately we have invented several keys identifying Terry. Terry answers Terry's phone. Terry reads mail addressed to "Terry." Terry answers to the word "Terry." Terry has a scraggly beard. No key identifies Terry uniquely, but taken together they often do.

In this chapter our domain is a set of elements that can be put in order in the same way that we can put numbers or words in order. The numbers 3, 10, 6, 1 are *out of order,* the numbers 1, 3, 6, 10 are *in increasing order.* (They are in decreasing order as: 10, 6, 3, 1.) Putting things in order is called **sorting**. We will find out how to sort things in chapter four.

This chapter is about different versions of the search problem. In the first section, our domain is unsorted and we can only get information by comparing things. We will analyze the simplest algorithm, *linear search.* In the second and third sections the domain is sorted. To solve this version of the problem we'll improve linear search to *jump search,* then we'll improve that to *binary search.* In the fourth section we'll explore what happens when we change the model in four important ways.

2.1 Linear Search

> 'Where shall I begin, please your Majesty?' he asked.
> 'Begin at the beginning,' the King said, very gravely,
> 'and go on till you come to the end: then stop.'
>
> Lewis Carroll, *Alice's Adventures in Wonderland*

Let's first assume that we know nothing about the list to be searched and the element we wish to search it for; let's walk through the entire analysis task sketched in chapter one.

The Problem

We are given a list, L, of n elements and one more element, X, and the problem is to decide whether X is in L. If X is in L we have to identify at least one element of L that it's equal to.

The Model

Our environment will be the default environment given in chapter one (page 13) plus the following assumptions.

- All elements of L are unique (this assumption simplifies analysis).

- We can compare X or any element of L with any element of L and this comparison will tell us that the two elements are equal, the first is less than the second, or the first is greater than the second.

- We can't find ordering information about X and the elements of L except by comparing elements.

Our goal is to minimize the number of "three-way" ($<$, $=$, and $>$) element-element comparisons done. This is the **comparison-based model**.

Note that, as with any model, merely defining it does not imply that all search problems are dominated by, or even proportional to, comparisons. This model only fits search problems on arrays. It implicitly assumes that array access has constant cost, that comparisons are proportional to overall run time, and that run time is the only thing that matters. The third model assumption rules out using anything but comparisons to find X in L. For example, in this restricted model we cannot assume that the elements of L are numbers, find their average, and use that to deduce something about X's location in L.

The Algorithm

The first thing to do with a problem is to *reduce it to something simpler.* This idea is so important and occurs in so many guises in analysis that it deserves a name:

> *The reduction strategy:* Try to reduce the problem to simpler subproblems, even if this results in many subproblems.

Mathematicians have a special way of saying the same thing: *reduce the problem to something already solved.* There's even a special mathematical joke expressing the idea: Alice and Bob have to complete two tasks in the minimum time possible. The first task is to make tea given kettles, cups, and teabags. Both do the obvious. The second task is the same except that the kettles are initially full. Bob makes tea as before except that he doesn't have to first fill his kettle. However Alice takes less time by emptying her kettle and observing that she has reduced the problem to one already solved!

We've already used this reduction strategy when designing HANOI (algorithm 1.1, page 16).

Now what could be simpler than the given search problem on n elements? Simple; the same search problem on $n - 1$ elements! In one comparison we can reduce our uncertainty about the position of X in L by at least one. Thus, there is a simple brute force and ignorance algorithm solving this problem: compare X to each element of L. This is *linear search.* (See algorithm 2.1.)

LINEAR_SEARCH($List, lower, upper, X$)
   { Look for X in $List[lower..upper]$.
   Report its position if found, else report 0.
   $upper \geq lower > 0$. }

   if $List[lower] = X$
      then return $lower$
      else
         if $lower = upper$
            then return 0
            else return LINEAR_SEARCH($List, lower + 1, upper, X$)

Algorithm 2.1

Analysis

In the next five subsections we'll find an upper bound on the worst cost of the algorithm, a lower bound on the worst cost of the problem, and then corresponding bounds on the average cost.

The Worst Cost

Let $f(n)$ be the number of comparisons LINEAR SEARCH does when finding X in a list of size n. The following recurrence models the worst cost of LINEAR_SEARCH.

$$f(n) = \begin{cases} 1 & n = 1 \\ f(n-1) + 1 & n > 1 \end{cases}$$

Since, if we only have one element in L then it costs one comparison to tell whether X is in L, and if we have $n > 1$ elements, then in one comparison we reduce the problem to the same problem but on $n - 1$ elements.

In analysis we often have to estimate the growth rate of a function defined by a recurrence. Sometimes we end with a recurrence because we started with a recursive algorithm. However many algorithms are naturally iterative and it's sometimes easier to model an iterative algorithm *as if* it were recursive. For example, algorithm 2.1 is an iterative version of LINEAR_SEARCH. The two versions of the algorithm do the same element-element comparisons and in the same order and both are modelled by the above recurrence.

```
LINEAR_SEARCH ( List, lower, upper, X )
    { Look for X in List[lower..upper].
    Report its position if found, else report 0.
    upper ≥ lower > 0. }

    index ← lower
    while upper ≥ index and List[index] ≠ X
        index ← index + 1
    if index > upper
        then return 0
        else return index
```

Algorithm 2.2

This is a simple recurrence and it is easy to see that its solution is $f(n) = n$. Since we already know the expected answer we can use induction to prove it. (Compare the proof on page 21.)

We wish to show that

$$f(n) = \begin{cases} 1 & n = 1 \\ f(n-1) + 1 & n > 1 \end{cases} \quad \Longrightarrow \quad f(n) = n$$

Basis step: $f(1) = 1$ so $f(n) = n$ when $n = 1$.

Inductive step: Suppose that for all $k < n$, $f(k) = k$. Then since $n > 1$, from the recurrence we must have that $f(n) = f(n-1)+1$. But $n > n-1$. Therefore $f(n) = (n-1)+1 = n$.

Hence, if the inductive assumption is true for all $k < n$ then it is true for n as well. Thus, the theorem is true for all n.

Now, what if we didn't know the exact form of $f(n)$? This is where induction falls to the ground with a loud crash. *Induction is only useful if we already know the answer.* This is like the difference between guessing and checking discussed in chapter one (page 53). Once we think we know the answer, we can use induction to check that it is correct.[1]

So if we've already guessed the answer why bother to check it? Well, we may have guessed wrong; checking reassures us that we're right. Also, if the proof fails then we *know* we guessed wrong and have to start over. Finally, producing a proof is like producing a lower bound; it forces us to think about what we're doing, and perhaps suggests a better, less problem dependent, way to do the same thing—a way that we can then use for other problems. Our first solutions are usually heavily problem dependent—we think of a solution based on simple cases then see what's wrong with it, refining the original solution to fit the general case by adding qualifications and extensions. But often there is a cleaner, less problem dependent, solution. Clean solutions are more likely to be useful elsewhere; the best algorithms have little to do with the original problem.

To solve a problem we can't allow it to intimidate us; we'll just attack it and bull our way through. Only after finding a solution will we look for ways to turn the direct assault into a clever flanking maneuver showing how best to outwit the enemy. Then this maneuver becomes part of our arsenal.

One alternative when we don't know the exact form of f is to iterate a few steps of the recurrence and try to guess the sum of the sequence of

---

[1]"You can always find truth with logic if you have already found truth without it." G. K. Chesterton, *The Man who was Orthodox.*

terms. Let's call this method *substitute and guess*. This example would go something like this:

$$
\begin{aligned}
f(n) &= f(n-1)+1 && [= f(n-1)+1] \\
&= \{f(n-2)+1\}+1 && [= f(n-2)+2] \\
&= \{\{f(n-3)+1\}+1\}+1 && [= f(n-3)+3] \\
&\;\;\vdots \\
&= f(n-i)+i && \text{(this is a guess)}
\end{aligned}
$$

| Long Pause | Why is this a guess and not a proof?

With this guess in hand we ask: when does this stop? The answer is: *at the boundary.* We want an i that makes $n-i$ equal to 1 (because we know the value of $f(1)$). So i must be $n-1$. Thus,

$$f(n) = f(n-(n-1))+n-1 = f(1)+n-1 = 1+n-1 = n$$

Now we can use this guess in a proof by induction if need be. This is a guess and not a proof because the ellipsis (the "...") hides an unbounded number of steps. Since we hope to convince other people of a fact using a proof, a proof must have a *finite* number of steps. If not, we would never finish convincing them of the fact!

Another way to solve recurrences is to guess the general form of the function then solve the equations the recurrence generates for that form. Let's call this method *guess and test*. For example, suppose we guess that f is linear. Thus, $f(n) = rn + s$ for some r and s. Then, from the boundary value of the recurrence, we know that

$$r + s = 1$$

From the recurrence itself we know that for all n greater than 1

$$rn + s = r(n-1) + s + 1$$

This implies that $r = 1$, which in turn implies that $s = 0$. Therefore $f(n) = rn + s = n$ is a solution to the recurrence with boundary value of 1 when $n = 1$.

| Long Pause | Will guess and test always work? Show that it will work for $f(n) = rn^2 + sn + t$ but not for $f(n) = rn^2 + s$.

So LINEAR_SEARCH uses up to n element-element comparisons; other comparisons don't count within the model. Is this worst case optimal? (Remember to add *"within this model,"* under your breath when claiming optimality.) Unsurprisingly, LINEAR_SEARCH has optimal worst cost ("within this model").

The Lower Bound on the Worst Cost

To prove that LINEAR_SEARCH has optimal worst cost we can show that if any algorithm tries to do the same job in less time (that is, if it tries to use fewer comparisons), then it must be *incorrect.* Thus, *if only element-element comparisons matter,* no algorithm is better than LINEAR_SEARCH in the worst case.

Suppose a search algorithm does $n - 1$ (or less) comparisons of X with the elements of L. Since there are n elements in L, it must have avoided comparing X with at least one element of L, say $L[i]$. We can now arrange it so that the algorithm answers that X is *not* in L when X is in fact in L by constructing the following input and watching the poor algorithm choke. Let L be a list of n different elements and let X equal $L[i]$. The hypothetical algorithm never compares X to $L[i]$ so it will decide, incorrectly, that X is not in L.

Since such an input is legal within our model, any algorithm that supposedly decides whether X is *not* in L in less than n comparisons must be incorrect. Since this hypothetical algorithm determines this fact it cannot be correct. Hence every algorithm to search for X in L must do at least n comparisons. This is a proof by contradiction.

| Pause | Do you believe this proof?

Such a seemingly obvious lower bound required a reasonable amount of effort. Unfortunately, *the above argument is wrong.* The first error is to assume that if an algorithm skips $L[i]$ on one run then it will always skip $L[i]$. The second, more subtle, error is to assume that the only way an algorithm can gain information about the elements of L is by comparing them with X. This is not correct because the algorithm can gain information by comparing elements of L *to each other.* The model does not disallow these comparisons.

We can patch the first error by observing that the algorithm doesn't have to skip the same i every time; once it skips some i then there is an input that it answers incorrectly.

The second error is more difficult to fix. We could restrict our model to only allow comparisons between X and elements of L but it would be better if we didn't have to unnecessarily restrict our results. Suppose an algorithm does $k \geq 0$ comparisons not involving X (the preprocessing stage) and then l comparisons of X with elements of L (the searching stage). We want to show that $k + l \geq n$.

| Pause | Couldn't an algorithm do something clever in the preprocessing stage so that it wouldn't have to compare X to a large number of elements?

Now, when we've finished the preprocessing phase we've split L into some number of pieces, say m. A "piece" is a set of elements every two of which have been connected by some sequence of comparisons. We start with n separate pieces and we need at least one comparison to connect any two pieces (and so decrease the number of pieces by one). Since there are now m pieces then we must have used at least $n - m$ comparisons to build them. Therefore, $k \geq n - m$.

| Pause | Show that $n \geq m \geq 1$ and that $m = n \iff k = 0$.

When we come to search with X we must compare X to at least one element from each piece, otherwise X may be in a piece we didn't look at. Thus $l \geq m$. Therefore, $k + l \geq n$. So, if we spend time making L easier to search then we will not spend less time than if we had just done a linear search for X.

Despite the two errors in our original argument we only need the last two paragraphs to establish the lower bound; they amount to saying that we can't avoid at least looking at the input. This is a simple lower bound argument—so simple that we can apply it to almost all problems, even to those that don't involve comparisons. This bound is the **input-output lower bound**.

| Pause | You might complain that there is nothing in the model about having two phases to the search. Show that it is not necessary to restrict the model.

Probability Theory

To talk about the average cost we first have to agree on how to describe uncertain events. **Probability theory** is all about expressing the uncertainty of complicated events in terms of the assumed probability of simpler events. Although the basic ideas go back to the sixteenth-century Italian mathematician Gerolamo Cardano, as a discipline probability theory is thought to have started in France in the seventeenth century when a gambler asked a mathematician to figure out the best way to bet when playing dice. The date was 1653; the gambler was Antoine Gombaud, the Chevalier de Méré; and the mathematician was Blaise Pascal. Besides mathematics, Pascal contributed to philosophy, experimental physics, and computer design (he built the first calculator). The programming language Pascal is named after him.

The *sample space* of an experiment is the set of all outcomes of the experiment. Let's agree to delimit sets using curly braces. The sample space of the "experiment" of tossing a coin is {heads, tails}; the sample space of the "experiment" of pulling a card from a deck of cards has fifty-two outcomes; the sample space of the "experiment" of whether my car will start tomorrow is {starts, doesn't start}.

You may object that a coin could fall on its edge, or that it could be tossed so hard that it enters earth orbit, or that it could fall into a volcano. No problem. All this means is that we didn't include all the possible outcomes of the experiment. Usually we will allow only a finite number of different outcomes for any experiment. For example, the tossed coin experiment could have the sample space {heads, tails, something else}.

An *event* is a subset of the sample space. An event is a set of outcomes, and an outcome is an instance of an event if it's in that set. For instance, when drawing a card we could be interested in the event of selecting a face card. There are sixteen outcomes that belong to the face-card event. Or perhaps we're interested in the five events: "a six," "a spade," "an ace," "any other card," or "any card." Several of these events share outcomes. If two events share no outcomes they are *disjoint*.

For each experiment we associate a probability with each event. The *probability* of an event is the ratio of the number of outcomes favorable to the event divided by the total number of possible outcomes. Let's adopt the convention that a bold-face P (**P**) means "the probability of." Thus, in our card example, the probabilities of the five events are:

$$\mathbf{P}(\text{a six}) = \frac{4}{52}, \quad \mathbf{P}(\text{a spade}) = \frac{13}{52}, \quad \mathbf{P}(\text{an ace}) = \frac{4}{52}$$

$$\mathbf{P}(\text{not a six and not a spade and not an ace}) = \frac{33}{52}, \quad \mathbf{P}(\text{a card}) = \frac{52}{52}$$

Two events are *independent* if the probability of each event does not depend on the other occurring. So if we toss a coin then pull a card, the event "heads" should be independent of the event "king of clubs." This is not the same as saying that the two events are disjoint. Alternately, two events are independent if the probability of their joint occurrence is the product of the probabilities of their separate occurrences. That is, "heads" and "king of clubs" are independent events if

$$\mathbf{P}(\text{heads and king of clubs}) = \mathbf{P}(\text{heads})\mathbf{P}(\text{king of clubs})$$

There are several things to note about the definition of probability. First, it assumes that there are only a finite number of possible outcomes; we may also define probabilities over infinite sample spaces. Second, it forces the probability of any event to be a number between zero and one. Third, it implies that the probability of any one of two disjoint events happening is the sum of the probabilities of the events. (This is the *sum rule.*) That is, if A and B are disjoint then

$$\mathbf{P}(A \text{ or } B) = \mathbf{P}(A) + \mathbf{P}(B)$$

Finally, it assumes that outcomes are equally likely—a concept we need probability to define!

Like any model of the world we start by making assumptions about the world then we begin calculating based on the model. If we gather evidence that the model is not adequately predicting real behavior, we change the model. In this case we would have to go back to the experiment and ask whether the assumption of equal likelihood of outcomes is reasonable. Perhaps we're playing cards with a cardsharp and our estimate of the likelihood of aces doesn't match their actual frequency!

By now you may have another objection: we may have no way to gather empirical data because the experiment may not be performable. Or it may be one of a kind. For example, in six billion years the sun will either go nova or it won't. We won't consider such experiments just yet. There are more objections to be made—as Pascal would say, probability is a dicey subject—but let's stop here for now.

The Average Cost

How many comparisons does LINEAR_SEARCH do on average? Before we can talk about an average input and the average behavior of an algorithm, we need to know the probability of occurrence of each possible input. Since we usually don't know this, let's assume that X is equally likely to be any of the elements of L. This is reasonable since, within our current model, we don't know anything about the elements of L. Note that this doesn't force X to actually be in L.

Pause | Why?

This assumption is an application of the following strategy:

> *The simplicity strategy:* When in doubt assume as little as necessary.

This strategy has several names: in science it is called Occam's razor, in statistics it is called the principle of indifference, and in systems design it is called the KISS (keep it simple, stupid) principle. (Perhaps instead of "sealed with a kiss" analysts should sign their love letters SWAK—simplicity will aid knowledge.)

Let's also assume that the only thing varying in the input is X's position in L, if it is in L. This assumption is reasonable because we are only interested in *those inputs that make* LINEAR SEARCH *behave differently* (that is, inputs requiring different numbers of comparisons). To see that this is so, suppose we let both X and L vary. Since our model ignores all attributes of the input elements except for their relative sizes, all LINEAR SEARCH cares about is the relative order of occurrence of the elements in L. It is not necessary to consider all possible Ls since all that matters to LINEAR SEARCH is *the number of elements that precede X in L* (if X is in L). No matter what the element is, it costs exactly one comparison to decide if it's equal to X. Also, the cost to find X varies only as X's position in L varies. Thus, we may treat L as fixed and allow X to vary its position in L, if it is in L.

Okay, let's think of the number of comparisons LINEAR SEARCH does as the outcome of an experiment. We have assumed two things:

- X is equally likely to be any element of L, and

- the only thing varying in the experiment is X's position in L, if it's in L.

There are $n + 1$ events: $X = L[1]$, $X = L[2]$, ..., $X = L[n]$, and $X \notin L$. These events are disjoint since within our model each element of L is unique. Thus all $n + 1$ probabilities are greater than or equal to zero and they must sum to one.

Pause | Why?

Since X is either in L or it isn't, and since all the probabilities sum to one, then

$$\mathbf{P}(X \notin L) = 1 - \sum_{i=1}^{n} \mathbf{P}(X = L[i])$$

Let k_i be the number of comparisons LINEAR SEARCH does when X equals $L[i]$. Let k_0 be the number of comparisons it does when $X \notin L$.

If X happens to equal $L[i]$ then LINEAR_SEARCH takes i comparisons to find it. So, $\forall i \leq n$, $k_i = i$. If X is not in L then LINEAR_SEARCH does n comparisons to determine this, so $k_0 = n$.

The **average** of n numbers is the sum of the numbers divided by n. So the average number of comparisons is the number of comparisons for each disjoint event weighted by the probability of that event. Let $f(n)$ be the average number of comparisons LINEAR_SEARCH uses to search a list of size n. Let p_i be the probability that X equals $L[i]$ and let p_0 be the probability that X is not in L. Then

$$f(n) = k_0 \mathbf{P}(X \notin L) + \sum_{i=1}^{n} k_i \mathbf{P}(X = L[i])$$

$$= n p_0 + \sum_{i=1}^{n} i p_i$$

Since X is equally likely to be anywhere in L (by assumption) then $\forall i, j \leq n$, $p_i = p_j$. Let this common probability be p. Thus $p_0 = 1 - np$. Therefore

$$f(n) = p_0 n + \sum_{i=1}^{n} i p$$

$$= p_0 n + p \sum_{i=1}^{n} i$$

$$= p_0 n + p \frac{n(n+1)}{2}$$

$$= p_0 n + \frac{(1 - p_0)}{n} \frac{n(n+1)}{2}$$

$$= \frac{n + 1 + p_0(n-1)}{2}$$

Since $1 \geq p_0 \geq 0$ then, with the *assumption* that X is equally likely to be any of the elements of L, we have that

$$n \geq f(n) \geq \frac{(n+1)}{2}$$

Now various choices for p_0 give us different averages (see table 2.1). As p_0 increases from 0 to 1 the average search time goes up linearly (see figure 2.1). As the table shows, if X is equally likely to be any of the elements of L and

- if X must be in L, then LINEAR SEARCH examines roughly half of L.

- if X is equally likely to not be in L as to be any one of the elements of L, then LINEAR SEARCH examines roughly half of L.

- if X is equally likely to be in L as to not be in L, then LINEAR SEARCH examines roughly three-quarters of L.

- if X cannot be in L, then LINEAR SEARCH examines all of L.

p_0	p	$f(n)$
0	$\dfrac{1}{n}$	$\dfrac{(n+1)}{2} \approx \dfrac{n}{2}$
$\dfrac{1}{n+1}$	$\dfrac{1}{n+1}$	$\dfrac{n(n+3)}{2(n+1)} \approx \dfrac{n}{2}$
$\dfrac{1}{2}$	$\dfrac{1}{2n}$	$\dfrac{(3n+1)}{4} \approx \dfrac{3n}{4}$
1	0	n

Table 2.1   Average cost of linear search

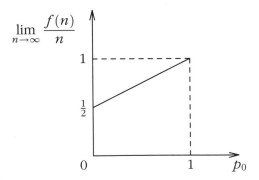

Figure 2.1   Average behavior of linear search for large n

In practice we may know a lot about the *probability distribution* of the chances of X being each element of L (that is, all $n + 1$ p_is). In that case the above analysis will have to be changed, just as our assumptions about the chance of aces change if we play cards with a cardsharp.

Although the average cost is important there are three problems with average cost analysis. First, the average cost is usually harder to find than the worst cost. Second, for the average to be meaningful we also need a measure of the spread of values around the average; we need a measure of *variance* as well as the average value. Finally, we usually have to guess the probability distribution, so the calculated average is just a guess. Fortunately there is often a way out of this last bind: we can *randomize* the algorithm to avoid the problem (see section 2.4, page 123).

The Lower Bound on the Average Cost

Given a problem, P, a model M, the set of algorithms, $\mathcal{A}_M$, solving P within M, together with the set of all size n instances of P, I_n, and a cost function $f_\mathcal{A}$,

$$\text{the lower bound on the average cost of } P = \min_{\mathcal{A} \in \mathcal{A}_M} \left\{ \sum_{I \in I_n} \mathbf{P}(I) f_\mathcal{A}(I) \right\}$$

where $\mathbf{P}(I)$ is the probability that I occurs.

Intuitively, the reason LINEAR SEARCH uses up to n comparisons is that any algorithm solving the problem must compare X to every element of L. Comparing elements of L can reduce these comparisons but only by replacing them with at least as many other comparisons. So let's break the proof that LINEAR SEARCH is optimal on average into two parts: first we'll assume that we can only compare X and elements of L, then we'll see that other comparisons cannot reduce the average number of comparisons needed.

First, suppose that every average case optimal algorithm can only compare X with every element of L. The only thing mattering to these algorithms is X's position in L, if it's in L. If every comparison must involve X then the sequence of comparisons determines one of the $n!$ ways of arranging the n elements of L. If X is equally likely to be any element of L, if it's in L, then for any arrangement of the elements of L the average search time is the same as LINEAR SEARCH. Thus, if all comparisons must involve X then LINEAR SEARCH has optimal average cost.

Pause Why does every arrangement give the same average?

Now we have to show that every comparison must involve X. We could show this using an argument similar to the one we developed for the lower bound on the worst cost. Instead, for variety, let's see how the probabilities change after a comparison between two elements of L and develop a proof by contradiction. Consider any algorithm comparing two elements of L, say $L[i]$ and $L[j]$. Suppose that $L[i] < L[j]$ (the case $L[i] > L[j]$ is symmetric). We want to show that we won't gain any information useful to us on average, so we are wasting the comparison.

Now, after the comparison, do we have any more reason to believe that X is likely to be in L? If so, then perhaps our algorithm could shorten its computation time on average. If the algorithm doesn't know that X lies between $L[i]$ and $L[j]$ then, because the events $X = L[i]$, $i = 1..n$, are independent, when we find that $L[i] < L[j]$, the probability that X is in L has not increased. X may be equal to $L[i]$, equal to $L[j]$, or unequal to both. Thus if anything is to improve then the algorithm must already know that X lies between $L[i]$ and $L[j]$ *before* the comparison of $L[i]$ with $L[j]$.

But if, before the comparison, the algorithm could infer that X lies between $L[i]$ and $L[j]$ then it had enough information to tell whether $L[i] < L[j]$ or whether $L[i] > L[j]$. (In our model $L[i]$ cannot equal $L[j]$.) Thus, the comparison between $L[i]$ and $L[j]$ is redundant. Thus, any algorithm comparing two elements of L cannot have optimal average cost.

Therefore every average case optimal algorithm can only compare X to elements of L. Finally, since the algorithm must also work in the worst case, it must compare X to every element of L. As we saw in the first part of the proof, all such algorithms cost the same as LINEAR SEARCH, so LINEAR SEARCH is optimal in the average case.

Programming

LINEAR SEARCH is optimal in the worst case and average case, but only within our narrow model; in practice we may further improve the algorithm.

First, although the recursive and iterative versions cost the same within the comparison-based model, in practice the iterative solution is superior in most languages. Thinking recursively helps a lot while developing ideas but few languages support cheap recursion.

Second, when coding algorithm 2.1 [p. 85] we are sometimes allowed to fiddle with L. If so, then we should place X after the last position in L. We can then get rid of the comparison in the while loop involving *index* and *upper*, since X will always be found. We pay for this savings with an extra element-element comparison, but only for unsuccessful searches. (Why?)

Adding X to the end of L as a **sentinel** in this way lets us do two things. We can test *index* against *upper* to determine whether we fell or were pushed out of the loop, and we avoid problems with languages, like Pascal, that don't allow partial evaluation of conditionals. In such older languages, both conditions in conjunctive "if" or "while" tests (tests like "A and B") are evaluated even if the first is found to be false (and similarly for disjuncts like "A or B").[2]

Third, sometimes not only can we change L, but also L will typically be indexed from 1 to n. In that case we can put X in $L[0]$. Then instead of counting *index* up from 1, we can count it down to 0. Now we can delete the while loop test involving *index* and *upper*, and we can delete the last test and just return *index*. (Why?)

Finally, in practice a search routine is often only a small part of a larger program. Thus we may know a lot about the kind of input it usually has to deal with, so we should adapt the algorithm to the special circumstances it finds itself in. For example, in a sequence of searches, the next element to be searched for is commonly near the previous one searched for. In this case we could keep track of where each search ends and start the next search near that point.

As you can see, we can improve many things in special cases. None of these nuances are part of the comparison-based model that we started with, and each may improve search time. However there are three reasons why we shouldn't worry about them until we've designed the algorithm.

First, each of the four improvements suggested above is special:

- recursive solutions may be faster than equivalent iterative solutions in some languages (or iteration may not be supported at all);

- often we cannot change L when searching it—L may be part of a larger structure that cannot be easily modified;

- in some languages we can't refer to the zeroth location of L because there is no zeroth location to refer to; and

- the search algorithm may be independent, so it must expect any input.

Second, worrying about special case improvements during design obscures the algorithm and makes programming errors more likely. For some reason many programmers never have time to do it right, but always have time to do it over.

_____

[2]People working on programming languages call partial evaluation of conditionals "short circuiting." It is part of the more general idea of "lazy evaluation:" don't evaluate something until you have to.

Finally, none of these changes affect the algorithm's growth rate—at most they change its run time by an additive or multiplicative constant. For large n, the worst cost of the (theoretical) algorithm and the (real) program will be similar. So the moral is to design a general purpose algorithm before looking for special case improvements.

2.2   Jump Search

> Intuitively, a reluctant algorithm for a
> problem P is one which wastes time in
> a way that is sufficiently contrived to
> fool a naive observer.
>
> Andrei Broder and Jorge Stolfi,
> *"Pessimal Algorithms and Simplexity Analysis,"*
> Sigact News, 16, 3, 49–53

Now let's assume that L is sorted in increasing order. We're given an element, X, and we have to determine whether X is in L. We could use LINEAR_SEARCH again but we have more information than before, so perhaps LINEAR_SEARCH is no longer optimal.

If we change LINEAR_SEARCH to test whether X is greater than each element (instead of equal to it) then for many inputs search time will improve. The way it is now, if X is not in L then we will always examine all of L, but if X is not in L and we check whether each element is greater than X then on average we will only have to examine half of L.

| Pause | Do you believe this?

Since L is in increasing order, if we ask whether X is greater than, say, $L[5]$ and it is, then, not only is X bigger than $L[5]$, but it is also bigger than $L[1]$ to $L[4]$ as well. So after only one comparison we have gained five pieces of information!

Of course, the outcome could have been $X = L[5]$ or $X < L[5]$, but those cases are cheaper than $X > L[5]$ in the worst case (unless $n < 10$). Immediately our danger antennae start quivering, since this would be too much of a good thing; in the worst case the outcome of the comparison will be that X is greater than $L[5]$.

However, the same rule does not hold for all elements of L. For example, if we query $L[n]$, then in the best case $X = L[n]$ or $X > L[n]$ and in both cases we can halt immediately. But in the worst case we would have found out only that $X < L[n]$. So, in the worst case, comparing X

with $L[n]$ will give us only one piece of information. Big deal. Thus, *if we try to be too greedy* we will lose in the worst case. Our task is to determine how greedy is too greedy.

| Pause | What's the best element to query so that *in the worst case* we gain as much information as possible? (See section 2.3, page 105.)

Consider the following scheme: choose a number $k < n$ and repeatedly ask whether X is greater than the next k^{th} element in L. That is, interrogate $L[1]$, $L[k+1]$, $L[2k+1]$, and so on. In this way, either we fall off the end of the list or at some time one of the probed elements is greater than or equal to X.

| Pause | Should we really start with $L[1]$?

If one element reports that X is less than it then we use LINEAR_SEARCH on the k elements between it and the last queried element. If we fall off the end of the list then we use LINEAR_SEARCH on the elements from the last probed element to the end of the list. This way we eliminate a large number of the comparisons done in LINEAR_SEARCH. Note that $k = 1$ is the same as LINEAR_SEARCH.

Now, in the worst case it's a bad idea to interrogate $L[1]$ for the same reason that it's a bad idea to interrogate $L[n]$. So let's modify the scheme to interrogate $L[k]$, $L[2k]$, $L[3k]$, and so on. This is *jump search*. $k = 1$ still behaves like LINEAR_SEARCH.

| Pause | In which sublist will X lie in the worst case?

How many comparisons does JUMP_SEARCH (algorithm 2.3) do in the worst case? At worst, X will lie in the penultimate sublist since all sublists are equally hard to search (except possibly the last, which can be no harder). The worst that could happen is that we have to get all the way to the end to find out that X lies in the previous sublist (if k divides n then the last sublist is the appropriate choice).

Thus, if $(m+1)k > n \geq mk$ then we will do up to m probes to find the sublist that X must lie in (see figure 2.2). We will then do at most $k-1$ comparisons to find X in that sublist. (Assuming three-way comparisons that is. Algorithm 2.3 uses two-way comparisons for ease of coding [the possible outcomes are $<$ and $\geq$], and it requires k two-way comparisons.)

JUMP_SEARCH (*List*, *lower*, *upper*, *jump*, X)
  { Look for X in *List*[*lower..upper*].
  Report its position if found, else report 0.
  List is sorted in increasing order.
  upper $\geq$ *lower* > 0; *upper* $-$ *lower* $+ 1 \geq$ *jump* ≥ 1. }

  index $\leftarrow$ *lower* $+$ *jump* $- 1$
  while *upper* $>$ *index* **and** $X >$ *List*[*index*]
    index $\leftarrow$ *index* $+$ *jump*
  if *upper* $>$ *index*
    upper $\leftarrow$ *index*
  LINEAR_SEARCH (*List*, *index* $-$ *jump* $+ 1$, *upper*, X)

Algorithm 2.3

Thus we expend at most $m + k - 1$ three-way comparisons where m satisfies the inequality

$$m + 1 > \frac{n}{k} \geq m$$

We can express inequalities like this compactly using floor and ceiling functions. The **floor** of x, $\lfloor x \rfloor$, is the largest integer less than or equal to x. The **ceiling** of x, $\lceil x \rceil$, is the smallest integer greater than or equal to x:

$$\lfloor x \rfloor = n \iff n + 1 > x \geq n \quad \text{and} \quad \lceil x \rceil = n \iff n \geq x > n - 1$$

Thus, for $\pi = 3.141 \cdots,$[3] $\lfloor \pi \rfloor = 3$ and $\lceil \pi \rceil = 4$. For $e = 2.718 \cdots$, $\lfloor e \rfloor = 2$ and $\lceil e \rceil = 3$. And for $\phi = 1.618 \cdots$, $\lfloor \phi \rfloor = 1$ and $\lceil \phi \rceil = 2$.

Figure 2.2 Probes executed by jump search

Let $f(n, k)$ be JUMP_SEARCH's worst case number of comparisons. We have established that

$$f(n, k) = m + k - 1 = \left\lfloor \frac{n}{k} \right\rfloor + k - 1$$

---

[3]Here are two mnemonics you can use to remember the digits of π (count the letters), they begin: "How I need a drink, alcoholic of course, after the heavy chapters involving quantum mechanics," Sir Arthur Eddington, and "Sir, I bear a rhyme excelling/In mystic force and magic spelling," Bertrand Russell, *A Mathematician's Nightmare.*

	Jump Size (k)									
n	1	2	3	4	5	6	7	8	best k	least cost
1	1								1	1
2	2	2							1 2	2
3	3	2	3						2	2
4	4	3	3	4					2 3	3
5	5	3	3	4	5				2 3	3
6	6	4	4	4	5	6			2 3 4	4
7	7	4	4	4	5	6	7		2 3 4	4
8	8	5	4	5	5	6	7	8	3	4

Table 2.2 Cost of jump search for different jump sizes

From table 2.2 we see that $k = 2$ is better than $k = 1$ in the worst case. The above analysis assures us that this is true for all larger n. Thus some choices of k are better than others. Also, looking at the table we see that the best k varies as n varies (the best values of $f(n,k)$ are boxed). This suggests that we should let k be a function of n instead of a constant. Which k should we choose?

Square Root Search

Now we'd like to find the best jump size. That is, we require

$$\min_{1 \leq k \leq n} \left\{ \left\lfloor \frac{n}{k} \right\rfloor + k - 1 \right\}$$

This seems difficult to do but, fortunately, there is no shortage of goodies in our analysis knapsack! The *second derivative* of a function is the derivative of the derivative of the function; it's the growth rate of the growth rate of the function. In terms of time, the derivative is speed and the second derivative is acceleration. We can often find the maximum or minimum of a differentiable function by setting its derivative to zero if the second derivative is not also zero.

In figure 2.3 the first derivative is zero at both the maximum point and the minimum point of the two functions shown. In the first graph the second derivative is negative, since the first derivative decreases across a max point (it's first positive, then zero, then negative). But in the second graph the second derivative is positive, since the first derivative increases across a min point (it's first negative, then zero, then positive). So we can use second derivatives to, er, differentiate maxima from minima.

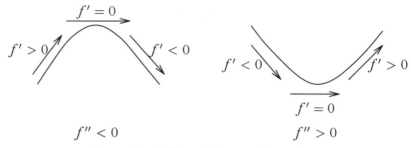

Figure 2.3   Differentiating up from down

Unfortunately we cannot just differentiate $f(n,k)$ because $f(n,k)$ is defined only when k is an integer, and $f(n,k)$ contains a floor function. How can we differentiate a function with floors? Well, what if we just ignore the floor and turn the function into a real-valued function defined over the real numbers? We will be off by no more than one comparison if we ignore the floor function and treat the minimization as

$$\min_{1 \le x \le n} \left\{ \frac{n}{x} + x \right\} - 1$$

| Pause | Can you prove this?

Consider the function $f(x) = n/x + x$ mapping real numbers to real numbers. Suppose the minimum of this function occurs at the point $x = r$. Then

$$\lceil r \rceil \ge r > \lceil r \rceil - 1 \implies \frac{1}{r} \ge \frac{1}{\lceil r \rceil} \implies \frac{n}{r} \ge \frac{n}{\lceil r \rceil} \implies \frac{n}{r} + r > \frac{n}{\lceil r \rceil} + \lceil r \rceil - 1$$

But the minimum occurs at r, so

$$\frac{n}{\lceil r \rceil} + \lceil r \rceil \ge \frac{n}{r} + r$$

Therefore

$$\frac{n}{r} + r + 1 > \frac{n}{\lceil r \rceil} + \lceil r \rceil \ge \frac{n}{r} + r$$

Therefore, if we can find the point at which the real-valued function is minimum, then taking the ceiling of this point provides a function value within one comparison of the minimum possible. (However this function value is not necessarily an integer.)

Now, if we have to minimize a function with a floor or ceiling we can use the following relations

$$\min_{x} f(x) \geq \min_{x} \lfloor f(x) \rfloor \quad \text{and} \quad \min_{x} \lceil f(x) \rceil = \lceil \min_{x} f(x) \rceil$$

(Because of our conventions on page xxvi, "$\min_{x}$" is short for "the minimum value where x ranges over the real numbers.")

[Pause] Why are these relations true?

Therefore we can find f', set it to zero, solve for x, then check that that point gives a minimum by seeing if $f'' > 0$.

$$f(x) = \frac{n}{x} + x \implies f'(x) = -\frac{n}{x^2} + 1$$

$$f'(x) = 0 \implies x^2 = n \iff x = \pm\sqrt{n}$$

$$f''(x) = \frac{2n}{x^3} \qquad \begin{cases} > 0 & \text{if } x = \sqrt{n} \\ < 0 & \text{if } x = -\sqrt{n} \end{cases}$$

Thus $x = \sqrt{n}$ gives the minimum. (See figure 2.4.)

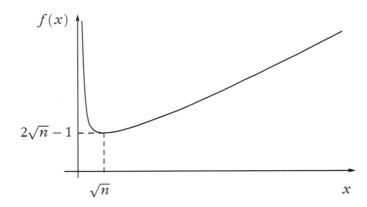

Figure 2.4 $f(x) = n/x + x - 1$

Thus we should probe every $\lceil\sqrt{n}\rceil^{th}$ element. This "square root search" is just JUMP_SEARCH for a particular value of k, so we can find its worst cost by substituting $\lceil\sqrt{n}\rceil$ for k in the worst cost of JUMP_SEARCH.

Let $\langle x \rangle$ be the **nearest integer** to x. (Note: This is undefined if $x = n + 1/2$.) It is possible to show that

$$\left\lfloor \frac{n}{\lceil \sqrt{n} \rceil} \right\rfloor = \begin{cases} \langle \sqrt{n} \rangle & \text{if } n = k^2 \text{ or } k(k+1) \\ \langle \sqrt{n} \rangle - 1 & \text{otherwise} \end{cases}$$

Thus square root search takes no more than $\langle \sqrt{n} \rangle + \lceil \sqrt{n} \rceil - 1$ comparisons to find X in L. Therefore we have cut n comparisons to roughly $2\sqrt{n} - 1$ in the worst case. This is a big improvement! Can we do better?

Note that the work is least when we balance the work we do in the probing phase with the work necessary to search a sublist. We don't want to do too much work either probing for the correct sublist or searching that sublist—and the two are nearly equal when we use about $\sqrt{n}$ probes, giving us a sublist size of about $\sqrt{n}$. This idea is so useful that we'll name it:

> *The balance strategy:* Given a problem that we can divide into related subproblems, make the subproblems equal in effort.

In every job there is some irreducible amount of work that must be done; if we try to get off too easily on one part of it we will just have to work that much harder on others. Symmetry tells us that the grass is always at least as brown on the other side of the fence. (This is the law of conservation of hassle.)

We can use the balance strategy to reduce the work even further. Intuitively, the first phase of the search pretends that there are only $\sqrt{n}$ elements; we're wearing $\sqrt{n}$-sized glasses—we can't see anything smaller than blocks of $\sqrt{n}$ elements. In the second phase we use normal-sized glasses—we can see every element. If we use three pairs of glasses, what size glasses should we use?

Suppose we do k comparisons with the first pair to find X to within n/k elements, then l comparisons with the second pair to find X to within n/kl elements, and finally, n/kl comparisons with the normal-sized pair. Balancing suggests that we let $k = l = n/kl$. This implies that $n = k^3$. Thus $k = l = n/kl = \sqrt[3]{n}$. Aha! The search now takes no more than roughly $3\sqrt[3]{n}$ comparisons! ($3\sqrt[3]{n}$ is less than $2\sqrt{n}$, $\forall n \geq 12$.)

| Long Pause | Extend this idea to get logarithmic time search. (Hint: Show that $\min\limits_{x} x \sqrt[x]{n} = e \ln n$. Recall that $n = e^{\ln n}$ and differentiate.)

Like all strategies, the balancing idea is not a cure-all. For example, how can we balance the work in the towers of Hanoi problem? Nevertheless, it is the principle behind several strategies in analysis, the best known is *divide and conquer*. We turn next to an important application of this strategy.

2.3   Binary Search

> Since most concepts of science are
> relatively simple (once you understand
> them), any ambitious scientist must, in
> self-preservation, prevent his colleagues
> from discovering that *his* ideas
> are simple too.
>
> Nicholas Vanserg,
> *"Mathmanship," The American Scientist,* 46, 3, June 1958

We left the last section with a search strategy that was an improvement over LINEAR_SEARCH. However we do not yet know how much more we can improve our worst cost. Now we're going to reduce the worst cost to $\lfloor \lg n \rfloor + 1$ comparisons using *binary search.* Binary search works by dividing the current sublist (the set of elements that could contain X up to this point) into almost equal halves. Since L is sorted we can easily do this by querying the middle element. Independent of the answer we then have to search *at most* half of the remaining list. As with LINEAR_SEARCH, BINARY_SEARCH can be recursive (algorithm 2.4) or iterative (algorithm 2.5).

BINARY_SEARCH($List, lower, upper, X$)
    { Look for X in $List[lower..upper]$.
    Report its position if found, else report 0.
    $List$ is sorted in increasing order. $upper \geq lower > 0$. }

    if $lower = upper$
        then
            if $X = List[lower]$
                then return $lower$
                else return 0
        else
            $mid \leftarrow \lfloor (lower + upper)/2 \rfloor$
            if $X > List[mid]$
                then return BINARY_SEARCH($List, mid + 1, upper, X$)
                else return BINARY_SEARCH($List, lower, mid, X$)

Algorithm 2.4

This is a natural generalization of JUMP_SEARCH. Instead of requiring that gap sizes between successive queries be fixed (although they may depend on n, once chosen they are all the same size) we allow their sizes to vary. Surely the early jumps should be large and the later jumps small—initially we have no idea where X is in L and finally we must narrow the possible sublist to one element. Since we can do only one comparison at a time, then, applying the balance strategy, every sublist will be half as big as the last. (The ability to use binary search divides the set of people into those who halve and those who halve-not.)

BINARY_SEARCH ($List, lower, upper, X$)
    { Look for X in $List[lower..upper]$.
    Report its position if found, else report 0.
    $List$ is sorted in increasing order. $upper \geq lower > 0$. }

$low \leftarrow lower$; $high \leftarrow upper$
while $high \geq low$
    $mid \leftarrow \lfloor (low + high)/2 \rfloor$
    case $List[mid]$
        $< X$:
            $low \leftarrow mid + 1$
        $= X$:
            return mid
        $> X$:
            $high \leftarrow mid - 1$
return 0

Algorithm 2.5

Let's analyze the iterative version of BINARY_SEARCH (algorithm 2.5). Let $f(n)$ be the worst cost to find X in n sorted things using BINARY_SEARCH then

$$f(n) = \begin{cases} 1 & n = 1 \\ f(\lfloor n/2 \rfloor) + 1 & n > 1 \end{cases}$$

since in one three-way comparison we eliminate *at least* $\lceil n/2 \rceil$ elements from consideration (see figure 2.5).

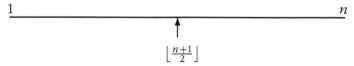

Figure 2.5 First probe of binary search

Pause Is this recurrence correct?

When we compare X to $L[\lfloor(n+1)/2\rfloor]$ one of three things can happen. If X is in L at all then either it's equal to the middle element, it's in the lower sublist of L, or it's in the upper sublist of L.

Now here's how to derive a recurrence modelling the worst cost of any algorithm that splits its task into three pieces. If $f(n)$ is the worst cost of the algorithm and we do some amount of work $g(n)$ to divide the problem into three pieces then

$$f(n) = \quad g(n) + \text{work to solve first piece} + \\ \text{work to solve second piece} + \text{work to solve third piece}$$

However, for BINARY SEARCH $g(n) = 1$ (the comparison to the middle element) and the three subtasks are disjoint. Further, the middle subtask involves no further work (it occurs when X is equal to the middle element). Therefore the worst cost satisfies the recurrence

$$\begin{aligned} f(n) &= \quad 1 + \max\{f(\text{size of first piece}), 0, f(\text{size of third piece})\} \\ &= \quad 1 + \max\{f(\lfloor(n+1)/2\rfloor - 1), f(n - \lfloor(n+1)/2\rfloor)\} \end{aligned}$$

Looking at table 2.3 we see that for $n \le 8$

$$\lfloor n/2\rfloor + 1 \ge \lceil n/2\rceil \ge \lfloor n/2\rfloor, \quad \lfloor(n+1)/2\rfloor = \lceil n/2\rceil, \quad \text{and} \quad \lceil n/2\rceil + \lfloor n/2\rfloor = n$$

These three relations are true for all n.

n	1	2	3	4	5	6	7	8
$\lfloor n/2\rfloor$	0	1	1	2	2	3	3	4
$\lceil n/2\rceil$	1	1	2	2	3	3	4	4

Table 2.3 Floors and ceilings of $n/2$

Pause Why is that true?

Now it's reasonable to assume that f is non-decreasing because it's unlikely that adding more elements will decrease the search time. If f is non-decreasing, the maximum value will be f of the size of the larger of the two remaining pieces. But

$$n - \lfloor(n+1)/2\rfloor = n - \lceil n/2\rceil = \lfloor n/2\rfloor$$

and

$$\lfloor(n+1)/2\rfloor - 1 = \lceil n/2\rceil - 1 \le \lfloor n/2\rfloor$$

Therefore the upper half is always at least as big as the lower half, so it will give the worst cost. Therefore

$$f(n) = 1 + f(\lfloor n/2 \rfloor)$$

Computing a few values we might guess that the solution of the recurrence is

$$f(n) = \lfloor \lg n \rfloor + 1$$

(See table 2.4; compare with table 1.3, page 27.)

n	1	2	3	4	5	6	7	8
$f(n)$	1	2	2	3	3	3	3	4

Table 2.4 Cost of binary search

Pause   Try to prove this before reading on.

Let's do some napkin math to get a feel for how fast the function grows. First, throw away the floor function to get

$$f(n) \leq \begin{cases} 1 & n = 1 \\ f(n/2) + 1 & n > 1 \end{cases}$$

We can do this because $n/2 \geq \lfloor n/2 \rfloor$ and we have assumed that f is non-decreasing, so $f(n/2) \geq f(\lfloor n/2 \rfloor)$. In fact, there is equality if n is even, so, if n is divisible by any power of two $\leq n$ (that is, if n is a power of two) we can substitute and guess

$$
\begin{aligned}
f(n) &= f(n/2) + 1 & [= f(n/2^1) + 1] \\
&= \{f(n/4) + 1\} + 1 & [= f(n/2^2) + 2] \\
&= \{\{f(n/8) + 1\} + 1\} + 1 & [= f(n/2^3) + 3] \\
&\ \ \vdots \\
&= f(n/2^i) + i & \text{(this is a guess)}
\end{aligned}
$$

It's clear what's going on here: every time we divide n by two we add one. We can divide n by two no more than $\lg n$ times before reaching one since $\lg n$ is the number of times we must multiply two by itself to get n. This would leave us with $\lg n$ ones added to $f(1)$. But $f(1) = 1$. Therefore

$$f(n) = f(1) + \lg n = \lg n + 1$$

Now as a check on our estimate let's prove that $f(n) = \lg n + 1$ for the simplified recurrence. This is easy to do by induction. We don't need to show all the steps except to note that

$$f(n/2) + 1 = (\lg(n/2) + 1) + 1 = (\lg n - 1 + 1) + 1 = \lg n + 1 = f(n)$$

Now since f is non-decreasing and $n = 2^{\lg n} \le 2^{\lceil \lg n \rceil}$, we know that $f(n) \le f(2^{\lceil \lg n \rceil})$. But we have just seen that $f(2^i) = i + 1$; therefore

$$f(n) \le \lceil \lg n \rceil + 1$$

Thus, BINARY_SEARCH never does more than $\lceil \lg n \rceil + 1$ comparisons.

This trick of turning a recurrence equality with a floor into an inequality with no floors is very useful. It will always work if f is non-decreasing.

$\boxed{Pause}$ What can we do if the recurrence involves $\lceil n/2 \rceil$?

This ballpark calculation[4] is good enough for most purposes but we can do better—we can determine the exact worst cost of BINARY_SEARCH for all n. We first expand the recurrence one step

$$
\begin{aligned}
f(n) &= f(\lfloor n/2 \rfloor) + 1 \\
&= f(\lfloor \lfloor n/2 \rfloor /2 \rfloor) + 1 + 1
\end{aligned}
$$

Yikes! How can we simplify $\lfloor \lfloor n/2 \rfloor /2 \rfloor$? It should be close to $n/4$ and calculation shows that it's equal to $\lfloor n/4 \rfloor$ for n up to 8. (Check this.)

$\boxed{Pause}$ Is $\lfloor \lfloor n/2 \rfloor /2 \rfloor = \lfloor n/4 \rfloor$?

When testing the equality we observe that both functions change value only at multiples of four (at least this is true for $n \le 8$; did you check?).

---

[4]Ballpark calculations are not calculations done in ballparks, but calculations to tell us whether we're in the ballpark (or way off base!).

BOB, WHO NEVER QUITE GOT THE KNACK
OF NAPKINING, RESORTED TO CUSTOM NAPKINS

Let $k = \lfloor n/4 \rfloor$, then $n = 4k + l$ where $4 > l \geq 0$. Therefore

$$\lfloor n/2 \rfloor = \lfloor (4k + l)/2 \rfloor = \lfloor 2k + l/2 \rfloor = 2k + \lfloor l/2 \rfloor \ \text{(since } 2k \text{ is an integer)}$$

$$\implies \lfloor \lfloor n/2 \rfloor /2 \rfloor = \lfloor (2k + \lfloor l/2 \rfloor)/2 \rfloor = k + \lfloor \lfloor l/2 \rfloor /2 \rfloor \ \text{(since } k \text{ is an integer)}$$

Now since $4 > l \geq 0$ then $2 > l/2 \geq 2$. Thus, $1 \geq \lfloor l/2 \rfloor \geq 0$. Therefore, $0 \geq \lfloor \lfloor l/2 \rfloor /2 \rfloor \geq 0$. So, $\lfloor \lfloor l/2 \rfloor /2 \rfloor = 0$. Thus, $\lfloor \lfloor n/2 \rfloor /2 \rfloor = k = \lfloor n/4 \rfloor$.

We can compress this argument to:

$$k = \lfloor n/4 \rfloor \ \implies \ k + 1 > n/4 \geq k$$

$$\implies \ 2k + 2 > n/2 \geq 2k$$

$$\implies \ 2k + 2 > \lfloor n/2 \rfloor \geq 2k$$

$$\implies \ k + 1 > \lfloor n/2 \rfloor /2 \geq k$$

$$\implies \ \lfloor \lfloor n/2 \rfloor /2 \rfloor = k = \lfloor n/4 \rfloor$$

| Pause | Use the same argument to show that $\lfloor \lfloor n/l \rfloor /m \rfloor = \lfloor n/lm \rfloor$.

Now we can proceed as before, but this time with exact values:

$$
\begin{aligned}
f(n) &= f(\lfloor n/2 \rfloor) + 1 & [= f(\lfloor n/2^1 \rfloor) + 1]\\
&= \{f(\lfloor n/4 \rfloor) + 1\} + 1 & [= f(\lfloor n/2^2 \rfloor) + 2]\\
&= \{\{f(\lfloor n/8 \rfloor) + 1\} + 1\} + 1 & [= f(\lfloor n/2^3 \rfloor) + 3]\\
&\;\;\vdots\\
&= f(\lfloor n/2^i \rfloor) + i & \text{(this is a guess)}
\end{aligned}
$$

It is straightforward to show that $\lfloor n/2^i \rfloor = 1$ precisely when $i = \lfloor \lg n \rfloor$ and therefore, $f(n) = \lfloor \lg n \rfloor + 1$. Therefore BINARY_SEARCH takes no more than $\lfloor \lg n \rfloor + 1$ comparisons.

$\lg n$ is an even better improvement over $\sqrt{n}$ than $\sqrt{n}$ is over n since n grows relative to $\lg n$ as 2^n grows relative to n. Although n is usually considered to be a slowly growing function, n is *exponentially greater* than $\lg n$ (see table 2.5 and figure 2.6). Can we improve our search time still more? Is $\sqrt{\lg n}$ possible? Is constant time possible?

n	Linear Search	Square Root Search	Binary Search
15	15	6	4
255	255	30	8
4095	4095	126	12
65535	65535	510	16
1048575	1048575	2046	20

Table 2.5 Growth rates of three search algorithms

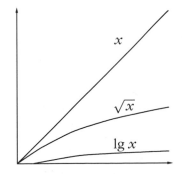

Figure 2.6 Searching better and faster

Decision Trees

We shall now see that binary search is optimal within the comparison-based model. Any algorithm in the comparison-based model that searches for X in L performs a sequence of comparisons. This sequence may vary depending on the input, but suppose that for any one input the sequence is always the same. Such an algorithm is **predictable**; it will always behave the same if given the same input.[5] Our lower bound will apply only to predictable algorithms in the comparison-based model that guarantee to find X in L.

In deriving the lower bound we shall see that any predictable search algorithm will do at least $\lfloor \lg n \rfloor + 1$ comparisons involving X. Any algorithm is free to compare elements of L but such comparisons are senseless—since L is sorted we already know their outcomes. Nevertheless, in proving a lower bound we must allow for all algorithms in the model, even silly ones. However we can't assume that every algorithm must do comparisons between elements of L so we don't bother to count such comparisons.

Consider any predictable search algorithm, let's call it $\mathcal{A}$. $\mathcal{A}$ must have a first comparison involving X and some member of L, say $L[i]$. Further, $\mathcal{A}$ is predictable, so no matter what the input is $\mathcal{A}$ always does this comparison first (amongst all comparisons involving X). If it turns out that $X = L[i]$ then $\mathcal{A}$ may halt since it now has proof that X is in L, and it knows where. Of course, $\mathcal{A}$ may choose to continue for some bizarre reason of its own, but we can't depend on it doing any further comparisons.

Now if $X \neq L[i]$ then $\mathcal{A}$ knows that either $X < L[i]$ or $X > L[i]$. In both cases it must proceed (it can only halt when it's found X or exhausted L) and eventually it must compare X to another element of L. However, $\mathcal{A}$ now has the option to make this second X comparison contingent on the outcome of the first X comparison. If $X < L[i]$ then suppose the new comparison is between X and $L[j]$, otherwise suppose it is between X and $L[k]$. Because $\mathcal{A}$ is predictable, i, j, and k are fixed, independent of the input.

At this point $\mathcal{A}$ is about to compare X with either $L[j]$ or $L[k]$. We could think of $\mathcal{A}$ as being in one of two states of mind depending on whether X is bigger or smaller than $L[i]$. After $\mathcal{A}$ makes the next comparison it can be in one of four states of mind. If we let each X comparison be a branch point and the two possible subsequent comparisons (if any) be two further branch points then we can produce a diagram of $\mathcal{A}$'s possible states of mind—without the need to keep them all in ours!

[5]Often "deterministic" is used instead of predictable. But as we shall discover in chapter seven, that choice leads to terrible nomenclature problems when we come to consider "non-deterministic" turing machines.

Call each comparison a **node** and call the comparisons that follow each node the **children** of that node. The collection of nodes together with the mapping telling which node is a child of another node is called a **tree**. A tree modelling the algorithm's possible branches after each comparison is called a **decision tree**. Trees are extremely important in computer science; they grow in the unlikeliest places—and for some reason always upside-down.

Each node of a decision tree may have no children, one child, or two children. The node representing the comparison of X with $L[i]$ has a left child if the algorithm does not halt after it compares X with $L[i]$ and it finds that $X < L[i]$. Similarly, it has a right child if the algorithm does not halt if $X > L[i]$. So the left and right children represent the branches the algorithm would take if $X < L[i]$, and if $X > L[i]$, respectively. For example, figure 2.7 gives the beginnings of two decision trees. The first models the first two possible comparisons of BINARY SEARCH and the second models a weird algorithm.

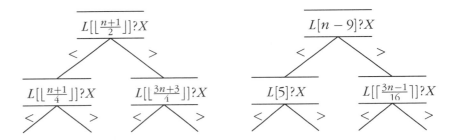

Figure 2.7 The beginnings of two decision trees

Trees that can have at most two branches at each node are **binary** trees. If we distinguish between left and right in a tree then the tree is **ordered** and the intuition is that we can order the children of a node. By analogy with living trees, a **rooted** tree is a tree with a special node called its **root** (although all our trees are upside down by that analogy). A childless node is a **leaf**. The **level** of a node in a rooted tree is the number of nodes on the path from the root to the node; the root has level zero. The **height** of a rooted tree is the level of the deepest leaf.

Now consider a decision tree representing the set of all possible sequences of comparisons that a particular search algorithm could perform. The tree's height plus one is an upper bound on how many comparisons the algorithm must do to find X in L.

| Pause | Why?

Also, there must be *at least* n nodes in the tree. If not then one ele-ment of L, say L[i], does not appear in any comparison in the tree. There-fore, there is no sequence of comparisons that tests whether X equals L[i]. Thus, there are inputs that the algorithm answers incorrectly. Thus every position in L must appear in at least one node in the tree (if the algorithm is correct!).

Pause   Why does this argument work here and not when it was used for the lower bound of LINEAR_SEARCH (page 88)?

Now if we can find a lower bound on the height of an n-node tree this will be a lower bound on the search problem. Now comes the clincher: as you may have guessed from figure 2.8 every height m rooted binary tree has at most $2^{m+1} - 1$ nodes.

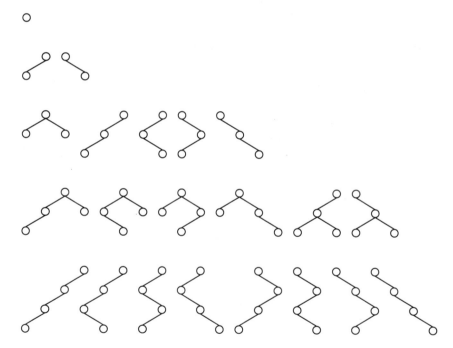

Figure 2.8   All ordered and rooted binary trees with up to four nodes

Pause   Can you prove this?

To prove this let's try induction on height. Suppose every binary tree of height less than m has no more than $2^m - 1$ nodes (the induction hypothesis). Now, like Gaul, every rooted binary tree of height m is divided into three parts: a root, a left subtree, and a right subtree (see figure 2.9). The height of both subtrees is at most $m - 1$. Hence, by the induction hypothesis, they each have at most $2^m - 1$ nodes. Thus the whole tree can have no more than $2(2^m - 1) + 1 = 2^{m+1} - 1$ nodes. This is an example of proof by **structural induction**; we are using induction by exploiting the recursive structure of binary trees.

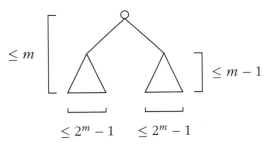

Figure 2.9 Every rooted binary tree has three parts

Now, since the number of nodes in the tree is greater than or equal to n then $2^{m+1} - 1 \geq n$. Thus $m + 1 \geq \lg(n + 1)$. But m is an integer, so $m + 1 \geq \lceil \lg(n + 1) \rceil$. Thus, if we consider the set of decision trees representing all search algorithms, then the *minimum possible height* is $\lceil \lg(n + 1) \rceil - 1$. Therefore there is at least one sequence of comparisons of length at least $\lceil \lg(n + 1) \rceil$ in any such decision tree. Hence any algorithm in the comparison-based model must do at least $\lceil \lg(n + 1) \rceil$ comparisons in the worst case.

Finally, observe that

$$\lceil \lg(n + 1) \rceil = \lfloor \lg n \rfloor + 1$$

$\boxed{Pause}$ Why is this true? (Hint: For which n does $\lceil \lg(n + 1) \rceil$ change value? See table 2.6.)

n	1	2	3	4	5	6	7	8
$\lceil \lg n \rceil$	0	1	2	2	3	3	3	3
$\lfloor \lg n \rfloor$	0	1	1	2	2	2	2	3

Table 2.6 Floors and ceilings of $\lg n$

Thus BINARY SEARCH has optimal worst cost within the comparison-based model.

The Average Cost

To find BINARY_SEARCH's average cost we need to assume two things about X and L. Let's assume that X is in L, and that X is equally likely to be anywhere in L. Now we can napkin to find an estimate. We will find X in one probe if it's the middle element, in two probes if it's the quarter or three-quarters element, in three probes if it's any one of four elements, and so forth (see figure 2.10). So within k probes we will have covered $2^k - 1$ elements. Since we eventually have to cover all n elements, k is about $\lg n$. Therefore, roughly speaking, the average will be near

$$\frac{1 \times 1 + 2 \times 2 + 3 \times 4 + 4 \times 8 + 5 \times 16 + \cdots + \lg n 2^{\lg n - 1}}{n} = \frac{1}{n} \sum_{i=1}^{\lg n} i 2^{i-1}$$

We will see later (page 120) that this is roughly

$$\frac{n(\lg n - 1)}{n} = \lg n - 1$$

So when X is in L and X is equally likely to be anywhere in L, then on average BINARY_SEARCH does about $\lg n$ comparisons—about the same as its worst cost. This isn't so surprising when we realize that about half the elements ($2^{\lg n - 1}$) take about $\lg n$ probes!

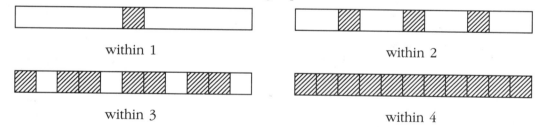

within 1

within 2

within 3

within 4

Figure 2.10 Elements covered by binary search when $n = 11$

Now let's find the average exactly. With our two assumptions, on probing $L[\lfloor (n+1)/2 \rfloor]$ (one comparison) the probability that X is in the lower half of L is $(\lceil n/2 \rceil - 1)/n$; the probability that X is in the upper half is $\lfloor n/2 \rfloor / n$; and the probability that X is equal to the middle element is $1/n$. Thus, BINARY_SEARCH's average cost satisfies the recurrence

$$f(n) = \begin{cases} 0 & n = 0 \\ 1 & n = 1 \\ \dfrac{\lceil n/2 \rceil - 1}{n} f(\lceil n/2 \rceil - 1) + \dfrac{1}{n} 0 + \dfrac{\lfloor n/2 \rfloor}{n} f(\lfloor n/2 \rfloor) + 1 & n > 1 \end{cases}$$

See table 2.7.

n	1	2	3	4	5	6	7	8
$f(n)$	1	3/2	5/3	2	11/5	7/3	17/7	21/8
$=$	1/1	3/2	5/3	8/4	11/5	14/6	17/7	21/8

Table 2.7 Average cost of successful binary search

| Pause | Why does this recurrence have two boundary values?

This recurrence looks armed to the teeth, but there's something special about it—both fs on the right are multiplied by their argument. Unfortunately the f on the left isn't. However we can make all of them the same type if we multiply everything by n.

| Pause | Can you guess the function from the first eight values given in table 2.7?

Multiplying by n yields the recurrence

$$nf(n) = \begin{cases} 0 & n = 0 \\ 1 & n = 1 \\ (\lceil n/2 \rceil - 1)f(\lceil n/2 \rceil - 1) + \lfloor n/2 \rfloor f(\lfloor n/2 \rfloor) + n & n > 1 \end{cases}$$

| Pause | Why didn't the boundary values change?

Since all the fs are now of the same type we can replace each of them by another function; perhaps we'll get lucky and see a pattern when things clear up a bit.

Replacing $nf(n)$ by a new function $g(n)$ yields the recurrence

$$g(n) = \begin{cases} 0 & n = 0 \\ 1 & n = 1 \\ g(\lceil n/2 \rceil - 1) + g(\lfloor n/2 \rfloor) + n & n > 1 \end{cases}$$

See table 2.8.

n	1	2	3	4	5	6	7	8
$g(n)$	1	3	5	8	11	14	17	21

Table 2.8 Cost of the transformed function

This recurrence looks a lot more docile, but it still has those threatening floors and ceilings. If only we could change them all into floors (or ceilings) perhaps there would be some pattern to exploit. Aha! Recall that

$\lceil n/2 \rceil - 1 = \lfloor (n-1)/2 \rfloor$. Also, this term must also occur in the expansion for $g(n-1)$! So what happens if we turn everything into floors and subtract two consecutive terms?

Subtracting $g(n-1)$ from $g(n)$ yields

$$
\begin{aligned}
g(n) - g(n-1) &= g(\lceil n/2 \rceil - 1) + g(\lfloor n/2 \rfloor) \\
&\quad - g(\lceil (n-1)/2 \rceil - 1) - g(\lfloor (n-1)/2 \rfloor) + 1 \\
&= g(\lfloor (n-1)/2 \rfloor) + g(\lfloor n/2 \rfloor) \\
&\quad - g(\lfloor n/2 \rfloor - 1) - g(\lfloor (n-1)/2 \rfloor) + 1 \\
&= g(\lfloor n/2 \rfloor) - g(\lfloor n/2 \rfloor - 1) + 1
\end{aligned}
$$

Replacing $g(n) - g(n-1)$ by a new function $h(n)$ yields

$$
h(n) = \begin{cases} 1 & n = 1 \\ h(\lfloor n/2 \rfloor) + 1 & n > 1 \end{cases}
$$

See table 2.9.

n	1	2	3	4	5	6	7	8
$h(n)$	1	2	2	3	3	3	3	4

Table 2.9 Cost of the next transformed function

Pause Why does this recurrence only need one boundary value?

Eureka! This recurrence is the same as that for the worst cost of BINARY_SEARCH. Thus, we just plug in the known result

$$
h(n) = \lceil \lg(n+1) \rceil
$$

Now we retrace our steps to get

$$
g(n) = g(n-1) + h(n) = g(n-1) + \lceil \lg(n+1) \rceil
$$

From which it follows that

$$
g(n) = \sum_{i=1}^{n} \lceil \lg(i+1) \rceil = \sum_{i=2}^{n+1} \lceil \lg i \rceil
$$

Therefore

$$f(n) = \frac{g(n)}{n} = \frac{1}{n} \sum_{i=2}^{n+1} \lceil \lg i \rceil$$

∞∞∞∞∞

We've finally cornered the function in a sum, but what's the value of the sum? Napkining we see that the sum can be no larger than $n \lceil \lg(n+1) \rceil$. (Why?) And since $f(n) = g(n)/n$, this means that $f(n)$ is no worse than $\lceil \lg(n+1) \rceil$. But we knew that, that's just the worst cost. Let's take a look at the first few terms of the sum

$$\sum_{i=2}^{n+1} \lceil \lg i \rceil = \overbrace{\lceil \lg 2 \rceil}^{=1} + \overbrace{\lceil \lg 3 \rceil + \lceil \lg 4 \rceil}^{=2} + \overbrace{\lceil \lg 5 \rceil + \lceil \lg 6 \rceil + \lceil \lg 7 \rceil + \lceil \lg 8 \rceil}^{=3} + \cdots$$

$$= 1 \times 1 + 2 \times 2 + 3 \times 4 + 4 \times 8 + \cdots$$

$$+ \lceil \lg(n+1) \rceil \times 2^{\lceil \lg(n+1) \rceil - 1} - \lceil \lg(n+1) \rceil \times ??$$

$$= \left(\sum_{i=1}^{\lceil \lg(n+1) \rceil} i 2^{i-1} \right) - \lceil \lg(n+1) \rceil \times ??$$

We know that the terms can't continue past $\lceil \lg(n+1) \rceil$. However, unless $n+1$ is a power of two, the sum will add too many terms. So we have to subtract some of them. And each of these terms will have the same value as $\lceil \lg(n+1) \rceil$.

Pause　How many terms do we have to subtract?

First, let's figure out the value of the sum of $i2^{i-1}$. (Look at the exercises on sums in chapter one to see why the following useful trick works.)

$$\sum_{i=1}^{k} i2^{i-1} = \sum_{i=0}^{k-1} (i+1)2^i$$

$$= \sum_{i=0}^{k-1} i2^i + \sum_{i=0}^{k-1} 2^i$$

$$= 2\sum_{i=0}^{k-1} i2^{i-1} + 2^k - 1$$

$$= 2\sum_{i=1}^{k} i2^{i-1} - k2^k + 2^k - 1$$

Now if we subtract the sum from both sides we'll have an expression for the sum! Therefore,

$$\sum_{i=1}^{k} i2^{i-1} = k2^k - 2^k + 1 = (k-1)2^k + 1$$

This trick works by renaming the terms of the sum, rearranging them, then subtracting rearranged parts. It will work for any bijective function (the bijective function does the renaming). Thus, if f is bijective then $\sum r_i = \sum r_{f(i)}$.

Now we have to figure out exactly how many terms to count to find the value of the original sum, $g(n)$. It's easy to show that the sum counts $2^{\lceil \lg(n+1) \rceil} - n - 1$ extra terms; thus

$$
\begin{aligned}
g(n) &= \sum_{i=1}^{\lceil \lg(n+1) \rceil} i2^{i-1} - \lceil \lg(n+1) \rceil (2^{\lceil \lg(n+1) \rceil} - n - 1) \\
&= (\lceil \lg(n+1) \rceil - 1)2^{\lceil \lg(n+1) \rceil} + 1 - \lceil \lg(n+1) \rceil (2^{\lceil \lg(n+1) \rceil} - n - 1) \\
&= (n+1)\lceil \lg(n+1) \rceil - 2^{\lceil \lg(n+1) \rceil} + 1
\end{aligned}
$$

Hence

$$f(n) = \frac{g(n)}{n} = \lceil \lg(n+1) \rceil - \frac{2^{\lceil \lg(n+1) \rceil} - \lceil \lg(n+1) \rceil - 1}{n}$$

Victory!

Finally, since $n = 2^{\lg n}$ it follows that

$$\frac{2^{\lceil \lg(n+1) \rceil} - \lceil \lg(n+1) \rceil - 1}{n} = 2^r - \frac{\lceil \lg(n+1) \rceil + 1}{n}, \quad \text{where } 1 \geq r > 0$$

So the average cost when $X \in L$ is disappointingly close to the worst cost; it's at most two comparisons less on average. Still, we've learned how to tame a pretty wild recurrence. To complete the analysis we have to find the average cost for $X \notin L$. It turns out that that average cost is also close to the worst cost.

The Lower Bound on the Average Cost

The previous analysis was a difficult cross-country walk; we saw the goal and simply hacked our way straight to it. As is often the case, this arduous pathfinding forced us to develop new tools to make our way easier; we now know how to solve a complicated recurrence and we know the values of two difficult sums. Now in developing a lower bound we're going to climb a tree to see the problem as a whole. After developing the lower bound proving BINARY_SEARCH optimal on average we'll see a much easier path to our previous goal. Our new vantage point will be decision trees.

Recall that we can model every search algorithm in the comparison-based model by a decision tree. Every such decision tree must have at least n nodes, and, since we have assumed that X is in L, every node is a possible outcome of the search algorithm. The cost of an outcome is the same as the level of the corresponding node plus one. (Why?) The sum of the levels of the nodes of a rooted binary tree is called its **path length**. So the average number of comparisons, if X must be in L and X is equally likely to be anywhere in L, is the same as the path length divided by n plus one. So we want to find the minimum possible path length of any rooted n-node binary tree.

Consider building an n-node tree from scratch so that its path length is as small as possible. After the root and the first level one node we have two places to put the next node. If we make it a child of the root it will add one to the path length, if we make it a child of the level one node it will add two to the path length. So let's make it a child of the root. The next node we add must be a level two node, but the following child can be level two or level three, so let's make it a level two node. Continuing in this way we see that the path length of this tree is

$$\sum_{i=1}^{n} \lfloor \lg i \rfloor = \sum_{i=1}^{n} (\lceil \lg(i+1) \rceil - 1)$$
$$= \sum_{i=1}^{n} \lceil \lg(i+1) \rceil - n$$
$$= (n+1)\lceil \lg(n+1) \rceil - 2^{\lceil \lg(n+1) \rceil} + 1 - n$$

This is a **greedy strategy**; we're trying to minimize path length by taking the best (in this case, smallest) bites we can at each step. Being as greedy as possible means assuming that locally optimal decisions make for globally optimal structures—in other words, living for the moment. In this case we toss caution to the winds and allow all nodes in each generation to have as many children as possible. Like real life. To see that this is best possible in this case, call a node in a binary tree **fertile** if it has two offspring. Now if any binary tree has a non-fertile node and if that node, or any other node in the same generation, has a grandchild then there is another tree with the same number of nodes with a smaller path length (see figure 2.11).

Pause   Why is this true?

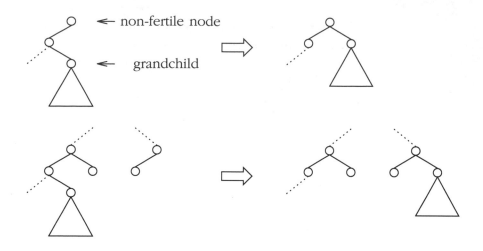

Figure 2.11 Reducing path length of binary trees with non-fertile nodes

So if an n-node binary tree has the smallest possible path length among all n-node binary trees then all its non-fertile nodes can be at most one level higher than the height of the tree.

Therefore the minimum average height of an n-node binary tree is

$$\lceil \lg(n + 1) \rceil - \frac{2^{\lceil \lg(n+1) \rceil} - \lceil \lg(n + 1) \rceil - 1}{n} - 1$$

Therefore a lower bound on the average cost of any successful search in the comparison-based model is

$$\lceil \lg(n + 1) \rceil - \frac{2^{\lceil \lg(n+1) \rceil} - \lceil \lg(n + 1) \rceil - 1}{n}$$

Exactly the same as the average cost of a successful BINARY_SEARCH! A similar analysis applies to unsuccessful searches. So BINARY_SEARCH is optimal, even on average.

Programming

Considering how slowly $\lg n$ grows and the size of most inputs there is little point trying to fine tune binary search. However, if it is to be used as a frequently called subroutine then there are some tricky speedups. For example, we can rewrite it to only test equality at the end of the search. (Still, if you feel the urge to optimize, lie down for a while, it will pass.) Although short, binary search is difficult to code correctly and, as we saw with LINEAR_SEARCH, the best thing to do is to develop the algorithm from general principles (argue inductively about the search) and only then think about tweaking the resulting program to exploit any special circumstances.

2.4   Changing the Model

> What is laid down, ordered, factual, is never
> enough to embrace the whole truth: life always
> spills over the rim of every cup.
>
> Boris Pasternak

Well, it seems that we've completely solved the searching problem: BIN-ARY_SEARCH is optimal in both the worst and average case. Unfortunately there are at least four important cases where we either can't or shouldn't use binary search:

- The data is either not sorted or not sortable.

- The data is sorted but it is structured in such a way that it does not cost the same to probe data in different parts of the structure.

- The data is sorted and probe costs are uniform but we know something about the possible values and we can exploit that information for faster performance.

- The data is static so we know all possible search requests in advance.

Let's look at one simple instance of each case in the next four subsections.

Randomized Linear Search

Suppose L is unsorted and X is known to be in L; LINEAR_SEARCH's worst cost is then $n - 1$, not n. If we have two processors to do the search then we can reduce the worst cost to $\lfloor n/2 \rfloor$ by dividing L into two parts and searching each in parallel. Unfortunately many machines have only one processor. Surprisingly, it is possible to get a similar effect on average with only one processor.

Suppose we have two versions of LINEAR_SEARCH: one searches from the left end of L and moves right, and the other searches from the right end of L and moves left (see figure 2.12). Both separately have the same average and worst cost as LINEAR_SEARCH. Now construct another algorithm that flips a coin and depending on the outcome decides to call one of the two versions of LINEAR SEARCH to do the search. (See algorithm 2.6.) What are the worst and average costs of this coin flip algorithm? In some sense they must be the same as those of the two subalgorithms, but can we *guarantee* them?

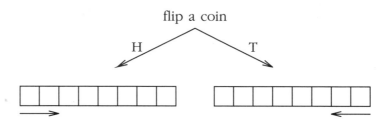

Figure 2.12   Coin flip linear search

Let's try to pick an input that will make the algorithm work as hard as possible. If we put X near either of the ends of L then there is a one in two chance that COIN FLIP SEARCH will find it quickly. On average, the

```
COIN FLIP SEARCH (List, lower, upper, X )
    { Look for X in List[lower..upper].
    Report its position if found, else report 0.
    upper ≥ lower > 0. }

    flip a coin
    if heads
        then
            index ← lower
            while upper ≥ index and List[index] ≠ X
                index ← index + 1
            if index > upper
                then return 0
                else return index
        else
            index ← upper
            while index ≥ lower and List[index] ≠ X
                index ← index − 1
            if lower > index
                then return 0
                else return index
```

Algorithm 2.6

worst place we could put X is right in the middle of L. Then, no matter which version of the algorithm is chosen, the worst cost will be $n/2$. But this is weird; the definition of worst cost we have been using assumes that there is a fixed worst cost. Here we seem to have a variable worst cost whose "average" is $n/2$. What's going on?

Algorithms that make decisions using random numbers are called **randomized algorithms;** randomized algorithms force us to rethink what we mean by average cost and worst cost. Given an algorithm $\mathcal{A}$, the set I_n of all inputs to $\mathcal{A}$ each of size n, and a cost function $f_\mathcal{A}$, the worst and average cost of $\mathcal{A}$ are defined as follows:

$$\text{worst cost}(\mathcal{A}) \;=\; \max_{I \in I_n} f_\mathcal{A}(I)$$

$$\text{average cost}(\mathcal{A}) \;=\; \sum_{I \in I_n} \mathbf{P}(I) f_\mathcal{A}(I)$$

where $\mathbf{P}(I)$ is the probability that I occurs.

These definitions don't work if $\mathcal{A}$ flips a coin because they assume that the only variation is *over the input space, I_n*. The coin flip algorithm shows that it is possible to have variation *over the algorithm space as well.* We can think of a randomized algorithm as a set of algorithms, one of which is picked at some point and, for each algorithm, the input can vary over the entire input space. (See figure 2.13.) For example, we can think of the coin flip algorithm as really being two algorithms, only one of which gets picked at run time.

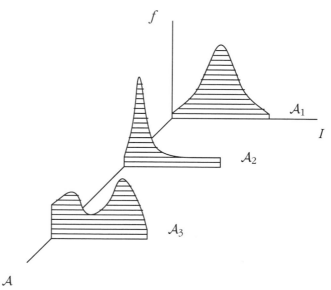

Figure 2.13 The algorithm space and the input space

Suppose a randomized algorithm, $\mathcal{A}$, flips a coin three times (or flips three coins), figure 2.14 shows the eight *predictable* algorithms belonging to $\mathcal{A}$'s algorithm class. Having "unrolled" $\mathcal{A}$ in this way we can extend our previous definitions of worst and average cost because the leaf algorithms are predictable. Since each is predictable, the worst cost of each of the eight leaf algorithms is well-defined. So $\mathcal{A}$'s worst cost should be the worst of the worst costs of each of the eight.

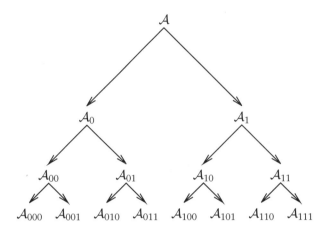

Figure 2.14   Algorithms produced by a three coin randomized algorithm

But now notice something important: *the worst cost of each leaf algorithm can occur for different inputs.* Suppose one leaf algorithm's worst cost occurs when the input is I_1, and suppose the worst costs of the other leaf algorithms occur for other inputs. If $\mathcal{A}$ is faced with I_1 then, assuming that $\mathcal{A}$ uses unbiased coins, there is a seven in eight chance that it will avoid that worst cost![6]

What does this mean to our analysis? Suppose we fix the input to be I, what is $\mathcal{A}$'s performance on I? *It is no longer fixed.* We now have an *expected* performance since no one can predict which version of $\mathcal{A}$ will actually be picked. This is the same idea as the average cost, so to distinguish between them let's use "expected" when it is for many algorithms and a fixed input, and "average" when it is for many inputs and a fixed algorithm. (Beware: Most books do not make this distinction; usually "expected" means the same as "average.")

---

[6]We don't even have to make all inputs equally likely, we can force any probability distribution we want.

So when the algorithm can be any one of a set of algorithms $\mathcal{A}_S$ and we cannot predict which algorithm is picked, then for a fixed input I, $\mathcal{A}_S$'s **expected cost** on I is

$$\text{expected cost}(\mathcal{A}_S, I) = \sum_{A \in \mathcal{A}_S} \mathbf{P}(A) f_A(I)$$

where $\mathbf{P}(A)$ is the probability of choosing the algorithm A from the set of algorithms $\mathcal{A}_S$.

And we should replace our definitions of worst and average cost by **worst expected cost** and **average expected cost**

$$\text{worst expected cost}(\mathcal{A}_S) = \max_{I \in I_n} \left\{ \sum_{A \in \mathcal{A}_S} \mathbf{P}(A) f_A(I) \right\}$$

$$\text{average expected cost}(\mathcal{A}_S) = \sum_{I \in I_n} \mathbf{P}(I) \left\{ \sum_{A \in \mathcal{A}_S} \mathbf{P}(A) f_A(I) \right\}$$

This definition of the worst expected cost is reasonable since it is the cost we can guarantee, independent of the outcomes of the coin flips.

Long Pause   Is it possible for the worst expected cost to be lower than the average cost?

For COIN_FLIP_SEARCH, $\mathcal{A}_S$ is of size two and the probability of picking each version is $1/2$. As we determined when analyzing LINEAR_SEARCH (page 92), the only variation in the input that matters is X's position in L, so here I_n is of size n. A little computation shows that the worst place we can put X (assuming that X is in L) is right in the middle of L. Thus, the worst expected cost, if X is always in L, is $n/2$. The "worst cost" is still $n - 1$, but it's now meaningless, since we can no longer predict when it will occur.

Pause   What happens if $X \notin L$?

Finally, if we can predict which algorithm gets picked (as happens, for example, when there is only one algorithm to choose from) then we may use the old definitions of the average and worst costs since the only variation is over the input space. But there really is no need because the old definitions are just a special case of the new ones.

Randomizing has three important practical consequences. First, *randomizing makes the average cost easier to predict*. This is important because, as we saw after analyzing LINEAR SEARCH, even if we calculate an "average" there is no guarantee that it will corresponds to anything in reality. To calculate the average of a predictable algorithm we have to guess the probabilities of each possible input. These guesses may well be wrong. Paradoxically, randomizing makes guessing unnecessary.

Second, by scrambling the algorithm's behavior we can guarantee that the algorithm's cost will be near its calculated average independent of its input! We've all had the frustrating experience of searching for a pair of matching socks and finding one only after looking at half the socks. To guarantee average search times we should always start the search by tossing all the socks into the air! *Randomizing decouples the algorithm's behavior from its input.* If previously a particular input caused really bad behavior now it can cause only average behavior.

RANDOMIZING

On the other hand, a predictable algorithm does well in a benign universe (for example, LINEAR SEARCH does well if X is always near the left end of L) but a randomized algorithm does not exploit that advantage. We could make it adapt to its input, but the better it adapts, the more it exposes itself to worst cases; an algorithmic catch-22. As Lewis Carroll pointed out: jam yesterday and jam tomorrow, but never jam today.

This apparent disadvantage of randomized algorithms becomes an advantage when we are working on problems that have only one instance (all the problems in chapter six have only one instance). When given a problem with only one instance (for example, is n prime?) a predictable algorithm does the same thing over and over again. But a randomized algorithm may respond differently every time it is called, even though the input is always the same. This can be used to great advantage; we'll consider this again in chapter six.

A worst case optimal predictable algorithm is like a koala. Koalas subsist almost entirely on eucalyptus trees and their physiology is specialized to take advantage of the peculiarities of these trees. However this extreme adaptation makes it easy for us to get rid of all koalas (just get rid of all eucalyptus trees!). A randomized algorithm is more of an all-rounder— like omnivorous humans; it doesn't necessarily exploit all that there is to exploit, but on average it doesn't do too badly, no matter what its environment. So, if you suspect that the universe is out to get you, randomize your behavior!

Searching Linked Lists

Now assume L is sorted, but the sorted order is kept indirectly. L is a list of n elements, with a helper array, *next*, of size n. There is a special index, *head*, which points to the smallest element in L; thus $L[head]$ is the smallest element in L. In figure 2.15 $head = 2$, so the smallest element is $L[2]$. Unlike previous lists, there is no necessary relation between $L[i]$ and $L[i + 1]$; for each i, the next largest element after $L[i]$ is $L[next[i]]$. The successor of the largest element is an index that cannot point to any element (any such value will do, let's call it **nil**) signifying the end of the list. In figure 2.15 $next[3] = $ **nil**, so the largest element is $L[3]$. Such a structure is called a ***singly linked list***. The array *next* is an array of ***pointers*** giving the sorted order of the list L.

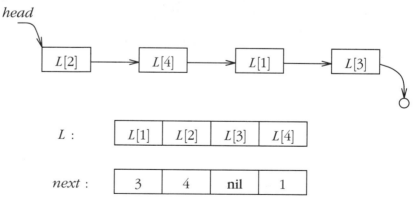

Figure 2.15 A singly linked list and its implementation

Linked lists are useful when we want to maintain a list in more than one order. For example, L could be a list of patients at a hospital ordered by name (the list order) with a secondary ordering by age (the linked list order). Given such a list we want to search for X in L. (Suppose, for example, that the chief resident doesn't want to find a patient by name, she wants to find a sixty-five year old patient.)

To find the ith largest element in a singly linked list we must follow i pointers (see figure 2.15). So the access time is proportional to the element's position. If a list access costs about as much as a comparison then we can't use binary search because it implicitly assumes that all probes cost the same. If comparisons are the only operations that matter then binary search is still a hot idea. But otherwise we have to change the model.

We can't avoid n comparisons and accesses in the worst case since X could be the largest element, but if the list is kept compactly in an array in positions 1 to n we can randomize to achieve a worst expected cost of $O(\sqrt{n})$. We will need **uniform**$(1, n)$—a procedure that returns an integer randomly chosen with uniform probability from the range 1 to n (each integer in the range is equally likely to be chosen).

The idea is to guess k locations for X. Of those k, find the largest one less than X. Then search the linked list for X from that element to the end of the list. See algorithm 2.7. This is like JUMP_SEARCH except that during the first phase of the search we're shooting in the dark; the k random elements are not necessarily in increasing order.

LINKED_LIST_SEARCH (*List*, n, *head*, *next*, *guesses*, X)
    { Look for X in the n element singly linked implicit list *List*.
    Report its position if found, else report 0.
    List is sorted in increasing order through *next*,
    List[*head*] is the smallest element of *List*, and
    the largest element of *List* has a *next* value of **nil**.
    $n \geq 1$ and *guesses* is the number of samples of *List* examined. }

    largest ← *head*
    for i **from** 1 **to** *guesses*
        j ← **uniform**$(1, n)$
        if $X > List[j]$ **and** $List[j] > List[largest]$
            largest ← j

    index ← *largest*
    while *next*[*index*] ≠ **nil and** $X > List[index]$
        index ← *next*[*index*]
    if $List[index] = X$
        then return *index*
        else return 0

Algorithm 2.7

For this algorithm, the worst thing to search for is an X greater than or equal to the largest element. So let's assume that X is the largest element; this will give us the algorithm's worst expected cost. Now, what's the best k? Assume that all n^k sequences of k random elements are equally likely to be chosen. Since each guess must be smaller than X, it's possible to show that the probability of finding X after at least i further comparisons is $(n-i)^k/n^k$. Therefore, the average number of comparisons involving X is

$$
\begin{aligned}
k + 1 + \sum_{i=0}^{n} \frac{(n-i)^k}{n^k} &= k + 1 + \frac{1}{n^k} \sum_{i=0}^{n} (n-i)^k \\
&= k + 1 + \frac{1}{n^k} \sum_{i=0}^{n} i^k
\end{aligned}
$$

Now, by induction on k it is possible to show that for large n

$$
\sum_{i=1}^{n} i^k = \frac{n^{k+1}}{k+1} - \frac{n^k}{2} + O(kn^{k-1})
$$

Therefore, for large n the average number of comparisons is

$$
\begin{aligned}
&= k + 1 + \frac{1}{n^k} \left(\frac{n^{k+1}}{k+1} - \frac{n^k}{2} + O(kn^{k-1}) \right) \\
&= k + 1 + \frac{n}{k+1} - \frac{1}{2} + O\left(\frac{k}{n} \right)
\end{aligned}
$$

Differentiating with respect to k we see that the minimum occurs when

$$
k \approx \sqrt{n} - 1
$$

Thus the best k is about $\sqrt{n}$. The worst expected cost is then $2\sqrt{n} + o(\sqrt{n})$ comparisons involving X. And this can be shown to be asymptotically optimal for the worst expected cost.

Interpolation Search

Given a sorted list L and an unknown element X, we know that to find X in L we cannot reduce the worst number of three-way comparisons below $\lfloor \lg n \rfloor + 1$. But perhaps we can reduce the average cost if we know the probability distribution of the universe of which L is a sample. Intuitively, we should be able to better guess X's probable location in L.

For example, if for romantic reasons we're searching a thick phone book for Montague Capulet, it's reasonable to look near the beginning of the phone book. If the first letter of a name occurs with uniform probability then Montague Capulet should appear about one ninth of the way in. Similarly, if there are many Capulets, then Montague Capulet should be near the middle of the list of Capulets.

Suppose that L is a sorted list of numbers. If L uniformly partitions the set of numbers then X should be near $L[[\lceil pn\rceil]]$ where

$$p = \frac{X - L[1]}{L[n] - L[1]}$$

is the average proportion of elements less than X. So $L[[\lceil pn\rceil]]$ is the element most likely to be near X. (For this to work we must already know that $L[n] \geq X > L[1]$.) Then we do the same thing for the appropriate sublist, and so on. This is *interpolation search.*

This algorithm is simple, but its analysis appears to be difficult. It is possible to show that it is $O(\lg\lg n)$ on average, but instead of analyzing it let's look at a more complicated algorithm, called *quadratic binary search,* that is also $O(\lg\lg n)$ on average but that is easier to analyze.

Quadratic binary search first probes $L[[\lceil pn\rceil]]$. If $X < L[[\lceil pn\rceil]]$ then it sequentially probes the elements

$$L[[\lceil pn - i\sqrt{n}\rceil]] , \quad i = 1, 2, 3, \dots$$

until it finds the smallest i for which $X \geq L[[\lceil pn - i\sqrt{n}\rceil]]$. Similarly, if $X > L[[\lceil pn\rceil]]$ then it sequentially probes the elements

$$L[[\lceil pn + i\sqrt{n}\rceil]] , \quad i = 1, 2, 3, \dots$$

until it finds the smallest i for which $X \leq L[[\lceil pn + i\sqrt{n}\rceil]]$.

Why do this? Well, when the jump search ends we know X's position to within roughly $\sqrt{n}$ elements. If the average number of comparisons that this process takes is constant (it's about two), then in a constant number of comparisons we've reduced the search space to the square root of the previous size. Now we do the same thing on the sublist, and so on. We can take the square root of n no more than $\lg\lg n$ times before reaching a constant since $n = 2^{\lg n} = 2^{2^{\lg\lg n}}$ and taking the square root of a number halves the exponent. So, since each iteration takes a constant number of comparisons on average and there are $\lg\lg n$ iterations on average, then, on average, quadratic binary search takes $O(\lg\lg n)$ comparisons.

Now, let's get technical and show that it only takes about two comparisons on average to reduce the sublist by a square root. The average number of comparisons before we bracket X on the first iteration is

$$\sum_{i=1}^{\sqrt{n}} i \, \mathbf{P}(\text{we use exactly } i \text{ probes to determine the sublist})$$

And this (see figure 2.16) equals

$$\sum_{i=1}^{\sqrt{n}} \mathbf{P}(\text{we use at least } i \text{ probes to determine the sublist})$$

Also, we know the probability is one when $i = 1$ and $i = 2$ since we always use at least the first two comparisons to bracket X. Thus the average value is

$$2 + \sum_{i=3}^{\sqrt{n}} \mathbf{P}(\text{we use at least } i \text{ probes to determine the sublist})$$

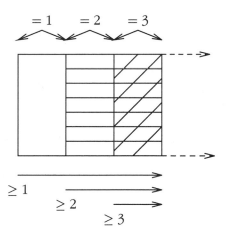

Figure 2.16 $\sum_i i\mathbf{P}(f(x) = i) \;=\; \sum_i \mathbf{P}(f(x) \geq i)$

Now, suppose $i \geq 3$. If we need i or more probes then the probability that X's actual location is more than $(i - 2)\sqrt{n}$ locations away—in either direction—from our guessed location of pn is

$$\mathbf{P}(pn + (i - 2)\sqrt{n} \;\geq\; \text{location of } X \;\geq\; pn - (i - 2)\sqrt{n})$$

Now it is possible to show, by using a relation called Čebyšev's ("shay-bee-shev") inequality (which we will develop in the next chapter, page 171), that

$$\mathbf{P}(pn + (i - 2)\sqrt{n} \geq \text{location of } X \geq pn - (i - 2)\sqrt{n}) \leq \frac{p(1 - p)n}{(i - 2)^2 n}$$

$$\leq \frac{1}{4(i - 2)^2}$$

since $p(1 - p) \leq 1/4$.

| Pause | Why is it true that $p(1 - p) \leq 1/4$?

Thus the average number of comparisons is less than

$$2 + \sum_{i=3}^{\sqrt{n}} \frac{1}{4(i - 2)^2} \quad < \quad 2 + \frac{1}{4} \sum_{i=1}^{\infty} \frac{1}{i^2}$$

$$= \quad 2 + \frac{1}{4}\frac{\pi^2}{6}$$

$$= \quad 2.4112 \cdots$$

(The bound on the sum of the squares of the reciprocals of the first n numbers is related to the *harmonic numbers* (see next chapter).)

So, quadratic binary search takes no more than about $2.5 \lg \lg n$ comparisons on average. It is possible to show that $\Omega(\lg \lg n)$ is necessary on average within a wide class of probability distributions.

Although interpolation search is exponentially better than binary search on average, it isn't always a good idea. First, in the worst case it can take n comparisons. Fortunately we can avoid this by interleaving a binary search with an interpolation search; this **interleaved algorithm** has a worst cost of $O(\lg n)$ and an average cost of $O(\lg \lg n)$. Second, on many machines, and for many applications, the arithmetic interpolation search needs to do takes more time than is saved in comparisons. So, in practice, interpolation search is not always much better than binary search.

Hashing

Finally, let's assume that we know all possible search requests, so we have complete knowledge of the data. For example, if a programming language has reserved words then they are fixed for all time when the language is created, so given a reserved word we only have to tell which it is. Now we could sort the words and use binary search whenever we need to identify a particular word, but since we know all possible words we should be able to reduce the search time considerably. However once again we have to leave the comparison-based model to do so.

Suppose there is some fast way to compute a number given any element of the search domain. This is reasonable if the domain is itself a set of numbers but it must also be possible for anything representable in a digital computer, since we must code it somehow to get it into the machine in the first place. So it's okay to assume that every element is now just a number. Assume further that each number is unique. It's stretching reality a little to assume that unique numbers can be computed quickly, but if all the elements are different then the numbers, theoretically at least, can be distinct.

Now in most imperative languages it is possible to access any array location in constant time.[7] Since all elements are now unique numbers we can use their values as array indices. Since every number is distinct, every element ends up in a unique array location. Finally, since computing these associated numbers is fast (by assumption), then to search for something we merely compute its associated number to produce an array index. This is a good solution if the array is about the same size as the search domain. Unfortunately the numbers can be very large, so the array can be impractically large. What to do?

If the numbers are wide apart then we can squish them into a smaller range to fit within a practical array size. This squishing operation is called *hashing*. In effect we first fingerprint all possible elements, then to search for any particular X we fingerprint the suspect, X, and quickly compare its fingerprint to those on file. If there is no match then X is not in the list; if there is a match then there may be many matches.[8] We now need to decide which, if any, of those matches is really X.

If the fingerprints of two different numbers are the same then we have a *collision*. (Imagine how annoyed the FBI would be if most of us had the same fingerprints.) We want a fingerprinting function

- that is easy to compute,

- whose values are easy to compare,

- that produces numbers of roughly the same size as the size of the search space, and

- that minimizes the number of collisions.

Such a function is called a *hash function*.

_____

[7]Technically, access times aren't constant for large arrays, but they are within an order of magnitude of each other so we can assume them to be constant.

[8]It is commonly believed that human fingerprints are unique; but even if they are, when fingerprints are taken they still get smudged and two different fingerprints can look alike after smudging.

There are two things to note. First, if we know the probability distribution of the elements of the domain then it is possible to show that searches take constant time *on average*. Of course, we have to spend preprocessing time building the hash array in the first place, but this is reasonable if we have a static set of input elements and a large number of queries to answer.

Second, in the most extreme case of foreknowledge we know all possible searches beforehand, as, for example, in the reserved words example. In that case we can build a hash array using **perfect hashing** so that *every* search takes constant time in the worst case! Building a perfect hash array is expensive, but this is the ultimate search algorithm if we want the fastest possible worst cost; we cannot improve on constant time. Because of its large set-up cost, perfect hashing is sensible only when the search domain does not change over many queries.

2.5   Coda—Apples and Oranges

> I don't know what I may seem to the
> world; but as to myself, I seem to have
> been only as a boy, playing on the
> seashore, and diverting myself, in now
> and then finding a smoother pebble
> or a prettier shell than ordinary, whilst
> the great ocean of truth lay all
> undiscovered before me.
>
> Isaac Newton, quoted in E. T. Bell,
> *Men of Mathematics*

So which search algorithm is "best?" During this chapter we have pretended that the number of comparisons done is proportional to the time taken. We have also agreed to say that one algorithm is "worse" than another if it takes more time to run. But there are other things to worry about. We have seen that binary search is "better" than linear search in both the worst and average case, but sometimes linear search is superior— if n is small or if the search is done rarely. Also, linear search is easier to code, so we get a working program faster and we have more faith that it's working properly. Binary search is difficult to get right the first time.

Further, we can only use binary search on a subset of the problems that linear search can solve. We cannot use binary search for any of the following: unsorted lists; linked lists, even if the linked list is sorted; hash arrays; multi-dimensional arrays, or any other non-linear structure;

multi-dimensional searches (searching on several keys) when many primary keys are the same; or any database changing so rapidly that it is too expensive to keep it sorted. Of course, in every case there are more sophisticated things we can do to the data to keep the search time low.

Generalizing the search problem, we could ask that if X is not in L then we at least get its nearest neighbors—that is, where would it be if it were in L? More generally, the search can be over many dimensions; this is the multi-dimensional search problem, and there are three versions of the problem: exact match, partial match, and range query. Other questions that we need to consider before coding a search procedure are: How static is L? Will searches be followed by insertions or deletions? Does L have to be in some order for reasons other than ease of searching? Are comparisons really expensive in this particular application? Is there anything special about the elements of the search domain that we can exploit to make the search faster? Is the search to be done in parallel with some other process? Is the search to be oblivious—that is, must each comparison be predetermined? (The advantage of an oblivious search is that it can be easily parallelized.) And so on, in infinite variety.

So which search algorithm is "best?" Well, the short answer is: best compared to what? Certainly if the search needs to be done often and there is a lot of data and the data is sortable and the data is not changing rapidly and the number of comparisons is proportional to the overall work then binary search is *exponentially* better than linear search. Other than that you have to decide for yourself. You should now have some of the tools to help you do so.

In this chapter we've seen the first practical uses of randomization in the algorithms for searching linked lists and for hashing. Randomization is of great practical importance and deep theoretical interest. It is connected to probability theory, information theory (we'll meet this in chapter four), lower bound theory, randomness (chapter six), and complexity theory (chapter seven). We will see several randomized algorithms in future, culminating in chapter six with a wonderful procedure to find primes fast.

This is the end of our first trek through the continent of analysis. We've grappled with a small cluster of related search problems and found optimal, or asymptotically optimal, solutions for them. Our next trek is through similar country. We will stay within the province of comparison-based problems but change emphasis from searching for something to searching for something with a particular property. That property is rank within some ordering.

Endnotes

Computational Ideas

Comparison-based model, linear search, jump search, binary search, interpolation search, quadratic binary search, hashing, perfect hashing, search keys, sentinels, reduction strategy, simplicity strategy, balance strategy, input-output lower bound, static versus dynamic data, average cost, trees, path length, decision trees, linked lists, pointers, predictable algorithms, randomized algorithms, interleaved algorithms, expected cost, worst expected cost, average expected cost.

Mathematical Ideas

- Solving recurrences by guessing a general solution involving several unknown constants then solving for the unknown constants using the recurrence.

- Finding the minimum of a differentiable function by differentiating and setting the derivative to zero, finding the turning point, then checking that it is a minimum by differentiating again and checking that the second derivative is positive.
  Note that a function may have a minimum when the derivative is undefined. Also, even if the derivative is zero, if the second derivative is also zero the turning point may be a maximum, minimum, or neither.

- Removing floors and ceilings in simple minimizations by examining the real-valued form of the function.

- Exploiting the fact that an algorithm's cost is usually non-decreasing to bound recurrences involving division by a constant.

- Using structural induction on recursively defined structures to prove properties of the structures.

- Simplifying recurrences involving floors and ceilings by turning all floors into ceilings (or conversely) and subtracting one value of the function from another to cancel common terms.

- Finding the values of sums by rearranging the terms of the sum with a suitable bijective function and subtracting similar terms.

Definitions

- *sample space:* The sample space of an experiment is the set of all outcomes of the experiment.

- *event:* An event is any subset of the sample space of an experiment.

- *probability:* The probability of an event among a finite set of events is the ratio of the number of ways the event can happen divided by the total number of ways any of the events can happen.

- *disjoint events:* Two events are disjoint if they do not share any outcomes.

- *independent events:* Two events are independent if the probability of one is not affected by whether the other happens.

- *boundary condition:* A boundary condition of a recurrence is any value of the function defined by the recurrence.

- *floor:* The floor of a number is the largest integer less than or equal to the number.

- *ceiling:* The ceiling of a number is the smallest integer greater than or equal to the number.

- *predictable algorithm:* A predictable algorithm always behaves the same if given the same input.

- *randomized algorithm:* A randomized algorithm modifies its behavior by flipping coins.

- *rooted tree:* A rooted tree is a tree with a special node, the root.

- *binary tree:* A binary tree is a rooted tree in which each node has at most two children.

- *ordered tree:* An ordered tree is a rooted tree in which we distinguish between the children of a node.

- *decision tree:* A decision tree models all possible sequences of comparisons of an algorithm.

- *leaf:* A leaf of a tree is a childless node.

- *fertile node:* A fertile node of a rooted tree is a node with the maximum possible number of children.

- *level:* The level of a node in a rooted tree is the number of nodes on the path from the root to the node; the root has level zero.

- *height:* The height of a rooted tree is the level of the deepest leaf.

- *path length:* The path length of a rooted tree is the sum of the levels of all nodes.

- *worst cost* $(\mathcal{A}) = \max\limits_{I \in I_n} f_\mathcal{A}(I)$

- $average\ cost(A) = \displaystyle\sum_{I \in I_n} \mathbf{P}(I) f_A(I)$

- $worst\ cost\ lower\ bound(A) = \displaystyle\min_{A \in A_M} \left\{ \max_{I \in I_n} f_A(I) \right\}$

- $average\ cost\ lower\ bound(P) = \displaystyle\min_{A \in A_M} \left\{ \sum_{I \in I_n} \mathbf{P}(I) f_A(I) \right\}$

- $expected\ cost(A_S, I) = \displaystyle\sum_{A \in A_S} \mathbf{P}(A) f_A(I)$

- $worst\ expected\ cost(A_S) = \displaystyle\max_{I \in I_n} \left\{ \sum_{A \in A_S} \mathbf{P}(A) f_A(I) \right\}$

- $average\ expected\ cost(A_S) = \displaystyle\sum_{I \in I_n} \mathbf{P}(I) \left\{ \sum_{A \in A_S} \mathbf{P}(A) f_A(I) \right\}$

Constants

- $\pi = 3.14159\ 26535\ 89793\ 23846 \cdots$

Notation

- $\mathbf{P}$ = the probability of

- {} = set delimiters

- $\lfloor x \rfloor$ = the floor of x

- $\lceil x \rceil$ = the ceiling of x

- $\langle x \rangle$ = the nearest integer to x

Tools

- $f(n) = \begin{cases} 1 & n = 1 \\ f(n-1) + 1 & n > 1 \end{cases} \qquad \Longleftrightarrow \qquad f(n) = n$

- The sum rule: If A and B are disjoint then $\mathbf{P}(A\ or\ B) = \mathbf{P}(A) + \mathbf{P}(B)$

- $\lfloor x \rfloor = n \iff n + 1 > x \geq n$

- $\lceil x \rceil = n \iff n \geq x > n - 1$

- $\langle x \rangle = \begin{cases} \lfloor x \rfloor & x < \lfloor x \rfloor + 1/2 \\ ? & x = \lfloor x \rfloor + 1/2 \\ \lceil x \rceil & x > \lfloor x \rfloor + 1/2 \end{cases}$

- $\displaystyle\min_x f(x) \geq \min_x \lfloor f(x) \rfloor, \quad \min_x \lceil f(x) \rceil = \lceil \min_x f(x) \rceil$

- $\displaystyle\min_{1\le x\le n}\left\{\frac{n}{x}+x\right\}=2\sqrt{n}$

- $\displaystyle\left\lfloor\frac{n}{\lceil\sqrt{n}\,\rceil}\right\rfloor=\begin{cases}\langle\sqrt{n}\,\rangle & \text{if } n=k^2 \text{ or } k(k+1)\\ \langle\sqrt{n}\,\rangle-1 & \text{otherwise}\end{cases}$

- $\displaystyle\min_{x} x\sqrt[x]{n}=e\ln n$

- $f(n)=\begin{cases}1 & n=1\\ f(\lfloor n/2\rfloor)+1 & n>1\end{cases}\qquad\Longleftrightarrow\qquad f(n)=\lfloor\lg n\rfloor+1$

- $\lfloor n/2\rfloor+1\ge\lceil n/2\rceil\ge\lfloor n/2\rfloor$

- $\lfloor(n+1)/2\rfloor=\lceil n/2\rceil$

- $\lceil n/2\rceil+\lfloor n/2\rfloor=n$

- $\lfloor\lfloor n/l\rfloor/m\rfloor=\lfloor n/lm\rfloor$

- $2^{\lceil\lg n\rceil}\ge n=2^{\lg n}\ge 2^{\lfloor\lg n\rfloor}$

- $\lfloor n/2^i\rfloor=1\iff i=\lfloor\lg n\rfloor$

- $\lceil\lg(n+1)\rceil=\lfloor\lg n\rfloor+1$

- The number of nodes of a height m rooted binary tree is at most $2^{m+1}-1$

- The height of an n-node rooted binary tree nodes is at least $\lfloor\lg n\rfloor$

- The path length of an n-node rooted binary tree nodes is at least $(n+1)\lceil\lg(n+1)\rceil-2^{\lceil\lg(n+1)\rceil}+1-n=(n+1)\lfloor\lg n\rfloor-2(2^{\lfloor\lg n\rfloor}-1)$

- The average path length of an n-node rooted binary tree nodes is at least $\lfloor\lg n\rfloor-\dfrac{2(2^{\lfloor\lg n\rfloor}-1)-\lfloor\lg n\rfloor}{n}$

- If f is bijective then $\displaystyle\sum r_i=\sum r_{f(i)}$

- $\displaystyle\sum_{i=1}^{n} i2^{i-1}=(n-1)2^n+1$

- $\displaystyle\sum_{i=1}^{n}\lceil\lg i\rceil=n\lceil\lg n\rceil-2^{\lceil\lg n\rceil}+1$

$$\bullet \; f(n) = \begin{cases} 0 & n = 0 \\ 1 & n = 1 \\ \dfrac{\lceil n/2 \rceil - 1}{n} f(\lceil n/2 \rceil - 1) + \dfrac{\lfloor n/2 \rfloor}{n} f(\lfloor n/2 \rfloor) + 1 & n > 1 \end{cases}$$

$$\Longleftrightarrow \; f(n) = \lceil \lg(n+1) \rceil - \frac{2^{\lceil \lg(n+1) \rceil} - \lceil \lg(n+1) \rceil - 1}{n}$$

$$\bullet \; f(n) = \begin{cases} 0 & n = 0 \\ 1 & n = 1 \\ f(\lceil n/2 \rceil - 1) + f(\lfloor n/2 \rfloor) + n & n > 1 \end{cases}$$

$$\Longleftrightarrow \; f(n) = (n+1)\lceil \lg(n+1) \rceil - 2^{\lceil \lg(n+1) \rceil} + 1$$

$$\bullet \; f(n) = \begin{cases} 0 & n = 0, 1 \\ \displaystyle \min_{0 < i < n} \{ f(i) + f(n-i) \} + n & n > 1 \end{cases}$$

$$\Longleftrightarrow \; f(n) = n(\lceil \lg n \rceil + 1) - 2^{\lceil \lg n \rceil} \quad (\text{problem 15, page 152})$$

$$\bullet \; \sum_{i=1}^{n} i^k = \frac{n^{k+1}}{k+1} - \frac{n^k}{2} + \frac{k n^{k-1}}{12} + O(k^2 n^{k-2}) \quad (\text{problem 16, page 152})$$

$$\bullet \; \sum_{i} i \mathbf{P}(f(x) = i) \; = \; \sum_{i} \mathbf{P}(f(x) \geq i)$$

Notes

Pierre de Fermat independently solved Pascal's original probability problem. Gerolamo Cardano preempted both mathematicians, but his work, done almost a century before, was ignored. Cardano, a lively figure in sixteenth century science, not only studied gambling he also gambled his fortune and his reputation away.

Randomized linked list search is adapted from "Analysis of a Randomized Data Structure for Representing Sets," Jon Louis Bentley, Donald F. Stanat, and J. Michael Steele, *Proceedings of the 19th Annual Allerton Conference on Circuit and System Theory,* 364–372, 1981. The lower bound was established in "Probabilistic Searching in Sorted Linked Lists," Tom Leighton and Margaret Lepley, *Proceedings of the 20th Annual Allerton Conference on Circuit and System Theory,* 500–506, 1982. The analysis of quadratic binary search is adapted from "Understanding the Complexity of Interpolation Search," Yehoshua Perl and Edward M. Reingold, *Information Processing Letters,* 6, 6, 219–222, 1977.

Exercise 1, page 144, is adapted from an illustration in *Programming Pearls,* Jon Louis Bentley, Addison-Wesley, 1986. Exercise 20, page 147, is adapted from *Combinatorial Search,* Martin Aigner, Wiley-Teubner, 1988.

Problem 24, page 154, is from "A General Class of Resource Tradeoffs," Jon Louis Bentley and Donna J. Brown, *Proceedings of the 21st Annual Symposium on the Foundations of Computer Science,* IEEE Computer Society, 217–228, 1980. It is generalized and completely solved in "Guessing Games and Distributed Computations in Synchronous Networks," J. van Leeuwen, N. Santoro, J. Urrutia, and S. Zaks, Carlton University technical report SCS-TR-96, June 1986. Problem 25, page 154, is adapted from "An Almost Optimal Algorithm for Unbounded Search," Jon Louis Bentley and Andrew C.-C. Yao, *Information Processing Letters,* 5, 82–87, 1976. For background on research problem 3, page 156, see "Ulam's Searching Game with Lies," Jurek Czyzowicz, Daniele Mundici, and Andrzej Pelc, *Journal of Combinatorial Theory, Series A,* 52, 62–76, 1989.

Further Reading

For a good book on the beginnings of probability, with some insight into Renaissance scholarship, see the stylish *Cardano: The Gambling Scholar,* Øystein Ore, Dover, 1953. Cardano wrote his book on games of chance in 1526.

For ways to speed up binary search see *Programming Pearls,* Jon Louis Bentley, Addison-Wesley, 1986. Be warned that even professional programmers get it wrong the first time; binary search is difficult to code correctly, especially if the programmer is trying to optimize its performance. Knuth in section 6.2.1 of *The Art of Computer Programming: Volume 3* points out that while binary search was first published in 1946, the first bug-free version only appeared sixteen years later. The following paper illustrates some of the difficulties of coding binary search: "Some Lessons Drawn from the History of the Binary Search Algorithm," R. Lesuisse, *The Computer Journal,* 26, 2, 154–163, 1983.

The study of finite sets of things belongs in discrete mathematics. As we've seen, a lot of analysis depends on discrete mathematics. For further background see the excellent *Concrete Mathematics: A Foundation for Computer Science,* Ronald L. Graham, Donald E. Knuth, and Oren Patashnik, Addison-Wesley, 1989.

For more on searching problems see *Combinatorial Search,* Martin Aigner, Wiley-Teubner, 1988. See also *Search Problems,* Rudolf Ahlswede and Ingo Wegener, Wiley, 1987, and for more practical problems see *Searching Algorithms,* Jiři Wiedermann, Teubner, 1987. For an analysis of one hash scheme see *Design and Analysis of Coalesced Hashing,* Jeffrey Scott Vitter and Wen-Chin Chen, Oxford University Press, 1987. As usual see also Knuth's *The Art of Computer Programming: Volume 3, Sorting and Searching,* Addison-Wesley, 1973.

Algorithmics: Theory and Practice, Gilles Brassard and Paul Bratley, Prentice-Hall, 1988, devotes a whole chapter to randomized algorithms.

For a comprehensive presentation of probability theory see *An Introduction to Probability Theory and Its Applications, Volume 1,* William Feller, Wiley, third edition, 1968. Although comprehensive, Feller is hard going for the novice, try also *Basic Probability Theory,* Robert Ash, Wiley, 1970.

Questions

> One must learn by doing the thing; for
> though you think you know it, you have
> no certainty until you try.
>
> Sophocles, *The Women of Trachis*

Exercises

1. We are to find a single bad card in a deck of about a thousand punched cards. Unfortunately, we can only find the bad card by running some subset of the cards through a program and seeing an erroneous answer. How many runs of the program does it take to find the bad card?

2. One day on the popular television game-show "The Artifice is Slight" Ms Minnie Mouse was given the chance to win a new car. Minnie would win the car if she could guess its price in one minute. She could ask only one kind of question, the format of which was that she would state a number and the obliging game-show host would tell her "lower" or "higher." Unfortunately, Minnie, a victim of overexcitement, guessed wildly and went home on foot. (This is a true story, only the names have been changed to protect the silly.)

   (a) What should Minnie have done?

   (b) What should Minnie have done if she had to guess the volume of the sun to the nearest liter?

3. What is wrong with the following argument?
   "BINARY_SEARCH shows that we can find an element in an ordered list in $O(\lg n)$ time, but these n elements must have been input at some point, so by the input-output lower bound BINARY_SEARCH must take $\Omega(n)$ time."

4. Suppose L is sorted. Find LINEAR_SEARCH's average cost if

(a) $X \in L$ (assume that X is equally likely to be any element of L).

(b) $X \notin L$ (assume that X is equally likely to be between any two consecutive elements of L).

5. There are many ways of reducing a problem to a collection of previously solved problems. Suppose we split the search problem for unsorted lists into two search problems, as in algorithm 2.8. Develop and solve a recurrence for the worst number of element-element comparisons.

```
LINEAR_SEARCH (List, lower, upper, X)
   { Look for X in List[lower..upper].
   Report its position if found, else report 0.
   lower > 0. }

   if lower > upper
      then
         return 0
      else
         mid ← ⌊(lower + upper)/2⌋
         if List[mid] = X
            then
               return mid
            else
               left ← LINEAR_SEARCH (List, lower, mid − 1, X)
               right ← LINEAR_SEARCH (List, mid + 1, upper, X)
               return max (left, right)
```

Algorithm 2.8

6. Rewrite algorithm 2.1, page 84, to recurse until there are no elements in the list left to search.

(a) Does the precondition of the algorithm change?

(b) Give a recurrence describing this algorithm's worst cost.

7. Consider finding LINEAR_SEARCH's average cost using an argument like that used for BINARY_SEARCH's average cost. If p is the probability that X equals any of the n elements of L then LINEAR_SEARCH's average cost is

$$f(n) = \begin{cases} 1 & n = 1 \\ 1 + (1 - p)f(n - 1) & n > 1 \end{cases}$$

(a) Solve this recurrence.

(b) What is wrong with this argument?

8. What happens if we replace the precondition

$$upper - lower + 1 \geq jump \geq 1$$

in algorithm 2.3, page 100, by the precondition $jump \geq 1$?

9. Show that $p(1 - p) \leq 1/4$.

10. Determine whether

(a) $\lceil x + n \rceil = \lceil x \rceil + n$.

(b) $\lfloor x + n \rfloor = \lfloor x \rfloor + n$.

(c) $\lceil x - n \rceil = \lceil x \rceil - n$.

(d) $\lfloor x - n \rfloor = \lfloor x \rfloor - n$.

11. Show that

(a) $\lfloor n/2 \rfloor + \lceil n/2 \rceil = n$.

(b) $\lfloor n/3 \rfloor + \lfloor (n + 1)/3 \rfloor + \lfloor (n + 2)/3 \rfloor = n$.

12. Show that

(a) $\lfloor \lfloor n/m \rfloor / l \rfloor = \lfloor \lfloor n/l \rfloor / m \rfloor = \lfloor n/lm \rfloor$.

(b) $\left\lfloor \dfrac{n + \lfloor \frac{n}{2} \rfloor}{2} \right\rfloor = \left\lfloor \dfrac{3n}{4} \right\rfloor$.

13. (a) Show that $\lfloor n/2^i \rfloor = 1 \iff i = \lfloor \lg n \rfloor$.

(b) If $\lceil n/2^i \rceil = 1$ what is i?

14. Show that

(a) $\lfloor \lg \lfloor x \rfloor \rfloor = \lfloor \lg x \rfloor$.

(b) $f(n) = \begin{cases} 1 & n = 1 \\ f(\lfloor n/2 \rfloor) + 1 & n > 1 \end{cases} \iff f(n) = \lfloor \lg n \rfloor + 1$.

15. Show that

(a) $\sqrt{n + 1} - \sqrt{n} = \dfrac{1}{\sqrt{n + 1} + \sqrt{n}}$.

(b) $\lceil 2\sqrt{n} \rceil - 1 \geq \left\lceil \displaystyle\sum_{i=1}^{n} \dfrac{1}{\sqrt{i}} \right\rceil \geq \lceil 2\sqrt{n} \rceil - 2$.

16. Solve the following two questions in either order.
    (a) Show that
        i. $\lceil (n+1)/k \rceil = \lfloor n/k \rfloor + 1$.
        ii. $\lceil \lg(n+1) \rceil = \lfloor \lg n \rfloor + 1$.
        iii. $\lceil \sqrt{n+1} \rceil = \lfloor \sqrt{n} \rfloor + 1$.
    (b) Develop conditions on f such that $\lceil f(n+1) \rceil = \lfloor f(n) \rfloor + 1$.

17. Suppose we can only afford c comparisons while searching a list. What is the maximum n that we can search using c comparisons in JUMP_SEARCH?

18. Here is a simple scale for weighing objects.

    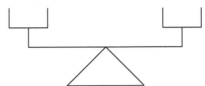

    Given a collection of objects of known weight we weigh an object by putting it in one pan and putting known weights in the other pan until the scale balances. It may happen that there is no way to do this if we may only place the given weights in only one pan.
    (a) If we can place the weights in *both* pans what is the minimum number of weights necessary to weigh an object whose weight is an (unknown) integer n?
    (b) Use decision trees to find a good lower bound.

19. We have n apparently identical gold coins. One of them is an amalgam and is lighter, but is otherwise indistinguishable from the others. We also have a balance with two pans as in the previous question, but without weights. So any measurement will tell us only if the loaded pans weigh the same or, if not, which one weighs more.
    (a) How many measurements are necessary and sufficient to find the false gold coin?
    (b) What happens if we don't know if the false coin is lighter or heavier?

20. We wish to test n people for syphilitic antigen. To this purpose we draw blood from each of them and label the samples. The Wasserman test tells whether blood contains syphilitic antigen. We may mix portions of the blood samples to conduct tests on several individuals simultaneously.
    How many tests are required to determine who has syphilis, if anyone?

Problems

1. Using the following definitions

$$\text{expected worst cost}(\mathcal{A_S}) \;=\; \sum_{\mathcal{A} \in \mathcal{A_S}} \mathbf{P}(\mathcal{A}) \left\{ \max_{I \in I_n} f_{\mathcal{A}}(I) \right\}$$

$$\text{expected average cost}(\mathcal{A_S}) \;=\; \sum_{\mathcal{A} \in \mathcal{A_S}} \mathbf{P}(\mathcal{A}) \left\{ \sum_{I \in I_n} \mathbf{P}(I) f_{\mathcal{A}}(I) \right\}$$

(a) Show that the expected average cost is the same as the average expected cost.

(b) Is the expected worst cost the same as the worst expected cost?

(c) Relate the following in order of size: worst cost, average cost, expected cost, expected worst cost, worst expected cost, expected average cost, and average expected cost.

(d) Why are "average worst cost" and "worst average cost" unimportant?

2. Consider the following randomized algorithm to search an unordered list of size n: generate a random number uniformly from the range 1 to n and start a linear search at that position, wrapping around the list until we return to the starting location.

(a) What is the worst cost of this algorithm?

(b) What is the probability of the worst cost occurring?

(c) What is the worst expected cost and average expected cost of this algorithm?

(d) Is this algorithm equivalent to first scrambling the list then searching it from left to right?

(e) We can think of LINEAR_SEARCH as making an assumption about where X will be in the list. LINEAR_SEARCH "assumes" that X will be near the left end of the list. What assumption is the randomized algorithm making?

(f) We can think of this randomized algorithm as selecting one of n versions of LINEAR_SEARCH at random. The coin flip algorithm presented in the text only selects one of two versions of LINEAR_SEARCH at random.

   i. Show that the two algorithms have the same worst expected cost.

   ii. What is the advantage of using the more complicated algorithm?

iii. Suppose that it is practical to generate $n!$ versions of LIN-EAR_SEARCH each using a different probe sequence. Consider a randomized algorithm that generates a random number in the range 1 to $n!$, then calls one of these algorithms. In what sense is this randomized algorithm best possible?

3. (a) Prove the following relations

i. $\min_x f(\lfloor x \rfloor) \geq \min_x f(x) \geq \lfloor \min_x f(x) \rfloor \geq \min_x \lfloor f(x) \rfloor$

ii. $\min_x f(\lfloor x \rfloor) \geq \lfloor \min_x f(\lfloor x \rfloor) \rfloor \geq \min_x \lfloor f(\lfloor x \rfloor) \rfloor \geq \min_x \lfloor f(x) \rfloor$

iii. $\lfloor \min_x f(\lfloor x \rfloor) \rfloor \geq \lfloor \min_x f(x) \rfloor$

iv. $\lfloor \min_x \lfloor f(x) \rfloor \rfloor = \min_x \lfloor f(x) \rfloor$

v. $\lfloor \min_x \lfloor f(\lfloor x \rfloor) \rfloor \rfloor = \min_x \lfloor f(\lfloor x \rfloor) \rfloor$

(b) Establish the relative order between the following

$$\min_x f(x) \qquad \min_x f(\lceil x \rceil) \qquad \min_x \lceil f(x) \rceil \qquad \lceil \min_x f(x) \rceil$$

$$\min_x \lceil f(\lceil x \rceil) \rceil \qquad \lceil \min_x f(\lceil x \rceil) \rceil \qquad \lceil \min_x \lceil f(x) \rceil \rceil \qquad \lceil \min_x \lceil f(\lceil x \rceil) \rceil \rceil$$

4. Show that $\lfloor \sqrt{n + \lfloor \sqrt{n} \rfloor} \rfloor = \langle \sqrt{n} \rangle$.

5. For this question you need to know that the minimum of a two-variable function $f(x, y)$ can be found by partial differentiation.

(a) Show that

$$\min \left\{ \sum_{i=1}^{k} x_i + n \left/ \prod_{i=1}^{k} x_i \right. \right\} = (k+1)n^{k+1}$$

where the minimum is taken over all sets of k positive real numbers x_1 to x_k and $\prod_{i=1}^{k} x_i$ is shorthand for $x_1 \times x_2 \times \cdots \times x_k$.

(b) Show that

$$\min \sum_{i=1}^{k-1} x_i / x_{i+1} = (k+1)x_1^{k+1}$$

where the minimum is taken over all sequences of k positive real numbers x_1 to x_k where $x_i > x_{i+1}$ and $x_k = 1$.

6. Suppose we have a list L, of n elements, drawn without replacement from a set S of m distinct things ($m \geq n$). We may compare any two elements of S but this comparison tells us only whether the two elements are equal.
Suppose that X is equal to an element of S and suppose that L is drawn from S (so X may or may not be equal to an element of L).

(a) What is the worst number of comparisons needed to decide whether X is in L?

(b) What is the average number of comparisons needed to decide whether X is in L? Assume that X is equally likely to be any element of S, and that L is equally likely to be any subset of S of size n.

(c) Give good lower bounds for both cases.

(d) Find the worst and average costs when S may have duplicated elements. Assume that S is partitioned into k sets of duplicates of multiplicities $m_1, m_2, \ldots, m_k$.

(e) Are the results different if S has no duplicates and L is drawn with replacement?

7. (a) What is the average time of JUMP_SEARCH if X is in L and X is equally likely to be any of the n elements in L?

(b) What is the average if X is not necessarily in L? (You must make an assumption about the probability of X not being in L.)

8. (a) Show that if we probe the first, the $(k+1)^{th}$, the $(2k+1)^{th}$, and so on, then JUMP_SEARCH's worst cost is $\lceil n/k \rceil + k - 1$.

(b) What is the best choice of k?

9. Recurrences involving both square roots and floors and ceilings are even harder than either separately. Consider

$$f(n) = \begin{cases} 0 & n = 0 \\ f(n + 1 - \lceil 2\sqrt{n} \rceil) + 1 & n > 0 \end{cases}$$

(a) Assume that f is non-decreasing. By constructing a recurrence with no ceiling function show that $f(n) \leq \lceil \sqrt{n} \rceil$.

(b) By considering $k = \lceil 2\sqrt{n} \rceil$ or otherwise show that $f(n) = \lfloor \sqrt{n} \rfloor$.

(c) Show that

$$g(n) = \begin{cases} 0 & n = 0 \\ g(n + 1 - \lfloor 2\sqrt{n} \rfloor) + 1 & n > 0 \end{cases} \implies g(n) = \lceil \sqrt{n} \rceil$$

10. Show that we cannot improve square root search in the worst case by using $k = \langle \sqrt{n+1} \rangle$ or $k = \lfloor \sqrt{n+1} \rfloor$ by showing that

(a) $\left\lceil \dfrac{n}{\lceil \sqrt{n} \rceil} \right\rceil = \langle \sqrt{n} \rangle$.

(b) $\left\lfloor \dfrac{n}{\lfloor \sqrt{n+1} \rfloor} \right\rfloor = \begin{cases} \langle \sqrt{n+1} \rangle - 1 & \text{if } n + 1 \text{ is a square} \\ \langle \sqrt{n+1} \rangle & \text{otherwise} \end{cases}$

11. Consider the following modification of JUMP_SEARCH: First choose two integers, k and l, as jump sizes. Interrogate every k^{th} element to bracket X to within k elements, then interrogate every l^{th} element of this sublist to bracket X to within l elements, then use linear search on this sub-sublist. (This assumes two-way comparisons.)

    (a) Show that the worst cost is $\lfloor n/k \rfloor + \lfloor k/l \rfloor + l$.

    (b) What are the best choices of k and l?

12. Show that

$$f(n) = \begin{cases} 0 & n \le 2 \\ \sqrt{n} f(\sqrt{n}) + n & n > 2 \end{cases} \implies f = O(n \lg \lg n)$$

13. Here is a modification of square root search: once we have located X to within roughly $\sqrt{n}$ elements we recursively use the square root search algorithm on the sublist. We can model this algorithm by the following recurrence on the real-valued function f

$$f(x) = \begin{cases} 2 & x = 2 \\ f(\sqrt{x}) + \sqrt{x} & x > 2 \end{cases}$$

    (a) By considering the recurrence, or otherwise, determine the order of the maximum depth of recursion of recursive square root search.

    (b) Give a close upper bound on the worst number of comparisons. Your upper bound should be within $o(\sqrt{n})$ of the actual upper bound. (Hint: This can be done without any analysis just by examining the recurrence.)

14. Consider the recurrence:

$$f(n) = f(g(n)) + r$$

We have seen three algorithms whose average costs fit this recurrence but which have three different growth rates. In linear search $g(n) = n-1$, in binary search $g(n) = n/2$, and in interpolation search $g(n) = \sqrt{n}$. The respective growth rates of f are $O(n)$, $O(\lg n)$, and $O(\lg \lg n)$.

    (a) If we want to design a search algorithm that is $O(\lg \lg \lg n)$ on average, what g should we look for?

    (b) What g makes $f = O(\lg \lg \lg \lg n)$?

15. We can use the average case lower bound on searching a sorted list to solve a difficult recurrence. As we have seen, we can decompose every rooted ordered binary tree into a root, a left subtree, and a right subtree (see figure 2.9, page 115). Now, over the set of all rooted binary trees with n leaves there is some smallest average height since there are only a finite number of such trees. Let $f(n)$ be the smallest sum of the levels of the leaves of such a tree. Then

$$f(n) = \begin{cases} 0 & n \le 1 \\ \min_{1 \le i \le n-1}\{f(i) + f(n-i)\} + n & n > 1 \end{cases}$$

(a) Explain why this recurrence is correct.

(b) This is a tough recurrence to solve but we already know the answer! Show that $f(n)$ is the same as the smallest path length of a rooted binary tree with n nodes. Hence,

$$f(n) = \lceil \lg n \rceil + 1 - \frac{2^{\lceil \lg n \rceil}}{n}$$

16. Show by induction on k that for large n

$$\sum_{i=1}^{n} i^k = \frac{n^{k+1}}{k+1} - \frac{n^k}{2} + \frac{kn^{k-1}}{12} + O(k^2 n^{k-2})$$

17. You are given two tokens of value r and s, respectively, and you may double the value of either token. However every doubling must result in a token of value at most t. Your mission, should you decide to accept it, is to maximize the value of the sum of the tokens if you may double n times.

18. Consider the following adaptive randomized list search. The algorithm searches an unsorted list from left to right or from right to left depending on the outcome of a coin toss. The coin is biased by the outcome of previous searches. Initially the coin is unbiased.
If the last search was unsuccessful then the coin's bias is unchanged.
Now consider the number of comparisons of a successful search:

  - if it's less than $n/2$, then the coin is linearly biased so that the next search has a higher probability of starting from the same side of the list;
  - if it's $n/2$, then the coin's bias is unchanged;
  - if it's more than $n/2$, then the coin is linearly biased so that the next search has a higher probability of starting from the opposite side of the list.

What is the average number of comparisons per search if we search for all n elements of the list in sequence?

19. For which n is the average number of comparisons to successfully find an element using algorithm 2.5, page 106, an integer?

20. (a) Assume that $\forall i \leq n$, $\mathbf{P}(L[i+1] > X > L[i]) = 1/(n+1)$. Show that the average time to find an element *not* in the list using iterative BINARY_SEARCH is given by the following recurrence:

$$f(n) = \begin{cases} 0 & n = 0 \\ 1 & n = 1 \\ \dfrac{\lceil n/2 \rceil}{n+1} f(\lceil n/2 \rceil - 1) + \dfrac{\lfloor n/2 \rfloor}{n+1} f(\lfloor n/2 \rfloor) + 1 & n > 1 \end{cases}$$

(b) Show that

$$f(n) = \lceil \lg(n+1) \rceil + 1 - \frac{2^{\lceil \lg(n+1) \rceil}}{n+1}$$

(c) Relate this result to the average time for a successful search.

21. The iterative binary search algorithm given uses three-way comparisons, but not all machines can do three-way comparisons in one step. Algorithm 2.9 may do better on those machines.

BINARY_SEARCH (*List, lower, upper, X*)
   { Look for X in *List[lower..upper]*.
   Report its position if found, else report 0.
   List is sorted in increasing order. *upper* $\geq$ *lower* > 0. }

   low $\leftarrow$ *lower* ; *high* $\leftarrow$ *upper*
   while *high* $>$ *low*
      mid $\leftarrow$ $\lfloor (low + high)/2 \rfloor$
      if $X >$ *List[mid]*
         then *low* $\leftarrow$ *mid* $+ 1$
         else *high* $\leftarrow$ *mid*
   if *List[low]* $= X$
      then return *low*
      else return 0

Algorithm 2.9

(a) Choose an appropriate operation to count, give a recurrence for the number of such operations as a function of n, and solve your recurrence.

(b) Find the algorithm's average cost.

22. There are several worst case optimal algorithms to search a sorted list; binary search is only one of the more convenient ones.

(a) Show that $n \leq 2^{\lfloor \lg n \rfloor + 1} - 1$.

(b) Show that a comparison of X and $L[i]$ where

$$2^{\lfloor \lg n \rfloor} \geq i \geq n - 2^{\lfloor \lg n \rfloor} + 1$$

can always be the first comparison of a worst case optimal search algorithm.

(c) As a function of n, how many different worst case optimal search procedures are there?

23. Suppose we are given a sorted list L of n elements, and we know that L contains k sets of duplicates of multiplicities $m_1, m_2, \ldots, m_k$, where $\sum_{i=1}^{k} m_i = n$. We wish to search L.

(a) Show that if $k = 1$ then one comparison suffices.

(b) Show that if $k = 2$ then two comparisons suffice.

(c) Show that if an element in the m_i class is less than an element in the m_j class $\forall i, j$ where $k \geq j > i$ then $\lceil \lg(k+1) \rceil$ comparisons are necessary and sufficient.

(d) If $k \geq 3$ is there any advantage if we only know that there are elements of multiplicity $m_1, m_2, \ldots, m_k$ but not their order?

24. You wish to determine the height, expressed in floors of a building, from which a human being dies if tossed out of a window on that floor. You have a building with n floors and you have a supply of k students. You are only allowed one operation to determine the lethal height: you may toss a student out of a window. If the student lives then he or she may be reused in another toss, but if the student dies then he or she cannot be reused.
Develop an algorithm to find the lethal height using the minimum number of tosses.

25. So far all our search algorithms search for elements in a bounded set.

(a) Show that you can find an integer in an *infinite range* in

$$\lceil \lg(n + 1) \rceil + 2 \lfloor \lg \lceil \lg(n + 1) \rceil \rfloor$$

comparisons where n is the (unknown) size of the integer.

(b) Prove a lower bound of $\sum_{i \geq 1} \lg^{(i)} n$, where $\lg^{(i)} n = \lg\lg \cdots \lg n$ (i times).

26. Transform randomized linked list search to a probabilistic guessing game on the integers and prove its optimality when searching for the largest element.

27. Prove the optimality of interpolation search within a model assuming a uniform distribution of the elements.

28. Exercise 2, page 144, assumes that Minnie can remember the two endpoints of the current reduced range as the search progresses. Effectively this means that Minnie must be able to remember $2 \lg n$ bits. Find a worst case optimal search algorithm that will work without calculating endpoints. Your algorithm may derive information from the value of the last probed point.

29. You are a robot facing an infinitely long wall and your task is to find a door in the wall. You are only allowed to walk along the wall to your left or to your right and at any time you may turn and walk in the opposite direction. Assume that the door is an (unknown) integer number of steps away.

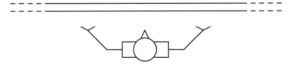

As a function of the (possibly unknown) distance to the door, what is the minimum number of steps you have to walk to find the door if

(a) you know that the door is to your left.

(b) you don't know where the door is but you know that it is n steps away.

(c) you don't know where the door is but you know that it is within n steps away.

(d) you neither know where the door is nor how far away it is.

30. You wish to find a record that you know is somewhere on one of m tapes. You could find the record by running through each tape but the tapes are very long and the record may be near the beginning of some tape. Assume that the desired record is the nth record of one of the tapes. But you don't know n.
Solve this problem by generalizing the solution to the previous problem to a robot searching for a door in m lanes.

Research

1. How many tests are required on average in exercise 20, page 147?

2. Find a worst expected case optimal algorithm to find the ith largest of a set of n things sorted in increasing order and implemented as a singly linked list in an array.

3. In some search problems we are not guaranteed a correct answer to all of our queries.

   (a) Suppose we know that we can be told up to k lies. What is the worst number of queries necessary to identify an element in a sorted list of size n?

   (b) What if we know that we will be told exactly k lies? (This has been solved exactly for $k \leq 2$, but only asymptotically for large k.)

4. How would we have to modify this chapter if our machines could compare three elements simultaneously and decide their relative order? We can now search a sorted list of n things in $\lceil \log_3 n \rceil$ time (how?) and there is an easy lower bound of $\lceil \log_6 n \rceil$ (why?). Which of these bounds can be improved? (This is not hard.) What is the best time for searching a sorted list if we have a comparator that can find the largest of three things simultaneously?

5. In this chapter we concentrated on searching for one thing in a list of n things. But what we really want to do is minimize the cost of searching for m things in a sorted or unsorted list of n things. For unsorted lists it is possible to show that

   (a) $2n$ comparisons are necessary and sufficient when $m = 2$.

   (b) $2n$ comparisons are necessary and $2n + 3$ comparisons are sufficient when $m = 3$.

   (c) $2n$ comparisons are necessary and $3n + 3$ comparisons are sufficient when $m = 4$.

   What are the exact results for (b) and (c)? What is the general case?

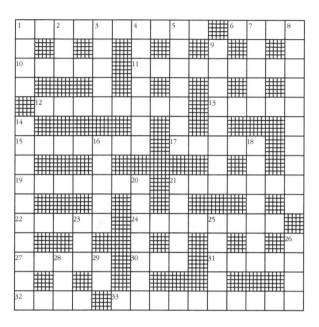

6. Across:

1 Hops are in every way to look. (4,6)
6 Nearly ready, without the article tinter sounds ominous. (4)
10 Kind expert exhibits pointer. (5)
11 Vegetable covering parchment. (9)
12 Southern way to kill takes hair short for the asian city. (8)
13 Fifty meet a common ending, love the language loosely. (5)
15 To subdivide give it as mercy. (7)
17 The romantic tale sounds like a joke. (5)
19 Wild bare gal solves your problems! (7)
21 Severe recipe begins with "Sauté. Stir." (7)
22 Seventy beheaded, and why not?, it's an occasion! (5)
24 As anticipated, they spat. Love's lost, get rid of the rat! (8)
27 ...And the home game holds nothing big at the ending. (5)
30 "Defensive language, lady". (3)
31 Nelson lost his head and sense of proportion. (5)
32 Corner a street without beginning or end. (4)
33 Unoriginal, but I drive a vet crazy. (10)

Down:

1 Enlist in following the little woman. (4)
2 One grand overdose shortly considers the remains. (3)
3 Gave the sack to the English then joined angles (obtuse). (5)
4 A throne on earth, no heart. One more—a hornet, maddened. (7)
5 We hear illegal clubbing overhead. (7)
7 Canadian territory is unruly, losing endless wood you know. (5)
8 Minor dazes in a tizzy truly disorders. (9)
9 Lays in as convoluted reasoning. (8)
14 Fairground dweller, but two for every integer. (6,4)
16 Bet it's strange to exist inside a bird. (5)
18 Set piece is a basic part. (7)
20 Rave, rage—lose our head. Mean! (7)
21 A short laugh after a mountain ray at the beginning... (5)
23 Complain until we sound hoarse. (3)
25 One cubic centimeter of air, polluted? About time! (5)
26 Part of a tree done badly. (4)
28 Adam's madam is darkening daily. (3)
29 Article for all nation's leaders. (2)

3

SELECTING

> The important thing in Science is not so much to obtain new facts as to discover new ways of thinking about them.
>
> William Lawrence Bragg, *Beyond Reductionism*

ONE OF the advantages of computers is that they allow us to collect, store, and retrieve enormous amounts of data. But data is not in itself useful; data is not information until it has been organized to some purpose. As you read this sentence, roughly one eighth of a billion light detector cells in each of your retinas are firing, trying to tell your brain something about the world. But each pixel by itself is meaningless; this enormous amount of data is worthless until it has been summarized and salient features have been selected and then communicated to the brain. (In humans this takes about one-thirtieth of a second, which is why the spokes of a car wheel appear to reverse at certain speeds.) It's curious that a sensory organ is useful only if it discards most of its sense data.

In chapter two we tried our hands at simple versions of searching for something; in this chapter we will examine simple versions of searching for something with a particular property. In chapter four we will consider ways to structure data to do both of these simple kinds of searches quickly. The particular property we concentrate on now is ranking within some ordering of the data. Given some data that can be put in order, we want to find the ith largest thing. This is the *selection problem*.

Selection is essential to make sense of the world. To avoid drowning in the never-ending information flood we're forced to summarize, simplify, and select.[1] For example, the health of the economy is typically expressed with a small set of numbers: cost of living index, gross national product, per capita income, and so forth. Each of these numbers is an amalgam of many separate indicators of economic well-being; each number is misleading in detail but each suggests general trends.

Similarly, given a file of numbers that is too large to keep, we want to save some of the information—we want to summarize the data. A good place to start is to find the largest, smallest, average, median, and mode. The **median** is the smallest value bigger than half of the numbers. The **mode** is the most frequent number. We could also find **percentiles**: n percent of all the numbers are smaller than the nth percentile; so fifty percent of all the numbers are smaller than the fiftieth percentile (the median).

The simplest way to find the ith largest is to sort the input then get the ith. This is a good solution if we have to select many things or if n is small (or both). But it isn't good if we only have to select a few things or if n is large, for, as we learn in the next chapter, we cannot sort n things in less than $\Omega(n \lg n)$ comparisons in the worst case (within the comparison-based model of chapter two), and there is no reason to suppose that we need this much work to select the ith. Intuitively, sorting is unlikely to be an optimal solution for the selection problem because we get much more information than we need. In fact, we will see that we can find the ith largest in *linear* work in the worst case.

3.1 Rankings

All our philosophy is a correction of the
common usage of words.

Georg Lichtenberg, *Vermischte Schriften*

We're going to be working with things that we can rank (or sort); what sets can we rank? Well, first, if one element precedes another, then the

---

[1] "Where is the Life we have lost in living?/ Where is the wisdom we have lost in knowledge?/ Where is the knowledge we have lost in information?" T. S. Eliot, *The Rock*.

second cannot also precede the first. Second, if of three elements the first precedes the second and the second precedes the third, then the first must precede the third. The first condition is **asymmetry** and the second is **transitivity**. If every two elements of a set are related, these are the simplest possible conditions guaranteeing that we can sort the set.

If we had asymmetry alone we would not always be able to put a set in order. Here's why: suppose we have three things a, b, and c, that obey the asymmetry condition, and suppose $a > b$. Where does c go? Asymmetry allows four cases:

$$c > a, \quad c > b \qquad c > a, \quad c < b \qquad c < a, \quad c > b \qquad c < a, \quad c < b$$

Three of these cases lead to rankings, but one case cannot fit any ranking. Transitivity ensures that that case cannot arise.

| Pause | Which case? What happens if there are four or more elements?

Strictly speaking, asymmetry and transitivity are not properties of elements, they're properties of *relations* between elements. A transitive asymmetric relation is called a **partial order**. For example, the relation "richer than" defined on the set of people is a partial order:

- If Alice is richer than Bob, then Bob is not richer than Alice (so "richer than" is asymmetric).

- If Alice is richer than Bob, and Bob is richer than Carol, then Alice is richer than Carol (so "richer than" is transitive).

| Pause | Is "sister of" a partial order? Is "cousin of" a partial order?

These orders are called "partial" to allow the possibility of two people whose relation we don't know. For example, Alice may really be richer than Bob but we can't know that unless we know how rich both are or unless we know that Alice is richer than someone who in turn is richer than Bob. It is even possible for two people to be unrelatable in our chosen relation. For example, if Alice and Bob are equally rich then neither is richer than the other. Again, consider the relation "ancestor of." This relation is a partial order, but there exist at least two people neither of whom is an ancestor of the other. Note that these relations are defined on the same set of things (the set of all people); we can define many different relations on the same set. In general, a **relation** on a set is just a set of ordered pairs of elements of the set. In normal speaking, we say that the first element of one such pair *is related to* the second element.

If every pair of elements in the set S is relatable by the partial order relation R, then R is a **linear order**, and we say that S is **orderable;** meaning that it is possible to rank the elements of S. For example, the middle partial order in figure 3.1 is a linear order.

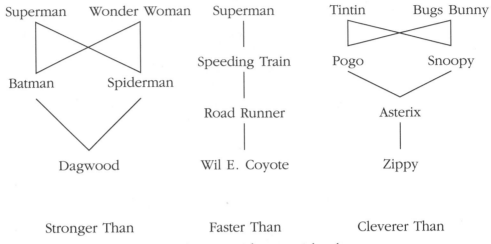

Figure 3.1 Three partial orders

Pause Is "funnier than" a linear order?

Let's call a partially ordered set a **poset** ("po-zet"), for short. For all future applications of posets let's assume that S is orderable by "less than," and that all elements of S are unique. Although S is orderable, we do not necessarily know the order of any two elements of S. However, since S is orderable, we know that every two elements are rankable. As we compare elements of S we gain information about the ordering of S.

We can draw posets using nodes to represent elements, and edges between the nodes to represent relationships, as in figure 3.1. We draw an edge connecting two nodes if we know their order, using relative height to indicate their order. The higher element is bigger. For clarity, we discard edges that we can deduce by transitivity (see figure 3.2). Sometimes it's awkward to draw posets using only downward pointing edges, but in that case we can add an arrow to make the direction of dominance explicit.

Long Pause Can we ever be forced to add an arrow to a poset drawing?

One poset is a **subposet** of another if all its relations are contained in the other. For example, in figure 3.2 all posets with three elements are subposets of the last (rightmost) poset with three elements. Thus, the poset consisting of n unrelated elements, called **singletons**, is a subposet of every poset with n elements.

Pause Why does this follow from the definition of subposets?

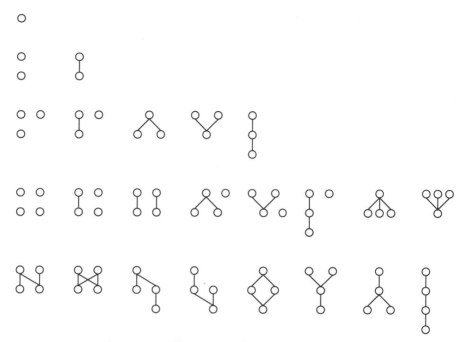

Figure 3.2 All posets with up to four elements

In this chapter and the next all problems are on an orderable set of n unique elements. We will continue to work within the comparison-based model. The problems will be of the general form: find the least number of three-way element-element comparisons necessary to build a particular poset starting with n singletons. In the following sections we will develop algorithms to find the largest element, the second largest, the largest and smallest, the ith largest, and then several ranks simultaneously.

Although order relations have to be transitive, arbitrary relations do not have to be. Here is an example from a part of mathematics called **game theory** showing that the relation "more popular than" is not necessarily transitive.[2] Marie Caritat, the Marquis de Condorcet, an eighteenth-century French mathematician who killed himself during the French Revolution, considered the following *voter's paradox:* Suppose Ronald, George, and Geraldine are running for president. There are three voters, Alice, Bob, and Carol. Alice prefers George to Geraldine, and Geraldine to Ronald.

---

[2]Game theory is about decision making in uncertain, risky, or competitive situations; it is largely the invention of the Hungarian-born American mathematician John von Neumann ("noy-man"), perhaps the brightest mathematical mind of this century.

Bob prefers Geraldine to Ronald, and Ronald to George. Carol prefers Ronald to George, and George to Geraldine.

Suppose they vote for two of the three in a primary, then vote for the third versus the winner of the primary. Let's say that the primary is between Ronald and George. Since Bob and Carol prefer Ronald to George then Ronald will win. Now Ronald goes up against Geraldine, and Geraldine wins. Therefore Geraldine > Ronald > George, right?

But, if we take a vote between Geraldine and George, George wins! Therefore Geraldine > Ronald > George > Geraldine!

| Pause | Suppose that Carol knows everyone's voting preference. Show that she can vote so that her second choice (George) wins instead of her third choice (Geraldine).

3.2   Finding the Best

> Selection is the very keel on which
> our mental ship is built.
>
> William James, *The Principles of Psychology*

How fast can we find the best wrestler among n wrestlers? As we saw in the voting example, transitivity and asymmetry do not always hold in real competitions because of the complexity of human interactions, however let's assume that the wrestlers are orderable by "better than." Also, let's assume that initially we know nothing about the wrestlers' fighting ability. Two wrestlers have to fight to determine their relative ability unless we can deduce that information by transitivity.

We can find the best wrestler with the following algorithm: let any two fight, then let the winner fight anyone who has not yet lost. Continue until everyone has fought. This takes $n - 1$ fights (see FIND_MAX, algorithm 3.1). Is this worst case optimal?

Proving optimality is a little difficult if we try to keep track of the eventual champion—because the champion could beat, say, Alice, without actually fighting her, by beating Bob, who has beaten, or will beat, Alice. Let's turn the question around and consider the *losers*. Only the eventual champion did not lose, so there must be $n - 1$ losers. Since $n - 1$ people must lose and each such loss is unique then there must be at least $n - 1$ fights. Similarly, finding the worst wrestler also requires $n - 1$ fights (though it seems cruel to do so!).

There are other ways to prove the same lower bound. To find the winner we must build a poset having one overall winner and $n - 1$ losers starting from a poset of n singletons. Let's say that a poset **solves** the problem

```
FIND_MAX ( List, lower, upper )
    { Find the index of the largest of List[lower..upper].
    upper ≥ lower > 0. }

    max ← lower
    for index from lower + 1 to upper
        if List[index] > List[max]
            max ← index
    return max
```

Algorithm 3.1

of finding the best, if when given the poset it is possible to determine the best with no further fights. Now call any poset solving the problem of finding the best a **max poset**. Figure 3.3 shows max posets for small n. When $n = 4$, for example, we must build one of the last five posets in the figure. Each of these posets solves the problem of finding the best of four things. However only one poset (the first of the five) is a subposet of all the others, so there is only one minimal poset with four nodes that delivers the best with no further fights (see figure 3.4). Note that this does *not* mean that the minimal poset is the cheapest to build, but only that no other poset can be cheaper, since the minimal poset is contained in them all.

Figure 3.3   All max posets with up to four nodes

Pause Find a poset containing the minimal max poset of four nodes that is as cheap to build.

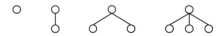

Figure 3.4   All minimal max posets with up to four nodes

Now, to build a poset solving the problem of finding the best we must connect it; that is, we must connect every wrestler by a chain of fights with every other wrestler. Otherwise there will still be at least two candidate winners, and either one could be better than all the others. Now just as in the lower bound argument for LINEAR SEARCH in the last chapter (page 88), connecting n wrestlers takes at least $n - 1$ fights. Therefore, finding the best requires at least $n-1$ fights in the worst case. So FIND MAX has optimal worst cost within the comparison-based model.

The Average Cost

How many comparisons does FIND MAX do on average? Well, FIND MAX does a comparison at every step so it does $n - 1$ comparisons on average. Since only comparisons count in our current model we could stop here, but by considering this seemingly innocuous problem we may find some tools that will be useful for harder problems.[3]

The only variation in the algorithm is in the number of assignments, so let's find the average number of assignments. While FIND MAX always does $n - 1$ comparisons the number of assignments it does depends on the ordering of the elements of L. If L is in decreasing order it does one assignment; if L is in increasing order it does n assignments.

Pause | So is the average number of assignments $(n + 1)/2$?

Since the actual values in L don't matter to FIND MAX (only their relative sizes influence the outcome of a comparison) then we may assume that L is one of the $n!$ arrangements of the numbers 1 to n; these are called the **permutations** of n things. (Note that FIND MAX cannot assume this about its input, but we can assume it to simplify our analysis of FIND MAX.) Also, lacking any information to the contrary, let's assume that all $n!$ permutations are equally likely.

Now consider the ith iteration of the loop. FIND MAX does an assignment only if $L[i]$ is the biggest of the first i elements of L. Since, by assumption, each permutation of L is equally likely, the probability of this happening should be $1/i$. On the other hand, if every permutation is equally likely then the elements being compared on the ith iteration could be any two elements, so the probability of one winning over the other should be $1/2$.

Pause | Is the probability $1/2$ or $1/i$?

_____

[3]"What is a weed? A plant whose virtues have not been discovered," Ralph Waldo Emerson, *Fortune of the Republic.*

It's tempting to think that if an event either happens or doesn't happen then the probability of the event is one-half. To see that this is not so consider the event of sneezing as you read this paragraph. This is an event that either happens or doesn't happen; but chances are that you will finish this paragraph without sneezing!

Now recall that the actual values in L don't matter to FIND_MAX, what matters is their relative sizes. As far as FIND_MAX cares, at the ith iteration any of the first i elements of L could be the best seen so far. Also, we've assumed that each permutation is equally likely, so the probability that $L[i]$ is bigger than all previous elements is $1/i$. Thus, with the assumption that each permutation is equally likely, the average number of assignments is

$$1 + \sum_{i=2}^{n} \mathbf{P}(L[i] > L[j] \ \forall \ j < i) \times 1 = 1 + \sum_{i=2}^{n} \frac{1}{i} \times 1 = \sum_{i=1}^{n} \frac{1}{i}$$

The sum of the reciprocals of the first n integers is called the nth **harmonic number;** it is symbolized by H_n.

How fast does H_n grow? Well, $i \leq 2^{\lceil \lg i \rceil}$, so $1/i \geq 1/2^{\lceil \lg i \rceil}$. Therefore, if $n = 2^k$ then

$$
\begin{aligned}
H_{2^k} &= 1 + \frac{1}{2} + \frac{1}{3} + \frac{1}{4} + \frac{1}{5} + \frac{1}{6} + \frac{1}{7} + \frac{1}{8} + \cdots + \frac{1}{2^k} \\
&\geq 1 + \left(\frac{1}{2}\right) + \left(\frac{1}{4} + \frac{1}{4}\right) + \left(\frac{1}{8} + \frac{1}{8} + \frac{1}{8} + \frac{1}{8}\right) + \cdots + \frac{1}{2^k} \\
&= 1 + \frac{1}{2} + \frac{2}{4} + \frac{4}{8} + \cdots + \frac{2^{k-1}}{2^k} \\
&= 1 + \frac{k}{2}
\end{aligned}
$$

Similarly, we can bound H_{2^k} from above using the inequality $1/i \leq 1/2^{\lfloor \lg i \rfloor}$.

$$
\begin{aligned}
H_{2^k} &= 1 + \frac{1}{2} + \frac{1}{3} + \frac{1}{4} + \frac{1}{5} + \frac{1}{6} + \frac{1}{7} + \frac{1}{8} + \cdots + \frac{1}{2^k} \\
&\leq 1 + \left(\frac{1}{2} + \frac{1}{2}\right) + \left(\frac{1}{4} + \frac{1}{4} + \frac{1}{4} + \frac{1}{4}\right) + \frac{1}{8} + \cdots + \frac{1}{2^k} \\
&= 1 + \frac{2}{2} + \frac{4}{4} + \frac{8}{8} + \cdots + \frac{2^{k-1}}{2^{k-1}} + \frac{1}{2^k} \\
&= k + \frac{1}{2^k}
\end{aligned}
$$

Combining the two bounds we see that

$$k + \frac{1}{2^k} \geq H_{2^k} \geq \frac{k}{2} + 1$$

Finally, $2^{\lceil \lg n \rceil} \geq n \geq 2^{\lfloor \lg n \rfloor}$ and H_n is an increasing function of n, therefore,

$$H_{2^{\lceil \lg n \rceil}} \quad \geq \quad H_n \quad \geq \quad H_{2^{\lfloor \lg n \rfloor}}$$

$$\implies \lceil \lg n \rceil + \frac{1}{2^{\lceil \lg n \rceil}} \quad \geq \quad H_n \quad \geq \quad \frac{\lfloor \lg n \rfloor}{2} + 1$$

Hence

$$H_n = \Theta(\lg n)$$

$\boxed{Pause}$ Why does this follow?

More exactly, Leonhard Euler ("oy-ler"), an amazing eighteenth-century Swiss mathematician,[4] showed that

$$H_n = \ln n + \gamma + \frac{1}{2n} + o\left(\frac{1}{n}\right)$$

where $\gamma = 0.577 \cdots$ is called *Euler's constant;* γ is the Greek letter gamma. See table 3.1.

n	1	2	3	4	5	6	7	8
H_n	1	1.500	1.833	2.083	2.283	2.450	2.592	2.717
$\ln n + \gamma + \dfrac{1}{2n}$	1.077	1.520	1.842	2.088	2.286	2.452	2.594	2.719

Table 3.1 An approximation to the harmonic numbers

Thus, with the assumption that each permutation of L is equally likely, FIND_MAX does an average of about $\ln n$ assignments.

---

[4]Euler, perhaps the most prolific mathematician of all time, produced so much mathematics that his complete works are still—after more than two centuries—not all published. He, like Beethoven, lost a sense during the latter part of his life without reducing his output (Euler his sight, Beethoven his hearing). Euler, in his depth and breadth, was a combination of Beethoven and Mozart; he calculated like a fish swims.

Statistics

Well, now we know the average number of assignments, but we don't know the likely variation in the number of assignments from one run to the next. Why is this important? Well, as mountain climbers, it isn't enough for us to know that our rope has an average thickness of ten millimeters. It is also comforting to know that its thickness doesn't vary between twenty millimeters and one millimeter! The area of mathematics that analyzes, summarizes, and interprets numerical data is called **statistics**.

One way to estimate the variation from one run to the next is to find the **variance** in assignments: that is, the average of the square of the differences of the numbers of assignments from the average. The variance of a set of numbers tells us something about the *spread* of the distribution of numbers. After raking a pile of leaves, the leaves' average position tells us roughly where the pile is, and the leaves' variance tells us roughly how spread out the pile is. The average and variance of a distribution summarize it by giving information on its location and spread; they are **statistics** of the distribution.

In figure 3.5 the flat distribution has a higher variance than the short squat distribution, and the short squat distribution has a higher variance than the tall thin one; the smaller the variance, the closer most numbers are to the average value. The square root of the variance is called the **standard deviation**. Since the standard deviation is the square root of the variance it's in the same units as the average, and so can be added and subtracted.

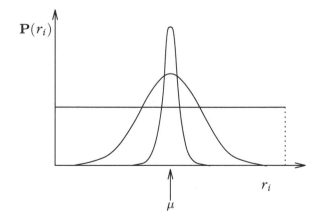

Figure 3.5 Three different distributions with the same average

A **random variable** is a function associated with an experiment that can take on numerical values of some property of the experiment. A random variable maps events onto real numbers; the probability that a random variable has the value r is the probability of the events that map to r. For example, if we measure people's tummy widths, the probability that one measurement will have a certain value is the probability of people's tummies being that wide.

The average of a random variable X is denoted by $\mu(X)$ (μ is the Greek letter mu, it stands for "mean") and its standard deviation is denoted by $\sigma(X)$ (σ is the Greek letter sigma, it probably stands for "standard"). Given an experiment producing n events and a random variable X associated with them that can take on one of n numbers $r_1, r_2, \ldots, r_n$ with probabilities $\mathbf{P}(X = r_1), \mathbf{P}(X = r_2), \ldots, \mathbf{P}(X = r_n)$, then

$$\mu(X) = \sum_{i=1}^{n} r_i \mathbf{P}(X = r_i)$$

$$\sigma^2(X) = \sum_{i=1}^{n} (r_i - \mu(X))^2 \mathbf{P}(X = r_i)$$

We shall soon see that at least seventy-five percent of a distribution lies within two standard deviations of the distribution's average using *Čebyšev's inequality,* a result named after the nineteenth-century Russian mathematician Pafnutiĭ Čebyšev (pronounced "shay-bee-shev," and often written "Chebyshev" or "Tchebycheff"). Besides being one of the founders of modern probability theory, Čebyšev was the first to improve our understanding of prime numbers beyond that of the Greeks, a subject we will meet again in chapter six.

Let X be a random variable and let f be a non-negative real-valued function then **Markov's inequality** states that

$$s\mathbf{P}(f(X) \geq s) \leq \mu(f(X))$$

Markov's inequality, named after the Russian mathematician Andreĭ Markov, follows from the definition of μ since

$$
\begin{aligned}
\mu(f(X)) &= \sum_{i=1}^{n} f(r_i)\mathbf{P}(X = r_i) \\
&= \sum_{i:f(r_i)<s} f(r_i)\mathbf{P}(X = r_i) \;+\; \sum_{i:f(r_i)\geq s} f(r_i)\mathbf{P}(X = r_i) \\
&\geq \sum_{i:f(r_i)\geq s} f(r_i)\mathbf{P}(X = r_i) \\
&\geq s \sum_{i:f(r_i)\geq s} \mathbf{P}(X = r_i) \\
&= s\mathbf{P}(f(X) \geq s)
\end{aligned}
$$

If X has finite variance then *Čebyšev's inequality* follows when we take $f(X)$ as $(X - \mu(X))^2/\sigma^2(X)$. From Markov's inequality we have that

$$t^2 \mathbf{P}\left(\frac{(X - \mu(X))^2}{\sigma^2(X)} \geq t^2\right) \leq \mu\left(\frac{(X - \mu(X))^2}{\sigma^2(X)}\right)$$

$$= \frac{\mu(X - \mu(X))^2}{\sigma^2(X)}$$

$$= \frac{\sigma^2(X)}{\sigma^2(X)}$$

$$= 1$$

In other words,

$$\mathbf{P}(\mu(X) + t\sigma(X) \geq X \geq \mu(X) - t\sigma(X)) \geq 1 - \frac{1}{t^2}$$

So, for example, taking $t = 2$ tells us that at least three-quarters of any distribution lies within two standard deviations of the distribution's average.

We've seen that FIND_MAX does H_n assignments on average, and H_n tends to $\ln n$ as n gets large. It is possible to show that the variance of the number of assignments is $H_n - H_n^{(2)}$ where $H_n^{(2)} = \sum_{k=1}^{n} 1/k^2$ and $H_n^{(2)}$ tends to $\pi^2/6$ as n gets large.[5] Thus the variance tends to $\ln n - \pi^2/6$ as n gets large. This variance is high relative to the average value so the distribution of the number of assignments is not localized near its average.

Thus, with the assumption that each permutation of L is equally likely, the average number of assignments FIND_MAX does is roughly $\ln n$ with a standard deviation of about $\sqrt{\ln n}$. Using Čebyšev's inequality we see that in at least three runs out of four the number of assignments will be between $\ln n - 2\sqrt{\ln n}$ and $\ln n + 2\sqrt{\ln n}$.

3.3 Finding the Second Best

> Symbolism is useful because it makes things difficult. . . in the beginning everything is self-evident, and it is hard to see whether one self-evident proposition follows from another or not.
>
> Bertrand Russell, *"Recent Work on the Principles of Mathematics,"*
> *International Monthly, 4, 84, 1901*

Now let's find the second best element of an orderable set. We wish to build posets like those in figure 3.6. There is a simple $2n - 3$ algorithm:

---

[5]Here's another surprising fact: as n grows, the probability that two randomly chosen positive integers less than n don't have any common factors tends to $6/\pi^2 = 0.607\cdots$.

find the best, discard it, then find the best of those remaining. Can we do better? Well, again thinking in terms of wrestling tournaments, anyone who lost to someone who was not the eventual champion cannot be the second best wrestler. So the only possible candidates for the second best wrestler are those wrestlers the eventual champion fought. But FIND_MAX (algorithm 3.1 [p. 165]) compares the eventual champion to as many as $n-1$ others. Since we need $n-2$ fights to decide the best of these second-raters, we cannot do better than $2n-3$. So $2n-3$ is optimal!

Figure 3.6 All minimal second-max posets with up to five nodes

Pause | Do you see anything wrong with this argument?

This argument has much to recommend it; it is seductive and widespread, but false. Here it is more starkly:

> *The necessity fallacy:* Our algorithm does something, therefore all algorithms solving the problem must do the same.

It's easy to fall into this state of sin because often we put a lot of effort into careful design of an algorithm, so we think that we have solved the problem in the best way possible. However, any such argument is *specious*. A lower bound must apply to *all* algorithms within the model that solve the problem, not just to particular kinds of algorithms.[6]

Okay, how much information about the second best can we gather while finding the best? FIND_MAX is a typical brute force and ignorance algorithm; it does nothing clever. In the worst case the eventual champion will be $L[1]$ or $L[2]$ and all $n-1$ other elements will be candidates for the second best, since they each lost to the eventual champion. However once again our trusty divide and conquer strategy comes to our rescue, showing us a better way. If we break the problem into two halves and use FIND_MAX on both halves, then we can find the second best with only $\lceil 3n/2 \rceil - 2$ fights!

Pause | Why is this true?

---

[6]However, when we're really stuck such lower bounds are better than nothing; we can restrict the model to only allow algorithms of the type we've designed.

After we find the overall winner there can only be at most $\lceil n/2 \rceil$ candidates for the second best. Why? Well, we've broken up the problem into finding the best of all elements up to $L[\lceil n/2 \rceil]$ and all elements from $L[\lceil n/2 \rceil + 1]$ on. This takes $\lceil n/2 \rceil - 1 + \lfloor n/2 \rfloor - 1 = n - 2$ fights. Suppose the two finalists are $L[i]$ and $L[j]$. Now we find the winner by letting $L[i]$ fight $L[j]$. Suppose $L[i]$ wins. Overall we've used $n-1$ fights. *But*, to find the second best we only need find the best of $L[j]$ and all the elements that lost to $L[i]$, because no element that lost to $L[j]$ can be the second best! See algorithm 3.2.

FIND_SECOND_MAX (*List, lower, upper*)
    { Find the index of the second largest of *List*[*lower..upper*].
    Break the list into two and find the largest of each half,
    then find the largest of the candidates for second largest.
    upper > *lower* > 0. }

    $mid \leftarrow \lfloor (lower + upper)/2 \rfloor$
    $index_1 \leftarrow$ FIND_MAX (*List, lower, mid*)
    $index_2 \leftarrow$ FIND_MAX (*List, mid* + 1, *upper*)
    if $List[index_1] > List[index_2]$
        then
            $List[index_1] \leftarrow List[index_2]$
            return FIND_MAX (*List, lower, mid*)
        else
            $List[index_2] \leftarrow List[index_1]$
            return FIND_MAX (*List, mid* + 1, *upper*)

Algorithm 3.2

Pause   Is $\lceil 3n/2 \rceil - 2$ fights worst case optimal?

Intuitively, this algorithm probably isn't optimal because in the second phase we recalculate a lot of information we already know. It would be better if we could reduce the size of the set of candidates in the second phase. But we can do this easily—just break the list into more pieces! See figure 3.7. If we break the list into quarters, the worst cost drops to $\lceil 5n/4 \rceil - 1$. If we break the list into eighths, the worst cost drops further to $\lceil 9n/8 \rceil$.

Pause   How far can this go?

Figure 3.7 Dividing a list into one, two, and four pieces

FIND_MAX is bad because at each iteration the current person fighting the current champion doesn't have a sporting chance. As FIND_MAX progresses through the list, the probability that the next wrestler beats the current champion decreases as $1/i$. So the probability that the current champion will be beaten rapidly approaches zero. It's as if you or I were to fight the world wrestling champion—we would probably lose. Now what would make the *last* fight as sporting as possible? In the absence of inside knowledge of the wrestlers' real strengths, the fairest thing is to have every two wrestlers beat an equal number of others before their fight. So the last two wrestlers should have beaten $(n-2)/2$ others each. Similarly, in the two fights leading up to the last fight the four wrestlers involved should each have beaten $(n-4)/4$ wrestlers, and so on.

Pause │ How many such rounds will be fought?

Carrying the above insights to their logical extreme, we build *binomial trees*. (See figure 3.8.) A height m **binomial tree** is

- a single node, if $m = 0$ or

- two height $m - 1$ binomial trees connected at their roots, if $m \geq 1$.

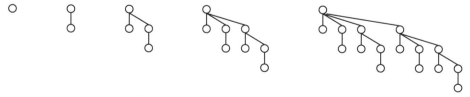

Figure 3.8 The first five binomial trees

A height m binomial tree has 2^m nodes, so an n-node binomial tree has height $\lg n$. These trees are called "binomial" because there are $\binom{\lg n}{l}$ level l nodes and the values of the choose function, $\binom{i}{j}$, are called **binomial**

coefficients. To show that a binomial tree has $\binom{\lg n}{l}$ level l nodes we can use the following binomial coefficient recurrence

$$\binom{i}{j} = \binom{i-1}{j} + \binom{i-1}{j-1}$$

To prove this recurrence recall that $\binom{i}{j}$ is the number of ways of choosing j things from i things. Now pick any of the i things. There are $\binom{i-1}{j}$ ways to exclude it from, and $\binom{i-1}{j-1}$ ways to include it in, the set of j things chosen.

This recurrence was known to the Chinese in ancient times but it's called **Pascal's relation** after the French mathematician Blaise Pascal, who popularized it in Europe in the seventeenth century. The set of binomial coefficients arranged in a triangle is called **Pascal's triangle** (see figure 3.9). Pascal's triangle makes clear the recursive creation of the binomial coefficients: every coefficient is the sum of two parent coefficients as given by Pascal's relation.

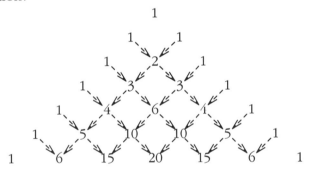

Figure 3.9 Pascal's triangle

By building binomial trees we can find the second best of n things using at most $n + \lceil \lg n \rceil - 2$ comparisons. To see this, assume that n is a power of two. First, we find the best by building a size n binomial tree. Then we find the second best by finding the best of the $\lg n$ candidates for the second best (these are the level one nodes of the tree). See algorithm 3.4.

Pause | Why are there $\lg n$ level one nodes?

One way to build the tree is to preserve dominance relationships by swapping subtrees so that the root of the binomial tree made up of the first 2^i elements in the list is in position 2^i, for i from 0 to $\lg n$ (see figure 3.10). Thus, after forming the binomial tree, the best is in location n and the $\lg n$ candidates for the second best are in locations $n - 2^i$, for i from 0 to $\lg n - 1$. See algorithm 3.3; the operation "$x \leftrightarrow y$" swaps the values of x and y, and the algorithm uses it to swap whole sublists.

BUILD_BINOMIAL_TREE ($List, lower, upper$)
  { Build a binomial tree on $List[lower..upper]$.
  $upper - lower + 1$ is a power of two. $upper \geq lower > 0$. }

  if $upper > lower$
    $mid \leftarrow \lfloor (lower + upper)/2 \rfloor$
    BUILD_BINOMIAL_TREE ($List, lower, mid$)
    BUILD_BINOMIAL_TREE ($List, mid + 1, upper$)
    if $List[mid] > List[upper]$
      $List[lower..mid] \leftrightarrow List[(mid + 1)..upper]$

Algorithm 3.3

Pause How can we extend this algorithm when n is not a power of two? (Hint: If $n = 2^i + j$ where $j < 2^i$, how can we eliminate j candidates?)

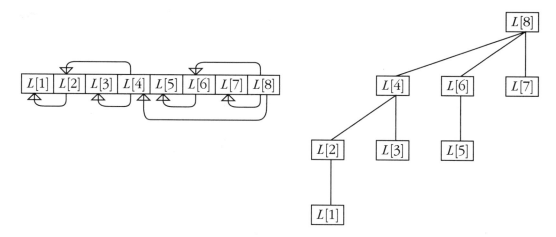

Figure 3.10 Representing a binomial tree implicitly in an array

BUILD_BINOMIAL_TREE is easy to analyze when n is a power of two. Let n be a power of two and let $f(n)$ be its worst number of comparisons, then

$$f(n) = \begin{cases} 0 & n = 1 \\ 2f(n/2) + 1 & n > 1 \end{cases}$$

which gives

$$f(n) = 2^{\lg n} - 1 = n - 1$$

| Pause | Solve the recurrence by considering the simpler recurrence $g(k) = 2g(k-1) + 1$. (This is the towers of Hanoi recurrence from chapter one, page 19.) |

We could also build the binomial tree explicitly using pointers, but that takes $O(n)$ more space (we need at least two pointers per element). A structure whose interpretation depends on the sequence of elements but not on explicit pointers is called an *implicit* structure. Although we have stored the binomial tree in an array it is *implicit* in the arrangement of the elements of the array. FIND_SECOND_MAX (algorithm 3.4) is good if we are short on space. However, saving space usually costs extra time (in this case, we use extra swaps, but in our current model only comparisons matter). This is a very common compromise—it's called the *space-time tradeoff*: more space for less time, more time for less space.

FIND_SECOND_MAX (*List, lower, upper*)
{ Find the index of the second largest of *List*[*lower..upper*].
First rearrange *List* to form a binomial tree
then find the largest of the candidates.
$upper - lower + 1$ is a power of two. $upper > lower > 0$. }

BUILD_BINOMIAL_TREE (*List, lower, upper*)

$2\_max \leftarrow upper - 1$
for i **from** 1 **to** $\lg(upper - lower + 1) - 1$
   if $List[upper - 2^i] > List[2\_max]$
      $2\_max \leftarrow upper - 2^i$
return 2_max

Algorithm 3.4

| Pause | Show that FIND_SECOND_MAX does up to $(n \lg n)/2$ swaps. (Hint: What's the appropriate recurrence?) |

The first phase of FIND_SECOND_MAX costs $n - 1$ comparisons. The second phase costs $\lg n - 1$ comparisons. So we use at most $n + \lg n - 2$ comparisons to find the second best of n things when n a power of two. Is this optimal?

Adversaries

To simplify the proofs of lower bounds for many problems we can create an **adversary**. An adversary is a fiend who tries to make all algorithms solving a problem work as hard as possible. This is hard to do if his nefarious stratagems only exploit the foibles of one particular algorithm, since, to give a lower bound on the problem, they must apply to all algorithms within the model that solve the problem. To make sure that the adversary is working within the model and not just exploiting a particular algorithm, let's shift attention from the algorithm to the input.

Think of the adversary as sitting between us and our data, and imagine that all possible size n inputs (all elements of I_n) are written on separate slips of paper. The adversary is armed with a paper shredder. When we ask for a decision that depends on the input he snickers to himself and works out which answer, among those still available to him, would make our task hardest. Then he gives us that answer and shreds all inputs inconsistent with it.

Note that he hasn't picked an input consistent with his answer, but he can produce one at any time since all the remaining slips are consistent with all his previous answers—they must be, they haven't been shredded. Thus, he's continually discarding subsets of I_n that he thinks would give us the least trouble; slowly winnowing out the wheat of inputs that make us work hard from the chaff of inputs that are easy for us. We're trying to pin him down to a definite input, and he's waffling as much as possible. Eventually, despite his most malicious efforts, we reduce the remaining slips of paper to just one, enabling us to halt.

| Long Pause | Can we use adversaries to prove lower bounds on the average cost of a problem?

Every lower bound on the worst cost of predictable algorithms that we've found so far is actually an adversary argument. For example, using three-way comparisons in binary search the adversary has three possible answers: X is equal to, less than, or greater than, the probed element. The algorithm decides which elements are probed, but the adversary decides what the outcome of each comparison will be. The adversary wants to make the algorithm probe as many elements as possible. As we have seen, one possible bad set of answers is to always respond that X is bigger than every element probed. Once we, through the adversary, have figured out what would be a bad outcome we can find an input that produces that outcome.

The strength of randomized algorithms is that letting the algorithm flip coins makes the adversary's job very difficult. No non-randomized adversarial strategy will always work against a randomized algorithm. Against a randomized algorithm the adversary is forced to give up predictable worst costs and look for worst expected costs.

Now, to turn the adversary into a proof of a lower bound we prove bounds on how long the computation must take by arguing that the adversary can force a particular amount of work no matter what an algorithm does. Of course, depending on how clever the adversary is, this bound may not be that good; to get a stronger bound we then have to define a more painstaking adversary. Because any adversary's bound follows by selecting subsets of the possible set of all inputs it is *independent* of any particular algorithm. Hence it is a lower bound on the difficulty of the *problem*.

To see how this works, consider the game of "Hangman." In this game, your opponent chooses a secret word and you try to guess it by guessing letters. If you guess a letter in the secret word, your opponent has to fill in all places in the word that the letter occurs. If your guessed letter isn't in the secret word, your opponent hangs one more part of a stick figure representing you. You lose if she manages to hang all ten parts of the stick figure. You win if you guess the word before she manages to fully hang you. So you get up to ten mistaken guesses. Usually your opponent picks a word and sticks to it. However she doesn't have to choose a word until she's forced to.

| Pause | How can your opponent do this?

Here's how: Your opponent is armed with a huge dictionary. Suppose she tells you that her secret word has six letters. But actually she hasn't chosen a word at all. This seems to be cheating, but she's honest in her own way; she won't ever tell you a lie. To make sure she never lies to you, she now crosses out all words in her dictionary that don't have six letters. If you first guess *e* (a sensible guess since it's the most common letter in English), she checks her dictionary to see if there are still some six letter words that don't have an *e*. If so, she tells you "no," and crosses out all words with *e*s. Next you guess *t*. (Another sensible guess; see table 4.8, page 261, in chapter four.) Again she scribbles in her dictionary and says "no." Frustrated, you guess *a* and receive another "no."

Suppose at some point you choose *i* and when she consults her list of remaining words, they all contain an *i*. If she's really painstaking she'll find the position where *i* occurs most frequently in the remaining words, cross out all those that don't have an i there, then tell you "yes," and give the position of the i. By this time you're three-quarters hung and things are looking very bad. By the time you get fully hung, you may have guessed only one of the six letters, and she *still* has a list of thirty possible words! When you demand to know the secret word, she innocently announces any one of them, just as though she had picked it before your first guess. (Three hard six letter words are: *cupful, fluffy,* and *plucky.*) Because she crosses out invalid words as she goes, you can never catch her out. Every time you play her, you lose—and badly.

THINGS WERE LOOKING BAD FOR BOB

Now that you know how she does it you can use your own dictionary and *prove* that no matter what ten guesses you make, there are always words that will not have had all their letters guessed. You have proved a lower bound, using the adversary's tactics. No matter what the letter guesser (the algorithm solving the problem) does, an arbitrary six letter word cannot always be guessed in ten tries.

The Lower Bound

Now let's build an adversary to prove FIND_SECOND_MAX optimal. First, to find the second best wrestler we must know who the best is. Why? Well, finding the second best is equivalent to finding a wrestler who has beaten all but one, and lost to that one. That one must be the best. So we cannot avoid knowing who the best is if we find the second best.

Pause | Suppose we have to find the third best, must we implicitly know who the best is?

Consider any algorithm that finds the second best and suppose the best wrestler fights k opponents. As we have already observed, when finding the best, at least $n - 1$ wrestlers must lose once. Now, every wrestler that loses to the best is a candidate for the second best, and all but one must lose again (to the second best). So of the n wrestlers, $n - 1$ of them must lose at least once, and $k - 1$ of those $n - 1$ must lose at least twice. Thus, there must be at least $n + k - 2$ fights. So, let's try to show that no matter what tricks an algorithm tries, in the worst case the best wrestler must fight at least $\lceil \lg n \rceil$ opponents.

| Long Pause | Instead of maximizing the number of winner fights, how about maximizing the number of candidate second best wrestlers?

The adversary wants to force any algorithm finding the best to stage as many fights as possible against the eventual champion. So he wants to make the number of wrestlers the winner of each fight has proved to be better than grow as slowly as possible. Recall that, by transitivity, the winner of a fight is not only better than the loser but is also better than everyone the loser is better than.

Let a wrestler's *strength* be the number of fighters the wrestler has proved to be at least as good as. Since every wrestler is at least as good as themselves then at the beginning of the tournament every wrestler's strength is one. At the end of the tournament there must be exactly one wrestler whose strength is the number of wrestlers, n. Now suppose Alice and Bob are about to fight, and suppose Alice's strength is a and Bob's strength is b. Obviously it doesn't matter who wins: the winner will then have strength $a + b$. (See figure 3.11.) However it does matter in terms of the growth rate of the winner's strength.

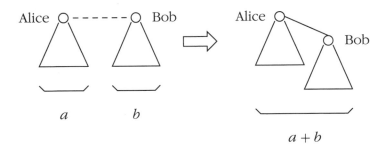

Figure 3.11 An intermediate fight while finding the best

| Pause | Who should the adversary let win?

The adversary wants to keep the growth in strength as small as possible. His task is made difficult because every fight has two fighters. If he lets

Alice win then Bob's strength stays the same but Alice's strength grows from a to $a + b$. If he lets Bob win then Alice's strength stays the same but Bob's strength grows from b to $a + b$. So the two relative growths in strength he must choose from are $(a + b)/a$ and $(a + b)/b$. And if $a \geq b$ then $(a + b)/b \geq (a + b)/a$. So the best he can do is to let the stronger wrestler win! (If $a = b$ he makes an arbitrary choice consistent with his previous choices.)

This argument seems to imply that the adversary is fixing the fights. Actually, he is keeping a list of all size n inputs that the algorithm has not yet forced him to disallow. Every time he makes a decision about the outcome of a fight he must discard all remaining inputs inconsistent with that decision. He discards subsets of the set of possible inputs (I_n), depending on what the algorithm does, to find an input forcing the eventual champion to fight as much as possible. (Here I_n is the set of all $n!$ possible rankings of the n wrestlers.)

Now, if $a \geq b$ then $2a \geq a + b$. So if the adversary forces the stronger wrestler of each match to always win then, from the algorithm's point of view, the best that could happen is that the strength of the strongest at most doubles. And it exactly doubles only when $a = b$. *Against this adversary no algorithm can more than double any wrestler's strength after only one fight.*

Since every wrestler's strength starts at one and at most doubles after each fight, then after k fights the strongest wrestler's strength is at most 2^k. Since the eventual champion's strength must equal or exceed the number of contestants, n, then there must be at least k fights where $2^k \geq n > 2^{k-1}$. Thus, no matter what an algorithm does, it must involve the eventual champion in at least $\lceil \lg n \rceil$ fights.

Therefore, finding the second best requires at least $n + \lceil \lg n \rceil - 2$ comparisons in the worst case. So FIND_SECOND_MAX has optimal worst cost within the comparison-based model.

3.4 Finding the Best and Worst

> It was the best of times,
> it was the worst of times.
>
> Charles Dickens, *A Tale of Two Cities*

Now let's find the best and worst wrestlers; that is, we want to produce minimal max-min posets like those in figure 3.12. We could use FIND_MAX twice to do this (invert the order of comparison to find the worst). This takes $2n - 3$ comparisons. Can we do better?

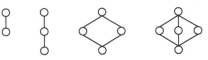

Figure 3.12 All minimal max-min posets with up to five nodes

Well, we just produced an optimal algorithm with divide and conquer, so let's try it again. Let's find the best and worst of n wrestlers by breaking the problem into two halves, recursively finding the best and worst of both halves (divide), then marrying the two subsolutions into a solution for the overall problem (conquer). See algorithm 3.5. (Divide and conquer means halving your cake and eating it too.)

FIND_MAX_MIN (*List, lower, upper*)
  { Find the indices of the largest and smallest of *List*[*lower..upper*].
upper $\geq$ *lower* > 0. }

  case *upper* $-$ *lower* $+ 1$
    $= 1$:
      return *lower, lower*
    $= 2$:
      if *List*[*lower*] $>$ *List*[*upper*]
        then return *lower, upper*
        else return *upper, lower*
    > 2 :
      $mid \leftarrow \lfloor (lower + upper)/2 \rfloor$
      $max_1, min_1 \leftarrow$ FIND_MAX_MIN (*List, lower, mid*)
      $max_2, min_2 \leftarrow$ FIND_MAX_MIN (*List, mid* $+ 1, upper$)
      if $List[max_1] > List[max_2]$
        then $max \leftarrow max_1$
        else $max \leftarrow max_2$
      if $List[min_1] > List[min_2]$
        then $min \leftarrow min_2$
        else $min \leftarrow min_1$
      return *max, min*

Algorithm 3.5

This algorithm is already better than $2n - 3$ for n as small as four since it finds the best and worst of four wrestlers in four fights, not five

$(= 2 \times 4 - 3)$. See figure 3.13; dashed lines indicate the next fight. Note that it doesn't matter who wins the first three fights, the posets that result have the same shape, but the last fight can have two different poset outcomes. However in both final posets it is easy to pick out the best and worst wrestlers. Both posets contain the minimal max-min poset for $n = 4$ as a subposet.

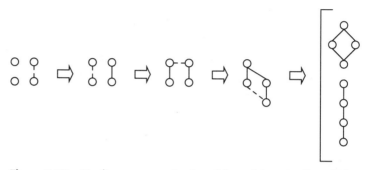

Figure 3.13   Finding max and min of four things in four fights

FIND_MAX_MIN leads to the recurrence

$$f(n) = \begin{cases} 0 & n = 1 \\ 1 & n = 2 \\ f(\lfloor n/2 \rfloor) + f(\lceil n/2 \rceil) + 2 & n > 2 \end{cases}$$

and it is possible to show that for $n \geq 2$

$$f(n) = \frac{3n}{2} - 2 + \begin{cases} \dfrac{n - 2^{\lfloor \lg n \rfloor}}{2} & n \leq 3 \times 2^{\lfloor \lg n \rfloor - 1} \\ \dfrac{2^{\lfloor \lg n \rfloor + 1} - n}{2} & \text{otherwise} \end{cases}$$

From this it is possible to show that $f(n) = 3n/2 - 2$ when $n = 2^i$ or $n = 2^i \pm 1$, and $f(n) = 5n/3 - 2$ when $n = 3 \times 2^i$. In figure 3.14 the straight line represents the cost of the naive algorithm and the two dotted lines are $5n/3 - 2$ and $3n/2 - 2$. The broken line, $f(n)$, lies between the two dotted lines, so the divide and conquer algorithm is always better than the naive algorithm. (For clarity, the horizontal scale is doubled.)

| Pause | Check that $f(n) = 3n/2 - 2$ when $n = 2^i$ or $n = 2^i \pm 1$.

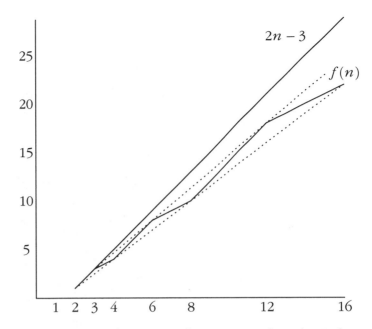

Figure 3.14 Finding max and min recursively and naively

So by using divide and conquer we've reduced the number of fights by roughly twenty-five percent when n is within one of a power of two. See table 3.2.

n	2	3	4	5	6	7	8	9	10	11	12	13	14	15	16
$2n - 3$	1	3	5	7	9	11	13	15	17	19	21	23	25	27	29
$f(n)$	1	3	4	6	8	9	10	12	14	16	18	19	20	21	22

Table 3.2 Cost of recursive max-min versus the naive algorithm

But wait a minute, something's wrong here. The algorithm takes eight fights to find the best and worst of six but from the table we see that we can manage with only seven fights! Instead of dividing six into two sets of three, divide them into two sets of sizes four and two. Finding the best and worst of four and two takes five fights altogether. Finding the overall best and worst takes two more fights (see figure 3.15). That takes seven fights

Figure 3.15 Two ways to find max and min of six things

in all, not eight! So although it's an improvement, algorithm 3.5 [p. 183] is not optimal.

Why does this happen? Divide and conquer is supposed to balance the work; shouldn't that always minimize the overall work done? Well, we want to minimize the *work*, not necessarily balance the *input sizes*. It is only coincidental that if we divide as closely as possible then we sometimes do the least work. Of course if we divide exactly then we always do the same amount of work on each recursion. But we can only divide exactly all the time when n is a power of two. Further, even if we always divide evenly we may still be doing more work than necessary.

| Pause | Since the algorithm is good when $n = 2^i$, what should we do if $n = 2^i + 2^j$? What does that decomposition suggest?

Figure 3.16 shows two ways to recursively divide six things into two parts. Although the three-three split is initially good (an exact split) it is later bad because each three makes a bad split, whereas the initially bad four-two split always splits well since both are powers of two. This is the source of the savings of one fight when $n = 6$.

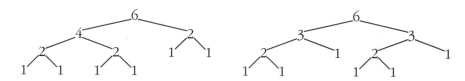

Figure 3.16   Two ways to recursively divide six things

Finally, because the algorithm is recursive, a small improvement for small n forces a large improvement for large n. If $n = 6$ costs seven and not eight, then $n = 12$ costs sixteen, not eighteen, $n = 24$ costs thirty-four, not thirty-eight, and so on, with an exponential improvement every time n doubles. Whenever we design a recursive algorithm we should pay careful attention to its performance for small n.

Designing Algorithms Using Recurrences

Many algorithms solve the same problem. Surprisingly we may stumble across new algorithms by examining a *recurrence* without thinking of any algorithm. Manipulation of the recurrence alone gives other forms of the recurrence that can then suggest new algorithms!

This sounds like a pretty goofy idea, but consider the recurrence

$$f(n) = \begin{cases} 0 & n = 1 \\ 1 & n = 2 \\ \min_{1 \le k \le n-1}\{f(k) + f(n-k)\} + 2 & n > 2 \end{cases}$$

This recurrence models the bizarre idea of trying out all possible ways of dividing n things into two sets, finding the best and worst of each of the two sets, then finding the overall best and worst. (See table 3.3; the best values are boxed.) Looking at the first few values we might guess that the minimum always occurs when $k = 2$. Suppose this is true, then

$$f(n) = \begin{cases} 0 & n = 1 \\ 1 & n = 2 \\ f(2) + f(n-2) + 2 & n > 2 \end{cases}$$

This recurrence suggests finding the best and worst of any two wrestlers (at a cost of $f(2)$), recursively finding the best and worst of the remaining wrestlers (at a cost of $f(n-2)$), then finding the overall best and worst in two more fights. See algorithm 3.6. This algorithm uses exactly $\lceil 3n/2 \rceil - 2$ fights.

				k						
n	1	2	3	4	5	6	7	8	best k	min cost
3	$\boxed{3}$	$\boxed{3}$							1 2	3
4	5	$\boxed{4}$	5						2	4
5	7	$\boxed{6}$	$\boxed{6}$	7					2 3	6
6	9	$\boxed{7}$	8	$\boxed{7}$	9				2 4	7
7	11	$\boxed{9}$	$\boxed{9}$	$\boxed{9}$	$\boxed{9}$	11			2 3 4 5	9
8	13	$\boxed{10}$	11	$\boxed{10}$	11	$\boxed{10}$	13		2 4 6	10
9	15	$\boxed{12}$	$\boxed{12}$	$\boxed{12}$	$\boxed{12}$	$\boxed{12}$	$\boxed{12}$	15	2 3 4 5 6 7	12

Table 3.3 Cost of finding the max and min

Pause   Why is this true?

FIND_MAX_MIN (*List, lower, upper*)
    { Find the indices of the largest and smallest of *List[lower..upper]*.
    upper ≥ *lower* > 0. }

    case *upper − lower* + 1
      = 1 :
        return *lower, lower*
      = 2 :
       if *List[lower]* > *List[upper]*
         then return *lower, upper*
         else return *upper, lower*
      > 2 :
       if *List[lower]* > *List[lower* + 1]
         then max_1 ← *lower* ; min_1 ← *lower* + 1
         else max_1 ← *lower* + 1 ; min_1 ← *lower*
       max_2, min_2 ← FIND_MAX_MIN (*List, lower* + 2, *upper*)
       if *List[max_1]* > *List[max_2]*
         then *max* ← max_1
         else *max* ← max_2
       if *List[min_1]* > *List[min_2]*
         then *min* ← min_2
         else *min* ← min_1
     return *max, min*

Algorithm 3.6

Since $f(2) = 1$, the recurrence is equivalent to the simpler recurrence

$$f(n) = \begin{cases} 0 & n = 1 \\ 1 & n = 2 \\ f(n-2) + 3 & n > 2 \end{cases}$$

This gives a bound of $\lceil 3n/2 \rceil - 2$ since every three fights remove two more wrestlers from consideration (there is one extra when n is odd). Figure 3.17 is a graph of the difference between this algorithm and the first algorithm, algorithm 3.5 [p. 183]. As the graph shows, the first algorithm uses $\lceil 3n/2 \rceil - 2$ fights only when n is within one of a power of two. If n is not a power of two then it does progressively worse than $\lceil 3n/2 \rceil - 2$, reaching a maximum relative bloat when n is three times a power of two.

Pause   Show that algorithm 3.5 [p. 183] does up to $n/6$ more comparisons than algorithm 3.6.

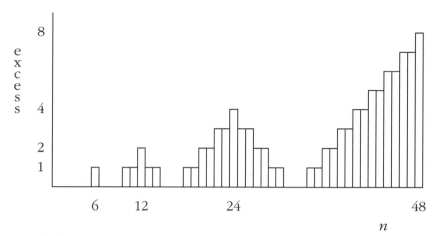

Figure 3.17 Extra fights done by divide and conquer max-min

The Lower Bound

Now let's show that $\lceil 3n/2 \rceil - 2$ is optimal by examining all possible states any algorithm solving the problem must go through. A lower bound derived this way is called a *state space lower bound.*

We need to track the elements who are still candidates to be the best (or worst). So there are four kinds of elements of interest (see figure 3.18):

- Novices: those who have not been compared.

- Winners: those who have won at least once and have not lost.

- Losers: those who have lost at least once and have not won.

- Moderates: those who have both won and lost at least once.

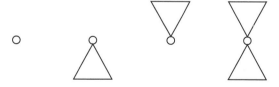

Figure 3.18 Four kinds of elements when finding max and min

Let the quadruple (i, j, k, l) represent the state of the n elements at any time, where i, j, k, and l are the numbers of novices, winners, losers, and moderates. Every algorithm finding the best and worst starts in the state $(n, 0, 0, 0)$ and ends in the state $(0, 1, 1, n - 2)$. We want to show that it is impossible to get from the first state to the last state without using at least $\lceil 3n/2 \rceil - 2$ comparisons.

Every comparison the algorithm does can only be one of ten kinds: novice and novice, novice and winner, and so on. No comparison involving a moderate element can decrease the minimum number of comparisons necessary to find the best and worst in the worst case, so we can ignore these four comparisons.

$\boxed{Pause}$ Do you believe this?

Table 3.4 lists the six remaining kinds of comparisons and their possible outcomes. The last three kinds of comparisons have two possible outcomes. For example, in the winner versus novice comparison, the first transition results if the novice lost and the second results if the novice won. See figure 3.19; in the first outcome the novice turns into a loser, in the second outcome the novice turns into a winner and the winner turns into a moderate.

	(i, j, k, l) Goes To							
V:V	$(i-2,$	$j+1,$	$k+1,$	l	$)$			
W:W	$(i,$	$j-1,$	$k,$	$l+1)$				
L:L	$(i,$	$j,$	$k-1,$	$l+1)$				
L:V	$(i-1,$	$j+1,$	$k,$	l	$)$ or	$(i-1,$	$j,$	$k,$	$l+1)$
W:V	$(i-1,$	$j,$	$k+1,$	l	$)$ or	$(i-1,$	$j,$	$k,$	$l+1)$
W:L	$(i,$	$j,$	$k,$	l	$)$ or	$(i,$	$j-1,$	$k-1,$	$l+2)$

Table 3.4 Comparison outcomes for the max-min problem

Now let's invent an adversary who forces every transition to be one of the left-hand outcomes in table 3.4. The simplest way to do that is to

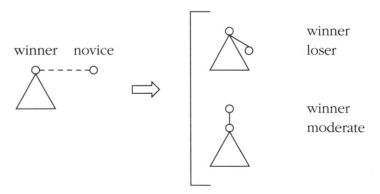

Figure 3.19 A winner fights a novice

have the adversary say that the outcome of comparing a winner with any-one but another winner is that the winner wins (and similarly, have losers lose). The adversary handles any other comparison arbitrarily but consistently with previous decisions. Against this adversary, any algorithm comparing a winner with a loser is wasting a comparison, since the adversary will always make the winner win. So against this adversary an algorithm can compare winners to losers till it's blue in the face and never get any closer to the state $(0, 1, 1, n - 2)$. So we can forget about winner versus loser comparisons.

| Pause | Does this explain why we can ignore comparisons involving moderates?

Table 3.5 lists the five remaining kinds of comparisons and the outcomes the adversary forces. Now observe something very interesting about this table: the first three kinds of comparisons preserve the sum $i + j + k$! Since initially $i + j + k = n$, and finally $i + j + k = 2$, then no matter what else an algorithm does it must do at least $n - 2$ winner versus winner and loser versus loser comparisons. (Alternately, only those two kinds of comparisons increase the number of moderates, and that number must increase from 0 to $n - 2$.)

	(i, j, k, l) Goes To
V:V	$(i - 2, \quad j + 1, \quad k + 1, \quad l \quad)$
L:V	$(i - 1, \quad j + 1, \quad k, \quad l \quad)$
W:V	$(i - 1, \quad j, \quad k + 1, \quad l \quad)$
W:W	$(i, \quad j - 1, \quad k, \quad l + 1)$
L:L	$(i, \quad j, \quad k - 1, \quad l + 1)$

Table 3.5 Simplified outcomes for the max-min problem

| Pause | Now show that comparisons involving moderates can't reduce the worst cost.

Further, the number of novices, i, must decrease from n to 0. But only the first three kinds of comparisons decrease i, and none of them decrease $i + j + k$. So none of them can be in the $n - 2$ previously counted! Therefore the algorithm must do at least $\lfloor n/2 \rfloor$ more comparisons since the fastest way to decrease i is to compare two novices. (It could use either of the two other kinds of comparisons, but they are slower.) Thus, overall any algorithm must do at least $n + \lfloor n/2 \rfloor - 2 = \lfloor 3n/2 \rfloor - 2$ comparisons. Finally, when n is odd we can only compare the last novice to a winner or loser, so we need one more comparison for a lower bound of $\lceil 3n/2 \rceil - 2$ comparisons to find the best and worst of n things.

| Pause | Show that $\lfloor 3n/2 \rfloor + n \bmod 2 = \lceil 3n/2 \rceil$. ($n \bmod m$ is the remainder on dividing n by m.)

Therefore, finding the best and worst requires $\lceil 3n/2 \rceil - 2$ comparisons in the worst case. So FIND_MAX_MIN has optimal worst cost within the comparison-based model.

3.5 Finding the ith Best

> As long as a branch of science offers an abundance of problems, so long it is alive; a lack of problems foreshadows extinction or the cessation of independent development.
>
> David Hilbert,
> *"Mathematical Problems,"*
> *Bulletin of the American Mathematical Society, 8, 438*

Finding the best was easy, finding the second best was harder; how hard is it to find the ith best? First, we'll design an algorithm (algorithm 3.8) to find the ith best quickly on average. Then we'll tighten it to produce another algorithm (algorithm 3.9 [p. 203]) to find the ith best quickly in the worst case.

We have to produce a poset like the one in figure 3.20. So we have to find an element splitting the list into two bags of sizes $i - 1$ and $n - i$. Beyond that division we don't care what order the elements are in, so sorting the whole list seems like overkill. How about divide and conquer again? Hmm, finding the "midpoint" of a list is the same as finding the median of the list and, intuitively, the median should be the hardest to select.

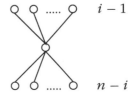

Figure 3.20 A minimal i^{th} best poset

The median—the $\lceil n/2 \rceil^{th}$ best—should be the hardest to select because it looks like selecting the ith is harder than selecting the $(i+1)^{th}$ and because we can reverse comparisons; selecting the ith best is exactly as hard as selecting the $(n-i+1)^{th}$ best. (See figure 3.21; note that there are two medians if n is even.) For a long time it was thought that the selection problem was in general $\Omega(n \lg n)$ because no one could find a better way to find the median than first sorting then choosing the median. Unfortunately, no one could find a lower bound that was better than linear. And that's good, because there isn't one.

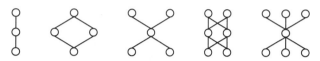

Figure 3.21   All minimal median posets with up to seven nodes

Okay, we probably can't find a midpoint easily; what if we find an arbitrary split? Let's choose an element and split the list based on this element. That is, compare the selected element—let's call it the *pivot*—with every other element in the list; larger elements go in one bag, the *top bag,* and smaller elements go in the other, the *bottom bag.* This is SPLIT, algorithm 3.7; it costs $n-1$ comparisons.

SPLIT (*List, lower, upper, pivot_loc*)
   { Split *List[lower..upper]* into two parts, those less than
   List[pivot_loc] on the left and those greater than it on the right.
   Return the pivot's new position.
   upper $\geq$ *pivot_loc* $\geq$ *lower* $>$ 0. }

   pivot $\leftarrow$ *List[pivot_loc]*
   List[lower] $\leftrightarrow$ *List[pivot_loc]* ; *pivot_loc* $\leftarrow$ *lower*
   for *index* **from** *lower* $+ 1$ **to** *upper*
     if *pivot* $>$ *List[index]*
        pivot_loc $\leftarrow$ *pivot_loc* $+ 1$
        List[index] $\leftrightarrow$ *List[pivot_loc]*
   List[lower] $\leftrightarrow$ *List[pivot_loc]*
   return *pivot_loc*

Algorithm 3.7

If we're lucky, the top bag will have exactly $i-1$ elements so the pivot will be the ith best. But even if the top bag has more than $i-1$ elements then we don't have much work to do to finish, since we only have to find the ith best *of the top bag.* Similarly, if j is the size of the top bag and j is less than $i-1$ then we only have to find the $(i-j)^{th}$ best *of the bottom bag.* So we are doing a kind of fuzzy binary search. Each "probe" costs $k-1$ comparisons, where k is the size of the current bag.

Finding the ith Best By Randomizing

FIND (algorithm 3.8) chooses a pivot and calls SPLIT to split the list around this element. The pivot could always be the worst (or best) of the remaining elements, and each call to SPLIT costs a linear number of comparisons. Thus, no matter what i is FIND is $O(n^2)$ in the worst case. Since FIND randomizes its pivot choice it doesn't have a predictable worst cost; the pivot is equally likely to be any list element. (See section 2.4, page 123, for a discussion of randomization.) Let's now show that FIND is linear on average and, because of randomization, no assumptions about the probabilities of the possible inputs are necessary.

FIND (*List, lower, upper, i*)
$\quad$ { Find the index of the ith largest of *List*[*lower..upper*].
$\quad$ *upper* $\geq$ *lower* > 0; *upper* $-$ *lower* $+ 1 \geq i \geq 1.$ }

$\quad$ *index* $\leftarrow$ **uniform**(*lower, upper*)
$\quad$ *pivot_loc* $\leftarrow$ SPLIT (*List, lower, upper, index*)
$\quad$ **case** *upper* $-$ *pivot_loc*
$\quad\quad$ $< i - 1$:
$\quad\quad\quad$ FIND (*List, lower, pivot_loc* $-1, i - upper + pivot\_loc - 1$)
$\quad\quad$ $= i - 1$:
$\quad\quad\quad$ **return** *pivot_loc*
$\quad\quad$ $> i - 1$:
$\quad\quad\quad$ FIND (*List, pivot_loc* $+ 1, upper, i$)

Algorithm 3.8

Let $f(n, i)$ be the average time FIND takes to select the ith best of n things. Because the pivot is chosen with uniform probability, it is the ith best with probability $1/n$. If the pivot is the ith best then FIND halts, otherwise it recurses on one of the two sublists. Suppose the pivot is in fact the kth best element. Since SPLIT costs $n-1$ comparisons then

$$f(n, i) = n - 1 + \frac{1}{n} \sum_{k=1}^{n-i} f(n - k, i) + \frac{1}{n} 0 + \frac{1}{n} \sum_{k=n-i+2}^{n} f(k - 1, i + k - n - 1)$$

We don't need boundary conditions for this recurrence because, by our convention, sums collapse to zero when their ranges are empty. So, for example, $f(1,1) = 0$, $f(2,1) = f(2,2) = 1$, $f(3,1) = f(3,3) = 7/3$, and $f(3,2) = 8/3$.

The two sums look a little less frightening if we change variables to $j = n - k + 1$.

$$f(n,i) = n - 1 + \frac{1}{n} \sum_{j=i+1}^{n} f(j-1,i) + \frac{1}{n} \sum_{j=1}^{i-1} f(n-j, i-j)$$

Now let $f(n)$ be the average cost of FIND averaged over all i. Then

$$f(n) = \frac{1}{n} \sum_{i=1}^{n} f(n,i)$$

(See table 3.6.)

n	1	2	3	4	5	6	7
$f(n)$	0	1	22/9	25/6	152/25	122/15	2522/245

Table 3.6 Average cost of FIND

Therefore,

$$nf(n) = \sum_{i=1}^{n} f(n,i)$$

$$= n^2 - n + \frac{1}{n} \sum_{i=1}^{n} \left\{ \sum_{j=i+1}^{n} f(j-1,i) + \sum_{j=1}^{i-1} f(n-j, i-j) \right\}$$

Gosh, this recurrence looks pretty awful. Fortunately we can rearrange the double sums—maybe they will then be easier to solve. The idea is called *swapping the sum order,* and figure 3.22 shows how it works.

Pause Show that $\displaystyle \sum_{i=1}^{n} \sum_{j=1}^{i-1} f(n-j, i-j) = \sum_{l=1}^{n-1} \sum_{k=1}^{l} f(l,k) = \sum_{j=1}^{n-1} \sum_{i=1}^{j} f(j,i)$.

$$\sum_{i=1}^{n}\sum_{j=1}^{i} f(i,j) = \sum_{k=1}^{n}\sum_{l=k}^{n} f(l,k)$$

$$\sum_{j=1}^{1} f(1,j) \quad = \quad f(1,1)$$

$$\sum_{j=1}^{2} f(2,j) \quad = \quad f(2,1) \quad + \quad f(2,2)$$

$$\vdots$$

$$\sum_{j=1}^{n} f(n,j) \quad = \quad f(n,1) \quad + \quad f(n,2) \quad +\cdots+ \quad f(n,n)$$

$$\| \qquad\qquad \| \qquad\qquad \|$$

$$\sum_{l=1}^{n} f(l,1) \qquad \sum_{l=2}^{n} f(l,2) \qquad \cdots \qquad \sum_{l=n}^{n} f(l,n)$$

Figure 3.22   Equivalence of double sums

Swapping the order of both double sums, we see that the two sums are the same!

$$n f(n) \quad = \quad n^2 - n + \frac{1}{n}\sum_{j=1}^{n-1}\left\{\sum_{i=1}^{j} f(j,i) + \sum_{i=1}^{j} f(j,i)\right\}$$

$$= \quad n^2 - n + \frac{2}{n}\sum_{j=1}^{n-1}\sum_{i=1}^{j} f(j,i)$$

$$= \quad n^2 - n + \frac{2}{n}\sum_{j=1}^{n-1} j f(j)$$

Therefore,

$$n^2 f(n) = n^3 - n^2 + 2\sum_{j=1}^{n-1} j f(j)$$

$\boxed{Pause}$ Check that $f(1) = 0$, $f(2) = 1$, and $f(3) = 22/9$.

Now what? This recurrence is much simpler than the first, but it's still pretty ghastly; how can we simplify it further? The biggest problem is the sum; such recurrences are called **full-history recurrences** because for every $i < n$, $f(i)$ contributes to $f(n)$. Now notice that most of the terms of the sum will appear in a recurrence for $f(n-1)$. So if we subtract the equivalent expression for $f(n-1)$ lots of terms will cancel.

Subtracting the $(n-1)^{th}$ term from the nth term and simplifying we see that,

$$n^2 f(n) - (n-1)^2 f(n-1) = n^3 - n^2 + 2 \sum_{j=1}^{n-1} j f(j)$$

$$- (n-1)^3 + (n-1)^2 - 2 \sum_{j=1}^{n-2} j f(j)$$

$$= 3n^2 - 5n + 2 + 2(n-1)f(n-1)$$

$$\Longrightarrow n^2 f(n) = (n^2 - 1)f(n-1) + 3n^2 - 5n + 2$$

Now we can quickly napkin f's order:

$$n^2 f(n) = (n^2 - 1)f(n-1) + 3n^2 - 5n + 2$$
$$< n^2 f(n-1) + 3n^2$$
$$\Longrightarrow \quad f(n) < f(n-1) + 3$$
$$\Longrightarrow \quad f(n) < 3n$$
$$\Longrightarrow \quad f(n) = O(n)$$

Thus, f is at worst linear! So FIND is $O(n)$ on average.

Having reached our goal we could stop here, but let's press on and see if we can find FIND's exact cost, we may find some more weapons that may be useful elsewhere. (Besides, in the heat of calculation we're not guaranteed to find a simple napkin bound.) Brace yourself for a further math attack.

Here is the recurrence again

$$n^2 f(n) = \begin{cases} 0 & n = 1 \\ (n^2 - 1)f(n-1) + 3n^2 - 5n + 2 & n > 1 \end{cases}$$

$\boxed{Pause}$ Why do we need a boundary value now?

MORE NAPKINS, PLEASE....

This recurrence would be easy to solve if it weren't for those pesky n^2 and n^2-1 factors; how can we get rid of them? Let's see if we can develop some insight by generalizing the recurrence. Consider the recurrence

$$f(n) = \begin{cases} f(1) & n = 1 \\ g(n)f(n-1) + h(n) & n > 1 \end{cases}$$

where g and h are arbitrary functions of n and $g(n)$ is non-zero for all $n > 1$. This is a **first-order linear recurrence**. First-order means that only one prior term, (in this case, $f(n-1)$) appears—a recurrence involving, say, $f(n-1)$ and $f(n-2)$, would be second-order. Linear means that none of the prior terms are higher powers—a recurrence involving, say, $f(n-1)^2$, would be quadratic.

Expanding a few terms we see that

$$\begin{aligned} f(n) &= g(n)f(n-1) + h(n) \\ &= g(n)g(n-1)f(n-2) + g(n)h(n-1) + h(n) \\ &= g(n)g(n-1)g(n-2)f(n-3) + \\ &\quad g(n-1)g(n)h(n-2) + g(n)h(n-1) + h(n) \end{aligned}$$

This isn't going anywhere, we need to cancel all those g functions somehow. But wait, nothing prevents us from doing just that!

Define the new function $f_1(n)$ where

$$f_1(n) = \frac{f(n)}{\displaystyle\prod_{i=2}^{n} g(i)}$$

where $\prod_{i=j}^{k} g(i) = g(j)g(j+1)\cdots g(k)$ and $\prod_{i=j}^{k} g(i) = 1$ if $j > k$.
($\prod$ is the Greek letter capital π; it stands for "product.") That is

$$f(n) = \begin{cases} f_1(1) & n = 1 \\ g(n)g(n-1)\cdots g(2)f_1(n) & n > 1 \end{cases}$$

Now substitute for $f(n)$ in the original recurrence to get:

$$g(n)g(n-1)\cdots g(2)f_1(n) = g(n)\{g(n-1)g(n-2)\cdots g(2)f_1(n-1)\}$$
$$+h(n)$$
$$\Longrightarrow f_1(n) = f_1(n-1) + \frac{h(n)}{g(n)g(n-1)\cdots g(2)}$$

Except for the messy fraction this is an easy recurrence, its solution is

$$f_1(n) = f_1(1) + \sum_{i=1}^{n} \frac{\frac{h(i)}{i}}{\prod_{j=2}^{i} g(j)}$$

If we can solve this then we can find f_1, and if we have f_1 then we have f.
This way of solving recurrences is the **transformation algorithm**.
   So let's change to this new function and see what happens. For our
particular recurrence $g(n) = (n^2 - 1)/n^2 = (n+1)(n-1)/n^2$ and $h(n) = (3n^2 - 5n + 2)/n^2$. So

$$\begin{aligned} f(n) &= g(n)g(n-1)\cdots g(2)f_1(n) \\ &= \frac{(n+1)(n-1)}{n^2} \times \frac{(n)(n-2)}{(n-1)^2} \times \frac{(n-1)(n-3)}{(n-2)^2} \times \cdots \\ &\quad \cdots \times \frac{(4)(2)}{(3^2)} \times \frac{(3)(1)}{(2^2)} \times f_1(n) \\ &= \frac{n+1}{2n} f_1(n) \end{aligned}$$

After substituting for f in the original recurrence and simplifying we see
that

$$f_1(n) = \begin{cases} 0 & n = 1 \\ f_1(n-1) + \dfrac{2(3n^2 - 5n + 2)}{n(n+1)} & n > 1 \end{cases}$$

Pause   Check this—especially the boundary value!

Thus,

$$
\begin{aligned}
f_1(n) &= \sum_{i=1}^{n} \frac{2(3i^2 - 5i + 2)}{i(i+1)} \\
&= 2\sum_{i=1}^{n} \frac{3i^2 - 5i + 2}{i(i+1)} \\
&= 2\sum_{i=1}^{n} \left(3 - \frac{8i - 2}{i(i+1)}\right) \\
&= 6n - 4\sum_{i=1}^{n} \frac{4i - 1}{i(i+1)}
\end{aligned}
$$

Napkining on this sum we see that

$$
\frac{4i - 1}{i(i+1)} < \frac{4i}{i(i+1)} = \frac{4}{i+1}
$$

so the sum is no bigger than about $16H_{n+1}$. So $f_1 \approx 6n - 16\ln(n+1)$ and therefore $f \approx 3(n+1) - 8\ln(n+1)$.

This approximation is already good enough for most purposes, but let's press on to the bitter end. To find the sum exactly we need *partial fractions.* Suppose r and s are two constants such that

$$
\frac{4i - 1}{i(i+1)} = \frac{r}{i} + \frac{s}{i+1}
$$

Then

$$
4i - 1 = r(i+1) + si = (r+s)i + r
$$

From this it follows that

$$
r = -1, \quad s = 5
$$

(We could also find r and s by substituting any two values of i into the equation defining the partial fractions and solving the resulting simultaneous equations.)

Hence,

$$
\frac{4i - 1}{i(i+1)} = \frac{5}{i+1} - \frac{1}{i}
$$

Therefore,

$$
\begin{aligned}
f_1(n) &= 6n - 4 \sum_{i=1}^{n} \left(\frac{5}{i+1} - \frac{1}{i} \right) \\
&= 6n - 20 \sum_{i=2}^{n+1} \frac{1}{i} + 4H_n \\
&= 6n - 20 \left(H_n - 1 + \frac{1}{n+1} \right) + 4H_n \\
&= 6n - 16H_n + 20 \frac{n}{n+1}
\end{aligned}
$$

Therefore,

$$
f(n) = \frac{n+1}{2n} f_1(n) = 3(n+1) - 8H_n \frac{n+1}{n} + 10 = O(n)
$$

Ah! The end of our quest. We should feel good about ourselves, we've just thought our way through a quite complicated problem; *cogito, ergo smug.* Although this has been a long and arduous hike, we've learned a lot about recurrences; we will put this knowledge to use later. As the psalmist says: though sorrow endureth for a night, yet joy cometh in the morning.

To sum up, FIND is at worst quadratic, linear on average, and, because of randomization, it doesn't have a worst case, only worst case executions.

Finding the ith Best Without Randomizing

Now let's design a worst case linear predictable algorithm to select any element. To find the ith we could find the best, the second best, and so on, until we get the ith. Alternately, we could pick any element, find its rank (by comparing it to every other element), and discard it if it's not the ith. Both algorithms are predictable. Further, both are quadratic in the worst case, since both use linear work, in the worst case, to discard only one element. The only things we can do are to find the rank of an arbitrary element, or to find an element of constant rank. But perhaps we can relax our probe and instead of going all the way and finding the exact rank of an arbitrary element we only find its rank to within a certain range. Something like "this element has rank in the range a to b." Can we use this weaker probe to find the ith more efficiently?

Can we modify FIND to select the ith best in linear time in the worst case without randomizing? To do so we have to guarantee that we discard a fixed proportion of the elements at each recursion. We cannot just choose our pivot randomly, we must choose a pivot dividing the list into two bags, where the smaller of the two is *always* some fixed fraction of the remaining elements.

We can guarantee to discard a fixed fraction if we choose the median at each recursion, since at each step we would discard half the elements. But to find the median we have to solve the selection problem! Instead, let's find a pivot that is provably close to the median (without knowing exactly how close) so that when we split with this pivot we will always discard at least some fixed fraction of the input.

So, how about this: choose a constant, c, take a sample of size n/c of the list and find the median of the sample, then split the list using the sample median as pivot. This guarantees that we will discard at least $n/2c$ elements. (Why?) Depending on how much work we do to find the sample median in the first place this may be all right. We must try to balance the work we do to find a pivot against the number of elements that we can then discard.[7] Unfortunately this requires us to find the median of n/c elements cheaply, which means we already know how to find medians cheaply!

Instead, let's divide L into fixed-sized groups, each of size c, find the median of each group, then recursively find the median of the list of n/c medians. This median of medians is not necessarily the median of L, but we can guarantee that if we use it to split L then we will always discard a fixed fraction of L. Now we split the list using the median of medians as pivot and recurse on the appropriate sublist. This is SELECT, algorithm 3.9.

| Pause | What fixed fraction can we guarantee to discard when $c = 5$?

To find the fraction discarded when $c = 5$ look at the posets in figure 3.23. This figure shows the median of medians for $n = 5, 15$, and 25, when the sample size is five (the highlighted circles are the medians of medians for each n). After finding the median of medians of twenty-five things we know that *at least eight* are bigger than the median of medians and *at least eight* are smaller than the median of medians. So if we wanted to find, say, the third best element, we know that it *cannot* be one of the eight elements smaller than the median of medians (because each of them is smaller than at least nine others). Therefore after splitting we will surely discard all eight of those elements less than the median of medians.[8]

---

[7]Note that FIND does no work (measuring in terms of comparisons) to select the pivot, but, in the worst case, it is only guaranteed to discard one element.

[8]This is a lower bound on the number of elements discarded. Depending on i we may discard more—for example, if $i = 3$ we discard seventeen—but independent of i, we're sure to discard at least these eight.

SELECT($List, lower, upper, i$)
  { Find the index of the ith largest of $List[lower..upper]$.
  Use the list $Medians[1..\lceil n/5 \rceil]$ as extra storage.
  $upper \geq lower > 0$; $upper - lower + 1 \geq i \geq 1$. }

  $n \leftarrow upper - lower + 1$
  for j **from** 0 **to** $\lfloor n/5 \rfloor - 1$
    $Medians[j+1] \leftarrow$ median of $List[(lower + 5j)..(lower + 5j + 4)]$
  if n is not a multiple of 5
    $Medians[\lceil n/5 \rceil] \leftarrow$ median of the remaining elements of $List$

  $index \leftarrow$ SELECT($Medians, 1, \lceil n/5 \rceil, \lceil n/10 \rceil$)
  Make $index$ the index of the corresponding element of $List$
  $pivot\_loc \leftarrow$ SPLIT($List, lower, upper, index$)
  case $upper - pivot\_loc$
    $< i - 1$:
      SELECT($List, lower, pivot\_loc - 1, i - upper + pivot\_loc - 1$)
    $= i - 1$:
      return $pivot\_loc$
    $> i - 1$:
      SELECT($List, pivot\_loc + 1, upper, i$)

Algorithm 3.9

Then repeat the entire rigmarole for the at most seventeen remaining elements. Thus we are doing a kind of fuzzy binary search for the third best thing. Instead of discarding half the elements at each step, we only discard roughly $3(n - 5)/10 + 2 = (3n + 5)/10$ elements at each step.

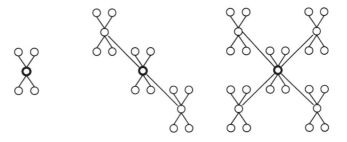

Figure 3.23   Median of medians of five, fifteen, and twenty-five things

It is possible to find the median of five elements in six comparisons so finding the $\lceil n/5 \rceil$ medians of five costs $6\lceil n/5 \rceil$ comparisons. SPLIT costs $n - 1$ comparisons, and recursively finding the median of medians costs $f(\lceil n/5 \rceil)$ comparisons. Finally, the algorithm recurses on at most $\lceil (7n - 5)/10 \rceil$ elements. So if $f(n)$ is the worst cost of SELECT on n elements, then

$$f(n) \leq f(\lceil n/5 \rceil) + f(\lceil (7n - 5)/10 \rceil) + 6\lceil n/5 \rceil + n - 1$$

This is not an equality because, depending on i and the ranks of the pivots found at each recursion, we may discard more elements, but never less.

This is a difficult recurrence to solve exactly. We can show that f is linear by **constructive induction.** First we assume that there is a constant r such that $f(n) \leq rn$ for all n beyond some constant. Then we plug the bound this gives into the recurrence and find bounds on r. Then we choose r bigger than those bounds, thus proving that there is such a constant. Here we go:

$$
\begin{aligned}
f(n) \ & \leq \ r\lceil n/5 \rceil + r\lceil (7n - 5)/10 \rceil + 6\lceil n/5 \rceil + n - 1 \\
& \leq \ r\left(\frac{n}{5} + 1\right) + r\left(\frac{7n - 5}{10} + 1\right) + 6\left(\frac{n}{5} + 1\right) + n - 1 \\
& \leq \ \left(\frac{r}{5} + \frac{7r}{10} + \frac{11}{5}\right) n + \frac{3r}{2} + 5 \\
& \leq \ \left(\frac{9r + 22}{10}\right) n + \frac{3r + 10}{2}
\end{aligned}
$$

After some further manipulations we find that $f(n)$ satisfies this inequality if $r \geq 23$ and $n \geq 380$. So the original induction can now go through as the theorem:

$$\forall n \geq 380, \quad f(n) \leq 23n$$

A more careful algorithm and a sharper analysis shows that the constant multiplier can be reduced to 3, for large n. This algorithm isn't particularly practical; the resulting program is complicated and so has high overhead. Because of high overhead the algorithm is worse than sorting until n is in the thousands. Unfortunately, not every simple question has a simple answer.

To wrap up, we know that $f = \Omega(n)$ because we have two lower bounds on selection problems (find the best and find the second best) and either one would do as a proof that the general selection problem cannot be easier than $\Omega(n)$. Therefore selecting the ith best is $\Theta(n)$ in the worst case in the comparison-based model.

3.6   The Partition Problem

> Mathematics is the tool specially suited
> for dealing with abstract concepts of any
> kind and there is no limit to its power
> in this field.
>
> P. A. M. Dirac, *The Principles of Quantum Mechanics*

We've now solved four selection problems, each of which could be of practical value (although, our version of SELECT isn't particularly practical); how hard is it to select several elements at a time?

In general, what is the worst cost to find the i_1 best elements, the i_2 next best elements, . . . , the i_k worst elements? This is the *partition problem.* Let's denote the worst case number of comparisons needed to solve this problem by $P(i_1, i_2, \ldots, i_k)$.

Recalling our division of problems by type (page 9) we see that selection is half a search problem (find the ith) and half a structuring problem (order the input to give the ith). So selection belongs between the previous chapter (on searching) and the next chapter (on sorting). More generally, we can think of searching as a partition problem where our input is a sorted list plus one more element and we have to produce a sorted list, and we can think of sorting as the particular partition problem in which each i_j is one. So searching, selecting, and sorting are all instances of partitioning.

To determine $P(i_1, i_2, \ldots, i_k)$ we must find the worst case number of comparisons necessary to build the poset shown in figure 3.24.   Exact

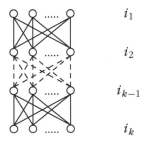

Figure 3.24   The partition problem

solutions are known for simple instances of the problem, but the general problem is unsolved. For example, we have seen that

best	$P(1, n-1)$	$=$	$n-1$
second best	$P(1, 1, n-2)$	$=$	$n + \lceil \lg n \rceil - 2$
best and worst	$P(1, n-2, 1)$	$=$	$\lceil 3n/2 \rceil - 2$
i^{th} best	$P(i-1, 1, n-i)$	$=$	$\Theta(n)$

The only other exact results known are (assume $n \geq 6$):

$$P(2, n-2) \quad = n + \lceil \lg(n-1) \rceil - 2$$

$$P(3, n-3) \quad = n + 2\lfloor \lg n \rfloor - \begin{cases} 3 & n \leq 2^{\lfloor \lg n \rfloor} + 2 \\ 2 & 2^{\lfloor \lg n \rfloor} + 2 < n \leq 5 \times 2^{\lfloor \lg n \rfloor - 2} + 2 \\ 1 & \text{otherwise} \end{cases}$$

$$P(2, 1, n-3) \quad = n + 2\lfloor \lg n \rfloor - \begin{cases} 3 & n \leq 2^{\lfloor \lg n \rfloor} + 1 \\ 2 & 2^{\lfloor \lg n \rfloor} + 1 < n \leq 5 \times 2^{\lfloor \lg n \rfloor - 2} + 1 \\ 1 & \text{otherwise} \end{cases}$$

$$P(1, 1, 1, n-3) = n + 2\lfloor \lg n \rfloor - \begin{cases} 3 & n = 2^{\lfloor \lg n \rfloor} \\ 2 & 2^{\lfloor \lg n \rfloor} < n \leq 5 \times 2^{\lfloor \lg n \rfloor - 2} \\ 1 & \text{otherwise} \end{cases}$$

Selecting the ith best is the problem of finding $P(i-1, 1, n-i)$. We could also select the i best elements in order or select them without regard to order (see figure 3.25). These three partition problems are

- i best elements: $P(i, n-i)$

- i^{th} best element: $P(i-1, 1, n-i)$

- i best elements in order: $P(1, 1, \ldots, 1, n-i)$

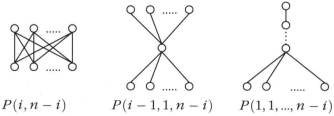

$\qquad P(i, n-i) \qquad\qquad P(i-1, 1, n-i) \qquad P(1, 1, ..., n-i)$

Figure 3.25 Three natural selection problems Darwin forgot

Now, if we know the best i elements in order then we know the ith, and if we know the ith then we know the best i elements[9] so,

$$P(1,1,\ldots,1,n-i) \geq P(i-1,1,n-i) \geq P(i,n-i)$$

We have seen that $P(1,n-1) = P(n-1,1)$; finding the best costs the same as finding the worst. This is a special case of a general *duality*:

$$P(i_1,i_2,\ldots,i_k) = P(i_k,\ldots,i_2,i_1)$$

a poset costs the same if it's turned upside down, forming its **dual**.

Note that a lower bound on any poset problem can be turned into a lower bound on the partition problem. For example, we can turn the lower bound on the best and worst selection problem into a lower bound for any partition problem:

$$P(i_1,i_2,\ldots,i_k) \geq \left\lceil \frac{3n}{2} \right\rceil - i_1 - i_k$$

Finally,

$$\sum_{j=1}^{k-1} i_j \left(\sum_{l=j+1}^{k} i_l \right) \geq P(i_1,i_2,\ldots,i_k) \geq \left(\sum_{j=1}^{k} i_j \right) - 1$$

The lower bound follows because we must at least connect the elements of any poset solving the partition problem. The upper bound is the number of relations we must establish between the elements of any poset solving the problem. We can always establish these relations by doing a comparison and ignoring any transitively induced relations. Of course by taking advantage of transitivity, a comparison can gain us much more than just one bit of information.

We will briefly meet the partition problem again near the end of the next chapter. It is a special case of an even more general (and even more difficult) poset problem.

3.7   Changing the Model

> A mind that is stretched to a new idea
> never returns to its original dimension.
>
> Oliver Wendell Holmes

Suppose we want to find the best wrestler but we only have a limited time to run the tournament. If we don't have time for $n-1$ fights what's the best we can do? Obviously we can no longer guarantee to find the best

---

[9]Interestingly, this last does not follow when n is odd and we have to find the median.

wrestler so we will have to find an "approximate best." Sometimes a near best is as good as the real thing. We will, however, want a guarantee that this wrestler is "near to" the best. What kinds of guarantees can we ask for?

Suppose an algorithm produces X while the best wrestler is really Y. Here are four kinds of guarantees we could ask for:

1. $X = Y$.

2. X's rank is "close" to Y's rank:

$$rank(X) \leq rank(Y) + \text{"small"}$$

3. X is "usually" Y:
$$\mathbf{P}(X = Y) \geq \text{"large"}$$

4. X's rank is "usually" "close" to Y's rank:

$$\mathbf{P}(rank(X) \leq rank(Y) + \text{"small"}) \geq \text{"large"}$$

The first three properties are special cases of the fourth: when "small" = 0 and "large" = 1 we get the first; when "large" = 1 we get the second; and when "small" = 0 we get the third. Note that the third guarantee does not imply the second guarantee; if $X \neq Y$ then X may be ranked far below Y. As figure 3.26 suggests, the first guarantee is a special case of the other three, and the second and third are special cases of the fourth.

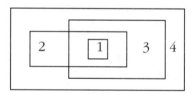

Figure 3.26   Strength of guarantees

Of the four kinds of guarantees we usually only ask for the first, but the others are important in practice. Let's call algorithms giving any of the last three guarantees **relaxed algorithms**. Relaxed algorithms are called different things depending on the guarantees they give. An algorithm giving the second guarantee is an **approximation algorithm**. An algorithm giving the third guarantee is a **probabilistic algorithm**. An algorithm giving the fourth guarantee is usually not even called an algorithm, it's a **heuristic**.

The difference between these algorithms and "normal" algorithms is difficult to pin down because what they're called often depends on how well analyzed they are. For example, a guarantee three algorithm is a probabilistic algorithm if we know the value of "large," but if we don't, it is only a heuristic. To make things more confusing, procedures are often called heuristics (or "rules of thumb") if their success depends on assumptions about the input. If the input does not satisfy those assumptions then the heuristic may not work.

We can ask for other kinds of guarantees. Since we usually want fast algorithms we could sacrifice almost everything to ensure speed on average. Let f be an algorithm's resource cost, and let I be an instance of the problem. Here are two kinds of guarantees stressing speed:

- We always find the best wrestler, and it may take a while but it is "usually" fast:

$$\mathbf{P}(f(I) \leq \text{"low"}) \ \geq \ \text{"large"} \quad \text{and}$$

$$0 \ < \ \mathbf{P}(f(I) \geq \text{"high"}) \ \leq \ \text{"small"}$$

- We "usually" find a wrestler fast, and if we do find one then that is the best wrestler, but sometimes we don't find a wrestler at all:

$$\mathbf{P}(f(I) \leq \text{"low"}) \ \geq \ \text{"large"} \quad \text{and}$$

$$0 \ < \ \mathbf{P}(f(I) = \infty) \ \leq \ \text{"small"}$$

To further complicate things, "usually" can apply to one problem instance or to all problem instances of a particular size. We can combine each of the four previous guarantees with these two guarantees to produce even more relaxed algorithms. We will untangle this snarl of ideas about algorithms in chapter seven.

Although they are usually harder to analyze than normal algorithms, relaxed algorithms are very important in computation and in everyday life. Speed and simplicity often beats accuracy and sophistication—especially if the quick solution is biased toward safety. Proofs are preferable but probability is practical. For example, imagine that Ug and Gug are having a quiet conversation sometime in the stone age when they both hear a soughing cough. Ug, an engineer, immediately takes to his heels, but Gug, a theorist, stays to investigate whether it really is a saber-tooth tiger or some natural phenomenon that just sounds a lot like a saber-tooth tiger. Be careful when shaping your tools—after you shape them, they shape you.

Here's a simple probabilistic algorithm to find the best: find the $n - m$ best elements then pick one at random. This costs m comparisons. This algorithm is correct one in $(n - m)$ times, and the average best rank is $(n - m)/2$. Note that a probabilistic algorithm is *not* necessarily a randomized algorithm. Instead of picking one of the $n - m$ candidates at random we could have, say, always picked the first one. Similarly, a randomized algorithm is *not* necessarily probabilistic. For example, FIND is randomized, but not probabilistic.

Here's a simple approximation algorithm to find the best: choose m elements at random then find the best. This costs $m - 1$ comparisons. What is the average rank of the best element found?

Let's model this problem as follows: draw m integers at random with replacement from the set of n integers $\{1, 2, \ldots, n\}$ to form a sample (that is, choose one at random, replace it, then choose the next at random). It is possible to show that the average best rank is

$$\frac{1}{\binom{m+n}{m}} \sum_{i=0}^{n} i \binom{m + i - 1}{m - 1} = \frac{mn}{m + 1}$$

As this result suggests, analyzing even simple relaxed algorithms can require sophisticated mathematics.

If we randomly choose about $\lg n$ elements, say, then for large n, with high probability the best element seen will be close in rank to the best element. This sampling idea is the basis of many estimation schemes. For example, to perform quality control in manufacturing it is cheaper to test only a few products out of many thousands. Besides being cheaper, sometimes we have no choice but to test only a few products since in some cases, like fuses, we won't know if they work unless we break them.

3.8   Coda—Artists and Artisans

The society which scorns excellence in plumbing because plumbing is a humble activity and tolerates shoddiness in philosophy because it is an exalted activity will have neither good plumbing nor good philosophy.

John W. Gardner,
Forbes, "Thought" page, August 1, 1977

In this chapter we used comparisons as our yardstick. Is the number of comparisons an algorithm does really indicative of its run time? There are two justifications for using comparisons as a measure of worth. First, sometimes comparisons dominate the algorithm's cost. For example, comparisons between long records in a large database are expensive. Second, even if comparisons are cheap, sometimes the number of comparisons done is still proportional to the work done, since the outcomes of the comparisons direct the algorithm's execution path. So sometimes comparisons are proportional to run time.

But often the number of comparisons an algorithm makes does not influence its run time. For example, the second FIND_SECOND_MAX does the minimum number of comparisons, but it does $(n \lg n)/2$ swaps. If a swap costs about the same as a comparison then swapping will dominate the algorithm's run time. The art in choosing a good model lies in identifying which operations will dominate, or be proportional to, the run time.

There are two kinds of scientists—the theoreticals and the practicals—and there is much unnecessary wrangling between the two. Theoreticals sneer that practicals cannot abstract from details, and practicals scoff that theoreticals aren't connected to reality. But both camps are trying to solve problems and in this they are mutually dependent. Too close an attention to practical detail hides important general solutions, but too close an adherence to theoretical issues hides handy pragmatic solutions. Besides its elegance, a model is only as good as its predictions. Don't confuse the thermometer with the heat.

Our next trek takes us into the province of sorting algorithms. Except for SPLIT and FIND, none of the algorithms presented in this chapter are particularly important in practice; but they illustrate useful algorithmic and analytic ideas. We will find a use for several of these insights in the next chapter. In particular, we will use SPLIT to design the most popular sorting algorithm known—quick sort.

Endnotes

Computational Ideas
Summarizing information, partial orders, posets, linear orders, poset diagrams, state space lower bounds, adversaries, the necessity fallacy, binomial trees, implicit structures, space-time tradeoff, the median problem, the partition problem, relaxed algorithms, approximation algorithms, probabilistic algorithms, heuristics, estimation.

Mathematical Ideas
- Finding the variance of a distribution.

- Designing algorithms by manipulating recurrences.

- Simplifying double sums by swapping them.

- Improving the performance of recursive algorithms by improving their base case performance.

- Optimizing divide and conquer algorithms by looking at all possible ways to divide the work.

- Solving first-order linear recurrences by transformation.

- Solving full-history recurrences by subtraction.

- Solving sums using partial fractions.

- Finding a function's growth rate by constructive induction.

- Pascal's triangle.

Definitions

- *relation:* a relation on a set is a set of ordered pairs of elements of the set. If R is a relation we can say either that aRb or $(a, b) \in R$.

- *asymmetric relation:* An asymmetric relation is a relation R for which aRb implies that $b\not R a$.

- *transitive relation:* A transitive relation is a relation R for which aRb and bRc implies that aRc.

- *partial order:* A partial order is an asymmetric and transitive relation.

- *linear order:* A linear order is a partial order under which all pairs of elements are related.

- *orderable set:* An orderable set is a set with a linear order on its elements.

- *singleton:* A singleton is an unrelated element.

- *poset:* A poset is a set with a partial order on its elements.

- *subposet:* One poset is a subposet of another if there is a relationship-preserving mapping from the subposet to the poset.

- *dual poset:* The dual of a poset is the poset with all relations reversed; if R is the relation, then aRb in a poset if and only if bRa in its dual.

- *minimal poset:* The minimal poset with property P is the smallest subposet of all posets with property P.

- *tail recursive algorithm:* A recursive algorithm is tail recursive if there is only one recursion and the call is at the end of the algorithm.

- *permutation:* A permutation of a set of things is a listing of them in some order; there are $n!$ permutations of n distinct things.

- *harmonic number:* The nth harmonic number is the sum of the reciprocals of the first n integers.

- *mode:* A mode of a sequence is any of the most frequent elements in the sequence (any of the elements with highest multiplicity).

- *median:* The median of an orderable set is the $\lceil n/2 \rceil^{th}$ best.

- *mean:* The mean of a set of numbers is its (arithmetic) average.

- *percentile:* The nth percentile of an orderable set is the smallest element larger than n percent of the elements of the set.

- *variance:* The variance of a set of numbers is the average of the square of the differences of the numbers from the set's average.

- *standard deviation:* The standard deviation of a set of numbers is the square root of the set's variance.

- *implicit structure:* An implicit structure is one whose interpretation depends on the order of elements, not on explicit pointers.

- *random variable:* A random variable is a real-valued function defined on the sample space (the set of events) of an experiment.

- *binomial tree:* A height m binomial tree is a single node if $m = 0$, and two height $m - 1$ binomial trees connected at their roots if $m \geq 1$.

- *binomial coefficient:* A binomial coefficient is another name for a value of the choose function, $\binom{n}{m}$.

- *linear recurrence:* A linear recurrence is a recurrence relating only first powers of the values of a function.

- *first-order recurrence:* A first-order recurrence is a recurrence relating each function value to only one previous function value.

- *full-history recurrence:* A full-history recurrence is a recurrence relating each function value to all previous function values.

- *partial fraction representation:* The partial fraction representation of a ratio of two polynomials is a decomposition of the ratio into a sum of proper rational functions of polynomials, where the denominators of these functions are the factors in the denominator of the ratio.

Constants

- $\gamma = 0.57721\ 56649\ 01532\ 86060 \cdots$

- $\pi^2/6 = 1.64493\ 40668\ 48226\ 43647 \cdots$

Notation

- μ = average

- σ = standard deviation

- $H_n = \displaystyle\sum_{i=1}^{n} \frac{1}{i}$

- $H_n^{(2)} = \displaystyle\sum_{i=1}^{n} \frac{1}{i^2}$

- $n \bmod m =$ the remainder on dividing n by m.

- $\displaystyle\prod_{i=1}^{n} f(i) = f(1)f(2)\cdots f(n)$

- $P(i_1, i_2, \ldots, i_k) =$ smallest number of comparisons needed to produce the corresponding partition poset

Conventions

- $m > n \implies \displaystyle\prod_{i=m}^{n} f(i) = 1$

Tools

- If n is a power of two, an n-node binomial tree costs $n - 1$ comparisons to build.

- $\displaystyle\sum_{i=1}^{n} \frac{1}{2^{\lfloor \lg i \rfloor}} = \lfloor \lg n \rfloor + \frac{n + 1 - 2^{\lfloor \lg n \rfloor}}{2^{\lfloor \lg n \rfloor}}$ (exercise 20, page 222)

- $\displaystyle\sum_{i=1}^{n-1} H_i = n(H_n - 1)$ (exercise 21, page 222)

- Tail recursive algorithms can be easily translated into iterative algorithms. (exercise 34, page 224)

- Euler's approximation: $H_n = \ln n + \gamma + \dfrac{1}{2n} + o\left(\dfrac{1}{n}\right)$

- $\displaystyle\sum_{i=1}^{n} \sum_{j=1}^{i} f(i,j) = \sum_{j=1}^{n} \sum_{i=j}^{n} f(i,j)$

- Pascal's relation: $\dbinom{n}{m} = \dbinom{n-1}{m} + \dbinom{n-1}{m-1}$

- $\displaystyle\lim_{n\to\infty} H_n^{(2)} = \dfrac{\pi^2}{6}$

- $\lfloor 3n/2 \rfloor + n \bmod 2 = \lceil 3n/2 \rceil$

- $\displaystyle\sum_{i=1}^{n} i \dbinom{m+i-1}{m-1} = \dfrac{mn}{m+1} \dbinom{m+n}{m}$

- $f(n) = \begin{cases} 0 & n = 1 \\ 1 & n = 2 \\ f(\lfloor n/2 \rfloor) + f(\lceil n/2 \rceil) + 2 & n > 2 \end{cases}$

  $\Longrightarrow f(n) = 3n/2 - 2 + \begin{cases} (n - 2^{\lfloor \lg n \rfloor})/2 & n \leq 3 \times 2^{\lfloor \lg n \rfloor - 1} \\ (2^{\lfloor \lg n \rfloor + 1} - n)/2 & \text{otherwise} \end{cases}$

- $f(n) = \begin{cases} 0 & n = 1 \\ 1 & n = 2 \\ f(n-2) + 3 & n > 2 \end{cases}$

  $\Longrightarrow f(n) = \lceil 3n/2 \rceil - 2$

- $f(n) = \begin{cases} 0 & n = 1 \\ 1 & n = 2 \\ \min\limits_{1 \leq k \leq n-1} \{f(k) + f(n-k)\} + 2 & n > 2 \end{cases}$

  $\Longrightarrow f(n) = \lceil 3n/2 \rceil - 2$

- $f(n) = n - 1 + \dfrac{1}{n^2} \sum\limits_{i=1}^{n} \left\{ \sum\limits_{j=1}^{i-1} f(n-j, i-j) + \sum\limits_{j=i+1}^{n} f(j-1, i) \right\}$

  $\Longrightarrow f(n) = 3n + 13 - 8H_n \dfrac{n+1}{n}$

- $n^2 f(n) = \begin{cases} 0 & n = 1 \\ (n^2 - 1)f(n-1) + 3n^2 - 5n + 2 & n > 1 \end{cases}$

  $\Longrightarrow f(n) = 3n + 13 - 8H_n \dfrac{n+1}{n}$

- $f(n) \leq f(\lceil n/5 \rceil) + f(\lceil (7n-5)/10 \rceil) + 6\lceil n/5 \rceil + n - 1 \Longrightarrow f = O(n)$

- Markov's inequality: If f is non-negative then $r\mathbf{P}(f(X) \geq r) \leq \mu(f(X))$

- Čebyšev's inequality: If X has finite variance then
  $\mathbf{P}(\mu(X) + r\sigma(X) \geq X \geq \mu(X) - r\sigma(X)) \geq 1 - \dfrac{1}{r^2}$

Notes

Euler's enormous paper production led one author to observe that if "publish or perish" were real, Euler would be alive today. Euler has a contemporary rival who may have already outdistanced him: Paul Erdös.

Finding the second best player (in a tennis tournament) was introduced as a serious problem in 1883 by Lewis Carroll, the author of *Alice in Wonderland*; Carroll pointed out that the runner-up is not always the second best player. The minimum number of games needed to find the second runner-up was recently solved by Martin Aigner; see *Combinatorial Search*, Martin Aigner, Wiley-Teubner, 1988. More than one hundred years after Carroll's complaint we still don't know the minimum number of games needed to find the third runner-up.

Exercise 16, page 221, was motivated by an observation in *Probability, Statistics and Truth*, Richard von Mises, Dover, republication, 1981. Problem 11, page 227, is adapted from "On Selecting the Largest Element In Spite of Erroneous Information," B. Ravikumar, K. Ganesan, and K. B. Lakshmanan, *STAC* 1986. Problem 15, page 227, is adapted from "Minimean Optimality in Sorting Algorithms," Ira Pohl, *Proceedings of the 16th Annual Symposium on the Foundations of Computer Science*, IEEE Computer Society, 71–74, 1975. Problem 16, page 228, is adapted from "Exact Balancing Is Not Always Good," Marc Snir, *Information Processing Letters*, 22, 97–102, 1986. Problem 18, page 228, and Problem 19, page 228, are discussed in *Combinatorial Search*, Martin Aigner, Wiley-Teubner, 1988. Exercise 36, page 225, and problem 20, page 228, are adapted from "Finding a Majority Among *n* Votes," M. J. Fischer and S. L. Salzberg, *Journal of Algorithms*, 3, 375–379, 1982. Problem 21, page 228, is from *The Art of Computer Programming: Volume 1, Fundamental Algorithms*, Donald E. Knuth, Addison-Wesley, second edition, 1973.

Further Reading

To find out more about game theory see *The Mathematics of Games and Strategy*, Melvin Dresher, Dover republication, 1981. The canonical reference is also the first book in the area: *Theory of Games and Economic Behavior*, John von Neumann and Oskar Morgenstern, Princeton University Press, 1947.

For a thoroughly researched history of the early development of statistics see *The History of Statistics*, Stephen M. Steigler, Harvard University Press, 1986. I strongly recommend *Probability, Statistics and Truth*, Richard von Mises, Dover, republication, 1981, as a gentle and impressive introduction to the foundations of probability theory. For a comprehensive history of the early development of probability theory see *A History of the Mathematical Theory of Probability*, Isaac Todhunter, Chelsea, 1865. The following book ties together game theory and probability at an elementary level *The Mathematics of Games and Gambling*, Edward Packel, The Mathematical Association of America, 1981.

One important early use of relaxed algorithms was in primality testing; see "Probabilistic Algorithms," Michael O. Rabin, in *Algorithms and Complexity: New Directions and Recent Results,* J. F. Traub (editor), 21–39, Academic Press, 1976. For further references see the further readings section of chapters six and seven. The following paper puts the analysis of one class of relaxed algorithms on a sound footing: "Probabilistic Computations: Toward a Unified Measure of Complexity," Andrew Chi-Chih Yao, *Proceedings of the 18th Annual Symposium on the Foundations of Computer Science,* IEEE Computer Society, 222–227, 1977.

For more on selection problems see *Combinatorial Search,* Martin Aigner, Wiley-Teubner, 1988. See also *Search Problems,* Rudolf Ahlswede and Ingo Wegener, Wiley, 1987. The following paper presented the mentioned $3n + o(n)$ median-finding algorithm: "Finding the Median," A. Schönhage, M. Paterson, and N. Pippenger, *Journal of Computer and System Sciences,* 13, 184–199, 1976. And the following paper gives the best known lower bound: "Finding the Median Requires $2n$ Comparisons," Samuel W. Bent and John W. John, *Proceedings of the 17th ACM Symposium on the Theory of Computing,* 213–216, 1985. Finally, the first paper on producing arbitrary posets is still rewarding reading: "The Production of Partial Orders," Arnold Schönhage, *Asterisque,* 38/39, 29–246, 1976.

The following books provide more analysis background and more detailed analysis, but all require advanced mathematics. *Probabilistic Analysis of Algorithms,* Micha Hofri, Springer-Verlag, 1987, studies properties of permutations. *Fundamentals of the Average Case Analysis of Particular Algorithms,* Rainer Kemp, Wiley-Teubner, 1984, concentrates on detailed analysis of random walk algorithms. *Generatingfunctionology,* Herbert S. Wilf, Academic Press, 1990. presents a detailed introduction to generating functions—an algebraic way to solve recurrences. *Mathematics for the Analysis of Algorithms,* Daniel H. Greene, and Donald E. Knuth, Birkhäuser, third edition, 1990, presents in-depth analysis of a few recalcitrant recurrences. *Combinatorial Enumeration,* Ian P. Goulden and David M. Jackson, John Wiley & Sons, 1983, builds an algebraic theory of enumeration functions and uses it to solve many problems; it also contains many worked examples.

For good analyses of sorting and selection problems see *Data Structures and Algorithms: Volume 1, Sorting and Searching,* Kurt Mehlhorn, Springer-Verlag, 1984, and *The Analysis of Algorithms,* Paul Walton Purdom, Jr. and Cynthia A. Brown, Holt, Reinhart and Winston, 1985; in particular, Purdom and Brown exhaustively analyze their version of SELECT.

As usual, see *The Art of Computer Programming: Volume 3, Sorting and Searching,* Donald E. Knuth, Addison-Wesley, 1973. Knuth exhaustively analyzes FIND_MAX both in the worst case and on average in *The Art of Computer Programming: Volume 1, Fundamental Algorithms.*

Questions

> Each problem that I solved became a
> rule which served afterwards to solve
> other problems.
>
> René Descartes, *Discours de la Méthode*

1. Consider a wheel with k equiangular spokes (each spoke is a diameter of the circle). Suppose the human visual system reacts to a visual stimulus after one-thirtieth of a second. Express speeds in revolutions per minute (rpm).

   (a) At what speeds must the wheel spin for it to appear motionless?

   (b) At what speeds must the wheel spin for it to appear to reverse?

2. To a mathematician, a relation is just a set of ordered pairs: the ordered pair (a, b) is in the set R if and only if aRb. Here are several properties of relations.

R is *reflexive* on S if	$\forall a \in S$	aRa.
R is *irreflexive* on S if	$\forall a \in S$	$a\cancel{R}a$.
R is *symmetric* on S if	$\forall a, b \in S$	$aRb \Longrightarrow bRa$.
R is *asymmetric* on S if	$\forall a, b \in S$	$aRb \Longrightarrow b\cancel{R}a$.
R is *transitive* on S if	$\forall a, b, c \in S$	aRb and $bRc \Longrightarrow aRc$.

   An *equivalence relation* is a reflexive, symmetric, and transitive relation.

   (a) Show that we can use money to define an equivalence relation on the set of all things.

   (b) Show that the order notation Θ induces an equivalence relation on the set of functions.

3. (a) If a relation is not reflexive, is it irreflexive?

   (b) If a relation is not symmetric, is it asymmetric?

   (c) Show that if a relation is asymmetric then it is irreflexive.

   (d) Show that if a relation is irreflexive and transitive then it is asymmetric.

4. Viewing a relation as a set of ordered pairs, show that a relation may be

(a)	reflexive,	symmetric, and	transitive
(b)	reflexive,	symmetric, and	not transitive
(c)	reflexive,	not symmetric, and	transitive
(d)	reflexive,	not symmetric, and	not transitive
(e)	not reflexive,	symmetric, and	not transitive
(f)	not reflexive,	not symmetric, and	transitive

5. Since a relation is just any set of ordered pairs, how many relations are there on n unlabelled nodes?

6. (a) Develop an adversary to show that $n - 1$ comparisons are necessary to find the best of n things in the worst case.

   (b) Develop an adversary to show that n comparisons are necessary in the worst case to search for an unknown in a list of n things.

7. (a) Design an optimal algorithm to find the median of three orderable elements (a sequence of poset diagrams showing comparisons will do).

   (b) Prove that this problem is equivalent to finding the best and worst of three elements.

   (c) Assume that each input permutation is equally likely. How many comparisons does your algorithm take on average?

   (d) Find *three* lower bound arguments to show that your algorithm has optimal worst cost.

8. $f(x, y)$ is a *mean* if the following properties hold:

$$\text{Intermediacy:} \quad \max(x, y) \geq f(x, y) \geq \min(x, y)$$
$$\text{Symmetry:} \quad f(x, y) = f(y, x)$$
$$\text{Homogeneity:} \quad f(rx, ry) = rf(x, y)$$

   (a) Show that the following eight functions are means:

   maximum: $\max(x, y)$ root mean square: $\sqrt{(x^2 + y^2)/2}$

   minimum: $\min(x, y)$ harmonic: $2xy/(x + y)$

   arithmetic: $(x + y)/2$ contraharmonic: $(x^2 + y^2)/(x + y)$

   geometric: $\sqrt{xy}$ heronian: $(x + \sqrt{xy} + y)/3$

   (b) Prove the inequality:

   contraharmonic $\geq$ root mean square $\geq$ arithmetic $\geq$ heronian $\geq$ geometric $\geq$ harmonic

(c) Why should we choose to use the arithmetic mean over any other mean?

9. Use the transformation algorithm to solve the recurrence

$$f(n) = \begin{cases} 1 & n = 1 \\ 2f(n-1) + 1 & n > 1 \end{cases}$$

10. We can use the insights behind manipulating double sums to find the value of single sums.

(a) In chapter two (page 120) we found that

$$\sum_{i=1}^{n} i 2^{i-1} = (n-1)2^n + 1$$

Demonstrate this result by considering figure 3.27.

$$\sum_{j=1}^{1} 2^0 \quad = \quad 2^0$$

$$\sum_{j=1}^{2} 2^1 \quad = \quad 2^1 \quad + \quad 2^1$$

$$\vdots$$

$$\sum_{j=1}^{n} 2^{n-1} \quad = \quad 2^{n-1} \quad + \quad 2^{n-1} \quad + \cdots + \quad 2^{n-1}$$

$$\| \qquad\qquad \| \qquad\qquad \|$$

$$\sum_{l=0}^{n-1} 2^l \qquad \sum_{l=1}^{n-1} 2^l \qquad \cdots \qquad \sum_{l=n-1}^{n-1} 2^l$$

Figure 3.27   Clever summing

(b) Use this insight to find

$$\sum_{i=1}^{n} i x^{i-1}$$

(c) Find the sum a third way by observing that

$$\frac{d}{dx} \sum_{i=0}^{n} x^i = \sum_{i=0}^{n} i x^{i-1}$$

11. Can *pivot_loc* be 1 in the first recursive call of FIND?

12. Let $f(n, i)$ be the average time FIND takes to select the ith best element from a list of n elements. Show that $f(n, i) = f(n, n - i + 1)$.

13. Consider the set of all $n!$ permutations of n orderable and distinct elements. Let $f(n, k)$ be the number of such permutations that cause FIND_MAX (algorithm 3.1, page 165) to perform exactly k assignments.
    Show that

    $$f(n, k) = \begin{cases} 1 & k = n \\ (n - 1)! & k = 1 \\ f(n - 1, k - 1) + (n - 1)f(n - 1, k) & n > k > 1 \end{cases}$$

    The numbers $f(n, k)$ are called *Stirling numbers of the first kind* after their inventor, the Scottish mathematician James Stirling. ($f(n, k)$ is the number of permutations of n things with k cycles.)

14. Show that a height m binomial tree has 2^m nodes.

15. Show that

    $$f(n) = \begin{cases} 0 & n = 1 \\ 1 & n = 2 \iff f(n) = \lceil 3n/2 \rceil - 2 \\ f(n - 2) + 3 & n > 2 \end{cases}$$

16. We have a jar of red and yellow jelly beans and we know that the ratio of red to yellow beans, r, is between one and two. Based on our ignorance of the real value of r, let's assume that r is equally likely to be any fraction between one and two. Then $\mathbf{P}(3/2 \geq r \geq 1)$ = 1/2. But $1 \geq 1/r \geq 1/2$. So $\mathbf{P}(3/4 \geq 1/r \geq 1/2)$ = 1/2. Hence $\mathbf{P}(2 \geq r \geq 4/3)$ = 1/2.

    (a) Following the above reasoning, what is $\mathbf{P}(3/2 \geq r \geq 4/3)$?
    (b) If there are twenty-nine jelly beans why can't seventeen of them be red?
    (c) What is wrong with this conclusion?
    (d) Does anything change if we know that there are no more than five hundred beans in the jar?

17. What is wrong with the following argument?
    "We have shown that $n - 1$ comparisons are necessary to find the best. By symmetry, $n - 1$ comparisons are necessary to find the worst. Therefore $2n - 2$ comparisons are necessary to find the best and worst."

18. What is wrong with the following argument?
    "In chapter two we showed that $\lfloor n/2 \rfloor + \lceil n/2 \rceil = n$, so $\lfloor n/4 \rfloor + \lceil n/4 \rceil = n/2$."

19. Show that

    (a) If n is three times a power of two then $n = 3 \times 2^{\lfloor \lg n \rfloor - 1}$.

    (b) If n is five times a power of two then $n = 5 \times 2^{\lfloor \lg n \rfloor - 2}$.

20. Show that $\displaystyle\sum_{i=1}^{n} \frac{1}{2^{\lfloor \lg i \rfloor}} = \lfloor \lg n \rfloor + \frac{n + 1 - 2^{\lfloor \lg n \rfloor}}{2^{\lfloor \lg n \rfloor}}$

21. Show that $\displaystyle\sum_{i=1}^{n-1} H_i = n(H_n - 1)$.

22. Show that

    (a) $\displaystyle\sum_{i=1}^{n} \frac{1}{i(i+1)} = \frac{n}{n+1}$

    (b) $\displaystyle\sum_{i=1}^{n} \frac{1}{i(i+1)(i+2)} = \frac{n(n+3)}{4(n+1)(n+2)}$

23. Given that $\displaystyle\sum_{i=1}^{n} \frac{1}{i(i+1)} = \frac{n}{n+1}$ show that $H_n^{(2)}$ lies between 1.5 and 2. (Its actual value as n tends to infinity is $1.64493\cdots$.)

24. Full-history recurrences can appear deceptively complicated because their name depends on how the recurrence looks and not on any property of the recurring function.
    Solve the following full-history recurrences

    (a) $f(n) = \begin{cases} 1 & n = 1 \\ \displaystyle\sum_{i=1}^{n-1} f(i) + 1 & n > 1 \end{cases}$

    (b) $f(n) = \begin{cases} 1 & n = 1 \\ \displaystyle\sum_{i=1}^{n-1} f(i) + n & n > 1 \end{cases}$

    (c) $f(n) = \begin{cases} 1 & n = 1 \\ \displaystyle\sum_{i=1}^{n-1} i f(i) + 1 & n > 1 \end{cases}$

    (d) $f(n) = \begin{cases} 1 & n = 1 \\ \displaystyle\sum_{i=1}^{n-1} i f(i) + n & n > 1 \end{cases}$

    To bound (d) recall that $\sum_{i=0}^{\infty} 1/i! = e$.

25. Show that $P(2,3) = 5$. (For the lower bound use figure 4.15, page 278.)

26. The proof outlined in the text of the lower bound for the problem of finding the best and worst ignores all comparisons involving moderates. Complete the proof. (Hint: Split the problem into two parts. First consider the adversary's effect on the number of moderates, then consider the number of novices.)

27. (a) Solve

$$f(n) = \begin{cases} c_1 & n = 1 \\ c_2 & n = 2 \\ \min_{1 \le i \le \lfloor n/2 \rfloor} \{f(i) + f(n - i)\} + c_3 & n > 2 \end{cases}$$

(b) Use your solution to bound the worst cost of finding the best, and also of finding the best and worst.

28. Modify algorithm 3.4, page 177, to work for arbitrary n. Your algorithm should still take $n + \lceil \lg n \rceil - 2$ comparisons.

29. Show that algorithm 3.4, page 177, uses $(n \lg n)/2$ swaps.

30. Let $f(n, m) = \binom{n}{m}$.

(a) Show that $f(n, m) = f(n, n - m)$.

(b) Show that

$$f(n, m) = \begin{cases} 0 & n < m \\ f(n - 1, m) + f(n - 1, m - 1) & n \ge m \end{cases}$$

(c) Interpret these results in terms of the number of ways of selecting m people from n people.

31. (a) Prove Pascal's relation algebraically: $\binom{n}{m} = \binom{n-1}{m} + \binom{n-1}{m-1}$

(b) Use Pascal's relation to show that an n-node binomial tree has $\binom{\lg n}{l}$ level l nodes.

32. Find the growth rates of

(a) $\displaystyle\sum_{i=1}^{\lg n} 1/2^{\lg i}$

(b) $2^{\sum_{i=1}^{\lg n} 2^{-\lg i}}$

33. Find $\min_i \{i + \lceil n/2^i \rceil\}$.

34. A *tail recursive* algorithm is a recursive algorithm that calls itself only at the end of the algorithm. The first LINEAR SEARCH (algorithm 2.1, page 84) presented in chapter two, for example, is tail recursive. Algorithm 3.6, page 188, is also tail recursive, and we can unravel it to get an iterative version, algorithm 3.10.

    (a) Why has the precondition changed?

    (b) Explain in English what this algorithm is doing.

    (c) What is this algorithm's worst cost?

FIND_MAX_MIN (*List, lower, upper*)
   { Find the indices of the largest and smallest of *List[lower..upper]*. *upper* > *lower* > 0. }

   if *List[lower]* > *List[lower* + 1]
      then *max* ← *lower* ; *min* ← *lower* + 1
      else *max* ← *lower* + 1 ; *min* ← *lower*
   for *index* **from** *lower* + 2 **to** *upper* − 1 **by** 2
      if *List[index]* > *List[index* + 1]
         then
            if *List[index]* > *List[max]* **then** *max* ← *index*
            if *List[min]* > *List[index* + 1] **then** *min* ← *index* + 1
         else
            if *List[index* + 1] > *List[max]* **then** *max* ← *index* + 1
            if *List[min]* > *List[index]* **then** *min* ← *index*
   if *upper* − *lower* + 1 is odd
      if *List[upper]* > *List[max]*
         then *max* ← *upper*
         else if *List[min]* > *List[upper]* **then** *min* ← *upper*
   return *max*, *min*

Algorithm 3.10

35. Consider finding the second best by splitting the problem into two parts of sizes k and $n - k$, finding the best of each, finding the overall best, then finding the best of the remaining candidates. To minimize this algorithm's worst cost we must find

$$n - 2 + \min_{0 < k < n} \left\{ \max_{0 < k < n} \{k, n - k\} \right\}$$

    (a) Explain why.

    (b) Minimize this expression.

36. Given a list of n elements, an element of the list is a *majority* if it appears more than $n/2$ times. Design an algorithm that is linear in the number of element-element comparisons in the worst case that will find a majority if one exists, and report that there is no majority if no such element exists.

Problems

1. Show that we can always draw a poset without having to use arrows.

2. What is the average number of assignments FIND_MAX does if of the n elements in L only k of them are different, and the number of copies are $m_1, m_2, \ldots, m_k$?

3. (a) Show that if we recursively divide n as equally as possible we will divide unequally up to $\lfloor n/2 \rfloor$ times. It may be helpful to consider the recurrence

$$f(n) = \begin{cases} 0 & n \le 1 \\ f(\lceil n/2 \rceil) + f(\lfloor n/2 \rfloor) + n \bmod 2 & n > 1 \end{cases}$$

   (b) Show that if splits do not have to be as close as possible that the number of bad splits is never more than $\beta(n) - 1$, where $\beta(n)$ is the number of ones in the binary representation of n (see table 3.7).

   (c) If all bad splits are equally bad, independent of the split size, and if we can split arbitrarily, what is the best split?

n	1	2	3	4	5	6	7	8	9	10	11	12
$\beta(n)$	1	1	2	1	2	2	3	1	2	2	3	2

Table 3.7   Number of ones in the binary representation of n

4. Let

$$f(n) = \begin{cases} 0 & n < 0 \\ 1 & n = 0 \\ \displaystyle\sum_{i=1}^{k} f(n - i) & n > 0 \end{cases}$$

Assume that $\lim_{n \to \infty} f(n)/f(n-1)$ exists and call it x. Show that

   (a) $k = 1$ implies $x = 1$.
   (b) $k = 2$ implies $x = \phi$.
   (c) $k = n$ implies $x = 2$.
   (d) $2 \ge x \ge 1$.
   (e) $k = -\log_x(2 - x)$.

5. Let $f(n)$ be the cost of the divide and conquer version of FIND_MAX_MIN (algorithm 3.5, page 183).
   Let $g(n) = f(n) - f(n-1)$.

   (a) Show that
   $$g(n) = \begin{cases} 1 & n = 2 \\ 2 & n = 3 \\ g(\lceil n/2 \rceil) & n > 3 \end{cases}$$

   (b) Show that for $n > 2$
   $$f(n) = \frac{3(2^{\lfloor \lg n \rfloor} - 2)}{2} + 1 + \begin{cases} 2(n - 2^{\lfloor \lg n \rfloor}) & n \le 3 \times 2^{\lfloor \lg n \rfloor - 1} \\ n - 2^{\lfloor \lg n \rfloor - 1} & \text{otherwise} \end{cases}$$
   $$= \frac{3n}{2} - 2 + \begin{cases} \dfrac{n - 2^{\lfloor \lg n \rfloor}}{2} & n \le 3 \times 2^{\lfloor \lg n \rfloor - 1} \\ \dfrac{2^{\lfloor \lg n \rfloor + 1} - n}{2} & \text{otherwise} \end{cases}$$

6. Consider the following recurrence
   $$f(n) = \begin{cases} 0 & n = 1 \\ 1 & n = 2 \\ f(2^{\lceil \lg n \rceil - 1}) + f(n - 2^{\lceil \lg n \rceil - 1}) + 2 & n > 2 \end{cases}$$

   (a) Show that $f(n) = \lceil 3n/2 \rceil - 2$ satisfies this recurrence.

   (b) This recurrence is implementable as a recursive algorithm finding the best and worst elements of an orderable set. How many levels does this algorithm recurse before it reaches a boundary value?

7. Show that all binomial coefficients are smaller than the middle binomial coefficient(s). That is, show that
   $$\max_{0 \le k \le n} \binom{n}{k} = \binom{n}{\lfloor n/2 \rfloor}$$

8. Develop an adversary using the state space lower bound idea to prove that $n + \lceil \lg n \rceil - 2$ comparisons are necessary to find the second best. Your adversary should keep track of the following four classes of elements: a *novice* has never been compared; a *winner* has won at least once and never lost; a *runner-up* has lost exactly once; a *loser* has lost at least twice.

9. Consider algorithm 3.4, page 177, our implicit implementation of binomial trees. Let $\nu(n)$ be the number of times two divides n (see table 3.8).

(a) Show that the parent of the element in location n is in location $n + 2^{\nu(n)}$.

(b) Show that the element in location n has $\nu(n)$ children.

(c) Show that the ith child of the element in location n is in location $n - 2^{i-1}$.

n	1	2	3	4	5	6	7	8	9	10	11	12
$\nu(n)$	0	1	0	2	0	1	0	3	0	1	0	2

Table 3.8 Number of times two divides n

10. An element is *maximal* in a poset if no element of the poset is larger than it; an element is *minimal* in a poset if no element of the poset is smaller than it. Let $max\#(P)$ and $min\#(P)$ be the number of maximal and minimal elements in the poset P.
    Demonstrate a lower bound of $\lceil 3n/2 \rceil - 2$ comparisons on the problem of finding the best and worst by considering the function $f(P) = max\#(P) + min\#(P)$.

11. (a) Show that if a selection algorithm can make up to k erroneous comparisons then we need at least $(k+1)n - 1$ comparisons to find the best.

    (b) Show that this is worst case optimal.

12. Consider finding the best and worst by dividing n into two pieces.

    (a) Prove that if we divide n into two pieces where at least one is even, then we do no worse than if we divide n into two odd pieces. (Note that we can only find a division of n into two odd pieces when n is even.)

    (b) Prove that if we divide n into two pieces of sizes 2 and $n - 2$, then we do no worse than if we use any other even number.

13. Show that $P(2,1,2) = 6$. (For the lower bound use figure 4.15, page 278.)

14. (a) Find $P(1,1,1,1,1,1,1)$.

    (b) Show that $P(3,1,3) \leq 10$.

15. (a) Show that algorithm 3.6, page 188, takes

$$3n/2 - 2 + (1/2n)(n \bmod 2)$$

comparisons on average.

(b) Show that this is optimal.

16. The following recurrence frequently arises in the analysis of divide and conquer algorithms (assume that f and g are non-decreasing):

$$f(n) = \begin{cases} 0 & n = 0 \\ \min_{0 \leq k \leq n-1} \{f(k) + f(n-k-1)\} + g(n-1) & n > 0 \end{cases}$$

(a) Establish conditions on f so that f obeys the following easier recurrence.

$$f(n) = \begin{cases} a & n = 0 \\ b & n = 1 \\ f(\lfloor n/2 \rfloor) + f(\lceil n/2 \rceil) + g(n-1) & n > 1 \end{cases}$$

(b) Solve this recurrence for $g(n) = c$ and $g(n) = n$.

(c) Find other instances of g that make this recurrence solvable.

(d) Establish conditions on f so that f obeys the following recurrence.

$$f(n) = \begin{cases} a & n = 0 \\ b & n = 1 \\ f(2^{\lceil \lg(n/3) \rceil} - 1) + f(n - 2^{\lceil \lg(n/3) \rceil}) + g(n-1) & n > 1 \end{cases}$$

17. Show that $\displaystyle\sum_{i=1}^{n} i \binom{m+i-1}{m-1} = \frac{mn}{m+1} \binom{m+n}{m}$.

18. Show that $P(2, n-2) = n + \lceil \lg(n-1) \rceil - 2$.

19. Use decision trees or adversaries to show that

(a) $P(i-1, 1, n-i) \geq \left\lceil \lg \dfrac{n!}{(n-i)!} \right\rceil$

(b) $P(i-1, 1, n-i) \geq n - i + \left\lceil \lg \dfrac{n!}{(n-i+1)!} \right\rceil$

20. (a) Show that finding a majority element in a list of n elements (see exercise 36, page 225), if one exists, costs no more than $3n/2+1$ comparisons in the worst case.

(b) Show that this is worst case optimal.

21. Show that the variance of the number of assignments FIND_MAX does is $H_n - H_n^{(2)}$.

22. Our analysis of FIND's average cost is for the average over all inputs and over all i. Find its average cost over all inputs but for a fixed i.

Research

1. Show that $P(i-1, 1, n-i)$ is unimodal and that the median is the most difficult element to select.

2. Call a selection problem an *order k* problem if $n-k$ elements can be in arbitrary order. We know the solution of all order one problems (there are only two: $P(1, n-1)$ and $P(n-1, 1)$ and they are duals) and all order two problems ($P(2, n-2)$, $P(1, 1, n-2)$, $P(1, n-2, 1)$, $P(n-2, 1, 1)$, and $P(n-2, 2)$). We know the solution of some order three problems: $P(3, n-3)$, $P(2, 1, n-3)$, and $P(1, 1, 1, n-3)$ and their duals, but we don't know any higher orders!
Complete the order three problems: find $P(1, 2, n-3)$, $P(2, n-3, 1)$, and $P(1, 1, n-3, 1)$. How about $P(1, 1, n-4, 1, 1)$?

3. How many posets are there with n elements? Observe that the number of allowed (i, j, k, l) states in the state space view of the max-min problem is a lower bound on the number of posets, since although many posets many have the same configuration, no poset can belong to two configurations.
Find the number of different kinds of posets allowed by the max-min problem and use that to bound the number of posets from below. For $n = 1$, 2, 3, and 4 the bounds are: 1, 2, 5, and 10. (This is not difficult.)
In general, we can use every lower bound argument on poset cost to establish bounds on the number of posets. Use this observation to find a tight lower bound on the number of different posets on n elements.

4. Call a problem *decomposable* if it is possible to model its cost function with the "try all decompositions" recurrence (page 187). Show that finding the best and finding the best and worst are the only decomposable partition problems. (Intuitively, for any other partition problem we amass too much information when answering the two subproblems, some of which is then thrown away to arrive at the overall answer.)

5. Suppose we want to find the ith best *or* the ith worst and we don't care which. Is this problem easier than finding the ith best? Intuitively, in the worst case an algorithm like FIND would have to divide the set of elements in half at each step, because if it favors one subset over another it will make our task easier.

6. Across:

1 Silly Ivan's trite relation's property. (10)
6 Powder the derelict alcoholic's stomach. (4)
10 Nursery companion has rhythm; the end but not the start. (5)
11 Gun, permit nervous shuffling. (9)
12 Limp front to back and I see it but it goes without saying. (8)
13 A set type will pose before tea. (5)
15 Wild eastern sea bird may come in. (5)
17 Be present as silicon returns. (2)
18 In what sounds like empty grave, end is encountered. (3)
19 As paper ages, with no pain cries. (5)
21 Tail first, at a dorm, enraged bull charges. Who? (7)
22 Dance with an unexpected ending. (5)
24 Shaky on a limb, I knock out tree. (8)
27 Deranged? So? Flirt sends flowers. (7)
28 They slip and skid and lives end disastrously. (5)
29 Erotic affirmation returned holding an unknown. (4)
30 Such rites I disturbed are methods that may not work. (10)

Down:

1 Name an element. (4)
2 My mastery takes sides. (9)
3 It certainly looks like she'll bombard. (5)
4 Just the usual senseless clay pit. (7)
5 Much about it is true. (6)
7 Also known as part of, inter alia, sacrament. (5)
8 The small company gets headless agitators and thinkers. (10)
9 Contains and contained by 13 Across. (8)
14 High quality particle's choices. (10)
16 Mapping a family tree member. (8)
18 Found in the middle, the press take opposing points. (7)
20 Briefly, submarine team to go down. (7)
21 Keep tabs on a lizard. (7)
23 A way to traverse a tree in repair. (5)
25 Styles are modest when backless. (5)
26 Egyptian goddess discovered on Atlantis Island? (4)

4

SORTING

I saw, when at his word the formless mass,
This world's material mould, came to a heap:
Confusion heard his voice, and wild uproar
Stood ruled, stood vast infinitude confin'd;
Till at his second bidding darkness fled,
Light shone, and order from disorder sprung.

John Milton, *Paradise Lost*

SO FAR we've explored two simple versions of the search problem mentioned in chapter one (page 9). In this chapter and the next we will tramp through simple versions of the structuring problem. As in chapters two and three, the property we will focus on is *linear order.* The sorting problem is to rank an orderable set.

Sorting is useful because it makes finding things, both by value and by rank, more efficient (imagine how useful a dictionary would be if the words weren't alphabetical). Sorting things can also suggest relationships between them. For example, sorting a list of names is a good way to see if any name is duplicated. In fact there is no better way to do this.

Here are a few of the things we might want to sort in daily life: playing cards, ideas, numbers, words, job offers, books, fruit, and socks. Obviously different things need different tactics. (How should we sort a million oranges by size?) Suppose we want to sort a thousand books so that each book is easy to find. There are many sort keys we could use: for instance, length, width, weight, binding, color, subject, author, and title. The actual sort key we use depends on what we find memorable and how many books it distinguishes; nobody remembers a book by its weight in micrograms even though this key is probably as good an identifier as author name. Faced with this multitude of things to sort and keys to sort by, we will, as usual, simplify things considerably so that we can get started.

Let's use the comparison-based model; we assume only that the input is orderable. Because sorting is a structuring problem, we also need some way to preserve the information we derive at each step. Initially, let's assume that we can preserve this information only by moving elements in the list. Later we will weaken this restriction and allow ourselves more work space.

So our problem is that

- we have a list of orderable elements, and

- we want a ranked list of the elements.

Our environment is that

- the list elements are all different (to simplify the analysis),

- we can derive order information only by comparing elements, and

- we can preserve order information only by swapping elements.

Our goal is to minimize the numbers of comparisons and swaps. This is the *comparison-swap model.*

As you can see this is a pretty restricted problem; we will consider more general structuring problems in the next chapter.

Input values don't matter to a sort algorithm in the comparison-swap model; only their relative sizes influence the outcome of a comparison. So when analyzing algorithms in this model we may assume that the input is a permutation of the numbers 1 to n. A sort algorithm in our model *cannot* assume this (and exploit that information to speed up the sort) but we can assume this abstraction to simplify analysis.

4.1   Strategies

'Tis distance lends enchantment to the view,
And robes the mountain in its azure hue.

Thomas Campbell, *Pleasures of Hope*

Before starting in on specific algorithms let's take a step back and look at the sorting problem from a distance. We want to put n things in order; what general strategies will do this? In our model there are only two things we can do to elements: compare them or move them.

Suppose we divide the input into two parts. There are only four properties this division can have; and of the four, only two are important. First, the two parts can be ranked or unranked relative to each other—all elements in one part can be smaller than all elements in the other, or not. Second, they can be ranked or unranked within themselves—all elements in one part can be in order, or not. (See figure 4.1; the figure uses height to suggest the sizes of input elements.) Thus there are six possible kinds of ranking.[1] Of these, only four are important; the other two do not yield sort algorithms. (Note that because we're considering only ranking, an algorithm can belong to more than one of the four groups depending on the sizes of the sublists and on whether the elements of a sublist are contiguous.)

The four important rankings are:

- The two parts are unranked relative to each other:

  - One part is sorted. This is an **insert sort**. Examples in this chapter are *linear insert sort, binary insert sort,* and *jump insert sort.*

  - Both parts are sorted. This is a **merge sort**. One example in this chapter is *merge sort.*

- The parts are ranked relative to each other:

  - Neither part is sorted. This is a **split sort**. One example in this chapter is *quick sort.*

  - One part is sorted. This is a **select sort**. Examples in this chapter are *bubble sort, linear select sort,* and *heap sort.*

Each of the four sort strategies is named after the most expensive stage of the sort. In a merge sort, merging costs more than splitting; in a split sort,

---

[1]The two other properties are that the two parts may have different sizes, and the elements in the two parts can be contiguous in the list, or not. Each choice of inter-part ranking, intra-part ranking, size, and contiguity leads to a sort algorithm.

splitting costs more than merging; in an insert sort, inserting costs more than selecting; and in a select sort, selecting costs more than inserting.

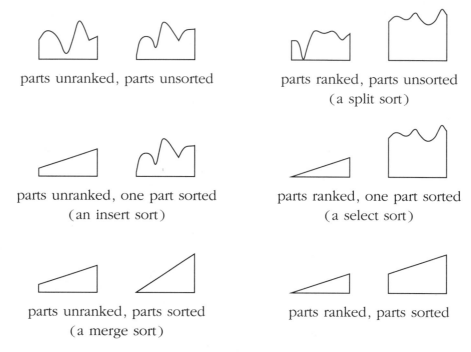

parts unranked, parts unsorted

parts ranked, parts unsorted
(a split sort)

parts unranked, one part sorted
(an insert sort)

parts ranked, one part sorted
(a select sort)

parts unranked, parts sorted
(a merge sort)

parts ranked, parts sorted

Figure 4.1 All possible reduction strategies

The merge sort and split sort strategies suggest recursive algorithms, since the two subproblems are similar. The insert sort and select sort strategies suggest iterative algorithms, since the two subproblems are different. In an insert sort, the elements in the sorted sublist have no special rank, so one way to insert sort is to repeatedly select any element of the remaining unsorted sublist and insert it in the already sorted sublist. In a select sort, the elements in the sorted sublist have special rank—any rank will do but the largest (or smallest) is easiest to find—so one way to select sort is to repeatedly select the largest of the remaining unsorted sublist and insert it in the already sorted sublist. The top left and bottom right strategies in the figure don't lead to sort algorithms; the first just divides the input, and the second assumes that the problem is already solved!

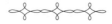

There are other ways to sort. For example, we can compare every pair of elements, then arrange elements based on the number of elements they're less than. This is a **count sort**. Since a count sort compares every pair of elements, it is $\Theta(n^2)$. Another way to sort is to repeatedly swap any two elements that are out of order relative to each other. This is a **swap sort**.

Further, we could leave the comparison-swap model entirely and use some special property of the input elements. For example, to sort oranges by size, fruit packers roll them between two slowly diverging pipes with a series of boxes below. Each orange rolls until the pipes diverge enough for it to fall into the box below. This is how industry sorts things by size when the things can roll. As you can see, cheating can provide really effective solutions; however, because it exploits something other than comparisons, it won't work for all inputs. We couldn't sort oranges so easily without gravity—we would have to fake it with suction, or something similar.

Within the comparison-swap model other sort strategies relax the intermediate sorting; in our classification we either sort or don't sort each part, but we can break each part into further parts and do the same. Generally speaking, within the comparison-swap model, count and swap sorts are the least efficient, insert and select sorts are moderately efficient, and merge and split sorts are the most efficient. One advantage of an insert sort over a select sort is that we can use it **on-line:** we can start sorting even before all elements are present. One advantage of a select sort over an insert sort is that we can always find the i largest elements even before the sort ends.

We will first consider swap sorts, then insert sorts, then select sorts, then merge sorts, and finally split sorts. Then we will find a lower bound on sorting in the comparison-swap model. Finally, we will speed up sorting by changing the model and assuming more about the input.

4.2   Swap Sorts

> Everything should be made as simple
> as possible, but no simpler.
>
> Albert Einstein, *Reader's Digest, October 1977*

One simple way to sort is to repeatedly scan the input, swapping any out of order elements. This is a *swap sort.* One simple swap sort continually scans the input, swapping out of order neighboring elements until none are left. This is BUBBLE_SORT (algorithm 4.1), so named because elements "bubble" up the list (from left to right).

Pause   Why is this guaranteed to sort the list?

```
BUBBLE_SORT (List, lower, upper)
   { Sort List[lower..upper] in increasing order.
   upper ≥ lower > 0. }

   for unsorted from upper downto lower + 1
      for index from lower to unsorted − 1
         if List[index] > List[index + 1]
            List[index] ↔ List[index + 1]
```

Algorithm 4.1

If, after some scan, no two neighboring elements are out of order, then the list is sorted. Further, whenever we meet the largest of the still unsorted elements we bubble it all the way up the list since, no matter where it is, it is always out of order with its neighbor. So while reducing disorder, after each scan BUBBLE_SORT at least puts the next largest element in its final position. So BUBBLE_SORT is really a disguised select sort.

The ith scan costs up to $n - i$ comparisons and there are $n - 1$ scans so BUBBLE_SORT can use up to

$$\sum_{i=1}^{n-1}(n - i) = \sum_{i=1}^{n-1} i = \frac{n(n - 1)}{2} = O(n^2)$$

comparisons and swaps.

It is possible to improve this algorithm but it's not worth the bother; BUBBLE_SORT is no better than any other sort algorithm we will invent in this chapter. And while simple to code, it is not much simpler than our next algorithm. BUBBLE_SORT is good only when the input is nearly sorted to begin with. Although sorting by swapping neighboring elements is natural it is not efficient—something that costs nothing isn't always worth the price.

The Average Cost

Since movement is in one direction only, as an element bubbles up the list we will eventually swap it with all smaller elements that initially were further up the list. Call the number of smaller elements initially to the right of each element its *inversions*. The sum of all inversions of all elements is a measure of how much work BUBBLE_SORT does. Now since BUBBLE_SORT only swaps neighbors, it only removes one inversion with each swap; so its number of swaps is exactly the number of inversions in the input. Assuming each permutation is equally likely, what's the average number of inversions?

Pause | Any ideas?

As previously observed, we may assume that the input is one of the $n!$ permutations of the integers 1 to n. The most inversions occur when the list is in decreasing order—n, $n - 1$, $n - 2$, ..., 1—and the number of inversions is then $\binom{n}{2}$, giving us the worst cost above. *Any* algorithm that removes only one inversion per swap will do up to $\binom{n}{2}$ swaps. The least inversions occurs when the list is in increasing order—1, 2, 3, ..., n—and the number of inversions is then zero.

Pause | So what's the average number of inversions?

The worst cost occurs when the input is in decreasing order, and the best cost occurs when the input is in increasing order. The sum of the inversions of these two inputs is $\binom{n}{2} + 0$. Hmm, the sum of the inversions of any input and its reverse will always be $\binom{n}{2}$. To see this, pick any two elements, i and j, and suppose $i > j$. Now consider any input and its reverse. If i is below j in one input, then i is above j in the other (see figure 4.2). So exactly one of these two inputs adds one to the sum of inversions of the two inputs. But there are $\binom{n}{2}$ choices for i and j. Therefore the sum of inversions of these two inputs must be $\binom{n}{2}$. Hence the average number of inversions for each of these paired inputs is $\binom{n}{2}/2$. Therefore the average number of inversions over all $n!$ inputs is $\binom{n}{2}/2$. So BUBBLE_SORT, along with all algorithms that only remove a constant number of inversions per swap, does $O(n^2)$ swaps on average.

Figure 4.2 Inversions in an input and its reverse

Pause | What's the average number of comparisons?

4.3   Insert Sorts

> And slowly answer'd Arthur from the barge:
> 'The old order changeth, yielding place to the new,
> And God fulfils himself in many ways,
> Lest one good custom should corrupt the world.'
>
> Alfred, Lord Tennyson, *The Passing of Arthur*

Our next strategy is to build a sorted sublist incrementally in one contiguous segment of the list. Let's put each new element in its correct place relative to the already sorted sublist. This is an *insert sort*. The ways we choose to select the next element, and to search for that element's correct relative position, determine the different types of insert sorts.

Linear Insert Sort

The simplest way to find the relative resting place of the next unplaced element is to use linear search. At the ith step, insert the next element into its correct position relative to the already sorted $i - 1$ elements. This costs at most $i - 1$ comparisons. Repeat for i from 2 to n (see algorithm 4.2). This is *linear insert sort*.

LINEAR_INSERT_SORT (*List, lower, upper*)
   { Sort *List*[*lower..upper*] in increasing order.
   upper $\geq$ *lower* $> 0.$ }

   for *sorted* **from** *lower* $+ 1$ **to** *upper*
      placeholder $\leftarrow$ *List*[*sorted*] ; *index* $\leftarrow$ *sorted* $- 1$
      while *index* $\geq$ *lower* **and** *List*[*index*] $>$ *placeholder*
      List[*index* $+ 1$] $\leftarrow$ *List*[*index*]
      index $\leftarrow$ *index* $- 1$
    List[*index* $+ 1$] $\leftarrow$ *placeholder*

Algorithm 4.2

The ith scan costs up to $i - 1$ comparisons and swaps and there are $n - 1$ scans. Thus, LINEAR_INSERT_SORT uses up to

$$\sum_{i=2}^{n}(i - 1) = \sum_{i=1}^{n-1} i = \frac{n(n - 1)}{2} = O(n^2)$$

comparisons and swaps.

As we saw with LINEAR_SEARCH (algorithm 2.1, page 84), if we can modify the list then we can improve implementations slightly by inserting the smallest possible element in position zero as a sentinel. But here we have to part company with the comparison-swap model since we need to know a smallest possible element without doing any comparisons.

If all $n!$ inputs are equally likely, it isn't hard to show that LINEAR_INSERT_SORT is also $O(n^2)$ on average. (Recall from chapter two that on average a linear search in a sorted list will examine roughly half the elements in the list.) Also, the number of swaps is the same as the number of comparisons in both the average and worst cases. So this is no real improvement over BUBBLE_SORT.

Binary Insert Sort

Instead of using linear search to insert why not use binary search? This is *binary insert sort*. Binary search takes up to $\lceil \lg(i+1) \rceil$ comparisons to insert the $(i+1)^{th}$ element, so the maximum number of comparisons of binary insert sort is

$$\sum_{i=0}^{n-1} \lceil \lg(i+1) \rceil = \sum_{i=1}^{n} \lceil \lg i \rceil = n \lceil \lg n \rceil - 2^{\lceil \lg n \rceil} + 1 = O(n \lg n)$$

(We found the value of this sum in chapter two, page 120.) See table 4.1.

n	1	2	3	4	5	6	7	8
$f(n)$	0	1	3	5	8	11	14	17

Table 4.1   Cost of binary insert sort

There's a big difference between n^2 and $n \lg n$; $\lg n$ grows so slowly in comparison to n that $n \lg n$ is "almost linear." For example, if n is a million, $n \lg n$ is about twenty million, but n^2 is a trillion. If n is a million and a comparison takes one microsecond then $n \lg n$ comparisons take about twenty seconds but n^2 comparisons take more than eleven and a half days.

This is a great improvement in the worst number of comparisons, but what about swaps? Since we're sorting in an array, then after we've used binary search to find the correct position of the ith element we still have to shift up to $i - 1$ elements to make room for it. So the sort still takes $\Omega(n^2)$ swaps in the worst case. We can reduce this by using extra indices to keep track of the correct relative positions of each element, but this is expensive because those positions can change after each insertion.

We can reduce the $\Omega(n^2)$ swaps to $O(n \lg n)$, in line with the number of comparisons, but to do so requires significantly more storage and more overhead per insertion. This insert sort is called *tree sort*.

4.4   Select Sorts

> A mathematician, like a painter or a poet, is a maker of patterns. If his patterns are more permanent than theirs, it is because they are made with *ideas*.
>
> G. H. Hardy, *A Mathematician's Apology*

Insert sorts work on one element at a time. But we can split the input in many ways, thereby producing many different algorithms. The next strategy carries on from the selection problem of the last chapter: instead of working on any old element, find the largest element and put it in its correct place, then repeat the process for the remaining elements (see algorithm 4.3). This is a *select sort*. One advantage of a select sort over an insert sort is that once we find a position for an element, it is in its final position. One disadvantage of a select sort over an insert sort is that it doesn't benefit from partially ordered inputs; also, a select sort must be done **off-line**—it can be done only when all elements are present.

LINEAR_SELECT_SORT (*List, lower, upper*)
   { Sort *List*[*lower..upper*] in increasing order.
   upper $\geq$ *lower* > 0. }

   for *unsorted* **from** *upper* **downto** *lower* $+ 1$
      next_max $\leftarrow$ *unsorted*
      for *index* **from** *lower* **to** *unsorted* $- 1$
         if *List*[*index*] $>$ *List*[*next_max*]
            next_max $\leftarrow$ *index*
      List[*unsorted*] $\leftrightarrow$ *List*[*next_max*]

Algorithm 4.3

Consider the ith iteration of the algorithm. At this point the largest $i - 1$ elements are already in order in the last $i - 1$ positions in the list.

LINEAR SELECT SORT repeatedly finds the largest of all remaining elements until there are none left. The ith iteration costs up to $n - i$ comparisons, therefore LINEAR SELECT SORT costs up to

$$\sum_{i=1}^{n-1}(n - i) = \sum_{i=1}^{n-1} i = n(n - 1)/2 = O(n^2)$$

comparisons. However LINEAR SELECT SORT uses only $O(n)$ swaps. The average number of comparisons and swaps are the same as their worst cost.

As with LINEAR INSERT SORT, one reason to use LINEAR SELECT SORT is that it's easy to get right the first time. Also, both algorithms are so simple that they have low overhead; so both are efficient for small n.

Heap Sort

Let's look a little more closely at the select sort strategy. At each step we find the largest of the remaining unordered elements. But we throw away lots of useful information after each scan since the next scan doesn't start with any information about the second largest (which is now the largest of the remaining elements). As we saw in chapter three, if we're careful, then after we have found the largest, the second largest can only be one of $\lceil \lg n \rceil$ elements, and we can identify these elements on our first pass through the input. So let's keep track of the relative order of elements when finding the largest and then use that information when finding the second largest on the next round, and so on. To do that we need a structure to retain information about the elements' order.

Now what should this structure be like? We could use binomial trees, as we did in the last chapter, but because the root has $\lceil \lg n \rceil$ children we will lose a lot of information every time we replace it. One way around this is to build a stronger structure that only allows a constant number of children for each element. Although the structure will have more information than a binomial tree (and so will cost more to build) it will be easier to modify as we remove elements. The simplest such structure has only one child per element—but in that case we have already sorted the elements! The next simplest structure allows up to two children per element; in other words, it's a binary tree.

A *heap* is a rooted binary tree such that the value of any node is at least as large as the values of its children. To use heaps to sort we need an algorithm to fix the heap after we remove the root (the largest element). Since the root of the adjusted heap will be the largest of the remaining elements we can repeat the process, each time picking the ripest fruit off the tree.

Now how can we fix the heap after we delete the root? Well, we know that the root of any subtree is at least as large as its children, so when we remove the root we can just replace it with the larger of its two children (see figure 4.3). But now we have a problem.[2] To make room for the value-10 node we have to change the value-6 node from being the left child of the new root to being its right child. (Alternately, we could make the value-10 node the right child.) Worse, the new root could have had two children already! How can we deal with that?

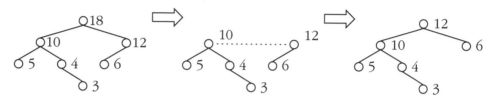

Figure 4.3   Fixing a heap after deleting its root

<u>Pause</u>   Any ideas?

We can avoid both problems by inventing a *placeholder* node, as we did in Linear_Insert_Sort. After deleting the root we pick a leaf (any leaf will do) and put it in the placeholder node—initially the root position. See step (1) of figure 4.4. (The point of using a leaf is that leaves don't have children, and, as you know, children complicate things.) At this point the tree may not be a heap because the new root is not guaranteed to have a larger value than its children.

<u>Pause</u>   Now what?

To guarantee that the root is larger than its children we could find the larger of the two children and compare it to the newly created root. If it's smaller than the root then the tree is a heap, if it's larger then we swap it with the root. See step (2); in the figure we have just swapped the nodes with values 3 and 16. Now we repeat the process for the placeholder node until we swap it with a leaf or find that it's larger than the next two children.

Now to sort, we first form a heap, then repeatedly remove the root and fix the heap after replacing the root with a leaf until we've reduced the heap to nothing. So we have two subproblems: creating a heap efficiently and fixing it efficiently.

_____

[2]". . . that's the way problems propagate their species. A problem left to itself dries up or goes rotten. But fertilize a problem with a solution—you'll hatch out dozens." N. F. Simpson, *A Resounding Tinkle.*

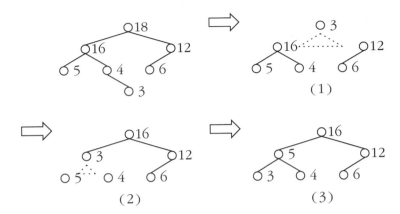

Figure 4.4   Fixing a heap after deleting its root: second try

Okay, let's ignore the first problem for a bit.[3] Suppose we already have a height m heap. Removing the root and letting a leaf "trickle-down" the heap costs at most two comparisons per level of the tree. So a trickle-down costs no more than $2m$ comparisons. Now, if we use any of the deepest leaves, *trickle-down never increases the height of the tree*. So if we start with a height m heap then we can force *each* trickle-down to take no more than $2m$ comparisons. Therefore the whole sort costs no more than $2nm$ comparisons. So we want m, the height of the heap, to be as small as possible.

Now let's get back to creating the heap in the first place. We want to minimize heap height. We saw in chapter two that a height m binary tree can have no more than $2^{m+1} - 1$ nodes: so the shortest possible n-node binary tree has height at least $\lfloor \lg n \rfloor$. What's more, there are trees of this height for all n. A *complete* binary tree is an ordered, rooted binary tree in which every non-leaf node has two children and with all its leaves on one level (see figure 4.5). A *left-complete* binary tree is a complete binary tree with zero or more of its rightmost leaves deleted (see figure 4.6). (As we shall see, forcing the heap to be left-complete leads to a very efficient sort.) The n-node left-complete binary tree has height $\lfloor \lg n \rfloor$; no n-node binary tree is shorter.

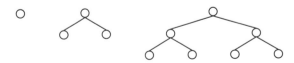

Figure 4.5   All complete binary trees up to height two

---

[3]"In skating over thin ice, our safety is in our speed."   Ralph Waldo Emerson, *"Prudence," New England Reformers.*

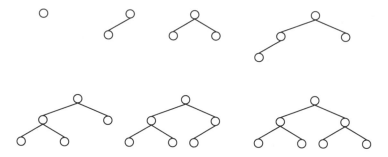

Figure 4.6 All left-complete binary trees up to height two

Pause Argue by induction that at least half the nodes of a left-complete binary tree are leaves. Is this true for every binary tree?

Now let's build a heap. There are two natural ways to do this: incrementally by adding leaves to an initially empty heap; and recursively by creating two subheaps and adding a root. Which is better, adding a leaf or adding a root? Since the heap is logarithmic and the incremental algorithm takes at most two comparisons per level, it will take no more than a logarithmic number of comparisons to add each leaf; so its cost is no worse than $O(n \lg n)$. But the recursive algorithm is trickier since roughly half the nodes will be leaves and we don't have to do anything to leaves—they are already "heaps." So the recursive algorithm begins by saving us half the work we would otherwise have to do! Is this enough to reduce the worst cost below $\Omega(n \lg n)$?

Well, let's see. The recurrence for the worst cost of the recursive algorithm is roughly

$$f(n) \leq 2f(n/2) + 2\lg n$$

After a few steps of substitute and guess we see that

$$
\begin{aligned}
f(n) \;&\leq\; \sum_{i=0}^{\lg n - 1} 2^{i+1} \lg(n/2^i) \\
&=\; 2 \sum_{i=0}^{\lg n - 1} 2^i (\lg n - i) \\
&=\; 2\lg n \sum_{i=0}^{\lg n - 1} 2^i - 4 \sum_{i=0}^{\lg n - 1} i2^{i-1} \\
&=\; 2\lg n(2^{\lg n} - 1) - 4((\lg n - 2)2^{\lg n - 1} + 1) \\
&=\; 2n \lg n - 2\lg n - 2n \lg n + 4n - 4 \\
&=\; 4n - 2\lg n - 4
\end{aligned}
$$

So although the top-down algorithm is $O(n \lg n)$, the bottom-up algorithm is linear!

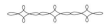

Here's the exact cost. Let $f(n)$ be the worst number of comparisons needed to fix an n-node left-complete heap. Both subtrees are heaps, but the root may have to trickle all the way down the heap to find its correct place. An n-node heap has height $\lfloor \lg n \rfloor$ and we do up to two comparisons per level, so $f(n)$ is $2\lfloor \lg n \rfloor$ unless n is a power of two, when it is one less. Therefore,

$$f(n) = 2\lfloor \lg n \rfloor - (\lfloor \lg n \rfloor - \lfloor \lg(n-1) \rfloor) = \lfloor \lg n \rfloor + \lfloor \lg(n-1) \rfloor$$

With the convention that $\lfloor \lg 0 \rfloor = 0$, this holds for all n. See table 4.2.

n	1	2	3	4	5	6	7	8	9	10	11	12
$f(n)$	0	1	2	3	4	4	4	5	6	6	6	6

Table 4.2 Cost to fix a heap

Let $g(n)$ be the worst cost of building an n-node left-complete heap using the recursive algorithm. If the heap has less than two nodes, there is nothing to do, and if it has two nodes, we must do one comparison. So $g(0) = g(1) = 0$ and $g(2) = 1$. Considering the two types of left-complete heap shapes (see figure 4.7) we see that for $n \geq 3$, g must satisfy

$$g(n) = f(n) + \begin{cases} g(n - 2^{\lfloor \lg n \rfloor - 1}) + g(2^{\lfloor \lg n \rfloor - 1} - 1) & n < 3 \times 2^{\lfloor \lg n \rfloor - 1} \\ g(2^{\lfloor \lg n \rfloor} - 1) + g(n - 2^{\lfloor \lg n \rfloor}) & n \geq 3 \times 2^{\lfloor \lg n \rfloor - 1} \end{cases}$$

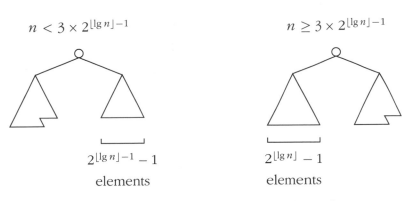

Figure 4.7 The two possible left-complete heap shapes

It is possible to show that g obeys the simpler recurrence

$$g(n) = \begin{cases} 0 & n \leq 1 \\ g(n-1) + \nu(n) + \nu(n-1) & n > 1 \end{cases}$$

where $\nu(n)$ is the number of times two divides n (see table 4.3).

n	1	2	3	4	5	6	7	8	9	10	11	12
$\beta(n)$	1	1	2	1	2	2	3	1	2	2	3	2
$\nu(n)$	0	1	0	2	0	1	0	3	0	1	0	2
$2\beta(n) + \nu(n)$	2	3	4	4	4	5	6	5	4	5	6	6
$g(n) = 2n - 2\beta(n) - \nu(n)$	0	1	2	4	6	7	8	11	14	15	16	18

Table 4.3 Binary functions and cost to build a heap

From this recurrence it is possible to show that the cost to build a left-complete heap is

$$g(n) = 2n - 2\beta(n) - \nu(n)$$

where $\beta(n)$ is the number of ones in the binary representation of n (see table 4.3). Finally, it is possible to show that

$$\forall n \geq 3, \quad 2\beta(n) + \nu(n) \geq 4$$

so for $n \geq 3$, $g(n) \leq 2n - 4$.

Already we can tell that heap sort will not be optimal; $g(4) = 4$ but we can build the heap in three comparisons—a four element heap is the same poset as a four element binomial tree. Table 4.4 lists the exact worst costs to build a heap for small n. Note that the best cost known for a ten element heap is twelve comparisons, but the best lower bound known is only eleven comparisons; so we don't know the exact cost for even as little as ten elements.

n	1	2	3	4	5	6	7	8	9	10
cost	0	1	2	3	5	6	8	8	10	(11,12)

Table 4.4 Exact cost to build a heap for small n

Now it's easy to use heaps to sort. Build a heap as a left-complete binary tree; this takes no more than $2n - 4$ comparisons. Then repeatedly remove the root, replacing it with any leaf until the tree is empty. This takes $O(n \lg n)$ comparisons since each trickle-down is logarithmic. So in all the sort is $O(n \lg n)$.

Programming

As with binomial trees in the last chapter, we can implement left-complete binary trees implicitly. This leads to a version of heap sort using no pointers and no extra space.

Left-complete binary trees are neat because we can represent them implicitly in an array with no wasted space and with no pointers by indexing the nodes in left-to-right level-by-level order. This ordering is called *level order*. If the heap begins at $L[1]$ then the left child of the node stored in $L[i]$ is in $L[2i]$ and the right child is in $L[2i + 1]$. Therefore, the parent of the node stored in $L[j]$ is in $L[\lfloor j/2 \rfloor]$ (see figure 4.8). More generally, we can put the heap anywhere in the array; it does not have to begin at location one. If it begins at $L[lower]$ then the appropriate access functions are:

$$\begin{aligned} left\_child(i) &= 2i - lower + 1 \\ right\_child(i) &= 2i - lower + 2 \\ parent(i) &= \left\lfloor \frac{i + lower - 1}{2} \right\rfloor \end{aligned}$$

We can use this array implementation for any ordered, rooted binary tree, but it's perfect for left-complete trees because it wastes no space. Further, these access functions can be implemented very efficiently: a multiply or divide by two is just a shift in binary. Finally, in an actual implementation these functions would be in-line macros, not separate procedures.

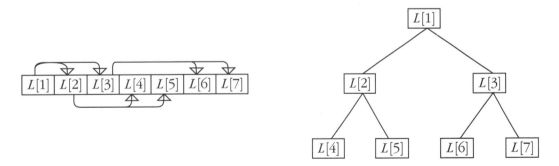

Figure 4.8   Representing a left-complete heap implicitly in an array

During the sort we can arrange to always have a left-complete tree when fixing the heap by always moving the *rightmost* leaf into the root position, $L[lower]$. As a bonus we can put the old root into the old location of the rightmost leaf (at the end of the array), and because roots come off the heap in decreasing order, the array will be in increasing order at the end of the sort. Truly an elegant use of resources!

We build the heap starting from n initially unordered elements in no more than $2n - 4$ comparisons by calling FIX_HEAP (algorithm 4.4) on $\lfloor n/2 \rfloor$, $\lfloor n/2 \rfloor - 1$, ..., 1 elements. Therefore HEAP_SORT (algorithm 4.5) takes no more than $O(n \lg n)$ comparisons in the worst case.

FIX_HEAP (*List, low, high*)
    { Create a subheap within *List[lower..upper]* in positions *low..high*.
    List[low..high] is already a heap except that
    the root node, *List[low]*, may be smaller than its children.
    lower and *upper* are global variables; they are used in
    the functions *left_child* and *right_child*.
    upper ≥ *high* ≥ *low* ≥ *lower* > 0. }

    root ← *low*
    if *high* ≥ *left_child(root)*
      if *high* ≥ *right_child(root)*
        then
          if *List[right_child(root)]* > *List[left_child(root)]*
            largest_child ← *right_child(root)*
        else
          largest_child ← *left_child(root)*
      if *List[largest_child]* > *List[root]*
      List[largest_child] ↔ *List[root]*
      FIX_HEAP (*List, largest_child, upper*)

Algorithm 4.4

A Theoretical Improvement

It may seem that heap sort is so elegant that there is no way to squeeze by with less comparisons. But we can. For example, observe that the elements on the path from the root to any leaf are in sorted order, so to find the position to insert a new element we can binary search along the path from the rightmost leaf to the root! If the heap currently has n elements then there are $\lfloor \lg(n+1) \rfloor$ elements along that path, so the search costs

$$\lceil \lg(\lfloor \lg(n+1) \rfloor + 1) \rceil = \lceil \lg \lceil \lg(n+2) \rceil \rceil$$
$$= \lceil \lg \lg(n+2) \rceil$$

comparisons. (Recall that $\lfloor \lg n \rfloor + 1 = \lceil \lg(n+1) \rceil$.) It can be shown that this is within two comparisons of optimality in the worst case. Of course, having found the insertion position this cheaply it still costs $\lceil \lg(n+2) \rceil$ shifts to add the new element. This can be further improved.

HEAP_SORT (*List*, *lower*, *upper*)
 { Sort *List*[*lower..upper*] in increasing order.
 First build a heap, then repeatedly replace the root
 with the next rightmost leaf using trickle-down.
 upper ≥ *lower* > 0. }

 smallest_parent ← $\lfloor (upper + lower - 1)/2 \rfloor$
 for *index* from *smallest_parent* **downto** *lower*
  FIX_HEAP (*List*, *index*, *upper*)

 for *index* from *upper* **downto** *lower* + 1
  List[*lower*] ↔ *List*[*index*]
  FIX_HEAP (*List*, *lower*, *index* − 1)

Algorithm 4.5

4.5   Merge Sorts

> All engineering is characterized by the engineer's
> dissatisfaction with the achievement of just a solution.
> Engineering seeks the *best* solution in established
> terms, within recognizable limitations, and making
> compromises required by working in the real world.
>
> E. Yourdon and L. Constantine, *Structured Design*

So far our sorts work incrementally and contiguously; at any time there is a sorted and contiguous sublist of elements, and we increase it by including one new element at a time from the as yet unsorted elements. However, divide and conquer suggests a more global strategy: split the problem into two or more large pieces, solve the subproblems, then marry the solutions to solve the original problem.

Let's consider insert sort yet again. The algorithm seems plausible enough at the beginning. We tend to think about small numbers of things; putting one thing in its correct place with respect to three (or five, or seven) other things does not seem that bad, but what about near the end of the sort?

Suppose we've already sorted a million elements. What happens when we only have two more elements to insert? These two elements go into the list one at a time and take, using linear search, about half a million comparisons each on average. (Switching to binary search improves this to about twenty comparisons each.) This seems like a bad way to insert the last two elements.

Pause Why?

If the last two elements were randomly chosen then the smaller one should be bigger than about one-third of the elements and the larger one should be bigger than about two-thirds. Suppose we first compare the last two elements and then insert them *as a pair* in the long list. That is, take the smaller of the two and use linear search to find its correct position, then search *from that point on* for the correct position of the larger of the two. On average, inserting the pair should only take about two-thirds of a million comparisons in all. So on average we expect to save about a third of a million comparisons!

Pause How many would we save on average if we were inserting three elements into a million?

This idea is an instance of a general design strategy that isn't widely used; it's a special case of the balance strategy introduced in chapter two.

> **The balanced run strategy**: Try to make the work done near the end of the algorithm's run equal to the work done near the beginning of the algorithm's run.

This strategy will not apply when the greedy strategy applies. Being greedy means not worrying about future work—just do the least work at each step. But greed does not always pay.

WHEN GREEDY ALGORITHMS GO BAD

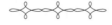

Where do the savings come from? Well, by comparing the last two elements first we can sequence the two searches; finding the correct position of the first reduces the average cost of inserting the next. In general, we want to insert m elements into a sorted list of size n. Instead of treating each of the m elements independently, we first sort them and then exploit the savings on future insertions by inserting them in order. Intuitively this should work best when $m = n$. So let's split the problem into two halves, sort the halves, then merge the sorted halves. This is LINEAR_MERGE_SORT (algorithm 4.6). LINEAR_MERGE_SORT uses the subsidiary algorithm LINEAR_MERGE (algorithm 4.7).

LINEAR_MERGE_SORT ($List, lower, upper$)
   { Sort $List[lower..upper]$ in increasing order.
$upper \geq lower > 0.$ }

  if $upper > lower$
     $mid \leftarrow \lfloor (lower + upper)/2 \rfloor$
     LINEAR_MERGE_SORT ($List, lower, mid$)
     LINEAR_MERGE_SORT ($List, mid + 1, upper$)
     LINEAR_MERGE ($List, lower, mid, upper$)

Algorithm 4.6

LINEAR_MERGE_SORT's worst cost is

$$f(n) = \begin{cases} 0 & n \leq 1 \\ f(\lfloor n/2 \rfloor) + f(\lceil n/2 \rceil) + n - 1 & n > 1 \end{cases}$$

This recurrence is nothing new. We've already solved several of its cousins in chapters two and three; for example, see the recurrence for $g(n)$ on page 117. Using the weapons we discovered in previous chapters it is not hard to show that

$$f(n) = n\lceil \lg n \rceil - 2^{\lceil \lg n \rceil} + 1 = O(n \lg n)$$

(See table 4.5.) How interesting—this is the same worst cost as BINARY_INSERT_SORT!

Pause   Solve the recurrence.

LINEAR_MERGE (*List, lower, mid, upper*)
   { Merge *List*[*lower..mid*] and *List*[*mid* + 1..*upper*],
where each is sorted in increasing order.
Use the array *Save*[*lower..upper*] as extra storage.
upper > *lower* > 0; *upper* ≥ *mid* ≥ *lower*. }

   next ← *lower* ; *lower₁* ← *lower* ; *lower₂* ← *mid* + 1
   while *mid* ≥ *lower₁* **and** *upper* ≥ *lower₂*
     if *List*[*lower₁*] > *List*[*lower₂*]
       then *Save*[*next*] ← *List*[*lower₂*] ; *lower₂* ← *lower₂* + 1
       else *Save*[*next*] ← *List*[*lower₁*] ; *lower₁* ← *lower₁* + 1
     next ← *next* + 1
   if *mid* ≥ *lower₁*
     then *Save*[*next..upper*] ← *List*[*lower₁..mid*]
     else *Save*[*next..upper*] ← *List*[*lower₂..upper*]
   List[*lower..upper*] ← *Save*[*lower..upper*]

Algorithm 4.7

LINEAR_MERGE_SORT is elegant but it requires twice as much storage as every other sort algorithm in this chapter (it needs the extra storage for LINEAR_MERGE). Further, since LINEAR_MERGE_SORT copies every two sublists to merge them, in practice it is often slower than HEAP_SORT. It is possible to merge with only a constant amount of extra storage but this complicates the algorithm. The increased complexity leads to higher overhead costs, which in turn slows the algorithm. This is a direct tradeoff between time and space; more space for less time and vice versa.[4] The space-time tradeoff is like the money-time tradeoff—the value of money is inversely proportional to the time you have to enjoy it. We will see more of the problem of balancing time with space in the next chapter.

n	1	2	3	4	5	6	7	8
$f(n)$	0	1	3	5	8	11	14	17

Table 4.5 Cost of merge sort

---

[4]"Nothing puzzles me more than time and space; and yet nothing troubles me less." Charles Lamb.

4.6   Split Sorts

> A moment's insight is sometimes
> worth a life's experience.
>
> Oliver Wendell Holmes, *The Professor at the*
> *Breakfast Table*

Keeping the idea of breaking up the input into two large chunks, our next idea might be to divide the parts once and for all—just like the change in philosophy from an insert sort to a select sort. To split the input once and for all we can choose an element, the *pivot,* and split the list into two pieces: those larger than the pivot and those smaller than the pivot. Then we sort each separately. Once an element has moved to the left (or right) of the pivot it remains to the left (or right) of the pivot. This algorithm is similar to FIND (algorithm 3.8, page 194) of the previous chapter, except that we have to recurse on both sublists instead of only one.

NATURE DISCOVERS RECURSION

In terms of balancing the work, it would be best if the pivot were the median of the list of elements, but, as we saw in chapter three, finding the median is not trivial. Instead let's choose a random element to be the pivot and use SPLIT (algorithm 3.7, page 193) to split the list around it. This is QUICK_SORT (algorithm 4.8). SPLIT decides which elements are less than the pivot (the left sublist) and which are greater (the right sublist). Notice that the pivot element is not used in either of the recursive calls since it is already in its final position. By analogy with merge sort, quick sort should really be called "split sort," but it earns its name because it's perhaps the fastest (on average) sorting algorithm in practice.

```
QUICK_SORT (List, lower, upper)
   { Sort List[lower..upper] in increasing order.
   upper ≥ lower > 0. }

   if upper > lower
      index ← uniform(lower, upper)
      pivot_loc ← SPLIT (List, lower, upper, index)
      QUICK_SORT (List, lower, pivot_loc − 1)
      QUICK_SORT (List, pivot_loc + 1, upper)
```

Algorithm 4.8

If we select pivots predictably then in the worst case the pivot will always be the largest (or smallest) element in every recursive call; so in the worst case we only sort one element after each call. Since each call takes linear time (because SPLIT takes linear time), QUICK_SORT could use up to $\Omega(n^2)$ comparisons. But because QUICK_SORT randomizes its pivot choice it doesn't have a predictable worst cost, only a worst expected cost. Also, by choosing the pivot randomly we don't have to assume anything about the input.

To find QUICK_SORT's average cost assume that there are n elements in the portion of the list from *lower* to *upper*. The following recurrence models QUICK_SORT's average number of comparisons

$$f(n) = \begin{cases} 0 & n \le 1 \\ n - 1 + \dfrac{1}{n} \displaystyle\sum_{i=0}^{n-1} (f(i) + f(n - i - 1)) & n > 1 \end{cases}$$

(See table 4.6.) SPLIT does $n - 1$ comparisons; QUICK_SORT chooses each element as pivot with probability $1/n$; and it calls itself recursively on both sublists. QUICK_SORT does no comparisons if the recursive call is to a sublist of zero or one elements.

n	1	2	3	4	5	6	7	8
$f(n)$	0	1	8/3	29/6	37/5	103/10	472/35	2369/140

Table 4.6 Average cost of quick sort

Long Pause How come this recurrence and the recurrence for FIND (page 194) both sum two recursions, yet FIND only recurses on one sublist while QUICK_SORT recurses on both sublists?

This recurrence isn't so bad, we solved a similar but tougher one in the last chapter (the average cost of FIND, page 194). First, the two terms of the sum give the same values, but in two different orders: $f(0) + f(1) + \cdots + f(n-1)$ and $f(n-1) + f(n-2) + \cdots + f(0)$. So the recurrence is equivalent to

$$f(n) = \begin{cases} 0 & n \leq 1 \\ n - 1 + \dfrac{2}{n} \displaystyle\sum_{i=0}^{n-1} f(i) & n > 1 \end{cases}$$

Now multiplying throughout by n we have that

$$n f(n) = n(n-1) + 2 \sum_{i=0}^{n-1} f(i)$$

$\boxed{Pause}$ What's become of the boundary values?

This is a full-history recurrence so we get rid of the sum by subtracting $f(n-1)$ from $f(n)$.

$$\begin{aligned} n f(n) - (n-1) f(n-1) &= n(n-1) + 2 \sum_{i=0}^{n-1} f(i) \\ &\quad -(n-1)(n-2) - 2 \sum_{i=0}^{n-2} f(i) \\ &= 2 f(n-1) + 2n - 2 \end{aligned}$$

Therefore,

$$n f(n) = (n+1) f(n-1) + 2n - 2$$

At this point we might try the following bit of napkin math: since $n+1 \approx n$ and $2n - 2 \approx 2n$, then

$$\begin{aligned} n f(n) &\approx n f(n-1) + 2n \\ \implies \quad f(n) &\approx f(n-1) + 2 \\ \implies \quad f(n) &\approx 2n \end{aligned}$$

So QUICK_SORT is linear on average!

$\boxed{Long\ Pause}$ Do you believe this?

Well, let's take a closer look. As we saw with FIND, this is a first-order linear recurrence with variable coefficients; so we can use the transformation algorithm we developed in the last chapter (page 199). Following that algorithm we transform the recurrence using the new function

$$g(n) = \frac{2f(n)}{n+1}$$

(page 199)

Pause Do the calculations to find this transformation for yourself.

Now the recurrence is

$$g(n) = \begin{cases} 0 & n = 1 \\ g(n-1) + \dfrac{4(n-1)}{n(n+1)} & n > 1 \end{cases}$$

Thus,

$$g(n) = 4 \sum_{i=1}^{n} \frac{i-1}{i(i+1)}$$

Napkining on this sum we see that $4H_{n+1} \geq g(n) \geq 2H_{n+1}$ since

$$\frac{i-1}{i(i+1)} < \frac{i}{i(i+1)} = \frac{1}{i+1}$$

$$\implies \quad g(n) \leq 4H_{n+1}$$

and

$$i \geq 2 \implies \frac{i-1}{i} \geq \frac{1}{2}$$

$$\implies \frac{i-1}{i(i+1)} \geq \frac{1}{2(i+1)}$$

$$\implies \quad g(n) \geq 2H_{n+1}$$

So $g = \Theta(H_{n+1})$. Therefore $f = \Theta(n \lg n)$. So our previous napkin simplification is wrong! We have to be careful when using our tools; overfamiliarity breeds contretemps. The $n+1$ factor, instead of an n, multiplying $f(n-1)$ makes it $\Theta(n \lg n)$, not $O(n)$. QUICK_SORT is $O(n \lg n)$ on average.

We can use partial fractions to find the exact result. Expanding into partial fractions we see that

$$g(n) = 4 \sum_{i=1}^{n} \left(\frac{2}{i+1} - \frac{1}{i} \right)$$

After some simplification we see that

$$g(n) = 4H_n - \frac{8n}{n+1}$$

Pause | Is this correct?

Therefore,

$$
\begin{aligned}
f(n) &= \left(4H_n - \frac{8n}{n+1} \right) \frac{n+1}{2} \\
&= 2(n+1)H_n - 4n \\
&= 2(n+1) \left(\ln n + \gamma + \frac{1}{2n} + o\left(\frac{1}{n}\right) \right) - 4n \\
&= 2n \ln n + (2n+2)\gamma + 2\ln n + 1 + \frac{1}{n} + o(1) - 4n \\
&= 2n \ln n - (4 - 2\gamma)n + 2\ln n + O(1)
\end{aligned}
$$

So although QUICK_SORT is at worst $O(n^2)$, it is $O(n \lg n)$ on average, and, because of randomization, this is true independent of its input; it does not have a predictable worst cost, only a worst expected cost.

Programming

This development is enough to write an efficient program but, mindful of Pope's advice,[5] let's consider some practical details.

First, we can improve performance by choosing the base case of the recursion carefully. Instead of recursing all the way down to sublists of one or two elements, we can stop short at sublists of ten or fifteen elements and use, say, LINEAR_SELECT_SORT, for these small sublists. (We considered the issue of choosing the base case of a recursive algorithm in chapter three, page 186). We can tune the sublist size we cut off at depending on our

---

[5]"True ease in writing comes from art, not chance,/ As those move easiest who have learn'd to dance." Alexander Pope, *An Essay on Criticism.*

system and language. Depending on the overhead cost of a recursion, this can greatly speed up the algorithm.

Further, why sort these small sublists at all? It's even better if we don't sort them during the run (that is, if we just recursively split the list and stop at small sublists). We can complete the job using an iterative sort, like LINEAR_INSERT_SORT, that is efficient when the list is nearly sorted. However, by doing so we give up the locality of sorting sublists that are all in the same page in fast memory. For large data sets, and depending on our machine configuration, this may outweigh the advantage of postponing sorting small sublists. As usual, the answer is that there is no final answer; in practice we have to get detailed information about our particular environment and tailor the algorithm to that environment.

Now what about space? At first blush it looks like the sort uses no extra space but actually it uses up to n extra locations to hold the stack that manages the recursions. (Stacks belong in the next chapter; for now we can think of them like vertical stacks of books where each book holds the left and right boundaries of the current sublist.) If we are a little more careful and always sort the *larger* sublist first then the stack depth is never more than $\lg n$. This works because we at least halve the remaining work to be done after sorting each sublist. This trick won't help if the algorithm is recursive, because the parent boundaries will still be on the stack; so if space is a serious concern we have to rewrite the algorithm iteratively and manage the stack ourselves.

Finally, how expensive are QUICK_SORT's calls to **uniform**? If they're very expensive on our machine, we might consider simulating the randomization step by taking a sample of the list elements, finding the median of that sample, and using it as the pivot for the splitting step. One popular way to do this is to find the median of the first, middle, and last list elements and use that as the pivot. One advantage of this method is that the algorithm is fast when the list is sorted to begin with.

If, to avoid spending time finding the sample median, we give up randomization altogether and just choose, say, the first element as the pivot, then in the worst case the algorithm is no better than BUBBLE_SORT! Further, the worst cost occurs for the most embarrassing case—when the list is already sorted. We can think of randomizing the algorithm as scrambling the input.[6] For instance, we can think of the call to **uniform** as just shifting the pivot element around. All other elements stay in the same place so each call to **uniform** stands for n different inputs. Is this equivalent to scrambling, since it's done recursively? Yes, because SPLIT preserves rela-

[6]Note that scrambling the input is not allowed if we need a *stable sort,* that is, if, for example, we have a sorted set of passenger names and flight numbers and we wish to sort by flight number while preserving the relative order of passenger names on each flight.

tive order between all elements less than the pivot and all elements greater than the pivot. So if the list was random to begin with, the two sublists are random after splitting.

4.7   Lower Bounds on Sorting

> A poem is never finished,
> only abandoned.
>
> Paul Valéry, quoted in W. H. Auden,
> *A Certain World*

We've now designed several sort algorithms, what's best possible? As usual, this depends on what we're looking for. Let's assume that only comparisons matter (or, equivalently, that comparisons adequately mirror the overall work done). What's the smallest number of comparisons needed to sort n elements in the comparison-swap model?

Well, the poset representing a sorted list of n elements contains every other poset on n elements as a subposet. So any lower bound we derive for poset production is also a lower bound on sorting. For example, as we saw in chapter three, finding the largest and smallest of n elements is equivalent to building a particular poset starting from the poset with no relations (a set of n singletons). This max-min poset is a subposet of the chain of n elements, in which all elements are related. So $\lceil 3n/2 \rceil - 2$ comparisons is a lower bound on sorting, since sorting is at least as hard as finding the largest and smallest. The sorted list of n elements solves the largest and smallest problem in the sense of chapter three—given the poset we can find the largest and smallest without any further comparisons. Table 4.7 lists the best upper bounds we have so far ($f(n)$ is the cost of binary insert sort) together with the lower bound on finding the largest and smallest for each n.

n	1	2	3	4	5	6	7	8
$f(n)$	0	1	3	5	8	11	14	17
$\lceil 3n/2 \rceil - 2$	0	1	3	4	6	7	9	10

Table 4.7   Cost of binary insert sort versus $\lceil 3n/2 \rceil - 2$

From the table we see that so far we have optimal algorithms to sort less than four elements. What is the optimal cost of sorting four elements? Can it be done in only four comparisons? Or is $\lceil 3n/2 \rceil - 2$ a weak lower bound?

Information Theory

In 1948, Claude Shannon, an American mathematician, published a paper outlining a mathematical theory of communication; this paper spawned a field now called information theory. Put simply, **information theory** is about the amount of surprise in a message. The headline: DOG BITES MAN, is less surprising than: MAN BITES DOG. Let's say that the second message carries *more information* than the first, since the chance of the second event is much smaller than the first (we hope!).

Writing a program that must handle n different possibilities is like playing the game of "Twenty Questions." In this game someone chooses something, unknown to us, and we have twenty tries to guess what it is by asking whether it has various properties (for example, "is it green?," "does it hang on a wall?," and "does it snuffle for truffles?"). In the worst case, every question at best eliminates only half the possible things the unknown could be. If we have narrowed the choices to only one possibility, then we don't need any questions. If there are two possibilities left, we need one question to tell which it is; if there are three left or four left, we need two questions, and so on

Similarly, how many "if" tests do we need to distinguish between n cases in a program? No tests for one case; one test for two cases; two tests for three cases and for four cases, and so on. Again, what is the minimum length in bits of an index for a size n array? An array of size one doesn't require any bits—if an element is in the array it can only be in the first location.[7] An array of size two requires one bit to distinguish between the first and second locations. Arrays of size three and of four require two bits, and so on.

In all three cases (game, program, and index) we want to distinguish among the elements of some domain of things. If every element of the domain is equally likely, then on average each question (or test, or bit) can *at best* only distinguish between two halves of the domain. Each question determines one *information bit.*

> **The information lower bound:** If an algorithm can use only binary decisions to distinguish between n possibilities then it must use at least $\lg n$ such decisions on average.

Since the worst cost of anything must be at least as bad as the average cost, this is also a lower bound on the worst cost.

Each of the above three examples assumes that the elements of the domain are equally likely (or equally surprising); what happens if some

---

[7]Technically, we require several bits just to show where the array starts in memory, but this is a constant overhead for all array locations.

elements are more likely than others? For example, there are about sixty thousand active words in English, but only forty-three of them account for almost half of all words spoken or written. Only nine account for one-quarter of all words used! (The words are: *and, be, have, it, of, the, to, will,* and *you.*) Even at the level of letters, English, along with all other natural languages, is disproportionate (see table 4.8). So a piece of English text is much more predictable than a random sequence of words. In the perverse view of information theory, the information content of a poem is much lower than that of a shopping list.

E	100	S	56	C	27	B	14	X	3
T	71	R	49	M	20	G	14	Z	2
A	64	H	42	F	20	V	10		
I	63	D	35	W	18	K	6		
O	56	L	35	Y	18	Q	4		
N	56	U	31	P	17	J	3		
space or punctuation = 166									

Table 4.8 Letter frequencies per thousand characters of English

Given an experiment with n disjoint events having probabilities p_1, p_2, ..., p_n, the **entropy** of the experiment is

$$H(p_1, p_2, \ldots, p_n) = -\sum_{i=1}^{n} p_k \lg p_k$$

where, by convention, we take $0 \lg 0$ as 0. Figure 4.9 shows the entropy function for an experiment with two disjoint events.

Information theory uses entropy as a measure of the uncertainty of the experiment; it tries to quantify the amount of surprise we would feel if any of the events occurred. Different events may be more likely than others; if a very likely event occurred we would be less surprised than if a less likely event occurred. Like every great idea, information theory is connected to other important ideas. This notion of entropy is related to that of the Austrian physicist Ludwig Boltzmann's definition of entropy in statistical mechanics (a branch of thermodynamics he essentially created in 1871).[8] Independently of Shannon, the American mathematician

---

[8]A brilliant yet tragic figure, Boltzmann killed himself in 1906, depressed partly by thirty years of unrelenting non-acceptance of his ideas by leading scientists of the time, He died just as physics was waking up to the deep importance of statistical mechanics in atomic theory; Planck and Einstein were to use his work to great effect in the twentieth century.

Norbert Wiener ("vee-ner"), a prodigy who finished his doctorate at eighteen, also derived the entropy function, as part of his seminal work on cybernetics.

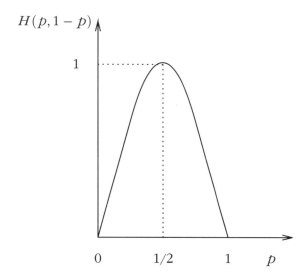

Figure 4.9 The entropy function for a two-event experiment

For fixed n, the experiment with the least uncertainty is the one in which one event is certain. It is possible to show that the entropy function is zero (its smallest value) if and only if one of the probabilities is one. Further, for fixed n, the experiment with the most uncertainty is the one with equally likely events. It is possible to show that the entropy function is $\lg n$ (its largest value) if and only if the probabilities are equal. (For example, figure 4.9 shows that the entropy of a coin flip is smallest when the coin always comes up heads (or tails); it's largest when the coin is unbiased.) Finally, if an experiment can be divided into two independent parts then the uncertainty of the experiment should be the sum of the uncertainties of the two parts. It is possible to show that the entropy of such an experiment is also the sum of the entropies of its two parts. From these three facts it is possible to show that, up to a constant factor, there is only one measure of uncertainty that obeys all three conditions; and that is the entropy function.

In chapter two we used decision trees to derive a lower bound of $\lceil \lg(n+1) \rceil$ on the worst number of comparisons needed to search a sorted list. Information theory gives the same lower bound without explicitly using decision trees. Since there are $n + 1$ possibilities (the unknown, X, is either one of the n elements of the list, L, or it's not in L) we must acquire at least $\lceil \lg(n + 1) \rceil$ bits of information. We can obtain each bit of information only by doing at least one comparison.[9]

This lower bound argument depends in a subtle way on the *statement* of the problem. For example, if we phrase the search problem as: "Is X in L?" (expecting the algorithm to answer yes or no), then we could say that the algorithm has to establish only *one* bit of information and so the information lower bound is one! But we feel that the problem as stated is *equivalent* to asking "Is X in L and, if so, where?"

| *Very Long Pause* | Are they equivalent?

We'll return to the difficult question of how much information we need to prove a result when we meet *zero-knowledge proofs* in chapter six (page 390), and again in chapter seven when we consider the question of knowledge and proof.

| *Pause* | Suppose that if X is not in the list we want to know whether X is less than $L[1]$ or greater than $L[n]$. Do we need $\lceil \lg(n + 2) \rceil$ comparisons?

Information theory gives lower bounds for searching, selecting, and sorting without having to examine the problem too closely. However, every silver lining has a cloud; the information lower bound isn't always good. For example, if L is unsorted we need at least n comparisons to search it. But information theory only says that we require at least $\lceil \lg(n + 1) \rceil$ bits. True. But not useful. In this case the information lower bound is weak.

One reason for this weakness is that when we model algorithms with decision trees (which is what we're doing when we apply the information lower bound) then *we allow too many algorithms.* For example, decision trees allow algorithms whose length is a function of the input! The definition of a decision tree does not require the tree's size to be bounded. Binary search probes the elements of L in a particular pattern; along any path from the root to a leaf there is a simple relationship between the indices of the elements probed. No matter what the search algorithm is, there must be some such pattern once the algorithm handles inputs of any size, is predictable, and is of bounded length. However, it is easy to imagine decision trees resulting from algorithms with no particular pattern (for example, see the beginning of the decision tree for the silly algorithm in figure 2.7, page 113). These algorithms *cannot* be of bounded length;

_____

[9]Since L is sorted, all of these comparisons must involve X; we already know the order of $L[i]$ and $L[j]$ for all i and j.

their length must grow with the size of the input. Such algorithms would be true random algorithms, if such things exist. We will return to this issue in chapter seven.

The Worst Cost

Information theory gives a good lower bound on the worst number of comparisons necessary to sort n things. If we only know that the input is orderable then there are $n!$ possible outcomes—each of the $n!$ permutations of n things. Since, within the comparison-swap model, we can only use comparisons to derive information, then from information theory $\lceil \lg n! \rceil$ is a lower bound on the worst number of comparisons necessary to sort n things.

How fast does $\lg n!$ grow? We can bound $n!$ from above by overestimating every term of the product, and bound it from below by underestimating the first $n/2$ terms (compare the analysis on page 29).

$$n! = n \times (n-1) \times \cdots \times 2 \times 1 \quad \begin{aligned} &\leq \overbrace{n \times n \times \cdots \times n \times n}^{n \text{ times}} = n^n \\ &\geq \underbrace{\frac{n}{2} \times \frac{n}{2} \times \cdots \times \frac{n}{2} \times \frac{n}{2}}_{n/2 \text{ times}} = \left(\frac{n}{2}\right)^{n/2} \end{aligned}$$

Therefore,

$$n^n \quad \geq \quad n! \quad \geq \quad \left(\frac{n}{2}\right)^{n/2}$$

$$\implies \quad n \lg n \quad \geq \quad \lg n! \quad \geq \quad \tfrac{1}{2}(n \lg n - n)$$

So, for example, 100! has between 85 and 200 decimal digits (remember to use the log base ten).

It follows that

$$\lg n! = \Theta(n \lg n)$$

Pause | Why does this follow?

So, sorting can cost up to $\Omega(n \lg n)$ comparisons. So algorithms like BINARY_INSERT_SORT, HEAP_SORT, and LINEAR_MERGE_SORT are asymptotically optimal.

We can improve the lower estimate by adapting Gauss's trick of pairing up large and small terms of $\sum_{i=1}^{n} i$ (page 35) to better estimate the product $\Pi_{i=1}^{n} i$. Observe that if $n - 1 \geq k \geq 0$ then

$$
\begin{aligned}
(k+1)(n-k) &= k(n-k) + (n-k) \\
&\geq k \times 1 + (n-k) \\
&= n
\end{aligned}
$$

Therefore,

$$
\begin{aligned}
(n!)^2 &= n \times (n-1) \times \cdots \times 2 \times 1 \times n \times (n-1) \times \cdots \times 2 \times 1 \\
&= \times \begin{array}{ccccc} n & \times & (n-1) & \times & \cdots & \times & 1 \\ 1 & \times & 2 & \times & \cdots & \times & n \end{array} \\
&\geq n \times n \times \cdots \times n = n^n \\
\Longrightarrow n! &\geq n^{n/2}
\end{aligned}
$$

This lower estimate improves the bounds to

$$
\begin{aligned}
n^n &\geq n! \geq n^{n/2} \\
\Longrightarrow n \lg n &\geq \lg n! \geq \tfrac{1}{2} n \lg n
\end{aligned}
$$

So 100! has between 100 and 200 digits.

Now we can improve the upper bound by using a more accurate over-estimate. For example, we can split $n!$ into $\sqrt{n}$ blocks of $\sqrt{n}$ terms each.

$$
\begin{aligned}
n! &= [n(n-1)\cdots(n-\sqrt{n}+1)] \times \\
&\quad [(n-\sqrt{n})(n-\sqrt{n}-1)\cdots(n-2\sqrt{n}+1)] \times \\
&\quad \cdots \times \\
&\quad [(n-(\sqrt{n}-1)\sqrt{n})(n-(\sqrt{n}-1)\sqrt{n}-1)\cdots(1)] \\
&\leq [n^{\sqrt{n}}] \times [(n-\sqrt{n})^{\sqrt{n}}] \times \cdots \times [(n-(\sqrt{n}-1)\sqrt{n})^{\sqrt{n}}] \\
&= [\sqrt{n}^{\sqrt{n}} \times \sqrt{n}^{\sqrt{n}}] \times [\sqrt{n}^{\sqrt{n}} \times (\sqrt{n}-1)^{\sqrt{n}}] \times \cdots [\sqrt{n}^{\sqrt{n}} \times 1] \\
&= \sqrt{n}^n \times ((\sqrt{n})!)^{\sqrt{n}}
\end{aligned}
$$

This upper estimate improves the bounds to

$$
\begin{aligned}
n^{n/2}((\sqrt{n})!)^{\sqrt{n}} &\geq n! \geq n^{n/2} \\
\longrightarrow \tfrac{1}{2} n \lg n + \sqrt{n} \lg((\sqrt{n})!) &\geq \lg n! \geq \tfrac{1}{2} n \lg n
\end{aligned}
$$

Since $10! = 3,628,800$ has 7 digits then $100!$ has between 100 and 170 digits.

In the same way, we can prove even better bounds, but they are harder to find. Instead we can derive close bounds with **integration**. The integral of a function with respect to x, if it exists, is the area between the function's graph and the x axis. Consider the graph of $\ln x$ shown in figure 4.10. The area of the shorter rectangle is $\ln n$ since its width is 1 and its height is $\ln n$. Similarly, the area of the taller rectangle is $\ln(n+1)$. Further, since $\ln x$ is an increasing function, the area of the taller rectangle is larger than the area under the curve from n to $n+1$, which is larger than the area of the smaller rectangle, which is larger than the area under the curve from $n-1$ to n. Thus, for all $n > 1$

$$\ln(n+1) > \int_n^{n+1} \ln x \, dx > \ln n > \int_{n-1}^n \ln x \, dx > \ln(n-1)$$

Adding all n of the inequalities bounding $\ln n$, we have that

$$\int_1^{n+1} \ln x \, dx > \ln n! > \int_0^n \ln x \, dx$$

The integral of $\ln x$ is $x \ln x - x$ plus a constant, so integrating we see that

$$(n+1)\ln(n+1) - n \quad > \quad \ln n! \quad > \quad n \ln n - n$$

$$\implies \quad \ln\left(\frac{(n+1)^{n+1}}{e^n}\right) \quad > \quad \ln n! \quad > \quad \ln\left(\frac{n^n}{e^n}\right)$$

Hence

$$e\left(\frac{n+1}{e}\right)^{n+1} > n! > \left(\frac{n}{e}\right)^n$$

Now recall that $e = \lim_{n \to \infty}(1+1/n)^{n+1}$, so $((n+1)/n)^{n+1} \approx e$. Therefore, $(n+1)^{n+1} \approx en^{n+1}$. Therefore,

$$n\left(\frac{n}{e}\right)^n > n! > \left(\frac{n}{e}\right)^n$$

So we've managed to bound $n!$ to within a factor of n. We can improve this bound to within a factor of roughly $\sqrt{2\pi n}$ using **Stirling's approximation:**

$$n! \approx \sqrt{2\pi n}\left(\frac{n}{e}\right)^n$$

(See table 4.9). This approximation, usually credited to James Stirling, an eighteenth-century Scottish mathematician, is mostly the work of the French-born English mathematician Abraham De Moivre.

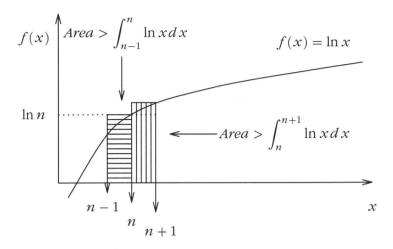

Figure 4.10 Using integrals to estimate $\lg n!$

Using Stirling's approximation we see that

$$
\begin{aligned}
\lg n! &= n \lg n - n \lg e + \tfrac{1}{2} \lg n + O(1) \\
&= n \lg n - n \times 1.44 \cdots + o(n)
\end{aligned}
$$

So 100! has roughly 157 digits (it has exactly 160 digits.)
In the worst case, sorting requires $\Omega(n \lg n)$ comparisons.

n	1	2	3	4	5	6	7	8
$\dfrac{n!}{\sqrt{2\pi n}(n/e)^n}$	1.084	1.042	1.028	1.021	1.016	1.013	1.011	1.010

Table 4.9 An approximation to the factorials

The Average Cost

To find a lower bound on the average number of comparisons necessary to sort, let's assume that all input permutations are equally likely. Consider any decision tree modelling a sort algorithm and associate equal probabilities to each leaf of the decision tree. This probability represents the chance that that leaf will be reached on a given input. Now we can use the lower bound on the average path length of a binary tree we found in chapter two (page 122) when we proved BINARY_SEARCH optimal on average.

If $f(n)$ is the average path length of an n-node binary tree then

$$f(n) \geq \lceil \lg(n+1) \rceil - \frac{2^{\lceil \lg(n+1) \rceil} - \lceil \lg(n+1) \rceil - 1}{n}$$

Since any decision tree modelling a sort algorithm must have at least $n!$ nodes then we have a lower bound on the average number of comparisons of any sort algorithm of at least

$$\lceil \lg(n!+1) \rceil - \frac{2^{\lceil \lg(n!+1) \rceil} - \lceil \lg(n!+1) \rceil - 1}{n!}$$

which is roughly $n \lg n$. So sorting costs $\Omega(n \lg n)$ comparisons, even on average.

4.8   Optimal Sorting

> Ah, but a man's reach should exceed his grasp,
> Or what's a heaven for?
>
> Robert Browning, *Andrea del Sarto*

What's the minimum number of comparisons needed to sort? Although binary search is optimal for searching, binary insert sort is only asymptotically optimal for sorting. The information lower bound for sorting five elements is $\lceil \lg 5! \rceil = 7$ but binary insert sort takes 8 comparisons, as does merge sort. See table 4.10.

n	1	2	3	4	5	6	7	8
$f(n)$	0	1	3	5	8	11	14	17
$\lceil \lg n! \rceil$	0	1	3	5	7	10	13	16

Table 4.10   Cost of binary insert sort versus $\lceil \lg n! \rceil$

Binary insert sort costs

$$\sum_{i=1}^{n-1} \lceil \lg(i+1) \rceil = 1 + \sum_{i=3}^{n} \lceil \lg i \rceil$$

but our current best lower bound is

$$\lceil \lg n! \rceil = \left\lceil \sum_{i=1}^{n} \lg i \right\rceil = 1 + \left\lceil \sum_{i=3}^{n} \lg i \right\rceil$$

Since there are $\lceil \lg(n+1) \rceil$ powers of two less than or equal to n and each power of two contributes the same to both sums (since their logs are integers), then our current best sort can potentially be up to $n - \lceil \lg(n+1) \rceil$ comparisons off for $n \geq 5$. Is the information lower bound weak, or are both sorts inefficient?

Well, let's see. Binary insert sort inserts the last two elements into sorted sublists of size three and then four (which costs two plus three comparisons). But perhaps we can apply the balanced run strategy here and insert them more carefully. Binary search is sensitive to the value of n. In terms of the work done per element, *binary search is most efficient when* $n = 2^i - 1$, *and it is least efficient when* $n = 2^i$. (See figure 4.11.) Is there some way to insert both of the last two elements into sorted sublists of size three?

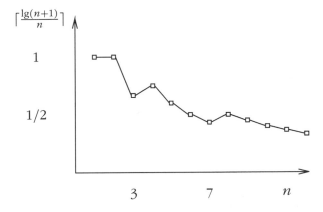

Figure 4.11 The relative efficiency of binary search

Since inserting into a list of size three is cheaper than inserting into a list of four, can we *partially* insert one element into a sublist of size three in such a way that we can *also* insert the next into a sublist of size three? If so, each element cost only two comparisons to insert! If we do this carefully then five elements take only seven comparisons to sort.

Here's the idea: build the poset ⅄, a binomial tree with four elements. This costs three comparisons. Now since this poset has a subset of three elements in order (relative to themselves) we can insert the remaining singleton element into the chain of three in two more comparisons using binary search. (See figure 4.12.) This results in only two different posets, both of which can be completed into a chain by binary searching the pendant element. This costs seven comparisons in all. We're still using binary search but we're using it *selectively*.

More generally, we can use this idea to sort ten elements as well. First pair the elements (using five comparisons) then form a binomial tree of size eight with four of the pairs, leaving one pair extra. (See the first poset in figure 4.13.) Now comes the key idea: because all the original

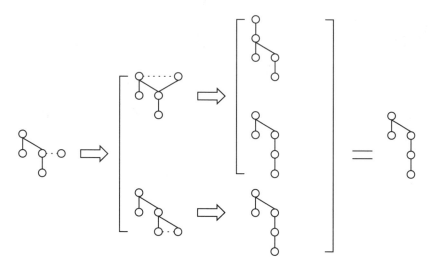

Figure 4.12 Sorting five elements in at most seven comparisons

winners of the pairing round each have one unique descendant we can
treat them as single nodes. That is, we can interpret a binomial tree of
size eight as a binomial tree of size *four* when each "node" of this tree is
really *two* nodes.[10] (These winner nodes are highlighted in figure 4.13.)
Interpreting the poset this way we can now "sort" it using the strategy we
just devised to sort five elements. And the result is the last poset in figure 4.13. This strategy of "folding" binomial trees into smaller binomial
trees to sort them can be generalized for arbitrary n.

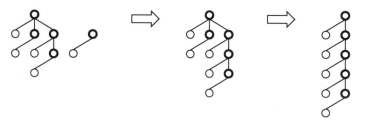

Figure 4.13 Sorting ten elements by first sorting five elements

Pause   How would you sort twenty elements?

_____

[10]We can also think of the binomial tree as a binomial tree of size *two*—that is, just a pair—
since the two sets of four descendants of each node better than four others each have the
same poset structures. Generalizing further, we can interpret a binomial tree of size 2^k as
a binomial tree of size 2^l, for all $l \leq k$. In the most general case, it is possible to show
that once two nodes have the same ancestor and descendant poset structures then they are
isomorphic with respect to the poset.

The general sort is called *merge insert sort.* First pair elements (using $\lfloor n/2 \rfloor$ comparisons) and recursively sort the $\lfloor n/2 \rfloor$ winners of the pairs, producing a chain of $\lfloor n/2 \rfloor$ elements with $\lfloor n/2 \rfloor$ pendant nodes (the losers). Then insert the $\lfloor n/2 \rfloor$ losers—including the extra element, if n is odd—into the chain. If $f(n)$ is the worst cost of merge insert sort then

$$f(n) = \begin{cases} 0 & n < 2 \\ 1 & n = 2 \\ f(\lfloor n/2 \rfloor) + g(\lceil n/2 \rceil) + \lfloor n/2 \rfloor & n > 2 \end{cases}$$

where $g(n)$ is the cost of inserting n pendant nodes.

Now to figure out $g(n)$ let's number the pendant nodes from bottom to top as is suggested in figure 4.14 (the figure shows only five pendant nodes), then merge insert sort inserts the pendant nodes in the order shown in table 4.11.

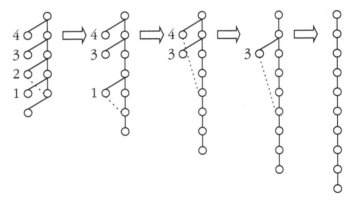

Figure 4.14 Merge insert sorting ten elements

If we let $h(k)$, $k = 1, 2, 3, \ldots$, be the sequence 0, 2, 4, 10, 20, 42, $\ldots$, then all pendant nodes numbered between $h(k-1)+1$ and $h(k)$ cost at most k comparisons to insert into the main chain.

```
                           2  1
                           4  3
                    10  9  8  7  6  5
              20 19 18 17 16 15 14 13 12 11
  42 41 40 39 38 37 36 35 34 33 32 31 30 29 28 27 26 25 24 23 22 21
```

Table 4.11 Insertion orders of pendant nodes

Let $h(k) \geq n \geq h(k-1)$, then

$$g(n) = \left(\sum_{j=1}^{k-1} j(h(j) - h(j-1)) \right) + k(n - h(k-1))$$

$$= kn - \sum_{j=0}^{k-1} h(j)$$

$$= kn - \left\lfloor \frac{2^{k+1}}{3} \right\rfloor$$

Now by induction on n we can show that

$$f(n) - f(n-1) = k \quad \Longleftrightarrow \quad \left\lfloor \frac{2^{k+2}}{3} \right\rfloor \geq n > \left\lfloor \frac{2^{k+1}}{3} \right\rfloor$$

Now

$$\left\lfloor \frac{2^{k+2}}{3} \right\rfloor \geq n > \left\lfloor \frac{2^{k+1}}{3} \right\rfloor$$

$$\Longleftrightarrow \quad \frac{2^{k+2}}{3} > n \geq \frac{2^{k+1}}{3}$$

$$\Longleftrightarrow \quad k+2 > \lg 3n \geq k+1$$

$$\Longleftrightarrow \quad k = \left\lceil \lg \frac{3n}{4} \right\rceil$$

Therefore,

$$f(n) - f(n-1) = \left\lceil \lg \frac{3n}{4} \right\rceil$$

So each element is inserted at an average cost of $\lceil \lg(3n/4) \rceil$ instead of $\lceil \lg(n+1) \rceil$; quite a savings! Therefore,

$$f(n) = \sum_{i=1}^{n} \left\lceil \lg \frac{3i}{4} \right\rceil$$

$$= n \lceil \lg(3n) \rceil - 2n - \left\lfloor \frac{2^{\lfloor \lg 6n \rfloor}}{3} \right\rfloor + \left\lfloor \frac{\lg 6n}{2} \right\rfloor$$

Table 4.12 shows that merge insert sort takes thirty comparisons to sort twelve elements, but $\lceil \lg 12! \rceil$ is twenty-nine. Is merge insert sort optimal for $n = 12$? Or is the information lower bound weak? Well, it has been shown by exhaustive search that it is not possible to sort twelve elements in twenty-nine comparisons, so merge insert sort does the minimum possible number of comparisons when $n = 12$. So, perhaps merge insert sort is optimal for all n? This question took twenty years to answer. Because merge insert sort depends on efficient merging, before answering the question let's see if we can improve merging.

n	1	2	3	4	5	6	7	8	9	10	11	12
$f(n)$	0	1	3	5	7	10	13	16	19	22	26	30
$\lceil \lg n! \rceil$	0	1	3	5	7	10	13	16	19	22	26	29

n	13	14	15	16	17	18	19	20	21	22	23	24
$f(n)$	34	38	42	46	50	54	58	62	66	71	76	81
$\lceil \lg n! \rceil$	33	37	41	45	49	53	57	62	66	70	75	80

Table 4.12 Cost of merge insert sort versus $\lceil \lg n! \rceil$

Binary Merging

Suppose $n \geq m$. What is the best way to merge two sorted lists of size n and m into one sorted list of size $n + m$? LINEAR_MERGE takes up to $n + m - 1$ comparisons. But when m is one, BINARY_SEARCH has optimal worst cost, and it costs no more than $\lceil \lg(n + 1) \rceil$ comparisons. Further, we can always binary search all m elements in the list of n elements. Let $M(m, n)$ be the worst cost of merging two sorted lists of size m and n. We've just established that

$$M(m, n) \leq m + n - 1$$

$$M(m, n) \leq m \lceil \lg(n + 1) \rceil$$

$$M(1, n) = \lceil \lg(n + 1) \rceil$$

Immediately we can tell that $m \lceil \lg(n + 1) \rceil$ is too high a cost when m is bigger than one, since to get it we ignore the order between the m elements and treat them independently. As we saw when developing LINEAR_MERGE_SORT, we can do better than that.

What about when $n = m$? Let's build an adversary for this merge problem. Let the two sorted lists be $L_1[1..n]$ and $L_2[1..n]$. The adversary's task is to intertwine the two lists in the merged list as much as possible. Why? Well, suppose the adversary allows $L_1[i - 1]$, $L_1[i]$, and $L_1[i + 1]$ to be consecutive in the merged list. Then an algorithm can avoid comparing $L_1[i]$ to *any* element of L_2 since, by transitivity, it can infer $L_1[i]$'s correct position in the merged list by only comparing elements of L_2 with $L_1[i - 1]$ and $L_1[i + 1]$. So the adversary aims for the final ordering

$$L_1[1] < L_2[1] < L_1[2] < L_2[2] < \cdots < L_1[n - 1] < L_2[n - 1] < L_1[n] < L_2[n]$$

This is easy to do; its strategy is to say that $L_2[i]$ is bigger than $L_1[j]$ if $i \geq j$.

Since for each i the algorithm must at least test whether $L_2[i] > L_1[i]$ (otherwise, against this adversary, it merges incorrectly) then in the worst case

$$M(n, n) \geq 2n - 1$$

So LINEAR_MERGE has optimal worst cost when $n = m$ and

$$M(n, n) = 2n - 1$$

More generally, it is possible to show that LINEAR_MERGE has optimal worst cost whenever $m \leq n \leq \lceil (3m + 1)/2 \rceil$. It is unknown whether it is optimal outside of this range.

| Pause | Show that $M(n - 1, n) = 2n - 2$.

Now suppose we're merging $L_1[1..m]$ and $L_2[1..n]$ and suppose the first comparison involves $L_1[1]$. Which element of L_2 should we compare it to first? If we compare it to $L_2[n]$ and $L_2[n]$ is smaller then we're done, but if $L_2[n]$ is larger we have learned almost nothing. If we compare it to $L_2[1]$ then for neither outcome will we finish the merge right away, but in both outcomes we have reduced the problem (to $M(m, n - 1)$ or to $M(m - 1, n)$). This safe but sure method leads to linear merge; is that the best we can do?

Intuitively, when m is much smaller than n, then on average the m elements will end up spread apart by about n/m elements each. So it seems reasonable to split L_2 into sublists of size n/m and probe each with selected elements of L_1. For example, we can binary search each element of L_1 in the sublist made up of every m^{th} element of L_2. Each element will take about $\lg(n/m)$ comparisons, and we may reduce the problem to $M(m, m)$, which costs $2m - 1$ further comparisons. So in all we may use about $m \lg(n/m) + 2m - 1$ comparisons. But it isn't clear how to guarantee this cost.

Intuitively, we want to tradeoff paying more for a comparison between $L_1[1]$ and $L_2[n]$ against our win when $L_1[1]$ is bigger than $L_2[n]$. Because that case is so easy (the merge is then finished) we're prepared to pay much more to get it. So, relative to $L_1[1]$, there is a "hardness gradient" across the length of L_2 that gets steeper the further along L_2 the comparison is. This suggests that comparing $L_1[1]$ with $L_2[\lceil n/2 \rceil]$, as binary search might suggest, is a bad idea. Coupled with the observation that on average the elements of L_1 will end up spaced apart by roughly n/m elements, this in turn suggests that the first comparison should be between $L_1[1]$ and $L_2[n/m]$. If $L_1[1]$ wins, we can discard the first n/m elements of L_2, reducing the problem to $M(m, n - n/m)$. If $L_1[1]$ loses, we binary search the first n/m elements of L_2 to find its final place, and merge the remaining

$m - 1$ elements into L_2 at a cost of $M(m - 1, n)$. In effect, we're guaranteeing that each element of L_1 costs at most about $\lg(n/m)$ comparisons to get rid of, one way or the other.

We have two optimal solutions to the merging problem—when $m = 1$ and when $m = n$. MERGE, algorithm 4.9, blends these two strategies based on the ratio of n to m. It uses BINARY_MERGE, algorithm 4.10. This algorithm is more complicated than the above description; to further reduce comparisons it plays tricky games with indices.

MERGE ($List_1, List_2, n, m$)
   { Merge $List_1[1..n]$ and $List_2[1..m]$,
   where each is sorted in increasing order.
   Return the merged array $List[1..(n + m)]$.
   Use *next* to keep track of the next free location in $List[1..(n + m)]$.
   $n \geq m > 0$. }

   next $\leftarrow n$
   while $n > 0$ **and** $m > 0$
     if $n > m$
       then
         next $\leftarrow$ BINARY_MERGE ($List_1, List_2, n, m, List, next$)
       else
         next $\leftarrow$ BINARY_MERGE ($List_2, List_1, m, n, List, next$)

   if $n = 0$
     then $List[(n + 1)..(n + m)] \leftarrow List_2[1..m]$
     else $List[(m + 1)..(n + m)] \leftarrow List_1[1..n]$
   return $List$

Algorithm 4.9

Let $f(m, n)$ be BINARY_MERGE's worst number of comparisons, then it is possible to show that

$$f(m, n) = \begin{cases} n + m - 1 & n < 2m \\ f(m, \lfloor n/2 \rfloor) + m & n \geq 2m \end{cases}$$

From this recurrence it is possible to show that BINARY_MERGE costs

$$m \left\lceil \lg \frac{n + m}{m} \right\rceil + \left\lfloor \frac{n}{2^{\lfloor \lg(n/m) \rfloor}} \right\rfloor - 1$$

BINARY_MERGE ($List_1, List_2, n, m, List, next$)
    { Merge $List_1[1..n]$ and $List_2[1..m]$,
    where each is sorted in increasing order.
    $List[next]$ is the next free location counting from the end of $List$.
    $n \geq m > 0.$ }

    $k \leftarrow 2^{\lfloor \lg(n/m) \rfloor} - 1$
    if $List_1[n-k] \geq List_2[m]$
        then
            $List[(next-k)..next] \leftarrow List_1[(n-k)..n]$
            $n \leftarrow n-k-1$; $next \leftarrow next-k-1$
        else
            $l \leftarrow$ BINARY_SEARCH ($List_1, n-k, n, List_2[m]$)
            $List[(next-l)..next] \leftarrow List_1[(l+1)..n]$
            $next \leftarrow next-n+l$; $List[next] \leftarrow List_2[m]$
            $n \leftarrow l$; $m \leftarrow m-1$; $next \leftarrow next-1$
    return $next$

Algorithm 4.10

The information lower bound for merging two sorted lists of size n and m is

$$\left\lceil \lg \binom{n+m}{n} \right\rceil$$

since there are $n+m$ positions in the output and the n elements can end anywhere in this list once they remain in order.

If $n \geq m$ it is possible to show that

$$\left\lceil \lg \binom{n+m}{n} \right\rceil + m \geq M(m,n) \geq \left\lceil \lg \binom{n+m}{n} \right\rceil$$

so BINARY_MERGE is within m comparisons of worst case optimality. Both bounds can be improved.

For small m the following exact results are known:

$$M(m,n) = n+m-1 \quad \forall m \leq n \leq \lceil (3m+1)/2 \rceil$$
$$M(1,n) = \lceil \lg(n+1) \rceil$$
$$M(2,n) = \left\lceil \lg \frac{7}{12}(n+1) \right\rceil + \left\lceil \lg \frac{14}{17}(n+1) \right\rceil$$
$$M(3,n) = \left\lceil \lg \frac{28}{43}(n+2) \right\rceil + \left\lceil \lg \frac{56}{107}(n+2) \right\rceil + \left\lceil \lg \frac{1}{17}(7n+13) \right\rceil$$

The result for $m = 3$ holds only for $n \geq 9$. The smaller values are

$$M(3,6) = 7, \quad M(3,7) = 8, \quad \text{and } M(3,8) = 8$$

Finally, $M(4,n)$ is known and very tight bounds are known for $M(5,n)$.

Beating Merge Insert Sort

Sadly, although merge insert sort is elegant and efficient, it isn't optimal. Let $S(n)$ be the worst cost to sort n elements. Although we don't know S we know that it must satisfy an infinite number of inequalities. For example, it must be that $S(n + 1) \leq S(n) + \lceil \lg(n + 1) \rceil$, otherwise it would be cheaper to sort $n+1$ elements by sorting n, then binary inserting one more element. Similarly, for all n and m we must have that

$$S(n + m) \leq S(n) + S(m) + M(m,n)$$

We can beat merge insert sort by splitting the input, sorting the pieces, then merging the pieces. The smallest known n for which this works is forty-seven, and the input is split into sublists of five and forty-two elements. This scheme will beat merge insert sort only for certain n; so far merge insert sort is unbeaten when n is near one-third of a power of two.

But even if we have an optimal algorithm to sort two sublists of k and $n - k$ elements for every $k > 0$, and an optimal algorithm to merge them, we do not necessarily have an optimal algorithm to sort n elements. When we recurse we may do *unnecessary work* that gets thrown away when we "marry" the two pieces. (Recall the problems with using divide and conquer to find the largest and second largest in chapter three). Thus we cannot guarantee to sort optimally by optimally sorting two sublists and optimally merging them. Of course we can always find an optimal sort for each n separately by testing all possible comparison sequences to find the shortest one that will sort that number of elements. Then we can imagine building an "optimal sort algorithm" by concatenating all of these special purpose algorithms and continually adding new special purpose optimal sorts for particular ns not yet covered. The first thing this "algorithm" would do is check the value of n and, depending on that value, branch to the appropriate special purpose sort. Of course such an "algorithm" may grow to be infinitely long, stretching both the meaning of the word "algorithm" and our credulity. It may well be that there is *no* optimal sort algorithm of bounded length.

Poset Production

The sorting problem is to find the worst cost of building the poset consisting of a chain of elements starting from n singletons. It is a special case of the partition problem discussed in the previous chapter. We know even less about the worst cost of building an arbitrary poset starting from n singletons. Figure 4.15 shows the reduced posets producible in five or less comparisons (ignoring duals). A **reduced** poset is a poset with no singletons (adding singletons cannot increase the cost). Table 4.16 lists the numbers of reduced posets that cost less than six comparisons, together with lower bounds for the numbers of posets costing six comparisons.

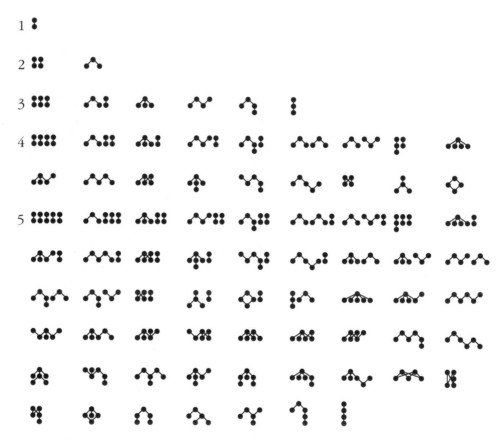

Figure 4.15 Posets producible in five comparisons (ignoring duals)

This is a frighteningly difficult problem; even the simplest assumptions about poset cost are suspect. For example, although adding a singleton to a poset cannot increase its cost, it can decrease it! Further, producing two copies of a poset simultaneously can cost less than producing each separately!

Number of Elements

		2	3	4	5	6	7	8	9	10	11	12	
	1	1											1
c	2		2	1									3
o	3		1	5	2	1							9
s	4			4	14	8	2	1					29
t	5			1	15	41	24	8	2	1			92
	6				11	$\geq$61	$\geq$124	$\geq$82	$\geq$28	8	2	1	$\geq$317
		1	3	11	47	255	1727	14954					

Figure 4.16 Number of reduced posets of various costs

4.9   Changing the Model

> As far as the laws of mathematics refer to reality, they are not certain; and as far as they are certain, they do not refer to reality.
>
> Albert Einstein, quoted in Fritjof Capra,
> *The Tao of Physics*

So far we've pretended that we don't know anything about the input except that it is orderable. But this is disingenuous; in practice, we often know a lot about the input and we can use that knowledge to build faster algorithms. In particular, the input is usually a set of numbers, or it can be easily transformed into a set of numbers. And computers are very good with numbers.

Distribute Sorts

If we know that the input is a list of numbers from a known range then we can sort in linear worst cost using a *distribute sort*.

Consider sorting a deck of cards. One way is to divide the pack into aces, kings, queens, and so forth, then sort each group of four cards. The first division takes only one pass since we know that there will only be thirteen kinds of cards, and we can put each card in one of thirteen separate bins. If we assume that we can tell in constant time what kind a particular card is then this pass takes linear time. Alternately, we could divide the pack into its four suits: hearts, diamonds, clubs, and spades, then sort the cards in each suit. Again the first division takes only one pass. In both cases, once we have completed the first phase the second phase does not disturb the order; once we've divided the pack into suits, ordering each suit does not remix the suits. The key point is that we *know* how many different kinds of cards there will be before the sort, and can plan accordingly.

Pause | Will both algorithms work if we have some number of cards from two packs? Will both algorithms work if we have some number of cards from an unknown number of packs?

Now suppose we have n integers, each with at most k digits. The two ways of card sorting suggest two ways of sorting the numbers. We could sort the integers on the most significant (leftmost) digit, then sort all numbers with the same leftmost digit on their second most significant digit, and so on. Or we could sort the integers on the least significant (rightmost) digit, then sort all numbers with the same rightmost digit on their second least significant digit, and so on. Do these two sorts cost the same?

Surprisingly, when sorting numbers it's better to sort from least to most significant digit. This distribute sort is called *radix sort*. See algorithm 4.11. This algorithm uses a lot of storage, but we can reduce it by using linked lists (see chapter two, page 129).

RADIX_SORT($List, lower, upper, digits$)
    { Sort the integers $List[lower..upper]$ in increasing order.
    Each integer is a decimal number in the range $0..10^{digits}$
    Use lists $Sublist[i]$ ($digits \geq i \geq 1$) as temporary storage.
    $upper \geq lower > 0$; $digits > 0$. }

    for i **from** 1 **to** $digits$
       make $Sublist[i]$ empty

    for i **from** $digits$ **downto** 1
       for $next$ **from** $lower$ **to** $upper$
          $k \leftarrow i^{th}$ digit of $List[next]$
          add $List[next]$ to $Sublist[k]$
       make $List$ empty
       for j **from** 1 **to** $digits$
          add $Sublist[j]$ to $List$

Algorithm 4.11

Note that radix sort will not work unless the numbers are in a *fixed* range 0 to m. If k is the largest number of digits then radix sort costs $O((n+m)k)$. This is usually described as a linear time algorithm because k is fixed, but note the hidden log factor; k must be at least $\log_b n$, where b is the base of the numbers.

4.10   Coda—Sorting Out Sorting

> It is an error to believe that rigor in proof is an enemy of simplicity. On the contrary we find it confirmed by numerous examples that the rigorous method is at the same time the simpler and the more easily comprehended. The very effort for rigor forces us to find out simpler methods of proof.
>
> David Hilbert, *"Mathematical Problems,"*
> *Bulletin of the American Mathematical Society, 8, 441*

Why study sorting in such detail? The version of the general structuring problem we've studied is simple but important. Sorting is a basic step in many algorithms; it is estimated that about one-quarter of all computer time is spent sorting.

As we have seen, a select sort is to an insert sort as a split sort is to a merge sort. Linear insert sort is just merge sort with only one element in one part; linear select sort is just quick sort with only one element in one part. All sorting algorithms presented in this chapter are variations of the same basic strategy: split the list into parts, sort each part, and merge the parts. Is there a better way?

Why bother trying to find the best possible sort? Obviously optimal sorting is not practical. We investigate it mostly because it would be interesting to know the minimum possible number of comparisons necessary to sort. Perhaps if we ever find out we will learn something important about algorithms. Probably though we will solve the problem only *after* we learn something important about algorithms!

———✧—✧—✧———

A good theory should be proscriptive, prescriptive, and prospective; it should tell us what cannot work, what has worked, and what may work. Theory is for designers and artisans, not mechanics. The two prongs of attack on the problem of understanding the universe are: the eminently practical versus the completely theoretical, and there is danger for us if we ignore either one for too long. Theoretical doesn't necessarily mean useless, but practical doesn't necessarily mean useful. Goethe said that what we do not understand we do not possess. The world is not as understandable as science would have us believe, but without science the world is not understandable at all. Science costs, but we have no better tool.

This is the end of our three treks through the provinces dominated by comparisons. Everywhere in these provinces we saw well-defined problems and clear-cut solutions with near-optimal performances; the roads are well-tended and well-travelled. In part two we strike out into stranger and more difficult territory. In the next chapter, the first chapter of part two, we continue with our structuring problem, but expand it a great deal to capture something of the complexity and dynamism of large applications.

Endnotes

Computational Ideas

Comparison-swap model, sorting, balanced run strategy, heaps, information lower bound, entropy, space-time tradeoff, placeholder nodes, trickledown, linear merge, binary merge, bubble sort, swap sort, linear insert sort, binary insert sort, linear select sort, heap sort, split sort, merge sort, quick sort, radix sort, distribute sort, count sort, merge insert sort.

Mathematical Ideas

- Using integrals to approximate sums of terms of an increasing function.

- Using Stirling's approximation to estimate $n!$.

- Bounding the number of swaps by counting inversions.

- Viewing search, select, and sort problems as variations of search, and using information theory to capture the informal notion of uncertainty in search.

Definitions

- *complete binary tree:* A complete binary tree is an ordered, rooted binary tree in which every non-leaf node has two children and with all its leaves on one level.

- *left-complete binary tree:* A left-complete binary tree is a complete binary tree with zero or more of its rightmost leaves deleted.

- *heap:* A heap is a rooted binary tree such that the value of any node is at least as large as the values of its children.

- *on-line algorithm:* An on-line algorithm can process its data as it appears.

- *off-line algorithm:* An off-line algorithm needs all its data before running.

- *stable sort:* A stable sort preserves the relative order between two elements whose keys have the same value.

Conventions
- $\lfloor \lg 0 \rfloor = 0$

- $0 \lg 0 = 0$

Constants
- $\lg e = 1.44269\ 50408\ 88963\ 40735 \cdots$

Notation
- $M(m, n) = $ smallest number of comparisons needed to merge two sorted lists of sizes n and m in the worst case.

- $S(n) = $ smallest number of comparisons needed to sort n things in the worst case.

Tools
- A permutation of n orderable elements has at most $\binom{n}{2}$ inversions and the average number of inversions over all permutations is $\binom{n}{2}/2$.

- A left-complete heap costs no more than $2n - 4$ comparisons to build.

- For any non-decreasing function f
$$\int_1^{n+1} f(x)dx \geq \sum_{i=1}^{n} f(i) \geq \int_0^{n} f(x)dx$$

- Stirling's approximation: $n! \approx \sqrt{2\pi n}(n/e)^n$

- $\int \ln x\, dx = x \ln x - x + r$

- $\left(1 + \dfrac{1}{n}\right)^{n+1} \approx e$

- $(n + 1)^{n+1} \approx en^{n+1}$

- Given n probabilities p_i, $\lg n \geq -\sum\limits_{i=1}^{n} p_k \lg p_k \geq 0$

- $g(n) = \lfloor \lg n \rfloor + \lfloor \lg(n-1) \rfloor +$

$$\begin{cases} g(n - 2^{\lfloor \lg n \rfloor - 1}) + g(2^{\lfloor \lg n \rfloor - 1} - 1) & n < 3 \times 2^{\lfloor \lg n \rfloor - 1} \\ g(2^{\lfloor \lg n \rfloor} - 1) + g(n - 2^{\lfloor \lg n \rfloor}) & n \geq 3 \times 2^{\lfloor \lg n \rfloor - 1} \end{cases}$$

$$\Longrightarrow g(n) = 2n - 2\beta(n) - \nu(n)$$

- $g(n) = \begin{cases} 0 & n \leq 1 \\ g(n-1) + \nu(n) + \nu(n-1) & n > 1 \end{cases}$

$$\Longrightarrow g(n) = 2n - 2\beta(n) - \nu(n)$$

- $f(n) = \begin{cases} 0 & n \leq 1 \\ f(\lfloor n/2 \rfloor) + f(\lceil n/2 \rceil) + n - 1 & n > 1 \end{cases}$

$$\Longrightarrow f(n) = n\lceil \lg n \rceil - 2^{\lceil \lg n \rceil} + 1$$

- $f(n) = \begin{cases} 0 & n \leq 1 \\ n - 1 + \dfrac{1}{n} \sum\limits_{i=0}^{n-1} (f(i) + f(n-i-1)) & n > 1 \end{cases}$

$$\Longrightarrow f(n) = 2(n+1)H_n - 4n$$

- $f(n) = \begin{cases} 0 & n \leq 1 \\ n - 1 + \dfrac{2}{n} \sum\limits_{i=0}^{n-1} f(i) & n > 1 \end{cases}$

$$\Longrightarrow f(n) = 2(n+1)H_n - 4n$$

- $nf(n) = n^2 - n + 2\sum\limits_{i=0}^{n-1} f(i) \Longrightarrow f(n) = 2(n+1)H_n - 4n$

- $nf(n) = (n+1)f(n-1) + 2n - 2 \Longrightarrow f(n) = 2(n+1)H_n - 4n$

- $g(n) = \begin{cases} 0 & n = 1 \\ g(n-1) + \dfrac{4(n-1)}{n(n+1)} & n > 1 \end{cases} \Longrightarrow g(n) = 4H_n - \dfrac{8n}{n+1}$

- $f(n) \leq 2f(n/2) + 2\lg n \Longrightarrow f = O(n)$

- $f(n) = n + \min\limits_{0 < i < n} \{f(i) + f(n-i)\} \Longrightarrow f(n) = n(\lceil \lg n \rceil + 1) - 2^{\lceil \lg n \rceil}$

- $f(n) = \begin{cases} 0 & n < 2 \\ 1 & n = 2 \\ f(\lfloor n/2 \rfloor) + g(\lceil n/2 \rceil) + \lfloor n/2 \rfloor & n > 2 \end{cases}$

$$\Longrightarrow f(n) = n\lceil \lg(3n) \rceil - 2n - \left\lfloor \tfrac{1}{3} 2^{\lfloor \lg 6n \rfloor} \right\rfloor + \left\lfloor \tfrac{1}{2} \lg 6n \right\rfloor$$

$$\bullet \; f(n, m) = \begin{cases} n + m - 1 & n < 2m \\ f(\lfloor n/2 \rfloor, m) + m & n \geq 2m \end{cases}$$

$$\implies f(n, m) = m(1 + \lfloor \lg(n/m) \rfloor) + \lfloor n/2^{\lfloor \lg(n/m) \rfloor} \rfloor - 1$$

Notes

For a proof that the entropy function is the only uncertainty measure with all the requisite properties of uncertainty see *Mathematical Foundations of Information Theory*, A. I. Khinchin, Dover, 1957.

Heap sort is the invention of J. W. J. Williams, and it was subsequently improved by Robert Floyd. See "Algorithm 232, Heapsort," J. W. J. Williams, *Communications of the ACM*, 6, 347–348, 1964, and "Algorithm 245, Treesort," R. W. Floyd, *Communications of the ACM*, 7, 701, 1964. The clever observation about improving heap insertion on page 248 is from "Heaps On Heaps," Gaston H. Gonnet and J. Ian Munro, *SIAM Journal on Computing*, 15, 964–971, 1986.

Quick sort is the invention of Antony Hoare. See "Quicksort," C. A. R. Hoare, *Computer Journal*, 5, 10–15, 1962. For an extensive theoretical analysis see *Quicksort*, Robert Sedgewick, Garland, 1980. For an excellent discussion of many of the practical details see *Algorithms from P to NP: Volume I, Design & Efficiency*, Bernard Moret and Henry Shapiro, Benjamin/Cummings, 1991.

The proof that linear merge is optimal whenever $m \leq n \leq \lceil (3m + 1)/2 \rceil$ can be found in "On the Optimality of Linear Merge," Paul Stockmeyer and F. Frances Yao, *SIAM Journal on Computing*, 9, 85–90, 1980. For further work on other optimality bounds see "Improving the Bounds on Optimal Merging," C. Christen, *Proceedings of the 19th Annual Symposium on the Foundations of Computer Science*, IEEE Computer Society, 259–266, 1978. See also "Merging of 4 or 5 Elements with n Elements," Jürgen Schulte Mönting, *Theoretical Computer Science*, 14, 19–37, 1981.

Binary merging is the invention of Frank Hwang and Shen Lin; see "A Simple Algorithm for Merging Two Disjoint Linearly-Ordered Sets," Frank Hwang and Shen Lin, *SIAM Journal on Computing*, 1, 31–39, 1972. Merge insert sort used to be called Ford-Johnson sort, and it was first described in "A Tournament Problem," Lester Ford and Selmer Johnson, *American Mathematical Monthly*, 66, 387–389, 1959.

The breakthrough on optimal sorting that took twenty years to find is the work of Glenn Manacher; it's described in "The Ford-Johnson Sorting Algorithm is Not Optimal," Glenn Manacher, *Journal of the ACM*, 26, 434–440, 1979. See also "Further Results on Near-Optimal Sorting," Glenn Manacher, *Proceedings of the 17th Allerton Conference on Communication, Control and Computing*, 949–960, 1979, and "Significant Improvements to the Ford-Johnson Algorithm for Sorting," T. D. Bui and Mai Thanh, *BIT*, 25, 70–75, 1985. There is much more known than can be fit into this tiny book; but even that is a mere spoonful of the ocean of sorting. You can be sure that this isn't the end of the saga.

The most recent breakthrough on the arbitrary poset cost problem is "On the Complexity of Partial Order Productions," Andrew Chi-Chih Yao, *SIAM Journal on Computing,* 18, 679–689, 1989. Yao shows that the average cost of a poset is of the same order as its worst cost and he gives a tight upper bound on poset cost by showing that a poset with l linear extensions can be produced in $O(n + \lg(n!/l))$ comparisons.

The comment that sorting accounts for one-quarter of all computer time is from "The Input/Output Complexity of Sorting and Related Problems," Alok Aggarwal, and Jeffrey Scott Vitter, *Communications of the ACM,* 31, 1116–1127, 1988.

The second part of problem 9, page 294, is from "An Asymptotically Optimal Algorithm for the Dutch National Flag Problem," James R. Bitner, *SIAM Journal on Computing,* 11, 2, 243–262, 1982. Problem 11, page 294, is from "Sorting and Searching in Multisets," J. Ian Munro and Philip M. Spira, *SIAM Journal on Computing,* 5, 1, 1–9, 1976. For further results see "Determining the Mode," David Dobkin and J. Ian Munro, *Theoretical Computer Science,* 12, 255–263, 1980.

Problem 13, page 294, is from "Optimal Sorting of Seven Element Sets," Ľubor Kollár, *Mathematical Foundations of Computer Science, Proceedings 1986,* J. Gruska, B. Rovan, and J. Wiedermann (editors), 449–457, Springer-Verlag, 1986. Problem 14, page 294, is from "On The Complexity of Computations Under Varying Sets of Primitives," David Dobkin and Richard Lipton, *Journal of Computer and System Sciences,* 18, 86–91, 1979.

Problem 18, page 295, was suggested by "Recursively Rotated Orders and Implicit Data Structures: A Lower Bound," Greg Frederickson, *Theoretical Computer Science,* 29, 75–85, 1985. For an amazing related result see "Developing Implicit Data Structures," J. Ian Munro, *Mathematical Foundations of Computer Science, Proceedings 1986,* J. Gruska, B. Rovan, and J. Wiedermann (editors), 168–176, Springer-Verlag, 1986.

Jump insert sort, discussed in problem 19, page 296, is more usually called shell sort after its inventor Donald Shell. For further references and the best bounds known see "Tight Lower Bounds for Shellsort," Mark Allen Weiss and Robert Sedgewick, *Proceedings of the 1st Scandinavian Workshop on Algorithm Theory,* R. Karlsson and A. Lingas (editors), 255–262, Springer-Verlag, 1988.

Problem 24, page 297, is from "A Unified Lower Bound for Selection and Set Partitioning Problems," David Kirkpatrick, *Journal of the ACM,* 28, 150–165, 1981. Problem 26, page 298, and problem 27, page 298, are from "Heaps On Heaps," Gaston H. Gonnet and J. Ian Munro, *SIAM Journal on Computing,* 15, 964–971, 1986.

Further Reading

There are several good introductions to information theory. I particularly recommend *A Diary of Information Theory,* Alfréd Rényi, John Wiley & Sons, 1984, and *An Introduction to Information Theory,* John R. Pierce, Dover, second edition, 1980. The original papers are reproduced in *The Mathematical Theory of Communication,* Claude E. Shannon and Warren Weaver, University of Illinois Press, 1963.

For a general book on the relation of information to computer science, see the non-technical and amusing *Silicon Dreams: Information, Man, and Machine,* Robert W. Lucky, St. Martin's Press, 1989. For a collection of recent papers on a few applications of information theory to contemporary computer science see *Complexity in Information Theory,* Yaser S. Mostafa (editor), Springer-Verlag, 1988. For a look at applications of information theory in physical science today see *Complexity, Entropy and the Physics of Information,* Wojciech H. Zurek (editor), Addison-Wesley, 1990.

The most comprehensive presentation of optimal sorting problems is *Combinatorial Search,* Martin Aigner, Wiley-Teubner, 1988. Recent sort algorithms adapt their behavior to their input using various measures of disorder; for further references, several new algorithms, and their analyses see *Sorting and Measures of Disorder,* Vladimir Estivill-Castro, doctoral dissertation, Research Report CS–91–07, Department of Computer Science, University of Waterloo, 1991. For recent advances in heap sorting see *Heaps,* Svante Carlsson, doctoral dissertation, Department of Computer Science, Lund University, 1986. For more background and analysis of quick sort see *Quicksort,* Robert Sedgewick, Garland, 1980. For advanced analysis of distribute sorts and related algorithms see *Lecture Notes on Bucket Algorithms,* Luc Devroye, Birkhäuser, 1986. *The Art of Computer Programming: Volume 3, Sorting and Searching,* Donald E. Knuth, Addison-Wesley, 1973, although dated, is the best overall reference for sorting.

Questions

> I hear, I forget;
> I see, I remember;
> I do, I understand.
>
> Chinese proverb

Exercises

1. Show that $\lfloor 3n/2 \rfloor + 1 = \lceil (3n+1)/2 \rceil$.

2. (a) What sorts of things are we referring to when we talk about "the model" under which some computation is performed?

(b) Suggest *three* models that capture (in a reasonable way) the complexity of doing a midterm examination. What things do your models ignore? For example, one measure of complexity might be the number of self-referential questions on the exam. This ignores, among other things, the possibility that the exam is written in a language you don't understand.

3. Define left-complete k-ary trees by analogy with left-complete binary trees. Given an implicit implementation of a left-complete k-ary tree in an array find an access algorithm that given any array location will return the location of its parent and the location of the ith of its k possible children. It may help to think of the locations in base k.

4. An *anagram* of a word is a word made up of the same letters as the first word. For example, *stop, tops,* and *pots* are anagrams. This also works for phrases: *a mop acted wroth?, come adopt wrath?, thaw to drop mace?, what actor moped?,* and *coadapt the worm?,* are anagrams of *compared to what?; flashy glamorisations, also hasty formalising, also flashy amortising, half simian's astrology,* and *stylish anagram folios,* are anagrams of *analysis of algorithms.*
You are given a list of words. Write an algorithm to test whether two words are anagrams of each other in this list of words. Your algorithm should be asymptotically optimal in the number of letter-letter comparisons.

5. Rewrite LINEAR_MERGE_SORT as an iterative algorithm.

6. Consider algorithm 4.12.

   (a) Will this algorithm sort any list?

   (b) What kind of algorithm is it in our classification of algorithms on page 234?

   (c) How many element-element comparisons does it do in the worst case?

   (d) How many element-element swaps does it do in the worst case?

   (e) How many element-element comparisons does it do on average? (You must make an assumption about the probabilities of possible inputs.)

   (f) How many element-element swaps does it do on average?

   (g) Find good lower bounds for the above four measures.

7. Show that $\displaystyle\sum_{i=0}^{k} \frac{i}{2^{i+1}} = 1 - \frac{k+2}{2^{k+1}}$.

```
SIMPLE_SORT (List, lower, upper)
    { Sort List[lower..upper] in increasing order.
    upper ≥ lower > 0. }

    unsorted ← true
    while unsorted
        swaps ← 0
        for index from lower to upper − 1
            if List[index] > List[index + 1]
                List[index] ↔ List[index + 1]
                swaps ← swaps + 1
        if swaps = 0 then unsorted ← false
```

Algorithm 4.12

8. Without using Euler's approximation show that

$$\ln n + 1 \geq H_n \geq \ln(n + 1)$$

9. (a) Show that for $i \geq 3$

$$\frac{1}{i + 2} > \frac{i - 1}{i(i + 1)} > \frac{1}{i + 3}$$

   (b) Find a, b, and c such that for all $i > c$

$$\frac{1}{i + a} > \frac{i - 2}{i(i + 1)} > \frac{1}{i + b}$$

10. Show that $f(n) = \begin{cases} 0 & n \leq 1 \\ f(\lfloor n/2 \rfloor) + f(\lceil n/2 \rceil) + n - 1 & n > 1 \end{cases}$

$$\Longrightarrow f(n) = n\lceil \lg n \rceil - 2^{\lceil \lg n \rceil} + 1$$

11. In the following r and s are arbitrary constants.
    (a) Given that

$$\int x^2 dx = \frac{x^3}{3} + r$$

without integrating show that

$$\int \sqrt{x} \, dx = \frac{2\sqrt{x^3}}{3} + s$$

(b) Given that

$$\int e^x dx = e^x + r$$

show that

$$\int \ln x\, dx = x \ln x - x + s$$

12. Show that $\left(\dfrac{en}{k}\right)^k \geq \dbinom{n}{k} \geq \left(\dfrac{n}{k}\right)^k$.

13. Show that

$$f(n) = n + \min_{1 \leq i \leq n} \{i \lg i + (n-i)\lg(n-i)\} \Longrightarrow f \approx n \lg n$$

14. Use constructive induction to find f's growth rate if

$$f(n) = f(n/a) + f(n - n/a) + O(n)$$

15. Find f's growth rate if
    (a) $f(n) \leq f(\sqrt{n}) + \lg \sqrt{n}$
    (b) $f(n) \leq \sqrt{n} f(\sqrt{n}) + \dfrac{n \lg n}{2}$

16. HEAP_SORT exploits the savings from finding the largest and second largest simultaneously. Design and analyze a sort that exploits the savings from finding the largest and smallest simultaneously. As with HEAP_SORT, to do this efficiently you will need to design a new structure.

17. Algorithm 4.13 is a first cut at a recursive linear merge. The algorithm can only use constant extra storage (not counting storage necessary to support the recursion). Finish the algorithm (including *precondition* and *initialwork*).

18. Algorithm 4.14 is an alternative to SPLIT (algorithm 3.7, page 193).

    (a) What does this algorithm do when *lower = upper*?

    (b) Is the output of algorithm 4.14 different from that of algorithm 3.7?

    (c) Show that algorithm 4.14 correctly splits *List*.

19. LINEAR_SELECT_SORT finds the next largest of the remaining elements without exploiting any information found in previous scans.

    (a) Explain why it is better in the worst case to break the list into two, find the largest of each part, then find the overall largest.

ZIPPER_MERGE(*List*, *lower*, *mid*, *upper*)
  { Merge *List*[*lower*..*mid*] and *List*[*mid* + 1..*upper*],
where each is sorted in increasing order.
Use only constant extra storage (not counting recursion support).
precondition. }

initialwork

if *List*[*lower*] > *List*[*mid* + 1]
   List[*lower*] $\leftrightarrow$ *List*[*mid* + 1]
ZIPPER_MERGE(*List*, *lower* + 1, *mid*, *upper*)

Algorithm 4.13

SPLIT(*List*, *lower*, *upper*, *pivot_loc*)
  { Split *List*[*lower*..*upper*] into two parts: those less than
List[*pivot_loc*] on the left and those greater than it on the right.
Return the pivot's new position.
upper $\geq$ *pivot_loc* $\geq$ *lower* > 0. }

pivot $\leftarrow$ *List*[*pivot_loc*]
List[*lower*] $\leftrightarrow$ *List*[*pivot_loc*]
low $\leftarrow$ *lower* ; *high* $\leftarrow$ *upper*
while *high* > *low*
   while *upper* $\geq$ *low* **and** *pivot* $\geq$ *List*[*low*]
      low $\leftarrow$ *low* + 1
   while *high* $\geq$ *lower* **and** *List*[*high*] > *pivot*
      high $\leftarrow$ *high* − 1
   if *high* > *low* **then** *List*[*low*] $\leftrightarrow$ *List*[*high*]
pivot_loc $\leftarrow$ *high* ; *List*[*lower*] $\leftrightarrow$ *List*[*pivot_loc*]
return *pivot_loc*

Algorithm 4.14

(b) *Quadratic select sort* divides the list into $\sqrt{n}$ pieces, finds the largest of each piece, then finds the overall largest. Explain why this improves the worst case.

20. To win a bet you want to find all words in an on-line dictionary that remain words when you append "s" and "ss." Eight such words are:

bra, care, deadline, marque, needle, ogre, posse, and *prince.* Suppose the dictionary is in sorted order. What is the most efficient way to find all such words?

21. Given an $n \times m$ array of numbers where each of the n rows of m numbers are sorted in increasing order from left to right.

    (a) Show that if we sort the numbers in each column in increasing order from top to bottom then the rows are still sorted in increasing order from left to right.

    (b) Will the rows still be in increasing order from left to right if we sort the columns in decreasing order from top to bottom?

22. Find the growth rate of the worst cost of a merge sort that splits the problem into three parts, solves the subproblems, then uses linear merge to recombine them.

23. While considering various ways to reduce a problem using divide and conquer you examine the following general recurrence:

$$f(n) = \begin{cases} a & n = 1 \\ bf(n/c) + dn & n > 1 \end{cases}$$

    (a) Solve the recurrence by assuming that n is a power of c.

    (b) Why is it reasonable to assume that n is a power of c?

    (c) What happens if $b = c$?

    (d) When is $f(n) = O(n^2)$?

Problems

1. Find f's growth rate if $f(n) \leq f(2^{\sqrt{\lg n}}) + 1$.

2. Consider the following game: Someone tells you a sequence of n decimal digits (0 to 9) and you are to produce the smallest n-digit number you can. You are allowed to choose the position of each digit on hearing it, but after choosing a position for the ith digit you cannot move it after hearing the $(i + 1)^{th}$.

    (a) What is your average score if you select each digit's position at random from the remaining positions?

    (b) What strategy produces the smallest average score?

3. We wish to sort a bag of n nuts and n bolts by size in the dark. We can compare the sizes of a nut and a bolt by attempting to screw one into the other. This operation tells us that either the nut is bigger than the bolt; the bolt is bigger than the nut; or they are the same size (and so fit together). Because it is dark we are not allowed to compare nuts directly or bolts directly.
   How many fitting operations do we need to sort the nuts and bolts in the worst case?

4. You are given a pile of n coins and you may flip the first $m \leq n$ coins as a group.

   (a) What is the least number of flips needed to make sure that the coins are all heads up in the worst case?

   (b) What is the least average number of flips needed to make sure that the coins are all heads up if each arrangement of heads and tails occurs with uniform probability?

   (c) What are the worst and average costs if the cost of each flip is proportional to the number of coins flipped?

5. What is the average number of comparisons of LINEAR_SELECT_SORT?

6. We have seen that

$$n f(n) \;=\; (n+1)f(n-1) + n \qquad \Longrightarrow \quad f = O(n \lg n)$$

and

$$n^2 f(n) \;=\; (n^2 - 1)f(n-1) + n^2 \quad \Longrightarrow \quad f = O(n)$$

   (a) Show that

   i. $(n-1)f(n) \;=\; (n+1)f(n-1) \qquad\qquad \Longrightarrow f = O(n)$

   ii. $n^2 f(n) \;=\; (n^2 - 1)f(n-1) + n \;\Longrightarrow f = O(\lg n)$

   (b) Find f's growth rate if

   i. $n^k f(n) = (n^k - 1)f(n-1) + n^l$

   ii. $n^k f(n) = (n^k + 1)f(n-1) + n^l$

7. Show that

   (a) $\displaystyle\sum_{i=1}^{\lfloor \lg n \rfloor} (n \bmod 2^i) = n = \sum_{i=0}^{\lfloor \lg n \rfloor} 2^i (\lfloor n/2^i \rfloor \bmod 2)$

   (b) $\displaystyle\sum_{i=1}^{n} i \bmod 2 = \lceil n/2 \rceil$

(c) $\displaystyle\sum_{i=1}^{n} i(i \bmod 2) = \lceil n/2 \rceil^2$

(d) $\displaystyle\sum_{i=1}^{n} \lfloor i/2 \rfloor (i \bmod 2) = \binom{\lceil n/2 \rceil}{2}$

8. Given that $\displaystyle\sum_{i=1}^{n} \lfloor i/2 \rfloor = \lfloor n^2/4 \rfloor$, show that $\displaystyle\sum_{i=1}^{n} \lceil i/2 \rceil = \lceil n(n+2)/4 \rceil$.

9. We are given a sequence of n pebbles colored red, white, or blue, and we have to arrange them so that all red pebbles precede all white pebbles, and all white pebbles precede all blue pebbles. We are allowed two operations: $color(i)$, which tells us the color of the ith pebble, and $swap(i, j)$, which swaps the ith and j^{th} pebbles.

   (a) Find an algorithm that minimizes the number of swaps if we are only allowed to test each pebble's color *once*. This is the *Dutch national flag problem.*

   (b) Find an algorithm that uses the least number of swaps on average where each of the 3^n pebble colorings are equally likely. Solve the problem using only a constant amount of extra space.

10. Show that $\displaystyle\binom{2n}{n} = \frac{2^{2n}}{\sqrt{\pi n}}(1 + O(1/n))$.

11. Throughout this chapter we have assumed that the input does not have duplicated elements. Show that if the input has duplicates of multiplicities $m_1, m_2, \ldots, m_k$ then sorting costs

$$O\left(n \lg n - \sum_{i=1}^{k} m_i \lg m_i + n\right)$$

12. Show that
    (a) $M(m,n) \;\leq\; M(m, n+1).$
    (b) $M(m+k, n) \;\leq\; M(m,n) + M(k,n).$
    (c) $M(m,n) \;\leq\; M(m, \lfloor n/2 \rfloor) + m.$

13. Show that the information lower bound on the average cost of sorting is achievable for $n \leq 6$ but not for $n = 7$.
    Show that any average case optimal sorting algorithm sorting seven elements needs at least $62416/(7!)$ comparisons.

14. The *element uniqueness* problem is to decide whether any two of n orderable elements are equal using only element-element comparisons. Show that the element uniqueness problem requires $\Omega(n \lg n)$ comparisons in the worst case.

15. (a) What is the smallest number of comparisons to decide whether one array is a permutation of another?

   (b) Can this bound be used to give a lower bound on sorting?

16. You have two arrays. The elements of each separate array are distinct. Viewing them as clockwise rings where the first location follows the last, what is the smallest number of comparisons needed to tell whether one array is a rotation of the other if

   (a) You know that they are rotations of each other.

   (b) You don't know that they are rotations of each other.

17. Many things influence the choice of one algorithm over another. Suppose you have an array of n elements, and you wish to rotate the list in a different sense to the last question. You wish to move the first $i < n$ elements to the end of the array and the last $n - i$ elements to the front of the array while otherwise preserving the elements' order. Design and analyze at least five algorithms to solve this problem. For each algorithm, consider

   - The amount of space it uses.
   - The number of element shifts it does.
   - The number of function calls and the depth of recursion (if your algorithm is recursive).
   - The order of accessing array elements. (For large arrays accessing widely separated elements might cause paging.)
   - How difficult it is to program.
   - How difficult it would be to understand someone else's program.

   Of your algorithms, which would be the most useful in the widest context? Is it optimal with respect to any of the above measures?

18. If a list is kept in an array and we have to insert and delete many elements when we search for them then it is undesirable to maintain sorted order. Let's keep the elements in sorted order but "forget" where the list begins. As we insert and delete elements we allow the list to rotate cyclically. From the beginning to some point, say i, we have i elements in increasing order, then from the $(i + 1)^{th}$ to the end we have $n - i - 1$ elements in increasing order, such that the nth is no bigger than the first, but we don't know i.

   (a) Show that we can find an element in a rotated list in at most $2\lceil \lg(n + 1) \rceil$ comparisons.

(b) Show that we can improve this worst cost to $\lceil \lg(n+1) \rceil + \lceil \sqrt{\lg n} \rceil$.

(c) Show that we require at least $\lg n + \sqrt{\lg n} + o(\sqrt{\lg n})$ comparisons in the worst case.

19. The trouble with local swap sorts is that they only reduce disorder locally; they only compare neighboring elements. Instead we should try to reduce disorder "in the large" before trying to reduce it "in the small."

Every sort algorithm can be rewritten so that it sorts $L[k]$, $L[k+l]$, $L[k+2l]$, ..., $L[k+\lfloor(n-k)/l\rfloor l]$, where $n \geq l \geq k$. Call this *l-sorting* (1-sorting is then just normal sorting).

Now we can write a sort that first $(n/10)$-sorts then 1-sorts, say. The two possible advantages of this sort are that after the $(n/10)$-sorting, several well-separated elements are in order relative to each other and their various contributions to the number of inversions are reduced. So, perhaps, the list is much less disordered when we come to 1-sort.

(a) Show that for any k and m, if a list is k-sorted and we m-sort then it is still k-sorted.

(b) Use this observation together with all integers of the form $2^i 3^j < n$ (where the increments diminish), to show that algorithm 4.15 sorts in $O(n \lg^2 n)$ in the worst case.

JUMP_INSERT_SORT($List, lower, upper$)
    { Sort $List[lower..upper]$ in increasing order. $upper \geq lower > 0$. }

    Generate the list $Jump[1..number]$
    for $index_1$ **from** $number$ **downto** 1
        for $index_2$ **from** $Jump[index_1] + 1$ **to** $upper$
            $save \leftarrow List[index_2]$
            $step \leftarrow index_2 - Jump[index_1]$
            while $step > 0$ **and** $List[step] > save$
                $List[step + Jump[index_1]] \leftarrow List[step]$
                $step \leftarrow step - Jump[index_1]$
            $List[step + Jump[index_1]] \leftarrow save$

Algorithm 4.15

20. Recall that $\beta(n)$ is the number of ones in the binary representation of n and $\nu(n)$ is the number of times two divides n. Show that

    (a) $\beta(n) + \beta(m) - \beta(n+m)$ is the number of carries on adding n to m in binary.

    (b) $\beta(n) + \beta(m) \geq \beta(n+m)$

    (c) $\beta(n-1) = \beta(n) + \nu(n) - 1$

    (d) $\beta(n) = \beta(n - 2^{\lfloor \lg n \rfloor}) + 1$

21. If $f(1) = 1$, show that

$$f(n) = n - \beta(n) + 1 \iff \begin{cases} f(n) = f(n-1) + \nu(n) \\ \\ f(n) = f(\lfloor n/2 \rfloor) + \lfloor n/2 \rfloor \end{cases}$$

22. If $f(1) = 1$, show that

$$f(n) = n \iff \begin{cases} f(n) = f(n-1) + 1 \\ \\ f(n) = f(\lfloor n/2 \rfloor) + \lceil n/2 \rceil \\ \\ f(n) = 2f(\lfloor n/2 \rfloor) + n \bmod 2 \end{cases}$$

23. (a) Show that the worst cost of fixing an n-node heap obeys the recurrence

$$f(n) = \begin{cases} 0 & n \leq 1 \\ f(n-1) + \nu(n) + \nu(n-1) & n > 1 \end{cases}$$

    where $\nu(n)$ is the number of times two divides n.

    (b) Show that $f(n) = 2n - 2\beta(n) - \nu(n)$, where $\beta(n)$ is the number of ones in the binary representation of n.

    (c) Show that for all $n \geq 3$, $f(n) \leq 2n - 4$

24. Show that

$$P(i-1, 1, n-i) \geq \begin{cases} n + i - 3 + \displaystyle\sum_{j=0}^{i-2} \left\lceil \lg \dfrac{n-i+2}{i+j} \right\rceil & \dfrac{n}{3} \geq i \geq 1 \\ \\ \left\lfloor \dfrac{3n+i+1}{2} \right\rfloor - 3 & \dfrac{n}{2} \geq i > \dfrac{n}{3} \end{cases}$$

25. If the elements we want to sort are long records we don't want to move the records unless we have to. If we can use more storage, we can maintain n pointers that we update after each comparison instead of moving the compared elements.

Given an array of records and an array of pointers pointing to their correct positions in sorted order, move the records into their sorted positions in the least number of moves.

26. By building an adversary, or otherwise, show that in the worst case inserting a new element into an n element heap can require $\lceil \lg \lg(n+2) \rceil - 2$ comparisons.

27. Show that we can extract the root of an n element heap and reorder the heap in no more than $\lg n + \lg^* n + O(1)$ comparisons. ($\lg^* n$ is the iterated logarithm function, defined in chapter one, page 51.)

28. By dividing by n we can transform the recurrence

$$f(n) = \begin{cases} 1 & n \leq 1 \\ \dfrac{n}{g(n)} f(g(n)) + n & n > 1 \end{cases}$$

to the recurrence

$$h(n) = \begin{cases} 1 & n \leq 1 \\ h(g(n)) + 1 & n > 1 \end{cases}$$

$h(n)$ counts the number of levels of recursion of $f(n)$.
Define $F(i,k)$ as follows

$$F(i,k) = \begin{cases} k & i = 0 \\ 2^{F(i-1,k)} & i > 0 \end{cases}$$

and define the iterated log function as follows

$$\lg^{(i)} n = \begin{cases} n & i = 0 \\ \lfloor \lg(\lg^{(i-1)} n) \rfloor & i > 0 \end{cases}$$

Let $\lg^* n$ be the smallest i such that $\lg^{(i)} n < 2$.

(a) Show that $\lg^{(i+1)} n = \lg^{(i)}(\lfloor \lg n \rfloor)$.

(b) Show that if $i \leq \lg^* n$ and $n \geq 2$ then $F(i, \lg^{(i)} n) \leq n$.

(c) Consider the following five recurrences. For each of the recurrences, $f_i(n) = 1$ when $n \leq 1$. Assume that the recurrences use only integer operations; that is, take a/b, $\sqrt{a}$, and $\lg a$ as $\lfloor a/b \rfloor$, $\lfloor \sqrt{a} \rfloor$, and $\lfloor \lg a \rfloor$, respectively.

$$f_0(n) = f_0(n-1) + n$$
$$f_1(n) = 2f_1(n/2) + n$$
$$f_2(n) = \sqrt{n} f_2(\sqrt{n}) + n$$
$$f_3(n) = \frac{n}{2^{\sqrt{\lg n}}} f_3(2^{\sqrt{\lg n}}) + n$$
$$f_*(n) = \frac{n}{\lg n} f_*(\lg n) + n$$

The transform of each recurrence is: $h_0(n) = h_0((\lg^{(0)} n) - 1) + 1$

$$h_1(n) = h_1(2^{(\lg^{(1)} n) - 1}) + 1$$
$$h_2(n) = h_2(2^{2^{(\lg^{(2)} n) - 1}}) + 1$$
$$h_3(n) = h_3(2^{2^{2^{(\lg^{(3)} n) - 1}}}) + 1$$
$$h_*(n) = h_*(\lfloor \lg n \rfloor) + 1$$

Rewrite the five recurrences using the function F and *no* explicit exponentiation. (Hint for the last recurrence: The argument of h_* on the right-hand side needs only to be $\Theta(\lfloor \lg n \rfloor)$.)

(d) Show that if $\lg^* n \geq i \geq 0$ and $n \geq 2$ then

$$h_i(n) = \begin{cases} 1 & n \leq 1 \\ h_i(F(i, \lg^{(i)} n - 1)) + 1 & n > 1 \end{cases}$$

$$\implies h_i(n) = O(i + \lg^{(i)} n)$$

Research

1. Show that there is no bounded length optimal sorting algorithm.

2. What is the best way to search for a phrase in a phrase dictionary? Assume that phrases are ordered alphabetically in the dictionary and that the only operations allowed on phrases are comparisons of the letters making up the phrases. Suppose we are searching for the phrase "the moon is a balloon." We can use binary search with the whole phrase but there may be better ways to do the search in less comparisons, since each such "comparison" seems to force twenty-one letter-letter comparisons. Such a search takes up to $n\lceil \lg(m+1)\rceil$ letter-letter comparisons if the phrase is n letters long and the dictionary is m phrases long.

   (a) Find a better algorithm or show that $n \lg m$ is asymptotically optimal.

   (b) Generalize your algorithm to match phrases that can occur as parts of other phrases.

3. Suppose we "sort" in such a way that for any element in the list we could guarantee that it was no more than c positions away from its correct location. Call this *c-sorting*. If $c = 0$ then we have the normal definition of sorting.
   Does c-sorting take appreciably less time than $\Omega(n \lg n)$ in the worst case?
   How can we search a c-sorted list optimally in the worst case?
   We can check that a list is sorted in $n - 1$ comparisons. How many comparisons are necessary to check that a list is c-sorted? How about a probabilistic check? Is it worthwhile to include such a check before attempting any sorting?

4. Find a sequence of shift values to sort in $O(n \lg n)$ using JUMP_INSERT_SORT or show that none is possible.

5. What is the exact cost to create a heap?

6. (a) Find $M(m, n)$ or show that it has no universal expression.

   (b) Find $S(n)$ or show that it has no universal expression.

   (c) How many comparisons does it cost to build an arbitrary poset on n elements in the worst case starting from n singletons?

7. Across:

1 Naive organizer effervesces before dinner end. (6,4)

6 Sound the rebuke? That's not hip. (3)

9 Join and put power in me. (5)

10 Sounds like Algernon cultivates a seaweed producer. (5,4)

11 Bad aim, peril for a regal moth. (8)

12 Losing its head sounds incorrect, but it's piercing. (5)

14 Best choose before mail gets sorted. (7)

16 Spanish nobelist embraced by smooch oaf. (5)

18 Accomplice backtracks about Northern trap. (7)

20 Beat, I rest at theater, man. (7)

21 Conrad ardently contains an invisible warning. (5)

23 Occasional sometimes goes with table. (8)

26 It is said some may shun addition. (9)

27 Greek's maybe, or maybe Magis on the move. (5)

28 Certainly sounds like any holds on nothing! (4)

29 Atavisms about accounts. (10)

Down:

1 Weapon failure. (4)

2 Stop oxygen rhythm with a pressure gauge. (9)

3 Example found in deception? There's loyalty for you! (5)

4 Misfire at a slip in space. (7)

5 In simple language, awkwardly carry back in the rear. (7)

6 Instrument of horrible pain with taboo ending. (5)

7 Endless tragic mimes come to stay. (10)

8 Pile order gives odd sop taken to heart. (4,4)

13 Establishes order without end. Come on after Paris. (10)

15 Fierce baboon or an emergency routine for men only! (8)

17 Quick! Look up! Technique has headless thing for company. (7)

19 A snake or lizard may possibly rile pet. (7)

20 Sort sounds like a series of mountains. (7)

22 Lacking treats, demonstrate evil spirit. (5)

24 Verdant desert island? Also, a sister holds the answer. (5)

25 The academic goal is a high place. (4)

PART TWO

Sea Change

⚜⚜⚜

Nothing of him doth fade,
But doth suffer a sea-change
Into something rich and strange.

William Shakespeare, *The Tempest, I, II*

NOW THAT we've got the basics we can look at more complicated, and more realistic, problems. The province of comparison-oriented problems that we've just left is only a microcosm of the continent of analysis; it's important because problems there are clear-cut so it happens to be well explored. Now we're going out into wilder domains. Our goal in subsequent chapters is to learn how to deal with complexity. In chapter five we look at the problem of solving problems with a complex system of related parts. In chapter six we examine the problem of solving problems on numbers. And in chapter seven we look back the way we've come and look forward to future exploration.

5

GRAPHS

Banach once told me, "Good mathematicians see analogies between theorems or theories, the very best ones see analogies between analogies."

Stanis law Ulam, *Adventures of a Mathematician*

I N THIS chapter we explore graphs. A graph is a collection of relationships between things. Graphs help us solve problems involving complex systems since we can describe many such systems in terms of the relationships between their parts. It's often easier to see what makes a problem difficult once the problem has been sufficiently abstracted, and this sometimes makes the problem easier to solve.

A *graph* is a mapping from a collection of nodes to itself. Two nodes are related if there is a link, or edge, between them. We won't consider relations where one node may be related to itself, or where two nodes can be related more than once. Graphs without these complications are called *simple graphs;* all of our graphs will be simple. Since only relations between nodes matter, we can think of nodes as beads and edges as strings joining them; so although the two figures in figure 5.1 look different, they are the same graph. There is a way to map each node in the first graph to a node in the second graph so that two nodes are related in the first graph if and only if they are related in the second graph. Such graphs are called **isomorphic.** Figure 5.2 shows all non-isomorphic graphs with up to three nodes. Unlike posets, relationships captured by graphs do not have to be order relations.

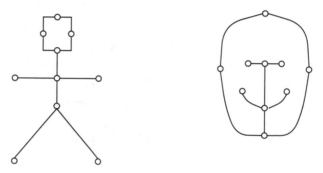

Figure 5.1   Two isomorphic graphs

Pause   Show that if we label the nodes in figure 5.1 then there are eight mappings between the two graphs that preserve node relations.

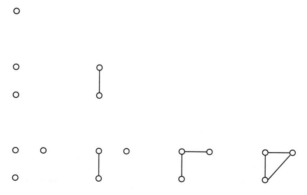

Figure 5.2   All graphs with up to three nodes

Stating a problem in terms of graphs often makes the problem easier. First, graphs encourage us to discard irrelevant detail—clearing away the undergrowth simplifies the problem. Second, the problem may be a disguised form of an already solved graph problem—in which case we can use the known solution. Alternately, we may find that the problem is equivalent to a hard graph problem—in which case we know we're in for a fight. Looking at a problem as a graph problem encourages us to ignore detail, and that makes problem abstraction and problem classification easier. Graphs encourage us to squint.

For example, the road system and the phone system look very different, but their main purpose is to get things from one place to another. We can model both as graphs if we think of a phone call as being the same as a car: their primary function is to get from one place to another.

Let's model places as nodes and connections between places as edges between the nodes. To allow for one-way streets we can put directions on the edges of the graph, making a *directed graph*. To allow for traffic limitations on streets and bridges, we can put numbers on a graph's edges, making a *network*.

When a bridge goes out, or a road is blocked, a traffic engineer wants to know if she still can route traffic to reach Manhattan. When a Canadian trunk line goes out, or a communications satellite malfunctions, a communications engineer wants to know if he still can route calls to reach Alaska. Both engineers want to know whether their networks are still *connected*. The traffic engineer wants to know the maximum traffic a network of roads can bear. The communications engineer wants to know how many calls can be placed at the same time. Both engineers want to find their network's *maximum flow*. When it rains, traffic flows change; when there is a solar flare, information flows change. Both engineers want to know their network's *cheapest paths*.

Since we can think of most systems as a collection of things with some spatial or temporal relationship between them, we can use graphs to model all sorts of complex systems. We can use them to model electrical circuits, communications networks, transportation networks, large molecules, large programs, economic systems, and industrial processes. Further, because of their generality, their applications are as diverse as their application areas: we can use them for task sequencing, routing design, chip layout, transportation analysis, and flow control.

We have already seen several kinds of graphs. A rooted binary tree is a graph with five properties: it is directed; it is connected; no node has more than two children; no node has more than one parent; and it has one node with no parent (the root). A singly linked list is also a graph; it's a rooted tree whose nodes have at most one child each. A poset is a graph too. It too is directed, but it may have several roots and each node may have many children.

Further, we can turn almost any problem into a graph problem. For example, here's one way to think of the towers of Hanoi problem as a graph problem: Think of it as a state-space problem (as in the max-min problem of chapter three), and describe a position by the number of disks on the three pegs. The problem is to transform $(n, 0, 0)$ into $(0, 0, n)$ in the smallest number of moves. This is equivalent to finding a particular kind of path in a particular kind of graph.

Again, consider a salesman who has to visit each of n cities and return to his starting city without visiting any other city twice. This problem can be turned into the problem of finding a path through a graph whose nodes are cities and whose edges are roads (or airline routes). Such a path is called a **hamiltonian cycle** after the nineteenth-century Irish mathematician William Hamilton, who designed a game around the problem in 1857. A graph that has a hamiltonian cycle is called **hamiltonian**. (See figure 5.3.) If we now add costs to the edges of the graph—making it a network—then finding a cheapest hamiltonian cycle of the network is called the **travelling salesman problem**. As we shall discover in the last chapter, this problem is probably quite hard;[1] currently, solutions for only a hundred cities can take millions of years! So if your problem on communications networks, chemical isomers, or integrated circuits, is equivalent to the travelling salesman problem, then you know you're in trouble.

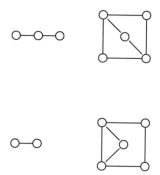

Figure 5.3 Two hamiltonian (top) and two non-hamiltonian graphs (bottom)

In contrast to the hamiltonian cycle problem, the first ever graph problem was also the problem of finding a particular kind of path; this time the path had to pass through every *edge* once before returning to its start. The problem has become known as the **Königsberg bridges problem,** after the city it was intended for. In 1736, seventy years before Hamilton's birth, Leonhard Euler solved this problem by showing that there was a simple

---

[1]Not to keep you in suspense any longer, both the hamiltonian cycle problem and the travelling salesman problem are $\mathcal{NP}$-complete.

test for any graph, and if the graph passed the test then it had at least one appropriate path, called an **eulerian cycle,** otherwise it did not. That test leads to a simple algorithm to find such cycles. So whereas finding hamiltonian cycles appears to be very hard, finding eulerian cycles is easy.

Graph problems are different from previous problems since there are now *two* input variables—the number of nodes (n), and the number of links (l). In this chapter we will take n as the number of nodes and l as the number of links, or edges.

5.1   Structures

> It is a profoundly erroneous truism. . . that we
> should cultivate the habit of thinking of what
> we are doing. The precise opposite is the case.
> Civilization advances by extending the number
> of important operations which we can perform
> without thinking about them.
>
> Alfred North Whitehead,
> *Introduction to Mathematics*

Before we design our graph algorithms we need to design some structures to hold our data. Our data is now more structured than the simple lists of chapters two, three, and four. Three things drive us to consider structures more complicated than lists.

First, so far we've concentrated on reducing the number of times we do one operation (an addition, an assignment, a comparison, a swap). But in this chapter we will build structures to reduce the overall work done when interrelated operations manipulate data; usually no single operation accurately reflects the overall work done.[2]

Second, so far we've assumed that our data is fixed, but more often our data is *dynamic,* it changes over time. We must now widen our model to include space as well as time; our model of cost should now include the structure's size, since with dynamic data it can grow and shrink. Let's take the number of elements in the structure as a measure of its size.

Third, so far we've implicitly assumed that we can analyze each problem instance independently of any others. This isn't realistic when we have a long sequence of actions and a set of operations to realize them, some of

---

[2] "There is more to life than increasing its speed." Mohandas K. Gandhi.

which may not be used in any one sequence. The worst cost of any one operation is no longer helpful; it's better to average over a representative sequence of operations. Instead of worrying only about the work done in a snapshot, we now have to average over the time the structure will be alive.

Let's assume that cost is proportional to the number of times any element in the structure is touched, used, or accessed over a sequence of operations. This is the *touch-based model.* Further, let's add one more dimension to the five dimensions of analysis we developed in chapter one (page 24); we now expand the input to include sequences of operations. Each operation separately has a worst cost, an average cost, and so on, and now we modify our cost function to reflect the cost of a sequence of operations. The best way to do that is to shift attention from the algorithm to the structure.

It often happens in complex algorithms that choosing a good structure clears some of the murkiness and makes it easier to see that the algorithm is correct. As applications become more complex, algorithm correctness grows in importance. Paradoxically, correctness is more important in computer science than even in mathematics; most theorems are used less than a million times a year, but many programs may be used a million times a day. In contrast to previous chapters, in this chapter whether an algorithm is correct will be a major issue.

A well-chosen structure lets us separate concerns so that neither its implementer nor its user has to worry about many things at once. This idea of *data abstraction* forces us to identify exactly what we can do to the data. It hides the data format from users of the structure (including the original programmer); it encourages application program modularity and simplicity; and it lets us change the implementation without changing application programs. These are powerful program simplifiers. Further, a well-chosen structure can reduce an algorithm's storage cost and overhead. Finally, a well-chosen structure makes algorithms easier to analyze.

Structures as Restaurants

Structures are like restaurants. If we think of manipulating data as shaping or cooking food, then in past chapters we cooked at home; now, because of the complexity of the meals, we're going to eat out. Whereas before we cooked everything ourselves, now we take the restauranteur's, the chef's, and the customer's, point of view. Each restaurant serves some collection of dishes. Each dish is the result of an operation on food (data). Some restaurants, like fast food chains, are strongly typed; we can't get any variation on the menu—the most we can do is discard things already given. Others, the really expensive ones, allow us to tell the chef exactly how to do our filet mignon. The restaurant is the structure, the chef is the implementation, the menu is the set of operations supported, the customer is the application, and the kitchen door is the information hider.

In previous chapters we didn't have a kitchen door hiding the implementation. Because we were the chefs, we were always in the kitchen and we paid obsessive attention to perfecting each dish. We built everything from scratch for each new dish, sometimes even going so far as the analogue of grinding our own flour. Until recently, programming didn't have a kitchen door either. But now we realize that with enormously complex applications, it's often better to package generic meals so that we can take them for granted. A further advantage is that packaging allows levels of restaurants, where, like cafeterias, one restaurant orders submeals from other restaurants then further packages them. For example, a heap is a structure, but heaps themselves can be used as an implementation of more general structures called *priority queues*. Further, heaps can themselves be implemented implicitly in an array, or with explicit pointers, or with arrays to simulate pointers.

IF STRUCTURES WERE RESTURAUNTS,
YOUR CODE WOULD BE A LEMONADE STAND.

In the past, if we wanted the best steak we surveyed all valid chefs and chose the one that did steak best (the model defines which chefs were valid and it defines what best means). But a meal consists of more than a steak, and the epicure will choose a restaurant that may not have the best steak, but which has good salads too. Also, in times past we were thinking of ourselves only as chefs, now we have to worry about the chef, the customer, and the restauranteur. Their interests do not always coincide.

For example, restauranteurs want to maximize their performance over a long sequence of customers. This shows how much more complicated our problems have become. The restauranteur must worry not only about the demands of one particular customer, but the demands of all customers where some customers may show up more often than others. We have to expand our notion of problem instance to encompass sequences of problem instances.

We can think of many problems in terms of operations on sets of elements. Given an element x and a structure S, tables 5.1 and 5.2 list some of the things we might want to do. If these operations are common, it would be foolish to rewrite them every time we write a new program using some or all of them. It's better to write and debug them once then forget about them. Learning judo, or any other martial art, is like slowly programming a subconscious computer that will control you in combat conditions. If you try to keep conscious control of all necessary subroutines, you will never master the complexity of movement needed for fast combat.

CREATE (S)	Make an empty structure and call it S
DESTROY (S)	Remove S
COPY (S)	Make a copy of S
UNION (S_1, S_2)	Join the structures S_1 and S_2
INSERT (x, S)	Add x to S
DELETE (x, S)	Remove x from S
FIND (x, S)	Find x, if it is in S
EMPTY (S)	Test whether S is empty
FULL (S)	Test whether S is full
FIND_SIZE (S)	Find the number of elements in S
FIND_STRUCTURE (x)	Find the structure to which x belongs

Table 5.1 Some general structure operations

Structures aren't interesting if the operations are independent of each other. If they're independent we can improve each operation without worrying about any others, as we have done in previous chapters. So let's focus on structures where two or more operations are interrelated. For example, Insert and Delete have opposite effects on Finds; the more we

Operations assuming timed elements

FIND_YOUNGEST(S)	Find the element earliest inserted in S
FIND_OLDEST(S)	Find the element last inserted in S
FIND_TIME(i, S)	Find the ith inserted element in S
FIND_AGE(x, S)	Find the time x was inserted in S
FIND_BEFORE(x, S)	Find the element in S inserted before x
FIND_AFTER(x, S)	Find the element in S inserted after x
GET_YOUNGEST(S)	Delete and return the earliest element in S
GET_OLDEST(S)	Delete and return the latest element in S

Operations assuming linear structures

INSERT_BEFORE(x, i, S)	Add x before the ith element in S
INSERT_AFTER(x, i, S)	Add x after the ith element in S
FIND_FIRST(S)	Find the first element in S
FIND_LAST(S)	Find the last element in S
FIND_POSITION(i, S)	Find the ith element in S
FIND_PLACE(x, S)	Find the position number of x in S
FIND_PREDECESSOR(x, S)	Find the element in S preceding x
FIND_SUCCESSOR(x, S)	Find the element in S following x
GET_FIRST(S)	Delete and return the first element in S
GET_LAST(S)	Delete and return the last element in S

Operations assuming orderable elements

SPLIT(x, S)	Partition S into two disjoint structures with all elements less than x in one structure
FIND_NEAREST(x, S)	Find the element in S closest to x in value
FIND_SMALLEST(S)	Find the smallest element in S
FIND_LARGEST(S)	Find the largest element in S
FIND_ORDER(i, S)	Find the ith largest element in S
FIND_RANK(x, S)	Find x's rank in S
FIND_SMALLER(x, S)	Find the largest element in S smaller than x
FIND_LARGER(x, S)	Find the smallest element in S larger than x
GET_SMALLEST(S)	Delete and return the smallest element in S
GET_LARGEST(S)	Delete and return the largest element in S

Table 5.2 Some special structure operations (for time, position, or rank)

Delete, the cheaper Find gets, the more we Insert, the dearer Find gets.[3] As usual, we have to compromise. No operation should be "too easy;" if something is very easy, something else may be very hard.

Some operations in the tables are expressible as combinations of more primitive operations in the table. Depending on the application, for efficiency we may choose to implement these secondary operations directly instead of composing two or more others.

For example, suppose we define a new operation on linear structures called "Join" that takes two linear structures and concatenates the elements of the second to the end of the first. We could implement $Join(S_1, S_2)$ as repeated calls to Get_First of S_2, Find_Place of the last element in S_1, and Insert_After that position. (Then delete the first element of S_2.) That is, repeated calls to the single command:

$$\text{Insert\_After}(\text{Get\_First}(S_2), \text{Find\_Place}(\text{Find\_Last}(S_1), S_1), S_1)$$

However, if we expect to do many Joins then it's better to write a faster, more direct, Join. On the other hand, if we also need "Reverse_Join," which appends the reversed form of S_2 to S_1, then we may be better off using variants of the first implementation for both operations since we would have to change it only slightly to do both. As you can see, there are many tradeoffs.

Pause | What are some tradeoffs in implementing an operation to reverse the elements of a linear structure?

We have to distinguish between how we *represent* data and how we *implement* algorithms manipulating the data. For example, table 5.3 shows the addition of seven and five expressed in binary and in decimal. There is nothing special about either representation of the numbers; for both representations we can implement addition by writing an addition algorithm. Further, having chosen an implementation, when we want to add we don't have to worry about how numbers are represented nor how addition is implemented.

We can implement every operation using a one-dimensional array. This must be true since in present-day computers all programs are eventually translated into nothing more than a very long list of binary numbers. More generally, we can implement all operations using *any* structure. The question is: Which operations will be efficient? Most applications only use a

_____

[3]Assuming that we don't delete more elements than we insert. We could conceivably have delete requests for elements that aren't there.

few operations, so our problem is to choose an implementation that best fits the collection of operations necessary for the current application. Let's call this collection of operations the application's **menu**.

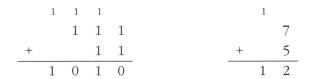

Table 5.3 Adding in binary and in decimal

Let's distinguish between *allowing* every operation—every implementation does this if expense is no object—and *supporting* an operation. Let's say that an implementation **supports** an operation if the operation is cheap with that implementation. In this chapter, an implementation supports an operation if the operation takes at most polylogarithmic time and the implementation uses at most linear space.

Even though two structures may have the same menu, the distribution of costs for each operation will, in general, be different. If the demand for an operation is very high in a particular application then we should choose the structure that supports it most cheaply, even if other structures are better overall. So we also have to take into account the demand for each operation; let's call this the menu's **profile**.

Suppose we keep data in no special order in a one-dimensional array. Here, Insert, Find_Oldest, Find_Youngest, Find_First, and Find_Last are, or can be made, constant time. But Copy, Find, Delete, Union, and so on, are linear. So this implementation supports the menu: Insert, Find_Oldest, Find_Youngest, Find_First, and Find_Last.

We can add Union to the menu by allowing pointers; each structure is now a collection of one or more one-dimensional arrays linked together. This takes more space but Union is now constant time while previously supported operations cost asymptotically the same. As a by-product, we can now Create and Destroy structures cheaply. So this new implementation supports the menu: Create, Destroy, Insert, Find_Oldest, Find_Youngest, Find_First, Find_Last, and Union. It's profile is a different matter; it depends on the distribution of the various numbers of each operation the particular application requires.

Pause | If a pointer is about the same size as an element, at most how much extra space does this implementation use?

Some menus are so popular that structures specifically supporting them have names. See table 5.4. A dictionary is the dynamic form of the simple search problem we worked on in chapter two, and a priority queue is the dynamic form of the first selection problem we worked on in chapter three. Given either of these structures we can solve the dynamic form of the sorting problem we worked on in chapter four. Of the structures in the table we are most interested in queues and partitions.

Structure	Menu
Stack	INSERT, GET_YOUNGEST
Queue	INSERT, GET_OLDEST
Priority queue	INSERT, GET_LARGEST
Mergeable queue	INSERT, GET_LARGEST, UNION
Dictionary	INSERT, DELETE, FIND
Partition	UNION, FIND_STRUCTURE

Table 5.4 Some common structures

5.2   Queues and Partitions

Sometimes it happens that a man's circle of horizon becomes smaller and smaller, and as the radius approaches zero it concentrates on one point. And then that becomes his point of view.

David Hilbert

The central property of many datasets is that one element is easiest to get at or serve. Usually, when the elements are served depends on when they were put into the collection. For example, queues at a bank, post office, bus stop, or check-out counter; and stacks of books, dishes, stereo equipment, or planes in a holding pattern. Although most of these examples are linear, in general they don't have to be. For example, in a stack of books, two or more books could be on one level. Once we get to that level we can pick any one next until all are gone, then we go to the next level.

If we always serve the oldest element of a structure first, the structure is a queue; if the youngest, a stack. A *queue* supports Insert, and Get_Oldest. A *stack* supports Insert, and Get_Youngest. If we serve elements depending

A QUEUE

on how important they are, the structure is a priority queue. For example, if a plane is low on fuel, it gets high priority, even if it arrives last. A *priority queue* supports Insert, and Get_Largest (or Get_Smallest).

A PRIORITY QUEUE

If we keep track of insertion times, or if the elements are from an orderable set, then we can make a priority queue act like either a stack or a queue. This is a general property of the three classes of special purpose structures sketched in table 5.2 [p. 313]. Potentially, we could use place, size, or time to order elements, depending on the native properties of the elements and the structure's implementation. We can't use place if the structure isn't naturally linear, or size if the elements aren't drawn from an orderable set, or time if we can't keep track of when elements are inserted. The point is that these things can be done but, depending on the structure and the elements, they may not be cheap. It is common to confuse the fact that a particular structure is naturally linear (for example a one-dimensional array is naturally linear) with the use to which it was put. For example, a structure that has to keep timed or orderable elements doesn't have to be linear, and a linear structure doesn't have to be able to retrieve elements' insertion times or their rank (if they are orderable) from their linear positions.

The algorithms in implementation 5.1 implement a stack using a one-dimensional array; we could implement it just as easily using a linked list, and the same is true for queues, but not for priority queues. Further, we could use either binary trees or binomial trees to implement each of the queues. And we can even implement all three queues implicitly.

Mergeable Queues

Now we want the menu: Create, Insert, Union, and Get_Largest; structures supporting these operations are **mergeable queues**. Merging two heaps by inserting all elements of one heap into the other can take $\Omega(n \lg n)$ time. We can reduce this to linear time by forgetting all relations and building a heap on the elements of both structures from scratch. (As we saw in the previous chapter, creating a heap from scratch takes linear time.) Finally, we could conceivably take a leaf from the larger heap, make it the root of the two heaps, and let it trickle down the newly created heap. This is logarithmic, but could be tricky to code.

Fortunately, we do know one structure that supports merging, at least for some sizes: a binomial tree. We can merge two binomial trees having the same power of two number of elements in constant time—just compare their roots and hang the smaller off the larger, making a binomial tree twice as large as the two original ones. Call a binomial tree where each node is at least as large as its children a **binomial heap**. (See figure 5.4.) We now have an implementation, but only for powers of two elements. Next we want to support general Union.

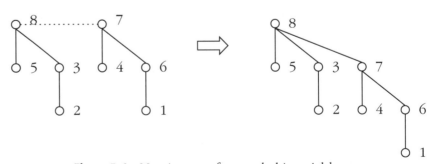

Figure 5.4   Merging two four-node binomial heaps

| Pause | How can we do this?

{ *Stack* is implemented as an array *Stack*[1..*stack_size*],
with youngest element *Stack*[*stack_top*], and oldest *Stack*[1].
stack_size ≥ 1; *stack_size* ≥ *stack_top* ≥ 0.
Initially *stack_top* is 0. }

INSERT (*element*, *Stack*)
  { Add *element* to *Stack*. }

   if FULL (*Stack*)
     then
       ERROR ("stack full")
     else
       stack_top ← *stack_top* + 1
       Stack[*stack_top*] ← *element*

GET_YOUNGEST (*Stack*)
  { Delete and return the most recent element in *Stack*. }

   if EMPTY (*Stack*)
     then
       ERROR ("stack empty")
     else
       element ← *Stack*[*stack_top*]
       stack_top ← *stack_top* − 1
       return *element*

EMPTY (*Stack*)
  { Test whether *Stack* is empty. }

   if *stack_top* = 0
     then return true
     else return false

FULL (*Stack*)
  { Test whether *Stack* is full. }

   if *stack_top* = *stack_size*
     then return true
     else return false

Algorithm 5.1

First, how can we Union two binomial heaps having different powers of two elements? Easy: Just keep them separate in a new structure! This new structure will have *two* binomial heaps. In general, we may want to Union two priority queues of sizes n and m, and neither n nor m will be powers of two. So we need to extend binomial heaps to work when n is not a power of two.

Call a set of trees a *forest*. A set of binomial trees is then a binomial forest. (See figure 5.5.) A *binomial queue* is a forest of binomial heaps, each with different powers of two elements. Since we can always decompose n uniquely into powers of two, let's make a binomial queue of size n have a binomial heap for each power of two in the binary representation of n.[4] (See figure 5.6.) This idea of taking a static structure and *dynamizing* it by decomposing the number of elements into powers of two (or any of several other decompositions) is widely applicable.

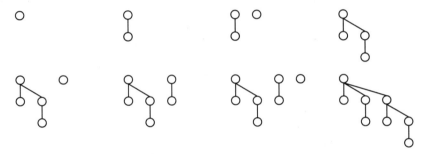

Figure 5.5   Binomial forests with one to eight elements

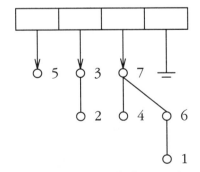

Figure 5.6   A seven-node binomial queue

---

[4]Since there are at most a logarithmic number of powers of two in the binary representation of n, there are at most a logarithmic number of binomial heaps in any binomial queue.

Now to Union two binomial queues we can start with the two smallest binomial heaps and work up to the largest. We can add their component binomial heaps as if they were binary numbers. (See figure 5.7 and compare with the binary addition in table 5.3, page 315.)

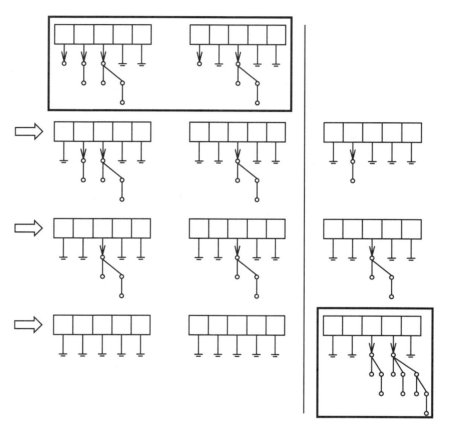

Figure 5.7 Merging two binomial queues of sizes seven and five

To Create a binomial queue, we just create a root. To Insert an element, we Create a binomial heap with the element as root, put the heap in a new binomial queue, then Union the two binomial queues. So binomial queues support Create in constant time, and Insert and Union in logarithmic time. To Get_Largest, we first scan the roots of each binomial heap in the binomial queue. That gives us the largest in logarithmic time. Then we delete its node and make all its children roots of new binomial heaps in a new binomial queue. Then we Union this new binomial queue with the original. Thus, binomial queues are mergeable queues; they support the menu: Create, Insert, Union, and Get_Largest.

Partitions

We now want the menu: Create, Find_Structure, and Union; structures supporting it are called *partitions* since the elements are partitioned into disjoint sets. We have a fixed universe of n elements and we want to maintain disjoint sets of elements; initially each element is in its own set. Let's use trees to implement the sets where each node points to its parent, and a root points to itself. Initially every node is in a set by itself (so it points to itself). Each tree's root will be the name of the tree and a Find_Structure on any node in a tree will follow a path from the node up to the root, thus finding the name of the set to which the node belongs.

Now, whenever we Find_Structure we are gaining information about ancestor relationships, so we can use that information to make the ancestors found on the way to the root children of the root. This way, when next we Find_Structure for one of these elements, or any of their descendants, we won't have as far to go to get to the root. So although a Find_Structure may take twice as long as it would if we didn't do any of this compressing, the compression will pay off over a long sequence of Find_Structures. Let's call such a Find_Structure a *compressing* Find_Structure.

One way to Union is to create a new set and copy all elements from both sets to the new set. But it's more efficient to just add the elements of the second set to the first (by making them point to the first root), then rename the first set. This saves us having to touch any of the elements of the first set. Further, since we do work proportional to the number of elements in the second set, we should add the elements of the *smaller* set to the larger, rather than vice versa. Finally, to avoid having to count the elements each time we Union (and so pay linear cost for each Union) we can keep track of the size of each set. Let's call such a Union a *weighted* Union.

When Unions are weighted, no tree is more than logarithmic in height; we've seen this idea before when finding the second largest in chapter three, and in the programming section of quick sort in chapter four. Implementing weighted Union and compressing Find_Structure as in implementation 5.2 can be shown to support the menu: Create, Find_Structure, and Union. Although several operations can be expensive, each operation averages at most logarithmic time over a sequence of n operations.

{ An implementation of two partition operations.
Size[*node*] is the size of the set with root *node*;
Parent[*node*] is *node* if *node* is the root of a set,
otherwise it is the parent of *node*. }

FIND_STRUCTURE(*node*)
    { Find the root of the set containing *node*,
    then compress the set using any information gained. }

    next ← *node*
    while *Parent*[*next*] ≠ *next*
      next ← *Parent*[*next*]
    root ← *next*

    next ← *node*
    while *next* ≠ *root*
      save ← *Parent*[*next*]
      Parent[*next*] ← *root*
      next ← *save*
    return *root*

UNION($node_1, node_2$)
    { Merge the sets containing $node_1$ and $node_2$. }

    $root_1$ ← FIND_STRUCTURE($node_1$)
    $root_2$ ← FIND_STRUCTURE($node_2$)
    if $root_1 = root_2$ **then return**

    sum ← $Size[root_1] + Size[root_2]$
    if $Size[root_1] > Size[root_2]$
      then
        $Parent[root_2]$ ← $root_1$; $Size[root_1]$ ← *sum*
      else
        $Parent[root_1]$ ← $root_2$; $Size[root_2]$ ← *sum*

Algorithm 5.2

5.3   Connecting Telephones

> The difference between a text without
> problems and a text with problems is like
> the difference between learning to read
> a language and learning to speak it.
>
> Freeman Dyson, *Disturbing the Universe*

Now we're ready to solve some graph problems. Nowadays all land-based communication networks (like the telephone system and cable television) are switching from copper wire to fiber-optic cable. Fiber-optic cable has much higher bandwidth;[5] it's almost wiretap proof; it needs less power to send information over the same distance; it's not affected by power surges or electromagnetic interference; it's thin and lightweight; and it doesn't rust. The present phone system has many inconsistencies and inefficiencies because it evolved from earlier systems. Let's take advantage of the change to redesign the phone system.

Each user has a phone and we want to connect them so that every user can talk to every other user. We want a communications network providing the most service to the user at the least cost to the phone company. Let's call this the *telephone problem.*

There are many ways of measuring "cost" and "service" and each definition leads to a different version of the problem. Let's assume that the most expensive thing is running a cable between two users. Also, let's assume that every phone can route calls from any phone directly connected to it to any other phone directly connected to it. So Alice can talk to Bob if there is a direct connection between them, or if she can talk to someone who can talk to Bob. Thus, connectivity is transitive.[6] Finally, let's assume initially that the time to place a call is proportional to the number of times the call must be rerouted to reach its destination. Call each rerouting a *hop*. Users want to minimize the number of hops their calls have to make, and the phone company wants to minimize the number of cables it has to lay.

Suppose there are only four users. Figure 5.8 shows all non-isomorphic graphs with four nodes; Now imagine that each graph is a map, each node is house, and each edge is a road. Let's say that when we reach a node by driving along an edge we **visit** it. A graph is **connected** if from any node

---

[5]The *bandwidth* of a communications channel is the amount of information the channel can carry per second.

[6]Current phones don't allow much call rerouting through them; the most we can do today is to have one of our phones route calls to another of our phones. But it's sure to happen eventually.

we can visit every other node by driving only along edges. That is, a graph is connected if there is a sequence of edges joining any two nodes. Six of the eleven graphs are connected. Thinking of graphs as beads and strings, a graph is connected if by picking up any bead, we pick up the whole graph. If a graph is disconnected we can decompose it into a number of **connected components**, each of which is itself a connected graph (with a smaller number of nodes). Of the five disconnected graphs in the figure, one has four components, one has three components, and three have two components each.

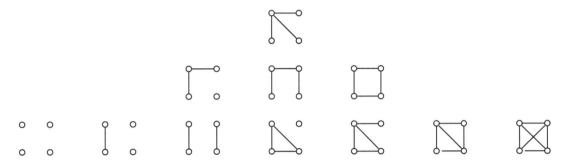

Figure 5.8 All graphs with four nodes

Now let n be the number of users. What's the least and most number of edges in a connected graph with n nodes? Well, since all our graphs are simple, no node can have more than $n - 1$ edges touching it. So there can't be more than $n(n - 1)$ edges in all. But each of these edges touches another node, so perhaps it's about half that number?

Pause | What's the largest number of connecting cables?

The most we can do is connect everyone to everyone else directly. So there is a cable for every two people, and the number of ways of choosing two things from n things is $\binom{n}{2}$. So the maximum number of edges is $n(n - 1)/2$. A graph is **complete** if it has the maximum number of edges (see figure 5.9). Since there are about half a billion phones in the world, to connect them in a complete graph would take about 125×10^{15} cables. With a world population of about five billion, this is about twenty-five million cables per person! This is the best solution for the users since every call is placed immediately, but it's too expensive for phone companies.

Pause | What's the smallest number of connecting cables needed?

Figure 5.9 All complete graphs with up to six nodes

Looking at figure 5.8 we might guess that a connected graph has at least $n - 1$ edges. Is this true? From the figure we see that a graph with $n - 1$ edges is not necessarily connected; there are three graphs with three edges, but only two of them are connected. Okay, suppose we start with a connected graph. We need to add at least one edge to connect a new node. Since a graph with one node has no edges, then, by induction, we need at least $n - 1$ edges to connect an n-node graph. A connected graph with n nodes and $n - 1$ edges is a **tree**. (See figure 5.10.)

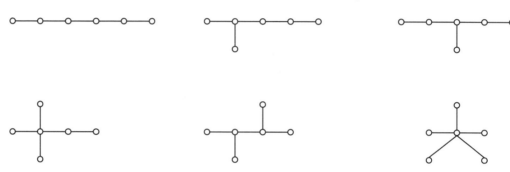

Figure 5.10 All trees with six nodes

Pause There is only one tree each with one, two, and three nodes, and there are two with four nodes; how many trees have five nodes?

So the smallest number of connecting cables is $n - 1$ and in that case the connection graph is a tree; if there are less than $n - 1$ cables then there is at least one unconnected user. Since we have assumed cost to be proportional to the number of cables, the phone company wants to connect users in a tree. Now, half a billion nodes is too many for mere intuition.[7] But the numbers grow too fast even for trees. Although there are only six trees with six nodes, there are forty-seven with nine nodes! So we cannot list all trees connecting half a billion nodes. Now that we've settled on trees, the telephone problem has become: Which tree would users like best?

_____

[7]There are 274,668 graphs with only nine nodes. In general, it is possible to show that asymptotically there are $O(2^{n^2/2}/n!)$ graphs with n nodes.

From the user's point of view the problem with some trees is that a call could have to hop many times. For example, if Alice and Bob live on opposite ends of the first tree in figure 5.10, a call from one to the other hops four times. Knowing all about divide and conquer, phone companies reduce hops by building substations to handle some of the routing. Each substation handles all the calls from a particular area, and it passes all calls to different areas up a chain of substations, each responsible for larger and larger regions. Substations are easier to build if they are all the same, so suppose each substation can handle k other substations.

Unfortunately although the number of hops goes down, a call can be potentially delayed at a substation roughly proportional to the largest number of calls a substation may have to handle. If we connect all n users in a chain, like the first tree in figure 5.10, then a call could have to hop roughly n times before reaching its destination. If the phone company builds one substation, the system will look like the last tree in figure 5.10. Every call goes to the substation and the substation routes it to the right user, so a call only hops once. But the maximum call delay is still proportional to n, and the substation has to handle too many users.

We can think of a chain as a height $n-1$ tree. If we build one substation, the delay is proportional to n. We can think of this as a height one tree; the substation is the root of the tree and the tree has n leaves (the users) all directly connected to the root. (See the second arrangement in figure 5.11.) If we can afford $k+1$ substations then we can build a height two tree: k substations each serving n/k users, and one substation, the root of the tree, serving those k substations. (See the third arrangement in figure 5.11.) The number of substations goes up (so the cost goes up), but the potential delay down (so the service goes up). Now the longest time to place a call is proportional to

$$k + \frac{n}{k}$$

A call is delayed proportional to n/k at whichever of the level one substations it goes to, and delayed proportional to k at the root substation. The cost of a return down the tree will be proportional to the same function. As we saw in the analysis of JUMP_SEARCH in chapter two, page 102, we can differentiate with respect to k to find the worst delay. $k + n/k$ is smallest when $k = \sqrt{n}$, and the minimum is $2\sqrt{n}$. This is better than the height one tree, but each substation must still handle $\sqrt{n}$ users.

If we can afford $k^2 + k + 1$ substations we can build a height three tree (see the third tree in figure 5.12); the worst delay is now proportional to

$$2k + \frac{n}{k^2}$$

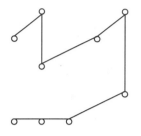 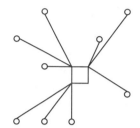 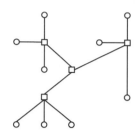

Figure 5.11 Three ways to connect nine users

A call is delayed proportional to n/k^2 at whichever of the level two substations it goes to, and delayed proportional to k at its level one substation and at the root substation. $2k + n/k^2$ is smallest when $k = \sqrt[3]{n}$, and the minimum is $3\sqrt[3]{n}$. Further, now each substation has to handle only $\sqrt[3]{n}$ users.

1 substation $k + 1$ substations $k^2 + k + 1$ substations

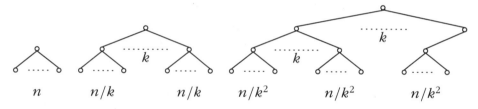

Figure 5.12 Thinking of the connection graph as a hierarchy

In general, if the tree has height m, there are $(k^m - 1)/(k-1)$ substations, and each level $m - 1$ substation has to handle up to n/k^m users. The worst delay is proportional to

$$mk + \frac{n}{k^m}$$

Pause | What k minimizes this function?

The smallest delay occurs when $k = \sqrt[m]{n}$, and the delay is then proportional to $m \sqrt[m]{n}$. To find the best such tree we have to find

$$\min_{m}\{m \sqrt[m]{n}\}$$

Let's differentiate with respect to m to find this function's minimum. First, let's put it in a more easily differentiable form

$$m \sqrt[m]{n} = m \sqrt[m]{e^{\ln n}} = m(e^{\ln n})^{1/m} = me^{(\ln n)/m}$$

Now,

$$\frac{d}{dm}(me^{(\ln n)/m}) = e^{(\ln n)/m} + m\left(\frac{d}{dm}\left(\frac{\ln n}{m}\right)\right)e^{(\ln n)/m}$$

$$= e^{(\ln n)/m} - \frac{\ln n}{m}e^{(\ln n)/m}$$

$$= e^{(\ln n)/m}\left(1 - \frac{\ln n}{m}\right)$$

This derivative is zero when $m = \ln n$ and the second derivative is positive there, so the function is smallest there.

Pause Check that the second derivative is positive when $m = \ln n$.

So the best performance is achieved by a tree of depth $m = \ln n$ and the tree has a branching factor of

$$k = \sqrt[m]{n} = n^{1/\ln n} = (e^{\ln n})^{1/\ln n} = e$$

Obviously we can't build substations that handle e callers! Fortunately we can approximate the best tree by branching two or three times. If the connection graph must be a tree this gives the most service to the users, since it minimizes the time to place a call, and the phone company has to lay no more than $2n$ cables.

Pause Why only a linear number of cables?

The real phone system isn't a tree because although trees are the cheapest connection graphs they aren't reliable; if any line goes out the graph becomes disconnected. Further, phone companies have to worry about things like the length of cables, their geographic placement, their bandwidth, their maintenance, their cost, and the best mix of satellite uplinks, land lines, and undersea cables. Finally, a substation is more expensive than a constant number of extra cables, so it isn't sensible to build $O(n)$ substations just to minimize the number of cables. However, no matter what the final system is, substations will still handle only a constant number of calls. This number is larger than e but still constant; and whenever substations only handle a constant number of calls the system will have a hierarchical structure.

5.4   Partially Sorting

> Important though the general concepts and
> propositions may be with which the modern
> industrious passion for axiomatizing and
> generalizing has presented us. . . nevertheless
> I am convinced that the special problems
> in all their complexity constitute the stock
> and core of mathematics. . .
>
> Hermann Weyl, *The Classical Groups*

When building a house we can't put on the roof before putting up the
walls. Similarly, there are a number of things to do before workers start
laying fiber-optic cable for the new phone system. They can't lay cable
until they put conduits in. They can't put conduits in until they dig guide
channels. And so on. However they can do several things at the same
time—for example, some can test new phones while others dig channels.
Our new problem is to arrange a set of dependent subtasks so that the
overall task can be done efficiently. This is the *sequencing problem*.

Let's model this problem with graphs. Let each task be a node and
connect a pair of nodes if one must be done before the other. This graph
must be directed; edges specify which nodes precede other nodes. Call a
directed graph a **digraph**, for short.

Imagine a graph is a road system. If, by driving only along edges, we
can start at one node and visit at least two other nodes before returning
to our start, then the graph is **cyclic**. A graph with no cycles is **acyclic**.
The **degree** of a node is the number of edges touching it. A **cycle** is a
connected graph in which every node has degree two. Five of the eleven
graphs in figure 5.8, page 325, are cyclic, but only one is a cycle; in each
of these graphs there is a subset of at least three users who can talk to
each other directly. Note that two connected nodes alone do not form a
cycle since neither node has degree two.

| Pause | Find a cyclic graph, a cycle, and an acyclic graph. |

Now what should a cycle be in a digraph? A digraph can have a cycle
when we remove the directions (for example, if, as some drivers do, we
pretend that one-way streets are two-way) but this may not be a cycle
in the directed version of the graph. Cycles should now be directed too.

Unlike undirected graphs, a digraph can have cycles of only two nodes, since these nodes can each have degree two. A directed acyclic graph has no directed cycles. Let's call a directed acyclic graph a **dag**, for short. All the digraphs in figure 5.13 are acyclic, even though the last is cyclic if we remove all directions.

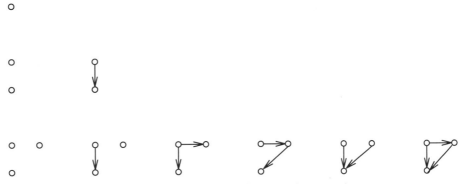

Figure 5.13 All dags with up to three nodes

Dags are like generalized rooted trees; the differences are that a node in a dag can have more than one parent and the dag can have more than one root.[8] A **root** of a digraph is any node of zero **indegree** (no node points to it); a **leaf** is any node of zero **outdegree** (it doesn't point to any node). For example, posets are dags; every maximal element is a root and every minimal element is a leaf. But not every dag is a poset. (One dag in figure 5.13 is not a poset, which is it?) Unlike arbitrary digraphs, every dag has at least one root and at least one leaf.

Pause   Why must a dag always have a root?

We can show that every dag has a leaf by contradiction. Suppose a dag doesn't have a leaf. This means that every node has non-zero outdegree. So no matter where we are in the graph we can always go forward. But there are only a finite number of nodes, so eventually we will hit a cycle. But a dag is acyclic, so we have a contradiction. So there must be at least one leaf. Similarly, there must be at least one root.

_____

[8]'So she went on, wondering more and more at every step, as everything turned into a tree the moment she came up to it.' Lewis Carroll, *Through the Looking-Glass*.

We can also talk about the **descendants** of a node in a dag: those nodes pointed to by the node or transitively pointed to by a node pointed to by the node. In sum, *if we take a node's-eye view then a dag looks like a rooted tree.* A **topological sort** of a dag is a listing of the nodes of the dag such that each node is listed before any of its descendants. Finding a topological sort is similar to sorting. When sorting, every node either precedes or succeeds every other node; here some nodes may be independent of other nodes. Further, when sorting we have to compare nodes to find their order; here we're given their order, but we may have some freedom in sequencing them since some pairs of nodes may have no special order.

Pause | Why is the sequencing problem equivalent to topologically sorting a dag?

Now how do we find a topological sort of a dag? Well, any root is fair game for the first node to be listed since no node precedes it (it has no ancestors). After we list a root, then what? Well, we can list all other roots, but there may be only one. Instead, imagine *removing* a root. (See figure 5.14.) After we remove a root and all its outgoing edges some other nodes may become roots. But will there always be a new root? Well no, but the reduced digraph is also a dag, so there will still be at least one root. (See figure 5.15.) We can then list this root and remove it, and so on, until there are no more nodes to remove.

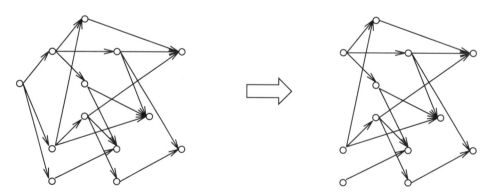

Figure 5.14   Removing a root can make more roots

Pause | Why is the reduced digraph a dag?

At any time there is a frontier of roots. There may be many roots but we don't care what order they are listed in, as long as none is listed before any

Figure 5.15 Removing a root doesn't necessarily make more roots

of its descendants. So we can use a set, *Roots*, to keep track of the frontier of as yet unlisted nodes. After removing a root we check its children (if any) to see if they have become roots. This way we won't list a node before any of its ancestors, so the listing produced is a topological sort of the dag. This is algorithm 5.3. (The algorithm uses the symbols "\" and "∪." $A \setminus B$ is the set of things in A that aren't in B; $A \cup B$ is the set of things in A or in B.)

TOPOLOGICAL_SORT(*Digraph*)
    { Find a topological sort of *Digraph*, if it has one;
    return the sort in *List*, a labelling of *Digraph*'s nodes.
    Use the sets *Roots* and *Children* as temporary storage. }

    Roots ← empty
    for each *node* ∈ *Digraph*
       if *node* is a root in *Digraph*
          Roots ← *Roots* ∪ {*node*}

    label ← 0
    while *Roots* is not empty
       next_node ← any element in *Roots*
       Roots ← *Roots* \ {*next_node*}
       label ← *label* + 1 ; *List*[*next_node*] ← *label*
       Children ← all children of *next_node* in *Digraph*
       Digraph ← *Digraph* \ {*next_node*}
       for each *node* ∈ *Children*
          if *node* is now a root in *Digraph*
             Roots ← *Roots* ∪ {*node*}

    if *Digraph* is empty
       then return *List*
       else return "*Digraph* is cyclic"

Algorithm 5.3

What happens if the digraph is cyclic? Well, what does that mean in our original sequencing problem? There must then be two tasks that each precede the other![9]

Pause | Why does our algorithm detect if the digraph has a cycle?

Programming

It's best to think of structures as *objects*. Packaging graphs lets us separate concerns and that makes algorithms easier to write, easier to prove correct, and easier to analyze. After getting a working algorithm we can then worry about tweaking it to improve it further—but only if absolutely necessary. As an object, a digraph has various attributes; for example: number of nodes (n), number of edges (l); sets containing all roots, leaves, edge labels, node labels; lists of each edge's nodes, each node's edges, each node's indegree, each node's outdegree, each node's parents, each node's ancestors, each node's children, each node's descendants, and so on. If it's a graph instead of a digraph, we need attributes like each node's degree, each node's neighbors, and so on. If it's a network we also need a set containing each edge's cost.

To represent the dag we could keep all nodes in an array, perhaps numbered from 1 to n, and associate the set, perhaps as a linked list, of the array locations of the nodes each node points to. The node's labels (if any) can be kept elsewhere, with pointers matching them to the appropriate array location. And we can implement the set of children of each node as a list, *Children*. This representation uses $O(n + l)$ space.

With *Children* we can find a node's children in time linear in the number of children; and we can initialize the list *Indegree* by running through the set of nodes and checking for any with no children. This takes $O(n)$ time. We can implement the set *Roots* using a stack or a queue, it doesn't matter, the algorithm will still be correct.

Pause | Why doesn't it matter for correctness? Does it matter for efficiency reasons?

With the representation choices in algorithm 5.4, TOPOLOGICAL_SORT's worst cost is $O(n + l)$, since we touch each node at most twice (once when we put it onto the stack and once when we take it off the stack) and we handle each edge at most once.

—————————————————

[9]"The beginner. . . should not be discouraged if. . . he finds that he does not have the prerequisites for reading the prerequisites." Paul Halmos, *Measure Theory.*

```
TOPOLOGICAL_SORT(Digraph)
    { Find a topological sort of Digraph, if it has one;
    return the sort in List, a labelling of Digraph's nodes.
    Indegree is a list of each nodes' indegrees, and
    Children is a list of each nodes' children.
    Use Stack as temporary storage. }

    CREATE(Stack)
    for node from 1 to NODES(Digraph)
        if Indegree[node] = 0 then INSERT(node, Stack)

    label ← 0
    while not EMPTY(Stack)
        next_node ← GET_YOUNGEST(Stack)
        label ← label + 1 ; List[next_node] ← label
        for each node ∈ Children[next_node]
            Indegree[node] ← Indegree[node] − 1
            if Indegree[node] = 0 then INSERT(node, Stack)

    if label = NODES(Digraph)
        then return List
        else return "Digraph is cyclic"
```

Algorithm 5.4

5.5   Exploring Graphs

> Thanks to the interstate highway system, it
> is now possible to travel across the country
> from coast to coast without seeing anything.
>
> Charles Kuralt, *A Life On the Road*

Now let's explore the phone system; we want to know things like: Does it have a cycle? Is it connected? If it isn't connected, what are its connected components? If it is connected, is it multiply connected? If it isn't multiply connected, what are its weakest points? We can already answer the first question since TOPOLOGICAL_SORT will report if a graph is cyclic, but what about the other questions? TOPOLOGICAL_SORT will not notice if the graph is disconnected (see figure 5.16).

Figure 5.16 Topological sort doesn't care about connectedness

Thinking of a graph as a system of roads, there are two natural ways of exploring a new city—adventurously (depth-first) and timidly (breadth-first). When exploring **depth-first** we go as far as possible along one path without revisiting any node, then backtrack to our last turning and go as far as possible down the next path, and so on, until we visit all nodes. When exploring **breadth-first** we spiral out from the known to the unknown, visiting all places within the same radius before venturing further.

If our home base is near the center of town, then going breadth-first means that we first visit all the tourist traps; going depth-first avoids tourist traps early on, since early on we're almost always visiting places near the fringe of town. In both modes the next place to visit is always near-by. (See figure 5.17). Imagine that each node is a bead and each edge is a piece of string, all the same length. Now pick up the bead representing

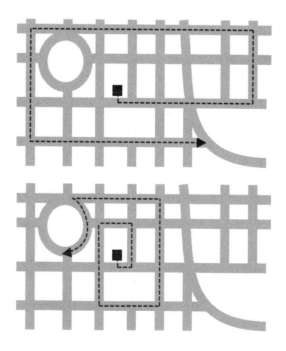

Figure 5.17 Exploring a town depth-first and breadth-first

the start node (see figure 5.18). When exploring breadth-first we first visit all beads on the level below the start bead, then all beads on the next level down, and so on. When exploring depth-first we run all the way down the graph and visit one of the leaf beads, then move up one level to the previous bead and run all the way down another path to a leaf bead, and so on.

Figure 5.18 Picking up a graph to explore it

If we go depth-first then to retrace our steps we need a stack. If we go breadth-first then to retrace our steps we need a queue. We can generalize this and make the strings of different lengths. Now we visit all nodes one level down *within a certain distance* and repeat for the rest of the graph. Thinking of the lengths as priorities, where longer strings imply lower priority for the pendant bead, leads to exploring the graph *priority-first*. This is how we really explore a new city—we first visit the places of most interest to us, say, friends, restaurants, and book stores, then we visit places of lesser interest, say, music stores, cinemas, and coffee houses, and so on.

Finding a topological sort of a dag is the same as exploring the dag breadth-first. We can think of it as visiting all roots in the dag, then all children of all roots, then all children of those nodes, and so on. Hmm, exploring a dag *depth-first* is just the reverse of topologically sorting the dag! When exploring a dag depth-first we drive all the way down to a leaf, visit it, then go back to the last turning and drive down to another leaf. The first nodes we visit are always leaves and, just as in TOPOLOGICAL SORT, there is always a frontier of as yet unvisited leaves. (See algorithm 5.5 and algorithm 5.6.)

Pause Does depth-first visit every node of a connected digraph starting from any node?

```
EXPLORE_BREADTH_FIRST(Graph, start)
    { Explore Graph breadth-first beginning at start;
    return the order in List, a labelling of the nodes.
    Use Queue and Type as temporary storage.
    Graph is connected; start is a node in Graph. }

    for each node ∈ Graph
        Type[node] ← unvisited

    CREATE(Queue)  ;  INSERT(start, Queue)
    Type[start] ← seen ; List[start] ← 1
    while not EMPTY(Queue)
        next_node ← GET_OLDEST(Queue)
        for each node ∈ Neighbors[next_node]
            if Type[node] = unvisited
                Type[node] ← seen
                List[node] ← List[next_node] + 1
                INSERT(node, Queue)
        Type[next_node] ← visited
    return List
```

Algorithm 5.5

Although depth-first must visit every node in a connected graph starting from any node, figure 5.19 shows that it does not necessarily visit every node in a connected digraph. If we start exploring from the top node in the figure then we will visit all nodes, but if we start from any other node then we won't visit all nodes. If the digraph in the figure had no top node then depth-first would never see all of the digraph. However we can make it visit all nodes by running it as many times as necessary, each time starting from a node that hasn't yet been visited.

Pause This works if we want to visit places (nodes) and not streets (edges). How can we guarantee to visit all streets?

If a graph is disconnected we can use EXPLORE_DEPTH_FIRST to find its connected components. Thus in linear time we can tell whether a graph is connected. Now almost anything we want to do to a graph requires at least linear time (just looking at all nodes and edges). So we can always *assume* that a graph is connected; the asymptotic cost of our algorithms will be the same.

```
EXPLORE_DEPTH_FIRST (Graph, start)
    { Explore Graph depth-first beginning at start;
    return the order in List, a labelling of the nodes.
    Use Stack and Type as temporary storage.
    Graph is connected; start is a node in Graph. }

    for each node ∈ Graph
        Type[node] ← unvisited

    CREATE (Stack)  ;  INSERT (start, Stack)
    Type[start] ← seen ; label ← 1
    while not EMPTY (Stack)
        next_node ← GET_YOUNGEST (Stack)
        List[next_node] ← label ; label ← label + 1
        for each node ∈ Neighbors[next_node]
            if Type[node] = unvisited
                Type[node] ← seen
                List[node] ← List[next_node] + 1
                INSERT (node, Stack)
        Type[next_node] ← visited
    return List
```

Algorithm 5.6

More generally, suppose P is a property and G is a graph. If in linear time we can test whether G has P, and if it doesn't then we also identify a largest subgraph that has P, then we can *always* assume that G has P. Because we can test for P in linear time, we can preprocess G to identify a largest subgraph that has P, and if that subgraph is G itself, we're done. Otherwise we remove the subgraph from G and test again. We can charge the work done at each step to the nodes in the subgraphs found and removed, so the whole process takes linear time. This reduction idea is very important; we will see it again in chapter seven.

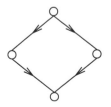

Figure 5.19 Depth-first doesn't always visit all nodes

5.6 Broadcasting Information

> To win one hundred victories in one
> hundred battles is not the acme of skill.
> To subdue the enemy without fighting
> is the acme of skill.
>
> Sun Tzu, *The Art of War*

Computers are comfortable with bits and bytes but humans are comfortable with sounds and sights. However, digitized sounds and sights take up an enormous number of bits and bytes. Besides letting more people talk to each other at the same time, high bandwidth communications channels let computers join the conversation.

Now that we have networked computers, we want to broadcast information from one node to all other nodes. How can we do this cheaply? This is the *information broadcast problem*. To solve it we must find a cheapest subgraph connecting all nodes. This subgraph must be a tree, since if we have a cycle we can delete an edge, and so lower its cost. This tree must be a spanning tree of the graph representing the communications system. A **spanning tree** is a tree with the same nodes as the graph, whose edges are a subset of the edges of the graph. Since a tree is minimally connected, a spanning tree uses the least number of edges to broadcast a message.

More generally, each communications channel has a cost and costs may vary from channel to channel (for example: posting a letter normally, sending it express, and faxing it). Alternately, each channel may have a length and we want to minimize the overall travel time. If the edges have numbers representing costs (capacities, lengths, or bandwidths) the graph is a *network*. To broadcast information efficiently we want a cheapest spanning tree of this network.

Now how do we find a cheapest spanning tree? If we divide the nodes of a network into two parts then any of the cheapest edges connecting a node in the first set with a node in the second set must be in a cheapest spanning tree of the network.

Pause   Why is this true?

Let's proceed by contradiction. Divide a network into two parts. Suppose A is one of the cheapest edges joining any two nodes in the two parts of the network. Is it possible that A is not in any cheapest spanning tree of the network? Well consider any cheapest spanning tree not containing A. A spanning tree is a tree, so it is connected. So there must be at least one edge in the tree connecting the two parts, call it B (see the first drawing in figure 5.20). Now add A to this tree. This creates a cycle since trees are minimally connected. Now delete B. This produces a new spanning tree.

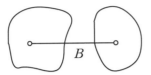 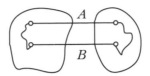 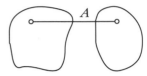

Figure 5.20   Dividing the nodes of a network into two

Pause   Why is this true?

Further, since all edges of the tree are the same except that we have substituted A for B, and since A is no more expensive than B, then we have another cheapest spanning tree. So if we divide a network into two parts then each of the cheapest edges joining the two parts must be in at least one cheapest spanning tree.

CHEAPEST_SPANNING_TREE (*Network*)
   { Find a cheapest spanning tree of *Network*,
   by building a tree incrementally. Return the tree in *Tree*.
   Use *Priority_Queue* as temporary storage.
   $Cost[node_1, node_2]$ is the cost of the edge joining
   $node_1$ and $node_2$; each edge has non-negative cost.
   Network is connected. }

   CREATE (*Priority_Queue*)
   for each $node_1 \in Network$
     CREATE ($\{node_1\}$)
     for each $node_2 \in Neighbors[node_1]$
       $edge \leftarrow (node_1, node_2)$
       INSERT ($edge, Cost[edge], Priority\_Queue$)

   CREATE (*Tree*)
   while not EMPTY (*Priority_Queue*)
     $(node_1, node_2) \leftarrow$ GET_LARGEST (*Priority_Queue*)
     if FIND_STRUCTURE ($node_1$) $\neq$ FIND_STRUCTURE ($node_2$)
       $Tree \leftarrow Tree \cup \{(node_1, node_2)\}$
       UNION($node_1, node_2$)
   return *Tree*

Algorithm 5.7

Now we have an algorithm: pick any node, the two sets are that node and all $n-1$ others. Examine all edges touching this node and greedily choose a cheapest edge. Change to the node on the other end of the chosen edge and look at all its edges, and so on. Keep adding edges as long as they don't form a cycle. (See algorithm 5.7.) We always have a tree, and if the network is connected the tree grows until all nodes are included. At this point it is a cheapest spanning tree of the network.

Alternately, at each iteration we can pick a cheapest edge no matter where it is in the network, as long as it doesn't make a cycle with the already included edges. We can use a priority queue to keep edges ordered by cost, and a partition to check for possible cycles. (See algorithm 5.8.) So the two ideas are to build a spanning tree, or build a spanning forest. Both algorithms are examples of the **greedy strategy**.

```
CHEAPEST_SPANNING_TREE (Network)
    { Find a cheapest spanning tree of Network,
    by building a forest incrementally. Return the tree in Forest.
    Use Priority_Queue and Type as temporary storage.
    Cost[node₁, node₂] is the cost of the edge joining
    node₁ and node₂; each edge has non-negative cost.
    Network is connected. }

    CREATE (Priority_Queue)
    for each node₁ ∈ Network
        CREATE ({node₁})  ;  Type[node₁] ← unseen
        for each node₂ ∈ Neighbors[node₁]
            edge ← (node₁, node₂)
            INSERT (edge, Cost[edge], Priority_Queue)

    CREATE (Forest)
    while there are unseen nodes
        (node₁, node₂) ← GET_LARGEST (Priority_Queue)
        Forest ← Forest ∪ {(node₁, node₂)}
        Type[node₁] ← seen
    return Forest
```

Algorithm 5.8

5.7   Distributing Flow

> Tallyrand once remarked that an idealist
> cannot last long unless he is a realist and
> a realist cannot last long unless he is an
> idealist. . . this observation speaks for the
> need to idealize real problems and to
> study them abstractly but it also says that
> the work of the idealist who ignores
> reality will not survive.
>
> Morris Kline, *Mathematics: The Loss of Certainty*

Things become both simpler and more complex when computers enter the conversation. A cheapest spanning tree is the cheapest way to connect all nodes, so if we want to broadcast a message to all nodes then it's the best way to do so. But if we want to send a message to a specific node, must we find a cheapest spanning tree of the whole network? The problem is that a cheapest spanning tree is cheapest among all spanning trees, but the path between any two nodes on a cheapest spanning tree is not necessarily the cheapest path connecting them. We now want to find the cheapest paths from one node to all other nodes.

Well how about trying the greedy strategy again? Unfortunately, greed is good if we have to find all paths, but isn't necessarily good for any one path; it's too short-sighted for that.[10] Shooting from the hip means sometimes shooting yourself in the foot. To see the importance of a properly designed routing algorithm consider the following incident in the history of electronic networks. The arpanet is the earliest such network. Unlike traditional communication networks, the arpanet (and now the much larger internet) runs itself; there is no central control. Instead, the net has protocols and machines on the net share the work of message subdivision, message routing, and message recreation and delivery. Unfortunately distributed control makes large distributed systems more like organisms than mechanisms; they can have viruses, fits, and plagues.

Unlike a phone call or physical mail, electronic mail may have a lot of protocol information added. Depending on size, a message may be divided into several pieces and routed all over the net. The target machine then reconstitutes these pieces into the original message. (See figure 5.21.) The net does not have fixed routes to send messages; routes are decided on demand to avoid congestion problems along well-travelled routes, and to reroute traffic when nodes go down. The machines that do

---

[10]"Alas, regardless of their doom/ The little victims play!/ No sense have they of ills to come,/ Nor care beyond today," Thomas Gray, *Ode on a Distant Prospect of Eton College.*

the routing are called *imps* (interface message processors). Imps calculate routing costs dynamically to allow for net changes.

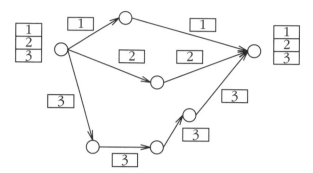

Figure 5.21 Delivering three parts of one electronic mail message

In 1972, one of the Los Angeles imps, let's call him Maxwell, experienced a memory fault. The fault caused him to tell his neighboring imps that there was a *negative* cost to send mail through him. So all of his neighbors immediately started sending all their mail through him. Worse, since imps calculate cost dynamically, all of his neighbors told *their* neighbors that they had a smaller cost than they really did. So, all of their neighbors started sending their mail through them! It was just like pulling the bathtub plug—and all the water in the world headed for the unsuspecting Maxwell. This rapidly brought the entire net down.

Now how can we find the cheapest path between nodes i and j in a network? In the worst case it seems difficult to find the cheapest path from i to j without finding the cheapest paths from i to all other nodes. So let's develop an algorithm to find the cheapest path from i to every other node. Looking at the problem this way makes it much easier. Since we're going to find all cheapest paths from i we may as well find them in the most convenient order.

So what's the most convenient first node? Well, right off we know the cheapest path to every node neighboring i whose connecting edge is cheapest among all nodes neighboring i. It must be the edge connecting them to node i! So now all of those nodes are done (and there must be at least one since the network is connected). What about the next most cheapest node? Well it must either be a node neighboring i (besides the cheapest ones) or a node next to one of the cheapest ones. So we need only find the cheapest among all those paths.

And now an algorithm follows naturally. At any time there is a frontier of nodes of various costs and none of these nodes' cost can decrease. To grow the frontier we look at the cost of all the nodes next to each of the nodes on the frontier. Eventually we will grow the frontier until we've used up all nodes, at which time we will know the cheapest paths from i to every other node in the network.

For the second (and subsequent) set of nodes we have to find the smallest of the following set of paths:

- i's neighbors, besides the ones already chosen, and

- those nodes next to any of i's neighbors, besides i itself.

The two hardest things to do are to find this node and then to update the estimated costs of all nodes neighboring it. We can use a priority queue to do the set maintenance. (See algorithm 5.9.) This algorithm is $O((n + l) \lg n)$.

CHEAPEST_PATHS (*Network, start*)
    { Find the cheapest path from *start* to each node in *Network*.
    On return, *Parent*[*node*] will be the node preceding *node*
    on the cheapest path from *start* to *node*,
    and *CostTo*[*node*] will be the cost of that path.
    Use *Priority_Queue* and *Type* as temporary storage.
    Cost[*node₁, node₂*] is the cost of the edge joining
    node₁ and *node₂*; each edge has non-negative cost.
    Network is connected; *start* is a node in *Network*. }

    CREATE (*Priority_Queue*)
    for each $node_1 \in Network$
        CostTo[$node_1$] ← ∞ ; *Type*[$node_1$] ← *unreached*
        for each $node_2 \in Neighbors[node_1]$
            edge ← ($node_1, node_2$)
            INSERT (*edge, Cost*[*edge*], *Priority_Queue*)
    CostTo[*start*] ← 0 ; *Type*[*start*] ← *reached*

    while not EMPTY (*Priority_Queue*)
        next_node ← cheapest unreached node in *Priority_Queue*
        Type[*next_node*] ← *reached*
        for each unreached $node \in Neighbors[next\_node]$
            edge ← (*next_node, node*)
            if *CostTo*[*node*] > *CostTo*[*next_node*] + *Cost*[*edge*]
                CostTo[*node*] ← *CostTo*[*next_node*] + *Cost*[*edge*]
                Parent[*node*] ← *next_node*
    return *Parent, CostTo*

Algorithm 5.9

5.8   Coda—Graph Therapy

> Any philosophy that can be put
> in a nutshell belongs there.
>
> Sidney J. Harris, *Leaving the Surface*

The two major lessons of this chapter are, first, that there is much more to efficiency than just speed, particularly since real algorithms have many different, and sometimes contrary, goals to achieve. Second, graphs encourage us to squint, and squinting helps us see the forest for the trees.

For economic reasons we have created complex electronic, power, and telecommunications networks whose second-order characteristics we don't understand. The only way we presently have to examine these characteristics is to experiment on the networks themselves. Similarly, in the sixties several governments experimented with seeding rain clouds. As we now know, the weather system is much too complex for this simple-minded experimentation to help. Our networks may in fact behave like the weather system; small local changes can have global effects. Graphs help us deal with this complexity.

As our systems become even more complex, we will become more like therapists than scientists. The basis of science is reduction: take a complex system, break it into pieces, understand the pieces, then put them back together again. But this doesn't work for some systems; if every piece depends on every other piece we cannot reduce the problem. Ultimately, an infinite universe is incomprehensible to finite beings, and poetry is our final defense. But in the meantime we must do our best. And our best is science.

There's something strange about graph properties and complexity: finding minimum cost paths in a graph is quadratic but, finding maximum cost paths appears to be exponential. Finding an eulerian cycle is quadratic, but finding a hamiltonian cycle appears to be exponential. Why such a big difference? This mystery will have to wait until chapter seven. In the next chapter we turn out attention to the province of numbers.

Endnotes

Computational Ideas

Data abstraction, modularization, separation of concerns, information hiding, touch-based model, dynamic structures, dynamization, depth-first exploration, breadth-first exploration, priority-first exploration, topological sort, greedy strategy, problem reduction.

Definitions

- *dictionary:* A dictionary supports Insert, Delete, and Find.

- *queue:* A queue supports Insert and Get_Oldest.

- *stack:* A stack supports Insert and Get_Youngest.

- *priority queue:* A priority queue supports Insert and Get_Largest (or Get_Smallest).

- *mergeable queue:* A mergeable queue supports Insert, Get_Largest, Create, and Union.

- *partition:* A partition supports Union and Find_Structure.

- *heap:* A heap is an implementation of a priority queue using a binary tree. This tree may be implicit or explicit.

- *graph:* A graph is a collection of relations between things; the things are represented by nodes and the relations between them are represented by edges joining the nodes.

- *isomorphic graphs:* Two graphs are isomorphic if there is a relation-preserving mapping between their nodes. G_1 and G_2 are isomorphic if there is a bijective function f such that for all nodes i and j in G_1, i is related to j in G_1 if and only if $f(i)$ is related to $f(j)$ in G_2.

- *subgraph:* A subgraph of G is a graph whose nodes are a subset of G's nodes, and whose edges are a subset of G's edges.

- *property P component:* A property P component of G is a largest subgraph of G with property P. For example, a connected component is a largest subgraph that is connected.

- *path:* A path in G is a sequence of edges of G connecting successive related nodes.

- *connected graph:* A graph is connected if every pair of nodes is joined by a path.

- *complete graph:* A graph is complete if there is an edge between every pair of nodes in the graph.

- *network:* A network is a graph with numbers on the edges.

- *indegree:* The indegree of a node in a digraph is the number of nodes that point to it.

- *outdegree:* The outdegree of a node in a digraph is the number of nodes it points to.

- *degree:* The degree of a node in a graph is the number of nodes it is related to.

- *cycle:* A cycle in G is a path in G such that no edge appears more than once and the first and last edges meet at the same node. In undirected graphs the cycle must connect at least three nodes. In directed graphs the edges of the cycle must have the same sense.

- *hamiltonian cycle:* A hamiltonian cycle of a graph is a cycle connecting all nodes in the graph such that each node except the start node appears once only.

- *eulerian cycle:* An eulerian cycle of a graph is a cycle connecting all nodes in the graph such that each edge appears once only.

- *hamiltonian graph:* A hamiltonian graph is a graph that has a hamiltonian cycle.

- *eulerian graph:* An eulerian graph is a graph that has an eulerian cycle.

- *cyclic graph:* A cyclic graph contains at least one cycle.

- *acyclic graph:* An acyclic graph contains no cycles.

- *tree:* A tree is a connected acyclic graph.

- *spanning tree:* A spanning tree of G is a subgraph of G on all the nodes of G that is a tree.

- *dag:* A dag is a directed acyclic graph.

- *root of a digraph:* A root of a digraph is a node of indegree zero.

- *leaf of a digraph:* A leaf of a digraph is a node of outdegree zero.

Notation
- $A \cup B =$ the set of things in A or in B.
- $A \setminus B =$ the set of things in A that aren't in B.

Tools
- Every dag has at least one root and at least one leaf.
- Every tree with n nodes has $n - 1$ edges.
- Every tree is minimally connected.
- Every tree with $n \geq 3$ nodes has at least two, and at most $n - 1$, leaves (degree one nodes).

Notes

The telephone problem and the motivation for the information broadcast problem were suggested by chapter five of *Computer Networks,* Andrew S. Tanenbaum, Prentice-Hall, second edition, 1988. The arpanet is named from its sponsor, DARPA: the U.S. Defense Advanced Research Projects Agency.

Partitions are also called disjoint set structures and union-find structures. A cheapest spanning tree is usually called a minimum spanning tree. A cheapest path is usually called a shortest path.

Hamilton was not the first to study what are now called hamiltonian graphs; he was preceded by Thomas Kirkman, an amateur mathematician. Euler solved the Königsberg bridges problem in 1736. Königsberg, formerly a Prussian city, is now Kaliningrad, a Russian naval station. Incidentally, David Hilbert, a famous mathematician who plays a pivotal role in chapter seven, was born in Königsberg in 1862.

Binomial queues, the invention of Jean Vuillemin, first appeared in "A Data Structure for Manipulating Priority Queues," Jean Vuillemin, *Communications of the ACM,* 21, 309–315, 1978. For a detailed analysis see "Implementation and Analysis of Binomial Queue Algorithms," Mark R. Brown, *SIAM Journal on Computing,* 7, 298–319, 1978.

The ideas behind the two cheapest spanning tree algorithms were first described in "Shortest connection networks and some generalizations," R. C. Prim, *Bell System Technical Journal,* 36, 1389–1401, 1957, and "On the shortest spanning subtree of a graph and the travelling salesman problem," J. B. Kruskal, *Proceedings of the American Mathematical Society,* 71, 48–50, 1956. The idea behind the cheapest paths algorithm was first considered in "A note on two problems in connexion with graphs," E. W. Dijkstra, *Numerische Mathematik,* 1, 269–271, 1959.

Exercise 11, page 352, is from "An Optimal Algorithm for Sink-Finding," K. N. King and B. Smith-Thomas, *Information Processing Letters,* 14, 109–111, 1982. Problem 6, page 353, was suggested by "Min-Max Heaps and Generalized Priority Queues," M. D. Atkinson, J.-R. Sack, N. Santoro, and Th. Strothotte, *Communications of the ACM,* 29, 996–1000, 1986. See also "A Note on the Construction of the Data Structure 'Deap'," S. Carlsson, J. Chen, and Th. Strothotte, *Information Processing Letters.* Problem 7, page 353, was suggested by Joe Culberson. Problem 8, page 353, was suggested by "Amortized Efficiency of List Update and Paging Rules," Daniel Sleator and Robert Endre Tarjan, *Communications of the ACM,* 28, 202–208, 1985. For further references related to problem 9, page 354, see "Implicit Data Structures for Fast Search and Update," J. Ian Munro and Hendra Suwanda, *Journal of Computer and System Sciences,* 21, 236–250, 1980. The name "beap" for bi-parental heap was coined by Edward L. Robertson.

Problem 10, page 354, was suggested by "A Class of Algorithms which Require Nonlinear Time to Maintain Disjoint Sets," Robert Endre Tarjan, *Journal of Computer and System Sciences,* 18, 110–127, 1979. Problem 11, page 354, is from "Developing Implicit Data Structures," J. Ian Munro, *Mathematical Foundations of Computer Science, Proceedings 1986,* J. Gruska, B. Rovan, and J. Wiedermann (editors), 168–176, Springer-Verlag, 1986. For references related to problem 12, page 354, see "Quick Gossiping by Conference Calls," Ákos Seress, *SIAM Journal on Discrete Mathematics,* 1, 1, 109–120, 1988. Research problem 3, page 356, was suggested by Ricardo Baeza-Yates.

Further Reading

For a thorough introduction to structures and their use in graph algorithms see *Data Structures and Network Algorithms,* Robert Endre Tarjan, The Society for Industrial and Applied Mathematics, 1983. For more on the design of dynamic data structures (for multi-dimensional dictionaries) see *The Design of Dynamic Data Structures,* Mark H. Overmars, doctoral dissertation, University of Utrecht, 1983. Also see the first half of *Data Structures and Algorithms: Volume 3, Multi-Dimensional Searching and Computational Geometry,* Kurt Mehlhorn, Springer-Verlag, 1984.

For a well-written introduction to elementary structures and their analysis see *Data Structures in Pascal,* Edward M. Reingold and Wilfred J. Hansen, Little, Brown and Company, 1986. For a more recent introduction see *Fundamentals of Data Structures in Pascal,* Ellis Horowitz and Sartaj Sahni, Computer Science Press, third edition, 1990.

For an introduction emphasizing abstract data types see *Data Structures with Abstract Data Types and Pascal,* Daniel F. Stubbs and Neil W. Webre, Brooks/Cole, second edition, 1989. For a more formal introduction to abstract data types see *Abstraction and Specification in Program Development,* B. Liskov and J. Guttag, MIT Press, 1986. Many recent programming languages implement abstract data types as independent objects; such languages are called *object-oriented,* since programs tend to be more data-driven (that is, we can think of the data as an active agent).

For a presentation of many structures, including advanced ones, see *Algorithms and Data Structures: Design, Correctness, Analysis,* Jeffrey H. Kingston, Addison-Wesley, 1990, and *Introduction to Algorithms,* Thomas M. Cormen, Charles E. Leiserson, and Ronald L. Rivest, McGraw-Hill/MIT Press, 1990.

For a recent survey of progress on partitions see "Data Structures and Algorithms for Disjoint Set Union Problems," Zvi Galil and Giuseppe F. Italiano, *Computing Surveys,* 1991. For recent work on the cheapest spanning tree problem and on the cheapest path problem see "Fibonacci heaps and their uses in improved network optimization algorithms," Michael L. Fredman and Robert Endre Tarjan, *Journal of the ACM,* 34, 596–615, 1987.

For a gentle introduction to elementary graph theory see *Graphs and Their Uses,* Øystein Ore, The Mathematical Association of America, 1963. For a more advanced introduction see *The Theory of Graphs and Its Applications,* Claude Berge, Wiley, 1962. One area of graph theory research important for computer science is random graph theory. For an amusing advanced introduction see *Graphical Evolution,* Edgar M. Palmer, John Wiley & Sons, 1985. For a more recent update see *Ten Lectures on the Probabilistic Method,* Joel Spencer, The Society for Industrial and Applied Mathematics, 1987.

Communications nets are endlessly fascinating. To learn more see *Computer Networks,* Andrew S. Tanenbaum, Prentice-Hall, second edition, 1988, and *Data Networks: Concepts, Theory, and Practice,* Uyless Black, Prentice-Hall, 1989. For an example of security issues for computer nets see the very readable *The Cuckoo's Egg,* Clifford Stoll, Doubleday, 1989. See also *Computers Under Attack: Intruders, Worms, and Viruses,* Peter J. Denning (editor), Addison-Wesley, 1990.

Questions

> I do not fancy this acquiescence in second-hand hearsay knowledge; for, though we may be learned by the help of another's knowledge, we can never be wise but by our own wisdom.
>
> Michel Montaigne, *Essays: Of Pedantry*

Exercises

1. Show that $\lceil n/2 \rceil \lfloor n/2 \rfloor = \lfloor n^2/4 \rfloor$.

2. A *k-ary tree* is a tree in which every internal node has exactly k children. Show that a k-ary tree with n nodes has $(k-1)(n-1) + k$ leaves.

3. Find the path length of a height m binomial tree.

4. Suppose elements are orderable. Consider a sorted one-dimensional array. Here Find_Smallest, Find_Rank, and Find_Largest are constant, and Find, Find_Next, and Find_Last are at worst logarithmic. Now we want to add the operation Split to the menu. (See table 5.1,

page 313.) This is easy if we allow pointers. After a sequence of Splits, the original monolithic sorted array has broken up into a collection of disjoint sorted arrays, with pointers showing where each begins and ends.

(a) Does the new structure support Find_Largest?

(b) Does the new structure support both Insert and Union?

5. Design a structure supporting Insert, Delete, Find, and Find_Rank, all in logarithmic time and linear space.

6. A rooted binary tree is *half-balanced* if every node either has two children or no children, and for every node the length of the longest path from the node to a leaf is at most twice the length of the shortest path from the node to a leaf.

(a) Show that a half-balanced tree has logarithmic height.

(b) Call a binary tree $1/k$-balanced if the ratio between the longest and shortest path as above is at most k. What is the height of a $1/k$-balanced tree?

7. Show that left-complete heaps do not support Find.

8. Call an ordered binary tree a *right-heap* if for every node both it and its left child are less than its right child.

(a) Does this structure support Find_Largest?

(b) This shows another way (besides heap-order) to organize the data in the nodes of an ordered binary tree. If every node has the same relation to its children as every other node, show that there are nineteen relations on ordered binary trees.

9. Show that if the costs are distinct then there is only one cheapest spanning tree.

10. Show that an even number of people will shake hands an odd number of times today.

11. Among n people, a *celebrity* is someone who everyone knows but who knows no one. To identify a celebrity, if one exists, you are allowed to ask questions of any of the n people, but only of the form: "Excuse me, do you know that person over there?" Assume that all answers given are correct. Minimize the number of questions you need to ask to determine the celebrity, if one exists, or to determine that no celebrity exists in a given set of n people.

12. (a) Show that a connected graph is eulerian if and only if all its nodes have even degree.

(b) Develop an algorithm to find an eulerian cycle in an arbitrary graph, if it has one.

13. Show that the complete graph on n nodes has $(n-1)!/2$ hamiltonian cycles.

14. Show that

$$n^2 f(n) = (n^2 - 1)f(n-1) + 2(n-1) \Longrightarrow f(n) = 2\frac{n+1}{n}H_n - 4$$

Problems

1. Given n nodes linked in a chain, adding one edge to form a cycle roughly halves the maximum distance between any two nodes. How many edges do you have to add to halve the maximum distance (the diameter of the graph) again?

2. A digraph is *strongly connected* if every pair of nodes is joined by a directed path.
Use depth-first exploration to find the strongly-connected components of a digraph.

3. An *articulation node* of a graph is a node whose removal disconnects the graph. A graph with no articulation nodes is *biconnected;* to disconnect it we must remove at least two nodes.
Use depth-first exploration to find the articulation nodes of a graph.

4. Develop an $O(n+l)$ algorithm to find the single source cheapest paths in a dag.

5. Show that binomial queues can be made to support Delete.

6. Design an implicit structure supporting Insert, Get_Largest, and Get_-Smallest, all in logarithmic time.

7. Describe an implementation of a structure supporting the following two operations on a set of real numbers in logarithmic time: insert two numbers and delete the (or a) pair of numbers that are closest in value.

8. Suppose we maintain pointers to both the beginning and the end of a linked list so that we can shift an element to either end of the list in constant time. Further suppose that Finds always start from the beginning of the list. Now we do the following sequence of operations starting with an empty list:

$\text{Insert}(x_1), \text{Insert}(x_2), \ldots, \text{Insert}(x_n),$
Repeat m times: $\text{Find}(x_1), \text{Find}(x_2), \ldots, \text{Find}(x_n).$

Compute the total cost of this sequence if after an element is found it is

(a) moved to the beginning of the list,

(b) moved to the end of the list.

9. A *beap* is a bi-parental heap: a child may have up to two parents and each parent may have up to two children. Each node is larger than its children, if any. (See figure 5.22.)

(a) Show how to implement a beap implicitly in a two-dimensional array so that it supports Insert, Delete, Find, Get_Largest, and Get_Smallest all in $O(\sqrt{n})$ time and no extra storage.

(b) Can any of these times be improved without using more storage?

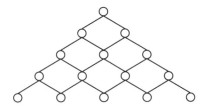

Figure 5.22 A beap

10. Consider the following recurrence

$$f(n) = \begin{cases} 0 & n = 1 \\ \max_{1 \le k \le \lfloor n/2 \rfloor} \{\lfloor \lg k \rfloor + 1 + f(k) + f(n-k)\} & n > 1 \end{cases}$$

(a) Show that $f = \Theta(n)$.

(b) Find $f(n)$.

11. Develop an implicit structure supporting Insert, Delete, and Find all in $O(\lg^2 n)$ time.

12. n theorists want to swap gossip. If every phone call is between two theorists, and if when two theorists talk they swap all the gossip they each know, what is the least number of calls necessary for everyone to know everything?

13. Consider a set merging process that starts with n singleton sets and does $n - 1$ merges. Let the cost of a merge be the size of the smaller set merged. Are the following two cost maximizing policies the same?

(a) Merge any set whose size is a power of two with any set of equal or smaller size.

(b) Merge any two sets whose sizes differ by at most one.

14. Prove the bounds on the implementation combinations shown in table 5.5. (Note: these are not bounds on the *problem*.) For example, for the third implementation first prove that $O(n \lg n)$ is an upper bound, then prove that for some constant c and for arbitrarily large n, there exist sequences of Union and Find_Structure operations requiring $cn \lg n$ steps.

Strategy		Bounds	
Union	Find	Upper Bound	Lower Bound
unweighted	uncompressed	$O(n^2)$	$\Omega(n^2)$
unweighted	compressed	$O(n^{3/2})$	$\Omega(n \lg n)$
weighted	uncompressed	$O(n \lg n)$	$\Omega(n \lg n)$
weighted	compressed	$O(n \lg^* n)$	

Table 5.5   Bounds on four implementations of partitions

Research

1. Consider the partition problem. The strategy of always choosing to make the elements of the smaller of the two sets elements of the larger set forces us to devote linear space just to record set sizes. What is the performance of a randomized implementation of Union that flips a coin to decide which set to union to the other?

2. Given a digraph, how hard is it to identify those nodes whose label is invariant over every topological ordering of the digraph? In a sense, these nodes are the most critical ones, since the whole ordering depends on them.

3. The following recurrence occurs in the analysis of the number of binary trees with a certain property, can you solve it?

$$f(n) = \begin{cases} 1 & n = 0 \\ f(n-1) + f(\lfloor n/2 \rfloor) & n > 0 \end{cases}$$

4. A *binary search tree* is a binary tree where the value of each node is greater than the value of its left child and less than the value of its right child. Usually a binary search tree deletion algorithm replaces the deleted node with the largest node in its left subtree. Instead, suppose we first flip a coin and either replace the node with the largest node in its left subtree, or with the smallest node in its right subtree. Can the tree become significantly unbalanced with this randomized deletion algorithm?

6

NUMBERS

There's safety in numbers.

Proverb

IN THIS chapter we concentrate on problems connected with numbers. Problems like these: How hard is it to raise a number to an integer power? To find common factors of two integers? To tell whether an integer is prime? To get the factors of a composite integer? To generate a random integer? To multiply two integers?

These problems involve all the digits of an integer, so we usually can't use a floating-point approximation. Further, the numbers may have hundreds of digits, but contemporary computers handle only a dozen digits directly in hardware. So we have to do arbitrary precision arithmetic in software (numerical analysis worries about errors caused by fixed precision). This means two things. First, addition, subtraction, multiplication, and division are no longer cheap since their costs increase with the number of digits of their arguments. Second, we should change our model and measure an input's "size" by the number of digits needed to represent it. Since computers are binary and the number of decimal digits is just a constant multiple of the number of binary digits, let's use the number of binary digits as our new measure of input "size." This is the **bit-cost model**.

| Pause | What's the constant multiple?

In previous chapters we agreed to estimate the difficulty of inputs by their size; previously, larger inputs meant more work in the worst case. How do we define the worst cost of a problem (and lower bounds on the problem) when the cost depends on divisibility properties of n? For example, consider testing n for primality by trying to divide by all smaller numbers. If n is even then after only one trial division we know that n is not prime—unless it's two. If n is divisible by three we halt after two trial divisions. In general, this algorithm's run time *is not non-decreasing in n*. Again, suppose we want to find the number of times two divides n. The run time of the obvious algorithm solving this problem is also not non-decreasing in n; it is low for odd numbers, and high for powers of two.

The difference with previous problems is that input size is an additive property; previously for all $n > m$ there was always an input of size n at least as hard as every input of size m. However when multiplicative properties of n matter, mere size can be irrelevant; if we're factoring, even numbers are easier than odd numbers; if we're finding the number of times two is a factor, even numbers are harder than odd numbers. *Unfortunately we don't know the factors of n beforehand.* Fortunately, if instead of thinking of individual inputs, we think of all k-bit inputs then, in general, the difficulty of the problems increases as k increases, as expected. All the usual intuitions hold once we stop talking about inputs of size n, and talk about inputs of length k $(= \lceil \lg n \rceil)$. Ideally, multiplicative problems on integers should have instances measured by their factorizations, since that will most influence algorithm cost. This is the first, but not the last, time that we ask ourselves: How hard is factoring?

In sum, in this chapter four things are different:

- arithmetical operations are no longer cheap,
- there is only one instance of value n,
- there are 2^k instances of length k,
- the size of an instance of value n is the length of n in binary, and

- the cost to solve a problem on an instance of value n may decrease when n increases in size, but will, in general, increase when n increases in length.

⊹⊱∙∘⊱∙∘⊰∙∘⊰⊹

In this chapter we will have to tussle with number theory; don't be afraid of the symbols. For example,

$$\forall n, \quad ((\exists m \; : \; n = 2m \vee n = 2m + 1) \wedge \neg(\exists m, k \; : \; n = 2m \wedge n = 2k + 1))$$

simply says that every integer is either even or odd. ($\wedge$ means "and," $\vee$ means "or," and $\neg$ means "not.") Mathematics is no more about symbols than mountain climbing is about ropes. Symbols only help us get to our goal—they can neither do the job for us nor are they indispensable—we could do without them, but the climb would be much harder.

6.1   Exponential Numbers

> I have yet to see any problem, however complicated, which when you looked at it in the right way, did not become still more complicated.
>
> Poul Anderson, *Call Me Joe*

Not all of the elementary operations we learned as children are optimal. How best can we evaluate m^n through a sequence of multiplications? Suppose the sequence of products we produce in generating m^n is m_1, m_2, ..., m_k. One sequence generating m^n is m, m^2, m^3, ..., m^n. This takes $n - 1$ multiplications. Can we reduce the number of multiplications?

How can we reduce m^n to a simpler problem? It doesn't seem to help if we relate m^n to k^n for some $k < m$; we can use the binomial theorem, but that means more than $n-1$ multiplications. But we can easily relate m^n to m^k for some $k < n$. If n is even, m^n is the square of $m^{n/2}$. So if n is even, find $m^{n/2}$ then square it. If n is odd, find $m^{\lfloor n/2 \rfloor}$, square it, and multiply by m. In other words

$$m^n = \begin{cases} 1 & n = 0 \\ m^{2\lfloor n/2 \rfloor} \times m^{n \bmod 2} & n > 0 \end{cases}$$

This is algorithm 6.1.

```
POWER(base, power)
    { Compute base^power.
    power ≥ 0 is an integer. }

    if power = 0
        then
            return 1
        else
            half ← POWER(base, ⌊power/2⌋)
            half ← half²
            if power is odd then half ← half × base
            return half
```

Algorithm 6.1

POWER finds m^n in $O(\lg n)$ multiplications since the recurrence counting the number of multiplications is

$$f(n) = \begin{cases} 0 & n = 1 \\ f(\lfloor n/2 \rfloor) + 1 + n \bmod 2 & n > 1 \end{cases}$$

which has solution

$$f(n) = \lfloor \lg n \rfloor + \beta(n) - 1$$

Here $\beta(n)$ is the number of ones in the binary representation of n, and is no more than $\lfloor \lg n \rfloor + 1$ (see table 6.1). So finding powers can be solved in a linear number of multiplications,[1] where "linear" means linear in $\lceil \lg(n+1) \rceil$, the length of the input, n.

n	2	3	4	5	6	7	8	9	10	11	12	13	14	15
$\lfloor \lg n \rfloor + \beta(n) - 1$	1	2	2	3	3	4	3	4	4	5	4	5	5	6

Table 6.1 Number of multiplications sufficient to find powers

Pause Why isn't f a function of n and m?

---

[1]Note that using the standard multiplication algorithm, each multiplication is quadratic in the length of the input (initially $\lceil \lg(n+1) \rceil$). This can be improved asymptotically.

This algorithm is either the oldest or second oldest in this book; it was known to the Indians more than two millenia ago and, in a related form, to the Egyptians almost *four* millenia ago. Later we'll see that this algorithm turning an exponential solution ($n - 1$ multiplications) into a linear solution ($2\lfloor \lg n \rfloor$ multiplications) is at the heart of an important cryptographic system.

If m changes and n is constant over a number of runs then it's worthwhile to find the cheapest way to raise a number to the power n. So what's the smallest number of multiplications necessary to find the nth power? Well consider $n = 15$. POWER finds m^{15} in six multiplications, but looking at table 6.1 we see that we can do it in five since we can find m^5 in three and can cube that in two more.

$$m^{15} = m^{3 \times 5} = (m^3)^5 = (m^5)^3$$

This is the same idea that we used in chapter three, when finding the best algorithm for the largest and smallest (page 185). The difference is that there we wanted the *sum* of the costs of two previous numbers and now we want the *product* of the costs of two previous numbers.

And this leads us to the factor algorithm: factor n then look at all possible ways to complete a multiplication from the combinations of factors.

In general we can build addition chains. An **addition chain** is a sequence of exponents starting with 1 such that every exponent in the sequence is the sum of two previous exponents in the sequence. Table 6.2 lists all powers reachable in seven multiplications.

k	Powers														
0	1														
1	2														
2	3	4													
3	5	6	8												
4	7	9	10	12	16										
5	11	13	14	15	17	18	20	24	32						
6	19	21	22	23	25	26	27	28	30	33	34	36	40	48	64
7	29	31	35	37	38	39	41	42	43	44	45	46	49	50	51
	52	54	56	60	65	66	68	72	80	96	128				

Table 6.2 Powers computable in exactly k multiplications

The binary algorithm is optimal for those n where $\beta(n) \leq 3$. But $n = 15, 23, 39$, and 135, show that the binary algorithm is not optimal when $\beta(n) = 4$. Alas, the factor algorithm is not optimal either—the smallest counterexample is $n = 33$. Further, it's natural to guess that squaring, whenever it's possible, is the only thing to do. Even this is false! When $n = 191, 701, 743$, and 1111, n costs the same as $2n$. It is possible to show that finding the optimal addition chain is $\mathcal{NP}$-complete (a term we'll meet in the next chapter) suggesting that the problem is probably difficult. This is a hard problem!

The factor algorithm shows that factoring the input would be beneficial. Again we're faced with the problem: How hard is factoring?

6.2   Common Numbers

> Life is a country that the old have seen,
> and lived in. Those who have to travel
> through it can only learn from them.
>
> Joseph Joubert

The **largest common factor** of two positive integers is the largest integer that divides both numbers exactly. So, the largest common factor of 12 and 6 is 6, the largest common factor of 12 and 7 is 1, the largest common factor of 12 and 8 is 4.

Finding the largest common factor of n and m is conceptually easy. We know from the **unique factors theorem** that every integer greater than one is uniquely expressible as a product of primes raised to integer powers. That is, for all $n > 1$ there exist unique integers $n_1, n_2, \ldots$, such that

$$n = 2^{n_1} 3^{n_2} 5^{n_3} 7^{n_4} 11^{n_5} \cdots$$

That mathematical busybody, Carl Friedrich Gauss, was the first to find a correct proof of this, the most fundamental of all theorems in arithmetic. Gauss proved the theorem in his thesis *Disquisitiones Arithmeticae*, in 1801.

From this theorem we know that the largest common factor of n and m is

$$2^{\min(n_1,m_1)} 3^{\min(n_2,m_2)} 5^{\min(n_3,m_3)} 7^{\min(n_4,m_4)} \cdots$$

where the m_is are the powers in the unique factorization of m. So we need only factor n and m and find the smaller of the two powers for each common prime factor. Again there is that pesky problem: How hard is factoring? Assuming factoring is hard, is there a cheaper way?

Pause   Any ideas?

Suppose $n \geq m$. What can we say about the largest common factor of n and m? Well, if $m = 0$ the largest common factor is n; if $m = 1$ the largest common factor is 1; and if m divides n the largest common factor is m. Finally, if both n and m are even then so is their largest common factor, and, if one or both are odd then so is their largest common factor.

Pause Can you generalize these observations?

If k divides both n and m then it divides $n - m$, because if k divides both then $n = ak$ and $m = bk$ for some constants a and b and, therefore, k divides $n - m = (a - b)k$. So if $f(n, m)$ is the largest common factor of n and m then

$$f(n, m) = \begin{cases} n & m = 0 \\ m & n = 0 \\ 1 & n \text{ or } m = 1 \\ f(n - m, m) & n \geq m > 1 \\ f(n, m - n) & m \geq n > 1 \end{cases}$$

This function will keep subtracting the smaller argument from the larger argument until hitting a boundary. (See figure 6.1.)

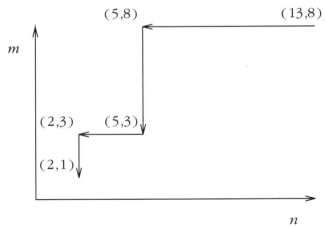

Figure 6.1 Finding the largest common factor of 13 and 8

Pause Must it hit a boundary?

We can do the same thing more quickly by just dividing m into n and finding the remainder. For all n and m there exist k and l such that

$$n = km + l \quad \text{where } m > l \geq 0$$

k is the **quotient** and l is the **remainder** of the division. (See figure 6.2.)

As we saw in the analysis of jump search (section 2.2, page 98), this is just another way of writing

$$n = \lfloor n/m \rfloor m + n \bmod m$$

So it must be that

$$f(n, m) = f(m, l) = f(m, n \bmod m)$$

and now we have the nice condition that the first argument is always at least as large as the second.

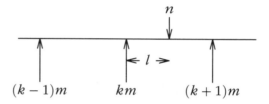

Figure 6.2   The quotient and remainder of n divided by m

Pause   Why?

Also, if m divides n exactly, that is, if $l = 0$, then $f(m, l) = m$. So we can simplify the recurrence considerably to

$$f(n, m) = \begin{cases} n & m = 0 \\ f(m, n \bmod m) & m > 0 \end{cases}$$

And this leads directly to an algorithm (algorithm 6.2).

LARGEST_COMMON_FACTOR(n, m)
    { Find the largest common factor of n and m.
$n \geq m \geq 0$. }

  if $m = 0$
     then return n
     else return LARGEST_COMMON_FACTOR($m, n \bmod m$)

Algorithm 6.2

This elegant algorithm is credited to that great Greek compiler of mathematics in antiquity, Euclid, although there is evidence that it dates from at least a century before his time. Being more than two millenia old, it is one of the oldest non-obvious algorithms known.

LARGEST_COMMON_FACTOR (algorithm 6.2) seems tricky to analyze. We'll eventually reach a boundary case since we're continually reducing both arguments, and since they are always non-negative integers we will eventually reach zero. But how long does it take? (See figure 6.3.) Well, what does the algorithm do? We start with n and m and reduce the problem to m and $n \bmod m$. Then we reduce that to $n \bmod m$ and $m \bmod (n \bmod m)$. If $n \geq m$, how big is $n \bmod m$ relative to n?

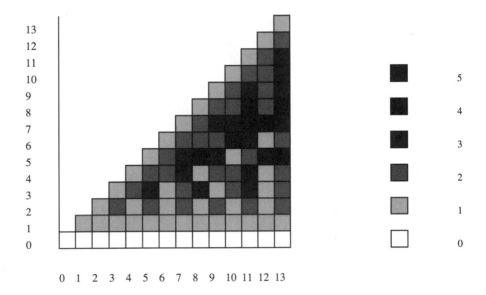

Figure 6.3 Number of divisions for small n and m

| Pause | Try to relate the two.

For all $x \geq 1$, $2\lfloor x \rfloor > x$ since, if $x \geq 1$ then,

$$2\lfloor x \rfloor \geq \lfloor x \rfloor + 1 > x \geq \lfloor x \rfloor$$

Therefore

$$
\begin{aligned}
n \geq m \implies\quad & n/m & \geq\quad & 1 \\
\implies\quad & 2\lfloor n/m \rfloor & >\quad & n/m \\
\implies\quad & m\lfloor n/m \rfloor & >\quad & n/2 \\
\implies\quad & n - n/2 & >\quad & n - m\lfloor n/m \rfloor = n \bmod m \\
\implies\quad & n/2 & >\quad & n \bmod m
\end{aligned}
$$

So in two iterations we have more than halved the first argument! And this is true for every two subsequent iterations. So we will stop after no more than about $2\lg n$ iterations.

Looking at table 6.3 we might guess that the largest number of iterations occurs when n is a fibonacci number (the largest values are boxed). This is true! It is possible to show that we do the largest number of divisions when m and n are consecutive fibonacci numbers. And the worst number of iterations is

$$\lceil \log_\phi \sqrt{5}n \rceil - 2$$

where $\phi = 1.618\cdots$ is the golden ratio.

n	1	2	3	4	5	6	7	8	9	10	11	12
max	1	2	3	3	4	3	4	5	4	4	5	5

n	13	14	15	16	17	18	19	20	21	22	23	24
max	6	5	5	5	5	6	6	5	7	5	6	5

Table 6.3 Maximum number of divisions for small n

6.3   Prime Numbers

> Pure Mathematics. . . need not really be concerned with the application of theory. There is no danger that someone will construct a rapidly converging Euler-Maclaurin series and threaten to destroy the world with it.
>
> Richard G. Hamlet,
> *Introduction to Computation Theory*

Finally we face the central problem squarely: How hard is it to factor a number or to find primes? The theory of primes is part of **number theory**, the study of the properties of integers. Perhaps the oldest, and most prestigious, branch of mathematics, number theory used to be the most pure of pure mathematics.

The simplest way to test whether n is prime is by the **sieve algorithm**: try to divide n by all numbers up to $\lfloor \sqrt{n} \rfloor$ (see figure 6.4). This algorithm goes back at least to Eratosthenes, a remarkable Greek astronomer and poet, who more than two thousand years ago calculated the earth's circumference to within two percent of its real value.

```
 1  2  3  4  5            1  2  3  4̸  5
 6  7  8  9  10           6̸  7  8̸  9  1̸0
11 12 13 14 15     ⟹    11 1̸2 13 1̸4 15
16 17 18 19 20           1̸6 17 1̸8 19 2̸0
21 22 23 24 25           21 2̸2 23 2̸4 25
```

```
 1  2  3  4̸  5            1  2  3  4̸  5
 6̸  7  8̸  9̸  1̸0          6̸  7  8̸  9̸  1̸0
11 1̸2 13 1̸4 1̸5     ⟸   11 1̸2 13 1̸4 1̸5
1̸6 17 1̸8 19 2̸0           1̸6 17 1̸8 19 2̸0
2̸1 2̸2 23 2̸4 2̸5          2̸1 2̸2 23 2̸4 25
```

Figure 6.4 Panning for primes

Pause   Assume that it takes k microseconds to divide two k-digit numbers. Roughly how long will the sieve take to find the 1,065-digit prime in figure 6.5?

The sieve can use up to $\lfloor\sqrt{n}\rfloor - 1$ divisions, so in the bit-cost model its worst cost is exponential in the length of the input ($\lceil \lg(n+1)\rceil$) since

$$\lfloor\sqrt{n}\rfloor - 1 = \Omega(\sqrt{2^{\lg n}}) = \Omega((\sqrt{2})^{\lg n})$$

Now consider the related problem of finding the number of times two divides n. This problem can be solved by a similar algorithm (try to divide by two, then four, and so on). But we can easily find the number of times two divides n by counting the number of trailing zeros in the binary representation of n (this begs the question of how we get such a representation). So if we have n in binary, finding the number of times two divides it is linear in the length of n.

Long Pause   If n is in trinary, powers of three factors are easy to find. How hard are they to find if n is in binary?

Is there a polynomial time primality test? That is, is there a polynomially checkable pattern to the primes? More exactly, is there some property of the representation of n that we can test in polynomial time that will be true if and only if n is prime? Well we don't know, but if we're willing to give up certainty we can test for *probable* primality with polynomial cost. But first we need some terms from number theory.

$$(2^{3539} + 1)/3 =$$

73796098201307225171782711424752769966406992611066
19267611608939891718261411195219291019313693834909
82766847861989655122674917393968130587829514313057
96489726066660396601455113545487696032021613786047
39678190791265595837888230533183069353598614418373
66855882806862688379176110552962626629416447849146
63043127327299572416775873260328538318677775758573
88313348767693230454881593789029774677138375143104
34260339455526629562477584638188948029810999272419
75469249961920962300161327832415657918219483072464
13064371974422537588315069791917933521235759000780
74622075861772974340085081499946707336416327925893
77144627990269571823358464168616611706888054984712
67236930944512264656164534699162419633046314148665
52321857691895960230071117582088132687611887380755
93564976176900029491437349453342290468209106578697
95686757670121149406155031547246128512609768035885
66734355505597767200432478724025353578867345462382
93142036593310331175158539571544734560818933417814
36048539882490795869343661381353636091810141863994
26964456547292271975820619495426338199733732972086
304686486497963

Figure 6.5 A big prime

Number Theory

If n divides $a - b$ let's denote that fact using the symbol "$\equiv$" as follows:

$$a \equiv b \quad (\mathrm{mod}\, n)$$

Modulo a multiple of n, a and b are the same; that is, a and b leave the same remainder on division by n. So, for example,

$$12 \equiv 0 \quad (\mathrm{mod}\, 2) \qquad 13 \equiv 28 \quad (\mathrm{mod}\, 3) \qquad 14 \equiv 6 \quad (\mathrm{mod}\, 4)$$

If n is an odd prime and m and a are less than n then a is a **modular square root** of m modulo n if

$$m \equiv a^2 \quad (\mathrm{mod}\, n)$$

Whenever such an a exists, m is a **modular square** modulo n. Every modular square has at least two modular square roots. From this we can show that for every odd prime n, exactly half the numbers from 1 to $n - 1$ are modular squares modulo n.

If

$$m \equiv a^b \quad (\bmod\, n)$$

then b is the base a **modular logarithm** of m modulo n. We can find a^b modulo n efficiently with MODULAR_POWER (algorithm 6.3). But there is no known way to easily find b given a^b modulo n. Similarly, generating modular squares is easy, but there is no known way to easily find modular square roots.

MODULAR_POWER($base, power, modulus$)
  { Compute $base^{power}$ mod $modulus$.
  $power \geq 0$ is an integer; $modulus \geq 1$ is an integer. }

  if $power = 0$
    then
      return 1
    else
      $half \leftarrow$ MODULAR_POWER($base, \lfloor power/2 \rfloor, modulus$)
      $half \leftarrow half^2$
      if $power$ is odd **then** $half \leftarrow half \times base$
      return $half$ mod $modulus$

Algorithm 6.3

Two numbers are **coprime** if their only common factor is 1 (so their largest common factor is 1). Let $\psi(n)$ be the number of positive integers less than, and coprime to, n. This is the **totient** ("toe-shent") function. The great Irish algebraist William Hamilton derived the name from the Latin *tot* (so many), by analogy with quotient, which is from the Latin *quot* (how many).

The **Euler-Fermat theorem** states that for every coprime n and m

$$m^{\psi(n)} \equiv 1 \quad (\bmod\, n)$$

Now if n is prime then all $n - 1$ smaller numbers are coprime to it, so $\psi(n) = n - 1$. So if n is prime then for all $m \neq n$

$$m^{n-1} \equiv 1 \quad (\bmod\, n)$$

That is, if n is prime then for all smaller m, m^{n-1} is one more than a multiple of n. This special case is called **Fermat's theorem**. The French mathematician Pierre de Fermat stated this special case in 1640, and the Swiss mathematician Leonhard Euler proved it in 1736. Euler proved the general theorem in 1760.[2]

It might seem reasonable to use Fermat's theorem to test whether n is even. Unfortunately a few numbers fake being prime with respect to this test for every m. The **Carmichael number** n is composite, yet for every $m < n$, m^{n-1} is one more than a multiple of n. The first three Carmichael numbers are: $561 = 3 \times 11 \times 17$, $1105 = 5 \times 13 \times 17$, and $1729 = 7 \times 13 \times 19$. These numbers are named after the American mathematician Robert Carmichael who pointed them out in 1909.

A special case of the following theorem was known to the Chinese mathematician Sun Tsŭ perhaps two millenia ago; Euler proved the general result in 1734. The **Chinese remainder theorem** states that if $n_1, n_2, \ldots, n_k$ are all pairwise coprime, then the k linear congruences

$$m \equiv a_1 \pmod{n_1}, \quad m \equiv a_2 \pmod{n_2}, \quad \ldots, \quad m \equiv a_k \pmod{n_k}$$

are simultaneously solvable and the solution is unique modulo $n_1 \times n_2 \times \cdots \times n_k$. We can prove this theorem by induction on k.

Building on work going back to 1792 by three mathematicians—the German Carl Friedrich Gauss, then the French Adrien-Marie Legendre, then the Russian Pafnutiĭ Čebyšev—in 1896 the French mathematician Jacques Hadamard and, independently, the Belgian mathematician Charles de la Vallée Poussin, proved the *prime number theorem*. The **prime number theorem** states that the number of primes less than n grows like

$$\frac{n}{\ln n}$$

So for large n the average distance between two consecutive primes near n is roughly $\ln n$. (See table 6.4.)

In 1940, improving on earlier results by Čebyšev, then the English mathematician G. H. Hardy and the Indian mathematician Srīnivāsa Rāmānujan, the Hungarian-born stateless mathematician Paul Erdös and the Polish-born American mathematician Mark Kac proved the **prime factors distribution theorem**: Let $f(m)$ be the number of different prime factors of m, then for all r

$$\lim_{n \to \infty} \frac{1}{n} \left| \{ m \le n \ : \ f(m) \le \ln \ln m + r\sqrt{\ln \ln m} \} \right| = \frac{1}{\sqrt{2\pi}} \int_{-\infty}^{r} e^{-x^2/2} dx$$

(Here $|A|$ means the size of the set A.) So for large n, on average, n has about $\ln \ln n$ different prime factors with a standard deviation of $\sqrt{\ln \ln n}$.

---

[2]An amateur mathematician, Fermat is famous for one outstanding unsolved problem: Is it true that for all $n > 2$ there are no solutions to the equation $k^n + l^n = m^n$. Although unproven, this belief is called *Fermat's last theorem*.

n	$\pi(n)$	$\pi(n)\ln n/n$
10^1	4	0.92103
10^2	25	1.15129
10^3	168	1.16050
10^4	1229	1.13195
10^5	9592	1.10431
10^6	78498	1.08448
10^7	664579	1.07117
10^8	5761455	1.06129
10^9	50847534	1.05372
10^{10}	455052512	1.04779

Table 6.4   An approximation to the number of primes

Finding Primes Probabilistically

We want to tell whether n is prime and we're willing to settle for a probabilistic algorithm (one that is only probably correct). Recall Nelson Cole's feat from chapter one (page 54):

$$2^{67} - 1 = 193707721 \times 761838257287$$

Either of these two factors certify that $2^{67} - 1$ is composite. Given either number we can tell that $2^{67} - 1$ is composite just by dividing. But to test n for primality we want "primality certificates:" numbers that attest to n's primeness with cheap checking. Do we need $\lfloor \sqrt{n} \rfloor - 1$ such certificates before we can decide that n is prime?

By the prime number theorem the primes are distributed as $1/\ln n$ so our test could be to just say that n is composite! For large n this algorithm is almost always right. But, you object, this test is independent of n; for every prime n it will be always wrong.

So how about this: with probability $1/\ln n$ say that n is prime. This algorithm is dependent on n, and for large n it is almost always right. But, you complain, although this algorithm depends on the size of n, it doesn't depend on any divisibility properties of n.

So how about this: pick an m at random from the range 2 to $\lfloor \sqrt{n} \rfloor$ and try dividing m into n. If m divides n then say that n is composite (and m is a factor), otherwise say that n is prime. But, you protest, this isn't a good idea; even when n is composite, m will almost always not divide n unless n has very many factors. And when n has many small factors it's easy to factor directly! Further, even if m is prime, chances are that m won't divide n. Finally, finding random primes is probably at least as hard as testing whether n is prime.

So how about this:[3] pick an $m < n$ at random and test whether m is coprime to n. This is fast with LARGEST_COMMON_FACTOR. But, you wail, this algorithm will almost always say that n is prime, and for most n it will be wrong. If n is composite it will almost surely not detect that fact because chances are that a randomly chosen m will be coprime to n, even if n is composite. Only if m has many small factors will m and n being coprime imply that n is prime with reasonable probability. Fortunately we have a condition that all prime numbers must obey, namely, from Fermat's theorem we know that if n is prime then for all m coprime to n, m^{n-1} is one more than a multiple of n.

So how about this: generate many random ms where $m < n$ and test whether m^{n-1} is 1 modulo n. This is fast with MODULAR_POWER. If any such m fails the test then n is composite, otherwise n is unlikely to be composite. (If n is indeed prime then if we choose $m < n$ there is no need to check that m is coprime to n, it must be.) Only Carmichael numbers will slip through, and they are rare: there are only two hundred and fifty-five of them less than one hundred million. As n keeps passing the test, our confidence that it is either prime or Carmichael increases. But, you sigh, n might be Carmichael.

Given n and m, let $k = (n-1)/2^{\nu(n-1)}$, where $\nu(n)$ is the number of times two divides n. Then n is a **base m pseudoprime** if

$$m^k \equiv 1 \quad (\bmod\, n)$$

or if there is an i between 0 and $\nu(n-1) - 1$ such that

$$m^{k2^i} \equiv -1 \quad (\bmod\, n)$$

Now here's the last test: pick many ms at random where $m < n$ and test whether n is a base m pseudoprime for each m. If n isn't pseudoprime for some m then n is composite, otherwise n is probably prime. This test is better than the last because not even Carmichaels can survive it in the long run. And we can repeat it as many times as we wish. (See algorithm 6.4.)

It is possible to show that if n is not pseudoprime then n is composite, but if n is pseudoprime then n may be prime or composite. Fortunately it is possible to show that if n is composite then n will fail the pseudoprime test for *at least half* of the integers $m < n$. So running the algorithm is like playing one round of Russian roulette where at least half of the

_____

[3] "An idea will not work unless you do." Oswald Avery.

bullet chambers have bullets; if n is indeed prime it has nothing to fear, but if it's composite there is a better than one in two chance that it will be shot. Of course a composite number could get lucky and pass the test over and over; we can't be sure that n is really prime just because it keeps passing this test. That's why we call the survivors pseudoprimes: they fake being primes (*pseudes* is Greek for *false*). The brilliant thing about pseudoprimes is that for the purposes for which they are used *they are as good as primes.*

PSEUDOPRIME(n)
  { Look for a witness to n's compositeness.
  $\nu(n)$ is the number of times two divides n.
  Return *composite* if n is found to be composite,
  otherwise return *pseudoprime*.
  $n \geq 3$ is odd. }

  guess ← **uniform**($2, n-1$)
  if MODULAR_POWER(*guess*, $\nu(n-1), n$) = 1
    return *pseudoprime*

  test ← $(n-1)/2^{\nu(n-1)}$
  for i **from** 0 **to** $\nu(n-1) - 1$
    power ← *test* $\times 2^i$
    if n divides MODULAR_POWER(*guess*, *power*, n) $+1$
      return *pseudoprime*

  return *composite*

Algorithm 6.4

6.4   Secret Numbers

> What is truth? said jesting Pilate, and
> would not stay for an answer.
>
> Francis Bacon *Essays: Of Truth*

The *secrecy problem* is about keeping secrets. How can we transport information in a network whose nodes are information producers and consumers (users) and whose edges are information transporters (communications channels)? To model this problem let edges be directed or undirected, with edge costs representing time, channel bandwidth, or cost of information loss. Suppose there is an edge joining Alice and Bob. If the edge is undirected then Alice and Bob trust each other, and they trust the channel. If the edge points from Alice to Bob then Alice distrusts either Bob or the channel, but Bob trusts both Alice and the channel. If the edge points both ways then neither Alice nor Bob trusts the other, or neither trust the channel. Note that Alice and Bob may trust each other yet they may have no secure edge joining them. Information can flow along all edges, regardless of edge direction, if any.

For example, when meeting a friend in private you trust both the friend and the channel (the private face-to-face conversation). When phoning a friend you trust the friend, but not the channel. When logging on to a computer or using a cash dispenser, you (usually) trust that the computer is who it says it is (which means that you trust both the channel and the respondent) but it doesn't trust you, until you give a password. When meeting or phoning an enemy you may trust neither the enemy nor the channel; or you may distrust the enemy but trust the channel. When two paranoiacs meet they trust neither each other nor the channel.

Pause | When in a bank do you trust someone claiming to be a teller? When logging on do you trust the program claiming to be the login program?

Since the secrecy problem involves information, communication, and ownership, almost every information exchange is an example. Nodes can be people, computer terminals, computers, cash dispensers, bank tellers, companies, governments, spies, databases, or cable companies. Edges can be copper wire, face-to-face speech, fiber-optic cable, smoke signals, telegrams, telephone calls, satellite links, letters, faxes, semaphores, reflecting mirrors, or radio waves.

The simplest problem is a one node network, but this is uninteresting—secrets are only fun if you share them. More generally, all undirected networks are uninteresting; since everyone trusts everyone else and all channels are secure, they are just communication problems and belong in the previous chapter. The two interesting versions of the two node problem are if one node distrusts the other, and if each node distrusts the other; this is the *authentication problem,* which we examine in the next section (page 385). The traditional secrecy problem is a three node problem where two nodes trust each other and both distrust the third. (Alternately, two nodes trust each other but not the channel connecting them.) See figure 6.6.

Cryptology is about systems that keep secrets; **cryptography** (from the Greek for *secret writing*) is about making such systems, and **cryptanalysis** is about breaking such systems. A **cryptosystem** should let one node send a message to another without a third understanding any part of the message. The sender can encrypt the message (the **plaintext**) into **ciphertext**, then send it to the receiver, who decrypts it back into plaintext. Meanwhile an attacker intercepts the ciphertext and tries to decrypt it. The three main issues are privacy, authentication of sender or receiver, and integrity of transmitted data.

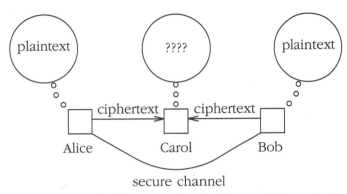

Figure 6.6 Alice and Bob trust each other but not their main channel

It's safest to assume that an attacker intercepts every message. In an ideal cryptosystem attackers cannot decrypt ciphertext. Further, in an ideal system attackers cannot change, replace, create, delay, block, repeat, misroute, or undetectably reorder messages. Finally, they cannot even derive information just because a message was sent. This last is difficult to mask cheaply. To mask it the sender must continually send unnecessary messages to the receiver, or randomly send encrypted empty messages. Of course, the empty ciphertexts must all be different, otherwise the attacker will realize they're just noise. Some, or all, of these cryptosystem attributes can rely on physical security, misdirection, and deception, as well as cryptographic security.

Now how do we accomplish all of these aims? Well there are three philosophies: we can lock the building (use a secure channel, and keep data unencrypted); lock the data (use an insecure channel, but encrypt data); or hide the data (keep data apparently unencrypted, but with a hidden message). Of course, the truly paranoid, being prudent, will quite sensibly lock the building and the data, then hide the data!

We can think of a cryptosystem as a mapping from the cross product of a message space and a function space to a ciphertext space. Choose a function f_c to encrypt and a function f_d to decrypt. c and d are called **keys**; they let us refer easily to the functions in the function space of the cryptosystem. Given a message m, encrypt it by applying f_c to form $f_c(m)$, the ciphertext. To decrypt the ciphertext apply f_d to form $f_d(f_c(m))$ to recover the plaintext, m. We want functions such that for all m in the message space:

$$f_d(f_c(m)) = m$$

Our aim, when wearing our cryptographer hats, is to choose the function space, and specific functions f_c and f_d, so that: c and d are easy to remember; f_c and f_d are easy to compute; and d is hard to find. When wearing our cryptanalysts hats, our task is to find d and break the system, or at least to find m from $f_c(m)$ without necessarily finding d.

Changing a key is usually much easier than changing the entire system—algorithms, file formats, communicating agents, communications channels, and communication protocols. Since these parts of the system can last a long time, and people are weak, it's best to assume that they are all compromised. In the old days, attacks were classified by the information attackers had. Nowadays, because changing keys is easy while changing systems is hard, we assume the attacker knows the encrypt and decrypt algorithms, and magically knows the plaintext corresponding to a polynomial number of ciphertexts.[4] So the attacker knows the function space, but not the keys, c and d. The system's security depends on the difficulty of deriving c and d even knowing all previous ciphertext/plaintext pairs.

Finally, let's assume that attackers cannot penetrate secure channels, and that secure channels have low bandwidth. It's reasonable to assume that secure channels can only carry small amounts of data, or large amounts infrequently, since otherwise there is no secrecy problem! For example, when Alice and Bob meet privately they have a (supposedly) secure conversation, perhaps to exchange keys, but when they part they must use their high bandwidth communications channels (the mail, their computers, their faxes) to exchange large amounts of data. More importantly though, naive dependence on a supposedly secure channel, agent, or place has been responsible for most major security breaches. No security system is proof against users who leave their passwords lying near their terminals, carry their authorization codes with their credit cards, or leave their spare door keys under their door mat. *Any system is penetrable if it depends on a secure channel.*

⊱✦⊰ ⊱✦⊰ ⊱✦⊰

Everybody keeps secrets. Some of the oldest civilizations used secret writing to keep their secrets. Egyptian hieroglyphs (from the Greek for *holy carvings*), initially the secret writing of priests, weren't decrypted until

---

[4]Polynomial in the message length that is. Usually the size of the message space is exponentially larger than the message length, so knowing a super-polynomial number of pairs makes breaking the system trivial in the sense that the attacker would be allowed to know *all* pairs—in which case, decryption is just table lookup.

the chance discovery of the Rosetta stone in 1799. The Spartans spirally wrapped a strip of parchment around a tapered rod called a scytale (Greek for *staff*) of secret diameter before writing the message on it. The conqueror of Gaul, Julius Caesar, also encrypted messages; this system cyclically mapped letters to the third letter on in the alphabet: *a* becomes *d, z* becomes *c.*

Over the millenia many systems have been thought unbreakable. Most have been broken. Before 1975 the cryptographer's main tools were substitution and transposition. Under substitution, plaintext symbols are replaced by one or more ciphertext symbols. Under transposition, only the ordering of the symbols is changed (see figure 6.7). Caesar used substitution and the Spartans used transposition.

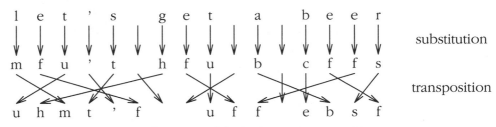

Figure 6.7 Substitution and transposition

A letter-for-letter substitution does not change the frequency of English letters. Since, as we saw in chapter four (page 261), the six most frequent letters in English are *e, t, a, i, o,* and *n,* it's easy to break any Caesar system given a long ciphertext by counting letter frequencies. A frequency attack will always break it if the message is long enough. Failing that, just knowing that the message is English and that a Caesar system is used, is enough to decrypt the message since there are only twenty-six choices.

| Pause | Dbo zpv sfbe uijt, j xpoefs? J tvqqptf tp. Jg zpv eje, uifo dpohsbuvmbujpot!

There is only one provably secure system known: a **one-time pad:** an infinite stream of random letters that are used to modify the message a letter at a time. Each random letter in the pad is used to modify one letter in the message and then thrown away. Both the sender and the receiver must have a copy of the pad. No amount of previous plaintext/ciphertext pairs can help attackers decrypt the current ciphertext; as far as they are concerned it is complete gibberish. Unfortunately, a one-time pad is expensive, and each key is as long as the message. Allegedly the Washington-Moscow hotline uses a one-time pad.

A cryptosystem's worth is primarily determined by how secure it is. Other things, like encrypting speed, secret key distribution, and data expansion, are important, but security is the main thing. To evaluate a system we need to know what sort of attacks it might be subjected to, and for how long. A system is secure enough if it can resist all attacks for an appropriate time. For instance, a ciphertext telling the army to demolish a city may need to be secure only for the time it takes to deliver and decrypt the ciphertext; the message may not need to be secret after that. This time period might be only a few minutes, so even an insecure system could be secure enough. Almost all major cities are less than ten minutes away from a submarine-based missile attack.

Most systems are only **computationally secure**. Their security relies on the probable cost of solving some problem. For instance, a nation wishing to send encrypted press releases to its embassies may regard as secure a system that can resist attack for a year; but that system is insecure if the nation wants to encrypt data for thirty years.

Secret Key Systems

Secret key systems are schizophrenic; they need secret, but common, keys. In a **secret key system**, all intended recipients have the same secret key the sender used to produce the ciphertext. Usually we can distribute secret keys securely—courier, armed guard, word of mouth—but where this is too slow, expensive, or awkward, secret key systems aren't good. Further, the more people who know the secret key the more insecure the system.

Before 1975, all known systems used a common secret key. These systems were generally combinations of several substitutions and transpositions; their strength depended on the number of transformations used, which was large relative to the numbers that had previously been employed. As computers entered the game it was easier to generate more, and more sophisticated, combinations, but because of computers these combinations were easier to break!

Although a lot of cryptology was done during the second world war, modern cryptology started in 1949 when Claude Shannon, the founder of information theory, proved results about security and unicity. Loosely speaking, the **unicity** of a system is the average length of a ciphertext such that it is the image of only one plaintext/key pair. Given a system, let c_n be a random ciphertext of length n, let m be its corresponding plaintext, and let k be a key. The unicity of a system is the smallest n such that

$$H(m) + H(k) = H(c_n)$$

where H is the entropy function defined on page 261 in chapter four. Note that because of redundancy the entropy of English is less than two bits per letter for long messages. (It would be five bits if English were not redundant.) A cryptosystem that always substitutes the same ciphertext for each plaintext letter is **monoalphabetic**. Shannon showed that for monoalphabetic cryptosystems the unicity point for English is between twenty and thirty letters. So any ciphertext longer than about thirty letters in a monoalphabetic system can be at most one message. A monoalphabetic system is fairly easy to break.

In 1973, the U.S. National Bureau of Standards advertised for a cryptosystem to establish a standard. The U.S. National Security Agency (NSA) was asked to help assess submissions.[5] The Bureau eventually chose a secret key algorithm designed at IBM.[6] IBM had invested seventeen person years trying, unsuccessfully, to break the algorithm, but critics felt that IBM, urged on by the NSA, had put a trapdoor in the algorithm to allow fast decryption without the secret key. (A **trapdoor** is a function that is easy to undo with an associated secret.) These claims were based on the secrecy surrounding the analysis of the non-linear tables, called S-boxes, in the system. This analysis is still secret.

Critics also felt that the key length, fifty-six bits, was too short. IBM suggested a one hundred and twenty-eight bit key, but the NSA vetoed this. Of course that made everybody suspicious. Some claimed that the NSA wanted keys long enough for normal security, but short enough for the NSA to break. Yet despite protests, nobody broke the system, so in 1977 it became the U.S. Data Encryption Standard (DES). Since then, the DES ("dez") has received massive government funding, and has been endorsed by most major banks and several large corporations. It has been implemented on a chip capable of encrypting and decrypting twenty million bits per second.

Despite many attacks, it has apparently remained unbroken for fourteen years now. Many institutions use it daily, rumors of insufficient key length and trapdoors notwithstanding. It is now known that longer keys do not make it significantly more secure; so it is possible that the NSA did not seriously weaken it. In sum, the DES is not publically broken, it is blindingly fast, and it is particularly useful for short term purposes where security

---

[5]The NSA is a heavily cloaked organization charged with protecting American secrets and penetrating foreign secrets. From their charter: "The Agency is charged with missions that are vital to the nation's security—producing foreign signals intelligence information, safeguarding U.S. communications systems, and providing computer security for the federal government." The NSA is so secret that even the number of NSA employees is secret; some say that NSA means "never say anything."

[6]IBM is a trademark of the International Business Machines Corporation.

needn't be absolute and secret key transfer is feasible. The caveats are that the U.S. Department of Defense never adopted it, the NSA no longer certifies it for federal use, its certification runs out in 1993, and it may not be recertified.

Public Key Systems

Before 1975 all systems linked the key and the decryption algorithm. If you gave away your secret key, you gave away your encryption. Further, if you encrypted something, you could later decrypt it. Since 1975 none of these are necessarily true. In 1975, Whitfield Diffie and Martin Hellman thought of a way to avoid the schizophrenia of a common secret key. In a **public key system** all users have *two* keys, one private one public. The private key is kept secret. The private key is for decrypting and the public key for encrypting. And neither key is derivable from the other.

To send ciphertext, Alice encrypts the message using Bob's public key as the encrypt key. Bob then uses his private key to decrypt the ciphertext. There is no need for a secure channel; there is no need for a common secret key; even Alice can't decrypt her own encrypted message; and Alice and Bob don't even have to know each other!

Let f_c and f_d be the encrypt and decrypt functions and let m be the message. We want

- $f_d(f_c(m)) = m$,

- f_c and f_d are both easy to compute, and

- knowing c does not help to find d.

A function f is **one-way** if $f(x)$ is easy to compute for all x, but for almost all y it is hard to compute an x such that $f(x) = y$. f is easy to do, but hard to undo (see figure 6.8); it's easy to put a letter into a public mailbox, but hard get one back out. Presently three potentially one-way functions exist: computing factors, modular square roots, and modular logarithms. In the language of the next chapter, it is possible to show that one-way functions exist if and only if $\mathcal{P} \neq \mathcal{NP}$. Since this question is still unresolved, we really don't know if public key systems exist, but the system in the next subsection looks like a good contender.

In a public key system, the attacker knows the encrypt key (the public key), and the encrypt algorithm. The attacker also knows the ciphertext. But the one-way function makes it computationally hard for the attacker to invert the encryption and recover the plaintext. When used in a public key system, a trapdoor built into the function makes this inversion easy, if the private key is known. It must be computationally hard to deduce the private key from the public key.

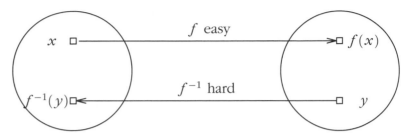

Figure 6.8 A one-way function

The **composition** of two functions f and g is the function fg where for all x

$$f(g(x)) = y \iff \exists z : g(x) = z \text{ and } f(z) = y$$

Two functions f and g **commute** if for all x in their common domain

$$f(g(x)) = g(f(x))$$

If f_c and f_d commute then for all messages m

$$f_c(f_d(m)) = m$$

so we can decrypt a message then encrypt it. (Note that this only makes sense if the ciphertext space is the same as the message space.)

If each user's encrypt and decrypt functions commute, then we don't have to distribute shared secret keys in advance. Alice puts a message in a box, locks the box with her lock, and sends the locked box to Bob. (See figure 6.9.) Bob locks the box with his lock and sends the doubly locked box to Alice. Alice unlocks her lock and sends the singly locked box to Bob. Now Bob unlocks his lock and opens the box. At no time is the box sent unlocked. Unfortunately in this protocol anyone can impersonate either Alice or Bob, since their private keys are secret.

Diffie and Hellman also gave a way for two users to generate a common secret key, and their method does not need a commutative public key system. Called **Diffie-Hellman key exchange**, the method begins with Alice and Bob agreeing on two large integers n and m, where $n > m$. Alice chooses a large integer a, computes m^a modulo n, and sends this to Bob. (This is easy to do using MODULAR POWER.) Similarly, Bob chooses

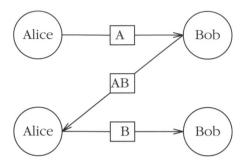

Figure 6.9 Alice passes a secret to Bob without shared keys

a large integer b, computes m^b modulo n, and sends this to Alice. Now Alice computes

$$(m^b \ (\mathrm{mod}\,n))^a \quad (\mathrm{mod}\,n)$$

and Bob computes

$$(m^a \ (\mathrm{mod}\,n))^b \quad (\mathrm{mod}\,n)$$

These two values are in fact the same since they both equal

$$m^{ab} \quad (\mathrm{mod}\,n)$$

And Alice and Bob can then use this as their common secret key. If finding modular logarithms is difficult, then it seems that attackers are stymied even though they know n, m, m^a modulo n, and m^b modulo n. Of course there could conceivably be some clever way to find the secret key without solving the modular logarithm problem.

A Factoring System

It used to be that finding primes and factoring integers was a hobby of harmless number theorists, but times have changed. In 1977, three computer scientists, American Ronald Rivest, Israeli Adi Shamir, and American Leonard Adleman produced a possibly secure public key system. They based their system, now called the RSA, on the presumed difficulty of factoring. Although the RSA has been patented, current RSA chips are slower than DES chips, and the U.S. government does not yet support the RSA as it does the DES.

Here's how it works: Alice chooses two large non-equal primes, k and l, say one hundred digits each, and computes $n = kl$. She then finds a large integer a, coprime to $\psi(n)$, the totient function of n, and computes b, the inverse of a modulo $\psi(n)$. That is,

$$ab \equiv 1 \quad (\mathrm{mod}\,\psi(n))$$

Therefore there is some i such that $ab = i\psi(n) + 1$. Alice's public key is (n, b); her private key is a.

To send Alice a secret message, Bob converts his message to a sequence of numbers, each less than n. Let one of these numbers be m. Bob computes m^b modulo n and transmits this ciphertext, call it c, to Alice. Alice computes c^a modulo n and recovers m since

$$
\begin{aligned}
c^a &= (m^b (\mathrm{mod}\, n))^a \\
&\equiv m^{ab} && (\mathrm{mod}\, n) \\
&= m^{i\psi(n)+1} && (\mathrm{mod}\, n) \\
&= m^{i\psi(n)} \times m && (\mathrm{mod}\, n) \\
&\equiv m && (\mathrm{mod}\, n)
\end{aligned}
$$

This system's security depends on the *presumed* difficulty of factoring. It replaces a secure channel with a (supposedly) secure cost. So far, all known attacks have been shown to be unlikely to succeed, but it has slight weaknesses. For example, for every public key, at least nine messages are unconcealable; that is, there are at least nine ms such that m^b modulo n is m. Worse, for a tiny number of choices of public keys, no messages are concealable! Fortunately it's possible to choose the parameters to guarantee that only nine unconcealable messages exist. And natural languages are so redundant that, as long as there are only a constant number of unconcealable messages, the system can simply check whether the ciphertext equals the plaintext and alert the sender to change the message. The RSA, with suitable parameters, appears to be computationally secure. Finally, there is a variant of it that is computationally equivalent to factoring.

A Knapsack System

Establishing the computational security of a system is difficult when the system has a trapdoor. Consider the **knapsack problem**: Given n tools each weighing an integer number of kilograms, and a knapsack that can carry m kilograms, is there a subset of the tools that will exactly fill the knapsack? This problem is probably computationally hard and there is more theoretical evidence that it is hard than there is that factoring or finding modular logarithms is hard.[7] So perhaps a knapsack-based public key system would be really secure.

In 1978, American computer scientists Ralph Merkle and Martin Hellman designed a system around the knapsack problem. In their system, Alice

_____

[7]In the language of the next chapter, factoring is only known to be in $\mathcal{NP}$, but knapsack is $\mathcal{NP}$-complete. The DES is not known to be based on an $\mathcal{NP}$-complete problem.

publishes a vector of integers, A. To send a message m to Alice, Bob converts m to a binary vector, B, and sends Alice $A \cdot B$, the inner product of two vectors A and B. The **inner product** of $A = (a_1, a_2, \ldots, a_n)$ and $B = (b_1, b_2, \ldots, b_n)$ is $a_1b_1 + a_2b_2 + \cdots + a_nb_n$. Carol, intercepting $A \cdot B$, must solve the knapsack problem to recover B. However Alice computed A to make this easy.

A **superincreasing** sequence is one in which each term is greater than the sum of all previous terms. That is, $a_1, a_2, a_3, \ldots,$ is superincreasing if

$$a_i > \sum_{j=1}^{i-1} a_j$$

It's easy to recover B from $A \cdot B$, if A is superincreasing,

$\boxed{Pause}$ Why is this easy?

But choosing A to be superincreasing lets Carol easily find B, so Alice chooses a superincreasing vector A' then disguises it to form A, her public key. Alice chooses two large coprime integers k and l, and masks A' by transforming it into the public A using

$$a_i \equiv l a_i' \pmod{k}$$

It was felt that the a_is are pseudorandomly distributed and this makes recovering B from $A \cdot B$ as difficult, in theory, as the knapsack problem. After receiving $m = A \cdot B$, Alice computes

$$\begin{aligned} m' &\equiv l^{-1}m &\pmod{k} \\ &\equiv l^{-1}\sum_{i=1}^{n} a_ib_i &\pmod{k} \\ &\equiv l^{-1}\sum_{i=1}^{n} l a_i'b_i &\pmod{k} \\ &\equiv \sum_{i=1}^{n} a_i'b_i &\pmod{k} \end{aligned}$$

then recovers B from $A' \cdot B$. Which is easy since A' is superincreasing.

Unfortunately, in 1982 Shamir broke this knapsack system, then Adleman broke the Graham-Shamir knapsack, a more secure iterated version of the knapsack, and in 1984 Ernest Brickell broke the iterated Merkle-Hellman knapsack. They broke these systems by exploiting the way A was formed, not by solving the knapsack problem in polynomial time.

6.5   Authentic Numbers

> What we call reality consists of a few iron
> posts of observation between which we fill in
> by an elaborate papier-mâché construction
> of imagination and theory.
>
> E. H. Gombrich, *Art and Illusion*

Authenticating authorship or validity is becoming increasingly important as an increasing amount of data is electronic. We authenticate others by personality characteristics: their faces at meetings, their voices over the phone, their signatures on checks. We test something that only the real person could know, do, or have: a face, a mannerism, a voice, a walk, a signature, a memory, a fact. Except for the last, these tests are irrelevant when communication is electronic, because they can be electronically forged. Computers makes impersonation easier than before, particularly when the only communication is electronic. How can we create a digital signature?

We want to verify that a message came from the alleged sender, went to the intended receiver, was not changed, and was received in the same sequence that it was sent. This is the *authentication problem.* Solving it would be useful in electronic funds transfer, in terminal sessions, in government agreements, and in court. The three main authentication situations are: with two-way trust (against an attacker); with one-way trust (user and a computer, a database, a bank, an institution); and with no trust (between governments, banks, companies, sleazy individuals). The difference between the secrecy problem and the authentication problem is the difference between maintaining privacy and maintaining integrity.

If Alice and Bob trust each other they can authenticate each other by sharing a secret key. Bob verifies that a message came from Alice if he can decrypt it using their common secret key. But impersonation is easy in a public key system since encrypt keys are public. However if the system is commutative we can sign messages. Suppose Bob wants to send Alice a signed message. Bob sends Alice a locked box containing a note and a locked box. He locks the outer box with Alice's public key, so only she can unlock it. And he locks the inner box with his private key, so only he could have locked it.

Specifically, let Bob's private key be f_d and let Alice's public key be f_c. Bob writes his message m, then forms $f_d(m)$. Then he attaches his name "bob" in plaintext, and encrypts the message "$f_d(m)$ bob" with Alice's public key, f_c. He then sends f_c("$f_d(m)$ bob") to Alice. (See figure 6.10; to suggest the two levels of encryption the secret message "msg" is double hatched, and the whole message, with signature, is single hatched.) Alice decrypts this with her private key. She now has "$f_d(m)$ bob" and sees that the (still unreadable) message claims to have come from Bob. She then uses Bob's public key on $f_d(m)$ to recover m. Thus she recovers the message and can be sure that it came from Bob; presumably, he is the only one who knows f_d.

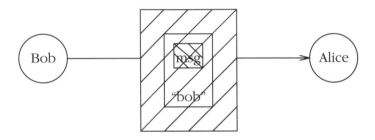

Figure 6.10 Bob signs messages with a commutative public key system

If Alice trusts Bob she can use this scheme to authenticate his messages. Note that Alice cannot later forge Bob's signature, since she still doesn't know his secret key. But if she doesn't trust him she can't convince Carol that the message came from him because he could say that someone stole his secret key. Of course if the system holds a user culpable for losing their private key then Alice wins the case.

Now consider a cash dispenser that processes a request to withdraw money from a bank account. Making this interaction secure is the *cash dispenser problem*. The dispenser sends the request to a central computer and the bank sends an acknowledgement approving the withdrawal. An attacker could record the acknowledgement, cut the connection to the bank, and withdraw more money by impersonating the bank and replaying its acknowledgement. To detect this we can time-stamp each valid acknowledgement.

To detect message modification, we can add a hash code dependent on every bit of the plaintext. To detect message repetition, we can make this code time-dependent. To detect message reordering, we can number messages or include the time. That won't prevent an attacker from impersonating the sender once, but the impersonation will be detected after the sender transmits the next message. We can reduce the chance of any impersonation at all by sending two (or more) time-dependent authentications with each message, where the second is the last authentication sent. This solves the cash dispenser problem.

Public Authentication

Sometimes authentication is necessary, but secrecy is not allowed. For example, suppose Alice, a Citibank customer, wants to withdraw money from a Deutschebank cash dispenser. Her request must be routed to a Citibank computer and back, possibly passing through nodes owned by other banks. A message containing the request, the destination bank, the dispenser's identification, and an authenticator from the dispenser, must be routed to Citibank. This is the *remote cash dispenser problem.*

There are numerous possible information leaks here. Alice's request has her identification, so if it is sent in plaintext any attacker can then raid her account. Even if the entire communications channel is secure, a trusted, but unscrupulous, Citibank employee could raid her account. Further, if the *amount* of the transaction is sent in plaintext then an attacker could glean information both about Alice and about Citibank. Given enough transactions, an attacker would learn a lot about both. So to be safe let's encrypt everything.[8]

But here's the problem: if the message authenticator is formed with a key known only to Deutschebank, then it must be replaced by an authenticator based on a secret key known to Deutschebank and Citibank. Citibank won't stand for this. If the authenticator is formed with a key known only to Citibank, then the message from the dispenser to Deutschebank must be partly plaintext, otherwise the routing information will be unreadable. So if the message is to be routed through intermediate nodes, it cannot be totally encrypted. More generally, sometimes intermediate nodes cannot encrypt and decrypt, or the eventual receiver does not want to trust intermediaries. Such trust would be unacceptable to the intermediaries as well, since it makes them potentially liable if there is a problem.

The more general problem occurs if Alice doesn't trust her bank. If a bank decides to keep tabs on its customers' accounts, it can learn a lot about their personal habits, and perhaps sell or otherwise exploit that information. It should be enough for Alice to use a smartcard (a credit-card sized computer) to anonymously prove that she is a valid customer, and that she has enough money to cover her withdrawal. This is the *anonymous credit problem,* which is an instance of the yet more general *privacy problem.* The privacy problem is more difficult than the traditional secrecy problem because we can derive a lot of indirect information by looking at

---

[8]In reality the information leak is even worse. In 1991, U.S. cash cards only have a four-digit "secret" authentication code. This is trivially crackable by anyone who works in the bank's computer center. The situation is just as bad for credit cards that let you make payments over the phone if you know the credit card number—on the assumption that only the card bearer would know the number; but of course anyone the card bearer buys from could memorize the number.

public information. With computers, processing large amounts of information is now easy, but our justice system has yet to catch up to the change. As a trivial example, some agencies ask for the last half of your social security number, others ask for the first half. They keep this information, and it may even be publically available if you know where to look. If someone were to get both pieces of information they could impersonate you. We're years away from a solution to the privacy problem.

❀❀❀❀❀

Now suppose the two countries of Avalon and Camelot wish to monitor each other's compliance with a ban on underground nuclear testing. Each country lets the other install underground devices detecting seismic activity. Each country wants to read outgoing messages to ensure that no other information is transmitted. Each country wants to authenticate received messages to ensure that the other country has not sabotaged their monitors. But an authenticator must also be readable to the monitored country! This is the *treaty compliance problem.*

A secret key system requires trust—something in noticeably short supply here. A public key system partially solves the problem since Avalon can give Camelot its decrypt key (and conversely). Avalonian devices on Camelot's territory encrypt their messages using Avalon's (secret) encrypt key; so Camelot can check them, but not forge them. Camelot can check that authenticators on outgoing messages are only that. However Avalon cannot convince another country, say Caerleon, that Camelot violated the treaty—Camelot may claim that the incriminating report from the device is a forgery.

We can solve this by having messages encrypted by equipment built by both countries. The collected data from an Avalonian device on Camelot's territory is first encrypted by Avalon's equipment, then forwarded to Camelot's equipment, which decrypts the message to check its authenticity. If it authenticates, Camelot further encrypts the message with its encrypt key, and transmits the doubly encrypted message to Avalon. The decrypt keys of both countries are public. Unfortunately Camelot can still claim that its secret key was compromised—and hence that incriminating reports are forgeries.

So we need a third country, say Caerleon. Each country has a public key device and each publish their decrypt key. In this arrangement, everyone knows their own encrypt key, but cannot know other encrypt keys without collusion. Camelot cannot claim a forgery since, presumably, Avalon doesn't know Caerleon's encrypt key. If Avalon and Caerleon gang up, Camelot can still authenticate messages, but can't prove that it isn't lying. Usually, the more arbiters, the higher the security becomes as the likelihood of full collusion falls. Another solution using *zero-knowledge proofs* (page 390) forces the possibility of sabotage to go to zero.

Covert Channels

The problem at the heart of all public authentication is that authentication allows *covert channels*. Suppose Alice and Bob are prisoners in separate cells and Carol, their captor, agrees to carry messages for them. Carol wants to fool one of them into accepting as genuine either a fake or a modified message. Bob and Alice know that Carol will try to deceive them, so they authenticate. Further, they know that each message must appear unencrypted otherwise Carol won't carry it. But they need to plan their escape. So they want to establish a **covert channel** between them in full view of their captor, Carol. They want their messages to carry covert information even though there is no overt information in them. In everyday life we do the same with a nudge, wink, sniff, or raised eyebrow.

Carol's problem is that authentication can depend on the receiver finding some prearranged structure or content in the message; so such information is always redundant. Her captives can always sacrifice some of this redundancy to establish a covert channel.

For example, Bob and Alice can use synonymous messages to convey covert information. Before being separated they agree to exchange three-bit messages. Of the eight possible messages, even parity messages mean zero, and odd parity messages mean one. To authenticate only, they agree beforehand on which of the four messages in each group will be accepted. So, for each of the two possible outcomes, there are four possible messages, but only one can be authentic. Carol, attempting substitution or modification, has a one in four chance of success.

Now to establish a one-bit covert channel, Bob and Alice agree beforehand on *two* messages from each group that will be accepted as authentic. One will be sent to indicate a covert one, and the other for a covert zero. The receiver now accepts any of four messages as authentic, so Carol now has a one in two chance of successful substitution or modification.

But if Carol can tell whether her deception attempts were successful, she would see the frequency of deception tending toward one-half, instead of one-quarter, as she expects. From this she can infer that there is a covert channel. So, in the long run, sacrificing authentication bits is detectable.

However, detecting a covert channel can apparently be made as hard as factoring. Take $n = klm$ where k, l, and m are large primes and

$$k \equiv l \equiv 3 \pmod 4, \qquad m \equiv 5 \pmod 8$$

These requirements ensure that n is not one of the instances that are known to be easy to factor.

Any modular square a^2 modulo n, where a^2 is coprime to n, has eight modular square roots. These square roots can be grouped into pairs—by considering their size and the sign of a special function called the *Jacobi function*. Alice and Bob agree on n, and as they both know its factors, they can quickly compute the modular square roots of a transmitted a^2. A message is sent as a^2 and is authenticated by also sending one of its modular square roots. It appears computationally hard to compute modular square roots.

Covert information is transmitted as the choice of the root sent, from the pair of roots chosen for use. That is, for any modular square, there will be eight modular square roots (not necessarily all distinct), divided into four pairs. One pair will be chosen as being the acceptable authenticators for the message. Of that pair, if the smaller root is received, the covert message is a zero, if the larger, a one. If any of the other six modular square roots, or any other number is received, the message is rejected as inauthentic.

However Carol can produce valid message/authenticator pairs by choosing a random a and squaring it modulo n; thereby sending a random covert message. To prevent this attack, Alice and Bob have to reduce the number of acceptable messages, so that Carol will have a low probability of choosing one. Of course this reduces the number of messages they can send. We seem to be in a box; there seems to be no way to prove validity without at least partially giving away the method of proof. Or is there?

Zero-Knowledge Proofs

During the Renaissance, mathematicians were in the same box; they wanted to prove that they could do something, but they didn't want rivals to know how, and so claim the credit. One standard way was to deposit the proof with a (supposedly) impartial third party. Unfortunately the third party could always secretly give the proof to one of their rivals. Or could claim it themselves, as l'Hôpital did with Bernoulli's limits theorem (see page 47). Can we prove something without giving away any details of the proof?

We can if we change the notion of a proof to a game. The game is to convince a verifier that something is true. In 1985, Shafi Goldwasser, Silvio Micali, and Charles Rackoff showed that it was possible to probabilistically prove that a theorem was provable without giving the proof. That same year, Oded Goldreich, Micali, and Avi Wigderson showed that if one-way functions exist then certain theorems that are probably hard have such proofs. [9]

This is like a Renaissance mathematician who claims to be able to solve any cubic equation and who offers as proof any number of verifications. In each verification the authenticator can choose any four coefficients of a cubic and the mathematician gives the solution to the equation. The verifier can easily check that each answer is indeed a solution of the equation chosen, but someone not knowing the general solution would be hard pressed to find each answer. The point is that this can always be made to work if the verifier's choices are random (unpredictable to the prover), and if there is an easy way to check a given answer. Once again we're confronted by a possible difference between *finding* and *checking*. In the last chapter we face this issue head on.

Old-style proofs inextricably linked the knowledge of a fact with its verification; if you had the proof you could check it, and vice versa. But, like the change in philosophy from secret key systems to public key systems, these new-style proofs distinguish between a fact and its verification. The differences between this kind of proof and older proofs are that a proof is interactive, not a static text, and proof is by being convinced with high probability, not certainty. Random numbers appear to be essential here. Both the verifier and the prover can use an infinite stream of random numbers.

Here's an example of such an interactive protocol called a ***zero-knowledge proof***. In a zero-knowledge proof the prover convinces the verifier that something is true without giving anything else to the verifier beyond that fact. That is, after the proof, the verifier is convinced of the result, but is no closer to understanding why it's true, and is no closer to being able to produce a proof of the result! This works if one-way functions exist.

Suppose I want to show you that a graph has property X. I encrypt the graph, give you the encrypted graph, and invite you to ask me one of two kinds of questions. One of the two kinds of questions ensures that I'm always encrypting the same graph, but because I'm using a one-way function even when given the answer to such a question you have no computationally feasible way to break the encryption. The other kind of question ensures that I can show that the graph has property X. During each round you can ask me either kind of question, either one of which I may have been able to fake answering without really knowing if the graph has property X *but not both together.*

You can randomly choose which of the two kinds of questions to ask me and I can't predict which of the two you will ask. So if I'm able to repeatedly answer correctly, then after some number of rounds (whatever

———————————————————————————
[9]These theorems are proofs of membership in $\mathcal{NP}$-complete languages.

number that is needed to exceed your prefixed probability bound) you will be convinced that the graph indeed has property X. But you will have learned nothing more than that because I re-encrypt the graph every time I answer one of your questions.

Y'KNOW, THERE'S A DIFFERENCE BETWEEN A ZERO – KNOWLEDGE PROOF AND A PROOF OF ZERO KNOWLEDGE...

Digital Signatures

Here's an example of how we can use zero-knowledge proofs to solve authentication problems. The **chromatic number** of a graph is the smallest number of colors needed to color its nodes so that no two neighboring nodes have the same color. Finding the chromatic number of a graph appears to be hard; even telling whether a graph can be colored with three colors appears to be hard. Like the knapsack problem, there is strong evidence that three-colorability is hard; in the language of the next chapter, graph three-colorability is $\mathcal{NP}$-complete. Let's see how we can use this problem to construct digital signatures.

First, we generate a random three-colorable graph. This is easy to do by growing a random graph that is always three-colorable. To add a new node, choose one of the three colors at random. This will be the new node's color. Now choose a random subset of the nodes that are differently colored and connect the new node to them. Add as many nodes as necessary to ensure security.

To use this graph in a signature scheme, we give the authenticator the graph and an encrypted form of its coloring. Since graph coloring is apparently hard, our ability to color the graph will be our signature. When being authenticated, we don't want to give away the coloring, or any information about it, for fear that an attacker will eventually learn enough to reproduce our signature. We don't even want *the authenticator* to be able to impersonate us.

Now here's how we can convince the authenticator that we can three color the graph. The authenticator lays the graph on a table and we secretly three-color its nodes then cover up the node colors. The authenticator picks a random pair of neighboring nodes and we tell the authenticator the colors of the chosen nodes to show that they are indeed different. Then we give the authenticator the decrypt key for the encryption we just used to verify that we're not lying. We then secretly and randomly permute the colors of all nodes; for example, by changing all reds to blues, blues to whites, and whites to reds. (For a fixed three-coloring, there are six permutations to choose from.) In effect, this erases the authenticator's (and any attacker's) memory. Then we invite the authenticator to ask another question. We repeat this as many times as necessary to convince the authenticator that we must know a three-coloring of the graph.

Intuitively, we aren't demonstrating knowledge of a fact, but of a process. No matter how much an attacker eavesdrops on the conversation, once we randomize there is no way the attacker can work back from the answers given to the process that must have been used to produce the answers. Of course few humans will be able to go through this process, but we can put the whole thing on a smartcard and have the smartcard go through the protocol with the electronic counterpart of the authenticator. At no time is an attacker (or the authenticator) given any information that can be later used to impersonate the smartcard bearer.

6.6   Random Numbers

> I cannot believe that God
> plays dice with the cosmos.
>
> Albert Einstein, *The Observer, "Sayings of the week,"*
> *5 April, 1954*

> God not only plays dice, He also
> sometimes throws the dice where they
> cannot be seen.
>
> Stephen Hawking, *Nature, 257, 1975*

So far we've assumed, and extensively used, random numbers. What are they? To begin with, which of the following sequences are random?

- 1, 1, 1, 1, 1, 1, 1, 1, 1, . . .
- 1, 2, 3, 4, 5, 6, 7, 8, 9, . . .
- 2, 7, 1, 8, 2, 8, 1, 8, 2, . . .
- 2, 3, 0, 2, 5, 8, 5, 0, 9, . . .
- 0, 5, 8, 8, 2, 3, 5, 2, 9, . . .
- 3, 3, 5, 4, 4, 3, 5, 5, 4, . . .

| Pause | Give this a few minutes thought.

Your answers for the first two sequences probably were: always one and the integers. With some background in mathematics you say that the third is the digits of *e*. With much more background in mathematics you say that the fourth is the digits of ln 10. With a lot of experience with puzzles you say that the last two *can be described as* the digits of 1/17 and the number of letters in English names of numbers. Is this cheating? Silly puzzles like these work by assuming a common experience base. Would the average person consider all but the first two random?

For each of these sequences we could not have guessed anything given only one or two digits, but we feel, somehow, that if we see nine digits the sequence must be the sequence we guessed. But every finite sequence can be the start of an infinite random sequence. Let's see if we can disentangle *random,* from its various synonyms: *typical, representative, arbitrary, haphazard, accidental, scrambled, aimless, patternless, senseless, causeless, independent, incidental, indeterminate, indescribable, undirected, uncontrolled, uncertain, unrelated, unordered,* and *unpredictable.*

One meaning is that something is random if we have no reason to prefer one state over another; another meaning is that one thing is apparently unrelated to another. As a consequence, if something is random it is not possible to describe it more briefly than to reproduce it. Another angle is that if something is random it is not possible to predict it. The two main properties are: equidistribution and unpredictability. The two are not the same. For example, a number can be equidistributed yet not random, as is shown by *Champernowne's number:*

$$0.12345\ 67891\ 01112\ 13141\cdots$$

This number is equidistributed but certainly not random! The English mathematician David Champernowne, then an undergraduate at Cambridge, invented it in 1933. Further, in physics, chaotic systems show that a system can be non-random yet not practically predictable.

In cryptology there is no such thing as a secure cryptosystem, only secure enough ones. No cryptosystem is secure if you can buy the key from one of the valid users of the system. Trusting computers does not solve this problem, for we are then trusting the makers of the system. Similarly, there is no such thing as a random number sequence, only random enough ones. If a number sequence passes all the tests we throw at it, it's "random."

Just as we say a cryptosystem is "secure enough" if we can't break it in polynomial time, we can say that if we can't predict the next number with better than uniform probability in polynomial time then it's "random enough." A sequence is *pseudorandom* if no future term can be predicted in polynomial time, given all past terms. Of course we need to be careful here, we really want *sequence*, since, for example, all the digits of π are predictable in the sense that we know that they are all less than ten!

Randomness is a particularly slippery concept since all large collections of things will have some order no matter how we arrange them. We know the order is there, but we can't get at it. For example the result proved below shows that of any group of six people, at least three don't know each other or at least three know each other. We know such a triplet exists, but we don't know which of the six they are. This is the first result in an area of combinatorial mathematics called **Ramsey theory**, named after the brilliant but short-lived English mathematician Frank Ramsey.

Here's the result: in every complete graph on six nodes whose edges are colored white or black there is either a set of three nodes connected only by white edges or one connected only by black edges. Call such a triangle a *monochrome triangle*. If a triangle isn't monochrome it's bichrome; we want to show that not all triangles can be bichrome in the complete graph on six nodes.

Pause   Try to prove this.

Well let's look at the four kinds of triangles. Two are monochrome and two are bichrome. Every bichrome triangle has two differently colored edges meeting at one node. Call these edges a bichrome pair; every bichrome triangle has exactly two bichrome pairs. Further, in a complete graph on six nodes every bichrome pair is contained in exactly one triangle. So the number of bichrome triangles is half the number of bichrome pairs.

Now how many bichrome pairs can the complete graph have? Well, there are at most six bichrome pairs meeting at each node. So there are at most thirty-six bichrome pairs. So there are at most eighteen bichrome triangles. But there are twenty triangles in all. So at least two must be monochrome.

Fair Random Numbers

As we've seen with zero-knowledge proofs, cryptology and randomness are deeply intertwined; one particularly strange result is in producing fair random numbers. Suppose Alice and Bob want to flip a coin to decide something over the phone. How can they do this fairly?

The idea is to have Alice send a locked box that needs two keys (that Alice has) to open it. Bob partially opens the box then Alice sends one of the two keys. If Bob can now open the box he wins the toss, if not then Alice wins.

Here's how it works: Alice chooses two large primes and sends their product to Bob. Bob tries to factor it; if he succeeds he wins, but chances are slim. He then checks that the product is not even, a prime, or a power of a prime. It is possible to show that these cases are easy to check, and if it is any of these Alice loses the toss. Then he chooses a number less than and coprime to the product. If this number, by chance, is a factor then he wins immediately (but, again, the chance is small). He then squares it modulo the product and sends the remainder to Alice.

Alice uses the Chinese remainder theorem to find two pairs of numbers that Bob's secret number could have been. She chooses one of the numbers and sends it to Bob. If Bob can now factor the product he wins the toss; if Alice sends Bob's secret number, then Bob has no more information and so cannot factor the product, so he loses the toss. If finding modular square roots is hard, Alice cannot win better than one in two times. If factoring is hard, Bob cannot win better than one in two times. So this protocol provides an unbiased coin flip.

6.7   Transforming Numbers

> Life is the art of drawing sufficient
> conclusions from insufficient premises.
>
> Samuel Butler

In 1979, Allan Cormack, a South African-born American physicist, and Godfrey Hounsfield, a British engineer, were awarded the Nobel Prize in medicine for a new device to look inside people. The device revolutionized medicine because surgeons can now see internal anatomy without having to cut. The device has since evolved into a CAT scanner: a computerized axial tomography scanner. It provides clear images of the body as if it were cut in two with a buzzsaw (*tomos* is Greek for *cut*). And it works in part because of a mathematical operation called a *Fourier transform*.

The idea is to take numerous x-rays of one slice of the body and reconstruct the tissues that must be there based on the intensities of the emerging x-rays. Dense material attenuates an x-ray more than tenuous material, so tissue containing calcium, like bone tissue, absorbs more of the ray than lung tissue. Figure 6.11 shows an x-ray generator rotating about a patient in a fixed plane as the x-ray detectors (the circles) detect the x-ray intensities. This produces a large file of position-intensity numbers. Like cryptanalysis, our job is to reconstruct the internals that must have given rise to this file.

Figure 6.11 Taking a tomograph

Since the first scanner, the basic reconstruction idea has been used to build scanners using ultrasound, positron emission (PET scanners), nuclear magnetic resonance (NMR scanners), and magnetic resonance imaging (MRI scanners). MRI scanners are even more useful than CAT scanners, since it's easier to increase resolution, to display three-dimensional images, and to differentiate between soft tissues—like brain tissue. More generally, the basic idea is used in signal acquisition or transmission systems—in radio astronomy, oceanographic seismology, astrophysics, nuclear fuel testing, electron microscopy, solar physics, and telephony. Further, the reverse idea can be used to target x-rays on a portion of the body for cancer therapy. Truly a useful invention.

Tomography involves many technical details; let's consider a simple reconstruction illustrating the general principles. Suppose our body is a two-dimensional open triangle and suppose we have only three non-parallel orientations for the x-ray generator (horizontal, vertical, and diagonal). See figure 6.12. Think of each x-ray path as a strip of film where the ray's detected intensity has been smeared over the length of the strip.

Overlaying these strips give us a rough idea of where the figure is since the intensities superimpose. This is called **back projection**.

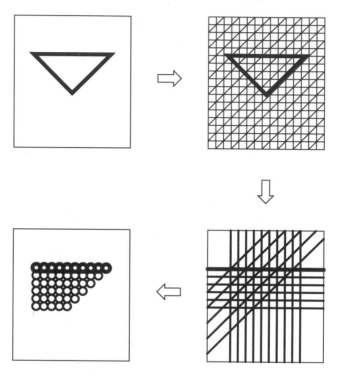

Figure 6.12   Recovering an object with filtered back projection

We can improve the back projected image by *filtering* each of the three sets of strips so that contributions that cannot be part of the figure are removed. For example, in the figure the horizontal strips happen to have the same orientation as one side of the triangle; this shows up clearly in the heavy horizontal line. From that we can deduce that many of the pixels turned on in the final figure, after superimposing the other two sets of strips, must be spurious smear effects. Instead of smearing the detected intensities over the entire length of the vertical and diagonal strips we can concentrate them only in the horizontal band we know the body must lie in. Similarly we can use information from the vertical strips to filter the horizontal and diagonal strips, and so on. The more orientations we have, the better our idea of the object's outline. But what about the interior blurring?

Suppose you've just bought a stereo system. Taken in by a glib salesrep you splurged on a graphic equalizer and skimped on speakers; your speakers only have woofers (heavy speakers that only respond to low frequency, or bass, sounds, and suppress high frequency, or treble, sounds). After lugging your stereo home and plugging it in, you're disappointed by the muffled sound. When you play a disk with lots of treble you hear almost nothing! Your system is producing wonderful sound but the woofer cuts off most of the high frequencies; they are mushed together into a blob of energy at the top end of the woofer's response range.

Fortunately you can salvage something. A graphic equalizer is like an extension of the amplifier's bass and treble controls. A good amplifier amplifies a sound by a constant amount independent of the sound's frequency. But, like sunglasses that differentially filter light, you can use the equalizer to differentially increase the treble response (that is, increase the energy the speakers get when given a high frequency sound) relative to the bass response. Now you can fiddle with the various responses over each frequency range the equalizer has, to differentially improve the speakers' response to high notes. This does not recreate the original sound stored on the disk, but with a finely divided equalizer, and enormous patience, you can make the sound close to the original (but at lower volume). The Fourier transform does the same thing. And we can use it for pictures as well as sound.

A blurred picture is like a muffled song. Instead of time varying frequencies, a picture has spatially varying "frequencies." The Fourier transform turns images into frequencies. Imagine walking across an image the size of football field. As you walk, your immediate neighborhood has a certain color. If the image is large, the next color will usually be close to the current color. But every time you reach an image boundary, the color may change abruptly. The rapidity of color change is like the frequency of sounds. A blurred image retains color variations close to the original colors but the abrupt color change signalling a boundary is lost. We want to recreate those boundaries (the high frequencies) with a filter function analogous to the settings on the graphic equalizer. We need a filter that undoes the blur.

This is an oversimplification of the intricacies involved in tomography. The Fourier transform itself is a complex business and like all complex things it has a real half and an imaginary half, which we examine next.

Fourier Transforms

In the nineteenth century, work on heat conduction by the French mathematician Joseph Fourier showed that any sound can be approximated as closely as we wish by adding pure tones—sine waves—of different frequencies, amplitudes, and phases. Think of these sine waves in terms of sound: amplitude roughly corresponds to loudness—high amplitude waves are loud—frequency roughly corresponds to pitch—high frequency waves are high pitched.

Humans are midway between elephants and rats. We hear only a tiny portion of the sounds either creature makes; most elephant sounds are too low pitched for us to hear, most rat sounds are too high pitched for us to hear. Most humans hear sounds only in the range 20 Hz to 20,000 Hz.[10] Similarly, we see only a small portion of the electromagnetic spectrum—the frequency of the portion we call visible light is about 10^{15} Hz (10^9 MHz, a billion megahertz). We cannot see using infrared radiation or anything lower, nor can we see using ultraviolet radiation or anything higher. If we could see seven orders of magnitude lower than visible light there would be no night; we would see by the light of radio and television waves.

We've already seen a transform—logarithms are transforms. Phones are transforms too: they convert sound waves into electrical pulses (or, nowadays, light waves) and reconvert those pulses back into sound waves. Our ears calculate another kind of transform; ears turn loudness (of sound waves) into frequency (of nerve impulses). Sound waves travel through the cochlea, a snail-like tube in the inner ear (*cochlea* is Latin for snail), and waves of different frequency excite different parts of the cochlea. All our senses transform sense intensity into nerve pulse frequency. Transforms are useful for many reasons—for faster computation, sound or picture compression, and noise resistance in transmission. Fourier transforms are important in signal analysis, and in communication and control problems.

Although for tomography we need the Fourier transform of a two-dimensional picture, let's work with the Fourier transform of a one-dimensional picture (a *scan-line*); the algorithm generalizes to arbitrary dimensions.

Let $\imath = \sqrt{-1}$. The complex number

$$z^j = e^{2\imath \pi j/n}$$

is an nth **root of unity**; if we raise it to the nth power we get 1 because of the wondrous equality:

$$e^{\imath \pi} = -1$$

Although there are either two or one n^{th} roots of unity on the real line, there are n n^{th} roots of unity on the complex plane.

Pause | When is there only one root of unity on the real line?

The **principal** roots of unity are the first $n - 1$ powers of $e^{2\imath\pi/n}$ (see figure 6.13). From the definition we see that z^j is periodic with period n;

---

[10]The Hertz (Hz), a frequency of one beat per second, is named after the tragically short-lived German physicist Heinrich Hertz, the discoverer of radio waves. On a piano, A above Middle C is about 440 Hz.

so, the principal roots of unity are the only roots of unity; higher powers wrap around modulo n since

$$
\begin{aligned}
z^{j+kn} &= e^{2\imath\pi(j+kn)/n} \\
&= e^{2\imath\pi j/n}e^{2\imath\pi kn/n} \\
&= z^{j}e^{2\imath\pi k} \\
&= z^{j}
\end{aligned}
$$

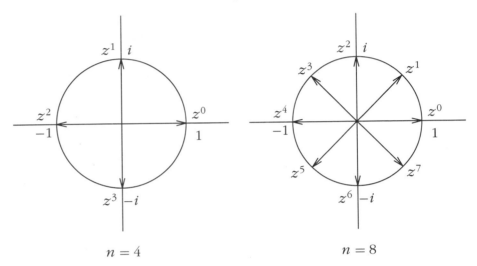

$n = 4$ $\qquad\qquad$ $n = 8$

Figure 6.13 Principal fourth and eighth roots of unity

A Fast Fourier Transform

The **discrete Fourier transform** of the n numbers,

$$
r_0, \quad r_1, \quad \ldots, \quad r_{n-2}, \quad r_{n-1}
$$

is the set of n complex numbers,

$$
f(z^j) = \sum_{k=0}^{n-1} r_k z^{jk} = \sum_{k=0}^{n-1} r_k e^{2\imath\pi jk/n}
$$

where $j = 0, 1, \ldots, n-1$. In our tomography application the r_is represent the intensities of n pixels in a scan-line, and the transformed points represent the (spatial) frequency components of the n pixels.

If we compute each of the transformed points in the obvious way then we use n^2 multiplications: n for each of the original n pixels. But, intuitively, we can do better because each coefficient captures information about the entire picture, so the coefficients should be related.

Suppose $n = 2^m$. Let's split the sum for each j into even and odd parts.

$$f(z^j) = \sum_{k=0}^{2^m-1} r_k z^{jk}$$

$$= \sum_{k=0}^{2^{m-1}-1} r_{2k} z^{2jk} + \sum_{k=0}^{2^{m-1}-1} r_{2k+1} z^{j(2k+1)}$$

$$= \sum_{k=0}^{2^{m-1}-1} r_{2k} z^{2jk} + z^j \sum_{k=0}^{2^{m-1}-1} r_{2k+1} z^{2jk}$$

Aha! The first sum is the Fourier transform of the sequence of points

$$r_0, \quad r_2, \quad \ldots, \quad r_{2^m-4}, \quad r_{2^m-2}$$

and the second is the Fourier transform of the points

$$r_1, \quad r_3, \quad \ldots, \quad r_{2^m-3}, \quad r_{2^m-1}$$

And this leads us directly to an algorithm (see algorithm 6.5).

FOURIER_TRANSFORM($Polynomial, n$)
  { Compute the Fourier transform of the n-degree $Polynomial$.
  $Polynomial$ is a list of coefficients indexed from 0 to $n - 1$.
  Use $Even$, Odd, $List_1$, and $List_2$ as temporary storage.
  n is a power of two. }

if $n = 1$
  then
    return $Polynomial[0]$
  else
    for j from 0 to $n/2 - 1$
      $Even[j] \leftarrow Polynomial[2j]$
      $Odd[j] \leftarrow Polynomial[2j+1]$
    $List_1 \leftarrow$ FOURIER_TRANSFORM($Even, n/2$)
    $List_2 \leftarrow$ FOURIER_TRANSFORM($Odd, n/2$)
    for j from 0 to $n - 1$
      $z \leftarrow e^{2i\pi j/n}$; $k \leftarrow j \bmod (n/2)$
      $Polynomial[j] \leftarrow List_1[k] + z List_2[k]$
    return $Polynomial$

Algorithm 6.5

If $g(n)$ is the worst number of multiplications when n is a power of two then

$$g(n) = \left\{ \begin{array}{ll} 0 & n = 1 \\ 2g(n/2) + n & n > 1 \end{array} \right.$$

So $g = O(n \lg n)$. This algorithm works for one dimension only; for two-dimensional pictures we can apply the algorithm twice, at a cost of $O(n^2 \lg^2 n)$.

6.8   Coda—Straight On Till Morning

> The disappointing fact is that while computer science welcomes some mathematical experts, and recommends that students of the subject have a dose of theory as "preventative mathematics" (in case of a later attack of Fundamental Difficulties), not very many practical computer scientists attempt to understand and apply the deep results of theory.
>
> Richard G. Hamlet,
> *Introduction to Computation Theory*

In this chapter we've looked at some of the oldest and some of the newest work in the analysis of algorithms. What have we learned? Well without previously "useless" number theory, contemporary cryptology wouldn't exist. Without Fourier transforms, or something similar, tomography would be much more inefficient, and may not even exist. The most abstruse theoretical work can have important practical applications. Theoretical is not a synonym for impractical. This is borne out again in zero-knowledge proofs; an apparently ridiculous idea that makes digital signatures possible.

Pseudoprime numbers and pseudorandom sequences are instances of another important development. The basic scheme is to take an idea and relax it, then use the relaxed instances in place of the original. This is a wonderfully liberating idea. But the problem with using relaxed instances, as we have seen with the fall of several knapsack cryptosystems, is that we're living in a house of cards, never knowing whether someone will break our system tomorrow. But then we've always lived in this house, it's just that we can see the cards now. Are finding factors, modular logarithms, or modular square roots really hard? So far we don't really know; the best we can say currently is that they seem to be.

Why do we have spies? Well usually stealing is cheaper than working. Most spying today isn't military or diplomatic—it's commercial, which means it affects us all directly. Public key cryptosystems threaten to take away spies' livelihood; information transmission can now be made effectively impenetrable. Of course once there are humans in the loop spies can still bribe or coerce them. There is the further danger that no public key system is based on a provably difficult problem.

Choosing the best cryptosystem for a particular application is hard. The strongest or fastest may not necessarily be the most useful. We have to tradeoff cryptographic strength, speed, implementation cost, and key management and distribution. If security must not be compromised at any cost, then use a one-time pad. The problem with a one-time pad is that many long keys must be secretly exchanged. If this is impractical, then most cryptographers would probably opt for DES; that's probably a safe choice where only short-term secrecy is required. Sometimes secret key exchange is impossible or impractical; in a network of n users, $O(n^2)$ keys must be distributed, and the addition of a new user requires that n new keys be securely distributed, to and from the other n nodes. Here a public key system is better.

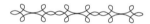

It's now a pressing matter to determine what we mean by a computationally hard problem. Now that we're using hard problems to protect our bank accounts, how do we know that they are really hard? We take up this, the last, topic in the next chapter. To answer it we will also have to answer the question posed in the first chapter—what is an algorithm? In the last chapter we explore the province of infeasible problems. We will find that the ideas behind interactive proofs and zero-knowledge proofs help clarify both questions.

Endnotes

Computational Ideas
Bit-cost model, largest common factor algorithm, sieve algorithm, certificates, computational primality, computational security, computational randomness, knapsack problem, covert channels, interactive proof, zero-knowledge proof, probabilistic acceptance.

Definitions
- *prime number:* A prime number is divisible only by itself and one.
- *coprime numbers:* Two numbers are coprime if they have no common factor other than one.

- *composite number:* A composite number is not prime.

- *imaginary number:* An imaginary number is a product of a real and the square root of -1.

- *complex number:* A complex number is a vector of two numbers, one real, one imaginary.

- n^{th} *root of unity:* A root of unity is a complex number that is one when raised to the nth power.

- *principal* n^{th} *root of unity:* A principal root of unity is one of the first $n - 1$ powers of $e^{2i\pi/n}$.

- *addition chain:* An addition chain is a sequence of numbers whose first element is 1 such that every number is the sum of two previous numbers.

- *quotient:* The quotient of a division is the largest number of times the divisor can be subtracted from the dividend and still leave a non-negative number; it's the floor of the dividend divided by the divisor.

- *remainder:* The remainder of a division is the difference between the dividend and the floor of the dividend divided by the divisor.

- *factor:* A factor of an integer is any integer that divides it leaving no remainder.

- *largest common factor:* The largest common factor of two integers is the largest integer dividing both numbers.

- *pseudoprime:* A base m pseudoprime is an n such that m^k is one more than a multiple of n or if there is an i between 0 and $\nu(n - 1) - 1$ such that m^{k2^i} is one less than a multiple of n (where $k = (n - 1)/2^{\nu(n-1)}$).

- *Carmichael number:* A Carmichael number is a composite integer n such that for all smaller m, m^{n-1} is one more than a multiple of n.

- *totient:* The totient of an integer is the number of positive integers less than, and coprime to, the integer.

- *modular square root:* A modular square root of an integer m modulo n is any integer a whose square is m more than some multiple of n.

- *modular square:* A modular square modulo n is the square of a modular square root modulo n.

- *modular logarithm:* A modular logarithm of m base a modulo n is any integer b such that a^b is m more than some multiple of n.

- *commutative functions:* Two functions f and g commute if for all x in their common domain $f(g(x)) = g(f(x))$.

- *function composition:* The composition of two functions f and g is the function fg where for all x

$$f(g(x)) = y \iff \exists z \ : \ g(x) = z \ \text{ and } \ f(z) = y$$

- *inner product:* The inner product of the vectors $A = (a_1, a_2, \ldots, a_n)$ and $B = (b_1, b_2, \ldots, b_n)$, written $A \cdot B$, is $\sum_{i=1}^{n} a_i b_i$.

- *superincreasing sequence:* A superincreasing sequence is one in which each term is greater than the sum of all previous terms.

- *pseudorandom:* A pseudorandom sequence is indistinguishable from a random sequence using up to a polynomial amount of time.

- *chromatic number:* The chromatic number of a graph is the smallest number of colors needed to color the nodes of the graph so that no two neighboring nodes have the same color.

Constants
- Champernowne's number = 0.12345 67891 01112 13141 $\cdots$

Notation
- $\wedge$ = and

- $\vee$ = or

- $\neg$ = not

- $|A|$ = the size of the set A

- $\equiv$ = equal remainders

- $\psi(n)$ = totient of n

- $\imath$ = $\sqrt{-1}$

Conventions
- the largest common factor of 0 and 0 is 0.

Tools
- The unique factors theorem: Every integer greater than one is uniquely expressible as a product of primes raised to integer powers.

- The Chinese remainder theorem: If n_1, n_2, ..., n_k are all pairwise coprime, then the k linear congruences $m \equiv a_i$ modulo n_i, $i = 1, 2, \ldots, k$, are simultaneously solvable and the solution is unique modulo $\prod_{i=1}^{k} n_i$.

- The Euler-Fermat theorem: $m^{\psi(n)}$ leaves remainder 1 modulo n.

- Fermat's theorem: If n is prime then for all $m \neq n$, m^{n-1} leaves remainder 1 modulo n.

- The prime number theorem: The number of primes less than n grows like $n/\ln n$.

- The prime factors distribution theorem: Let $f(m)$ be the number of different prime factors of m, then for all r

$$\lim_{n \to \infty} \frac{1}{n} \left| \{ m \leq n : f(m) \leq \ln \ln m + r \sqrt{\ln \ln m} \} \right| = \frac{1}{\sqrt{2\pi}} \int_{-\infty}^{r} e^{-x^2/2} dx$$

- $f(n) = \begin{cases} 0 & n = 1 \\ f(\lfloor n/2 \rfloor) + 1 + n \bmod 2 & n > 1 \end{cases}$

  $\implies f(n) = \lfloor \lg n \rfloor + \beta(n) - 1$

- $n = \lfloor n/m \rfloor m + n \bmod m$

- The largest common factor of n and m is the same as the largest common factor of m and n modulo m.

- $n \geq m \implies n > 2(n \bmod m)$

- $e^{i\pi} = -1$

- $g(n) = \begin{cases} 0 & n = 1 \\ 2g(n/2) + n & n > 1 \end{cases} \implies g = O(n \lg n)$

Notes

Gerolamo Cardano, one of the early contributors to probability theory, also invented an encrypting device, called a Cardano grille.

The reference for the $\mathcal{NP}$-completeness of the addition chain problem is "Computing Sequences with Addition Chains," Peter Downey, Benton Leong, and Ravi Sethi, *SIAM Journal on Computing*, 10, 3, 638–646, 1981.

The unique factors theorem is also called the fundamental theorem of arithmetic; the largest common factor is also called the greatest common divisor; coprime numbers are also called relatively prime numbers; modular squares are also called quadratic residues; and modular logarithms are called discrete logarithms.

The 1,065-digit prime in figure 6.5, page 368, is the largest found by a general algorithm. It was found by François Morain with a network of ten workstations in about six weeks time. See "Distributed Primality Proving and the Primality of $(2^{3539}+1)/3$," François Morain, *Advances in Cryptology: Eurocrypt '90,* I. B. Damgård, editor, 110–123, Springer-Verlag, 1991.

The elegant proof of the existence of monochrome triangles in the complete graph of six nodes is adapted from *On the Shape of Mathematical Arguments,* A. J. M. van Gasteren, Springer-Verlag, 1990.

Covert channels are the invention of Gus Simmons, who calls them subliminal channels; see "The Prisoners Problem and the Subliminal Channel," Gus Simmons, *Advances in Cryptology: Proceedings of Crypto 83,* 51–67, Plenum Press, 1984.

The result that all languages in $\mathcal{NP}$ have zero-knowledge proofs is from "Proofs That Yield Nothing But Their Validity and a Methodology of Cryptographic Protocol Design," Oded Goldreich, Silvio Micali, and Avi Wigderson *Proceedings of the 27th Annual Symposium on the Foundations of Computer Science,* IEEE Computer Society, 174–187, 1986. The use of zero-knowledge proofs for digital signatures is from "Zero Knowledge Proofs of Identity," Uriel Feige, Amos Fiat, and Adi Shamir, *Proceedings of the 19th Annual ACM Symposium on the Theory of Computing,* 210–217, 1987. The discussion of zero-knowledge in the text avoids many technical details, the most important of which is that there are *three* versions of zero-knowledge: computational, statistical, and perfect. The text uses the weakest (the computational) version. For more references see the further reading sections of this and the next next chapter.

Factoring numbers finds its way into a variety of problems, for example in the computation of fast Fourier transforms; see "Number-Theoretic Transforms of Prescribed Length," Creutzburg and Tasche, *Mathematics of Computation,* 46, 1986.

As an illustration of the universality of mathematics, Fourier developed Fourier series to model heat conduction. Nowadays, Fourier series are used in everything from consumer electronics to radio astronomy. We now know that Gauss preempted Fourier, but, as with many of his results, he did not publish his work. Gauss' motto was *Pauca sed matura* (Latin for *Few, but ripe*). Until recently it was thought that James Cooley and John Tukey were the inventors of the Fourier transform, but, once again, Gauss was there first. The reference for Gauss' early discovery of both Fourier series and the fast Fourier transform is "Gauss and the History of the Fast Fourier Transform," *IEEE ASSP Magazine,* 1, 4, 14–21, 1984. Incidentally, six years before he was to invent his famous transform, Fourier was outward bound from Egypt on a French ship that the British navy then hijacked. The Rosetta stone, which the British later used to finally decrypt hieroglyphics, was also on that ship.

A new transform appears likely to replace the Fourier transform as the king of the hill—wavelet transforms. See "A New Wave in Applied Mathematics: A technique called wavelets may upstage Fourier analysis in a multitude of applications—from CAT scanning to locating subs," *Science,* 249, 858–859, August 1990, and "Wavelet theory sets out the welcome mat," *SIAM News,* 23, 8–9, September 1990. For a technical presentation see "Continuous and Discrete Wavelet Transforms," Christopher E. Heil and David F. Walnut, *SIAM Review,* 31, 628–666, 1989.

Problem 3, page 414, is from "The Complexity of Finding Cycles in Periodic Functions," Robert Sedgewick, Thomas G. Szymanski, and Andrew C. Yao, *SIAM Journal on Computing,* 11, 376–390, 1982.

Further Reading

For more background on tomography see *The Physical Principles of Computed Tomography,* William R. Hendee, Little, Brown and Company, 1983, and *Image Reconstruction from Projections: The Fundamentals of Computerized Tomography,* Gabor T. Herman, Academic Press, 1980. Fourier transforms now belong almost totally to signal analysis, so to find out more about digital filtering you need to read *Discrete-Time Signal Processing,* Alan V. Oppenheim and Ronald W. Schafer, Prentice-Hall, 1989. Computer graphics and computer vision also make heavy use of Fourier (and other) transforms; see *Digital Image Processing,* Rafael C. Gonzalez and Paul Wintz, Addison-Wesley, second edition, 1987.

Although dated, the best general introduction to number theory is *An Introduction to the Theory of Numbers,* G. H. Hardy and E. M. Wright, Oxford University Press, 1954. For an elementary introduction see *Elementary Theory of Numbers,* William J. LeVeque, Addison-Wesley, 1962. The following survey paper gives a broad overview of primality testing algorithms: "Number-Theoretic Algorithms," Eric Bach, *Annual Review of Computer Science,* 4, 119–172, 1990. See also "Factorization and Primality Tests," John D. Dixon, *The American Mathematical Monthly,* 91, 333–352, 1984, and the comprehensive *Prime Numbers and Computer Methods of Factorization,* Hans Riesel, Birkhäuser, 1985. The following gives a good number-theory oriented introduction to cryptology and a useful introduction to recent factoring algorithms: *A Course in Number Theory and Cryptography,* Neal Koblitz, Springer-Verlag, 1987.

The two original references for probabilistic primality testing still repay reading: "Probabilistic Algorithms," Michael O. Rabin, in *Algorithms and Complexity: New Directions and Recent Results,* J. Traub (editor), 21–39, Academic Press, 1976, and "A Fast Monte Carlo Test for Primality," R. Solovay and V. Strassen, *SIAM Journal on Computing,* 6, 84–85, 1977. See also an erratum list to the last article *SIAM Journal on Computing,* 7, 118, 1978.

Randomness is deeply related to an area of research called algorithmic information theory (also called Kolmogorov complexity). Algorithmic information theory deals with the difficulty of describing an algorithm to solve a problem—it focuses on the minimum length of any algorithm solving the problem—so it could equally well be called algorithmic complexity theory. The following book will become the standard reference for algorithmic information theory: *An Introduction to Kolmogorov Complexity and Its Applications,* Ming Li and Paul M. B. Vitanyi, Addison-Wesley, to appear, 1992. See also "Kolmogorov's Contributions to Information Theory and Algorithmic Complexity," Thomas M. Cover and Peter Gacs, IBM Research Report. The canonical reference for Ramsey theory is *Ramsey Theory,* Ronald L. Graham, Bruce L. Rothschild, and Joel H. Spencer, John Wiley & Sons, 1980.

For more background on cryptanalysis, particularly during the second world war, see *The Codebreakers: The Story of Secret Writing,* David Kahn, Signet, 1973. Alan Turing, the central figure of the next chapter, played a major role in early cryptanalysis, see *Alan Turing, The Enigma of Intelligence,* Andrew Hodges, Unwin, 1983. There are several books on covert intelligence organizations, see *The Puzzle Palace: A Report on NSA, America's Most Secret Agency,* James Bamford, Houghton Mifflin, 1982, and *Secret Service: The Making of the British Intelligence Community,* Christopher Andrew, Heinemann, 1985.

The following two books are both excellent and they provide further background on cryptology: *Public Key Cryptography,* Arto Salomaa, Springer-Verlag, 1990, and *Modern Cryptology: A Tutorial,* Gilles Brassard, Springer-Verlag, 1988. Brassard continues to update cryptologic advances in "The Cryptology Column," in *Sigact News.* Brassard's book lists 250 references. In particular see the references to David Chaum's work; Chaum has done a lot of work on the privacy problem mentioned in the text, particularly for digital cash and smartcards. For physical implementations of smartcards see "Smart Cards," Robert McIvor, *Scientific American,* 152–159, November 1985.

For more background on zero-knowledge proofs see *Uses of Randomness in Algorithms and Protocols,* Joe Kilian, MIT Press, 1990, and "Zero Knowledge and the Department of Defense," Susan Landau, *Notices of the American Mathematical Society,* 35, 1, 5–12, 1988.

For encyclopedic analysis of random number generation, factoring, and primality testing see *The Art of Computer Programming: Volume 2, Seminumerical Algorithms,* Donald E. Knuth, Addison-Wesley, second edition, 1981. Knuth devotes more than forty pages of analysis to the largest common factor algorithm alone.

Questions

> What but the wolf's tooth whittled so fine
> The fleet limbs of the antelope?
> What but fear winged the birds, and hunger
> Jeweled with such fine eyes the great goshawk's head?
>
> Robinson Jeffers, *The Bloody Sire*

Exercises

1. Alice wants to give her bike to Bob. But their schedules make it impossible for them to meet. If both Alice and Bob have bicycle locks, can Alice let Bob have her bike without anyone stealing it?

2. One night you happen to be burgling a house for a desirable collection of analysis books. The house has two floors and you know the collection is on one of the two floors. You also know that it will take you five minutes to search one floor. After finding the collection it will take you ten minutes to cart away all the books. It takes five minutes to get from either floor to the other. However this house has an alarm system and you know that after you break in you will only have twenty minutes before the police come. Fortunately you happen to have a coin in your pocket. What should you do?

3. Your brilliant but erratic friend has found an algorithm that can solve an arbitrary exercise in this book in ten minutes flat. Unfortunately, her incomprehensible algorithm only works one time in a hundred; if it doesn't work within ten minutes it never will. Fortunately, her algorithm can be repeated on the same exercise as many times as you like, and each time it has a one in a hundred chance of solving the exercise. If the average exercise takes you an hour to solve using your normal algorithm (if you manage to solve it), and if you only solve one exercise in five using it, is it worthwhile to switch to your friend's algorithm exclusively?
Now suppose you work in a team of ten and everyone in the team currently uses your algorithm to solve exercises. Is it worthwhile for all of you to switch to your friend's algorithm? Is it worthwhile for any of you to switch to your friend's algorithm?

4. Show that every two consecutive fibonacci numbers are coprime.

5. Find the principal value of i^i.

6. Show that

$$f(n) = \begin{cases} n \lg n & n \text{ even} \\ n^{1.5} & n \text{ odd} \end{cases} \implies f = O(n^2)$$

7. Let

$$f(n) = \begin{cases} 3n^2 & n \text{ prime} \\ 2n \lg n & n \text{ composite} \end{cases}$$

$$g(n) = \begin{cases} n^2/20 & n \text{ even} \\ n^3/\lg n & n \text{ odd} \end{cases}$$

(a) Is $f = O(g)$?

(b) Is $g = O(f)$?

8. Suppose n is prime. When does n^2 divide $2^n + 1$?

9. Show that

(a) $\displaystyle\prod_{i=1}^{n}(1 + x_i) \geq \sum_{i=1}^{n} x_i$

(b) $\displaystyle\prod_{i=1}^{n}(1 - x_i) \leq \sum_{i=1}^{n} x_i$

(c) $\sqrt{n} \geq n^{1/\sqrt{n}} - 1$

10. Alice and Bob are two users of a public key system and Alice wants to sign her messages to Bob as in the text. Alice's public key is (n_1, a) and Bob's private key is (n_2, b). But in general $n_1 \neq n_2$.

(a) Why does this complicate the exchange given in the text?

(b) Design a protocol surmounting the problem.

11. [Not Completely Serious: I] Your mission, should you decide to accept it, is to decrypt the following message we intercepted: "Ink, leather, sausage, roulette, muffin, watch, fly, coffee, waltz, hieroglyphics!" Sources tell us it is a congratulatory message to one of their agents.

12. [Not Completely Serious: II] Your mission, should you decide to accept it, is to decrypt the following message we intercepted: "Carry on indefinitely else we become a laughingstock. Do not stupidly hijack a plane off the airstrip, security is not somnolent! Otherwise we will be forced to render you inoperative." Sources tell us it is a list of places to be infiltrated. So far places beginning with the letters D, G, S, H, and R have been hit, and we know that there are also targets in places beginning with N and M. Where will they hit next?

13. A number is *square-free* if it is not divisible by the square of a prime. Show that a Carmichael number is square-free.

14. Show that a Carmichael number must have at least three prime factors.

15. Paul Erdös found a new proof of the result that there is always a prime between n and $2n$ when he was eighteen. Given this result, show that there are always at least three k digit primes for each k.

16. Show that

$$f(n) = \begin{cases} 0 & n = 1 \\ f(\lfloor n/2 \rfloor) + 1 + n \bmod 2 & n > 1 \end{cases}$$

$$\implies f(n) = \lfloor \lg n \rfloor + \beta(n) - 1$$

Problems

1. Suppose the probability that PSEUDOPRIME reports that n is pseudoprime given that n is in fact composite is less than one half. (It's actually much less than one half.) What is wrong with the following statement?

"The probability that n is in fact composite given that PSEUDOPRIME reports that n is pseudoprime is less than one half."

2. Let m be a product of k coprime integers m_1 to m_k; call these k integers our *divisors*. Represent $n < m$ as the sequence of its k remainders modulo each divisor. For example, using the five divisors 13, 15, 16, 17, and 19, one thousand is represented as the sequence (12, 10, 8, 14, 12).

   (a) Can every $n < m$ be represented?

   (b) Can $n < m$ have more than one representation?

   (c) How hard is it to add two such integers?

   (d) How hard is it to subtract two such integers?

   (e) How hard is it to multiply two such integers?

   (f) How hard is it to test the equality of two such integers?

   (g) Why is this a useful way to do arithmetic if we have k parallel processors?

   (h) How hard is it to compare two such integers?

   (i) How hard is it to divide two such integers?

3. Given a function f mapping values of a finite domain onto itself and an element of the domain x, the sequence

$$f(x), \quad f(f(x)) = f^{(2)}(x), \quad f(f(f(x))) = f^{(3)}(x), \quad \ldots$$

will eventually repeat. We want to find the smallest n such that $f^{(n)}(x)$ has already appeared in the sequence.

(a) Show that this can be solved in no more than $3n$ function evaluations.

(b) Show that if we can use m storage locations to remember previous values then the problem can be solved in no more than

$$n(1 + O(1/\sqrt{m}))$$

function evaluations.

Research

1. Many secrecy problems can be simplified. Figure 6.14 shows two main ways to simplify them, a problem may be *reduced* or *condensed.* We can *reduce* a secrecy problem if it has two or more disconnected components. We can *condense* a secrecy problem if a clique of two or more nodes trust each other pairwise, and every node in the clique distrusts (or mutually distrusts) some node not in the clique. How many irreducible and non-condensible secrecy problems are there on n nodes?

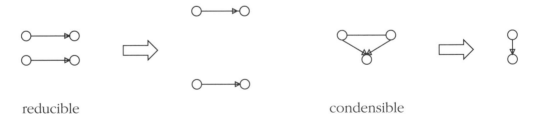

reducible   condensible

Figure 6.14   Reducible and condensible secrecy problems

2. Table 6.2, page 361, lists those powers that are computable in n multiplies.

(a) What is the minimum number of multiplications we can do?

(b) If we wish to minimize the *sum* of the partial products generated in finding m^n what is the best we can do?

INFEASIBILITY

We shall not cease from exploration
And the end of all our exploring
Will be to arrive where we started
And know the place for the first time.

T. S. Eliot, *Little Gidding*

IN CHAPTER one we set out on a journey; now we return to the beginning to ask some difficult questions. What is an algorithm? What is a proof? What is a hard problem? How can we identify hard problems? How can we solve them? Throughout this book we've been designing, analyzing, and redesigning algorithms without clarifying the idea of an algorithm. We've now built many algorithms; what's common to all of them? In this last chapter we'll explore the generally accepted notion of an algorithm. Then we'll see what's wrong with it. While doing so we'll meet

$\mathcal{NP}$-complete problems—practical problems that are strongly suspected to be computationally hard. Then we'll look for ways to climb even this mountain chain of hard problems. Finally we'll grapple with problems that are not solvable using *any* algorithm in the current algorithmic model.

First though we have to understand algorithms. And to do so we have to detour into **computability theory**. The difference between computability theory and complexity theory is that complexity theory asks: "How cheaply can this be computed?" and "How hard is this to compute?" computability theory asks: "When can this be computed?" and "Can this be computed at all?"

Our story first takes us to the heart of the idea of an algorithm. What is it? The story begins with a brilliant mathematician named David Hilbert one Wednesday morning, nearly a century ago.

7.1   Remembrance of Times Past

> History with its flickering lamp stumbles
> along the trail of the past, trying to reconstruct
> its scenes, to revive its echoes, and kindle
> with pale gleams the passion of former days.
>
> Winston Churchill, *Speech, 12 November, 1940*

1900 was an eventful year. As the old century died, three seminal things happened—Sigmund Freud published a book, Max Planck presented a paper, and David Hilbert gave a talk. Today many people have heard of Freud and Planck, but few have heard of Hilbert.

In 1900, Freud published his *The Interpretation of Dreams,* a work that was to become his magnum opus and the start of psychoanalysis. Freud's lifelong ambition was to build a scientific psychology that would explain all mental activities as the effects of prior causes. In October of that year Planck presented his theory of the quantum of action in a seminar at the University of Berlin. Planck's hypothesis explained some puzzling experiments in black body radiation and it led almost directly to the quantum theory. And the quantum theory forced a revolution in physics in the same way that Freud's radical views of human nature forced a revolution in psychology. Besides the philosophical implications of a discrete world, the quantum theory laid the groundwork for nuclear physics and all that that entails for our world.

Freud deliberately set out to change his world. Planck eventually realized that classical physics had to change in fundamental ways. Both started an enormous change in the way we view the world. Hilbert didn't want to change the world; he just wanted to keep his beloved mathematics safe from harm. But what he started on the morning of Wednesday, August 8th, 1900, was to destroy forever the idyllic mathematical world he lived in. And although he would never would know it, it was also the start of computer science.

At the turn of the century mathematics was under attack. For five thousand years mathematicians had been at play, madly inventing the future of their discipline with little thought to possible inconsistencies between different parts of mathematics. Over the centuries various people had complained that there was no proof that some new technique would work, but no one took them seriously. Besides, the German mathematician Georg Cantor had just invented set theory and it seemed to put everything on a firm logical footing.

Unfortunately mathematicians were about to be kicked over the precipice. Serious contradictions had been found in what was, until then, unquestioned mathematical "truth." In 1900 David Hilbert, the most important mathematician of his time, arguably the most famous German mathematician after Gauss, decided that the best way to restore mathematics was to treat it as a game in which you manipulated symbols by fixed rules without thinking of any possible meaning the symbols could have. This *formalist* school of mathematics is dominant today.

Epitomizing this idea, Bertrand Russell, an English mathematician and philosopher, was to write one year later:

> Pure mathematics consists entirely of such asseverations as that, if such and such a proposition is true of *anything,* then such and such a proposition is true of that thing. It is essential not to discuss whether the first proposition is really true, and not to mention what the anything is that of which it is supposed to be true. . . . If our hypothesis is about *anything* and not about some one or more particular things, then our deductions constitute mathematics. Thus mathematics may be defined as the subject in which we never know what we are talking about, nor whether what we are saying is true.

Russell didn't say it, but strict formalism, by not letting semantic interpretations influence how or when rules are applied, supposedly guarantees that whenever we prove something we're *sure* it's correct. That was the whole point. And in pursuit of it, Hilbert, along with most of the mathematical world, was prepared to *give up meaning.* By the late thirties Hilbert's scheme was widely accepted and the defense had been synthesized into a retreat to *formal systems.*

A *formal system* is a finite set of assumed truths, called **axioms**, and a finite set of rules, called **inference rules**. The idea is to isolate all of the intuitive, unprovable, or undefinable parts of an investigation in the set of axioms and to use the rules on the axioms to infer new results called **theorems**. We can then use the rules on the axioms plus any inferred theorems to infer more theorems. A *proof* of a theorem in a formal system is a demonstration of a sequence of inferred theorems starting only with the axioms and using only the inference rules and ending with the theorem. The purpose of formal systems was to gain surety and freedom from contradiction.

Now let's listen to Hilbert winding up his address to the Second International Congress of Mathematicians in Paris, August 1900:

> We hear within us the perpetual call: There is the problem.
> Seek its solution. You can find it by pure reason, for in mathematics there is no *ignorabimus* ["we shall not know"].

To spur on the gathered mathematicians to rectify his beloved mathematics Hilbert suggested twenty-three problems for the new century. One problem, the second, was to establish that arithmetic was **consistent,** meaning that, under the accepted rules of arithmetic, it is not possible to generate a contradiction.

In 1931, Kurt Gödel ("guer-dle"), a twenty-four year old Moravian graduate student at the University of Vienna, showed that if any system as "powerful" as arithmetic is consistent, then it cannot be **complete**—meaning that some true statements are unprovable in the system! Since then it has been shown that many formal systems are consistent—but none are interesting! Today we don't know whether arithmetic is consistent; all we can say is that if it is, then there are true things we cannot prove in it. This is similar to the uncertainty principle in quantum mechanics, enunciated by the German physicist Werner Heisenberg just four years earlier, in 1927: we can find the exact position of a subatomic particle, or we can find its exact velocity, but we can't do both together. So much for *ignorabimus.*

To see something of the intricacies involved in Gödel's proof consider *Russell's paradox,* named after Bertrand Russell, who invented it in 1902: If a plumber fixes the pipes of all people who don't fix their own pipes, who fixes the plumber's pipes? The crux of this problem is that something doesn't exist just because we talk about it.[1] Similarly, can an all-powerful being make a stone so big that it can't lift the stone? One answer is: What is it lifting the stone off of?

The consistency problem was only Hilbert's second problem; his first problem was the continuum problem. When Cantor invented set theory,

---

[1] "[Yossarian] had decided to live forever or die in the attempt." Joseph Heller, *Catch-22.*

one of his first, and most startling, results was that there is more than one infinity. Taking the number of integers as the first infinity, and using a proof method called *diagonalization,* Cantor showed that there were more real numbers than there were integers. But no one knew if there was an infinity between the number of integers and the number of reals. Hilbert's first problem was to settle this question, and the belief that there was no such infinity became known as the **continuum hypothesis**.

In 1938, Gödel partly solved the problem by showing that it couldn't be proved false from Cantor's axioms of set theory; Gödel was forced to assume that Cantor's set theory was consistent, since it was not (and still is not) possible to prove that it is. Then in 1963 the American mathematician Paul Cohen showed that it couldn't be proved true from Cantor's axioms. Thus Gödel showed that it isn't disprovable, and Cohen showed that it isn't provable! The continuum hypothesis is **independent** of the usual axioms of set theory. If set theory is consistent to begin with, then we can assume the continuum hypothesis true or false and still have a consistent set theory! So much for that problem.

To avoid known paradoxes, Cantor's theory was modified and extended by the German mathematicians Ernst Zermelo then Abraham Fränkel, and together with a widely-accepted axiom invented by Zermelo called the **axiom of choice,** is referred to as ZFC (Zermelo-Fränkel set theory plus the axiom of choice). Like the continuum hypothesis, the axiom of choice is independent of the other axioms, but it leads to bizarre results. For example, anyone accepting the axiom of choice (as most contemporary mathematicians do) has to accept that it is possible to dissect a sphere and produce a sphere of twice the volume! The formalist school was resisted by a group of mathematicians called constructivists (sometimes called intuitionists) who, led by the Dutch mathematician Luitzen Brouwer, wanted to toss infinite sets and rebuild mathematics from the bottom up starting from the integers and applying only finite operations to them. This effort continues today in the work of the late American mathematician Errett Bishop and his school.

7.2 Models of Computation

> All human knowledge begins with
> intuitions, proceeds to concepts, and
> ends in ideas.
>
> Immanuel Kant

Another of Hilbert's problems (the tenth) was to find a "finitary way" to solve any diophantine equation. A *diophantine equation* is a polynomial equation in n unknowns that can have only integer solutions; named after the early Greek algebraist Diophantus, thought to have lived either in the first or third century. Hilbert actually wanted more; he wanted a "finitary way" to solve *any* mathematical problem. Something like directions in a cookbook—only more precise: name these variables; construct those equations; solve for x, y, and z. In short, he wanted something he didn't have a name for, he wanted an algorithm. Hilbert, and his contemporaries, thought that such an algorithm must exist; they thought the difficulty with finding it was that it was surely very complicated.

In 1970, twenty-seven years after Hilbert's death, Jurii Matijasevič ("mat-ya-say-vich"), a twenty-two year old student at the University of Leningrad, found a brilliant proof using, of all things, fibonacci numbers, showing that this problem is **computationally unsolvable**—no such algorithm can exist. Matijasevič, building on work by American mathematicians Martin Davis, Julia Robinson, and the American philosopher Hilary Putnam, could do this because, during the seventy years between Hilbert's formulation and Matijasevič's solution, mathematicians had been furiously working on an *appropriate model* under which the tenth problem made sense.

What had been developed in the years between Hilbert's statement of the problem and its final solution by Matijasevič was a precise and widely-accepted definition of an *algorithm.* A lot of the credit for this revolution in understanding goes to the then twenty-four year old English mathematician after whom the formalized notion was named—Alan Turing—and the formalized notion of what an algorithm is has come to be called a *turing machine.*

As you may have surmised, this brief history has skimped on the details of this exciting story, not least of which is that although we now use turing machines as our paradigm of algorithms, it could possibly have been the pet formalism of any one of several French, Austrian, American, or Russian theorists. Other formalisms that might have had the honor are: (Jacques) Herbrand functions, (Kurt) Gödel functions, (Alonzo) Church calculus, (Stephen) Kleene functions, (Emil) Post systems, or (Andreĭ) Markov algorithms. Some of these theorists were kept from lionization by accident; for example, Post lost his left arm at twelve and suffered from recurring bouts of manic-depression, and Herbrand died in a mountaineering accident at twenty-three. (Perhaps in alternate universes where Herbrand or Post developed their ideas, computer scientists build their theories on Herbrand functions or Post systems.) All of these formalisms have the same computational ability as turing machines.

As an example of the interrelatedness of the work of these giants, Turing developed his famous machines to answer yet another of Hilbert's problems—the *decision problem*—that, in modern terms, asked whether there is an algorithm deciding the truth or falsity of any mathematical statement. This problem was vanquished independently by Church and by Turing in 1936; no such algorithm exists. What's more, the result is provable from Gödel's work on incompleteness in 1931! It's miraculous that all these ways of looking at computation are the same.

All of these theorists made major contributions to logic and to mathematics as a whole, and, almost as a side effect, because they were forced to, they codified what it meant for something *to be computable.* This is surprising when you consider that in the thirties, when most of this work was done, there were no computers for them to abstract from. In fact there is evidence that the brilliant Hungarian-born American mathematician John von Neumann, who is often credited with the central ideas of present day computers, developed them based on Turing's thought. This whole program can be traced back to Hilbert's call and it continues today in logic, philosophy, and computer science.

However turing machines came about we should be grateful to their creator since without a flexible model of computation we would not be able to come to grips with $\mathcal{NP}$-completeness. We would have no *model* to distinguish feasible from infeasible algorithms.

Why Should You Care?

Suppose you are a programmer at Yoyodyne Propulsion Labs and your boss asks you to find an efficient algorithm to generate a routing of wires on a new chip they're developing. Of course, costs being what they are and the world being what it is, Yoyodyne wants a routing using the least amount of wire; reasoning, no doubt soundly, that the less they pay for the chip and the more they charge for a copy of it, the more money they will make. As is also the way of the world, your job's existence is a function of Yoyodyne's profit margin.

So, you work on this problem and come up with a crude brute force algorithm—all the clever algorithmic tricks you learned in previous chapters failed. You couldn't find a way to avoid testing large numbers of the possible combinations. Unfortunately the chip has sixty-four pin connectors. Even though you managed to cut the cost of trying each combination of connections to one second, your algorithm takes 2^{64} seconds to run. Recall the towers of Hanoi problem from chapter one. Even assuming a computer capable of testing a pin assignment in a billionth of a second, your program will still take roughly six hundred years to run.

What to do? Do you tell your boss you can't solve the problem? You could get fired. Do you tell your boss that *it is impossible* to do better, so there's no point firing you? She might not fire you but she'd need proof. Besides, Yoyodyne frowns on bosses who don't produce; so, even if you could prove that it can't be done faster, she'll want results anyway. What to do?

Programmers were put in exactly that position about forty years ago. The digital computer had finally been invented and big business, big government, and big armies wanted it put to work. Unfortunately, nobody knew that some problems are computationally harder than others; some are so hard as to be unsolvable in practice. So programmers were asked to produce efficient algorithms for problems that we know as *the travelling salesman problem, the knapsack problem,* and *the graph colorability problem,* little knowing that such problems seem to be computationally hard.

So we have four questions: Are some problems much harder than others? If so, which ones? How much harder are they? And if they are much harder, what do we do? To begin answering these questions we next look at the history of understanding feasible problems. As we see next, today "feasible" is identified with "has a polynomial solution."

Why Polynomials?

In 1965, Jack Edmonds, a mathematician now at the University of Waterloo, and, independently, Alan Cobham, now at an IBM research center, gave a definition of a feasible problem: A problem is feasible if it has a solution whose cost is at most polynomial. Here's why:

- Polynomials are closed under composition and addition.
  This corresponds to our intuitive feeling that if we have two feasible algorithms then we can use one as a subroutine of the other to obtain another feasible algorithm (closure under composition), and, if we run them one after the other then we will also obtain a feasible algorithm (closure under addition).

- All sequential digital computers are *polynomially related.*
  That is, if we can solve a problem in $f(n)$ time on one machine we can solve it in some polynomial of $f(n)$ time on another machine. Thus, if a problem has a polynomial solution on any current digital computer, then it has a polynomial solution on any other digital computer. Therefore, it makes sense to call a problem polynomial, independent of the particular machine it is run on.[2]

_____

[2]Perhaps Shakespeare would say: What's in a mainframe? A computer by any other name would be as fleet.

- In general, a polynomial algorithm will do a feasible amount of work. Conversely, in general, if an algorithm is exponential (or worse) then it is feasible for small inputs only.

This last observation is an empirical one and it does not hold in all cases. For example, as we see next, an algorithm called *simplex* is fast in practice but exponential in the worst case. Conversely, most polynomial algorithms that grow faster than a cubic are almost useless. However, we can at least say that most exponential algorithms grow too fast for us to solve them for any reasonable size. The theory of hard problems is still young; *it is a first approximation only.* Similarly, we say that one algorithm is "worse" than another if its worst cost is larger; but, as we've seen in previous chapters, in practice many other things can be important.

Are Exponentials Really So Bad?

In 1947, the American mathematician George Dantzig published an algorithm solving optimization problems expressible as linear programs. A **linear program** is a collection of constraints in n variables, each of which is linear in each of the variables, together with a linear function to be maximized. Many optimization problems can be phrased as linear programs; in particular, Dantzig used his algorithm to solve logistics problems for the U.S. Air Force. Dantzig's algorithm, called *simplex,* was a great step forward since, in practice, it was much faster than previous brute force algorithms. However it is possible to show that simplex's worst cost is exponential in the number of variables (but these inputs are rare in practice). The search was on for an algorithm with a "more reasonable" worst cost.

In 1979, the Russian mathematician Leonid Hačijan ("kha-chi-yan") building on work by other Russian theorists A. Juriĭ Levin, N. Z. Shor, D. B. Judin, and A. S. Nemirovskiĭ, proved that an algorithm, called the *ellipsoid algorithm,* was polynomial. The ellipsoid algorithm is like a multidimensional binary search. Unfortunately the degree of the polynomial is too high for real problems, and simplex, although exponential in the worst case, is fast in practice. In 1984, Narendra Karmarkar, a computer scientist at AT&T Bell Labs, improved the ellipsoid algorithm to run well in practice. Called *projective scaling,* Karmarkar's algorithm is polynomial; it outperforms the ellipsoid algorithm; and it is competitive with simplex on practical problems. Since then several new polynomial time algorithms have been proposed, and these new algorithms beat simplex as the problem size grows.

So although simplex is exponential, the linear programming problem is polynomial. This difference is important because *no computer can perform more than about 10^{15} switches per second.* Beyond that speed, the frequency of visible light, the energy needed for the switching will break the chemical bonds holding solids together. Since we're already in the 10^9 operations per second range we can expect at best a million-fold speedup. But what's a factor of a million to an exponential algorithm? 2^n grows by a factor of better than a million whenever n increases by twenty. And that is the difference between exponentials and polynomials; although different computers have different speeds, exponentials grow so fast that they dwarf these differences.[3]

7.3   Turing Machines

> The final test of a theory is its capacity to solve the problems which originated it.
>
> George Dantzig, *Linear Programming and Extensions*

Now let's try to recreate Turing's thoughts about computation in 1936. In those days, a formal system, as defined on page 417, was not yet well-defined, for there was as yet no agreed upon meaning for computation. This was essential because to say unequivocally that something was true, Hilbert wanted a "finitary way" (an algorithm) to be used. This, for instance, was why the number of axioms and the number of inference rules had to be finite; Hilbert stipulated that there must be algorithms to decide whether something is an axiom, whether something is an inference rule, and whether one statement followed from another. Only so could he be assured that a theorem, once proved in a formal system, was correct. To solve Hilbert's decision problem, and to put bite into then still some-what vague idea of a formal system, Turing had to answer the question: What does it mean to compute something?

Consider solving a problem, proving a theorem, or writing an algorithm, with pencil and paper. Obviously some things don't matter. It doesn't (or shouldn't) matter what color the paper is; whether we write left to right, right to left, or up and down; or whether we're making marks with a pencil, pen, brush, lipstick, typewriter, or car tire. It doesn't even matter if we're using paper; we can perceive symbols in other ways (say, by hearing them spoken, or by feeling them as in braille), and we can alter them or add to them without writing (say, by speaking them, or by acting them as in mime or charades). What matters is that we're perceiving symbols

---

[3]Since we're dreaming about speed, *nothing* can happen faster than about 10^{-23} seconds; this is the time light takes to cross the diameter of a proton. 10^{23} is only one hundred million times faster than 10^{15}, and 2^n eats up that whenever n increases by twenty-seven.

fixed on some medium, and we can create or delete symbols, perhaps based on symbols already there, plus some thinking.

Since the medium doesn't matter, let's fix on paper and pencil. We don't need two-dimensional paper; our paper can be a tape divided into squares. This lets us ignore inessential details like how to handle margins and line spacing. Also, we can restrict our symbols so that each fits within one square; so there is only one symbol per square. Now we can make the number of different symbols finite, because if there were an infinite number of symbols it would take us an infinite time to distinguish between them. Further, let's extend the tape to infinity to make sure there is enough paper. It is only necessary for us to be able to move left or right on this tape and look at symbols. Now we can reduce "looking at symbols" to looking at one symbol at a time. In sum, we can reduce ourselves to:

- moving left one square,

- moving right one square,

- staying in the current square,

- reading the symbol on the current square,

- erasing the symbol on the current square, and

- writing a symbol on the current square.

We decide which of these operations to do next based on the symbol on the current square and our current state of mind.

Now how do we model "states of mind?" Again, some things don't matter. It doesn't (or shouldn't) matter whether it's a nice day; whether we are happy or sad; or whether we are in Fiji, in Guatemala, or on the first Mars mission. Let's assume that we have only a finite number of possible states of mind.[4] Now we can reduce "solving the problem" to reaching any one of a particular set of states previously designated as *accept states*. We can solve a problem that requires an answer by reaching an accept state and taking whatever is left on the tape as the "answer." So now we have two more operations:

- change state depending on the current symbol and current state, and

- stop when we reach any accept state.

We begin with the problem written out on the tape, using the symbols we've fixed. Since we may have to read all these symbols to solve the

---

[4]This might seem reasonable because our brains have only a finite number of atoms, but the issue is still clouded because an atom can be in an infinitude of quantum states.

problem, the problem must be finitely describable. Further, once we get going we don't stop to revise our thinking process. Nothing new occurs to us beyond our original finite thought process and the finite description of the problem. Both of these assumptions are debatable as models of human thought.[5]

Now how do we handle "guessing?" It seems as if there is a difference between guessing (intuition, creativity, insight) and mere routine manipulation. But if there are only a finite number of options there is no difference in ability if we disallow guessing since we can always try all possibilities; it will merely take us longer. So there is no difference in ability, but it's not clear whether there is a difference in speed. So let's make two kinds of machines: the normal kind executes a fixed program and the other kind does the same but can also guess (always correctly!). The first kind corresponds to what we've called a predictable algorithm throughout this book, but the second is magic.

An Exercise in Self-Control

In sum, a *turing machine* is a no-frills digital computer. There are two kinds of machine: normal and magical. A normal turing machine can read one square at a time of an infinitely long tape, and it can be in any one of a finite number of states. For each possible state and symbol on the current tape square it can write a symbol belonging to a finite set of symbols, move left one square, or move right one square. It has no choice at each step in its computation; it can follow only one branch. Finally, it stops if it reaches an accept state, but it may never reach an accept state for a particular input.

The definition of an algorithm given in chapter one (page 13) is restrictive; turing machines give us a prescriptive definition of algorithms. The definition in chapter one tells us what an algorithm is not; a turing machine tells us what an algorithm is.[6]

A magical, or *non-deterministic*, turing machine is like a normal one that can follow an arbitrary number of branches at each step. We can think of it as a computer that can simultaneously perform an *arbitrary* number of different computation paths (sequences of states and tape moves dependent on the input). This is different from a parallel computer; a parallel

---

[5]There are other, more philosophical, questions: Are symbols necessary for any computation, or just necessary for human understanding of the computation? Is there a difference between the machine and the program? Is there a difference between following a list of instructions and creating it? What does it mean to "understand" what the machine is doing?

[6]"She was a phantom of delight/ When first she gleam'd upon my sight;/ . . . And now I see with eye serene/ The very pulse of the machine." William Wordsworth, *Perfect Woman*.

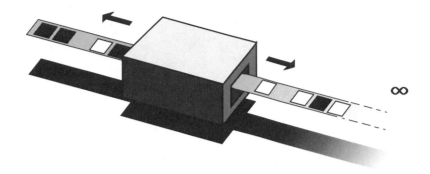

Figure 7.1 A turing machine

computer has only a constant number of processors, so it can't work on an arbitrary number of things simultaneously. For a technical reason that we use later (page 436), it is desirable (and possible) to configure a magical machine so that at each branch in its computation path it has to choose between only two alternatives, even if we have to make the two alternatives the same. So we can think of its computation paths as a binary computation tree. Since it essentially follows all computation paths in its computation tree, a magical turing machine accepts an input if *any* computation path ends in an accept state.

We can also think of a magical turing machine as a normal turing machine with a magic guessing module. The guesser first *guesses* a correct computation path, then the normal part of the machine performs the guessed computation. ("Non-determinism" is a misleading name; it should be called either "infinite parallelism" or "magic.")[7]

There is no difference in the ability of the two kinds of machines— whatever we can do with one we can do with the other. But it is not clear whether there is a difference in speed; perhaps magical machines are always faster. If there is a difference in speed between these two classes of machines then, roughly speaking, it should correspond to a difference between guessing and searching. The central question in theory today is whether there is a difference.

We can use turing machines as our model of computation where time is measured as the number of state transitions the machine goes through,

---

[7]Turing did not add non-determinism to his machines; that had to wait until 1959 when Michael Rabin ("rah-been") and Dana Scott did so for technical reasons. Rabin, a German-born Israeli computer scientist now at Harvard and the Hebrew University in Israel, is one of the originators of probabilistic algorithms. Both Rabin and Scott are major contributors to theory, and both were students of Alonzo Church at Princeton. Scott is an American computer scientist now at Carnegie-Mellon University.

and space is the number of tape squares it reads or writes. A computation runs in **polynomial time** if the number of state transitions is a polynomial of the length of the input (and similarly for space).

Granted that it's reasonable to classify problems depending on whether their worst cost is polynomial, why should we concentrate on turing machines? Why not something more powerful? Or why not a real machine? Well, first, if we try to model real machines we sink into a swamp of detail (for example, clock cycle counting). Turing machines are just plain simpler. Second, our theory cannot be too dependent on any real machine for then it is applicable only to that machine. Also, which company's machine do we pick as the standard machine? And finally, there aren't any more powerful machines. Although apparently primitive, turing machines are polynomially related to every other known digital computing device. All computers are created equal, up to a polynomial.

After sixty years of trying to find a stronger model of computation, computer scientists now accept the **Church-Turing hypothesis**: every algorithm can be described by (or implemented on, or is equivalent to) a turing machine. This is not a provable hypothesis since it depends on our intuitive understanding of the word "algorithm." But if we accept it, there is no point working only with turing machines; that's like trying to debug a program from its machine code—it's possible but tedious, prone to error, and dull. Instead, from now on let's accept the Church-Turing hypothesis and write algorithms in a decent language, as we've done in previous chapters. By the Church-Turing hypothesis all such algorithms are realizable on a turing machine. Further, there is no longer any need to refer to turing machines at all; let's just say "algorithm" and be done with it.

7.4   Birth of $\mathcal{NP}$-Completeness

> And what rough beast, its hour come round at last,
> Slouches towards Bethlehem to be born?
>
> W. B. Yeats, *The Second Coming*

Now that we've settled on a model of computation, let's formalize the Edmonds-Cobham intuition that a problem with a polynomial solution is "easy," and one whose every solution grows faster than every polynomial is "hard." Since we've decided to call polynomial computations easy, our first approximation to a notion of hardness is to ignore polynomial transformations.

Let's say that problem P_1 is **polynomially transformable** to problem P_2 if we can transform *any* instance of P_1 into some instance of P_2 in polynomial time. Thus, in principle, we could solve any instance of P_1 by transforming the instance, in polynomial time, into an instance of P_2, then solving the instance of P_2.

So *if* P_2 is easy then P_1 is also easy—because we can solve any of P_1's instances by turning it, in polynomial time, into an instance of P_2. If P_2 is hard we cannot say that P_1 is hard; there may be some other way to solve P_1. But we can at least say that it is *no harder* than P_2. So let's denote the polynomial transformability of P_1 to P_2 as

$$P_1 \leq P_2$$

To prove that P_1 is polynomially transformable to P_2 we have to find a polynomial time algorithm that transforms any instance of P_1 into an instance of P_2. If we can also polynomially transform P_2 to P_1 then the two problems are **polynomially equivalent**. They cost the same, up to a polynomial. And this is true irrespective of whether they are easy or hard.

| Pause | Suppose $P_1 \leq P_2$. Let I_1 be an instance of P_1, and let I_2 be the instance of P_2 produced by the transformation. Is it possible for I_2 to be exponentially longer than I_1?

So far, almost all problems that are solvable on normal machines before the heat-death of the universe when their inputs are of size a million are polynomial. Let's say that these problems are in $\mathcal{P}$, the class of problems solvable in polynomial time. Formalizing the Edmonds-Cobham intuition, let's say that a problem is **computationally hard** if it isn't in $\mathcal{P}$; that is, if it does not have a polynomial time solution.

Many problems belong to a possibly larger class than $\mathcal{P}$. These problems are in $\mathcal{NP}$, the class of problems solvable in polynomial time, but on magical machines. $\mathcal{P}$ is a subset of $\mathcal{NP}$, since a normal algorithm is just a magic one that doesn't guess. But it is unknown whether $\mathcal{P}$ equals $\mathcal{NP}$. The term $\mathcal{NP}$ is short for "$\mathcal{N}$on-deterministic $\mathcal{P}$olynomial time," *not* "non-polynomial;" that would make sense only if $\mathcal{P} \neq \mathcal{NP}$, and even then it's false since $\mathcal{P}$ is a subset of $\mathcal{NP}$.

$\mathcal{NP}$-Complete Problems

Now that we've clarified what we mean by a hard problem, let's see if we can identify them. First, let's fix a finite set of two or more symbols as our **alphabet**. (Any non-empty finite set will do.) A finite sequence of symbols of the alphabet is a **string**; a set of strings is a **language**; a set of languages is a **class**. Let's use uppercase italic letters for languages and calligraphic uppercase letters for classes. Now that we've settled on an alphabet, the class of all languages with a particular property means the subset of languages, within the set of all languages over our chosen alphabet, that have that property.

Now we're ready for problems. Here is the **satisfiability problem:** Given a set of strings of upper- and lowercase letters, where if one form of a letter appears in a string its other form does not, is it possible to select one letter from each string, without selecting both the upper- and lowercase versions of some letter? For instance, the set of strings

$$\{ \text{AbC, Ac, aBc, bC} \}$$

is satisfiable (for example, choose A from the first two strings, B from the third, and C from the fourth), while the set

$$\{ \text{ab, aBc, Abc, AB} \}$$

is not.

Pause How many letter choices satisfy the first example? How would you find a satisfying choice in general?

Turning this into a language acceptance problem, we pose the problem of **satisfiability acceptance:** Given a string made up of strings of letters separated by a special symbol, tell whether it is in the set of such strings that are satisfiable. For instance, the string

$$\text{AbC\#Ac\#aBc\#bC}$$

belongs in the language, but the string

$$\text{ab\#aBc\#Abc\#AB}$$

does not.

We can also phrase the acceptance problem as a problem in logic: Can a given conjunctive proposition composed of disjunctions of variables, where each variable can have only one of two logical values (true or false), ever be true (be *satisfied*)? For example, to a logician the above two examples would be: Are either of the two following propositions satisfiable?

$$(\bar{\alpha} \vee \beta \vee \bar{\gamma}) \wedge (\bar{\alpha} \vee \gamma) \wedge (\alpha \vee \bar{\beta} \vee \gamma) \wedge (\beta \vee \bar{\gamma})$$

and

$$(\alpha \vee \beta) \wedge (\alpha \vee \bar{\beta} \vee \gamma) \wedge (\bar{\alpha} \vee \beta \vee \gamma) \wedge (\bar{\alpha} \vee \bar{\beta})$$

Satisfiability acceptance is in $\mathcal{NP}$ since for any instance we can always guess a suitable sequence of letters, then verify, in polynomial time, that that sequence satisfies the instance.

Long Pause What if there is no satisfying sequence?

Satisfiability is an abstraction of an important problem: How can we tell that our beliefs are consistent? For example, suppose that two of the many beliefs we have about the world are:

- All grass is green.

- All hay is grass.

Then when we try to add the belief

- All hay is brown.

we no longer have a consistent set of beliefs.

Notice that it is easy to check our beliefs for consistency if the only possible inconsistency is between pairs of beliefs. It's easy, for instance, to detect inconsistency in any set of beliefs, no matter how large, if we only had to worry about finding pairs like

- All grass is green.

- Some grass is brown.

This only requires work at most quadratic in n, the number of beliefs. However, when inconsistencies can depend on an arbitrary number of beliefs the subsets that we have to check grows as 2^n. And so far we seem to have no better way to check than to examine all possible combinations of beliefs to see if any are inconsistent.

The acceptance problem is better than the original problem because it is a *decision problem.* (See the list of problem types in chapter one, page 9.) We construct the decision problem so that it is no harder than the optimization problem we really want to solve. So if we manage to prove that the decision problem is hard, then we know that the optimization problem is at least as hard. Also, analyzing only decision problems lets us ignore the size of the output since it is always either "yes" or "no." In some optimization problems we could confound the inherent hardness of the problem with the time necessary just to list its solution; for example, in the towers of Hanoi problem we need exponential time to list the solution. Once we get the supposedly simple case of decision problems straight we can worry about more complex kinds of problems.

Further, many optimization problems can be feasibly solved if their associated decision problem can be feasibly solved. For example, in chapter six (page 392) we used the graph colorability problem to construct digital signatures. If deciding whether a graph can be colored with a particular number of colors is easy, then *finding* a graph's chromatic number is also easy. All we have to do is ask whether the graph can be colored with $\lfloor n/2 \rfloor$ colors. If yes, then we ask whether the graph can be colored with $\lfloor n/4 \rfloor$ colors, otherwise we ask whether the graph can be colored with $\lfloor 3n/4 \rfloor$ colors. And so on. This gives us the graph's chromatic number after at most a logarithmic number of uses of the solution of the decision problem. So determining the optimal coloring is (up to a polynomial) no harder than deciding whether a particular number of colors suffice.

Given a language acceptance problem P and a class of problems C, P is *C-hard* if it is at least as hard as every problem in C. If P is also in C then P is *C-complete*.

This meaning of the word "complete" rightly baffles the non-initiate of *recursive function theory*, that part of mathematics developing the properties of the functions developed by Herbrand, Gödel, and Kleene. "Complete" is used here to mean that a solution to any problem in the set can be applied to all others in the set. It is different from the notion of complete proof systems discussed earlier. Unfortunately tradition requires one word to mean two different things.[8]

To avoid constantly saying that a particular language acceptance problem is hard, let's just say that the language in question is hard, since all we'll be doing with languages is trying to accept them. We've defined hardness in the class $\mathcal{NP}$ up to a polynomial transformation, so the language L is *$\mathcal{NP}$-complete* if:

- L is $\mathcal{NP}$-hard.
  That is, given a polynomial algorithm accepting L, then for *every* language in $\mathcal{NP}$ there is a polynomial algorithm accepting it.

- L is in $\mathcal{NP}$.
  That is, given a string we can tell whether it is in L in polynomial time.

It seems difficult to prove the first property since we must prove it for every language in $\mathcal{NP}$. Fortunately, in 1971 Stephen Cook, an American-born Canadian computer scientist now at the University of Toronto, showed that if satisfiability is solvable in polynomial time, then *all* problems in $\mathcal{NP}$ are solvable in polynomial time! Therefore, using the Edmonds-Cobham notion of hardness, *satisfiability is at least as hard as any other problem in $\mathcal{NP}$*. At about the same time, Leonid Levin, a Russian-born American computer scientist, then in Russia and now at Boston University, independently proved a similar result. This is the *Cook-Levin theorem*.[9]

---

[8]'When I make a word do a lot of work like that,' said Humpty Dumpty, 'I always pay it extra.' Lewis Carroll, *Through the Looking-Glass.*

[9]The Cook-Levin theorem might be stated: I can't get no satisfaction soon. An obvious corollary of a well-known theorem by the Rolling Stones.

Cook showed how to polynomially transform any instance of any problem in $\mathcal{NP}$ into an instance of the satisfiability problem in such a way that the original problem instance has a solution if and only if the satisfiability instance has a solution. Thus, we can polynomially transform every problem in $\mathcal{NP}$ to satisfiability. Therefore, up to a polynomial transformation, satisfiability is at least as hard as every other problem in $\mathcal{NP}$. So satisfiability is $\mathcal{NP}$-hard. And since satisfiability is in $\mathcal{NP}$, satisfiability is $\mathcal{NP}$-complete.

Pause — Why is it useless to show that given an instance of the satisfiability problem, we can polynomially transform it to an instance of some other problem in $\mathcal{NP}$?

So to show that a problem in $\mathcal{NP}$ is $\mathcal{NP}$-complete we only need show that the problem is at least as hard as satisfiability. Further, once we have proved that some problem, say P, is at least as hard as satisfiability then, given a new candidate problem, we can try to show that it is at least as hard as satisfiability *or* P. So the more problems we prove to be $\mathcal{NP}$-complete, the more ammunition we have to prove the next candidate problem $\mathcal{NP}$-complete!

This idea rose to prominence in 1972 when Richard Karp, an American computer scientist now at the University of California, Berkeley, expanded the set of known $\mathcal{NP}$-complete problems by showing that many important and well-known problems are $\mathcal{NP}$-complete. $\mathcal{NP}$-complete problems are *the hardest* problems in $\mathcal{NP}$, and they are suspected to be computationally hard. So far the only known way to solve them is by trying some large fraction of all combinations of the input. It is generally believed, but not proven, that we will never have a better algorithm.

$\mathcal{P} \neq \mathcal{NP}$

If a problem is in $\mathcal{NP}$ then it means roughly that checking a given solution takes polynomial time. But *finding* a solution in the first place seems hard. If $\mathcal{P} = \mathcal{NP}$ then it suggests that every problem that is easy to check is also easy to solve! Hard to believe! But $\mathcal{P}$ may equal $\mathcal{NP}$ and $\mathcal{NP}$-complete problems may still be too hard in practice. Ideally, we'd like to find not only that $\mathcal{P} = \mathcal{NP}$, but that $\mathcal{NP}$-complete problems are solvable with practical (say, less than cubic) algorithms. This is unlikely considering how long we've been trying.

On the other hand, the linear programming problem was long thought to have only exponential solutions, then the ellipsoid algorithm came along and showed that the problem is polynomial. So we have to be careful.

However, even without proof, the average efficiency of simplex could have led us to believe that linear programming really was easy, we just hadn't found a polynomial solution yet.

If a genius finds a short proof of a theorem that's been open for hundreds of years, everyone can check the proof. Naturally, if a theorem *has* no short proof then it's not unreasonable that we need a genius to find a proof of the theorem. But does it take a genius to find a proof of the theorem if we know that checking a proof of the theorem is easy? This is the question of whether $\mathcal{P}$ equals $\mathcal{NP}$ if we replace theorem by problem, proof by algorithm, short by polynomial, and long by exponential.

Suppose we keep score on a problem. Every time we solve a new instance of it we enter the instance and its solution in an ongoing table. If there is a pattern to the table entries then that pattern will help us predict some structure in the solution to a new instance. And that will reduce the computational cost of the problem, if we can test an instance for the pattern in a reasonable time. If no such pattern exists, or if there is a pattern only for a small portion of the entries, or if the pattern is widespread but it costs too much to test an instance for it, then each new instance requires an almost exhaustive search of the exponentially many possible cases.

So our questions are: If the problem is $\mathcal{NP}$-complete, must there be a pattern to the entries? If there is a pattern, is it polynomially testable? If there is a polynomially testable pattern, will we ever find it? It is arguable that if none of the solutions of the instances of a problem have something in common that we can test in a feasible amount of time, then it isn't a "problem" at all! To us it's just an arbitrary collection of instances.

7.5   Working out the Hierarchy

> Mathematicians are like Frenchmen:
> whatever you say to them they translate
> into their own language and forthwith
> it is something entirely different.
>
> Johann Wolfgang von Goethe,
> *Maximen und Reflexionen*

In 1964, work by Juris Hartmanis and Richard Stearns, then at the General Electric Research Laboratories, followed by work of Michael Rabin, then Manuel Blum, formalized the notion that we've studied all through this book—the *complexity* of computing something. The idea is to identify all problems that can be solved using a particular amount of resources (for example, linear, quadratic, polynomial, exponential). Each such class of problems is a **complexity class**. $\mathcal{P}$ and $\mathcal{NP}$ are complexity classes. Trying to understand what's special about $\mathcal{NP}$-complete problems (What makes them so hard? Are they really hard?), let's define some more complexity classes of languages. We're about to explore the structure of a poset of interrelated classes of languages ordered by containment.

First let's define two problems that we grew intimate with in the last chapter to use as examples. **Compositeness acceptance** is the problem of accepting the language of bit strings that are composite numbers when interpreted as binary numbers. Similarly define **primeness acceptance**. The compositeness problem is in $\mathcal{NP}$ since for any n we can guess $k < n$ and check (in polynomial time) that k divides n. And although it isn't as easy to see why, the primeness problem is also in $\mathcal{NP}$.

$co\mathcal{NP}$ and $\mathcal{P}space$

The **complement** of a language is the set of strings over the alphabet that aren't in the language. For example, compositeness and primeness are complements. The class of languages whose complements are in $\mathcal{P}$ is called $co\mathcal{P}$; the class of languages whose complements are in $\mathcal{NP}$ is called $co\mathcal{NP}$. Now $co\mathcal{P} = \mathcal{P}$, but we don't know whether $co\mathcal{NP} = \mathcal{NP}$. The question is interesting because its answer may tell us whether $\mathcal{P} = \mathcal{NP}$.

Pause | Why is $co\mathcal{P} = \mathcal{P}$?

It is possible that $co\mathcal{NP} = \mathcal{NP}$ yet $\mathcal{P} \neq \mathcal{NP}$. However closure under complementation restricts which problems can be $\mathcal{NP}$-complete. For example, both compositeness and primeness are in $\mathcal{NP}$, so both are in $co\mathcal{NP}$. Now, it is possible to show that if *any* $\mathcal{NP}$-complete problem is in $co\mathcal{NP}$ then $co\mathcal{NP} = \mathcal{NP}$. So compositeness can't be $\mathcal{NP}$-complete unless $co\mathcal{NP} = \mathcal{NP}$. But this doesn't mean that either problem is in $\mathcal{P}$.

$\mathcal{P} = \mathcal{NP}$ if and only if some $\mathcal{NP}$-complete problem has a polynomial solution. Even if the complement of every $\mathcal{NP}$-complete problem is also in $\mathcal{NP}$ (that is, if $co\mathcal{NP} = \mathcal{NP}$) that does not mean that any of them are in $\mathcal{P}$. In sum, $co\mathcal{NP} = \mathcal{NP}$ implies some restrictions on $\mathcal{NP}$-complete problems and their complements, and $co\mathcal{NP} \neq \mathcal{NP}$ implies that $\mathcal{P} \neq \mathcal{NP}$.

Pause | Why is this true? (Hint: $co\mathcal{P} = \mathcal{P}$.)

The class of languages accepted with a polynomial amount of space is called $\mathcal{P}space$. It is possible to show that this is the same as those languages accepted in polynomial space on a magical machine, so $\mathcal{P}space$ is about as big a complexity class as we can ever care about in practice; even if we wanted to solve a problem outside of $\mathcal{P}space$, we couldn't. It is possible to show that

$$\mathcal{P} \subseteq \mathcal{NP} \subseteq \mathcal{P}space$$

$\mathcal{PP}$, $\mathcal{BPP}$, $\mathcal{ZPP}$, and $\mathcal{RP}$

Unlike infallible algorithms, we make mistakes. For example, courts can make two types of errors: convict the innocent and acquit the guilty; statisticians call these type one and type two errors. Can we use this more realistic view of decision making in computation? In 1977, John Gill, then a student of Manuel Blum, developed the theory needed to talk about this idea.

A *probabilistic turing machine* is a non-deterministic turing machine that accepts an input if two-thirds or more of its possible computation paths on the input end in accepting states.[10] The actual proportion of acceptances isn't important, as long as it's above one-half.

The class of languages accepted in polynomial time by a probabilistic algorithm is called $\mathcal{PP}$ (for probabilistic polynomial time). It is possible to show that

$$\mathcal{P} \subseteq \mathcal{NP} \cup co\mathcal{NP} \subseteq \mathcal{PP} \subseteq \mathcal{P}space$$

Now consider the class of languages where for each language L there is a probabilistic turing machine such that for every string over the alphabet:

- the string is in L if and only if at least two-thirds of the machine's computations accept the string, and

- the string is not in L if and only if at least two-thirds of the machine's computations reject the string.

This class is called $\mathcal{BPP}$ (for bounded-error probabilistic polynomial time).

Ideally, the justice system should never make errors, but in practice we try to make as few type one errors (incorrect convictions) as possible, and pay the penalty of increasing the chance of type two errors (incorrect acquittals). The subclass of $\mathcal{BPP}$ whose languages are accepted in polynomial time by probabilistic algorithms that never accept strings not in the language, and that may reject strings in the language, but only at most

---

[10]As we observed in chapter three, page 209, in this book a probabilistic turing machine is not necessarily a randomized one (it does not necessarily use random numbers), and a randomized turing machine is not necessarily a probabilistic one (it does not necessarily make mistakes).

one-third of the time, is called $\mathcal{RP}$ (for random polynomial time). It is possible to show that

$$\mathcal{P} \subseteq \mathcal{RP} \subseteq \mathcal{NP} \cap \mathcal{BPP}$$

The probabilistic primality test we developed in chapter six (page 372) shows that compositeness is in $\mathcal{RP}$; if the algorithm's input is prime, it will not lie, it will say "pseudoprime," but if its input is composite, it may not say "composite."

The justice system tries to reduce the number of wrongful convictions even though that means an increase in the number of wrongful acquittals. But the chance of wrongful conviction is never zero. To reduce that risk we have appeals courts; each successive trial is meant to be a completely independent test of the defendant's innocence. Further, prosecutors also get to repeat trials, so we also reduce the chance of wrongful acquittal. As a statistician would say, we can reduce the chances of *both* types of error if we increase the sample size. This simple yet powerful idea leads us to look for algorithms that we can repeat. By rerunning such an algorithm we can reduce the chance that we make a type one *or* type two error as much as we wish. The more we repeat it and get the same result, the higher our confidence grows that it isn't making an error.

So the class we're most interested in is the intersection of $\mathcal{RP}$ and $co\mathcal{RP}$; it is called $\mathcal{ZPP}$ (for zero error probability). It is possible to show that the primeness problem is in $\mathcal{ZPP}$ and

$$\mathcal{P} \subseteq \mathcal{ZPP} = \mathcal{RP} \cap co\mathcal{RP} \subseteq \mathcal{NP} \cap co\mathcal{NP} \subseteq \mathcal{PP} \subseteq \mathcal{P}space$$

$\mathcal{IP}$

In 1985, László Babai of the Eötvös University in Hungary and the University of Chicago, and, independently, Shafi Goldwasser, Silvio Micali, both of MIT, and Charles Rackoff of the University of Toronto, published a revolutionary idea—that of *interactive proof.*

An **interactive proof** is a game with two players: a prover and a verifier; say, Alice and Bob. Alice is infinitely powerful and she wants to convince Bob that a particular string belongs to a particular language. Bob can do only a polynomial amount of work to verify Alice's claims, and both players can use a (shared or private) stream of random numbers. Since Bob can take only polynomial time, Alice's messages must be polynomial in length (he couldn't read longer messages). Bob and Alice take turns sending messages to each other, and Bob accepts his input if Alice can convince him with overwhelming circumstantial evidence that his input belongs in the language he is supposed to accept.

The class of languages for whom membership can be decided by an interactive proof is called $\mathcal{IP}$. It contains both $\mathcal{NP}$ and $\mathcal{BPP}$ since we get $\mathcal{NP}$ if we disallow random numbers, and we get $\mathcal{BPP}$ if we disallow interaction. See algorithm 7.1 for an example interactive algorithm. Since determining whether two graphs are non-isomorphic is known not to be in $\mathcal{NP}$, this algorithm shows that $\mathcal{NP}$ is a proper subset of $\mathcal{IP}$.

GRAPH_NON-ISOMORPHISM ($Graph_1, Graph_2, k$)
   { Interactively determine that $Graph_1$ is not isomorphic to $Graph_2$. $k \geq 1$ is the prefixed number of rounds. }

repeat
   <u>verifier</u>:
   privately and randomly choose $i \in \{1, 2\}$
   randomly permute $Graph_i$ to obtain an isomorphic graph $Graph$
   write $Graph$ on a tape visible to the prover
   <u>prover</u>:
   determine that $Graph$ is isomorphic to $Graph_j$, $j \in \{1, 2\}$
   write j on a tape visible to the verifier
   <u>verifier</u>: **if** ($i \neq j$) **then** reject and halt
until k rounds
<u>verifier</u>: accept and halt

Algorithm 7.1

In 1990, Carsten Lund, Lance Fortnow, Howard Karloff, all of the University of Chicago, Noam Nisan of MIT, and Adi Shamir of the Weizmann Institute in Israel, showed that every language in $\mathcal{P}space$ has an interactive proof. Thus, $\mathcal{IP} = \mathcal{P}space$! (See figure 7.2.)

Intuitively, this amazing result says that almost any problem we will ever want to solve has a cheap probabilistic verification. (Of course, it doesn't tell us how to find that verification.) Intuitively, $\mathcal{NP}$ is the class of languages with feasible proofs of membership, and $\mathcal{IP}$ is the class of languages with feasible *probabilistic* proofs of membership. In previous chapters we've seen the power of letting our algorithms err a little (for example, in primality testing), but interaction adds even more power. Adding probabilism grows the space of feasible problems from $\mathcal{P}$ to $\mathcal{BPP}$, but adding interaction as well we hit the roof, $\mathcal{P}space$!

In 1988, Michael Ben-Or, of the Hebrew University of Israel, Shafi Goldwasser, her then student Joe Kilian, both of MIT, and Avi Wigderson of the Hebrew University of Israel, introduced interactive proof systems with *two* provers. Here, two all-powerful non-communicating provers convince a

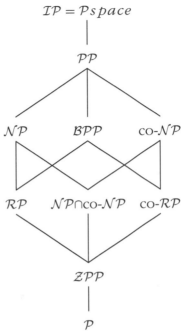

Figure 7.2 Complexity classes ordered by containment

probabilistic polynomial time verifier in polynomial time that a particular string belongs to a particular language. In 1990, Babai, Fortnow, and Lund showed that a class of *provably infeasible* languages have two-prover interactive proof systems. (Languages that require exponential time on even the magical kind of turing machine are definitely infeasible.) This further demonstrates the power of randomization together with interaction in feasible provability.

Unsolvable Problems

There are problems even harder than those we've seen so far. Some are so hard they aren't even solvable! This is like trying to climb a mountain so tall that we would be in orbit halfway up. With our normal definition of "climbable" such a mountain is "unclimbable." To repeat the moral we drew from Russell's paradox: not everything we can say necessarily makes sense; just because we can state a problem doesn't mean we can solve it. Historically, the unsolvable problems were the first class of hard problems to be identified. To find out more let's examine some of Cantor's work on set theory.

Cantor's first triumph was in finding a good definition for equal sizes of sets, even when sets are infinite. His definition, and the one accepted today, is that two sets, finite or infinite, have the same size if there is a bijective function mapping elements of one set onto the other. From this it follows that the set of positive and negative integers is the same size as the set of positive integers, even though one is a subset of the other! (See table 7.1.) As we saw with the infinite apples problem in chapter one, page 47, infinity is a dangerous place. Let's call a set with as many elements as the integers *countably infinite*.

| Pause | Is the set of all integers bigger than four countably infinite?

$$1 \quad 2 \quad 3 \quad 4 \quad 5 \quad 6 \quad 7 \quad 8 \quad 9 \quad 10 \quad \cdots$$
$$\updownarrow \quad \updownarrow \quad \updownarrow \quad \updownarrow \quad \updownarrow \quad \updownarrow \quad \updownarrow \quad \updownarrow \quad \updownarrow \quad \updownarrow \quad \cdots$$
$$1 \quad -1 \quad 2 \quad -2 \quad 3 \quad -3 \quad 4 \quad -4 \quad 5 \quad -5 \quad \cdots$$

Table 7.1 The set of positive and negative integers is countably infinite

Cantor's second triumph was to show that not every infinite set is countable. Imagine a square array of zeros and ones. Take the top left to bottom right diagonal of this array and complement every entry on the diagonal. When looked at as a row, this complemented diagonal cannot be any row in the array. (See table 7.2.) This also works for infinite arrays once there are countable number of rows. Here's why: If the number of rows is countably infinite then we can index them with the integers. For any row i, its ith entry must differ from the ith entry of the complemented diagonal. Therefore, by induction, the complemented diagonal must differ from every row, and so cannot be in the array. This is Cantor's proof by *diagonalization;* he used it to show that the set of real numbers is uncountable, and so is "bigger than" the set of integers.

Now let's show that there are computationally unsolvable problems. First, for every function we can phrase a problem that asks us to compute the function for an arbitrary argument. Now consider the subset of problems that can be described by *boolean* functions on the integers; that is, the set of functions f such that $f(n)$ is either zero or one. Suppose the set of all such functions is countably infinite. Then there is a correspondence between each function and each integer. Thus we can index the functions with the integers, say with subscripts. Let's make each function be a row in an infinite array whose columns are the integers. So f_i would be the ith function in this list, and its jth entry would be the value $f_i(j)$, which is either zero or one. We want to show that at least one boolean function cannot be in this array.

row								
1	[0]	1	1	1	0	0	1	1
2	1	[0]	1	1	0	1	0	0
3	1	1	[1]	0	1	1	1	1
4	0	1	0	[1]	0	0	1	0
5	0	0	1	1	[1]	0	0	1
6	1	1	0	0	0	[1]	0	1
7	0	0	1	1	1	1	[0]	0
8	0	1	1	0	0	0	1	[1]

new row	1	1	0	0	0	0	1	0

Table 7.2 Constructing a complemented diagonal

This is easy to do by complementing the diagonal. That produces a boolean function defined on the integers, so it should be in the array. But it can't be because for any function in the array, say f_i, $f_i(i)$ will differ from the ith value in the complemented diagonal. So the set of boolean functions, which is only a tiny subset of the set of all functions, is uncountable. Now if every program is a finite string of symbols, each chosen from a single finite alphabet, then it is possible to show that the set of all programs is countably infinite. So there are more problems than there are programs to solve them. Thus, at least one function is not describable as the output of any program, and so is computationally unsolvable.

Long Pause Why is the set of all programs countably infinite? (Hint: Think of the lengths of the programs. Another hint: Let k be the number of possible symbols in the alphabet. Think of base k numbers.)

Similarly, Turing used the same idea to show that for any program that claims to be able to tell if any program will stop, we can build a problem showing that the program cannot always tell. We might call this constructed problem a *Dirty Harry problem*. In the film *Dirty Harry,* Clint Eastwood tells someone that he can run, but he can't hide; the Dirty Harry problem tells the program: "You can run, but you can't decide."

There is a definite hierarchy of hard problems. Unlike $\mathcal{NP}$-complete problems, which are only suspected to to be exponential, there are solvable problems that are provably exponential. Further, there are solvable problems that are even worse than exponential, and there are unsolvable problems that are even worse than other unsolvable problems! For example, **Presburger arithmetic** is the formal system of the positive integers together with addition and equality alone. Deciding whether a statement in this extremely simple system is true is *doubly exponential* (2^{2^n}) in the length of the statement. This is such a ridiculous amount of time that there is no point even trying to solve the problem. Problems in the class "relativized unsolvable" are so difficult that they aren't even solvable if certain other unsolvable problems were magically solved by an oracle!

In sum, complexity theory has managed to classify problems into:

> unsolvable
> > relativized unsolvable (oracle machines)
>
> solvable
> > provably infeasible (example: Presburger arithmetic)
> > probably infeasible (example: satisfiability)
> > feasible
> > > hard (normal optimization problems)
> > > easy (normal computer science problems)
> > > > randomized easy (example: primality testing)
> > > > really easy (example: sorting)

Some things can't be done—either easily or at all.

7.6 Solving Hard Problems

> There is no such word as 'impossible'
> in my dictionary. In fact, everything
> between 'herring' and 'marmalade'
> appears to be missing.
>
> Douglas Adams,
> *Dirk Gently's Holistic Detective Agency*

Well we seem to have hit a brick wall. We've managed to show that some problems we need solved are probably too hard to solve. What to do? Over the course of this book we've discovered several algorithmic strategies, but none reduce the worst cost of an $\mathcal{NP}$-complete problem from exponential to polynomial. Our only way out is to relax our requirements.

- Relax the problem—use approximation algorithms and settle for an okay solution. This works well for some problems.

- Relax the solution—use randomized algorithms and give up predictability. This often reduces the worst cost to the average cost.

- Relax the method—use probabilistic algorithms and give up total correctness. This powerful idea is only now finding wider application.

- Relax the architecture—use parallel computation and give up sequentiality. This is the wave of the present.

- Relax the machine—use analog computation and give up digital computation. Some problems can be "solved quickly" using analog devices. This may be the wave of the future.

7.7   What Is an Algorithm?

> To think the thinkable—that
> is the mathematician's aim.
>
> C. J. Keyser

We started this trek in chapter one asking ourselves about models. Here, at the end of our trek, we're asking ourselves the same question, only now about models of computation instead of models of problems. Since at least the great seventh-century Arabic algebraist abu Ja'far Muḥammad ibn Mûsâ al-Khwârizmî, who gave his name to the word "algorithm," we've been trying to decide what an algorithm is. Based on theorist's intuitive understanding of a "finitary way" (needed for formal systems), when we ask for an algorithm to solve a problem, we usually have in mind something with the following five basic properties:

- Boundedness: it stops.

- Correctness: it finds the right answer to the problem.

- Predictability: it always does the same thing if given the same input.

- Finiteness: it can be described in a finite number of steps.

- Definiteness: each step has a well-defined meaning.

As programmers and analysts we want three further properties that theorists used to consider secondary:

- Feasibility: efficient algorithms mean that we can run more programs or solve bigger problems.

- Clarity: clear algorithms are easier to code and easier to prove correct.

- Brevity: short algorithms mean less coding and greater confidence in correctness.

Note that an algorithm can be unpredictable yet non-randomized; for example, race conditions in real-time computation, parallel computation, or distributed computation. And, in theory, an algorithm can be non-randomized yet non-deterministic, since a non-deterministic turing machine does not use random numbers; but such magic algorithms appear to exist only in our imagination. So, we have three kinds of unpredictability arising from random numbers, random interactions in asynchronous computation, and magic. From now on let's ignore the magic.

Clarity and brevity are too complex, and still a little too ill-defined, for further discussion here; other important, but even more ill-defined, properties are wide-applicability, modifiability, modularity, portability, expressibility, and elegance. Of the eight primary and secondary properties, above all else, as analysts we want feasibility; previously that wasn't thought necessary, only desirable. Within the past decade, in the interest of feasibility, useful algorithms have been found that aren't correct or predictable in the strict senses of the words. Can we, perhaps, gain by giving up boundedness as well? If we stay within our current model of computation, it is unlikely that we can give up finiteness or definiteness anytime soon.

Probabilistic algorithms tradeoff a little non-correctness for a lot of speed. Can we tradeoff a little non-boundedness for even more speed in parallel? We've inherited a view of the world from Hilbert's attempt to save mathematics that is skewed toward exact results. This dependence was necessary to get us this far—we now understand computation much better because of our theory—but Hilbert's view may have outlived its usefulness. It was reasonable in the days of sequential machines to define an algorithm as terminating and correct. For, the program implementing that algorithm would be run on only one machine and we naturally wanted it to stop and to give the right answer. But if you only do what you've always done, you'll only have what you've always had.

The problem with parallel computers presently is that we usually try to make them run one algorithm split into little pieces. This forces us to make independent processors work on the problem in concert and that forces us to make them communicate. Which is okay on the old-style von Neumann single processor machines, but in massively parallel machines, communication costs more computation. Perhaps we haven't fully exploited parallel computers yet because we still live in Hilbert's shadow.

A parallel machine can run many instances of one algorithm. This is particularly easy when the algorithm is randomized, since each instance can then be syntactically the same, except for a sequence of coin flips. So on a parallel machine it is not unreasonable to have non-bounded algorithm instances. All we care about is that at least one be guaranteed to stop, or failing that, that chances are good that at least one will stop in a specified time. With such a bound in hand we can start the family of algorithm instances and if none terminate in the time period we can kill them all and start over. Further, we can do the same thing on sequential machines. (In fact, in some sense that's what we do now whenever we use a randomized algorithm: we're running one instance of an algorithm family of instances.)

Finally, what does it mean to say that an algorithm gives the "right" answer? We develop a program specification then say that the program is correct if we can verify that the program satisfies the specification. But the specification is itself a "program," albeit in logic and intended to be run on sophisticated analog computers called "humans." Who checks the humans? It doesn't help to automate this checking, for who checks the checker? The Romans faced this problem millenia ago—Caesar's wife must be above suspicion, for who watches her watchers? If relaxing correctness, boundedness, and predictability can increase average feasibility, the gain seems worth the cost, particularly on parallel machines. These are unsettling ideas, but if we can't give up a possession, we don't possess it, it possesses us. Winston Churchill used to say that perfectionism is spelled "paralysis."

In sum, there appear to be five reasonable algorithmic dimensions: *feasibility, correctness, boundedness, predictability,* and *randomizedness.* The last dimension is binary: an algorithm either uses random numbers or it doesn't. But for the other four dimensions we can ask for a continuum of behavior. For instance, for the feasibility dimension an algorithm can be: always feasible, feasible on most inputs, feasible on a fixed subset of inputs, usually infeasible even for fixed inputs, or always infeasible. And similarly for correctness, boundedness, and predictability.

With these dimensions in mind, there seem to be six natural kinds of algorithm.

Classical algorithm:

- May be very slow.
- Never lies.
- Always stops.
- Always predictable.

- Doesn't use random numbers.

Heuristic algorithm:

- Always fast, if it stops.
- May not solve the problem. (Usually this is dependent on the input and the condition is usually difficult to check.)
- May not stop.
- May not be predictable.
- Sometimes uses random numbers.

Approximation algorithm:

- Always fast.
- Gives a "near" answer to the posed problem, or the answer to a "near" problem.
- Always stops.
- Always predictable.
- May use random numbers.

Randomized algorithm:

- Usually fast.
- Never lies.
- Always stops.
- Usually unpredictable. (Often uses sampling.)
- Uses random numbers.

Probabilistic algorithm:

- Always fast.
- Usually tells the truth.
- Always stops.
- May be unpredictable.
- May use random numbers.

Ergodic algorithm:

- Always fast, if it stops.

- Usually tells the truth.

- May not stop.

- Unpredictable. (Each repetition is independent.)

- Uses random numbers.

The odds are that $\mathcal{P} \neq \mathcal{NP}$, and even if not, it's unlikely that all problems in $\mathcal{NP}$ will have feasible solutions. This suggests that we should start reducing the importance of correct, bounded, predictable, and sequential algorithms in favor of more radical algorithms that are less safe, but more feasible. This is perhaps the end of an era. As with Kent in *King Lear,* we must now shape our old course in a country new.

7.8   What Is a Proof?

> Mathematical thinking is, and must remain, essentially creative. To the writer's mind this conclusion must inevitably result in an at least partial reversal of the entire axiomatic trend of the late 19th and early 20th centuries, with a return to meaning and truth as being the essence of mathematics.
>
> Emil Post,
> *invited address to the American Mathematical Society, 1944*

What is a proof? A proof is something that convinces us of something. The kind of proof that Turing tried to capture is a static, finite one; a proof that could be written down. In old-fashioned proofs, the proof is first given then we verify it. Interactive proofs are different. An interactive proof is never given; it comes about during a conversation between us and a prover. The prover claims to be able to prove something, and we interrogate the prover to validate that claim. Like the change in philosophy between the first four chapters and chapter five—when we were forced to consider dynamic structures—proofs can now be dynamic. For simplicity, classical theory ignores time, but we no longer can.

In interactive proofs both the prover and the verifier can use random numbers, and proof is by overwhelming circumstantial evidence. As verifiers we aren't really testing the prover, we're testing the prover's *consistency*. If the prover is always consistent then the most reasonable hypothesis is that the prover really knows the fact we want to establish. This is close to the way we do science, where the prover is the universe.[11] Further, it is close to the way we do real proofs and write real programs, despite the formalist's view that a proof or algorithm, once found, is something fixed, finite, comprehensible, and obvious. In fact, as we've seen throughout this book, proving a theorem or solving a problem is more usually like making a horseshoe; first we bang on the molten metal, let it cool into a fixed shape, then if it's not right we reheat it and bang some more.

In real life, provers can convince, and often have convinced, others of a result partly because of the prover's reputation at being good at proofs! Further, there are theorems that are so long that no one can understand all the details at once. For example, the finite simple groups classification theorem stretches across more than thirty years, depends on the work of more than one hundred mathematicians, and sprawls over more than ten thousand pages in various journals. In what sense is this theorem "proven?" For most people, mathematicians included, accepting this theorem is an act of faith.

Further, as we discovered in chapter six (page 390), in interactive proofs the prover doesn't necessarily have to tell us anything about the proof itself. Such *zero-knowledge proofs* are proofs that a proof probably exists! In 1988, Manuel Blum, Paul Feldman, and Silvio Micali showed that there is no connection between interactive proofs and zero-knowledge proofs! A zero-knowledge proof can be published once the prover and verifier share a common random string. Since an interactive proof does not have to be zero-knowledge, this shows that zero-knowledge and interaction are independent ideas. Zero-knowledge proofs show that there is an enormous distinction between "knowing how" and "knowing that."

Finally, are interactive and zero-knowledge proofs finite? Well, currently they are, because we choose a threshold before the proof begins and we accept the proof once the prover's answers have increased our confidence above that threshold. But, just as we relaxed algorithms in the previous section, we can relax the new proofs so that there is a chance that we are not convinced for any finite number of rounds. These proofs are "finite" in the sense that over many trials of proving things we will be satisfied within

---

[11]The Nobel laureate American physicist Richard Feynman ("fine-man") pictured the scientist's task as intermittently watching an infinitely large and infinitely long chess game and trying to figure out the rules.

a certain number of rounds. Is this a proof? Certainly Hilbert, and perhaps several contemporary logicians, would reject it; but in computer science we've learned to be more flexible. We've already seen that Hilbert's original program is flawed; Gödel showed that any sufficiently strong formal system is incomplete. Besides, ultimately we want to solve problems and we use whatever works.

Now we've turned Hilbert-style proofs completely on their head. First, proofs are no longer necessarily finite. Second, proofs are no longer necessarily a fixed thing, but a process. Third, proofs are no longer necessarily built on formal systems; since we may never see a "proof" (in the traditional sense) we may have no idea what system, if any, the prover used or is using. Finally, zero-knowledge proofs strike at the heart of our intuitive understanding of the word "proof;" we don't just want to be convinced, we want to understand. Although the conviction that something is true can be used to deduce aspects of a new problem, it is only understanding that gives us insights that we can take to other problems, and so solve them better or faster. Without some short description of what's important in a problem, we feel cheated even if given its solution, since we cannot use the experience to help us solve new problems. Like an enormous rubber ball, formalist mathematics picked up speed in the eighteen nineties, hit a brick wall in the thirties and forties and, now in the nineteen nineties, after forty years to absorb the impact and suitably deform, is headed back the way it came.

Speculations

The first wave of work on computability made the notion of a proof rigorous; something can be proved if it can be decided by a classical algorithm in a formal system. Now we're changing the notion of provability by relaxing the class of algorithms and relaxing the requirements of formal systems. Our new view is that something can be proved if there is a feasible relaxed algorithm that decides it, where decides is meant in the statistical sense of adding strong confirmation to it. So this is both an extension and a contraction: an extension of the idea of algorithm, and a contraction from computable to feasible, where feasible is now random polynomial time rather than polynomial time. This new attitude can apply to proof theory in three ways:

- by changing the notion of algorithm it changes the notion of solvability, which is a cornerstone of proofs in formal systems;

- by splitting the notion of proving into generation and verification, it is shifting the emphasis away from formal systems to the verification act; and,

- by shifting the emphasis from computable to feasible, it suggests that we try to determine what theorems can be "feasibly proved."

This is a natural progression; the only surprise, perhaps, is that it took a hundred years to reach this stage. The Church-Turing hypothesis came about in an attempt to answer Hilbert's questions about solvability. Once everyone agreed on a suitable notion of solvability, it was possible to show that some of Hilbert's questions were computationally unsolvable. *The Church-Turing hypothesis represents an upper bound on computability.* But not everything computable is necessarily feasible. Now our task is to refine our ideas about computability to better model feasible computation.

Every theorem has an infinite number of proofs in a formal system; let's now focus on the *shortest* proof. We can always find a shorter proof of any theorem in a formal system by building a new formal system with a larger alphabet, or by taking the theorem as an axiom. So let's fix some particular formal system. Can we use the new insights about proofs to bound the length of any proof of a theorem in the formal system? For example, perhaps we can prove that any proof of $\mathcal{P} = \mathcal{NP}$ is too long for feasible proof in any reasonable formal system. (Perhaps $\mathcal{P} = \mathcal{NP}$, but the shortest proof is beyond our reach! The universe can be quite snide at times.) If so, and if the lower bound is very large, we should forget about trying to prove $\mathcal{P} = \mathcal{NP}$.

Of course it still may be important to try to prove that $\mathcal{P} = \mathcal{NP}$ because one-way functions, useful in cryptology, exist only if $\mathcal{P} \neq \mathcal{NP}$. But for impossibly long proofs, perhaps the length of the proof makes it a good approximation to a one-way function. Perhaps there's a relation between the length of such a result and the cost of the algorithms found. That is, even if $\mathcal{P} = \mathcal{NP}$, it could be that the proof is so long that most resulting algorithms, although polynomial, are impractical. And therefore functions that approximate one-way functions would exist.

From Gödel's work we know that for any formal system strong enough to contain arithmetic, we cannot have upper bounds on the length of a proof of every theorem, because then membership in that formal system is solvable. On the other hand, we cannot prove a non-trivial lower bound on the length of the proof of a theorem in *every* formal system, because we can always make the theorem an axiom in a new formal system. So the question is: Given a theorem T and a formal system F, can we prove a lower bound on the length of the shortest proof of T in F? Further, if we could prove that the shortest proof of T in F is impossibly long, would we be justified in accepting T? Finally, could such results, if any!, be extended to bound the length of programs?

We can now, perhaps, define some adjectives that theorists commonly use but never define. All of the following definitions are relative to a fixed formal system: A theorem with many short proofs is *trivial*. A theorem with one short proof is *deep*. A proof is *elegant* when it is short and all other proofs of the theorem are much longer. A proof is *tedious* or *straightforward* when it is long but all auxiliary theorems needed in the proof are trivial. A proof is *ugly* or *uninspired* when it is just as long as its information content. We say that a brute force case analysis "is not enlightening" because we want to find patterns that shorten our descriptive and predictive task. It does not help us if those "patterns" are as long as the thing described!

On page 442 we saw how far complexity theory has classified problems; can we do the same thing for theorems? So far proof theory refines which proof systems are complete, sound, or consistent, without saying which theorems within a proof system are easy or hard. Formalism has carried us far, but there is as yet no formal definition of "infeasible theorem" analogous to "infeasible problem." Perhaps questions like whether $\mathcal{P} = \mathcal{NP}$ or whether Fermat's last theorem is true, aren't independent or unsolvable, as some presently believe, they're just infeasible. Can we refine provable into feasible and infeasible, as in complexity theory? Computability was the key used to make provability rigorous. Now we need formal definitions of easy and hard provability.

⁂

What is knowledge? Philosophers have been struggling with this question for millenia; but our complexity theory may shed new light on the problem. Suppose I want to identify a positive integer and I have three pieces of information. The first says that the number is even, the second says that the number is greater than one million, and the third says that the number is less than two million. Putting them all together narrows the search considerably, but if I had to choose only one of the three, I'd prefer to know the third (the upper bound). The upper bound gives more information than the other two.

Now suppose the third piece of information was that the number is a counterexample to a notoriously difficult conjecture like Fermat's last theorem. This piece of information *is almost useless*. It has hidden any information in an almost inaccessible place. Now consider the same problem again, with the same three pieces of information, but with the third "hidden" in the above way. Does the third still give more information than the other two?

Currently, interactive proofs and zero-knowledge proofs assume an infinitely powerful prover. But if we want applicable results then we must bound the prover's power. Now suppose a bounded prover says that she can prove a result with zero-knowledge. If we can prove that the shortest proof of the result she is claiming to be able to prove is *too long for her to have proven* then we have the option of disbelieving her even if she may have otherwise convinced us! (Perhaps we should have proofs of the prover's power?) Further, suppose there are two zero-knowledge provers, the first more powerful than the second. Suppose the first proves to the second that a result is true. If this result is within the first prover's power, but not the second's, then *the second prover cannot prove this result to us!*

So far, proof theory in logic has had little impact on proofs in science; formal systems are about deductions *from* a theory, but science is also about inductions *to* a theory. Faced with a number of phenomena, the scientist constructs a theory to explain and predict these phenomena; we might think of this as constructing a verifiable algorithm to generate predictions. This algorithm is useless if it is as long as the number of phenomena, or if it takes too long to compute a prediction. The joy we feel over short but comprehensive theories like general relativity or quantum chromodynamics is due to the surprise we feel over their enormous explanatory power; they are short statements explaining a large number of apparently unrelated phenomena. A brief explanation can be easily and quickly remembered, communicated, and extended. Given an apparently arbitrary collection of phenomena, how can we tell if they have a brief explanation?

We now have theories of complexity, probability, information, and the beginnings of a theory of algorithmic information, but what we want, and have always wanted, is a theory of knowledge. How do we know what we know, and how can we find out more? We need a computational epistemology. The ingredients appear to be: probability, randomness, conviction, probabilistic verification, bounded computation, probabilistic computation, protocols, cryptology, interaction, information, and inaccessible information. Going into the new century we are in the same position as Hilbert was at the turn of this century, but we're no longer confused about proofs or algorithms, we're confused about knowledge.

7.9 Coda—The End of the Beginning

> This is not the end. It is not even the beginning of the end. But it is, perhaps, the end of the beginning.
>
> Winston Churchill,
> *Speech on the fall of Egypt, 10 November, 1942*

Taking a generation as thirty years, we have had civilization for less than two thousand generations; and of those, the last three have seen the largest increase in power of them all. The only thing we can be sure of is that there will be change, and change at an ever increasing rate. This generation may well be the last before the term "generation" ceases to have meaning as the base measure of change. Our society is undergoing enormous technological changes and the computer is at the center of them all; if not as a direct cause then as an irreplaceable helper. Analysis has been somewhat parochial in the past, if only because the simplest problems weren't understood for many years. Now that some of the basic features of the field have emerged, it's time to apply this new-found knowledge to wider domains.

Today computers are everywhere, and they are moving deeper into the infrastructure and further from sight all the time. The analysis chores are therefore many. Diversification has already gone so far that a list of applications would merely be a list of every thing and every process in our society. But some major current thrusts are toward massively parallel computation, distributed computation, computational experimental physics, and computational number theory. And, of course, technological change continues apace in materials science, biotechnology, computer technology, optoelectronics, and space exploration and development. People in solid state physics, agriculture, molecular biology, engineering, materials science, business, architecture, and law desperately need your expertise and your creative solutions to their problems.

What is theory for? The computer scientist is an uneasy alliance of theorist and engineer. Theory forces classification, and classification makes identification and prediction easier. A theory is the condensate of experience; a condensed statement of what is common to many seemingly different things. The best theoretical work suggests practical analogues that aren't as exact as the theory specified, but which work well in practice. Often these pathbreaking applications are hard to find without theory guiding our steps. Theory is also good preventive medicine; some things can't be done, either easily or at all. The tree of theory grows by budding new twigs of conjecture at the cutting edge of the subject. If these conjectures are fruitful, the tiny twig grows into a main branch of the tree, with many new twigs of its own. To take but one example, the revolution in our understanding of proofs and algorithms will have ramifications all over computer science. And perhaps even in science in general. And that's what theory is for.

As Hilbert's epitaph says:

> Wir müssen wissen.
> Wir werden wissen.
> [We must know. We shall know.]

And what of analysis? Well, some trends are fairly clear, as analysts we should: look for solutions that are "good enough" (forget about exact answers all the time); look at sequences of instances rather than a single instance; look for adaptive solutions (allow the machine to mis-solve problem instances initially); allow randomness; and exploit parallelism more fully.

In chapter one we thought that $\mathcal{NP}$-complete problems formed a huge mountain chain deep in the interior of the continent of analysis. Now we know that they're just a hillock somewhere near the beach; we really haven't travelled very far at all. It's a large and complex universe and there is much to explore. This book described the beginning of a neverending story; there are frontiers everywhere—and there always will be. Do your share to make those frontiers grow.

A new breed of explorers are now trekking through the continent of analysis, bringing with them new tools and new techniques. To progress they have jettisoned some of the old ways and the old ideas. They keep secrets; they prove things without giving proofs; and they use randomness profusely. Having discovered a mountain in the way of progress they've lightened their conceptual burdens; they've dropped some of the classical ideas about algorithms to get fast solutions. These brave souls are prepared to have their algorithms sometimes fail, sometimes lie, and sometimes never return! It's an exciting time.

Welcome to the beginning.

Endnotes

Definitions

- *axiom:* An axiom is a statement whose truth is assumed.

- *inference rule:* An inference rule is a rule used to deduce new statements from a collection of statements.

- *formal system:* A formal system is a finite set of axioms and a finite set of inference rules.

- *theorem:* A theorem is a deduced statement of a formal system.

- *proof:* A proof of a theorem in a formal system is a (possibly empty) sequence of theorems deduced using only the inference rules starting only with the axioms and ending with the theorem.

- *consistency:* A formal system is consistent if it is not possible to prove two contradictory theorems within the system.

- *completeness:* A formal system is complete if all true theorems expressible in the formal system are provable in the system.

- *independence:* A statement is independent of a formal system if the system's consistency is not changed by assuming the statement either true or false.

- *continuum hypothesis:* The continuum hypothesis postulates that the number of real numbers is the next infinity after the number of integers.

- *axiom of choice:* The axiom of choice postulates that it is possible to choose one element from each of an infinite set of infinite sets.

- *computationally unsolvable problem:* A problem is computationally unsolvable if no algorithm solving it can exist.

- *linear program:* A linear program is a collection of constraints in n variables, each of which is linear in each of the variables, together with a linear function to be maximized. Solving linear programs is called linear programming.

- *Church-Turing hypothesis:* The Church-Turing hypothesis postulates that every algorithm can be described by a turing machine.

- *polynomial transformability:* One problem is polynomially transformable to another if we can transform any instance of the first into some instance of the second in polynomial time.

- *polynomial equivalence:* Two problems are polynomially equivalent if each can be polynomially transformed into the other.

- *computational hardness:* A problem is computationally hard if it does not have a polynomial time solution.

- *alphabet:* An alphabet is a finite non-empty set of symbols.

- *string:* A string is a finite sequence of symbols of some alphabet.

- *language:* A language is a set of strings over some alphabet.

- *complement of a language:* The complement of a language is the set of strings, over some alphabet, that aren't in the language.

- *class:* A class is a set of languages over some alphabet.

- *complement of a class:* The complement of a class is the set of languages, over some alphabet, that aren't in the class.

- *closed set:* A set is closed under relation R if A is in the set and ARB implies that B is in the set.

- *complexity class:* A complexity class is a class of languages each of which can be accepted by a turing machine using a particular amount of resources.

- *hardness with respect to a class:* A language is C-hard if it is at least as hard to accept as every language in the class C.

- *completeness with respect to a class:* A language is C-complete if it is C-hard and it is in the class C.

- *Cook-Levin theorem:* The Cook-Levin theorem states that the satisfiability problem is at least as hard as every other problem in $\mathcal{NP}$.

Notes

Russell's quote on page 417 appeared in "Recent Work on the Principles of Mathematics," Bertrand Russell, *International Monthly,* 4, 84, 1901. Cantor in his 1891 paper was not the first to use diagonalization; six years earlier Paul du Bois-Reymond used it to construct a function growing faster than any function in any countably infinite set of functions. But the nefarious use made of this construction is Cantor's.

The demonstration that simplex is exponential in the worst case can be found in "How Good is the Simplex Algorithm?," Victor Klee and G. J. Minty in *Inequalities-III,* O. Shisha (editor), Academic Press, 1972. Incidentally, Karmarkar's early proof that his algorithm was superior had the flavor of a zero-knowledge proof. Because of its enormous economic potential, AT&T wanted to keep the algorithm secret, but it wanted other companies to think it useful enough to pay for it. The strategy they decided on was to allow other companies to benchmark the object code form of the algorithm and keep the source code secret.

The example of the satisfiability problem in terms of letters is from the excellent article "Combinatorics, Complexity, and Randomness," Richard M. Karp, in *ACM Turing Award Lectures: The First Twenty Years, 1966–1985,* ACM Press, 1987.

Three basic references for the subsection on interactive proofs are: "The knowledge complexity of interactive proof-systems," Shafi Goldwasser, Silvio Micali, and Charles Rackoff, *SIAM Journal on Computing,* 18, 186–208, 1989. "The polynomial time hierarchy has interactive proofs," Carsten Lund, Lance Fortnow, Howard Karloff, and Noam Nisan, electronic mail announcement, December 1989, to appear, 1991. "$\mathcal{IP} = \mathcal{P}space$," Adi Shamir, *Proceedings of the 31st Annual Symposium on the Foundations of Computer Science,* IEEE Computer Society, 11–15, 1990.

The paper showing that there is no connection between interactive proofs and zero-knowledge proofs is "Non-Interactive Zero-Knowledge and Its Applications," Manuel Blum, Paul Feldman, and Silvio Micali, *Proceedings of the 20th Annual ACM Symposium on the Theory of Computing,*

103–112, 1988. The paper establishing the two-prover interactive proof result is "Multi-prover interactive proofs: How to remove the intractability assumptions," Michael Ben-Or, Shafi Goldwasser, Joe Kilian, and Avi Wigderson, *Proceedings of the 20th Annual ACM Symposium on the Theory of Computing,* 113–131, 1988.

Exercise 1, page 459, contains an extension of a game called the X of X game, which I first heard from Kellogg Booth. In the game, players take turns challenging the others to guess X when told, for example, that the X of X is "David and Solomon" (this is a hard one; hint: think of the Bible). Part of the exercise was also prompted by a question in *Introduction to Computation Theory,* Daniel I. A. Cohen, John Wiley & Sons, revised edition, 1990.

Further Reading

One of the seminal papers in computability theory (and by extension, complexity theory) is "On Computable Numbers with an Application to the Entscheidungsproblem," Alan M. Turing, *Proceedings of the London Mathematical Society, series 2,* 42, 230–265, 1936/37. A correction appeared in the same journal: 43, 544–546, 1937. This paper is well worth reading even today. For an excellent collection in English of the original papers on computability see *The Undecidable: Basic Papers On Undecidable Propositions, Unsolvable Problems, And Computable Functions,* Martin Davis (editor), Raven Press, 1965. For a more recent collection see *Philosophy of Mathematics,* Paul Benacerraf and Hilary Putnam (editors), Cambridge University Press, second edition, 1983.

For an excellent introduction to logic and its relation to computability see *A Profile of Mathematical Logic,* Howard Delong, Addison-Wesley, 1970. For a well-written advanced introduction to set theory see *Naive Set Theory,* Paul Halmos, Springer-Verlag, 1960. See also the first half of the delightful book *Set Theory and Metric Spaces,* Irving Kaplansky, Chelsea Publishing Company, second edition, 1977. To appreciate the depth of the axiom of choice and the paradoxes it leads to see *The Banach-Tarski Paradox,* Stan Wagon, Cambridge University Press, 1985. Recent work on constructivist mathematics before Bishop died is presented in *Constructive Analysis,* Errett Bishop and Douglas Bridges, Springer Verlag, 1985.

For an excellent introduction to computability theory see *Computability: Computable Functions, Logic, and the Foundations of Mathematics,* Richard L. Epstein and Walter A. Carnielli, Wadsworth & Brooks/Cole, 1989. For an elementary presentation of Gödel's theorem see *Godel's Theorem Simplified,* Harry J. Gensler, University Press of America, 1984.

For an introduction to computation theory (the study of computational machines—as distinct from computability, the study of models of computation) see *Introduction to Automata Theory, Languages, and Computation,*

John E. Hopcroft and Jeffrey D. Ullman, Addison-Wesley, 1979; or *Theory of Computation,* Derick Wood, Harper & Row, 1987.

The standard reference for infeasibility is the excellent *Computers and Intractability: A Guide to the Theory of $\mathcal{N}P$-Completeness,* Michael R. Garey and David S. Johnson, W. H. Freeman, 1979. Johnson continues to update the field in his periodic "The $\mathcal{N}P$-Completeness Column: An Ongoing Guide," in *The Journal of Algorithms.*

There is one large book solely on the travelling salesman problem. See *The Traveling Salesman Problem: A Guided Tour of Combinatorial Optimization,* Eugene L. Lawler, J. K. Lenstra, A. H. G. Rinnooy Kan, and D. Shmoys, John Wiley & Sons, 1985. For more on optimization see *Discrete Optimization,* R. Gary Parker and Ronald L. Rardin, Academic Press, 1988. For a well-written introduction needing only rudimentary background see *Linear Programming,* Vašek Chvátal, W. H. Freeman, 1983.

The two seminal papers on $\mathcal{N}P$-complete problems are "The complexity of theorem proving procedures," S. A. Cook, *Proceedings of the 3rd Annual ACM Symposium on the Theory of Computing,* 151–158, 1971; and "Universal'nyĭe perebornyĭe zadachi," (Universal search problems), in Russian, Leonid Levin, *Problemy Peredači Informatsiĭ,* 115–116, 1973. (English translation in *Problems of Information Transmission,* 9, 265–266, 1973.)

For further information on the finite simple groups classification theorem see "The Enormous Theorem," Daniel Gorenstein, *Scientific American,* 104–115, December 1985.

For more on structural complexity theory see the well-done *Structural Complexity I,* José Balcázar, Josep Díaz, and Joaquim Gabarró, Springer-Verlag, 1988. The authors continue with more advanced material, including brief introductions to interactive proofs and algorithmic information theory, in *Structural Complexity II,* Springer-Verlag, 1990.

For more on interactive proof systems see *Computational Models of Games,* Anne Condon, MIT Press, 1990. For more on zero-knowledge proofs see *Uses of Randomness in Algorithms and Protocols,* Joe Kilian, MIT Press, 1990. For an amusing and incisive overview with great stories and new results see "Email and the unexpected power of interaction," László Babai, *Proceedings of the 5th Annual ACM Structure in Complexity Theory Conference,* 30–44, 1990.

⁓⁓⁓⁓⁓

Besides the turing machine, Turing is important for other contributions to mathematics, computers, computer science, and biochemistry. He invented the Turing test in artificial intelligence; he designed and built one of the first digital computers; he worked on biological development; and he worked on cryptography too! Alan Turing was a stunningly original mind.

Science is about people. It's sad that otherwise educated people know Voltaire, Beethoven, and Picasso, but not Gauss, Euler, Cantor, Hilbert, Turing, or Gödel. A few know the classical scientists Galileo, Mendel, Darwin, Newton, Maxwell, and Mendeleev, but don't know the classical mathematicians Leibniz, Fermat, Abel, Fourier, Cauchy, Lagrange, Galois, Riemann, and Poisson. Even those who know recent scientists like Bohr, Watson, Crick, Einstein, Feynman, Hawking, Bell, Josephson, and Prigogine don't know recent mathematicians like Poincaré, Rāmānujan, von Neumann, Dantzig, Kolmogorov, Erdös, Pólya, Cohen, Gorenstein, Friedman, Shannon, and Faltings, or recent computer scientists like Cook, Levin, Karp, Blum, Rabin, Hartmanis, Markov, Yao, Knuth, Razborov, Lovász, Minsky, and McCarthy, to name but a few. These, and others like them, are the people who have given us our civilization; they are at least as important as writers, musicians, and painters. Do your part to see that they are not forgotten.

A hagiography would be out of place here, so I will merely urge you to read about those few who have already been written about: *Gauss: A Biographical Study,* W. K. Bühler, Springer-Verlag, 1981. *Georg Cantor: His Mathematics and Philosophy of the Infinite,* Joseph Warren Dauben, Harvard University Press, 1979. *Hilbert,* Constance Reid, Springer-Verlag, 1970. *Reflections on Kurt Gödel,* Hao Wang, MIT Press, 1987. *Alan Turing: The Enigma of Intelligence,* Andrew Hodges, Unwin, 1983.

Questions

> We cannot call that hope which may be resisted and overthrown by adversity, for as light shines most in darkness, even so hope must remain unshaken in the midst of toil.
>
> Miguel de Cervantes Saavedra,
> *Persiles and Sigismunda*

Exercises

1. "Short" is indeed short, "polysyllabic" is also polysyllabic. Call words that describe themselves *homologous* and words that don't describe themselves *heterologous.*

   (a) Classify "neologistic," "rarefactional," "intempestive," and "dasypygal."

(b) Is "heterologous" heterologous or homologous?

(c) Find ten homologous words.

(d) Find ten heterologous words.

(e) Find five words that fit the schema: the X of X is X. (Trivial answers like the misspelled word "mispelling" are disallowed.)

2. Let P be a problem.

(a) If P isn't in $\mathcal{NP}$, is P not in $\mathcal{P}$?

(b) If P isn't in $\mathcal{P}$, is P not in $\mathcal{NP}$?

3. Suppose P_1 and P_2 are problems and P_1 is polynomially transformable to P_2.

(a) If P_1 is in $\mathcal{P}$, is P_2 in $\mathcal{P}$?

(b) If P_2 is in $\mathcal{P}$, is P_1 in $\mathcal{P}$?

(c) If P_1 is $\mathcal{NP}$-complete, is P_2 $\mathcal{NP}$-complete?

(d) If P_2 is $\mathcal{NP}$-complete, is P_1 $\mathcal{NP}$-complete?

(e) If P_2 is polynomially transformable to P_1, are P_1 and P_2 $\mathcal{NP}$-complete?

(f) If P_1 and P_2 are $\mathcal{NP}$-complete, is P_2 polynomially transformable to P_1?

(g) If P_1 is in $\mathcal{NP}$, is P_2 $\mathcal{NP}$-complete?

4. Show that polynomial transformability is a partial order over $\mathcal{NP}$, and that polynomial equivalence is an equivalence relation over $\mathcal{NP}$.

5. Show that $\mathcal{P} \subseteq co\mathcal{NP} \cap \mathcal{NP}$.

6. The *symmetric difference* of two sets is the set of elements in the union of the sets that is not in the intersection. Call two sets *equal almost everywhere* if their symmetric difference is finite. Show that equal almost everywhere is an equivalence relation on all sets over a fixed alphabet.

7. Show that $\mathcal{P}$ and $\mathcal{NP}$ are closed under almost everywhere equality.

8. Suppose there are an infinite number of $\mathcal{NP}$-complete problems. Can there be a problem in $\mathcal{NP}$ that needs more than a polynomial number of polynomial transforms before we arrive at an instance of satisfiability?

9. Assume the Church-Turing thesis. Consider a physical digital computer M that solves an instance of a problem P, then builds a physically smaller copy of itself. Index the sequence of machines built as $M_0, M_1, M_2, \ldots$, where the first machine is M_0.

(a) Can M_0 ever stop for any instance of the problem P if P is a computationally unsolvable problem?

(b) Suppose one of these machines solves some problem P, but it can't build a smaller copy of itself because of physical limits. Is this machine the smallest possible machine that solves P?

(c) Suppose the problem P is for the machine to build a smaller copy of itself; so all that each machine is doing is building a smaller copy of itself. Is the smallest machine produced the smallest possible machine that solves P?

10. Call a language *polynomial* if there is a turing machine that accepts it in polynomial time. Show that

(a) Every finite language is polynomial.

(b) The complement of a polynomial language is polynomial.

(c) The union of two polynomial languages is polynomial.

(d) The intersection of two polynomial languages is polynomial.

11. Show that the set of all subsets of a countably infinite set is uncountable.

12. David Hilbert has a hotel with a countable infinity of rooms. Suppose the hotel is full.

(a) Show that if one new guest shows up then Hilbert can find an empty room.

(b) If a countable infinity of new guests show up can Hilbert find room for them all?

(c) Prove that if an uncountable number of new guests show up then Hilbert cannot find room for them all.

Problems

1. Hilbert's Hotel II: The Return of the Guests.
Show that if a countable infinity of sets each of a countable infinity of guests show up then Hilbert can find room for them all even though his hotel is already full.

2. What is wrong with the following argument?
Let's enumerate all real numbers between zero and one to show that there are only a countable infinity of them.
There are a finite number of one-digit reals between zero and one:

$$0.0 \ 0.1 \ 0.2 \ \ldots 0.7 \ 0.8 \ 0.9$$

There are a finite number of two-digit reals between zero and one:

$$0.00 \ 0.01 \ 0.02 \ \ldots \ 0.97 \ 0.98 \ 0.99$$

In general, for every n there are a finite number of n-digit reals between zero and one. From the previous question we know that a set made of a countable infinity of sets, each of which is at most countably infinite, is countably infinite. So there are a countable infinity of real numbers between zero and one.

3. Call a function that assumes a value for each element of its domain a *total* function. Given a countably infinite set of total functions, construct a total function that grows faster than every function in the set. That is, find a function f such that if g is in the set then $\lim_{n \to \infty} f(n)/g(n)$ is not bounded.

4. An *independent set* of a graph is a subset of its nodes no two of which are connected. Show that deciding whether a graph has an independent set of at least k nodes is $\mathcal{NP}$-complete.
   You may assume that the following problem is $\mathcal{NP}$-complete: deciding whether a graph has a subset of at least k nodes where every two nodes in the subset are connected in the graph. Such a subset is called a *clique*.

5. A *dominating set* of a graph is a subset of its nodes where every node of the graph is either in the subset or is a neighbor of at least one node in the subset. Show that deciding whether a graph has a dominating set of at most k nodes is $\mathcal{NP}$-complete.
   You may assume that the following problem is $\mathcal{NP}$-complete: deciding whether a graph has a subset of at most k nodes where for every edge of the graph at least one of its nodes is in the subset. Such a subset is called a *node cover*.

Research

1. Is deciding whether two graphs are isomorphic $\mathcal{NP}$-complete?

2. As we have seen, the classical notion of an algorithm is only one extreme of an entire continuum of hypothesis testers. In scientific tests of hypotheses some experiments give more confirmation to a hypothesis than others but confirmation theory is still in its infancy. Clarify the intuitive idea of an algorithm and classify all possible algorithms.

3. Are there useful theorems and sets of formal systems such that there is an easy proof of the theorem in one formal system, but no easy proof of its negation in any other formal system within the set of formal systems chosen? That is, are some theorems so hard that we can't find a proof of the theorem *or its negation* in any reasonable time? By this measure, theorems independent of the formal system would be the hardest, since they can be neither proved nor disproved in the system.

4. Prove that it doesn't matter whether $\mathcal{P} = \mathcal{NP}$.

A poem should begin in delight and end
in wisdom.

Robert Frost

Besides this, unexampled wonders have
been seen here performed by God, the
sea has been opened, a cloud has shown
you the road, the rock has given forth
water, manna has rained, and everything
has contributed to your greatness, the
remainder must be done by you.

Niccolò Machiavelli, *The Prince*

It is not incumbent on you to
complete the work, but neither
art thou free to desist altogether.

Rabbi Tarfon, *Tractate of the Fathers, 2:21, The Mishna*

The past is but the beginning of a
beginning, and all that is and has been is
but the twilight of the dawn.

H. G. Wells, *Essays: The Discovery of the Future*

The Road goes ever on and on
Down from the door where it began.
Now far ahead the Road has gone,
And I must follow, if I can,
Pursuing it with eager feet,
Until it joins some larger way
Where many paths and errands meet.
And whither then? I cannot say.

J. R. R. Tolkien, *The Lord of the Rings*

MATHEMATICAL BACKGROUND

A.1 Basics

Statements

In the following, P and Q are statements.

$\exists x, P(x)$ there is an x for which P is true

$\forall x, P(x)$ for all x for which P is true

$P(x) \implies Q(y)$ if $P(x)$ is true then $Q(y)$ is true

$P(x) \iff Q(y)$ if $P(x)$ is true then $Q(y)$ is true, and vice versa

The important thing to remember is that the implication $P(x) \implies Q(y)$ does not say anything about the truth of P or Q; it says something about the relation between the truth values of P and Q. If $P(x) \implies Q(y)$ is true it says that *if* P happens to be true for x then Q must be true for y. Alternately, it says that *if* Q happens to be false for y then P must be false for x. The second form is equivalent to the first, and is called the implication's *contrapositive.*

Sets

In the following, A and B are sets and $\{x \ : \ P(x)\}$ means the set of things for which P is true.

$a \in A$ a is an element of A

$A \subseteq B$ A is a subset of B $\iff \forall x, \ \ x \in A \implies x \in B$

$A \cup B$ the union of A and B $= \{x \ : \ x \in A \text{ or } x \in B\}$

$A \cap B$ the intersection of A and B $= \{x \ : \ x \in A \text{ and } x \in B\}$

$A \setminus B$ the set difference of A and B $= \{x \ : \ x \in A \text{ and } x \notin B\}$

Induction

It's important to try to prove things because patterns for small n can mislead us. For example, $n^2 + n + 41$ is prime for $n = 0, 1, 2, \ldots, 39$. Perhaps $n^2 + n + 41$ is prime for all n? No, it's composite for $n = 40$.

Or consider the factors of $x^n - 1$:

$$
\begin{aligned}
x^1 - 1 &= (x - 1) \\
x^2 - 1 &= (x - 1)(x + 1) \\
x^3 - 1 &= (x - 1)(x^2 + x + 1) \\
x^4 - 1 &= (x - 1)(x + 1)(x^2 + 1) \\
x^5 - 1 &= (x - 1)(x^4 + x^3 + x^2 + x + 1) \\
x^6 - 1 &= (x - 1)(x + 1)(x^2 + x + 1)(x^2 - x + 1)
\end{aligned}
$$

Perhaps $x^n - 1$ always factors into terms involving coefficients no larger than 1? No, this is true for n up to 104, but $x^{105} - 1$ contains a factor with a term of $2x^{41}$ and a term of $2x^7$.

On the other hand it is true that $x - 1$ always divides $x^n - 1$.

One way of gaining the surety that a proof gives is called *induction*. Induction is like any other proof method except that it is restricted to statements about the integers and when proving such a statement we are allowed to assume the truth of all statements for smaller integers.

For example, suppose we want to show that 9 always divides $25^n + 3n - 1$.

Basis step: when $n = 1$, $25^n + 3n - 1 = 27$, so our hypothesis is true when $n = 1$.

Inductive step: Suppose that 9 divides $25^k + 3k - 1$ for all $k < n$.

We now want to show that 9 then divides $25^n + 3n - 1$ and, if we need to, we're allowed to assume that 9 divides $25^k + 3k - 1$ for every k smaller than n.

Well,

$$
\begin{aligned}
25^n + 3n - 1 &= 25 \times 25^{n-1} + 3(n - 1) + 3 - 1 \\
&= 25 \times 25^{n-1} + 25 \times 3(n - 1) - 24 \times 3(n - 1) + 2 \\
&= 25(25^{n-1} + 3(n - 1) - 1) - 24 \times 3(n - 1) + 27 \\
&= 25(25^{n-1} + 3(n - 1) - 1) - 9(8(n - 1) - 3)
\end{aligned}
$$

But $n > n - 1$, so 9 divides the first term. Thus 9 divides both, hence 9 must divide $25^n + 3n - 1$.

Therefore, if 9 divides $25^k + 3k - 1$ for all $k < n$, then 9 also divides $25^n + 3n - 1$. And since 9 divides $25^1 + 3 - 1$, then 9 always divides $25^n + 3n - 1$.

Functions

An integer function f maps elements of a set of integers D with elements of a set of integers R, with the restriction that no element of D can map to more than one element of R. D is the *domain* of the function, and R is its *range*.

- *one-to-one:* f is one-to-one if $f(n) = f(m)$ implies that $n = m$.
- *onto:* f is onto if $\forall n \in R$, $\exists m \in D$ such that $f(m) = n$.
- *bijection:* f is bijective if it is one-to-one and onto.
- *non-decreasing:* f is non-decreasing if $n > m$ implies that $f(n) \geq f(m)$.
- *increasing:* f is increasing if $n > m$ implies that $f(n) > f(m)$.
- *real-valued:* f is real-valued if $f(n)$ may be a real number; that is, $f(n)$ is not restricted to being an integer.

Integer Functions

- The *floor function:* $\lfloor x \rfloor$ = the greatest integer less than or equal to x.
- The *ceiling function:* $\lceil x \rceil$ = the smallest integer greater than or equal to x.
- The *nearest integer function:* $\langle x \rangle$ = the nearest integer to x. (This is not really a function unless we decide to always round up or down.)

Powers and Logarithms

$$x^0 = 1$$
$$x^{-a} = 1/x^a$$
$$x^{a+b} = x^a \times x^b$$
$$x^{a-b} = x^a/x^b$$
$$x^{ab} = (x^a)^b$$

If $x > 1$ then the *logarithm to the base x of y*, written $\log_x y$, is the power to which we must raise x to get y. Therefore,

$$x^z = y \iff z = \log_x y$$

$\lg y$ is the log base two of y; $\ln x$ is the log base e of y.

It follows that

$$z^{\log_x y} = y^{\log_x z}$$

Using the relations

$$y = z^{\log_z y} = x^{\log_x y} \quad \text{and} \quad x = z^{\log_z x}$$

we can show that

$$\log_x y = \frac{\log_z y}{\log_z x}$$

With this relation we can change to any base, for example

$$\lg x = \frac{\ln x}{\ln 2}$$

Factorials

n factorial, $n!$, counts the number of ways we can arrange n distinct things.

$$n! = \begin{cases} 1 & n = 0 \\ 1 \times 2 \times \cdots \times (n-1) \times n & n > 0 \end{cases}$$

We have n choices for the first thing, $n - 1$ for the second, $n - 2$ for the third, and so on. Each arrangement is a *permutation*.

n choose k, $\binom{n}{k}$, counts the number of ways we can choose k things from n distinct things.

$$\binom{n}{k} = \begin{cases} 0 & k > n \\ \dfrac{n!}{k!(n-k)!} & n \geq k \geq 0 \end{cases}$$

The *falling factorial*, $n!_k$, counts the number of ways we can choose and then arrange k things out of n things.

$$n!_k = \frac{n!}{(n-k)!} = n(n-1)(n-2)\cdots(n-k+1)$$

Note that

$$\binom{n}{k} = \frac{n!_k}{k!}$$

and that

$$\binom{n}{k} = \binom{n}{n-k}$$

It is straightforward to show *Pascal's relation*

$$\binom{n}{k} = \binom{n-1}{k} + \binom{n-1}{k-1}$$

$\binom{n}{k}$ is also known as a *binomial coefficient* because it is the coefficient of the term $x^k y^{n-k}$ in the expansion of $(x + y)^n$.

Stirling's Approximation

$$n! = \sqrt{2\pi n} \left(\frac{n}{e}\right)^n e^{f(n)/12n}$$

where $1 > f(n) > 0$. Therefore,

$$n! = \sqrt{2\pi n} \left(\frac{n}{e}\right)^n (1 + o(1))$$

Harmonic Numbers

$$H_n = \sum_{i=1}^{n} \frac{1}{i} = \ln n + \gamma + \frac{1}{2n} + \frac{1}{12n^2} + \cdots$$

$$H_n^{(2)} = \sum_{i=1}^{n} \frac{1}{i^2} \to \frac{\pi^2}{6} = 1.64493\cdots$$

A.2 Algebra

The Binomial Theorem

The *binomial theorem* is

$$(x + y)^n = \sum_{i=0}^{n} \binom{n}{i} x^i y^{n-i}$$

Two important special cases are

$$(x + 1)^n = \sum_{i=0}^{n} \binom{n}{i} x^i$$

and

$$2^n = (1 + 1)^n = \sum_{i=0}^{n} \binom{n}{i}$$

The last relation says that the number of ways we can select i people from n people, where i ranges from 0 to n, is 2^n.

We can differentiate the binomial theorem with respect to x and substitute $x = 1$ to obtain an important sum

$$\sum_{i=0}^{n} i \binom{n}{i} = n2^{n-1}$$

Another way to see this is to count the number of ways we can select any number of people, where one person is special (say, the chair of a committee), from a set of n people. We could select someone to be the chair (n ways) then fill the remaining $i - 1 = 0$, or 1, or 2, ..., or $n - 1$ slots (2^{n-1} ways). So there are $n2^{n-1}$ ways to select $k \leq n$ people, one of whom is special. Alternately, we could first decide how many people are to be selected (say i), then there are $\binom{n}{i}$ ways to choose i people, and i ways to choose one of them to be special. So there are $\sum_{i=0}^{n} i \binom{n}{i}$ ways to do this. So the two expressions are equal.

Partial Fractions

Sometimes it is useful to be able to take a rational polynomial function (a ratio of two polynomials) and resolve it into "proper fractions." This process is called finding *partial fractions*.

For example, we would like to do the reverse of the following

$$\begin{aligned}
\frac{1}{x-1} + \frac{2}{x+1} + \frac{x+1}{x^2+1} &= \frac{x+1+2(x-1)}{x^2-1} + \frac{x+1}{x^2+1} \\
&= \frac{3x-1}{x^2-1} + \frac{x+1}{x^2+1} \\
&= \frac{(x^2+1)(3x-1) + (x+1)(x^2-1)}{x^4-1} \\
&= \frac{4x^3 + 2x - 2}{x^4-1}
\end{aligned}$$

To do this we factorize the denominator and write an equation summing each of the separate factors. Let r, s, t, and u be such that

$$\frac{4x^3 + 2x - 2}{x^4 - 1} = \frac{r}{x-1} + \frac{s}{x+1} + \frac{tx+u}{x^2+1}$$

Suppose we don't know r, s, t, and u. But we know that if they satisfy the equation then they must satisfy other conditions. Multiplying throughout by $x^4 - 1$ we get that

$$4x^3 + 2x - 2 = r(x+1)(x^2+1) + s(x-1)(x^2+1) + (tx+u)(x^2-1)$$

And now substituting various values for x gives us conditions that r, s, t, and u must satisfy (for example, substituting 1 and -1 for x give us r

and s). From these equations we can solve for r, s, t, and u, thereby giving us the partial fraction form of

$$\frac{4x^3 + 2x - 2}{x^4 - 1}$$

In general, we reduce the rational function to lowest terms by dividing the denominator into the numerator as many times as it can go, factorizing the remaining proper fraction, and expressing it as a sum of partial fractions. Each partial fraction is $P(x)/Q(x)$ where the degree of each $P(x)$ (the polynomial with the unknown constants) is one less than the degree of $Q(x)$, where $Q(x)$ is one of the factors of the factorization. Then we solve for each $P(x)$.

A.3   Real Analysis

Limits

$$\lim_{x \to r} f(x) = s$$

means that $f(x)$ can be kept as close to s as desired by keeping x sufficiently close to, but not necessarily equal to, r. In symbols:

$$\lim_{x \to r} f(x) = s \iff$$

$$\forall t > 0 \, \exists u > 0 : \ \forall x \neq r, \quad r + u > x > r - u \implies s + t > f(x) > s - t$$

Intuitively, the definition says that no matter how small someone requires the difference between the function value and the limit value to be, we can always find a point near r satisfying that condition

The limit as x tends to infinity of $f(x)$ is s if no matter how close we want $f(x)$ to be to s we can always find a big enough x making it that close. In symbols:

$$\lim_{x \to \infty} f(x) = s \iff$$

$$\forall t > 0 \, \exists u > 0 : \ x > u \implies s + t > f(x) > s - t$$

One limit is so important that it has its own name:

$$
\begin{aligned}
e^x &= \lim_{n \to \infty} \left(1 + \frac{x}{n}\right)^n \\
&= 1 + \frac{x^1}{1!} + \frac{x^2}{2!} + \frac{x^3}{3!} + \frac{x^4}{4!} + \cdots \\
&= 1 + x + \frac{x^2}{2} + \frac{x^3}{6} + \frac{x^4}{24} + \cdots
\end{aligned}
$$

The number $e = 1 + 1 + \frac{1}{2} + \frac{1}{6} + \frac{1}{24} + \cdots = 2.718 \cdots$ is so important that base e logarithms have a special symbol, ln.

f is *continuous* at r if

$$\lim_{x \to r} f(x) = f(r)$$

It is possible to show that

$$
\begin{aligned}
\lim_{x \to r} (-f(x)) &= -\lim_{x \to r} f(x) \\
\lim_{x \to r} f(x) &= s & \Longleftrightarrow \quad & \lim_{x \to r} (f(x) - s) = 0 \\
\lim_{x \to r} f(x) &= s & \Longleftrightarrow \quad & \lim_{x \to r} t f(x) = ts \\
\lim_{x \to r} f(x) &= s \neq 0 & \Longrightarrow \quad & \lim_{x \to r} 1/f(x) = 1/s
\end{aligned}
$$

$$
\begin{aligned}
\lim_{x \to r} (f(x) \pm g(x)) &= \lim_{x \to r} f(x) \pm \lim_{x \to r} g(x) \\
\lim_{x \to r} (f(x) \times g(x)) &= \left(\lim_{x \to r} f(x) \right) \times \left(\lim_{x \to r} g(x) \right) \\
\lim_{x \to r} (f(x)/g(x)) &= \left(\lim_{x \to r} f(x) \right) / \left(\lim_{x \to r} g(x) \right) \quad (\text{if } \lim_{x \to r} g(x) \neq 0) \\
\lim_{x \to r} f(g(x)) &= f(\lim_{x \to r} g(x)) \quad (\text{if } f \text{ continuous at } \lim_{x \to r} g(x))
\end{aligned}
$$

Differentiation

The *derivative* of f at x is

$$f'(x) = \lim_{r \to 0} \frac{f(x + r) - f(x)}{r}$$

This limit, if it exists, measures the growth rate of the function near x. The steeper the function is near x the faster it's increasing and the larger is its derivative. The derivative must be zero when f is constant, because f is not changing in value anywhere; and it must be constant when f is linear, because f is changing uniformly.

$$f(x) = s \Longrightarrow f'(x) = 0 \quad \text{and} \quad f(x) = sx + t \Longrightarrow f'(x) = s$$

The derivative is also denoted df/dx or d/dx of f since it's the limit of a difference in x divided into the corresponding difference in f (taking d for "difference").

It is possible to show that

$$
\begin{aligned}
f(x) &= g(x) \pm h(x) & \Longrightarrow \quad & f'(x) = g'(x) \pm h'(x) \\
f(x) &= g(x)h(x) & \Longrightarrow \quad & f'(x) = g(x)h'(x) + g'(x)h(x) \\
f(x) &= \frac{g(x)}{h(x)} & \Longrightarrow \quad & f'(x) = \frac{h(x)g'(x) - h'(x)g(x)}{h^2(x)} \\
f(x) &= g(h(x)) & \Longrightarrow \quad & f'(x) = g'(y)h'(x) \ (\text{where } y = h(x))
\end{aligned}
$$

To find the derivative we *differentiate* the function. Let's differentiate the two functions $f(x) = x^2$ and $g(x) = x^n$ $(n \geq 2)$.

$$
\begin{aligned}
f'(x) && g'(x) \\
= \lim_{r \to 0} \frac{f(x+r) - f(x)}{r} &\qquad = \lim_{r \to 0} \frac{g(x+r) - g(x)}{r} \\
= \lim_{r \to 0} \frac{(x+r)^2 - x^2}{r} &\qquad = \lim_{r \to 0} \frac{(x+r)^n - x^n}{r} \\
= \lim_{r \to 0} \frac{2rx + r^2}{r} &\qquad = \lim_{r \to 0} \frac{nrx^{n-1} + r^2(\text{some terms})}{r} \\
= \lim_{r \to 0} (2x + r) &\qquad = \lim_{r \to 0} (nx^{n-1} + r(\text{some terms})) \\
= 2x &\qquad = nx^{n-1}
\end{aligned}
$$

The Chain Rule

The chain rule: if $f = g(y)$ and $y = h(x)$ then

$$
f'(x) = g'(y)h'(x) = \frac{dg}{dy}\frac{dy}{dx}
$$

where $g'(y)$ is the derivative of g with respect to y.

Suppose we want to differentiate $f(x) = (x^3 - x)^2$. Let $y(x) = x^3 - x$, so $f(y) = y^2$ (and so, $f(x) = x^6 - 2x^4 + x^2$). By the chain rule

$$
\begin{aligned}
f'(x) &= f'(y)y'(x) \\
&= 2y(3x^2 - 1) \\
&= 2(x^3 - x)(3x^2 - 1) \\
&= 6x^5 - 8x^3 + 2x
\end{aligned}
$$

The same result follows by direct differentiation of f with respect to x.

We can use the chain rule to show that

$$
f(x) = e^{\sqrt{x^2 + x}} \implies f'(x) = \frac{2x + 1}{2\sqrt{x^2 + x}} e^{\sqrt{x^2 + x}}
$$

Using the chain rule, the derivative of x^s where s is a positive or negative real number is sx^{s-1}. Also using the chain rule, the derivative of $e^{g(x)}$ where g is any differentiable function is $g'(x)e^{g(x)}$. (In particular, the derivative of e^x is e^x; this is what makes it so special.) Finally, the derivative of $\ln x$ is $1/x$. Note that, since $\lg x = \ln x / \ln 2$, the derivative of $\lg x$ is $1/(x \ln 2) = (\lg e)/x$.

l'Hôpital's rule

The limit of the ratio of two functions is *indeterminate* if both functions go to zero or both go to infinity. The following rule sometimes helps to evaluate indeterminate limits.

l'Hôpital's rule: if f and g are differentiable, $\lim_{x \to \infty} f(x) = \infty$, $\lim_{x \to \infty} g(x) = \infty$, and $\lim_{x \to \infty} f'(x)/g'(x)$ exists, then

$$\lim_{x \to \infty} \frac{f(x)}{g(x)} = \lim_{x \to \infty} \frac{f'(x)}{g'(x)}$$

Partial Differentiation

We can differentiate a function of two variables f with respect to one variable, x, by treating the other variable, y, as a constant. This is the *partial derivative* of f with respect to x, and is symbolized f_x. Similarly, we can find f_y. From these we can find f_{xx}, f_{xy}, and f_{yy}. (Note: It is possible to show that if f is continuous then $f_{xy} = f_{yx}$, so the order of differentiation does not matter for continuous functions.)

If $x = r, y = s$ is a solution of the simultaneous equations

$$f_x = 0 \text{ and } f_y = 0$$

then (r, s) is a minimum point of f if both $f_{xy}^2 - f_{xx}f_{yy}$ and f_{xx} are greater than zero at (r, s).

A.4   Sums

The sum of $n - k + 1$ terms of a sequence is written

$$\sum_{i=k}^{n} a_i = a_k + a_{k+1} + a_{k+2} + \cdots + a_n$$

Properties

$$\sum_{i=k}^{n} c a_i = c \sum_{i=k}^{n} a_i$$

$$\sum_{i=k}^{n} (a_i \pm b_i) = \sum_{i=k}^{n} a_i \pm \sum_{i=k}^{n} b_i$$

$$\sum_{i=k}^{n} (a_i - a_{i-1}) = a_n - a_{k-1}$$

If f is any bijective function then

$$\sum_{i=k}^{n} a_i = \sum_{j=f(k)}^{f(n)} a_j$$

Note that in general

$$\sum_{i=k}^{n}(a_i \times b_i) \neq \left(\sum_{i=k}^{n} a_i\right) \times \left(\sum_{i=k}^{n} b_i\right)$$

and

$$\sum_{i=k}^{n}(a_i/b_i) \neq \left(\sum_{i=k}^{n} a_i\right) / \left(\sum_{i=k}^{n} b_i\right)$$

Arithmetic Sums

Using the above properties we have that

$$\sum_{i=1}^{n} 1 = n$$

$$\sum_{i=1}^{n} 1 = \sum_{i=1}^{n}(i - (i - 1))$$
$$= n - 0$$
$$= n$$

We can use this idea for more difficult problems. For example,

$$\sum_{i=1}^{n} i = \frac{n(n+1)}{2}$$

We can get this result in at least two ways.
Method 1:

$$\sum_{i=1}^{n} i = 1 + 2 + \cdots + n$$
$$+ \quad \sum_{i=1}^{n} i = n + (n-1) + \cdots + 1$$
$$= (n+1) + (n+1) + \cdots + (n+1)$$
$$= n(n+1)$$
$$\implies \sum_{i=1}^{n} i = \frac{n(n+1)}{2}$$

Method 2:

$$
\begin{aligned}
n^2 &= n^2 - 0^2 \\
&= \sum_{i=1}^{n} (i^2 - (i-1)^2) \\
&= \sum_{i=1}^{n} (2i - 1) \\
&= 2\sum_{i=1}^{n} i - \sum_{i=1}^{n} 1 \\
&= 2\sum_{i=1}^{n} i - n
\end{aligned}
$$

$$
\implies \sum_{i=1}^{n} i = \frac{n(n+1)}{2}
$$

Using the second technique we can show that

$$
\sum_{i=1}^{n} i^2 = \frac{1}{6}(2n^3 + 3n^2 + n) = \frac{n(n+1)(2n+1)}{6}
$$

In sum,

$$
\sum_{i=0}^{n} 1 = \frac{(n+1)}{1}, \quad \sum_{i=0}^{n} i = \frac{(n+1)(n)}{2}, \quad \sum_{i=0}^{n} i(i-1) = \frac{(n+1)(n)(n-1)}{3}
$$

In general,

$$
\sum_{i=0}^{n} i!_k = \frac{(n+1)!_{k+1}}{k+1}
$$

where $i!_k = i!/(i-k)! = i(i-1)(i-2)\cdots(i-k+1)$ is the falling factorial.

Geometric Sums

$$
\sum_{i=0}^{n} x^i = \begin{cases} n+1 & x = 1 \\ \dfrac{1 - x^{n+1}}{1 - x} & x \neq 1 \end{cases}
$$

A simple way to convince yourself that the second part is true is to do a few steps of the division.

Another proof follows from evaluating

$$(x - 1)\sum_{i=0}^{n} x^i = \sum_{i=0}^{n}(x^{i+1} - x^i)$$

$$= \sum_{j=1}^{n+1}(x^j - x^{j-1})$$

$$= x^{n+1} - x^0$$

$$= x^{n+1} - 1$$

If $x \neq 1$, dividing by $x - 1$ gives us the result. (What happens if $x = 1$?)

Arithmetico-Geometric Sums

$$\sum_{i=0}^{n} i x^{i-1} = \begin{cases} n(n+1)/2 & x = 1 \\ \dfrac{n x^{n+1} - (n+1)x^n + 1}{(x-1)^2} & x \neq 1 \end{cases}$$

We can find this sum by observing that from the definition of limits, differentiation distributes over addition. That is,

$$\frac{d}{dx}(f + g) = \frac{df}{dx} + \frac{dg}{dx}$$

Thus,

$$\sum_{i=0}^{n} i x^{i-1} = \sum_{i=0}^{n} \frac{d}{dx}(x^i)$$

$$= \frac{d}{dx}\left(\sum_{i=0}^{n} x^i\right)$$

$$= \frac{d}{dx}\left(\frac{x^{n+1} - 1}{x - 1}\right)$$

$$= \frac{n x^{n+1} - (n+1)x^n + 1}{(x-1)^2}$$

In particular, substituting $x = 2$ and simplifying, we see that

$$\sum_{i=0}^{n} i 2^{i-1} = n2^n - 2^n + 1$$

What is $\displaystyle\sum_{i=0}^{n} i/2^i$?

Asymptotics of a Special Sum

It is useful to know the following asymptotic approximation:

$$\sum_{i=1}^{n} i^k = O\left(\frac{n^{k+1}}{k+1}\right)$$

A.5 Probability

Probability theory attempts to find the uncertainty of events relative to other, more primitive, events. *Events* are subsets of a set called the space of outcomes of an experiment. An *experiment* is anything that has one or more outcomes, all of which are known in advance: for example, flipping a coin, rolling a die, measuring a height, or drawing a card.

The *probability* of an event E, written $\mathbf{P}(E)$, is the ratio of the number of events favorable to the event divided by the number of all possible events. Since this definition doesn't make much sense when there are an infinite number of outcomes, it is better to say that the probability of an event E out of a sample space S is any set of numbers that obey the following *axioms of probability:*

1. For all events E, $\mathbf{P}(E) \geq 0$.

2. $\mathbf{P}(S) = 1$.

3. If E and F are disjoint events then $\mathbf{P}(E \cup F) = \mathbf{P}(E) + \mathbf{P}(F)$.

Let $\bar{E}$ be the event complementary to the event E. That is, if E occurs then $\bar{E}$ didn't occur, if $\bar{E}$ occurs then E didn't occur. Since these events are disjoint and $E \cup \bar{E} = S$, it follows that

$$\mathbf{P}(\bar{E}) = 1 - \mathbf{P}(E)$$

Also, using the axioms we can show that if E and F are not disjoint then

$$\mathbf{P}(E \cup F) = \mathbf{P}(E) + \mathbf{P}(F) - \mathbf{P}(E \cap F)$$

by using the equality

$$E \cup F = (E \cap F) \cup (E \cap \bar{F}) \cup (\bar{E} \cap F)$$

Conditional Probability

The *conditional probability* of E given F, is the probability that E will occur given that F has occurred. It is written $\mathbf{P}(E|F)$, and it is defined as

$$\mathbf{P}(E|F) = \frac{\mathbf{P}(E \cap F)}{\mathbf{P}(F)}$$

Note that $\mathbf{P}(F)$ cannot be zero since we're told that F has occurred at least once, so its probability is non-zero.

The following theorem gives us a way to reverse conditional probabilities. *Bayes' theorem:*

$$\mathbf{P}(E|F) = \frac{\mathbf{P}(F|E)\mathbf{P}(E)}{\mathbf{P}(F)}$$

More generally, for n events $E_1, E_2, \ldots, E_n$, Bayes' theorem states that

$$\mathbf{P}(E_i|F) = \frac{\mathbf{P}(F|E_i)\mathbf{P}(E_i)}{\displaystyle\sum_{j=1}^{n} \mathbf{P}(F|E_j)\mathbf{P}(E_j)}$$

Independence

The events E and F are *independent* if

$$\mathbf{P}(E \cap F) = \mathbf{P}(E)\mathbf{P}(F)$$

Note that if E and F are independent then the conditional probabilities are the same as the unconditional probabilities. That is, if E and F are independent and neither event has zero probability then

$$\mathbf{P}(E|F) = \mathbf{P}(E) \quad \text{and} \quad \mathbf{P}(F|E) = \mathbf{P}(F)$$

Random Variables

A *random variable* is a real-valued function defined on the events of an experiment whose value depends on the outcomes of the experiment. For example, if when flipping a coin, our only two outcomes are heads or tails, we can define a random variable whose value is 0 if the outcome of the experiment is tails and 1 if it's heads.

Average and Variance

The *average* of a random variable X, denoted by $\mu(X)$, tells us something about the *location* of the values of X. The *variance* of a random variable X, denoted by $\sigma^2(X)$, tells us something about the *spread* of the values of X. The smaller the variance, the closer most values are to $\mu(X)$. The square root of the variance is called the *standard deviation.*

Given an experiment with n events and a random variable X associated with them that can take on one of n values $r_1, r_2, \ldots, r_n$ with probabilities $\mathbf{P}(X = r_1)$, $\mathbf{P}(X = r_2)$, $\ldots$, $\mathbf{P}(X = r_n)$, then

$$\mu(X) = \sum_{i=1}^{n} r_i \mathbf{P}(X = r_i) , \quad \sigma^2(X) = \sum_{i=1}^{n} (r_i - \mu(X))^2 \mathbf{P}(X = r_i)$$

Note that $\mu(X)$ is a fixed number and not a random variable, so

$$\begin{aligned} \sigma^2(X) &= \mu(X - \mu(X))^2 \\ &= \mu(X^2 - 2X\mu(X) + \mu(X)^2) \\ &= \mu(X^2) - 2\mu(X)\mu(X) + \mu(X)^2 \\ &= \mu(X^2) - \mu(X)^2 \end{aligned}$$

Markov's Inequality

If $X \geq 0$ and $r > 0$

$$r P(X \geq r) \leq \mu(X)$$

Čebyšev's Inequality

Applying Markov's inequality to the random variable $Y = (X - \mu(X))^2$ we get

$$P(\mu(X) + r\sigma(X) \geq X \geq \mu(X) - r\sigma(X)) \geq 1 - \frac{1}{r^2}$$

B

MANIPULATING ORDER NOTATION

B.1 The Sum Rule

Given the a functions $f_1, f_2, \ldots, f_a$, where a is a constant, if $f_i = O(g_i)$, $\forall i \leq n$, then

$$\sum_{i=1}^{a} f_i = O(g_m)$$

where g_m is the fastest growing of the functions $g_1, g_2, \ldots, g_a$.

This rule helps us analyze programs that have a sequence of parts with different run times. For example, consider the following algorithm

FARBLE (n)
    Segment 1
    Segment 2
    Segment 3

Suppose Segment 1 costs $O(n)$ steps, Segment 2 costs $O(n^2)$ steps and Segment 3 costs $O(n \lg n)$ steps. Then, by the sum rule, FARBLE's run time is $O(n^2)$.

Here is the proof of the rule. Let c_i and n_i be the constants specified by the definition for each of the O relations. Let g_m be the fastest growing function and let

$$n_0 = \max_{1 \leq i \leq a} \{n_i\} \quad \text{and} \quad c_0 = \max_{1 \leq i \leq a} \{c_i\}$$

Then for all $n \geq n_0$,

$$
\begin{aligned}
\sum_{i=1}^{a} f_i(n) &\leq \sum_{i=1}^{a} c_i g_i(n) \\
&\leq \sum_{i=1}^{a} c_0 g_i(n) \\
&\leq \sum_{i=1}^{a} c_0 g_m(n) \\
&= a c_0 g_m(n)
\end{aligned}
$$

Since $a c_0$ is a constant (this is why a must be a constant), this is $O(g_m)$. A similar proof works for Ω, and thus also for Θ.

B.2   The Product Rule

If $f_i = O(g_i)$, $\forall i \leq a$, where a is a constant, then

$$
\prod_{i=1}^{a} f_i = O(\prod_{i=1}^{a} g_i)
$$

For example, consider the following algorithm

JUMBLE(n)
   for i **from** 1 **to** n
      for j **from** 1 **to** $n - i$
         MUMBLE(j)

If MUMBLE(j) takes $O(j)$ time, then it takes $O(n)$ time, and JUMBLE calls MUMBLE $O(n)$ times each time the outer loop iterates. Since $n - i \leq n$, and the outer loop iterates $O(n)$ times, then by the product rule, JUMBLE's cost is $O(n \times n \times n) = O(n^3)$.

Note that we cannot say immediately that JUMBLE takes $\Omega(n^3)$ time, since the inner loop does not always execute n times. Nor does MUMBLE require $\Omega(n)$ time for each j. In general, the product rule for Ω is trickier to apply, and it often fails. It is usually safer to go back to the definition. In this case, we could get a lower bound on the run time by showing that

$$
\sum_{i=1}^{n} \sum_{j=1}^{n-i} c j = \Theta(n^3)
$$

B.3   Sample Algorithm Analyses

Now let's analyze a few sample algorithms.

Consider the following program fragment

> for i from 1 to n
>   for j from i to n
>   for k from i to j
> $m \leftarrow m + i + j + k$

Let's analyze this from the inside out. The run time is dominated by the time taken in the fourth line, since it is the one most frequently executed *and* each of the other lines takes constant time per iteration. The run time depends on n only; all other variables in the program fragment are computed in terms of n.

The fourth line requires three additions (and an assignment), so it takes constant time per iteration. That is, we assume that the time to do the additions does not depend on the values of m, i, j, or k, and thus the time for this statement does not depend on n.

Now, i ranges from 1 to n, so the program fragment executes n times; the first loop executes $O(n)$ times. Next, j ranges from i to n, so the last two lines execute $O(n)$ times whenever the outermost loop executes. Finally, k ranges from i to j, so the fourth line executes $O(n)$ times whenever the j loop executes.

This nesting suggests the product rule; the run time is

$$O(n \times n \times n \times c) = O(n^3)$$

where c is a constant.

But is it $\Theta(n^3)$? To be $\Theta(n^3)$, it must be $\Omega(n^3)$. Notice that k ranges from i to j, which is often only a small number. Thus, we cannot say that the k loop iterates $\Omega(n)$ times for each value of i and j in the program. But for many values of i and j it will iterate more than $n/2$ times.

We will show that for $\Omega(n^2)$ different (i, j) pairs, the last line will execute $\Omega(n)$ times. When $i \leq n/4$ and $j \geq 3n/4$, the k loop will iterate at least $n/2$ times. But there are $n/4$ different values of $i \leq n/4$, and for each of those values of i, there are $n/4$ different values of $j \geq 3n/4$. So $i \leq n/4$ while $j \geq 3n/4$ at least $n^2/16$ times.

Since for each of these $n^2/16$ cases, the k loop executes at least $n/2$ times, we can establish a lower bound on the number of times the fourth line executes of at least $n^3/32$. Indeed, it executes many more times than this, but to establish $\Omega(n^3)$, we only need this lower bound. That is, if

$f(n)$ is the number of times the last line executes in terms of n, then $f(n) \geq n^3/32$. This means that the program indeed requires $\Theta(n^3)$ time.

We can calculate the exact number of additions done in the fourth line as follows:

$$\sum_{i=1}^{n} \text{number of additions done on } i^{th} \text{ iteration of loop 1}$$

The number of additions done on the ith iteration is

$$\sum_{j=i}^{n} \text{number of additions done on } j^{th} \text{ iteration of loop 2 for a given } i$$

The number of additions done on the jth iteration for a fixed i is

$$\sum_{k=i}^{j} \text{number of additions done on } k^{th} \text{ iteration of loop 3}$$

The number of additions done on the kth iteration is always three, for any k. Thus, the last sum is

$$\sum_{k=i}^{j} 3$$

The total number of additions is then

$$\sum_{i=1}^{n} \sum_{j=i}^{n} \sum_{k=i}^{j} 3$$

Note the correspondence with the loop structure of the program fragment.

We expand the sums one at a time from the right (that is, the innermost sum first). The last sum is $3(j - i + 1)$.

Now we can plug this into the middle sum to obtain

$$\sum_{j=i}^{n} 3(j - i + 1) = 3\sum_{j=i}^{n} j - 3\sum_{j=i}^{n} i + 3\sum_{j=i}^{n} 1$$

The third sum is $3(n - i + 1)$ and the second sum is $3i(n - i + 1)$, since i does not depend on j. But what do we do with the first sum? Well, notice that

$$\sum_{j=i}^{n} j = \sum_{j=1}^{n} j - \sum_{j=1}^{i-1} j$$
$$= \frac{n(n+1)}{2} - \frac{(i-1)i}{2}$$

Putting all of this together we find that the number of additions done on the ith iteration is

$$3\left(\frac{n(n+1)}{2} - \frac{i(i-1)}{2}\right) - 3i(n-i+1) + 3(n-i+1)$$

Plugging this into the outermost sum gives the total number of additions as

$$\sum_{i=1}^{n}\left(3\left(\frac{n(n+1)}{2} - \frac{i(i-1)}{2}\right) + 3i(n-i+1) + 3(n-i+1)\right)$$

Now simplify the above exact result and compare with our estimate. (Previously we estimated a lower bound of $n^3/32$ iterations, which implies about $n^3/10$ additions.)

B.4 Algorithms That Call Subroutines

Now let's analyze programs that call subroutines, where the subroutine may be the program itself.

Here's an example.

```
for i from 1 to n
    FARBLE(i)
```

How long does this fragment take? Well that depends on how long FARBLE takes to execute, which in turn could depend on FARBLE's argument, i. Just executing the loop and making the subroutine call will require $\Theta(n)$ time; allocating stack space for each call and saving variables takes a constant amount of overhead for every call, regardless of the size of i.

Now suppose FARBLE(i) takes $f(i)$ time. Then the total time required by this fragment, including the subroutine calls, is

$$g(n) + \sum_{i=1}^{n} f(i)$$

where $g(n) = \Theta(n)$ is the loop overhead time.

If we analyze FARBLE, and find, say, that $f(i) = \Theta(i)$, then the execution time of this fragment is

$$\Theta\left(g(n) + \sum_{i=1}^{n} i\right) = \Theta(n^2)$$

Note what we did; we used i as a representative function of the set $\Theta(i)$. (Can this be justified? Why can't we just apply the sum rule?)

Let us look at this a bit more carefully. To show that the result is $\Theta(n^2)$, we need to show the result is both $O(n^2)$ and $\Omega(n^2)$.

Since $f(i) = \Theta(i)$ then $f(i) = O(i)$. Therefore there exist constants n_0 and c such that $f(i) \le ci$, for all $i \ge n_0$. It follows by induction that for all $n > n_0$

$$
\begin{aligned}
\sum_{i=n_0}^{n} f(i) &\le \sum_{i=n_0}^{n} ci \\
&= \sum_{i=1}^{n} ci - \sum_{i=1}^{n_0-1} ci \\
&= \frac{cn(n+1)}{2} - \frac{c(n_0-1)n_0}{2}
\end{aligned}
$$

This is indeed $O(n^2)$ but that does *not* prove our desired result. We have ignored the values of $f(i)$ for $1 \le i < n_0$. The total time for the fragment is

$$
\sum_{i=1}^{n} f(i) = \sum_{i=1}^{n_0-1} f(i) + \sum_{i=n_0}^{n} f(i)
$$

and so far we have only computed the second sum on the right-hand side. We can't bound the first sum using the definition of O, because for $i < n_0$, $f(i)$ does not have to be less than c_i.

However, all is not lost because the sum $\sum_{i=1}^{n_0-1} f(i)$ is just some constant, say c_1. Why? Because n_0 is a constant! Thus, the run time of the fragment is

$$
\begin{aligned}
\sum_{i=1}^{n} f(i) &= \sum_{i=1}^{n_0-1} f(i) + \sum_{i=n_0}^{n} f(i) \\
&= c_1 + \sum_{i=n_0}^{n} f(i) \\
&\le c_1 + \frac{cn(n+1)}{2} - \frac{c(n_0-1)n_0}{2} \\
&= \frac{cn^2}{2} + \frac{cn}{2} + c_2
\end{aligned}
$$

where $c_2 = c_1 - cn_0(n_0-1)/2$ is a constant.

Thus the run time is $O(n^2)$. Now show that the run time is $\Omega(n^2)$.

Now let's generalize this result. Suppose FARBLE's execution time is $f = O(g)$ for some g. Then we want to show that the program fragment as a whole takes $O(ng(n))$ time. Will this work? Read on, the answer may surprise you. If f is non-decreasing, then $\forall i \leq n$, $f(i) \leq f(n)$. Thus

$$\sum_{i=1}^{n} f(i) \leq \sum_{i=1}^{n} f(n) = nf(n)$$

then, by the sum rule, $nf(n) = O(ng(n))$. But in general, we may not know that f is non-decreasing so we must rely on the definition of O.

Since $f = O(g)$, we know there must exist constants n_0 and c such that $f(n) \leq cg(n)$, $\forall n \geq n_0$. Then, the run time of the program fragment is

$$
\begin{aligned}
\sum_{i=1}^{n} f(i) &= \sum_{i=1}^{n_0-1} f(i) + \sum_{i=n_0}^{n} f(i) \\
&= c_1 + \sum_{i=n_0}^{n} f(i) \\
&\leq c_1 + \sum_{i=n_0}^{n} cg(i) \\
&= O(\sum_{i=n_0}^{n} g(i))
\end{aligned}
$$

Now, if g is non-decreasing, then $g(n) \geq g(i)$, for $n \geq i$. Thus,

$$
\begin{aligned}
\sum_{i=n_0}^{n} cg(i) &\leq \sum_{i=n_0}^{n} cg(n) \\
&\leq cng(n) \\
&= O(ng(n))
\end{aligned}
$$

(If g is *decreasing*, then the conclusion does not hold, but decreasing functions rarely occur in the usual algorithm analysis context).

Now try a similar proof for Ω.

Well I hope your proof failed, because the result isn't true! The O conclusion may not hold for decreasing functions. When we change the "$\leq$" to a "$\geq$" for the Ω proof, this remark will also switch direction; the result for Ω will not hold for *increasing* functions g.

Since $f = \Omega(g)$, we know there must exist constants n_0 and c such that $f(n) \geq cg(n)$, $\forall n \geq n_0$. Then, the run time of the program fragment is

$$\sum_{i=1}^{n} f(i) \;=\; \sum_{i=1}^{n_0-1} f(i) + \sum_{i=n_0}^{n} f(i)$$

$$=\; c_1 + \sum_{i=n_0}^{n} f(i)$$

$$\geq\; c_1 + \sum_{i=n_0}^{n} cg(i)$$

$$=\; \Omega\!\left(\sum_{i=n_0}^{n} g(i)\right)$$

Now, if g is increasing, this result *may not* be $\Omega(ng(n))$! The reason is, if we try to finish the proof in a manner similar to that used for the O result, then we do *not* have

$$\sum_{i=n_0}^{n} cg(i) \geq \sum_{i=n_0}^{n} cg(n)$$

For example, suppose $f(n) = 2^n = \Omega(2^n)$. Then

$$\sum_{i=1}^{n} f(i) \;=\; \sum_{i=1}^{n} 2^i$$

$$=\; 2^{n+1} - 2$$

$$\leq\; 2 \times 2^n$$

But $2 \times 2^n \neq \Omega(n2^n)$. One way of understanding this is that exponential functions grow so fast that only the last term of the sum makes any real difference to the overall cost; that is, the program fragment's run time is determined largely by the last call to FARBLE, when FARBLE takes exponential time.

RECURRENCES

C.1 Simple Recurrences

Recurrences give the value of a function at a point in terms of its value at other points. For example,

$$f(n) = f(n/2) + 1$$

This is like a recursive program without a termination condition; it does not completely specify the function. To complete the specification we need a *boundary condition;* that is we need the function's value at some specific points. In algorithm analysis, these points are usually small values of n, such as 1 or 2. To complete the function we might have

$$f(1) = 1$$

One way to solve this is to start at the boundary and compute a sequence of values of $f(n)$. That is,

$$
\begin{aligned}
f(1) &= 1 \\
f(2) &= f(1) + 1 = 2 \\
f(4) &= f(2) + 1 = 3 \\
f(8) &= f(4) + 1 = 4
\end{aligned}
$$

Now we try to find a pattern then prove the pattern correct by induction. As we shall see, recurrences usually make induction easy. First, though, notice something a bit unnerving about the set of values we have computed—we skipped $f(3)$, $f(5)$, $f(6)$, and $f(7)$.

If we have an algorithm, such as binary search, then it should work on seven elements. However, if we assume that bigger inputs can't take less time to solve than smaller inputs then the algorithm's cost is non-decreasing, so $f(8) \geq f(7) \geq f(4)$. Therefore the value we obtain won't be off by much.

What are these easy to obtain values? In the above, we see that we have solutions for $n = 1, 2, 4$, and 8, which are all powers of 2 and which can be written as 2^0, 2^1, 2^2, and 2^3. It appears that $f(2^k) = k + 1$ would be a good guess. Let's try that guess in an inductive proof.

Basis step: $f(1) = 1$, by the boundary condition, which satisfies our assumption for $k = 0$. That is, $f(2^0) = 0 + 1$.

Inductive step: Assume $f(2^k) = k + 1$ for some $k > 0$. Then $f(2^{k+1}) = f(2^k) + 1$ by the definition of our recurrence. Using our induction hypothesis for $f(2^k)$, we then have that $f(2^{k+1}) = (k+1)+1 = k+2$, which agrees with the inductive assumption for $k + 1$. So, by induction, we conclude that $f(2^k) = k + 1$ for all $k \geq 0$.

Alternately, instead of working from the bottom up, we could work from the top down. Suppose our recurrence is

$$f(n) = \begin{cases} 27 & n = 1 \\ 2f(n/4) + n & n > 1 \end{cases}$$

Before going on, try to guess the answer using the bottom up approach. (Hint: sometimes it pays not to simplify too much.)

Now for the top down approach. This approach is usually the easier way for more complicated recurrences.

$$\begin{aligned} f(n) &= 2f(n/4) + n \\ &= 2(2f(n/4^2) + n/4) + n \end{aligned}$$

Multiplying out we have that

$$f(n) = 2^2 f(n/4^2) + n/2^1 + n/2^0$$

Stating it in this form makes the pattern clearer. Again using the definition, we can substitute for $f(n/4^2)$ and simplify to obtain

$$f(n) = 2^3 f(n/4^3) + n/2^2 + n/2^1 + n/2^0$$

At this point we guess that the pattern is

$$f(n) = 2^k f(n/4^k) + n/2^{k-1} + n/2^{k-2} + \cdots + n/2^1 + n/2^0$$

We can make this look simpler by expressing it as a sum.

$$f(n) = 2^k f(n/4^k) + \sum_{i=0}^{k-1} n/2^i$$

Now what? Well, first we assume that $n = 4^k$. Then, it follows that $n/4^k = 1$, and using the boundary condition $f(1) = 27$, we can substitute

$$f(n) = 27 \times 2^k + \sum_{i=0}^{k-1} n/2^i$$

where $n = 4^k$.

Again, keep in mind that we have only guessed this pattern, not proven it. Use induction to prove this result now.

To reduce the sum, we note that n does not depend on i and so can be factored out. Thus,

$$\sum_{i=0}^{k-1} n/2^i = n \sum_{i=0}^{k-1} 1/2^i$$

Now the sum looks like the geometric sum. Thus,

$$\sum_{i=0}^{k-1} 1/2^i = \sum_{i=0}^{k-1} (1/2)^i = (2 - 1/2^{k-1})$$

Therefore

$$f(n) = 27 \times 2^k + n(2 - 1/2^{k-1})$$

where, we must remember, $n = 4^k$.

Although for asymptotic analysis we would in general just ignore the fraction, let's treat it carefully this once. Note that $1/2^{k-1}$ is equal to $2/2^k$ and $n = 4^k = 2^{2k}$. Thus $2^k = \sqrt{n}$. So simplifying the expression for $f(n)$, we get

$$
\begin{aligned}
f(n) &= 27\sqrt{n} + 2n - 2n/\sqrt{n} \\
&= 27\sqrt{n} + 2n - 2\sqrt{n} \\
&= 2n + 25\sqrt{n} \\
&= O(n)
\end{aligned}
$$

C.2 Recursive Algorithms

Here is a recursive algorithm that draws some lines (assuming a graphics device) on a lattice of integer coordinates:

```
DOODLE( n, m )
   if  n > 0
      DRAW_LINE( n, n, m, m )
      DRAW_LINE( n, m, n, m )
      DOODLE( n − 1, m )
```

How long does DOODLE(n, n) take to finish doodling as a function of n? Well, DOODLE either does nothing, when $n = 0$, or it draws two lines and then calls itself recursively with n reduced by one. To estimate its run time, let's compute the number of lines drawn. We will *assume* that the time to draw a line is independent of its length. (Is this realistic?)

Let $f(n)$ be the number of lines DOODLE draws when called with a first parameter n. Then

$$f(n) = \begin{cases} 0 & n = 0 \\ f(n-1) + 2 & n > 0 \end{cases}$$

This is slightly different from our two previous recurrences—here we only subtract one from n, rather than divide it by a constant. However, we can still use either the top down approach or the bottom up approach. For example

$$
\begin{aligned}
f(n) &= f(n-1) + 2 \\
     &= f(n-2) + 2 + 2 \\
     &= f(n-3) + 2 + 2 + 2 \\
     &= f(n-k) + 2k \\
     &= f(n-n) + 2n \\
     &= 2n
\end{aligned}
$$

where the last is obtained by plugging in the boundary condition. Thus DOODLE's run time is $\Theta(n)$.

If we assume that the run time is proportional to the length of the lines drawn, then the problem becomes more difficult. The length of the first line is $\sqrt{2}(n - m)$ and the length of the second line is 0. Thus, DOODLE's drawing time will be

$$f(n) = \begin{cases} 0 & n = 0 \\ f(n-1) + \sqrt{2}(n-m) + 1 & n > 0 \end{cases}$$

because if nothing is drawn it's reasonable to assume that no drawing time is required and the 1 is the time I arbitrarily pick to draw a point (the line of length 0). I will leave this to you to puzzle out.

Here is another recursive function:

```
QUIBBLE(n)
  if n = 0
    then return 1
    else return QUIBBLE(n − 1) + QUIBBLE(n − 1)
```

If we let $f(n)$ count the number of additions, then

$$f(n) = \begin{cases} 0 & n = 0 \\ 2f(n-1) + 1 & n > 0 \end{cases}$$

This leads to

$$\begin{aligned}
f(n) &= 2f(n-1) + 1 \\
&= 2(2f(n-2) + 1) + 1 \\
&= 4f(n-2) + 2 + 1 \\
&= 2^3 f(n-3) + 2^2 + 2^1 + 2^0 \\
&= 2^k f(n-k) + \sum_{i=0}^{k-1} 2^i \\
&= 2^n f(0) + \sum_{i=0}^{n-1} 2^i \\
&= 2^n - 1
\end{aligned}$$

Verify this result by induction.

Finally, here is a generic divide and conquer algorithm:

```
D_AND_C(L)
  if |L| > 1
    in |L|² steps divide L into thirds L₁, L₂, L₃
    D_AND_C(L₁)
    D_AND_C(L₂)
    D_AND_C(L₃)
```

If we let $n = |L|$, and let $f(n)$ be the run time for D_AND_C when called with L, then the amount of time required is

$$f(n) = \begin{cases} c & n = 1 \\ 3f(n/3) + n^2 & n > 1 \end{cases}$$

where c is a constant. Then

$$\begin{aligned} f(n) &= 3f(n/3) + n^2 \\ &= 3^2 f(n/3^2) + 3(n/3)^2 + n^2 \\ &= 3^k f(n/3^k) + n^2 \sum_{i=0}^{k-1} (1/3)^i \\ &= c3^k + n^2 \left(\frac{1 - (1/3)^k}{1 - 1/3} \right) \\ &= \Theta(n^2) \end{aligned}$$

C.3 A Tricky Example

Sometimes a recurrence looks difficult but it can be transformed into a simpler one very easily.

Consider

$$f(n) = \sqrt{n} f(\sqrt{n}) + O(n)$$

Let $g(n) = f(n)/n$. Then,

$$g(n) = g(\sqrt{n}) + O(1)$$

Let $h(n) = g(2^{2^n})$. Then,

$$h(n) = h(n - 1) + O(1)$$

Therefore,

$$h(n) = O(n)$$

This implies that,

$$g(n) = O(\lg \lg n)$$

And so,

$$f(n) = O(n \lg \lg n)$$

Now solve the recurrence again by trying the transformations in the reverse order.

C.4   A Long Example

Consider the following recurrence

$$f(n) = \begin{cases} 1 & n = 1 \\ 8 & n = 2 \\ 3f(n/2) + 4f(n/4) + 3n & n > 2 \end{cases}$$

We shall show that

$$f(2^n) = 2^n(3 \times 2^n - 2)$$

so,

$$f(n) = O(n^2)$$

The only kind of recurrences we need to know to solve the above problem are *linear recurrences in one variable with constant coefficients*, and these are the easiest ones to solve. These recurrences are

$$c_1 f(n) + c_2 f(n - 1) + \cdots + c_a f(n - a) = g(n)$$

where the c_is are constants and $g(n)$ is some function of n. We are given a boundary values, where a is a constant.

First we ignore $g(n)$ and solve the equation

$$c_1 f(n) + c_2 f(n - 1) + \cdots + c_a f(n - a) = 0$$

This is the *homogeneous equation* of the recurrence. Since any solution to the homogeneous equation can be added to a solution to the general equation yielding yet another solution to the general equation (why?) we really have a family of solutions and our task is to identify the most general solution.

The homogeneous equation of a linear recurrence with constant coefficients has a solution proportional to r^n where r is some non-zero constant. So we try $f(n) = r^n$, yielding the equation

$$c_1 r^n + c_2 r^{n-1} + \cdots + c_a r^{n-a} = 0$$

Dividing by r^{n-a} we get the *characteristic equation* of the recurrence

$$c_1 r^a + c_2 r^{a-1} + \cdots + c_a = 0$$

This is a polynomial in r of degree a. Suppose this equation has solutions $r_1, r_2, \ldots, r_a$. If these a solutions are all different then the solution to the homogeneous equation is a linear combination of each of them. That is, it is equal to some constant times r_1 + some constant times r_2 + $\cdots$ + some constant times r_a. (There is a complication if some of the solutions are the same.)

Once we solve the homogeneous equation we guess a solution for the general equation depending on $g(n)$. Usually $g(n)$ is a polynomial in n, let's say of degree i, and the general solution will contain a polynomial of n of degree i whose coefficients we determine by substituting the a boundary values.

This may sound complicated but it's easy after you do a few. It is important to know how to solve linear recurrences with constant coefficients because they're the simplest and because many recurrences can be transformed into them (and so solved). A common technique with complicated recurrences is to try to reduce them to a simpler recurrence.

Here is the recurrence again

$$f(n) = \begin{cases} 1 & n = 1 \\ 8 & n = 2 \\ 3f(n/2) + 4f(n/4) + 3n & n > 2 \end{cases}$$

Trying a few iterations of substitution we get bogged down with the $3n$ term. The $3n$ makes things messy, so let's transform the recurrence by dividing by n. Consider the function $g(n) = f(n)/n$, then

$$g(n) = \begin{cases} 1 & n = 1 \\ 4 & n = 2 \\ \dfrac{3}{2}g(n/2) + g(n/4) + 3 & n > 2 \end{cases}$$

Note that the boundary values have changed.

Now we transform again. It would be nice to "take logs" and transform $n/2$ and $n/4$ to $n-1$ and $n-2$, respectively. This is easy to do. Consider the function $h(n) = g(2^n)$, then

$$h(n) = \begin{cases} 1 & n = 0 \\ 4 & n = 1 \\ \dfrac{3}{2}h(n-1) + h(n-2) + 3 & n > 1 \end{cases}$$

This is a linear recurrence with constant coefficients! (Note that the boundary values have changed again.)

(Could we have done these two transformations in the reverse order? What could we try if we had $n/2$ and $n/3$ instead of two powers of 2? Hint: think about transforming to a function of *two* variables.)

The characteristic equation of this recurrence is

$$r^2 - \frac{3r}{2} - 1 = 0$$

which has solutions 2 and $-1/2$. Thus we look for solutions to the general equation of the form

$$h(n) = a2^n + b\left(\frac{-1}{2}\right)^n - 2$$

The extra term "3" of the recurrence is a polynomial of degree 0 so we try a polynomial of degree 0, for example, "c", and we get that $c = (3/2)c+c+3$, which has solution $c = -2$.

Now we substitute in the two boundary values, yielding the simultaneous equations

$$a + b - 2 = 1 \implies a + b = 3$$
$$2a - \frac{b}{2} - 2 = 4 \implies 4a - b = 12$$

Solving, we have that
$$a = 3, \quad b = 0$$

Thus, $h(n) = 3 \times 2^n - 2$. So $f(2^n) = 2^n(3 \times 2^n - 2)$.

We could have continued to transform $h(n)$ into the function h_1 where $h_1(n) = h(n) + 2$, giving us the recurrence

$$h_1(n) = \begin{cases} 3 & n = 0 \\ 6 & n = 1 \\ \frac{3}{2}h_1(n-1) + h_1(n-2) & n > 1 \end{cases}$$

this recurrence has no constant added term! Thus it is already homogeneous and has a simple solution.

You're probably asking yourself "How do I known which transforms to try?" Unfortunately so far the only answer is: experience. For example, in the last transformation to h_1, experience tells us that a homogeneous recurrence is easier to solve than a non-homogeneous one. So we look for a constant c such that if we substitute $h_1(n) = h(n) + c$ then the recurrence for h_1 would be homogeneous. Since $h_1(n) = h(n)+c$ is equivalent to $h(n) = h_1(n) - c$, the only way the recurrence for h_1 could be homogeneous is if

$$(h_1(n) - c) = \frac{3}{2}(h_1(n/2) - c) + (h_1(n/4) - c) + 3$$

And this can happen only when $c = 2$. This is really all that we did when we found the solution of the non-homogeneous equation above.

BIBLIOGRAPHY

Aggarwal, Alok and Vitter, Jeffrey Scott; "The Input/Output Complexity of Sorting and Related Problems," *Communications of the ACM,* 31, 1116–1127, 1988.

Ahlswede, Rudolf and Wegener, Ingo; *Search Problems,* Wiley, 1987.

Aho, Alfred V., Hopcroft, John E., and Ullman, Jeffrey D.; *The Design and Analysis of Algorithms,* Addison-Wesley, 1974.

Aigner, Martin; *Combinatorial Search,* Wiley-Teubner, 1988.

Andrew, Christopher; *Secret Service: The Making of the British Intelligence Community,* Heinemann, 1985.

Ash, Robert; *Basic Probability Theory,* Wiley, 1970.

Atkinson, M. D., Sack, J.-R., Santoro, N., and Strothotte, Th.; "Min-Max Heaps and Generalized Priority Queues," *Communications of the ACM,* 29, 996–1000, 1986.

Baase, Sara; *Computer Algorithms: Introduction to Design and Analysis,* Addison-Wesley, second edition, 1988.

Babai, László; "Email and the unexpected power of interaction," *Proceedings of the 5th Annual ACM Structure in Complexity Theory Conference,* 30–44, 1990.

Bach, Eric; "Number-Theoretic Algorithms," *Annual Review of Computer Science,* 4, 119–172, 1990.

Balcázar, José, Díaz, Josep, and Gabarró, Joaquim; *Structural Complexity I,* Springer-Verlag, 1988.

Balcázar, José, Díaz, Josep, and Gabarró, Joaquim; *Structural Complexity II,* Springer-Verlag, 1990.

Bamford, James; *The Puzzle Palace: A Report on NSA, America's Most Secret Agency,* Houghton Mifflin, 1982.

Bell, Eric Temple; *Men of Mathematics,* Simon and Schuster, 1937.

Bell, Eric Temple; *Mathematics: Queen and Servant of Science,* Mathematical Association of America, republication, 1987.

Benacerraf, Paul and Putnam, Hilary (editors); *Philosophy of Mathematics,* Cambridge University Press, second edition, 1983.

Ben-Or, Michael, Goldwasser, Shafi, Kilian, Joe, and Wigderson, Avi; "Multi-prover interactive proofs: How to remove the intractability assumptions," *Proceedings of the 20th Annual ACM Symposium on the Theory of Computing,* 113–131, 1988.

Bent, Samuel W. and John, John W.; "Finding the Median Requires $2n$ Comparisons," *Proceedings of the 17th ACM Symposium on the Theory of Computing,* 213–216, 1985.

Bentley, Jon Louis; *Writing Efficient Programs,* Prentice-Hall, 1982.

Bentley, Jon Louis; *Programming Pearls,* Addison-Wesley, 1986.

Bentley, Jon Louis; *More Programming Pearls: Confessions of a Coder,* Addison-Wesley, 1988.

Bentley, Jon Louis and Brown, Donna J.; "A General Class of Resource Tradeoffs," *Proceedings of the 21st Annual Symposium on the Foundations of Computer Science,* IEEE Computer Society, 217–228, 1980.

Bentley, Jon Louis, Stanat, Donald F., and Steele, J. Michael; "Analysis of a Randomized Data Structure for Representing Sets," *Proceedings of the 19th Annual Allerton Conference on Circuit and System Theory,* 364–372, 1981.

Bentley, Jon Louis and Yao, Andrew C.-C.; "An Almost Optimal Algorithm for Unbounded Search," *Information Processing Letters,* 5, 82–87, 1976.

Berge, Claude; *The Theory of Graphs and Its Applications,* Wiley, 1962.

Bishop, Errett and Bridges, Douglas; *Constructive Analysis,* Springer Verlag, 1985.

Bitner, James R.; "An Asymptotically Optimal Algorithm for the Dutch National Flag Problem," *SIAM Journal on Computing,* 11, 2, 243–262, 1982.

Black, Uyless; *Data Networks: Concepts, Theory, and Practice,* Prentice-Hall, 1989.

Blum, Manuel, Feldman, Paul, and Micali, Silvio; "Non-Interactive Zero-Knowledge and Its Applications," *Proceedings of the 20th Annual ACM Symposium on the Theory of Computing,* 103–112, 1988.

Brassard, Gilles; "Crusade for a Better Notation," *Sigact News,* 17, 1, 1985.

Brassard, Gilles; *Modern Cryptology: A Tutorial,* Springer-Verlag, 1988.

Brassard, Gilles; "The Cryptology Column," ongoing in *Sigact News.*

Brassard, Gilles and Brately, Paul; *Algorithmics: Theory and Practice,* Prentice-Hall, 1988.

Brown, Mark R.; "Implementation and Analysis of Binomial Queue Algorithms," *SIAM Journal on Computing,* 7, 298–319, 1978.

Brown, Noll, Parady, Smith, Smith, and Zarantonello; Letter to the editor, *American Mathematical Monthly,* 97, 214, 1990.

Bühler, W. K.; *Gauss: A Biographical Study,* Springer-Verlag, 1981.

Bui, T. D. and Thanh, Mai; "Significant Improvements to the Ford-Johnson Algorithm for Sorting," *BIT,* 25, 70–75, 1985.

Carlsson, Svante; *Heaps,* doctoral dissertation, Department of Computer Science, Lund University, 1986.

Carlsson, S., Chen, J. and Strothotte, Th.; "A Note on the Construction of the Data Structure 'Deap'," *Information Processing Letters.*

Christen, C.; "Improving the Bounds on Optimal Merging," *Proceedings of the 19th Annual Symposium on the Foundations of Computer Science,* IEEE Computer Society, 259–266, 1978.

Chvátal, Vašek; *Linear Programming,* W. H. Freeman, 1983.

Cohen, Daniel I. A.; *Introduction to Computation Theory,* John Wiley & Sons, revised edition, 1990.

Condon, Anne; *Computational Models of Games,* MIT Press, 1990.

Cook, S. A.; "The complexity of theorem proving procedures," *Proceedings of the 3rd Annual ACM Symposium on the Theory of Computing,* 151–158, 1971.

Cormen, Thomas M., Leiserson, Charles E., and Rivest, Ronald L.; *Introduction to Algorithms,* McGraw-Hill/MIT Press, 1990.

Cover, Thomas M. and Gacs, Peter; "Kolmogorov's Contributions to Information Theory and Algorithmic Complexity," IBM Research Report.

Creutzburg and Tasche; "Number-Theoretic Transforms of Prescribed Length," *Mathematics of Computation,* 46, 1986.

Czyzowicz, Jurek, Mundici, Daniele, and Pelc, Andrzej; "Ulam's Searching Game with Lies," *Journal of Combinatorial Theory, Series A,* 52, 62–76, 1989.

Dauben, Joseph Warren; *Georg Cantor: His Mathematics and Philosophy of the Infinite,* Harvard University Press, 1979.

Davis, Martin (editor); *The Undecidable: Basic Papers On Undecidable Propositions, Unsolvable Problems, And Computable Functions,* Raven Press, 1965.

de Bruijn, N. G.; *Asymptotic Methods in Analysis,* Dover, reprinted, 1981.

Delong, Howard; *A Profile of Mathematical Logic,* Addison-Wesley, 1970.

Denning, Peter J. (editor); *Computers Under Attack: Intruders, Worms, and Viruses,* Addison-Wesley, 1990.

Devroye, Luc; *Lecture Notes on Bucket Algorithms,* Birkhäuser, 1986.

Dewdney, A. K.; *The Turing Omnibus,* Computer Science Press, 1989.

Dijkstra, E. W.; "A note on two problems in connexion with graphs," *Numerische Mathematik,* 1, 269–271, 1959.

Dixon, John D.; "Factorization and Primality Tests," *The American Mathematical Monthly,* 91, 333–352, 1984.

Dobkin, David and Lipton, Richard; "On The Complexity of Computations Under Varying Sets of Primitives," *Journal of Computer and System Sciences,* 18, 86–91, 1979.

Dobkin, David and Munro, J. Ian; "Determining the Mode," *Theoretical Computer Science,* 12, 255–263, 1980.

Downey, Peter, Leong, Benton, and Sethi, Ravi; "Computing Sequences with Addition Chains," *SIAM Journal on Computing,* 10, 3, 638–646, 1981.

Dresher, Melvin; *The Mathematics of Games and Strategy,* Dover, republication, 1981.

Epstein, Richard L. and Carnielli, Walter A.; *Computability: Computable Functions, Logic, and the Foundations of Mathematics,* Wadsworth & Brooks/Cole, 1989.

Estivill-Castro, Vladimir; *Sorting and Measures of Disorder,* doctoral dissertation, research report CS–91–07, Department of Computer Science, University of Waterloo, 1991.

Feige, Uriel, Fiat, Amos, and Shamir, Adi; "Zero Knowledge Proofs of Identity," *Proceedings of the 19th Annual ACM Symposium on the Theory of Computing,* 210–217, 1987.

Feller, William; *An Introduction to Probability Theory and Its Applications, Volume 1,* Wiley, third edition, 1968.

Fischer, M. J. and Salzberg, S. L.; "Finding a Majority Among n Votes," *Journal of Algorithms,* 3, 375–379, 1982.

Floyd, R. W.; "Algorithm 245, Treesort," *Communications of the ACM,* 7, 701, 1964.

Ford, Lester and Johnson, Selmer; "A Tournament Problem," *American Mathematical Monthly,* 66, 387–389, 1959.

Frederickson, Greg; "Recursively Rotated Orders and Implicit Data Structures: A Lower Bound," *Theoretical Computer Science,* 29, 75–85, 1985.

Fredman, Michael L. and Tarjan, Robert Endre; "Fibonacci heaps and their uses in improved network optimization algorithms," *Journal of the ACM,* 34, 596–615, 1987.

Galil, Zvi and Italiano, Giuseppe F.; "Data Structures and Algorithms for Disjoint Set Union Problems," *Computing Surveys,* 1991.

Gardner, Martin; *aha! Insight,* Scientific American/W. H. Freeman, 1978.

Garey, Michael R. and Johnson, David S.; *Computers and Intractability: A Guide to the Theory of $\mathcal{NP}$-Completeness,* W. H. Freeman, 1979.

Gensler, Harry J.; *Godel's Theorem Simplified,* University Press of America, 1984.

Goldreich, Oded, Micali, Silvio, and Wigderson, Avi; "Proofs That Yield Nothing But Their Validity and a Methodology of Cryptographic Protocol Design," *Proceedings of the 27th Annual Symposium on the Foundations of Computer Science,* IEEE Computer Society, 174–187, 1986.

Goldwasser, Shafi, Micali, Silvio, and Rackoff, Charles; "The knowledge complexity of interactive proof systems," *SIAM Journal on Computing,* 18, 186–208, 1989.

Gonnet, Gaston H. and Baeza-Yates, Ricardo; *Handbook of Algorithms and Data Structures,* Addison-Wesley, second edition, 1991.

Gonnet, Gaston H. and Munro, J. Ian; "Heaps On Heaps," *SIAM Journal on Computing,* 15, 964–971, 1986.

Gonzalez, Rafael C. and Wintz, Paul; *Digital Image Processing,* Addison-Wesley, second edition, 1987.

Gorenstein, Daniel; "The Enormous Theorem," *Scientific American,* 104–115, December 1985.

Goulden, Ian P. and Jackson, David M.; *Combinatorial Enumeration,* John Wiley & Sons, 1983.

Graham, Ronald L., Knuth, Donald E., and Patashnik, Oren; *Concrete Mathematics: A Foundation for Computer Science,* Addison-Wesley, 1989.

Graham, Ronald L., Rothschild, Bruce L., and Spencer, Joel H.; *Ramsey Theory,* John Wiley & Sons, 1980.

Greene, Daniel H. and Knuth, Donald E.; *Mathematics for the Analysis of Algorithms,* Birkhäuser, third edition, 1990.

Gries, David and Levin, G.; "Computing Fibonacci Numbers (and Similarly Defined Functions) in Log Time," *Information Processing Letters,* 11, 68–69, 1980.

Halmos, Paul; *Naive Set Theory,* Springer-Verlag, 1960.

Hardy, G. H. and Wright, E. M.; *An Introduction to the Theory of Numbers,* Oxford University Press, 1954.

Harel, David; *Algorithmics: The Spirit of Computing,* Addison-Wesley, 1987.

Heil, Christopher E. and Walnut, David F.; "Continuous and Discrete Wavelet Transforms," *SIAM Review,* 31, 628–666, 1989.

Hendee, William R.; *The Physical Principles of Computed Tomography,* Little, Brown and Company, 1983.

Herman, Gabor T.; *Image Reconstruction from Projections: The Fundamentals of Computerized Tomography,* Academic Press, 1980.

Hight, Donald W.; *A Concept of Limits,* Dover, 1977,

Hoare, C. A. R.; "Quicksort," *Computer Journal,* 5, 10–15, 1962.

Hodges, Andrew; *Alan Turing, The Enigma of Intelligence,* Unwin, 1983.

Hofri, Micha; *Probabilistic Analysis of Algorithms,* Springer-Verlag, 1987.

Hopcroft, John E. and Ullman, Jeffrey D.; *Introduction to Automata Theory, Languages, and Computation,* Addison-Wesley, 1979.

Horowitz, Ellis and Sahni, Sartaj; *Fundamentals of Computer Algorithms,* Computer Science Press, 1978.

Horowitz, Ellis and Sahni, Sartaj; *Fundamentals of Data Structures in Pascal,* Computer Science Press, third edition, 1990.

Hwang, Frank and Lin, Shen; "A Simple Algorithm for Merging Two Disjoint Linearly-Ordered Sets," *SIAM Journal on Computing,* 1, 31–39, 1972.

Johnson, David S.; "The $\mathcal{NP}$-Completeness Column: An Ongoing Guide," ongoing in *The Journal of Algorithms.*

Kahn, David; *The Codebreakers: The Story of Secret Writing,* Signet, 1973.

Kaplansky, Irving; *Set Theory and Metric Spaces,* Chelsea Publishing Company, second edition, 1977.

Karp, Richard M.; "Combinatorics, Complexity, and Randomness," in *ACM Turing Award Lectures: The First Twenty Years, 1966–1985,* ACM Press, 1987.

Kemp, Rainer; *Fundamentals of the Average Case Analysis of Particular Algorithms,* Wiley-Teubner, 1984.

Kernighan Brian W. and Plauger, P. J.; *The Elements of Programming Style,* McGraw-Hill, second edition, 1978.

Kernighan Brian W. and Plauger, P. J.; *Software Tools in Pascal,* Addison-Wesley, 1981.

Khinchin, A. I.; *Mathematical Foundations of Information Theory,* Dover, 1957.

Kilian, Joe; *Uses of Randomness in Algorithms and Protocols,* MIT Press, 1990.

King, K. N. and Smith-Thomas, B.; "An Optimal Algorithm for Sink-Finding," *Information Processing Letters,* 14, 109–111, 1982.

Kingston, Jeffrey H.; *Algorithms and Data Structures; Design, Correctness, Analysis,* Addison-Wesley, 1990.

Kirkpatrick, David; "A Unified Lower Bound for Selection and Set Partitioning Problems," *Journal of the ACM,* 28, 150–165, 1981.

Klee, Victor and Minty, G. J.; "How Good is the Simplex Algorithm?," in *Inequalities-III,* Shisha, O. (editor), Academic Press, 1972.

Knuth, Donald E.; Blindern lecture notes on computer science, 1972 (unpublished).

Knuth, Donald E.; *The Art of Computer Programming: Volume 1, Fundamental Algorithms,* Addison-Wesley, second edition, 1973.

Knuth, Donald E.; *The Art of Computer Programming: Volume 2, Seminumerical Algorithms,* Addison-Wesley, second edition, 1981.

Knuth, Donald E.; *The Art of Computer Programming: Volume 3, Sorting and Searching,* Addison-Wesley, 1973.

Koblitz, Neal; *A Course in Number Theory and Cryptography,* Springer-Verlag, 1987.

Kollár, Ĺubor; "Optimal Sorting of Seven Element Sets," *Mathematical Foundations of Computer Science, Proceedings 1986,* Gruska, J., Rovan, B., and Wiedermann, J. (editors), 449–457, Springer-Verlag, 1986.

Kronsjö, Lydia; *Computational Complexity of Sequential and Parallel Algorithms,* John Wiley & Sons, 1985.

Kronsjö, Lydia; *Algorithms: Their Complexity and Efficiency,* John Wiley & Sons, second edition, 1987.

Kruskal, J. B.; "On the shortest spanning subtree of a graph and the travelling salesman problem," *Proceedings of the American Mathematical Society,* 71, 48–50, 1956.

Lagarias, J. C.; "The $3x + 1$ Problem and Its Generalizations," *American Mathematical Monthly,* 92, 3–23, 1985.

Lakatos, Imre; *Proofs and Refutations: The Logic of Mathematical Discovery,* Cambridge University Press, 1976.

Landau, Susan; "Zero Knowledge and the Department of Defense," *Notices of the American Mathematical Society,* 35, 1, 5–12, 1988.

Lawler, Eugene L., Lenstra, J. K., Rinnooy Kan, A. H. G., and Shmoys, D.; *The Traveling Salesman Problem: A Guided Tour of Combinatorial Optimization,* John Wiley & Sons, 1985.

Leighton, Tom and Lepley, Margaret; "Probabilistic Searching in Sorted Linked Lists," *Proceedings of the 20th Annual Allerton Conference on Circuit and System Theory,* 500–506, 1982.

Lesuisse, R.; "Some Lessons Drawn from the History of the Binary Search Algorithm," *The Computer Journal,* 26, 2, 154–163, 1983.

LeVeque, William J.; *Elementary Theory of Numbers,* Addison-Wesley, 1962.

Levin, Leonid; "Universal'nyĭe perebornyĭe zadachi," (Universal search problems), in Russian, *Problemy Peredači Informatsiĭ,* 115–116, 1973. English translation in *Problems of Information Transmission,* 9, 265–266, 1973.

Li, Ming and Vitanyi, Paul M. B.; *An Introduction to Kolmogorov Complexity and Its Applications,* Addison-Wesley, to appear, 1992.

Liskov, B. and Guttag, J.; *Abstraction and Specification in Program Development,* MIT Press, 1986.

Lucky, Robert W.; *Silicon Dreams: Information, Man, and Machine,* St. Martin's Press, 1989.

Lund, Carsten, Fortnow, Lance, Karloff, Howard, and Manacher, Glenn; "The Ford-Johnson Sorting Algorithm is Not Optimal," *Journal of the ACM,* 26, 434–440, 1979.

Manacher, Glenn; "Further Results on Near-Optimal Sorting," *Proceedings of the 17th Allerton Conference on Communication, Control and Computing,* 949–960, 1979.

Manber, Udi; *Introduction To Algorithms: A Creative Approach,* Addison-Wesley, 1989.

Mason, John, Burton, Leone, and Stacey, Kaye; *Thinking Mathematically,* Addison-Wesley, 1982.

McIvor, Robert; "Smart Cards," *Scientific American,* 152–159, November 1985.

Mehlhorn, Kurt; *Data Structures and Algorithms: Volume 1, Sorting and Searching,* Springer-Verlag, 1984.

Mehlhorn, Kurt; *Data Structures and Algorithms: Volume 2, Graph Algorithms and NP-Completeness,* Springer-Verlag, 1984.

Mehlhorn, Kurt; *Data Structures and Algorithms: Volume 3, Multidimensional Searching and Computational Geometry,* Springer-Verlag, 1984.

Mönting, Jürgen Schulte; "Merging of 4 or 5 Elements with n Elements," *Theoretical Computer Science,* 14, 19–37, 1981.

Morain, François; "Distributed Primality Proving and the Primality of $(2^{3539}+1)/3$," *Advances in Cryptology: Eurocrypt '90,* Damgård, I. B. (editor), 110–123, Springer-Verlag, 1991.

Moret, Bernard and Shapiro, Henry; *Algorithms from P to NP: Volume I, Design & Efficiency,* Benjamin/Cummings, 1991.

Mostafa, Yaser S. (editor); *Complexity in Information Theory,* Springer-Verlag, 1988.

Munro, J. Ian; "Developing Implicit Data Structures," *Mathematical Foundations of Computer Science, Proceedings 1986,* Gruska, J., Rovan, B., and Wiedermann, J. (editors), 168–176, Springer-Verlag, 1986.

Munro and J. Ian and Spira, Philip M.; "Sorting and Searching in Multisets," *SIAM Journal on Computing,* 5, 1, 1–9, 1976.

Munro, J. Ian and Suwanda, Hendra; "Implicit Data Structures for Fast Search and Update," *Journal of Computer and System Sciences*, 21, 236–250, 1980.

Nisan, Noam; "The polynomial time hierarchy has interactive proofs," e-mail announcement, December 1989, to appear 1991.

Oppenheim, Alan V. and Schafer, Ronald W.; *Discrete-Time Signal Processing*, Prentice-Hall, 1989.

Ore, Øystein; *Cardano: The Gambling Scholar*, Dover, 1953.

Ore, Øystein; *Graphs and Their Uses*, The Mathematical Association of America, 1963.

Overmars, Mark H.; *The Design of Dynamic Data Structures*, doctoral dissertation, University of Utrecht, 1983.

Packel, Edward; *The Mathematics of Games and Gambling*, The Mathematical Association of America, 1981.

Palmer, Edgar M.; *Graphical Evolution*, John Wiley & Sons, 1985.

Parker, R. Gary and Rardin, Ronald L.; *Discrete Optimization*, Academic Press, 1988.

Perl, Yehoshua and Reingold, Edward M.; "Understanding the Complexity of Interpolation Search," *Information Processing Letters*, 6, 6, 219–222, 1977.

Péter, Rósza; *Playing With Infinity*, Dover, 1957.

Pierce, John R.; *An Introduction to Information Theory*, Dover, second edition, 1980.

Pohl, Ira; "Minimean Optimality in Sorting Algorithms," *Proceedings of the 16th Annual Symposium on the Foundations of Computer Science*, IEEE Computer Society, 71–74, 1975.

Pólya, George; *How To Solve It*, Princeton University Press, second edition, 1957.

Pólya, George; *Mathematics and Plausible Reasoning: Volume 1, Induction and Analogy in Mathematics*, Princeton University Press, 1954,

Pólya, George; *Mathematics and Plausible Reasoning: Volume 2, Patterns of Plausible Inference*, Princeton University Press, second edition, 1968.

Prim, R. C.; "Shortest connection networks and some generalizations," *Bell System Technical Journal*, 36, 1389–1401, 1957.

Purdom, Paul Walton, Jr. and Brown, Cynthia A.; *The Analysis of Algorithms*, Holt, Reinhart and Winston, 1985.

Rabin, Michael O.; "Probabilistic Algorithms," in *Algorithms and Complexity: New Directions and Recent Results*, J. F. Traub (editor), 21–39, Academic Press, 1976.

Ravikumar, B., Ganesan, K., and Lakshmanan, K. B.; "On Selecting the Largest Element In Spite of Erroneous Information," *STAC* 1986.

Reid, Constance; *Hilbert,* Springer-Verlag, 1970.

Reingold, Edward M. and Hansen, Wilfred J.; *Data Structures in Pascal,* Little, Brown and Company, 1986.

Rényi, Alfréd; *A Diary of Information Theory,* John Wiley & Sons, 1984.

Riesel, Hans; *Prime Numbers and Computer Methods of Factorization,* Birkhäuser, 1985.

Roberts, Eric S.; *Thinking Recursively,* John Wiley & Sons, 1986.

Russell, Bertrand; "Recent Work on the Principles of Mathematics," *International Monthly,* 4, 84, 1901.

Salomaa, Arto; *Public Key Cryptography,* Springer-Verlag, 1990.

Sawyer, W. W.; *What is Calculus About?,* The Mathematical Association of America, 1961.

Schönhage, Arnold; "The Production of Partial Orders," *Asterisque,* 38/39, 29–246, 1976.

Schönhage, A., Paterson, M. and Pippenger, N.; "Finding the Median," *Journal of Computer and System Sciences,* 13, 184–199, 1976.

Sedgewick, Robert; *Quicksort,* Garland, 1980.

Sedgewick, Robert; *Algorithms,* Addison-Wesley, second edition, 1988.

Sedgewick, Robert, Szymanski, Thomas G., and Andrew C. Yao; "The Complexity of Finding Cycles in Periodic Functions," *SIAM Journal on Computing,* 11, 376–390, 1982.

Seress, Ákos; "Quick Gossiping by Conference Calls," *SIAM Journal on Discrete Mathematics,* 1, 1, 109–120, 1988.

Shamir, Adi; "$\mathcal{IP} = \mathcal{P}space$," *Proceedings of the 31st Annual Symposium on the Foundations of Computer Science,* IEEE Computer Society, 11–15, 1990.

Shannon, Claude E. and Weaver, Warren; *The Mathematical Theory of Communication,* University of Illinois Press, 1963.

Simmons, Gus; "The Prisoners Problem and the Subliminal Channel," *Advances in Cryptology: Proceedings of Crypto 83,* 51–67, Plenum Press, 1984.

Sleator, Daniel and Tarjan, Robert Endre; "Amortized Efficiency of List Update and Paging Rules," *Communications of the ACM,* 28, 202–208, 1985.

Smith, Jeffrey D.; *Design and Analysis of Algorithms,* PWS-Kent, 1989.

Snir, Marc; "Exact Balancing Is Not Always Good," *Information Processing Letters,* 22, 97–102, 1986.

Solovay R. and Strassen, V.; "A Fast Monte Carlo Test for Primality," *SIAM Journal on Computing,* 6, 84–85, 1977. See also an erratum list in *SIAM Journal on Computing,* 7, 118, 1978.

Solow, Daniel; *How to Read and Do Proofs,* John Wiley & Sons, second edition, 1990.

Spencer, Joel; *Ten Lectures on the Probabilistic Method,* The Society for Industrial and Applied Mathematics, 1987.

Steigler, Stephen M.; *The History of Statistics,* Harvard University Press, 1986.

Stewart, Ian; *The Problems of Mathematics,* Oxford University Press, 1987.

Stockmeyer, Paul and Yao, F. Frances; "On the Optimality of Linear Merge," *SIAM Journal on Computing,* 9, 85–90, 1980.

Stoll, Clifford; *The Cuckoo's Egg,* Doubleday, 1989.

Stubbs, Daniel F. and Webre, Neil W.; *Data Structures with Abstract Data Types and Pascal,* Brooks/Cole, second edition, 1989.

Tanenbaum, Andrew S.; *Computer Networks,* Prentice-Hall, second edition, 1988.

Tarjan, Robert Endre; "A Class of Algorithms which Require Nonlinear Time to Maintain Disjoint Sets," *Journal of Computer and System Sciences,* 18, 110–127, 1979.

Tarjan, Robert Endre; *Data Structures and Network Algorithms,* The Society for Industrial and Applied Mathematics, 1983.

Todhunter, Isaac; *A History of the Mathematical Theory of Probability,* Chelsea, 1865.

Turing, Alan M.; "On Computable Numbers with an Application to the Entscheidungsproblem," *Proceedings of the London Mathematical Society, series 2,* 42, 230–265, 1936/37. A correction appeared in the same journal: 43, 544–546, 1937.

van Gasteren, A. J. M.; *On the Shape of Mathematical Arguments,* Springer-Verlag, 1990.

van Leeuwen, J., Santoro, N., Urrutia, J., and Zaks, S.; "Guessing Games and Distributed Computations in Synchronous Networks," Carlton University technical report SCS-TR-96, June 1986.

Vitter, Jeffrey Scott and Chen, Wen-Chin; *Design and Analysis of Coalesced Hashing,* Oxford University Press, 1987.

von Mises, Richard; *Probability, Statistics and Truth,* Dover, republication, 1981.

von Neumann, John and Morgenstern, Oskar; *Theory of Games and Economic Behavior,* Princeton University Press, 1947.

Vuillemin, Jean; "A Data Structure for Manipulating Priority Queues," *Communications of the ACM,* 21, 309–315, 1978.

Wagon, Stan; *The Banach-Tarski Paradox,* Cambridge University Press, 1985.

Wang, Hao; *Reflections on Kurt Gödel,* MIT Press, 1987.

Weiss, Mark Allen and Sedgewick, Robert; "Tight Lower Bounds for Shellsort," *Proceedings of the 1st Scandinavian Workshop on Algorithm Theory,* Karlsson, R. and Lingas, A. (editors), 255–262, Springer-Verlag, 1988.

Wiedermann, Jiři; *Searching Algorithms,* Teubner, 1987.

Wilf, Herbert S.; *Algorithms and Complexity,* Prentice-Hall, 1986.

Wilf, Herbert S.; *Generatingfunctionology,* Academic Press, 1990.

Williams, J. W. J.; "Algorithm 232, Heapsort," *Communications of the ACM,* 6, 347–348, 1964.

Wood, Derick; *Theory of Computation,* Harper & Row, 1987.

Yao, Andrew Chi-Chih; "Probabilistic Computations: Toward a Unified Measure of Complexity," *Proceedings of the 18th Annual Symposium on the Foundations of Computer Science,* IEEE Computer Society, 222–227, 1977.

Yao, Andrew Chi-Chih; "On the Complexity of Partial Order Productions," *SIAM Journal on Computing,* 18, 679–689, 1989.

Zurek, Wojciech H. (editor); *Complexity, Entropy and the Physics of Information,* Addison-Wesley, 1990.

"Gauss and the History of the Fast Fourier Transform," *IEEE ASSP Magazine,* 1, 4, 14–21, 1984.

"A New Wave in Applied Mathematics: A technique called wavelets may upstage Fourier analysis in a multitude of applications—from CAT scanning to locating subs," *Science,* 249, 858–859, August 1990.

"Wavelet theory sets out the welcome mat," *SIAM News,* 23, 8–9, September 1990.

SYMBOL INDEX

NAME INDEX

SUBJECT INDEX